Learning:

Interactions

Learning:

Interactions

Melvin H. Marx, Editor

University of Missouri, Columbia

The Macmillan Company

Collier-Macmillan Limited, *London*

First Printing

Library of Congress catalog card number: 79-81552

THE MACMILLAN COMPANY
COLLIER-MACMILLAN CANADA, LTD.,
TORONTO, ONTARIO

Printed in the United States of America

Foreword

The three volumes in this set were planned to provide comprehensive, up-to-date coverage of the wide range of behavioral functions generally referred to as learning. Obviously such an enterprise can be only partially achieved within the various limitations necessarily imposed upon the editor and writers. But it is my hope that we have achieved a reasonably satisfactory treatment of a wide sector of the very broad spectrum of learning problems. The books were planned on the premise that it is no longer possible for one psychologist to be fully expert in all of the areas of so broad and diversified a field as learning. Expert coverage of the major facets of the field has therefore been attempted by having a large number of separate authors each contribute a section on his own special subject. Variations in the time of receipt of the final manuscripts within each volume account for some differences in the nature and scope of literature coverage by the various authors.

Here I will briefly indicate some of the general considerations that were used in planning the volumes and then describe the specific intent of each of the volumes. More detailed descriptions of the particular volumes are provided in the introductions to them. The introductory sections are also designed to orient the reader in each subject matter by brief surveys of relevant background materials.

The general intent of each of the several sections in a volume is to present the highlights of the special subject matter. Each section has therefore been written by a psychologist who is himself an active researcher in the field.

The books are aimed at the advanced undergraduate. The question that was suggested to each author as the criterion for coverage and level of difficulty was, "What should a college senior graduating with a major in psychology know about this subject?" Each section was intended to be an independent, self-sufficient unit, including introductory or orienting material, a review of the major propositions and principles in the area, discussion of key questions and salient contributions, and finally some consideration of the future, with special regard to critical research needs.

The three volumes may be differentiated, briefly, as to their content and objectives. *Learning: Processes* is intended to emphasize the *description* of behavioral changes commonly called learning, and closely related fundamental behavioral phenomena (transfer, retention, stimulus generalization). *Learning: Interactions* is intended to emphasize the *interrelationships* between behavior changes produced by behavior itself

v

("learning") and certain intimately connected functions (motivation, perception, concept formation, and personality) as well as how such behavior changes operate across phyla and how they are neurophysiologically mediated. *Learning: Theories* is intended to emphasize the *interpretation* of the fundamental learning processes, ordered in terms of the type of theoretical method used, or of key constructs.

A word about the technical organization of the sections. In order to make the books maximally useful each section has been given a high degree of self-sufficiency. The glossary, suggested further readings, and references for each section are placed at the end of that section. There is a minimal degree of overlap in these materials. A comprehensive index, with extensive cross-referencing, should help to tie the sections together.

The symbols S (for subject) and E (for experimenter) have been used throughout the books because of the great frequency with which these terms occur.

I am grateful to a number of persons for their aid in the preparation of these volumes. The specific acknowledgments to publishers and authors for their kind permission to reprint materials are given in each volume. My colleagues have been generous with their time and helpful with their critical suggestions. Most of all, I wish to express my deepest gratitude to my wife, Kathleen, for her indefatigable assistance in the effort required to keep the contributors writing and in the endless technical details involved in the preparation of each volume for the publisher. I hope that the appearance of the volumes will be partial repayment to her for her patience and perseverance throughout the many long hours she has spent on this project.

M. H. M.

Columbia, Missouri

Preface

Overview of Volume

This book represents an attempt to portray certain salient aspects of the myriad interrelationships between learning and a variety of other behavioral processes. It is hoped that this kind of emphasis will fill a gap in the textbook literature. Availability of the book should enable the interested instructor to assign topics that are normally not found in textbooks but that are of central importance in helping us to understand how learning, as a broad and persistent influence on practically all aspects of human behavior especially, interacts with other behavioral functions.

The first four parts of the book are concerned with behavioral processes of varying levels of complexity. Interactions of learning with the fundamental behavioral functions of motivation and perception are treated in the first two parts. The next part treats of the interaction of learning with problem solving and concept attainment, which collectively may be described as "thinking." The fourth part treats of the interaction of learning with the very complex process of human socialization.

The final two parts are concerned with a different kind of interaction. Part V takes up the problem of relating learning across the very wide spectrum of phylogenetic differences in organisms. Part VI is concerned with the somewhat more specific problem of how learning is mediated by the nervous system of the higher organisms particularly.

Pervasiveness of Learning

The influence of prior behavior, and its consequences, upon subsequent behavior is usually accepted, in a more or less general manner, as a definition of learning. Viewed in this way, learning is so obviously a pervasive and ubiquitous influence in behavior that its importance need not be labored. The ability to benefit (or suffer) from past experience is often regarded as the hallmark of animal life, and some of the research described in the last two parts of this volume (comparative psychology and neurophysiology of learning) provides documentation for this point of view.

Although learning thus defined is quite clearly of major significance in its own right, much of its theoretical, and especially its practical, significance arises from the way in which it serves to influence other, sometimes more complex behavioral processes. Those selected in this volume for detailed treatment are by no means unique;

alternative processes (for example, psycho-therapy, behavior modification, and so on) might well have been selected. Nevertheless, the ones selected do represent *focal* processes and conditions whose interactions with the broad process of learning do in fact encompass a very large proportion of the critical interfacing of past experience and present behaviors.

Mutuality of Interactions

A basic theme of the present volume is the proposition that each of the behavioral functions treated can be shown to have a mutual interaction with learning, the relatively enduring changes in behavior that are attributable to behavior itself. To put this proposition another way, each of the fundamental behavioral functions can be said not only to have significant learned components—that is, to be influenced by learning—but also to contribute significantly to learning itself—that is, to have an important effect on learning.

Broadly defined as activating factors in behavior, motives are obviously learned as well as unlearned; they are assuredly influenced by past behavior. To look again at the other side of the same coin, they are also important determinants of learning, although their exact role in this regard needs to be more clearly delineated than is at present possible. Certainly the questions raised in Part I concerning the relationship between motivating and learning functions are real ones. But there is a solution to them that may be outlined briefly. For example, consider the apparent paradox of the *simultaneous* motivating and reinforcing properties of an implicit response (r_g), discussed later in Part I. This problem may be simply resolved by recognizing the synonymity of the terms *reinforcing* and *motivating*. In other words, if reinforcement is viewed as primarily a motivational function, with only incidental learning (associative or habit-forming) properties, there is no paradox left. The mutuality of learning and motivation is maximally expressed by this kind of theoretical solution, a somewhat radical one not generally considered by learning-motivation theorists.

Our mode of perceiving as well as the content of our perception is, quite clearly, markedly influenced (although not completely influenced, or solely influenced) by our past experience. At the same time, how and what we learn are markedly and necessarily influenced by both the mode and content of our perception. These interactions are amply illustrated by the discussion in Part II.

The dependence of thinking (more specifically identified within this volume as "problem solving" and "concept attainment") in all its ramifications upon prior experience is quite evident, and is documented with frequent illustrations in the section on this topic. If prior experience is severely limited (independent of "native" endowment, so far as that can be separately measured), thinking is also severely handicapped—with regard to mode as well as content. Learning provides not only the basic materials but also many of the obstacles for thinking (see the "functional fixedness" experimentation of Duncker, described in Part III). The influence of thinking on learning, insofar as these can be defined independently, is somewhat less clear—and largely so because of the difficulty in conceptually separating the two processes. That is to say, thinking can well be included as a kind of learning—and whether it is or not is an entirely arbitrary decision. Nevertheless, there can be no question but that certain of the products of thinking have significant influences upon the kind and degree of learning that the higher organisms at least reveal. And so this interaction can scarcely be counted as an exception to our general proposition of mutual interaction, even if it is admittedly somewhat less distinct than the others.

Although there are basic disagreements as to the scope and exact manner of the operation of the influence, there is no argument as to the fact that learning, or the persisting effects of environmental stimulation and the behaviors relevant thereto, plays a significant part in the development and the organization of personality and social behavior. On the other hand, although commonly ignored or controlled by learning researchers, personality variables quite often also influence learning. It is quite probable, moreover, that their influence is widely operative for animal as well as human Ss, although little effort has as yet been exerted to investigate this problem. The recent extensive research on effects of experimenter bias in animal as well as human research is suggestive on this count.

The situation for the comparative psychology and the neurophysiology of learning is a little different. Upon reflection, however, it is evident that there is mutuality of interactions also between these conditions and learning. It is apparent that learning varies more or less directly with phylogenetic level, and particularly with the development of the higher (cortical) brain centers. The influence of learning upon phylogenetic level is much less apparent. However, if comparative psychology may be considered to be, at least in part, a reflection of inherited (phylogenetic) differences, then the interaction becomes clear. It is generally agreed that heredity and environment interact, and perhaps so intimately as to make impossible their complete separation in behavioral matters. The influence of heredity upon learning is so patent as not to require much in the way of elaboration; the observations of the ethologists, reviewed in Part V, offer eloquent testimony on this point. We cannot say that learning, here identified as the effects of environmental variables, has a *direct* effect upon heredity, in the extreme sense posited by Lamarck's "inheritance of acquired characteristics," which is still without acceptance by ge-

neticists, in the Western world at least. Nevertheless, there are two ways in which an indirect effect exists. First, and most important, the manner and scope of the operation of genetic factors depend very much upon environmental conditions and are in many respects mediated by means of the organism's behavioral responses to the environment, and thereby via his learning. Second, the selection process which contributes so heavily to the direction of evolution is very importantly influenced by learning, so that organisms which behave more effectively, with regard to their particular environment (that is, learning more efficiently), will tend to survive and therefore reproduce and pass on their hereditary factors to future generations.

The interaction of learning and neurophysiology is evident when one considers the fact that (1) learning quite clearly depends upon neurophysiological processes, and (2) the neuroanatomical structures underlying the neurophysiology of learning are themselves presumably altered by the behavior involved in that learning. The present state of this fast-moving field of investigation is thoroughly reviewed in Part VI.

Significance of Learning Interactions

Generally speaking, the significance of learning lies primarily in its interactions with affective and cognitive variables. Although some of the details of these interactions are described in the following parts of this book, a great deal of research is still needed, particularly with regard to the affective interactions, before a reasonably complete picture can be drawn.

Learning may thus be viewed, in terms of practical affairs, as a kind of handmaiden to certain other, more immediately meaningful problems—socialization, personal adjustment, academic and occupational adjustment, and the like. Moreover, much the same role is played by the other fundamental behavioral processes, such as perception and motivation. Each of these may be studied in its own right, as a fundamental behavioral process, and indeed must be so studied for effective scientific advancement; but each contributes to the adjustment of the organism primarily in terms of more molar functions and inter-relationships.

A closer look at this duality of interaction is instructive. For purposes of exposition, the dichotomy between relatively molar and relatively molecular types of inter-actions between learning and other behavioral processes may be assumed, but in point of fact we need to recognize that what is involved here, as in most other biological functions, is a continuum. It should be recognized, also, that research on various facets of these interactions can proceed at any level of complexity, or molarity. Nevertheless, it is probably true that the most effective relationships, caus-

ally, are those at the more molecular level of analysis. If this is so, then this level of analysis must be vigorously researched. The products of recent neurophysiological research, summarized in Part VI, provide effective testimony as to the promise of this kind of molecular approach. It is particularly important that the student recognize the significance of such research, and the danger of neglecting it, because he is much less likely to neglect the more molar level of analysis which is so much closer to his normal everyday interests.

This prefatory statement has deliberately been kept simple and general. Pursuance of more detailed questions would rather quick-ly lead us to problems of definition and theory—which are intensively covered in the *Learning: Theories* volume of this set and need not be duplicated here. The detailed treatments that compose the pres-ent volume will therefore serve to fill out this sketchy outline of the role of learning interactions in behavior.

M. H. M.

Contents

Learning:

Interactions

Interactions with Motivation

Robert C. Bolles

University of Washington

Introduction: Learning and Motivation[1]

It is possible to conceive of many ways in which the processes involved in motivation and those involved in learning might interact with each other. At one extreme we might suppose that the various phenomena that are ordinarily regarded as motivation are in reality all based upon learning processes. That is, it is possible to dismiss all our present *concepts* of motivation and to account for the *facts* of motivation in terms of already familiar principles of learning. At the other extreme we might invert the process and attribute little or no role to what are customarily thought to be learning processes and account for all learning phenomena in terms of our familiar concepts of motivation. We will see in what follows that both these logical possibilities actually offer considerable attraction. But most behavior theorists appear to favor some middle ground between these extreme positions and prefer to explain behavior by invoking both motivational and learning concepts. As we proceed, two questions should be kept in mind. One is the extent to which the phenomena of learning may be logically and perhaps more profitably construed or interpreted or translated into motivational concepts, and the second is

the extent to which the phenomena we ordinarily think of as being motivation can reasonably and profitably be reduced to those concepts which we already use in explaining the phenomena of learning.

Historical Background

Some of the relationships between motivation and learning are rather intricate, and it probably will be helpful to begin by gaining a little historical perspective. In the early days of behavior theory (approximately through the late 1930's) the most dominant and powerful theoretical statements were those based on the principles of classical conditioning, for example, Watson (1919), Smith and Guthrie (1921), and Hull (1930). In all these early theoretical statements the emphasis was almost entirely on learning, and relatively little attention was paid to motivation. Part of this neglect was due to the fact that relatively little was known about the many motivation effects that seem important to us today; little was known about deprivation conditions or about the effects of the quality or quantity of food the animal receives in the goal box. The acquisition of new responses was a

[1] Supported by research grant GB-5694 from the National Science Foundation.

much older historical problem, and accordingly, it received greater attention. Another reason for the neglect of the motivation area was that much of what was known about motivation was interpreted in a way which did not require the introduction of new principles. For example, the stimuli arising from deprivation (such as stomach contractions or hunger pangs) were assumed to be just like the stimuli arising from the external environment. That is to say, hunger, thirst, and sexual excitement were all regarded as being no more than characteristic stimulus conditions to which appropriate adaptive behavior might become conditioned. Thus if the hungry rat explores its environment and seeks food, it is merely because such exploratory and food-seeking behaviors have become conditioned to the stimuli arising from the hunger state. Such conditioning was assumed to be in no way different from the conditioning, for example, of a left-turn response in a maze to the stimulus configuration present at the choice point; the same principles of classical or Pavlovian conditioning were assumed to apply. We shall see a little later that this position (which involves essentially a denial of the concept of motivation) is still defended today by such able theorists as Estes (1958).

Classical conditioning provided the dominant theoretical base for learning theory during the 1920's and 1930's, but its supremacy was by no means unchallenged by other theoretical positions. Thorndike's account of trial-and-error learning, based on his famous "law of effect" (Thorndike, 1911), provided one important challenge. However, it was characteristic of Thorndike that although he had a great deal to say about motivation and stressed concepts such as "set," "want," and "interest," the motivational aspects of his theory always played a secondary role to the laws of learning themselves. So although Thorndike differed in many important ways from Pavlov in regard to the nature of learning, and particularly the hypothesized mecha-

nisms involved, the two theorists had relatively similar and extreme solutions to the learning-motivation interaction problem: Motivation was assumed to be of minor importance.

Early in the present century there was a diverse group of theorists who shared very little in their views about the mechanisms of learning, but did share a common faith that motivation was of the utmost importance in the explanation of human and animal behavior. Freud is a good example of this point of view. For Freud the all-important aspects of the human personality were motivational; learning and, indeed, all the psychological activities of the individual, such as perception and memory, occurred in the service of the individual's motives. We need not consider here the details of Freud's theory of personality organization, or how he conceptualized the basic motives of the individual; it is sufficient to emphasize that he regarded motives as coming first. Freud indicated the importance of motivation in *The Interpretation of Dreams* (1900). This early date marks Freud as our first motivation theorist. It cannot detract from Freud's historical significance that his work was restricted to a rather special realm of psychological problems and lacked scientific rigor; his ideas have had enormous impact. Two of these ideas in particular have provided a background for all subsequent theorizing about motivation. One is that all behavior, even apparently meaningless behavior such as dreams and slips of the tongue, has a determinant cause, and the other is that these psychological causes are motivational, acting like physical forces in producing their effects.

A typical Freudian explanation would postulate some basic source of motivational energy, such as a sexual impulse or a feeling of guilt which had to express itself, and then proceed to show how the individual's behavior, perception, and personality became altered through experience so that the original sexual impulse could be expressed in a disguised form or the guilt feeling could either be covered over (repressed) or expressed in some acceptable manner. In all cases, Freud assumed, the unacceptable impulses or feelings are disguised or distorted in a way that makes their expression acceptable to the individual and to those around him. Any successful adjustment is likely to be learned with experience and to become a relatively fixed pattern of expression. If such patterns became too fixed, too inflexible, then the structure of the personality and the individual's behavior might lose the adaptive advantage that they once had, and the result could be a fixation, a neurosis, or a general inability to deal with contemporary problems. The important point is that at a time when few behavior theorists were speaking about motivation, Freud and his followers were expressing an altogether different picture of the learning-motivation interaction: Motivation was all important, and learning occurred primarily to solve the individual's motivational problem.

Other early theorists who emphasized the importance of motivation, particularly in humans, are McDougall (1908), Lewin (1922), and Tolman (1932). It was Tolman who was primarily responsible for getting motivational phenomena into the laboratory.

To summarize this historical outline, we may note that by the end of the 1930's two types of interaction between the processes of learning and those of motivation had been recognized. On the one hand, there were theorists who discounted the importance of motivational phenomena as such, and who either followed Pavlov in ignoring motivational problems altogether or followed Guthrie in seeking to explain the apparent motivation of behavior in terms of ordinary conditioning processes.

By the end of the 1930's several events conspired to show that some alternative position regarding learning and motivation was needed. This need was met by Clark L. Hull and his students. Their views soon came to dominate behavior theory in much the same way that those of Pavlov and his followers had just previously. Hull was the first theorist to attribute anything approaching equal importance to motivation and learning; both were essential components of his theory of behavior.

Certainly one of the reasons Hull shifted from classical conditioning theory to his own type of behavior theory was the evident failure of the former to account for a variety of learning phenomena, especially those in which an important role for motivation was indicated. For example, it had become apparent (Brogden, Lipman, and Culler, 1938; Mowrer and Lamoreaux, 1942) that Pavlovian conditioning principles were quite unable to explain the acquisition of avoidance behavior. It was also evident by this time (Finch, 1938) that salivary conditioning in the dog, the simplest Pavlovian procedure, was successful only if the dog was hungry. This fact was undoubtedly known to Pavlov, but he evidently attached no particular significance to it.

What we find in these two examples is not only that it is necessary for the animal to be appropriately motivated, by fear on the one hand and hunger on the other, but that the motivation condition is part and parcel of the learning. Without the motivation there is no learning, and what the animal learns, as Freud had indicated, is some means of dealing with its specific motivational state. Hull's pivotal position in the history of these problems is indicated by the fact that he himself was originally a conditioning theorist and at first attached very little importance to motivational concepts, treating them in almost precisely the same way that Pavlov had (Hull, 1930, 1931). But then in the span of a few years Hull introduced not just one but two important motivational concepts, drive (D) and incentive (K). Because the conceptual properties of D and K are quite different, and because their relationship to other processes involved in learning are quite different, we will take them up separately, drive first.

Hull's Drive Concept

The theoretical construct of drive (D) grew out of a pair of experiments conducted by Perin (1942) and Williams (1938). The results of these experiments gave form to the motivation-learning interaction in Hull's behavior theory, so it will pay us to look at them in a little detail. Williams trained four groups of rats to press a bar to obtain food. The different groups were given different numbers of reinforcements ranging from five to ninety. All Ss were trained under 22 hrs. of food deprivation and when the response had received the specified number of reinforcements, extinction was begun, also under 22 hrs. of food deprivation. The extinction results are shown in the upper curve in Figure 1-1. Perin's study was very similar: several groups of animals were extinguished after

receiving different numbers of reinforcements for the identical response, and were trained under 22 hrs. of food deprivation. The crucial difference was that extinction was carried out under 3 hrs. of deprivation. The extinction results are given in the lower curve of Figure 1-1.

There are two features of these curves that should be noted. One is the regular increase in resistance to extinction with increasing number of reinforcements. The inference Hull drew from this was that the strength of the underlying habit was a continuously increasing function of the number of reinforcements. This change in habit was presumed to reflect a permanent change in the organism's nervous system and to be independent of the transient state of deprivation. The second important feature of the Perin-Williams data is that the strength of motivation (hours of deprivation) prevailing at the time of testing, during extinction in this case, does have an important effect on the strength of the response, and this effect is primarily to potentiate the existing habit. Hull noted that strength of behavior under high and

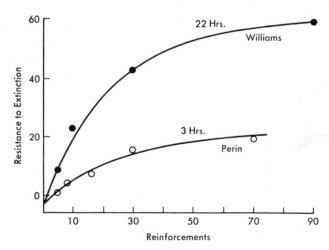

Figure 1-1. The data of Perin and Williams showing how resistance to extinction depends upon both deprivation conditions (D) and the number of reinforcements (S^{H}R). (Adapted with permission from Perin, C. T. Behavioral potentiality as a joint function of the amount of training and the degree of hunger at the time of extinction. *J. exp. Psychol.*, 1942, **30,** 93–113.)

under low motivation maintains an approximately constant proportion, and accordingly, he asserted that the permanent habit factor and the momentary motivational factor combined multiplicatively to determine the strength of the observed response.

On the question of the interaction between learning and motivation, Hull's tentative solution was a very simple and elegant one; drive and habit are independent. Although the strength of drive determines the level of overt performance, it does not affect the rate or rapidity with which the habit is acquired—the latter is only a function of the number of reinforcements. The speed with which a habit is built up is a function of the number of reinforcements only and does not depend on the animal's motivation.

There are two other ways in which the concepts of drive and habit are interrelated in Hull's (1943) theory of behavior. For one, Hull had abandoned by this time his earlier reliance on Pavlovian principles for providing a sufficient account of learning. And, in particular, he had abandoned the idea that a response became associated with a stimulus simply by contiguity. Instead he postulated, as Thorndike had before him, that there was a special class of events, reinforcers, which were necessary to produce learning. More specifically, he postulated that reinforcement would occur whenever there was a reduction in drive. Thus Hull had accomplished in one brilliant stroke a synthesis of conditioning principles with the view of the earlier motivation theorists that the acquisition of adaptive behavior allowed an animal to solve its motivation problems. For example, if an organism's immediate problem was a food deficit, then any response that the animal made which led to food, to eating, and to a subsequent reduction in drive would be more likely to recur when that situation arose again. Therefore it could be said that, at least in one sense, the animal learns in order to solve its motivational problems. But, on the other hand,

the mechanism whereby this came about was not in itself motivational. The animal does not "seek" a solution to its problems; rather, adaptation was made an intrinsic part of the learning process.

The final feature of Hull's drive theory which we must note because it bears on the question of the relationship between learning and motivation is his assumption that all the directionality of behavior was determined by the habit component and that the drive component acted merely as a numerical multiplier (what a mathematician would call a scalar). Drive could multiply the strength of the directed habit vector but did not itself affect the direction of behavior. Thus, rather than speaking of the animal as being hungry or thirsty or motivated in some other way, the Hullian speaks of the animal as being food-deprived or water-deprived, and thinks of this condition as acting as a *source* of drive, which facilitates or energizes whatever behavior is most likely to occur in a given situation. Prior to learning, the behavior may or may not be relevant to the motivating condition. Drive, D, is a general, nondirectional, nonspecific motivator.

In the quarter century since Hull wrote *Principles of Behavior* (1943) it has become increasingly clear that his $D \times H$ formula is too restrictive. The directionality of the animal's motivation in a given situation appears to be acquired too rapidly, more rapidly than the instrumental behavior. It is also clear that a great deal of animal motivation and probably most of human motivation involves goals that are of little biological significance. It has also become apparent that in many instances an organism's motivation changes over a series of trials as a consequence of encountering the goal object. And certainly there is an important sense in which man, and even lower animals, can anticipate the nature, quality, and quantity of goal objects. Thus it appears necessary to supplement the generalized motivator D with, or to substitute for it, a more specific motivating factor, incentive. This factor can be assumed to be a learned source of motivation, dependent on the specific nature of the goal object and the animal's previous experience with it, thus accounting for our impression that an animal can anticipate a goal object.

Hull's Incentive Concept

In a remarkable series of theoretical papers written during the 1930's, Hull postulated a simple S-R mechanism with the desired functional properties of an incentive motivator. For reasons not entirely clear, relatively little use was made of this incentive motivation principle until many years later. Hull himself did not give it prominence until 1952. However, it has gradually superseded the drive concept in importance. Part of the reason for its recent popularity is that as experimental findings related to the drive concept accumulated, it became apparent that many of the motivational functions originally attributed to drive could be explained better in terms of incentive motivation. At the same time, a variety of other phenomena were discovered which at the outset urgently called for an incentive-motivation interpretation. Let us consider how Hull's assumed incentive-motivation factor was supposed to work.

Hull (1930, 1931) proposed that in any instrumental learning situation the final response, the one that terminates behavior in the situation, is generally some sort of consummatory response or goal response, R_G. After a number of trials R_G should become conditioned to the environmental stimuli present at the goal so that, for example, the animal should be more likely to eat in a goal box where he has eaten before than in a novel situation. After R_G has become conditioned to stimuli in the goal box, it will tend to be elicited by all those stimuli in the experimental situation that are similar to those that exist at the

goal box. Now, ordinarily, the consummatory response will not be able to occur anywhere except in the goal box because food is not present elsewhere. But we may hypothesize that certain fractional parts of the consummatory response, such as salivation and small mouth movements, can occur and will occur anywhere in the experimental situation where there are stimuli similar to those that exist at the goal. This fractional, conditionable part of R_G may be designated r_G.

A simple illustration of this mechanism in operation is an animal learning to turn left in a T-maze to obtain food. After the animal has gone to the left, R_G will become conditioned to the stimuli that are characteristic of the left goal box plus the characteristic extramaze cues in that area. On a subsequent trial, when the animal is at the choice point and hesitantly looks to the left and to the right, the stimuli which it can see to the left are more likely to be like those in the left goal box, hence more likely to evoke r_G and therefore more likely to motivate an approach response.

There is a rather delicate point here which we have to treat with some care. It was said that the occurrence of r_G "motivates" the animal to approach. Some theorists (for example, Mowrer, 1960) have said that if these anticipatory reactions have been associated in the past with pleasurable events, then they themselves become pleasurable and the organism will tend on that account to preserve them. In the T-maze the animal can preserve r_G by approaching the stimuli that evoke it. Such stimuli are said by Mowrer to produce a positive emotion which he calls "hope," and he postulates that hope motivates whatever response the animals makes or may be starting to make. Mowrer therefore has an incentive theory of motivation which not only incorporates a motivational principle, but also, as we shall see later, places almost the entire burden of explaining behavior upon such incentive factors and the emotions associated with them. Mowrer thus solves the motivation-learning interaction question by putting virtually the entire explanatory burden upon his motivational concepts and attaching relatively little importance to learning principles.

On the other hand, we may conceive of the incentive phenomenon in stimulus-response terms without invoking any concept of motivation. When Hull first proposed the r_G mechanism, he conceived of it purely in conditioning terms. The r_G was a response which was conditionable, just as any overt response might be, and the proprioceptive feedback from r_G (designated s_G) was assumed to play a role essentially like that of any other stimulus in the situation. The stimuli that evoke r_G are more like those in the presence of which approach behavior is reinforced than those that occur on the other side of the choice point; hence the approach response will become more strongly conditioned to them. This purely associative interpretation of the incentive mechanism once again offers an extreme solution to the interaction problem by reducing all motivational phenomena and hypothesized mechanisms to basic stimulus-response principles and to the laws of learning. However, we shall see in Chapter 3 that a number of behavioral findings make it at least plausible to attribute a motivational function to the r_G mechanism. And, indeed, this is what the majority of theorists who have worked with it have assumed.

Whether we think of incentive mechanisms as motivational, or as having only associative effects on instrumental behavior, it is clear that incentive effects depend on learning. The animal must have made the consummatory response, and must have made a particular consummatory response, for a particular r_G to occur in the situation. Hence, before the hypothetical r_G-s_G motivation mechanism can become operative, it is necessary for the animal to have had at least one previous trial. Most often (as we shall see in Chapter 3) the effect of suddenly changing the conditions of reinforcement is

to produce fairly rapid alterations in behavior. This behavioral adjustment is evidently learned too; it usually takes a few trials—more than one, but fewer trials than are generally required for the acquisition of an instrumental response.

Hull's Secondary-Reinforcement Concept

There is another intimate interaction, involving r_G, between Hull's incentive-motivation factor and learning. The occurrence of r_G, in addition to supplying incentive motivation for an instrumental act, also provides, according to Hull (1952) and Spence (1951), secondary reinforcement. Because r_G immediately precedes primary reinforcement, its occurrence (or, actually, the occurrence of s_G) should be a secondary reinforcer. Consider again the animal that runs to the choice point in a T-maze and looks to the left where it encounters stimuli similar to those existing in the left-hand goal box where it has previously eaten. The occurrence of r_G at the choice point actively reinforces the preceding response, running down the stem of the T-maze. On a subsequent trial we may expect still more vigorous r_G's so that not only will the animal be more likely to turn to the left and run into the left goal box, but also it should run faster down the stem of the T-maze because it has received secondary reinforcement on the previous trials for doing so. The whole sequence of behavior will be tightly integrated by the combined action of enhanced motivation for ongoing behavior and reinforcement of the preceding behaviors.

There are some puzzling features of this analysis. For one thing, we may wonder how it is possible that the occurrence of r_G (or its stimulus consequence, s_G) can be both reinforcing and motivating at the same time. There is a more serious difficulty, however. We may wonder whether there is not some redundancy in the analysis. If we grant that the sudden elicitation of r_G is in fact reinforcing, then we may question the necessity of postulating that it is also motivating. Having postulated r_G, a partial occurrence of R_G, at the choice point, and then the full realization of R_G in the left-hand goal box, can we not account purely on the basis of reinforcement not only for the acquisition of left turning, but also for the integration of the whole response chain? In other words, if we analyze in sufficient detail the sources of reinforcement for the various elements of the response chain, is it necessary to add any motivational concepts to the analysis in order to explain the phenomenon? On the other hand, if we have such a sufficiently flexible and learning-dependent motivational factor as the Hull-Spence incentive motivator, is it necessary to invoke the secondary-reinforcement concept, or indeed, any reinforcement concept to explain the acquisition of the behavior? Specifically, if we think of the animal as having a little incentive motivation as it runs down the stem, somewhat more as it turns to the left and runs in that direction, and a great deal of incentive motivation as it enters the goal box and approaches the food, is it then necessary to talk about the reinforcement of these different responses in the chain?

One leading theorist (Mowrer, 1960) has contended that reinforcement is a superfluous concept as it is ordinarily invoked, and that what appears to be the learning of instrumental behavior can be explained on the basis of motivational factors. Mowrer has observed that most of the responses that we end up "teaching" an animal in learning experiments are already quite strong in its repertoire, and that what we are really teaching the animal is better thought of as emotions, that is, theoretical constructs such as hopes and fears which are like incentives in that they facilitate all concurrent behavior. Mowrer contends that we do not teach the rat to press the bar; it already knows how. What we teach the rat is to *want* to press the bar.

The opposite point of view, the position that we do not need a concept of motivation if we are willing to consider in sufficient detail the various sources of reinforcement, especially secondary reinforcement, that prevail in the situation, has been most ably defended by Skinner and his followers. Indeed, Skinnerian psychologists have relatively little use for any motivational concept. The function of depriving an animal of food is not to make him hungry or to make food an incentive, but simply to make food a reinforcer. When an animal is hungry—that is, when food is a reinforcer—we can reinforce eating, or an approach to food, or any instrumental response upon which the presentation of food is made contingent. By introducing stimulus changes between different responses, we can build a chain of behavior, because each of the stimulus changes will rapidly come to acquire secondary reinforcing value of its own. Again we can account for the tight integration of a chain of behavior and we can account for virtually all the simpler phenomena that have traditionally been explained in terms of either drive principles or incentive principles.

In Chapter 4 we will consider some other instances of motivated behavior that raise a number of theoretical questions. For example, what happens when reinforcement is suddenly withheld? Is the resulting alteration of behavior just a new facet of incentive motivation; does it represent the limiting case of a small amount of reinforcement or the limiting case of long-delayed reinforcement? Or does it introduce a new class of events based on some frustration mechanism? Although earlier theorists treated frustration as though it were simply another source of drive, like food or water deprivation, now there appears to be sufficient similarity between frustration and incentive motivation that it seems fruitful to introduce a hypothetical mechanism, r_F, analogous to r_G, to explain frustration phenomena (Amsel, 1958).

We shall also consider in Chapter 4 the case of aversive motivation and discuss some possible negative incentive factors which are analogous to r_G and r_F. Relatively little theoretical work has been done on this problem, but we shall consider whether it may be profitable to think of a negative emotional factor, r_E, which may be thought of as an anticipatory escape response. The r_E symbol has already been introduced by Spence (1958) and others to symbolize fear, but fear has almost invariably been conceptualized as a source of drive. We will see in Chapter 4 that fear too may be more profitably reconceptualized as an anticipatory response, a kind of negative incentive.

But before we come to these relatively new developments we must examine in the next two chapters what is now known about drive and what is now known about incentive motivation.

2

Drive:
Motivation Independent
of Learning

Since 1943, when Hull proposed his solution to the drive-habit problem, a great deal of work has been carried out to test it, and it is now possible to come to some relatively certain conclusions regarding the validity of Hull's formulation. Let us consider some of this evidence briefly, and let us begin by considering some of the studies that have been addressed specifically to the question of whether drive and habit really are independent.

The Independence of Drive and Habit

Davenport (1965) has recently described an extensive systematic analysis of learning curves of rats under 3, 22, or 42 hrs. of food deprivation. He fitted learning curves of the mathematical form required by Hull's theory to the trial-by-trial performance of individual animals and found, just as Perin and Williams had before, that whereas deprivation time determined the level of performance ultimately achieved by the animals, it had no effect upon the rate at which the animals approached their asymptotic performance levels. Other in-

vestigators working with other response measures and with different kinds of learning situations have generally found the same pattern of results, which suggests rather convincingly that if we look just at learning curves, we will find that drive and habit are independent in the way that Hull had first proposed on the basis of the Perin-Williams data.

There is a second class of experiments which bears upon the same theoretical question. In these studies the typical procedure is to train two groups of Ss, one under high deprivation conditions and one under low deprivation conditions. Then, when the behavior has become established, extinction is begun. Each group is split in extinction, half being extinguished under the same conditions as in acquisition while the other half is extinguished under the other conditions. Presumably if the animal's motivation during acquisition affects the strength of the habit, then there should be some asymmetry in performance during extinction. Unfortunately for Hull's assumption of independence, various types of asymmetrical pattern have frequently been reported. Asymmetrical results, or carry-over effects, have been the rule, particularly where the speed of a running response has been investigated. Typical results are those of Barry (1958), shown in Figure 2-1.

It has been suggested that one factor here is that whereas animals may acquire habits at the same rate under high and under low deprivation conditions, it is quite likely that somewhat different habits are acquired. More precisely, it seems probable that animals trained under high deprivation conditions learn to run, to move rapidly and vigorously, whereas animals trained under low deprivation learn to proceed down the alley at a leisurely pace. Then when extinction begins under the altered deprivation conditions, an animal will tend to carry into the extinction period of the experiment the particular habits which it had previously learned in the situation (see Figure 2-1). In short there seems to be a carryover attributable indirectly to the different prior deprivation conditions. To the extent that this is true, it is no longer possible to say that what the animal learns is independent of his state of deprivation at the time he learns it. And to this extent there is a very real and probably complicated interaction between motivation and learning rather than the simple picture of independence which Hull proposed.

In conclusion, the direct attempts to assess the independence of learning and motivation within the framework of Hull's theory lead us to two conclusions. One is that the rate of learning is independent of deprivation conditions, but the second conclusion is that animals under different deprivation conditions are likely to learn somewhat different responses. Thus, Hull's simple multiplicative D × H equation does not appear to be valid.

The Energizing Function of Drive

Instrumental Behavior. There is now an overwhelming mass of evidence to indicate that the probability and the vigor of an instrumental response increase as the severity of the relevant deprivation condition is increased. At least this much of Hull's multiplicative equation appears to hold true. It seems to make relatively little

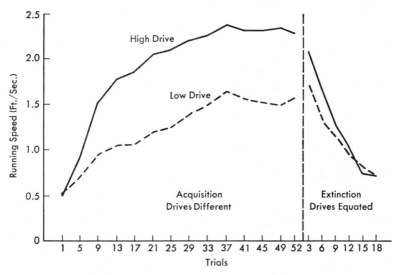

Figure 2-1.   Runway performance in acquisition and extinction as a function of the deprivation conditions in acquisition. (Reprinted with permission from Barry, H., Effects of strength of drive on learning and on extinction. *J. exp. Psychol.*, 1958, **55**, 473–481.)

difference whether we measure the latency of an instrumental response, its resistance to extinction, or the force with which it is executed; in each case we appear to find a direct relationship between the severity of deprivation and the strength of the instrumental response. The same pattern is found with hungry and thirsty animals and with those escaping from electric shock (Trapold and Fowler, 1960).

One limitation to this conclusion has to be noted, however. The energization of behavior best mirrors the severity of the deprivation conditions in simple situations in which only one response, such as running down an alley or pressing a bar, is involved. As soon as the situation is made more complicated so that we are concerned with the relative performance of two or more well-learned responses, such as turning left and turning right in a T-maze or approaching black and white doors in a discrimination problem, then the effects of deprivation conditions become harder to predict. Spence (1956) and others who have defended the Hullian drive concept have pointed out that in these more complicated situations there is competition between the correct and the incorrect responses, so that the expected effect of increasing drive should depend on the relative strength of the two habits. For example, suppose that the habit of the correct response is the strongest one in the animal's repertoire and the animal is successfully making the required discrimination. Then, because drive is supposed to multiply all existing habits indiscriminately, increasing deprivation should give the correct response a greater advantage than it previously had over the incorrect response. As a result, discrimination performance should improve with increasing deprivation. On the other hand, if the animal is performing at or near a chance level, implying that the habit of the correct response is not the strongest one, then an increase in deprivation may lead to decrements in discrimination performance, or to no difference at all.

This prediction from Hull's theory has not always been supported by experimental findings, however. Indeed, it is possible to find in the literature almost any kind of deprivation effect one might imagine in complicated learning situations. Unfortunately, these failures of the Hullian D × H model to predict the facts of behavior have led to few alternative formulations. Logan (1960) has sought to retain the basic D × H equation by reconceptualizing Hull's concept of habit. For Logan, different vigors of responding represent separate habits. Thus, the animal that is trained under severe deprivation conditions and runs quickly is said to have acquired a different habit from one trained under low-severity conditions that runs slowly. The picture is complicated somewhat by the fact that as the animal runs a series of trials, its speed or vigor of responding is likely to vary from one trial to the next, so that we have to conceive of the animal acquiring not a single habit but a whole group of habits, which may have different strengths if they have received different numbers of reinforcements. It is also worth pointing out, to anticipate some arguments we shall come to shortly, that the burden of explaining motivational effects in Logan's theory lies not so much upon the drive concept as upon the concept of incentive. So although Logan's neo-Hullian theory might be thought of as bolstering the somewhat strained energization hypothesis, it actually lends more support to alternative formulations, specifically, those couched in terms of an incentive concept.

An Associative Account of Energization. There is another interpretation of energization which is built not on these failures of Hull's scheme to explain the data, but on a consideration of those situations where Hull's formula seems to work best. The basic idea, originally stated by Guthrie (1935) and others in terms of classical conditioning principles, has been given its most recent and sophisticated treatment by Estes (1958, 1961). Estes' argument is this:

We may suppose that accompanying any given deprivation state there will be certain characteristic internal stimuli and that as the deprivation conditions become more severe, these "deprivation stimuli" will become a more prominent part of the total stimulus situation. (They will be, as Estes describes it, more likely to be "sampled.") If we assume further that an animal learns certain instrumental responses in the presence of these stimuli, such as pressing a bar or running down an alley for food, then the prevailing deprivation stimuli should acquire some associative control over the instrumental response in question. Following such an experience, or a number of such experiences, we may expect deprivation to produce all those responses that in the past have led to food (including, perhaps, some very general response tendencies, such as merely being active). If animals are trained under more severe deprivation conditions, the probability of the response should increase correspondingly as the deprivation stimuli become an ever-larger portion of the total stimulus pattern. Estes' proposed mechanism readily accounts for the fact that the probability of an instrumental response increases (or, what amounts to the same thing, the latency decreases) with deprivation.

This treatment of the energization problem has been extended by the introduction of what Estes calls "satiation stimuli," which have the property that responses become conditioned to them which are generally incompatible with most instrumental behavior. Such responses might include lying down, resting, and grooming. Thus, when there is a reduction in severity of deprivation conditions, we are able to predict with Estes' model that the animal's behavior should show a corresponding drop in performance. It should be emphasized that Estes' solution to the learning versus motivation problem is conceptually very simple; like Guthrie before him, he simply contends that what we have come to call motivation can be accounted for by already established principles of learning.

Although Estes' solution to the learning-motivation problem can probably be defended as well as any other solution now available to us, we may note that there are at least two serious difficulties with it. It is designed principally to explain the effect of deprivation conditions on the *probability* of an instrumental response, because the chief explanatory principle in Estes' system is the probability that certain stimuli, including deprivation and satiation stimuli, will be sampled by the organism. It is difficult to see how this model can account for the differences in the vigor, strength, or speed of instrumental responses that are now known to depend on deprivation conditions. Very hungry rats are not only more likely to go down an alley for food than less hungry ones, they are also likely to run more energetically (Cicala, 1961). The second difficulty with Estes' model is that too much of a burden is put on deprivation produced stimuli, especially in view of the fact that the experiments specifically designed to look for such stimuli have failed to find them. We shall examine some of these studies shortly and discover that the great bulk of the evidence seems to require an incentive motivation explanation rather than one couched in terms of deprivation- and satiation-produced stimuli.

General Activity. The brilliance of Hull's D × H formulation was that it tied together in a simple, systematic way a variety of motivation phenomena which had previously been very difficult to relate. One phenomenon which had been known from the very earliest days of animal research was that if animals are confined to activity wheels, their spontaneous running in the wheels increases as the severity of deprivation increases. Here we have a case of an apparent energization of behavior in the absence of any apparent relevance of the behavior to either the deprivation conditions or the reinforcement conditions. That is, it is not apparent how running in the wheel could be a learned response which would increase in probability as deprivation became more severe. Earlier theorists were reduced to making statements such as "where the deprived animal has no direct access to food, it engages in restless, food-seeking behavior."

Hull's drive theory can make sense of this phenomenon if we regard running as one of the animal's more probable responses when it lives in the wheel. Increasing deprivation should increase D and should therefore increase the strength of this highly probable response. The idea that running in a wheel is an aimless, pointless, apparently random kind of activity is entirely consistent with Hull's postulation of a general nondirective multiplier of the strength of ongoing behavior.

In the last few years, however, a variety of evidence has come forth which indicates that running in activity wheels is not unrelated to reinforcement. For example, Finger, Reid, and Weasner (1957) have shown that if animals are confined to a separate box for 1 hr. after coming out of activity wheels before they are given their daily food, they run significantly less than control animals that are fed, as usual, in the wheels. Finger et al. argue that if the animals would happen to run just prior to the regular feeding time, then when this activity was followed by feeding, the tendency to run would be reinforced. If this happens, and the Finger et al. data indicate that it does, we cannot regard running in an activity wheel as general activity in the sense of being unrelated to reinforcement; indeed it begins to appear to be a kind of instrumental food-getting behavior even though the contingency between the response and reinforcement is neither arranged nor intended by E.

In a follow-up study (Finger et al., 1960) animals were maintained under 3-hr. food deprivation conditions, and, as before, the animals in the control groups were fed immediately after having been in the wheels, whereas animals in the experimental groups were removed from the wheels, put in a waiting box for 1 hr., and then fed. Under these conditions the experimental group showed no increase in activity over successive test days, but the control group in which there could arise a contingency between running and eating did show a sizable increase in running behavior. The purpose of this study was to determine whether deprivation periods so short that they ordinarily produce no increase in activity could provide the basis for reinforcement by feeding. They evidently could. Note too the implication that putting animals in activity wheels to "become adapted" to the wheels will not prevent the activity-feeding pattern from developing, because even if food is constantly available they are sure to incur voluntary 3-hr. deprivations, and such deprivations now seem to be sufficient for the reinforcement of wheel running.

There remains the question of whether in addition to this reinforcement aspect of general activity there may also be a motivational aspect which is still consistent with the traditional view of generalized activation. It has been found that deprivation produces a pronounced increase in running even under circumstances where the animal is never fed in the wheel but simply confined there for perhaps a day after the deprivation has been imposed (Duda and Bolles, 1963). It seems that in the absence of any opportunity for reinforcement by food, the activity of the animal is directly correlated with weight loss and independent of how (that is, on what kind of a deprivation schedule) the weight was lost (Duda and Bolles, 1963; Finger, 1965; Treichler and Collins, 1965). One possibility that should not just be dismissed is that running in wheels is reinforcing in its own right and that it becomes more reinforcing for the rat as its deprivation becomes more severe. It has also been suggested that this is the case for the reinforcing effect of stimulus change (Tapp and Simpson, 1966).

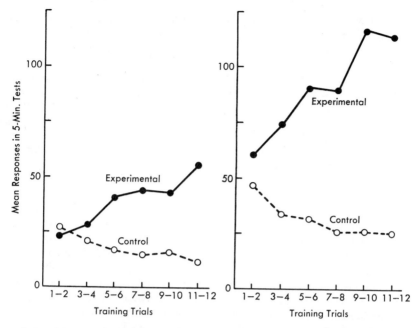

Figure 2-2.   Changes in spontaneous activity during a 5-min. change in stimulation (left side: quiet, light; right side: noise, dark) that regularly preceded feeding (experimental groups) or that was uncorrelated with feeding (control groups). (Reprinted with permission from Sheffield, F. D., and Campbell, B. A. The role of experience in the "spontaneous" activity of hungry rats. *J. comp. physiol. Psychol.*, 1954, **47**, 97–100.)

An experiment reported by Sheffield and Campbell (1954) has had an important effect on our thinking about general activity. Their Ss were tested not in the usual activity wheel, but in a "tilt cage," a cage balanced at the center so that any body movement within the cage would activate switches placed under different quadrants. The Ss were fed once a day at a fixed time, and just preceding feeding there was a 5-min. stimulus change involving both auditory and visual background stimuli. Sheffield and Campbell reported a gradual increase in activity for all Ss, but a particularly marked increase in activity in response to the 5-min. feeding signal. Control Ss showed adaptation to these same stimulus changes when they were presented randomly in time with respect to feeding (see Figure 2-2). Subsequently, it has been discovered that rats maintained in an isolated and homogeneous environment actually show a *decrease* in tilt cage activity in the absence of environmental-stimulus changes (Teghtsoonian and Campbell, 1960). It appears that the rat's activity in situations such as the tilt cage depends in large measure on some type of external stimulation and that in the absence of reinforcement by feeding, activity measured in the tilt cage is likely to decrease rather than increase during the first 72 hrs. or so of deprivation.

If these studies of hungry rats lead us to question the original conception of drive inducing increased activity levels, then the studies with other species of animals and those using other kinds of deprivation pose a still greater challenge to this traditional position (Campbell and Cicala, 1962; Campbell et al., 1966; Cornish and Mrosovsky, 1965). Moreover, experimental comparisons of different activity-measuring devices have led to a welter of conflicting results. There seems, in short, to be no generality of general activity. The original findings with hungry rats in activity wheels now appear to be limited rather specifically to hunger, to rats, and to activity wheels! Even within this much restricted domain there is still the problem of how much of the increase in activity with hunger can be attributed to purely motivational effect and how much of it to learning.

The Summation and Substitution of Different Sources of Drive

There is another implication of Hull's treatment of the general activity problem, namely, that different sources of drive, such as food deprivation and water deprivation, ought to be more or less interchangeable. For example, if a habit learned on the basis of food deprivation and food reinforcement does not depend specifically on hunger as the source of drive, it ought to be possible to satiate the animal for food and reinstate the behavior in full strength with water deprivation. The only complication here would be that the reinforcer would also have to be appropriately shifted from food to water (otherwise extinction would begin). Alternatively, it ought to be possible to extinguish the animal on a hunger-learned response while under water deprivation and obtain comparable levels of extinction performance. Both types of studies have been reported, and the results, in general, tend to support the drive-substitution hypothesis (Elliott, 1929; Teel, 1952; Webb, 1949).

Another variation of this experimental procedure would be to keep the animal hungry and use food as reinforcement but have an additional "irrelevant" source of drive, such as thirst, operating simultaneously. (The thirst is called irrelevant here because there is no water reinforcement in the test situation.) According to Hull's conception of generalized drive, the two sources of drive, one relevant and the other irrelevant, should *summate* to produce a greater response strength than obtained with just the relevant source of drive alone. Early tests of this proposal (for example, Kendler, 1945) gave some support to the drive-summation proposal, but subsequent investigations (for example, Bolles and Morlock, 1960; Levine, 1956; Siegel, 1946) have found inhibitory effects of irrelevant deprivation on instrumental responses. These inhibitory effects appear to be particularly strong in the case of irrelevant hunger and relevant thirst. It is apparent that the effects of irrelevant hunger are different from those of irrelevant thirst.

All these early studies involving the summation and substitution of hunger and thirst have been questioned on methodological grounds by Verplanck and Hayes (1953). They indicated that there is an interaction between hunger and thirst; when the rat is food-deprived, it voluntarily reduces its intake of water. It therefore becomes unclear to what extent the rat that is nominally hungry may also be thirsty. Conversely, if the rat is deprived of water, it will voluntarily reduce its food intake, again making impossible a clear separation of hunger and thirst. A further complication is that the physiological mechanisms whereby hunger and thirst interact are probably quite different when the animal is hungry and when it is thirsty. Thus, it may be that the "hungry" rat reduces its water consumption because it needs the normal amount of water only if it is required to eat the very dry food rats are usually fed. On the other hand, the "thirsty" rat may refrain from eating the normal amount because without water dry food becomes aversive. The situation is still further complicated by the findings of Cizek (1961) that food-deprived rabbits show a great increase rather than a decline in water intake. Here the interaction of hunger and thirst evidently involves still other mechanisms than those we have suggested.

Two conclusions seem clear. One is that it is extremely difficult to separate the motivational effects of food and water deprivation in either substitution or summation experiments without a better understanding of the physiological mechanisms involved in hunger and thirst. The second conclusion is that it now seems extremely hazardous to attribute a nondirective or general motivating effect to either hunger or thirst. It would seem that in both cases the motivation does have directionality. Indeed, Kendler, who was one of the first to argue in favor of summation of different sources of drive, soon came to the conclusion that the phenomena require some type of incentive interpretation, one couched in terms of r_G (Kendler, Karasik, and Schrier, 1954). Some incentive mechanism appears to be necessary to handle the active avoidance of food by thirsty animals. This is only the first of several instances we shall find where a series of studies originally undertaken with the intent of supporting the generalized-drive concept has turned out instead to provide support for an incentive-motivation concept.

There have also been a number of drive-summation studies combining an appetitive source of drive, usually hunger, with an aversive source of drive (for example, Ley, 1965). These studies have yielded inconsistent results and have, in general, failed to support the notion that unrelated sources of drive summate.

Drive-Reduction Hypothesis of Reinforcement

Perhaps the most controversial of all the attributes Hull hypothesized for D is that drive reduction constitutes reinforcement. It is clear that much of the time this hypothesis describes what we observe. Suppose, for example, we have a hungry animal. It makes a response that procures food, it eats, the hunger diminishes, and its motivation diminishes. Under these conditions we find that any instrumental response upon which obtaining the food is made contingent will be reinforced. But, of course, in this typical learning situation many observable events and many hypothetical mechanisms are confounded. We do not know whether the crucial reinforcing event is the reduction in motivation that follows ingestion (as Miller, Sampliner, and Woodrow, 1957, propose) or whether food in the stomach signals that the animal's food deficit is soon to be made up. (Note that the animal runs out of motivation, or becomes satiated, long before any substantial part of the meal can get to the body tissues and actually alleviate the physiological deficit.) Perhaps it is the act of ingestion or the taste of food in the mouth that constitutes the crucial reinforcing event.

Although there is an extensive literature on all these possibilities, we note here just one pair of studies, which are concerned with the reinforcing effects of saccharin. Sheffield and Roby (1950) and Sheffield, Roby, and Campbell (1954) have demonstrated that hungry animals will learn an instrumental response, running in an alley, in order to drink saccharin, which has no nutritive value and which should therefore not change the animal's drive state. Moreover, because the reinforcing effect of saccharin does not seem to extinguish with repeated testing, it would appear that the results of the saccharin studies cannot be explained simply on the ground that this substance is a secondary reinforcer.

Sheffield's interpretation, and indeed the usual interpretation, of this type of finding is that the source of reinforcement here is the occurrence of eating or drinking itself rather than the ultimate biological effects of these consummatory behaviors. And again it would appear that a type of experimentation designed to test an implication of Hull's drive concept has carried us away from the generalized-drive notion and toward a view that attributes a crucial role to the consummatory response.

There is also a variety of circumstances in which learning occurs, presumably through reinforcement, while nothing that can reasonably be called drive reduction is occurring. For example, there is the case of rats learning to run a T-maze to get into a part of the apparatus that they can explore (Montgomery and Segall, 1955). Premack (1962) has shown that an animal will learn an instrumental response that unlocks an activity wheel so that it can run. It defies common sense to suppose that running in the activity wheel can reduce any drive or eliminate any source of drive. Sheffield, Wulff, and Backer (1951) demonstrated that sexually naive male rats would learn to run in an alley in order to get to a receptive female. Such learning was demonstrated even under the unusual condition that ejaculation was not permitted. Again, it seems much more reasonable to suppose that drive, in the form of sexual excitement, was increasing during the course of learning rather than being reduced, yet learning occurred.

The importance of consummatory behavior, and/or the immediate stimulus consequence of consummatory behavior, is clearly shown by all these examples. It is becoming increasingly attractive to think of reinforcement in terms of R_G, and, to the extent that the animal can make some anticipatory consummatory response, to think of motivation in terms of r_g. Such an interpretation is entirely consistent with the fact that eating is ordinarily reinforcing if we are willing to assume that the ingestion of food does not eliminate or diminish the animal's motivation but, instead, produces some type of excitement, or perhaps some type of pleasurable sensation, and that it is this latter event which really constitutes reinforcement (Sheffield, 1966). Such a "drive-induction" theory of reinforcement has even been suggested by Miller (1963), who had for years attempted to defend Hull's original drive-reduction hypothesis.

Drive Discrimination

Curiously perhaps, some of the strongest evidence against the drive concept comes from those studies which have sought to demonstrate the existence of stimuli accompanying hunger and thirst, sometimes designated drive stimuli, or s_D. We may introduce this curious turn of events by considering a paradox presented by a set of four so-called drive-discrimination studies, all of which were conducted in the attempt to clarify the role of these hypothetical drive stimuli. The first of these studies, interestingly enough, was conducted by Hull himself in 1933. Hull's apparatus is shown in the upper left-hand corner of Figure 2-3. Animals were made hungry and thirsty on alternate days. When hungry, the animal was required to go to the left to the goal box to find food, and when thirsty to go in the opposite direction for water. Following an error, the animal could correct his run by going all the way back around the circle to enter the goal box from the correct side. Hull was able to obtain the discrimination, but performance on the task was relatively poor and required a great number of trials before any statistical significance was attained. Approximately 600 trials were required to get a modicum of discrimination performance. Hull must have been somewhat puzzled by the animal's poor discrimination performance, because he had asserted that these stimuli, the stimuli arising from hunger and thirst conditions, must surely be discriminable if the animal is to survive under normal circumstances. Certainly we know that animals eat when they are hungry and drink when they are thirsty and not vice versa. So part of our puzzle is that which confronted Hull: Why did his animals perform so poorly?

The next part of the puzzle is supplied by an early study by Leeper (1935), who used essentially the same procedure as Hull. He made his animals alternately hungry and thirsty, but used a different-shaped appara-

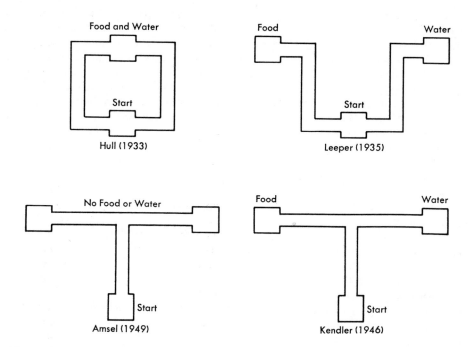

Figure 2-3.   Schematic diagram of apparatus used in four drive discrimination experiments.

tus, shown in the upper right-hand corner of Figure 2-3. Leeper argued that of course the animals had no trouble in discriminating hunger from thirst but had been confused in Hull's study about the location of food and water because they were to be found in the same location on alternate days. Leeper therefore merely "unfolded" the apparatus so that food and water would be located in different places. Although Leeper's explanation of his own success is not entirely convincing, he was able to get much faster discrimination learning than Hull had obtained. Within thirty-five trials the animals were performing quite accurately. In other words, in Leeper's experiment the discrimination was a very easy one for the animals to learn.

Our understanding of the drive-discrimination situation was not improved for several years until Kendler (1946) introduced a new variation of the Hull-Leeper procedure. Kendler's Ss were run in a simple T-maze, shown in the lower right-hand part of Figure 2-3, but were required to perform under the following unusual conditions. They were trained both hungry and thirsty at all times. On alternate days S was forced by a barrier at the choice point to one side where, both hungry and thirsty, it found water and drank. On the other days it was forced to the opposite side where, still both hungry and thirsty, it ate. After only twenty-eight trials Kendler introduced the crucial test condition; he made half of the Ss hungry and half of them thirsty. On a free choice the overwhelming majority chose the appropriate side. Here, again, we have a very easy discrimination, as common sense would predict, but our paradox deepens: In view of the fact that Kendler's Ss were both hungry and thirsty on all training trials, how can we account for the attachment of the different drive stimuli to the appropriate turning responses? To pose the puzzle concretely, imagine that on a given day when S is both hungry and thirsty, so that presumably the stimuli arising from both hunger and thirst are present, the animal turns left and eats. What is to prevent the left-turn response from being equally conditioned to both the s_D for hunger and the s_D for thirst? In spite of the apparent impossibility of the problem, the discrimination was actually a quite simple one to learn.

To complete our puzzle we must consider a study reported by Amsel (1949). Amsel argued that if there are stimuli arising from hunger and thirst, it ought to be possible differentially to attach different responses to them, as previous investigators had tried to do, but without the complication of S eating or drinking in the test situation. He arranged this by using an escape situation in which both hunger and thirst were irrelevant as far as reinforcement was concerned, but in which S was required to turn in one direction on days when it was hungry and in another direction on days when it was thirsty. Then Ss were trained alternately hungry and thirsty. Amsel's apparatus is shown in the lower left-hand corner of Figure 2-3. Amsel's Ss did ultimately learn, but it was, like Hull's problem, extremely difficult. Hundreds of trials were required and even then only a moderate level of discrimination performance was attained. Other investigators using procedures similar to Amsel's have likewise obtained only a very low order of discrimination performance (for example, Bailey, 1955; Levine, 1953).

Our puzzle is complete and the paradox it presents is this: All four of these illustrative experiments ought to have obtained comparable results because all were looking for the same thing, all imposed similar motivation conditions on their animals; yet in two cases we have extremely difficult discrimination problems and in two cases we have very easy, almost trivial, discrimination problems. What is it about the pattern of experimental procedures that

distinguishes between the easy problems and the hard ones? One possible answer is that in the easy discriminations eating and drinking occurred in goal boxes that were spatially separated, whereas in the difficult problems there either was no conditioning of the consummatory response (in Amsel's study) or the different consummatory behaviors occurred in the same environmental situation. In other words, it appears that what is important for easy drive discrimination is the opportunity for the different consummatory responses to become conditioned to different intra- and extramaze cues. It would follow that when easy drive discrimination is obtained, it must be based on differential evocation of r_G mechanisms, because in the absence of differential conditioning of r_G, when the animal must rely just on s_D, the discrimination is an extremely difficult one. A number of other studies that have been done in the attempt to isolate or describe drive-produced stimuli, s_D, also appear to be consistent with this interpretation. The more different the stimuli are at the food and water locations, the easier the discrimination becomes.

Summary

We have only briefly surveyed the evidence (a more extensive review is available in Bolles, 1967), but the conclusion seems clear. As attractive as Hull's drive concept appeared to be initially, the various specific hypotheses defining and describing it have failed to hold together systematically and have failed to be supported by the evidence accumulated over the last twenty-five years. Undoubtedly some of these failures could be set right simply by modifying the original hypotheses (for example, by substituting a drive-induction hypothesis for Hull's drive-reduction hypothesis of reinforcement). But the overall strain upon the drive concept is too great. Apparently either the drive concept must be given up entirely or its hypothetical structure must be drastically altered. Most of the major theorists who defended Hull's original concept, in the days when its defense seemed reasonable, have chosen the second alternative and introduced modifications of the original formulation. For example, in 1953 Brown adhered closely to Hull's conception; in fact, he clarified it considerably. But by 1961 Brown had moved away from the position that drive was produced by food and water deprivation, and the like, to the broader position that it could be produced by any of several learned sources of motivation as well. Incentive-motivation factors were subsumed under the heading of drive. Thus, drive became synonymous with the total motivation of the organism. With this approach drive naturally had to be given considerably different functional properties from those Hull had given it, and from those that Brown himself had spelled out so clearly in 1953. For one thing it was apparent that the drive-learning interaction problem had been altered, for now drive was explicitly stated to depend, at least in part, on learning.

A similar strategy was apparent in Miller, Sampliner, and Woodrow's (1957) attempt to rescue the drive-reduction hypothesis of reinforcement. Miller stated that the saccharin-drinking studies of Sheffield and others did not necessarily invalidate the drive-reduction hypothesis. If we measure drive not in terms of the organism's need, as Hull had done, but in terms of its subsequent motivation to consume food, then the consumption of saccharin is drive-reducing, because its consumption does lead to a reduction of subsequent food intake. The only inference possible from

such an argument is that drive is now to be considered virtually synonymous with motivation itself. Similarly, for the case of defensive eyelid conditioning, Spence (1958) has designated as drive whatever it is (and it is far from clear what it is) that motivates the response. Because it is so uncertain what motivates the eyeblink, Spence too, in effect, has pooled the unlearned and learned sources of total motivation.

There are too many sorts of evidence that are not only difficult to account for in terms of any conception similar to Hull's D, but that seem to call for an incentive-motivation approach, one based on r_G mechanisms and one based on the organism's own prior learning. This is the kind of motivational construct we shall now consider. As we do so we shall be encountering an entirely new kind of learning-motivation interaction, one in which the sources of motivation are assumed from the outset to involve learning.

It should be noted, finally, that the evidence we have just reviewed permits us to dismiss certain types of solutions to the general interaction problem. The kinds of evidence that appear to call for an incentive motivation principle are damaging not only to Hull's solution of the interaction problem, which separates the generalized motivation principle from a directional habit concept, but also to those who would dismiss the motivation principle altogether, as Guthrie (1935) and Estes (1958) have tried to do by accounting for the apparent energization of behavior in terms of the stimuli that accompany the motivation conditions. Such an approach simply does not square with the facts; we appear to need some type of an incentive-motivation construct.

3

Incentive: Motivation Based on Learning

There is a variety of evidence pointing to the need for some sort of incentive-motivational factor. We have seen in the previous chapter that there are certain kinds of experimental situations, such as the so-called drive-discrimination problem, in which the various kinds of experimental results that are reported seem to make sense only when viewed in terms of an incentive-motivation factor, and more specifically, a factor based upon the anticipatory r_G mechanism. There is also a great deal of evidence showing that an animal's motivation in a given situation is very largely specific to that situation. For example, when an animal has learned to eat in a given environment, it eats readily, with a short latency, and eats a quantity of food that is (if the animal is given enough time) approximately sufficient to maintain itself until the next day. Because the animal's food consumption approximately matches its deficit we are inclined to think of this in terms of drive, that is, deprivation-induced motivation. However, if we require the animal to eat in a novel situation, we find that it is much less ready to do so; its latency to eat is much longer and eating terminates before the animal has made up its deficit. It is only after a number of days

with the test procedure, that is, after a certain number of trials, that the animal's food consumption rises to an acceptable level. It appears as though the readiness to eat and the amount eaten are in fact *learned* aspects of behavior, and are in large part governed by the situation in which the behavior occurs. The effects of situational factors and prior learning on consummatory behavior are so impressive that no distinction was made in the preceding chapter between the energizing of consummatory behavior and the energizing of instrumental behavior. We may assume that consummatory behavior is much like instrumental behavior in that it may have some unconditioned strength in a given situation, but that it is customarily raised to great strength only through reinforcement.

The best-established motivational effects are precisely those that involve either instrumental or consummatory behavior that has been previously reinforced. We saw in the preceding chapter that when the contingencies between the response and reinforcement are removed, as in the general activity situation or in drive-summation experiments, then the evidence for a motivational interpretation begins to collapse. It is therefore somehow fitting that we should move on in our treatment of motivation by considering the effects of varying reinforcement conditions, for it is the conditions of reinforcement that govern incentive motivation. Let us begin by surveying briefly some of the data that have been collected in recent years showing how the strength of an instrumental response varies with the amount of reinforcement.

Amount of Reinforcement

It has been widely reported that the strength of an instrumental response increases with increasing amount of reinforcement. Not only the probability but also the vigor of the response increases, as shown by Pereboom and Crawford (1958) and Marx and Brownstein (1963), who measured the speed of running in an alley on those trials on which Ss engaged in no competing behavior so that the time measure was a measure of how fast Ss were actually running.

We also know that if we shift the amount of reinforcement an animal receives during the course of training, there will be a fairly rapid corresponding shift in the strength of the reinforced response. The classic experiment of Crespi (1942) demonstrates this effect (see Figure 3-1). Notice first that there is a correspondence between the amount of reinforcement given during the first nineteen trials and the speed of running. This relationship has been found in a multitude of similar studies, so we may conclude that there is a rough analogy between this incentive effect and the deprivation effect reported by Perin and Williams. The shapes of the acquisition curves suggest that the amount of reinforcement should be thought of as a motivational variable which simply multiplies the strength of the predominant response tendency.

On the twentieth trial Crespi switched the animals receiving small amounts and large amounts of food to the same intermediate amount. The behavior of these switched groups rapidly reached a level of performance which was appropriate to the new amount of reinforcement, and, presumably, to the new level of incentive motivation. Notice that the shift in running times following a shift in the amount of reinforce-

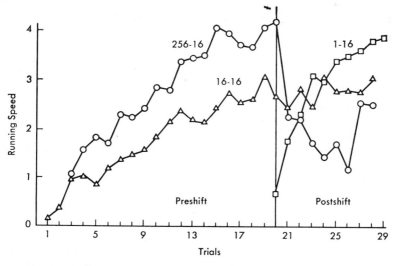

Figure 3-1. Speed of running as a function of amount of reinforcement. (Adapted with permission from Crespi, L. P. Quantitative variation of incentive and performance in the white rat. *Amer. J. Psychol.*, 1942, **55**, 467–517.)

ment occurs more rapidly than can reasonably be attributed to any change in the running habit itself, but it does not occur as rapidly as when deprivation is changed. Again we have a type of evidence that seems to require that the amount of reinforcement variable be regarded as motivational.

It has also been frequently found that behavior strength can change within a series of daily trials when motivation conditions are switched, as though the animal were adjusting to a new level of incentive motivation (for example, Bolles and Morlock, 1960; Collier and Marx, 1959). Some Es prefer to eliminate such transient effects by giving Ss just one trial a day. Spear and Pavlik (1966) have reported that the highly distributed trial procedure leads to somewhat different results in some cases.

At one point Spence (1956) considered the possibility that incentive motivation might grow as a result of the animal's cumulative experience with reinforcement, larger amounts of reinforcement leading to a more rapid accumulation. One implication is that different amounts of reinforcement should generate learning curves that rise at different rates and ultimately approach a common asymptote. Estes and Suppes (1959) made a similar proposal on the grounds that larger magnitudes of reinforcement should increase the probability of appropriate stimuli being sampled in the goal box. However, the rapidity of behavioral changes when the amount of reinforcement is changed and the continuing divergence of the learning curves with different amounts of reinforcement (for example, Champion and Smith, 1966) indicate that this is not the case. Spence also suggested in 1956 that incentive motivation was a function of the vigor of r_G, and that a sudden increase in the amount of reinforcement led to the rapid acquisition of a correspondingly more vigorous r_G. This proposal seems more in line with the available evidence. In any case, there seems to be little question that in a simple one-

response situation in which there is relatively little competition with the criterion response, the conditions of reinforcement, specifically the amount of reinforcement, affect behavior through the operation of a motivational factor. This factor, designated K by Hull (1952) and Spence (1951), is assumed to multiply with H, just as D was alleged to do.

In more competitive situations, such as discrimination problems and maze-learning problems, the analysis is considerably more complicated. Usually it is found that when animals are given more reinforcement they tend to run faster, but discrimination is not necessarily learned sooner. Occasionally, however, it has been reported that the rate of acquisition increases systematically with the amount of reinforcement (for example, Clayton and Koplin, 1964).

It appears that differential incentive effects are facilitated if animals have experienced some contrast in amount of reinforcement. Lawson (1957) discovered that if separate groups of animals are trained on a discrimination problem with each group receiving either a large or a small amount of reinforcement, then relatively small differences attributable to this variation are found. But if all animals are run under both high and low amounts of reinforcement, then large differences show up (for example, Morrison and Porter, 1965). On the other hand, if the stimuli to be discriminated are themselves made relevant to the amount of reinforcement variable, then the discrimination becomes much simpler. Greene (1953) reported, for example, that if rats eat large amounts of food in a black box and small amounts of food in a white box, then a black-white discrimination is readily acquired. In the absence of intramaze cues Ss are still able to solve the problem, presumably by the use of extramaze cues. Reynolds and Anderson (1961) and Davenport (1963), among others, have demonstrated that rats will rapidly learn to go to the side of a T-maze which provides the greater amount of reinforcement. This kind of result is extremely difficult to explain without the assumption of some type of r_G mechanism.

In the typical study of the amount of reinforcement there are a number of dimensions of the consummatory behavior that must necessarily be partly confounded, such as the amount of time in the goal box, the amount consumed, the rate of consumption, and the amount of consummatory behavior. The small amount of data available to unravel these tangled variables (for example, Goodrich, 1960) suggests that the critical variable is likely to be the total amount of consummatory activity. This confounding can be overcome to some extent by using sucrose solutions so that the amount of consummatory behavior can be equated for all groups and differences in reinforcement can be produced by variation in sugar concentration. Typically, it is found that as sugar concentration increases, the strength of the instrumental response increases accordingly (Collier and Siskel, 1959; Young and Shuford, 1955), although there may be a reversal at the highest concentrations. The reversal probably reflects something like a satiation effect; if the animal drinks very much of a highly concentrated solution, it is likely to consume an appreciable number of calories and its stomach may also become filled with water that is drawn in to dilute the excess sugar. Unfortunately for any such simple physiological account of the satiation effect, similar effects can be found with saccharin, which has little physiological effect upon the body (Collier, 1962).

When sugar concentrations are shifted suddenly there may be large contrast effects (Collier and Marx, 1959); however, such shifts in performance are generally slower and the carryover effects very much more pronounced with sucrose solutions than with dry food (Ison, 1964). What is needed to integrate sucrose studies with food studies is some kind of analysis which will make some allowance for the different behavioral effects produced by drinking sweet solutions, on the one hand, and

chewing dry food, on the other. Logan (1960) has suggested one way to view this problem by proposing that different amounts of reinforcement produce qualitatively different r_G's. When the amount of reinforcement is shifted there will be a competition between the r_G established from the previous reinforcement conditions and the rapidly strengthening r_G being produced by the new conditions. To test this hypothesis Logan ran animals under continuously varying amounts of reinforcement. He reports that the performance level is about the same as that which would be obtained with a constant amount of reinforcement equal to the mean amount (Logan, Beier, and Kincaid, 1956; Yamaguchi, 1961). Logan's interpretation is also consistent with his finding that when speed of running is measured in different portions of the runway, the incentive effect is seen most clearly in those portions closest to the goal, where presumably, r_G-evoking stimuli are most like those existing at the goal. This result has not always been verified, however (Goodrich, 1959). Considered altogether, the effects of varying amounts of reinforcement appear to give strong support to an r_G-based mechanism of incentive motivation.

Delay of Reinforcement

It has been found almost universally that when there is a delay of reinforcement there will be a decrement in instrumental behavior. This effect has been known for a long time and has been observed in a wide variety of apparatus (Cooper, 1938; Hunter, 1913; Muenzinger and Fletcher, 1937; Warden and Haas, 1927). Two effects were apparent in these early studies. One was that if the delay was incurred in the goal box itself there was relatively little disruption of the instrumental response leading to the goal box. The simplest explanation of this finding seems to be that because the goal box has been associated with eating it acquires secondary reinforcing powers so that the part of the response chain which leads to the goal box is immediately reinforced by secondary reinforcement. What the animal does subsequently to waiting out the delay interval has relatively little effect as far as reinforcement of the first member of the response chain is concerned. On the other hand, if the animal is delayed in a special delay chamber located before the goal box, then it is less able to tolerate a delay, presumably because any dissimilarity of the delay box and the goal means that there could be less secondary reinforcement.

The second early discovery was that the animal's behavior in the delay chamber was related to its subsequent performance of the instrumental response. If the animal balked or became emotional, then these reactions might generalize throughout the apparatus and impair the execution of the instrumental response. Both of these aspects of the delay situation were to receive further and more careful attention.

Students of Hull and Spence have systematically investigated the secondary reinforcement aspect of the delay situation. In one series of studies (Grice, 1948; Perin, 1943; Perkins, 1947) an attempt was made to eliminate as much of the secondary reinforcement effect as possible in the delay situation. The most successful of these attempts, by Grice, made use of a black-white discrimination in which S was required to enter either a black or a white chamber, each of which led to a gray chamber and then to the final gray goal box. The black and white sides were randomized, of course, so that S had no kinesthetic or visual cues at the choice point that were similar to or relevant to those which existed in the goal box. In other words, the discrimination situation was experimentally isolated from the reinforcement situation. Under these conditions Grice found an extremely slow acquisition of the discrimination for all delay periods beyond 5 sec. (see Figure 3-2).

Spence (1947) has interpreted these studies to mean that all learning with

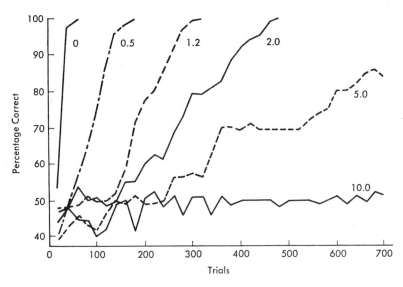

Figure 3-2. Acquisition of a black-white discrimination as a function of the delay of reinforcement (in seconds). (Reprinted with permission from Grice, G. R. The relation of secondary reinforcement to delayed reward in visual discrimination learning. *J. exp. Psychol.*, 1948, **38**, 1–16.)

delayed reinforcement involves the operation of immediate secondary reinforcement. If the animal is able to learn under delayed primary reinforcement, it must be because there is some secondary reinforcement which provides immediate strengthening of the response. If there is little opportunity for secondary reinforcement, as was evidently the case in Grice's study, then even a minimal delay of primary reinforcement will make acquisition of the instrumental response virtually impossible.

One interesting implication of Spence's analysis is that whereas quantity of reinforcement can be unequivocally viewed as an incentive motivating factor, it is not so clear that delay of reinforcement should be considered in the same way. The decrements in performance incurred with delay seem to represent not so much losses of motiva-tion as failures of reinforcement, and particularly as a failure of the secondary reinforcement asserted to be necessary to institute response chains.

Spence (1956) also described another series of studies done under his supervision which was addressed to the question of what happens during the delay interval and how this behavior affects the preceding instrumental response. Spence describes a study by Harker (1956) in which rats were trained to press a bar for food which arrived either after 1 sec. (approximately the minimal delay of reinforcements in bar-press situations) or after 10 sec. Harker found not only that the delay Ss performed at a lower level but also that their acquisition proceeded much more slowly (see Figure 3-3). Now if the effect of delay was to change the animal's motivation, then the

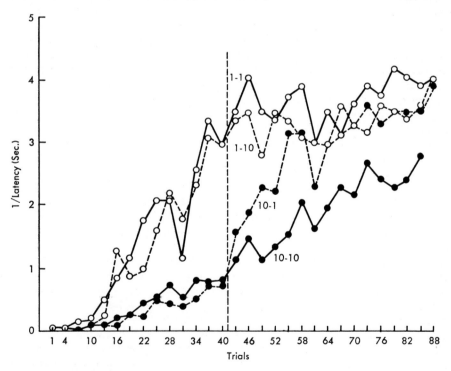

Figure 3-3. The effects of delays of 1 sec. and 10 sec. in reinforcement, and the effects of suddenly shifting delay conditions. (Adapted with permission from Harker, G. S. Delay of reward and performances of an instrumental response. *J. exp. Psychol.*, 1956, **51**, 303–310.)

learning curves should have proceeded to their own asymptotes at the same rate, as Perin and Williams had found with deprivation conditions and Crespi had found with amount of reinforcement.

Harker also reported the casual observation that animals under the delay conditions became distracted, that is, they could not wait at the food cup during the delay interval, and it appeared as though the behavior which distracted them from attending to the food cup came to interfere with the bar-press response. Carlton (1954) tried to determine the role of this competing behavior by running a group of animals in an apparatus similar to Harker's but much narrower so as to restrict the animal's behavior. A second group of animals was tested in a larger box, like Harker's, in which more competing behavior could occur. Carlton's results (see Spence, 1956) tended to support a competing response, that is, a nonmotivational interpretation. We may conclude that at least part of the delay-produced decrement in the strength of an instrumental response is due to behavior originally occurring during the delay generalizing throughout the apparatus to compete with the instrumental response.

A further clue to whether delay of reinforcement operates as a motivational factor or whether it just involves associative processes can be obtained by doing a Crespi-type experiment, that is, shifting the delay from short to long and vice versa to see how behavior follows the shifts. Harker's experiment included such shifts in reinforcement conditions. He found that animals shifted from long to short delay showed increased strength of the instrumental response, but he also found that this shift required about fifteen trials. Moreover, when the shift was from 1 sec. to 10 sec., from short to long delay, there was no apparent decrement in the strength of the bar-press response. Lawrence and Hommel (1961) have also reported that once a discrimination has been acquired in a delayed

reinforcement situation, the delay can be lengthened without producing a serious decrement in performance. It would appear that whatever the animal learns under moderate or short delays remains intact once it has been acquired even when very long delays are introduced later. This certainly does not seem like a motivational effect. On the other hand, an earlier study by Logan (1952) reported very gradual shifts in discrimination performance following both lengthening and shortening of delays. Logan used a forced trial procedure and a somewhat different type of task, however, so his results might be expected to differ from Harker's. Logan, Beier, and Ellis (1955) ran a group of rats in an alley under conditions where the delay of reinforcement was varied randomly between long and short. This group ran considerably faster than a group consistently fed with a delay equal to the mean of the variable delay. Performance under the variable conditions was, in fact, almost equal to that of a group run under the shortest delay conditions. This effect too appears to be something other than the kind of motivational effect we are accustomed to, and quite different from what Logan et al. (1956) found when they randomly varied the amount of reinforcement.

It is well known that appreciable delays can be instituted in bar-pressing situations and that, far from showing a failure of responding, animals tend to show increased response strength. We have to use a little caution in analogizing between the operant and the discrete trial situations, however. First of all, when animals are trained on a fixed interval schedule—for example, a 1-min. schedule—which would be a prohibitive delay in most discrete trial situations, they are customarily started with immediate reinforcement, and the time requirement is gradually increased so that the 1-min. interval is approached gradually. Furthermore, the animal can fill the 1-min. interval with a series of responses. Also, as training proceeds it begins to make a temporal discrimination. Evidence of temporal discrimination is shown when the rate of responding increases toward the end of the fixed interval so as to produce the well-known scallop effect. A situation more clearly analogous to the discrete trial problem would be one in which the animal is on a *multiple* schedule where it must press the bar on some reinforcement schedule in order to get onto a fixed interval schedule. The question then becomes how performance on the first component of the multiple schedule varies as a function of the severity of the fixed interval schedule. The answer seems to be that it makes relatively little difference, although what difference there is usually is in the appropriate direction: the more stringent the fixed interval schedule, the less reinforcing it is to get onto such a schedule (Kelleher and Gollub, 1962). This finding appears to hold even in cases where the animal is required to refrain from pressing the bar for a given interval of time, such as 20 sec. Here the animal may be required to press the bar on a fixed-ratio schedule to produce a light (which is usually called a secondary reinforcer) in the presence of which the animal must refrain from pressing the bar for 20 sec. in order to set up food reinforcement. Animals are able to acquire such complicated behavior, although it naturally takes extensive training. Here we have a situation perhaps more analogous to the discrete trial delayed-reinforcement procedure in that the animal cannot do anything very constructive during the delay interval; it certainly cannot press the bar, for to do so would only postpone reinforcement further. The question that arises is how learning is possible on such a multiple schedule. It is true that the light or other cue which signals the onset of the second part of the multiple schedule may serve as a secondary reinforcer because it is present at the time the food is delivered, but how can its presence maintain any semblance of coordinated behavior over appreciable periods of time, and how can the animal

master *chained* schedules in which there are no external cues to signal the different components?

Ferster (1953) has argued that in all such cases what occurs is a sequence of responses which the animal uses to fill the time interval. The animal constructs a chain of irrelevant or incidental responses which, although they have no real bearing upon reinforcement, do present a series of stimulus changes. We may suppose that each stimulus change acts as a source of secondary reinforcement for prior members of the chain, so that collectively they help bind the sequence of responses together. The only point at which primary reinforcement enters the picture is in maintaining the last element of the chain. Because the only leverage E has in the situation is the timing of primary reinforcement, the only prediction that can be made is that whatever responses the animal engages in over the delay interval, they will serve, at least approximately, to fill the interval.

It is also possible to explain the acquisition of a time-consuming instrumental response—as happens, for example, when the animal runs in a very long alley—by invoking the response chaining mechanism. It is known that the rat can bridge an appreciable temporal gap with relatively little disruption in the acquisition of such a continuing response. The explanation here is that the animal initiates the running response at the start of the alley and proceeds to continue running until it gets to the point of primary reinforcement. Even though the delay interval may be 10 sec. or more with a suitably long alley, the animal is engaged in a series of responses all of which happen to be the same. This homogeneous chain of responses enables it to bridge a long gap between the initiation of the response and reinforcement. In the case of homogeneous chains there is not the necessity for secondary reinforcements throughout the sequence that Ferster's (1953) analysis of heterogeneous chains requires. However, we may still suppose that the more similar the long alley is to the goal box, the faster the rat will run it.

Just as it is possible to shift an animal from a multiple schedule of reinforcement to a chain schedule of reinforcement by withdrawing the cue lights to indicate where in time the animal is, so it is also apparently possible to withdraw secondary reinforcing stimuli in a discrete trial situation once a response has been acquired under delay conditions and still find that the animal is able to bridge the gap (Myers, 1958). Moreover, Renner (1963) has found that although secondary reinforcing stimuli facilitate the acquisition of running in a delayed reinforcement situation, such stimuli provide no advantage to an animal learning the response without the delay, which we might expect if we conceive of a secondary reinforcer as providing incentive motivation. Hence, although such stimuli may be necessary for the establishment of a response under delayed reinforcement, they do not seem to be very critical in maintaining the response once it has been established.

The secondary reinforcement interpretation of the effects of delay is further strengthened by experimental data when the discriminanda differ in the same manner as the goal boxes—for example, if the animal is required to approach a black area in order to gain access to a black goal box, then a black-white discrimination is very rapidly acquired (Eninger, 1953; Grice and Goldman, 1955). But it has also been found that the mere discriminability of the goal boxes themselves is an important factor in a discrimination problem. Thus, Lawrence and Hommel (1961) have shown that simply using two goal boxes which are clearly distinguishable from each other but unrelated to the cues that exist at the choice point makes the discrimination problem much simpler. Indeed, Lawrence and Hommel ran a group in which Ss were reinforced in a white box but had to run down a black alley to get there, and found that this procedure greatly facilitated the discrimination learning.

It is not easy to summarize this complex problem area because there are about half a dozen partly interrelated theoretical mechanisms that have been proposed to account for the delay-of-reinforcement effect. The data available at this time do not lend overwhelming support to any one of these theoretical interpretations, nor do they permit us to exclude any one of them. Let us simply review what these alternatives are.

1. *A genuine effect of delaying primary reinforcement.* Spence (1947) and Hull (1952) proposed that the stimuli to which an instrumental response ultimately becomes conditioned leave traces that persist for some seconds after the original stimuli are gone. These traces fade in time so that with greater delay of primary reinforcement the traces will be fainter, and certainly less similar to the original. When the original stimuli are encountered again on a subsequent trial, there will be a generalization decrement in the instrumental response.

2. *Incentive motivation.* We may think of environmental stimuli which resemble those present in the goal box as eliciting r_G. However, if primary reinforcement is delayed, there will result less conditioning of r_G to goal-box stimuli because the onset of these stimuli will not be contiguous with the occurrence of R_G. If we attribute motivational properties to the occurrence of r_G, then we have an incentive motivational explanation of the delay effect. Spence regarded delay-induced incentive motivation as being essentially the same factor as that produced by the amount of reinforcement, but Hull (1952) postulated two separate incentive factors which, he assumed, merely multiplied together with D and H to determine the strength of the instrumental response. As a further subheading, we may consider an associative type of r_G, one which does not act as a multiplicative motivational factor but rather simply provides additional associative control for the instrumental response.

3. *Secondary reinforcement.* It is possible to conceive of the r_G mechanism as operating not as a purely associative factor, or as a motivator, but as a mechanism for reinforcing the early members of the response

chain that lead the animal to those stimuli to which r_G has been conditioned. In this view, the strength of the response is governed not by the strength of r_G that is elicited on a given trial but rather by the extent to which r_G has occurred on previous trials so as to provide reinforcement.

4. *Competing responses.* The decrement produced by delay may be explained without having recourse to any of the previous mechanisms, simply by observing that during delay the animal engages in irrelevant behavior, behavior such as exploring the apparatus and perhaps chewing on the food-delivery mechanism. To the extent that such responses generalize to the rest of the apparatus, we may expect that they will occur there too, and in so doing compete with the instrumental response.

5. *Response chaining.* That behavior occurs at all when reinforcement is delayed requires some explanation. The most common assumption is that the animal fills the time interval during which no particular behavior is reinforced by engaging in a series or chain of responses that are more or less adventitiously reinforced when primary reinforcement finally occurs at the end of the chain. The full theoretical implications of the chaining interpretation have not been very carefully examined, but it is conceivable that the incentive motivation mechanism and the secondary reinforcement mechanism can both be subsumed under this heading (Bolles, 1967).

6. *Frustration.* One further theoretical account of the delay phenomenon remains to be described, namely, the possibility that many of the experimental findings regarding the delay of reinforcement can be interpreted most adequately by introducing a new anticipatory mechanism which we may conceptualize as frustration. We will consider this possibility in the next chapter.

The Relation of Incentive to Drive

With essentially no data upon which to base such a proposal, Hull (1952) suggested

that incentive motivation (K) and D and H should all be multiplied together to determine the strength of the instrumental response. Later, on the basis of a study by Ramond (1954), Spence (1956) proposed that the proper mathematical relationship was additive rather than multiplicative. That is, D and K should add together and their sum should multiply habit. A number of experiments have been done in the attempt to test these two alternative formulations (for example, Ehrenfreund and Badia, 1962; Pavlik and Reynolds, 1963; Reynolds, Marx, and Henderson, 1952). The bulk of the evidence suggests that Spence's additive formulation is better than Hull's multiplicative formula.

Ramond (1954) and Renner (1963) have reported data suggesting that when K is varied by changing the delay of reinforcement, D and K still combine additively. Moreover, Logan (1960) has suggested, on the basis of a study in which delay and amount of reinforcement were both varied, that these two components of incentive motivation combine additively.

One further interaction between D and K has to be considered. It has been reported fairly consistently that when deprivation is reduced to zero, the effect of incentive motivation disappears (Seward and Procter, 1960). It seems, then, that the additive formula requires some adjustment because when D equals zero no amount of K seems to be capable of producing an appreciable sum of total motivation. It has been suggested (Black, 1965) that K be reconceptualized so that it becomes itself a function of deprivation. Thus, when deprivation is minimal, both D and K would approach zero. This strategy would permit the additive relationship between D and K to be retained. But in view of the general theoretical failure of D to explain what it is supposed to explain, this proposal does not seem very attractive. Indeed, all investigations of the relationship between D and K would seem to have dubious value. Note that when the hypothetical relationship between D and K is examined what is actually being studied is the interaction between two experimental procedures, deprivation time and amount of reinforcement. It is not the interaction between D and K themselves that is being studied; the latter are merely theoretical constructs. If it should become necessary to consider deprivation conditions as one of the several determinants of K, then the old problem of how D and K combine will become a new problem requiring for its solution a specification of how all the various determinants of K combine to produce the organism's total motivation.

Giving particular cogency and importance to this argument is the quite recent discovery that the incentive value of food, or water, does indeed increase with deprivation. Revusky (1967) fed rats grape juice while hungry and milk while nearly satiated. When these Ss were later given a preference test between the two foods they showed a clear preference for the grape juice, the food consumed while hungry. Using a somewhat different technique, Kurtz and Jarka (1968) forced animals to one goal box of a T-maze when they were hungry and to the other goal box, where they received exactly the same food reward, when they were nearly satiated. On subsequent free trials the animals tended to run to the "hungry side" of the maze. Mendelson (1966) has obtained analogous results using a brain stimulation procedure. Hypothalamic stimulation in an area that makes rats hungry had no effect on T-maze performance when it was administered in the maze, but facilitated performance when it was given in the goal box so that the rats, which were satiated, ate there. Comparable results have been found using thirst (Mendelson, 1967; Revusky, 1968). Although all these findings can probably be given alternative interpretations, taken together they give strong support to the unifying assumption that K is a function of deprivation.

The Status of r_G

Although most theorists who invoke it as an explanatory device probably do not consider r_G to be any more than a theoretical construct, a few investigators (for example, Lewis, Butler, and Diamond, 1958; Miller and DeBold, 1965) have actively searched for observable evidence of r_G. The attempts to measure the occurrence of salivation and to correlate it with the theoretically required occurrence of r_G have, in general, not been very successful. Hence, it cannot be said that r_G has been located, much less that it has the observable properties that have been assigned to it. Although some theorists may be discouraged at the failure to "find" r_G, the majority are probably not too concerned. It has proved to be an extremely valuable explanatory device, and theorizing with it has produced a rich experimental literature that might not have existed otherwise.

The status of r_G presents not only an interesting empirical question, but some rather crucial theoretical questions as well. For example, can we generalize the original concept by supposing not only that it may be a fraction of a consummatory response but that it may also be a fraction of any response which occurs in the goal box? Miller (1935) proposed such a modification and obtained some evidence for it. He required rats to adopt unusual postures while eating in the goal box, and found that the instrumental response leading to the goal box was either facilitated or interfered with in accordance with whether the instrumental response was compatible or incompatible with the behavior required in the goal box. Another theoretical possibility is to redefine r_G so that it is not so much an anticipatory consummatory response as an anticipation of the orienting and approach behavior that occurs in the goal box. If the principal thing that the animal does in the goal box is to run forward to food, then we might expect this response to generalize quite readily to other parts of the apparatus, which would account quite nicely for the fact that incentive motivation appears to work best when it calls for the animal to run forward to the incentive.

We may extend the r_G concept by noting the proposal made by Spence and others that r_G may become conditioned not only to external stimuli, cues in the maze and in the general environment which in some sense tell the animal *where* to go, but also to response-produced cues, such as proprioceptive feedback from the animal's own responses. This powerful conception, which has been promoted primarily by Mowrer (1960), would help account for the fact that the animal in some sense knows *what* to do. Maintaining the appropriate postures and making the appropriate responses leads, in this view, to proprioceptive feedback, which produces incentive motivation for the behavior in question.

Although there remains considerable doubt about the actual existence of r_G, there is little doubt that it has served admirably in the explanation of a host of behavioral phenomena. Hull (1952) himself gave a lucid account of how an r_G-incentive mechanism could deal with the latent learning effect. His account deals especially well with the case in which a rat is permitted to explore a T-maze for some time and is then passively placed in a distinctive goal box where, for the first time, it eats. On the next trial the rat shows a significant tendency to run toward the goal box where it had been fed (Seward, 1949). Moltz (1957) has given an r_G interpretation of a similar "latent extinction" effect: a previously learned response is markedly weakened following a short series of passive placements into the now empty goal box. Trapold and Bell (1964) have found similar "latent" shifts in performance following passive placement in a goal box containing new amounts of reinforcement.

The procedural feature that should be emphasized in these studies is that an instrumental response is strengthened or weakened in accordance with reinforcing events that happen to the animal independently of its making the response in question. The animal evidently learns two things in such situations (and presumably in all learning situations); one is the instrumental response (that is, a connection between the response and its controlling stimulus) and the other is some kind of connection between reinforcement and the stimuli that precede or accompany reinforcement. In effect, the animal learns both how to get to the reward and where and what the reward is. These latent learning experiments and related studies suggest that the second kind of learning can occur independently of the first, that is, that there is an incentive motivation mechanism independent of S's instrumental response learning.

Summary

It may be profitable to conclude this chapter with a summary of the assumptions typically made about the r_G-incentive mechanism and a word or two about the current status of each assumption.

1. *Incentive motivation is based upon the occurrence of some compatible fraction of the consummatory response.* Although it seems likely that the consummatory response, R_G, plays some part in the phenomenon of incentive motivation, the evidence surveyed in the preceding section indicates that this assumption may be too restrictive and difficult to defend by independent evidence. It seems safer and more descriptive at this point to leave open the question of mediation and refer to the hypothetical incentive motivator as just that—the incentive factor—rather than to make the gratuitous assumption of an r_G mechanism.

2. *The incentive factor becomes associated with stimuli that immediately precede or accompany reinforcement.* There seems to be little question about this assumption, although very little is known about details of the relationship, for example, whether

the stimuli should precede or accompany reinforcement for optimum association.

3. *This association is established by classical conditioning.* Although this assumption is very widely accepted, there is not much substantial evidence for it. Some writers have suggested that the incentive factor is acquired through reinforcement (Logan and Wagner, 1965; Spence, 1956), and at least one has proposed, in a manner reminiscent of early Hull, that it can be acquired through the long-delayed after-effects of the consummatory response, that is, by need reduction (Revusky, 1967). On the other hand, Morse and Skinner (1958) have suggested that although the incentive factor may be established by the use of Pavlovian *procedures*, it may actually involve the formation of an associative element quite different from the usually conceived conditioned S-R connection. They propose that there may be a direct functional connection between stimuli and reinforcers. Although Morse and Skinner do not develop the implications of this idea, it is certainly a novel and refreshing alternative to traditional modes of thought about what is learned when learning occurs. At the other end of the speculation-description continuum is the policy of Bower and Trapold, which is to emphasize the experimental procedures involved. They simply refer to the acquisition of the incentive factor as noncontingent learning, that is, learning that occurs when reinforcement is not contingent upon S's behavior (Bower and Grusec, 1964; Bower and Kaufman, 1963; Trapold, 1966).

4. *Once the incentive factor is established, it can be aroused by either the stimuli to which it has been conditioned or by any similar stimuli.* Although this assumption appears to be general to all associative psychology, and correspondingly quite safe, it should still be recognized as an assump-

tion. Moreover, there are instances where it appears to fail, for example, the failure of incentive motivation in satiated animals. There have also been a number of failures to obtain latent learning effects and related incentive motivation effects (for example, Gonzalez and Diamond, 1960; Koppman and Grice, 1963) in situations where they would be expected.

5. *The stimuli that arouse the incentive factor lead to motivation of any response that occurs in their presence.* There is relatively little agreement outside of the Hull–Spence camp about this assumption. A number of theorists would contend that it is unnecessary to introduce the concept of motivation here; the stimuli themselves can provide sufficient control over behavior so that no additional assumption of motivation is needed. Others would argue that behavior is motivated but that motivation gives behavior direction as well as energy (Bindra, 1968). These basic issues are far from settled.

6. *All of the previous assumptions are as applicable to aversive motivation as to appetitive motivation.* This is quite a new idea, and it has not been widely incorporated into existing theoretical statements. Fear, which is what we are talking about, is customarily regarded as a source of drive rather than as a variety of incentive motivation, even though fear-drive theorists generally consider it to be a learned source of drive (Brown and Farber, 1968). Rescorla and Solomon (1967) have started to make the transition to incentive theory, however. They argue that there are conditionable danger signals which arouse fear and therefore motivate avoidance behavior, and that there are also conditionable safety signals that can inhibit fear and thus reduce avoidance behavior. We will return to these problems in the next chapter.

4

Negative Incentives

The idea of a conditionable, fractional consummatory response has proved to be extremely fruitful in explaining appetitive behavior. It is therefore not surprising that the basic idea has been extended far beyond its original application. In the present chapter we will consider some of these extensions. Specifically, we will consider the anticipatory mechanisms that have been proposed to explain first frustration and then escape and avoidance behavior.

Frustration

It has been known for some time that delayed reinforcement can produce not only the decremental effects we noted in the last chapter, but also incremental effects. When animals are delayed part way through a chain of behavior, for example, in the middle of the runway, it is only that part of the behavior chain that *precedes* the delay that shows a decrement. When the animal is finally permitted to run from the delay chamber to the goal box, it may run with greater speed and shorter latency than control animals without the delay (Brown, Gentry, and Kaplan, 1948; Holder, Marx, Holder, and Collier, 1957). Amsel (1958)

has suggested that this anomalous finding is attributable to frustration. Amsel explains the predelay inhibition of behavior as caused by the introduction of competing responses which occur in anticipation of frustration in the delay box. The facilitation of postdelay behavior is attributed to a short-term increase in motivation which results from the motivational state produced by frustration.

Amsel postulates that there is some innate frustration response, R_F, which occurs when food is withheld or delayed and that this response becomes conditioned to stimuli present where the animal is detained. He handles the anticipatory form of frustration, r_F, in much the same way that Hull originally accounted for anticipatory consummatory behavior, that is, by assuming that some fractional or anticipatory part of the frustration reaction occurs whenever the animal is in the presence of stimuli similar to those that were present when it was thwarted. (We will refer here to the procedure of withholding or delaying reinforcement as "thwarting" and to the hypothetical or observed consequences of this procedure as "frustration.")

The use of frustration theory by Amsel (1962, 1967) and others to account for delay of reinforcement effects (and partial reinforcement effects) is a relatively new development, but a frustration effect has been known for some time in situations where reinforcement is withheld altogether. This original frustration phenomenon had been noted by a number of early investigators. It appears that when the extinction of an instrumental response first begins, the response tends to have greater vigor and a shorter latency than it had during the last part of acquisition. It is as if the animal were activated by a new kind of excitement, a new increment in total motivation, during the first few trials of extinction; and these effects are attributed to frustration.

There has been some discussion (for example, Lawson and Marx, 1958; Marx, 1956) about whether these effects are most profitably interpreted as motivational. Certainly there must be many instances in the prior history of the animal when the execution of a given piece of behavior failed to achieve reinforcement but then when it responded again more vigorously, for example, pressing the bar a little more forcefully, reinforcement was forthcoming. Thus, the animal may have had many opportunities in the past to learn that more vigorous responding pays off when less vigorous responding fails. In this connection, Marx (1956) has described a study in which rats were trained to respond less vigorously following a failure of reinforcement. Moreover, it was found that this effect was nearly as easy to get as, and was nearly equal in magnitude to, the more typical increase in vigor found under the usual training and thwarting conditions.

One other effect of frustration has been very widely accepted, namely, that it leads to aggressive behavior (Dollard et al., 1939); for many years it has been largely taken for granted that there is an intimate connection between frustration and aggression. However, in recent years even this assumption has been questioned on the grounds that, at least for human Ss, there is ample opportunity to learn that aggression is of instrumental value whenever thwarted. There is now a fair amount of experimental evidence to indicate that when aggression leads to no direct reward, frustration does not necessarily lead to aggression (Buss, 1966; Feshbach, 1964).

Of considerable theoretical interest are the cases where the effects of frustration are manifest on an instrumental response other than the one that is thwarted. The first report of this type was by Amsel and Roussel (1952), who used a procedure in which rats were trained to run a two-unit alley for food. The animals were required to run one unit of the alley to the first goal box; then after they had eaten there, they could move on to the second unit and a second goal box, where a second piece of food was presented. After the running response had been established, food was withheld from the first goal box on half of the trials, whereas on the other half of the trials, food was still present in the first goal box as before. In a sense each animal served as its own control to indicate the effect of presenting versus withdrawing reinforcement in the first goal box. A small but consistent and significant increase in speed was found in the second unit of the alley, presumably as a consequence of the thwarting in the first goal box on frustration trials. Here, then, running in the second part of the apparatus shows a frustration effect even though that response has not been thwarted.

Because r_F is a relatively new theoretical construct, we have a certain amount of choice in the functional properties we hypothesize for it. One possibility is to think of frustration as aversive, as a negative incentive factor which leads directly to the inhibition of behavior in the presence of stimuli that are similar to those to which the frustration response has been conditioned. But if we follow this line, then some special mechanism has to be introduced to account for the postdelay increment in behavior. One test of the aversiveness of frustration (Wagner, 1963) has produced equivocal results; it remains to be shown that it is aversive. On the other hand, if we think of r_F as the residual part of the full-blown frustration response that occurs with thwarting, and if we view it as contributing to the animal's total motivation in the same way that r_G does, then we have a mechanism to account for the postdelay increment in behavior, but we have to invoke competing behavior or some other device to explain the predelay decrements.

That some form of anticipatory frustration occurs, and that it is aroused by stimuli similar to those in the thwarting situation, is supported by a number of findings. For example, Lambert and Solomon (1952) found greater excitation in animals that were extinguished closer to the goal box than in those that were extinguished some distance from it. Such goal-gradient effects do not always materialize, however (Wagner, 1961). Amsel and Ward (1954) and Amsel and Prouty (1959) replaced the postdelay part of the alley with a choice situation that was arranged so that on frustration trials S had to take one side to obtain food, whereas on trials when food is present in the first box, that is, on nonfrustration trials, the second reinforcement was contingent upon making the opposite response. This discrimination was learned and appeared to depend upon some immediate consequence of frustration rather than any consequence of the prior ingestion of food.

It is known that following training with delayed reinforcement the instrumental response sometimes shows greater resistance to extinction than following immediate reinforcement (Crum, Brown, and Bitterman, 1951; Fehrer, 1956; Sgro and Weinstock, 1963), but not always (Tombaugh, 1966). Such a finding can be given several interpretations, but it is most commonly construed as indicating the operation of competing responses. The argument is that during the delay period the animal engages in many kinds of behavior which compete with the instrumental response. Ultimately, however, this behavior extinguishes because the animal is reinforced for persisting. Then during extinction, when primary reinforcement is no longer available, the frustration which would normally occur without the prior frustration-tolerance training is not so likely to occur, and competing behavior is not so likely to compete with the instrumental response.

The same type of analysis has been applied to a number of nonreinforcement phenomena, including discrimination learning and various extinction and partial reinforcement effects (Amsel, 1962). Amsel's analysis assumes, first, that anticipatory frustration responses become conditioned to stimuli in the situation, and second, that with continued training the feedback from such responses, s_F, becomes part of the total stimulus pattern controlling (or motivating) the appropriate instrumental behavior.

Even some of the apparent failures to obtain frustration effects tend to support an r_F analysis. For example, Wist (1962, 1963) reported that in a well-insulated runway, constructed so that there was a minimum of external cues, there was no incremental effect of thwarting, which is what might be expected if we assume that r_F is ordinarily elicited by stimuli arising from the environment.

The original frustration conception, until the time of Amsel's recent work, made it a source of drive. But the more we find out about frustration and the conditions under which it occurs, the more it appears to resemble incentive motivation. It becomes increasingly clear that in order to account for the various associative properties of frustration and the way in which it varies as experimental conditions are varied, frustration must have an anticipatory form; it is also clear that frustration depends upon what happens in the goal box.

This general pattern in the development of motivation theory—from drive to incentive—has by now encompassed most of the field, but there is one area still predominantly regarded in terms of drive. We may expect that the transition will soon occur there too, so that it will come in time to be treated primarily in terms of some type of fractional anticipatory mechanism. This remaining area is the rapidly growing and very complex one of defensive behavior. We will not attempt to cover the whole area, but only certain parts of it where the introduction of an anticipatory escape concept might clarify some phenomena that have so far resisted explanation.

Escape Behavior

All the questions that we have considered regarding appetitive behavior have analogies with defensive behavior, that is, escape and avoidance behavior. Unfortunately, the number of analogous experiments is

rather severely limited. Let us start with a study by Campbell and Kraeling (1953) in which animals were trained to escape different intensities of shock. It appears that animals not only perform better but also learn more quickly as shock intensity increases (see Figure 4-1). In commenting upon this result, Spence (1956) has raised the question of whether habit and motivation (drive) may not be interdependent in aversive learning situations. The failure of independence seems certain if one interprets the motivation in the shock-escape situation as a source of drive, which is what Spence tried to do. However, it is not just that the habit built up faster with the stronger shocks in the Campbell and Kraeling study; the animals under the greater shock intensity performed markedly better even on the first trial. Apparently the intensity of shock is one of the determinants of the nature and

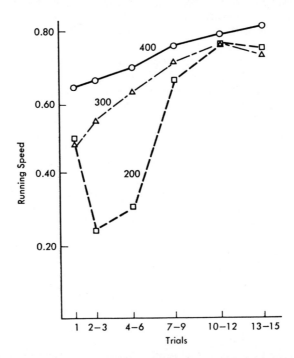

Figure 4-1. The strength of a running response as a function of drive level (voltage) and reinforcement (voltage reduction). (Reprinted with permission from Campbell, B.A., and Kraeling, D. Response strength as a function of drive level and amount of drive reduction. *J. exp. Psychol.,* 1953, **45,** 97–101.)

strength of the animal's innate responses to shock. Apparently the response selected to be the escape response was already a strong unconditioned reaction to the intense shock. Rats under strong shock intensity are inclined to leap about and run and jump, and thus they have a tremendous initial advantage over animals under low shock who may simply poke at the floor and squeal and engage in behavior which is incompatible with the required running response (Kimble, 1955). In other words, just as different deprivation conditions seem to call forth qualitatively different behaviors, so certain responses are in some sense appropriate to a given intensity of shock.

Another important finding reported by Campbell and Kraeling is that performance in the escape situation is clearly a function of the amount of reinforcement (the drop in voltage) produced by the instrumental response. Woods, Davidson, and Peters (1964) have reported a similar finding in an instrumental water escape situation. Woods et al. ran rats with a given water temperature in the alley and a different temperature in the goal box. It was possible to isolate experimentally the drive component (temperature in the alley) from the amount of reinforcement (temperature differential between alley and goal box), and it turned out that the amount of reinforcement was by far the more important of the two factors. Indeed, drive per se had relatively little effect upon the animal's response strength once allowance was made for the amount of reinforcement. These results suggest that the conditions of reinforcement are of the utmost importance in the instrumental escape situation and the effects that they have upon the strength of the instrumental response warrant very careful further consideration.

Bower, Fowler, and Trapold (1959) have described a Crespi-type of experiment using reduction of electric shock as the reinforcer. Different groups received different amounts of shock reduction until after

a few trials, when the reinforcement conditions were switched. The results indicated a rather rapid adjustment in running speed to levels appropriate to the postshift conditions. The transition in response strength required about ten trials. Unfortunately for an incentive motivation interpretation, this was approximately the number of trials the initial learning had required, so that we do not have very substantial support for an incentive interpretation of the results. However, perhaps we can assume that the initial acquisition of the running response in the Bower et al. study reflected not a build-up of habit strength per se, but a build-up of negative incentive motivation. What we are proposing here is a position similar to that previously suggested by Mowrer (1960), namely, that in the escape situation what the animal learns is not so much an instrumental running habit, but the acquisition of a negative incentive factor which involves the motivation of running. This proposal would account for Campbell and Kraeling's results too.

We may suggest a concrete reference for the anticipatory escape response; it is, we assume, an anticipatory running-away response. What we propose is analogous to the situation of the hungry rat at the point at which it enters the goal box and approaches food. The anticipatory response here very much resembles the instrumental response itself, which we may suppose is running forward and seizing the food. We may suppose further that this resemblance is not just coincidental, but that it is an essential part of incentive motivation. In the aversive case, we assume that there must be, again, a high degree of compatibility between the instrumental response, running away (which is the usual escape response in most experimental situations), and the anticipatory form of the escape response. One consequence of this formulation is that taking flight should be the most easily acquired escape response for the rat, and this in fact appears to be the case.

Now it turns out that rats are also able to acquire a bar-press response to terminate shock, and this response too is acquired extremely rapidly. The rat can learn to press a bar to escape shock just as rapidly as it learns to run, and the latency of this response soon becomes extremely short. The fact that the rat can learn an operant bar-press response that is quite incompatible with running away would seem to rule out the kind of incentive motivation explanation of escape behavior that has just been proposed. The usual interpretation of escape learning is, of course, that termination of shock is a very powerful reinforcer which reinforces any arbitrary operant (or instrumental) response we may choose; bar-pressing is simply a convenient response, and any other could be learned as readily. Unfortunately for this usual interpretation, the so-called learning is too good! It occurs in too few trials and the latency of the response is too short (Bolles and McGillis, 1968). Thus, in fewer than ten trials, rats may begin to show response latencies in the order of 0.1 sec., and in thirty trials they may be down to 0.05 sec. It is not reasonable to argue that any operant can be generated so rapidly. It is much more plausible to suppose that what the animal is doing, in fact, is *freezing* while holding on to the bar. When the shock comes on, the animal gives a reflexive lurch which has the effect of terminating the shock very rapidly. *S* cannot very well freeze while shock is on unless it is already holding on to the bar. Observation of rats in the bar-press escape situation indicates that this is just what they do, and, indeed, the main problem with bar-press escape training is getting the rat to emit genuine operant responses.

It is apparent that in bar-press studies, and in most aversive situations, the rat has another extremely strong unconditioned response to aversive situations, namely, freezing. And we may propose, therefore, that freezing is also one of the anticipatory escape responses of the rat. We are sug-gesting that in the case of the rat there is a repertoire of two responses, one running away and the other freezing, in either of which the animal may engage when it is frightened. We suggest that it is not an accident that all the escape training procedures that have been reported in the literature involve one or the other of these two types of behavior.

Avoidance Behavior

Miller (1948) shocked rats in a white compartment and then trained them to escape the white compartment by running through a doorway into a neighboring black compartment. The animals were then placed in the white compartment in which they had been shocked, but no more shocks were presented, and the door to the black compartment was shut. In order to open the door, *S*s were required to make an instrumental response which consisted of rotating a small wheel. About half of the *S*s froze and refused to turn the wheel or do anything else. The other half of the *S*s, however, did make the wheel-turning response, and when the door opened they made their way out of the white compartment. Trial-by-trial performance indicated learning of this new response. Subsequently the wheel-turning response was extinguished and *S*s were required to press a bar in order to open the door. This response was also learned. The ordinary interpretation of Miller's results is that the white compartment where the shock had been presented had come to elicit fear; since fear is a source of drive, any response which gets the animal out of the frightening situation reduces fear, reduces drive, and is therefore learned.

But consider the behavior exhibited by the animal in this situation. On the one hand, a great deal of freezing occurred, one of the animal's unconditioned responses to fear, and the animals fled from the white compartment whenever they were permitted to do so, exhibiting the other unconditioned response to fear. In addition, we may note that the responses that were required of the animals, turning the wheel and pressing the bar, were perhaps not in any strict sense arbitrarily chosen operants. Thus, in reporting the study, when Miller was discussing possible improvements in the procedure, he suggested that the acquisition of the "new response" would proceed much better if the situation were arranged so that the required response would be topographically similar to the old escape response. He suggested having the animals climb over a hurdle in order to leave the white compartment on the grounds that this would generalize better to the subsequently required wheel-turning and bar-pressing behavior.

Allison, Larson, and Jensen (1967) have recently discovered another difficulty in the interpretation of Miller's classic study. They simply measured the probability of rats staying in a white box or moving into a black box. As Miller had reported, there was no initial color preference, but when the animals were given a few electric shocks a very strong bias developed; they showed a strong preference for the black box. Even rats that had been shocked in the black box stayed there rather than cross over to the white box, where they had never been shocked. It appears that Miller's results can be obtained only when rats are tested running from white to black, and that had he counterbalanced colors he would have had no "new learning" to report. Finally, our own observation of rats in a situation like Miller's is that they approach the wheel and the bar in the attempt to climb out of the apparatus through the hole in which these devices are mounted. It would seem that the responses that the rat acquires are not strictly new and are not strictly arbitrary operants, but bear a strong resemblance to its anticipatory escape responses. Perhaps a crucial test is provided by the avoidance learning situation that does not require the animal to

leave the situation in which fear is elicited but merely requires it to turn off a fear-eliciting signal, such as a buzzer or a light, that precedes shock. Only one relevant study with adequate controls has been reported so far, and it gave entirely negative results (Baron, 1959).

Most theorists would maintain that an animal can learn an arbitrary operant, any convenient instrumental response, in order to turn off the warning signal and avoid shock. But let us look at the situation in which avoidance learning has been reported. When the situation is arranged so that the animal can make a continuous forward-moving locomotion response (a close replica of the taking-flight response), as in a running-wheel avoidance, avoidance learning occurs extremely rapidly and the performance level is extremely high. Moreover, it seems that the acquisition of avoidance in this situation is relatively independent of the other experimental contingencies usually associated with avoidance experiments, such as escape from shock and termination of the warning stimulus (Bolles, Stokes, and Younger, 1966). The best avoidance learning, of course, occurs in one-way situations like that of Theios and Dunaway (1964) in which, if the animal does not freeze, learning proceeds to a high level in only a few trials.

In the shuttle box situation, S is again free to locomote—that is, to make a response like the innate unconditioned response to fear—but it unfortunately cannot really leave the situation. The shuttle box requires S to return to the very situation from which it has just escaped. Accordingly, we should expect two findings, moderately good acquisition and a great deal of freezing. Both are commonly reported in shuttle box experiments.

The only other common avoidance learning situation is the Skinner box, and there the rat has notorious difficulty in acquiring efficient avoidance behavior (D'Amato and Schiff, 1964; Meyer, Cho, and Weseman, 1960). The rat acts the same as in the escape situation; it freezes while holding the bar. Sometimes it is fortunate enough to hold the bar in a manner which produces an avoidance when the warning stimulus comes on, but more frequently it freezes throughout the presentation of the warning stimulus and gives a reflexive lurch when the shock comes on. The characteristic outcome of bar-press avoidance studies with rats is that they endure innumerable brief shocks rather than generalize their responding to the presumably fear-eliciting stimulus and terminate it.

We are suggesting that, as in the case of escape, an animal learning an avoidance response must necessarily learn a response that is compatible with, or even a replica of, one of its innate defensive reactions. We are proposing that it is not possible to teach a rat, for example, to groom itself in order to avoid shock, or even to escape shock. We are proposing that it is impossible to teach a pigeon to peck a key in order to avoid shock, or even to escape shock.

A number of references have been made here to "fear," and a parenthetical comment should be made about that tortured concept. One type of fear concept or another is introduced by virtually all theorists dealing with these problems. Unfortunately they do not all seem to refer to the same events and hypothesized processes. Sometimes "fear" refers to a postulated increase in drive; sometimes it is that entity, whatever it is, whose reduction produces learning. At other times it may be a hypothetical or a measured state of the automatic nervous system, such as increased heart rate. For some theorists it is patently an emotion, or a subjective state of mind. Although the author personally has no doubt at all that physiological and even subjective effects of aversive stimulation can be found, he does have grave doubts that such effects can help provide an adequate explanation of defensive behavior (escape and avoidance). Hence, when I speak of fear I am referring to the animal's species-specific defense reactions and noth-

ing more. Fear is the response strength of these anticipatory escape and freezing responses (in the rat). If the situation permits such behavior the animal will take flight or freeze. If flight takes the animal to a situation which does not evoke flight or freezing, then fear can be said to have been reduced. If the situation does not permit flight, then r_E remains strong and fear can be said to be high. In spite of whatever biological utility it may have, freezing is generally maladaptive in the laboratory, because it is self-perpetuating and fails to change the situation. In short, the only properties we need to assign to fear are that it be conditionable and that it lead to flight and/or freezing. How do we know that the animal is frightened if it does not take flight or freeze?

Punishment

There is now reason to believe that learning in a punishment situation is considerably different from what has commonly been supposed. Recent reviews of the punishment literature (Church, 1963; Solomon, 1964) have emphasized that punishment can have quite varied and apparently unpredictable effects upon behavior. It surely is not the case that punishment just weakens the response upon which the punishing stimulus is made contingent. There are situations in which punishing a response appears to strengthen it (Brown, Martin, and Morrow, 1964; Fowler and Miller, 1963).

Consider the Fowler and Miller study. They trained rats to run an alley for food. At the goal, just prior to receiving food, one group of animals was shocked on the back feet and another group was shocked on the front feet. During the course of training the front-foot Ss ran progressively slower than a control group that received no shock. This is what one would ordinarily expect of punishment because the traditional view of punishment is that it is supposed to weaken a response. However, the remarkable finding reported by Fowler and Miller is that Ss shocked on the back feet ran progressively *faster* than the control group. The interpretation proposed for this striking result is that hind-foot shock innately elicits running or lurching forward, whereas front-foot shock innately elicits startle or withdrawal. The speed of running in the alley is determined by the reinforcing effect of food plus a generalization of the response elicited by shock throughout the apparatus. Animals who are shocked in the front feet run slower than the controls because there is a tendency for startle or withdrawal to be evoked by all stimuli that are similar to those existing at the goal. In the same way, the animals shocked on the back feet run faster than the controls because the lurching forward behavior also generalizes throughout the apparatus.

These results suggest the following interpretation. Whenever punishment has an effect upon instrumental behavior it is because S tends to make precisely that response which the punishing stimulus elicits. If the punishing stimulus has freezing as an immediate consequence, then freezing is the response the animal will learn and it will presumably interfere successfully with whatever response the animal was making at the time it was punished. If this is the case then the punishment will be effective in inhibiting the punished response. But if the animal's response to the punisher is to leap or jump away, then that response will be learned. If the punisher elicits withdrawal, which it frequently does, then any approach response will be effectively inhibited. To summarize the findings from a wide variety of punishment studies (Bolles, 1967), the organism can learn through punishment only that specific response which the punisher elicits.

Some writers have noted this anticipatory aspect of punishment-induced responses (for example, Logan and Wagner, 1965); whatever response the punisher elicits will move back in time to anticipate punishment. But earlier writers have imposed no restriction upon what responses the punisher may elicit, and hence, upon what its ultimate effects may be. There is a remarkable similarity, however, between punishment-elicited behavior and our two proposed anticipatory escape responses. In practice, punishment either produces freezing or flight, although flight here may involve either withdrawal backward or running away forward.

There is little evidence to indicate that an incentive analysis of punishment effects can be applied in a systematic manner, but the possibility appears to warrant further investigation. If punishment effects can be subsumed under the broad category of defensive behavior and handled in the same manner as escape and avoidance, and if these apparently diverse situations can all be treated in terms of negative incentives, we will indeed have a powerful explanatory concept.

It will be noted that aversive motivation, like incentive motivation, can be treated either as a motivational principle or as a purely associative element in the regulation of appetitive behavior. If we think of a negative incentive factor produced by an anticipatory freezing or withdrawal response being conditioned to whatever stimuli elicit such behavior innately, we can probably account for any defensive behavior by making a sufficiently critical analysis of the stimuli which impinge upon the animal at a given moment without ever having to invoke a motivational factor per se. There is nothing particularly new about this type of approach; it was suggested many years ago by Seward (1943). Seward suggested (he was speaking only of the appetitive case) that r_G might provide enough stimulus control over an instrumental response that the response could occur without requiring habit strength of its own. Seward (1952, 1956) has continued to propose various forms of negative incentive concepts.

More recently, Mowrer (1960) has presented a unitary treatment of appetitive and aversive behavior by means of complementary emotionlike incentive factors, "hope," on the one hand, and "fear," on the other. In Mowrer's analysis avoidance and punishment learning are given essentially identical treatments, the principal difference between the two being that in the case of punishment the negative incentive, or fear, becomes conditioned to proprioceptive feedback from the punished response. Thus the animal finds that the initiation of the response which was punished produces the unpleasant fear

emotion and so refrains from continuing the response. In the case of avoidance the fear is elicited either by external stimuli from which the animal seeks to free himself, or else by the stimulus consequences of not responding in a particular manner so that the animal initiates some other response which gets rid of the fear (Mowrer and Keehn, 1958). We are free, of course, to think of other possible mechanisms that can relate punishment, avoidance, and escape, but it seems likely that if any theoretical device can encompass these different aversive paradigms, it will have to be some form of negative incentive.

Glossary

activation. A theoretical principle of motivation, according to which the strongest ongoing response or habit is made still stronger as motivation is increased.

anticipatory response. A theoretical response, usually assumed to be a conditionable fraction of the consummatory response, which permits S-R theory to account for animals apparently being able to anticipate reinforcement.

appetitive behavior. Behavior that is motivated by positive reinforcement. Also, the conditions that produce this motivation.

associative. Involving stimuli, responses, and reinforcers, but not motivation.

aversive behavior. Behavior motivated by negative reinforcement. Also, the conditions, usually painful stimuli, that produce this motivation.

avoidance behavior. Behavior presumably reinforced either by the nonoccurrence of aversive stimuli or by the withdrawal of conditioned aversive stimuli.

classical conditioning. A procedure emphasizing the contiguity of stimuli. Also a theoretical process for obtaining learning with this procedure. Synonymous with Pavlovian conditioning.

consummatory response. Certain specific responses such as eating, copulating, and exploring which have been given various theoretical functions; for example, their occurrence reinforces prior responses, they are biologically important, and they lead to satiation.

contiguity. Spatial and temporal closeness of stimuli; usually assumed to be necessary for the response elicited by one stimulus to be conditioned to the other, and sometimes assumed to be sufficient for such learning.

defensive behavior. Generic term for escape and avoidance behavior as well as other learned and innate reactions to aversive stimuli.

deprivation. Any procedure that prevents normal food or water intake. Sometimes, by extension, *deprivation* is applied to other areas to produce sensory deprivation or sexual deprivation, but the motivating effects of these deprivations remain uncertain.

direction of behavior. What S is doing. There is a common vague implication about the direction of behavior persisting until some goal is reached.

drive. Originally, a vague concept of a motivating force. According to Hull and his followers, a theoretical construct which contrasts with incentive in being undirectional, in being unlearned, and in having a physiological basis.

energization. The activation of a habit.

escape. Behavior reinforced by withdrawal or termination of a negative reinforcer.

frustration. Behavioral change following thwarting. Also, the theoretical factor assumed to produce these changes.

general activity. Diffuse behavior, for example, running in an activity wheel, which is usually assumed not to be dependent upon reinforcement.

goal. The object or place which permits a consummatory response to occur; its availability is made contingent upon the occurrence of the operant or instrumental response to be learned.

habit. A theoretical construct in Hull's system which is a permanent change in the nervous system that multiplies with motivation to determine the strength and directionality of behavior.

incentive. A theoretical construct which contrasts with drive in being specific to a particular reinforcer, learned, and having a psychological basis. Also, sometimes the conditions of reinforcement such as amount and delay.

instrumental behavior. Behavior which is acquired (or acquirable) through positive or negative reinforcement. (Synonymous with operant behavior.)

learning. More or less permanent changes in behavior attributable either to reinforcement or to classical conditioning.

mechanism. Any theoretical principle, either physiological or behavioral, that is designed to explain some behavioral phenomenon.

motivation. The theoretical factors other than learning, such as drive and incentive, that contribute to the strength of behavior and give it direction.

Pavlovian conditioning. See classical conditioning.

punishment. A procedure that makes the presentation of an aversive stimulus contingent upon the occurrence of a particular response. The purpose is to weaken the response, and sometimes it does.

r_G, r_F, and r_E. Anticipatory responses associated, respectively, with appetitive, frustration, and escape behavior. Commonly assumed to provide a mechanism for incentive motivation.

reinforcer. A stimulus that can strengthen a response or a habit. If presentation of a stimulus strengthens the response upon which its occurrence is contingent, it is said to be a positive reinforcer; if withdrawal of the stimulus strengthens the response, it is said to be a negative reinforcer.

secondary reinforcer. A stimulus that acquires its reinforcing power by having been contiguous with another reinforcer.

thwarting. A procedure that is assumed to produce frustration; it involves blocking or delaying a previously learned appetitive response.

References

Allison, J., Larson, D., & Jensen, D. D. Acquired fear, brightness preference, and one-way shuttlebox performance. *Psychon. Sci.*, 1967, **8**, 269–270.

Amsel, A. Selective association and the anticipatory goal response mechanism as explanatory concepts in learning theory. *J. exp. Psychol.*, 1949, **39**, 785–799.

Amsel, A. The role of frustrative nonreward in noncontinuous situations. *Psychol. Bull.*, 1958, **55**, 102–119.

Amsel, A. Frustrative nonreward in partial reinforcement and discrimination learning: some recent history and a theoretical extension. *Psychol. Rev.*, 1962, **69**, 306–328.

Amsel, A. Partial reinforcement effects on vigor and persistence: advances in frustration theory derived from a variety of within-subjects experiments. In K. W. Spence & J. T. Spence (Eds.), *The psychology of learning and motivation.* New York: Academic Press, 1967.

Amsel, A., & Prouty, D. L. Frustrative factors in selective learning with reward and nonreward as discriminanda. *J. exp. Psychol.*, 1959, **57**, 224–230.

Amsel, A., & Roussel, J. Motivational properties of frustration: I. Effect on a running response of the addition of frustration to the motivational complex. *J. exp. Psychol.*, 1952, **43**, 363–368.

Amsel, A., & Ward, J. S. Motivational properties of frustration: II. Frustration drive stimulus and frustration reduction in selective learning. *J. exp. Psychol.*, 1954, **48**, 37–47.

Bailey, C. J. The effectiveness of drives as cues. *J. comp. physiol. Psychol.*, 1955, **48**, 183–187.

Baron, A. Functions of CS and US in fear conditioning. *J. comp. physiol. Psychol.*, 1959, **52**, 591–593.

Barry, H., III. Effects of strength of drive on learning and on extinction. *J. exp. Psychol.*, 1958, **55**, 473–481.

Bindra, D. Neuropsychological interpretation of the effects of drive and incentive-motivation on general activity and instrumental behavior. *Psychol. Rev.*, 1968, **75**, 1–22.

Black, A. H. Cardiac conditioning in curarized dogs: The relationship between heart rate and skeletal behavior. In W. F. Prokasy (Ed.), *Classical conditioning*. New York: Appleton-Century-Crofts, 1965.

Bolles, R. C. *Theory of motivation*. New York: Harper & Row, 1967.

Bolles, R. C., & McGillis, D. B. The non-operant nature of the bar-press escape response. *Psychon. Sci.*, 1968, **11**, 261–262.

Bolles, R. C., & Morlock, H. Some asymmetrical drive summation phenomena. *Psychol. Rep.*, 1960, **6**, 373–378.

Bolles, R. C., Stokes, L. W., & Younger, M. S. Does CS termination reinforce avoidance behavior? *J. comp. physiol. Psychol.*, 1966, **62**, 201–297.

Bower, G. H., Fowler, H., & Trapold, M. A. Escape learning as a function of amount of shock reduction. *J. exp. Psychol.*, 1959, **58**, 482–484.

Bower, G., & Grusec, T. Effect of prior Pavlovian discrimination training upon learning an operant discrimination. *J. exp. anal. Behav.*, 1964, **7**, 401–404.

Bower, G., & Kaufman, R. Transfer across drives of the discriminative effect of a Pavlovian conditioned stimulus. *J. exp. anal. Behav.*, 1963, **6**, 445–448.

Brogden, W. J., Lipman, E. A., & Culler, E. The role of incentive in conditioning and learning. *Amer. J. Psychol.*, 1938, **51**, 109–117.

Brown, J. S. Problems presented by the concept of acquired drives. In *Current theory and research in motivation: a symposium*. Lincoln: Univer. of Nebraska Press, 1953.

Brown, J. S. *The motivation of behavior*. New York: McGraw-Hill, 1961.

Brown, J. S., & Farber, I. E. Secondary motivational systems. *Ann. Rev. Psychol.*, 1968, **19**, 99–134.

Brown, J. S., Martin, R. C., & Morrow, M. W. Self-punitive behavior in the rat: Facilitative effects of punishment on resistance to extinction. *J. comp. physiol. Psychol.*, 1964, **57**, 127–133.

Brown, W. L., Gentry, G., & Kaplan, S. J. The effect of intra-maze delay: I. Delay enforced by a revolving wheel. *J. comp. physiol. Psychol.*, 1948, **41**, 258–268.

Buss, A. H. Instrumentality of aggression, feedback, and frustration as determinants of physical aggression. *J. pers. soc. Psychol.*, 1966, **3**, 153–162.

Campbell, B. A., & Cicala, G. A. Studies of water deprivation in rats as a function of age. *J. comp. physiol. Psychol.*, 1962, **55**, 763–768.

Campbell, B. A., & Kraeling, D. Response strength as a function of drive level and amount of drive reduction. *J. exp. Psychol.*, 1953, **45**, 97–101.

Campbell, B. A., Smith, N. F., Misanin, J. R., & Jaynes, J. Species differences in activity during hunger and thirst. *J. comp. physiol. Psychol.*, 1966, **61**, 123–127.

Carlton, P. L. Response strength as a function of delay of reward and physical confinement. Unpublished M.A. thesis, State Univer. of Iowa, 1954. Cited by Spence, 1956.

Champion, R. A., & Smith, L. R. Predicting discrimination learning from differential conditioning with amount of reinforcement as a variable. *J. exp. Psychol.*, 1966, **71**, 529–534.

Church, R. M. The varied effects of punishment on behavior. *Psychol. Rev.*, 1963, **70**, 369–402.

Cicala, G. A. Running speed in rats as a function of drive level and presence or absence of competing response trials. *J. exp. Psychol.*, 1961, **62**, 329–334.

Cizek, L. J. Relationship between food and water ingestion in the rabbit. *Amer. J. Physiol.*, 1961, **201**, 557–566.

Clayton, K. N., & Koplin, S. T. T-maze learning as a joint function of probability and magnitude of reward. *Psychon. Sci.*, 1964, **1**, 381–382.

Cofer, C. N., & Appley, M. H. *Motivation: Theory and research*. New York: Wiley, 1964.

Collier, G. Some properties of saccharin as a reinforcer. *J. exp. Psychol.*, 1962, **64**, 184–191.

Collier, G., & Marx, M. H. Changes in performance as a function of shifts in the magnitude of reinforcement. *J. exp. Psychol.*, 1959, **57**, 305–309.

Collier, G., & Siskel, M., Jr. Performance as a joint function of amount of reinforcement and interreinforcement interval. *J. exp. Psychol.*, 1959, **57**, 115–1120.

Cooper, J. B. The effect upon performance of introduction and removal of a delay within the maze. *J. comp. Psychol.*, 1938, **25**, 457–462.

Cornish, E. R., & Mrosovsky, N. Activity during food deprivation and satiation in six species of rodent. *Anim. Behav.*, 1965, **13**, 242–248.

Crespi, L. P. Quantitative variation of incentive and performance in the white rat. *Amer. J. Psychol.*, 1942, **55**, 467–517.

Crum, J., Brown, W. L., & Bitterman, M. E. The effect of partial and delayed reinforcement on resistance to extinction. *Amer. J. Psychol.*, 1951, **64**, 228–237.

D'Amato, M. R., & Schiff, D. Long-term discriminated avoidance performance in the rat. *J. comp. physiol. Psychol.*, 1964, **57**, 123–126.

Davenport, J. W. Spatial discrimination and reversal learning involving magnitude of reinforcement. *Psychol. Rep.*, 1963, **12**, 655–665.

Davenport, J. W. Distribution of M and i parameters for rats trained under varying hunger drive levels. *J. genet. Psychol.*, 1965, **106**, 113–121.

Dollard, J., Doob, L. W., Miller, N. E., Mowrer, O. H., & Sears, R. R. *Frustration and aggression.* New Haven: Yale Univer. Press, 1939.

Duda, J. J., & Bolles, R. C. Effects of prior deprivation, current deprivation and weight loss on the activity of the hungry rat. *J. comp. physiol. Psychol.*, 1963, **56**, 569–571.

Ehrenfreund, D., & Badia, P. Response strength as a function of drive level and pre- and postshift incentive magnitude. *J. exp. Psychol.*, 1962, **63**, 468–471.

Elliott, M. H. The effect of change of "drive" on maze performance. *Univer. of California Publ. Psychol.*, 1929, **4**, 185–188.

Eninger, M. V. The role of generalized approach and avoidance tendencies in brightness discrimination. *J. comp. physiol. Psychol.*, 1953, **46**, 398–402.

Estes, W. K. Stimulus-response theory of drive. In M. R. Jones (Ed.), *Nebraska symposium on motivation.* Lincoln: Univer. of Nebraska Press, 1958.

Estes, W. K. Growth and function of mathematical models for learning. In *Current trends in psychological theory.* Pittsburgh: Univer. of Pittsburgh Press, 1961.

Estes, W. K., & Suppes, P. Foundations of linear models. In R. R. Bush & W. K. Estes (Eds.), *Studies in mathematical learning theory.* Stanford: Stanford Univer. Press, 1959.

Fehrer, E. Effect of amount of reinforcement and of pre- and post-reinforcement delays on learning and extinction. *J. exp. Psychol.*, 1956, **52**, 167–176.

Ferster, C. B. Sustained behavior under delayed reinforcement. *J. exp. Psychol.*, 1953, **45**, 218–224.

Feshbach, S. The function of aggression and the regulation of aggressive drive. *Psychol. Rev.*, 1964, **71**, 257–272.

Finch, G. Hunger as a determinant of conditional and unconditional salivary response magnitude. *Amer. J. Physiol.*, 1938, **123**, 379–382.

Finger, F. W. Effect of food deprivation on running-wheel activity in naive rats. *Psychol. Rep.*, 1965, **16**, 753–757.

Finger, F. W., Reid, L. S., & Weasner, M. H. The effect of reinforcement upon activity during cyclic food deprivation. *J. comp. physiol. Psychol.*, 1957, **50**, 495–498.

Finger, F. W., Reid, L. S., & Weasner, M. H. Activity changes as a function of reinforcement under low drive. *J. comp. physiol. Psychol.*, 1960, **53**, 385–387.

Fowler, H., & Miller, N. E. Facilitation and inhibition of runway performance by hind- and forepaw shock of various intensities. *J. comp. physiol. Psychol.*, 1963, **56**, 801–805.

Freud, S. *The interpretation of dreams.* 1900. In A. A. Brill (Ed.), The basic writings of Sigmund Freud. New York: Modern Library, 1938.

Gonzalez, R. C., & Diamond, L. A test of Spence's theory of incentive-motivation. *Amer. J. Psychol.*, 1960, **73**, 396–403.

Goodrich, K. P. Performance in different segments of an instrumental response chain as a function of reinforcement schedule. *J. exp. Psychol.*, 1959, **57**, 57–63.

Goodrich, K. P. Running speed and drinking rate as functions of sucrose concentration and amount of consummatory activity. *J. comp. physiol. Psychol.*, 1960, **53**, 245–250.

Greene, J. E. Magnitude of reward and acquisition of a black-white discrimination habit. *J. exp. Psychol.*, 1953, **46**, 113–119.

Grice, G. R. The relation of secondary reinforcement to delayed reward in visual discrimination learning. *J. exp. Psychol.*, 1948, **38**, 1–16.

Grice, G. R., & Goldman, H. M. Generalized extinction and secondary reinforcement in visual discrimination learning with delayed reward. *J. exp. Psychol.*, 1955, **50**, 197–200.

Guthrie, E. R. *The psychology of learning.* New York: Harper & Row, 1935.

Harker, G. S. Delay of reward and performance of an instrumental response. *J. exp. Psychol.*, 1956, **51**, 303–310.

Holder, W. B., Marx, M. H., Holder, E. E., & Collier, G. Response strength as a function of delay in a runway. *J. exp. Psychol.*, 1957, **53**, 316–323.

Hull, C. L. Simple trial-and-error learning. *Psychol. Rev.*, 1930, **37**, 241–256.

Hull, C. L. Goal attraction and directing ideas conceived as habit phenomena. *Psychol. Rev.*, 1931, **38**, 487–506.

Hull, C. L. Differential habituation to internal stimuli in the albino rat. *J. comp. Psychol.*, 1933, **16**, 255–273.

Hull, C. L. *Principles of behavior.* New York: Appleton-Century-Crofts, 1943.

Hull, C. L. *A behavior system.* New Haven: Yale Univer. Press, 1952.

Hunter, W. S. Delayed reactions in animals and children. *Behav. Monogr.*, 1913, No. 2.

Ison, J. R. Acquisition and reversal of a spatial response as a function of sucrose concentration. *J. exp. Psychol.*, 1964, **67**, 495–496.

Kelleher, R. T., & Gollub, L. R. A review of positive conditioned reinforcement. *J. exp. anal. Behav.*, 1962, **5**, 543–597.

Kendler, H. H. Drive interaction: I. Learning as a function of the simultaneous presence of the hunger and thirst drives. *J. exp. Psychol.*, 1945, **35**, 96–109.

Kendler, H. H. The influence of simultaneous hunger and thirst drives upon the learning of two opposed spatial responses of the white rat. *J. exp. Psychol.*, 1946, **36**, 212–220.

Kendler, H. H., Karasik, A. D., & Schrier, A. M. Studies of the effect of change of drive: III. Amounts of switching produced by shifting drive from thirst to hunger and from hunger to thirst. *J. exp. Psychol.*, 1954, **47**, 179–182.

Kimble, G. A. Shock intensity and avoidance learning. *J. comp. physiol. Psychol.*, 1955, **48**, 281–284.

Koppman, J., & Grice, G. R. Goal-box and alley similarity in latent extinction. *J. exp. Psychol.*, 1963, **66**, 611–612.

Kurtz, K. H., & Jarka, R. G. Position preference based on differential food privation. *J. comp. physiol. Psychol.*, 1968, **66**, 518–521.

Lambert, W. W., & Solomon, R. L. Extinction of a running response as a function of distance of block point from the goal. *J. comp. physiol. Psychol.*, 1952, **45**, 269–279.

Lawrence, D., & Hommel, L. The influence of differential goal boxes on discrimination learning involving delay of reinforcement. *J. comp. physiol. Psychol.*, 1961, **54**, 552–555.

Lawson, R. Brightness discrimination performance and secondary reward strength as a function of primary reward amount. *J. comp. physiol. Psychol.*, 1957, **50**, 35–39.

Lawson, R., & Marx, M. H. Frustration: theory and experiment. *Genet. Psychol. Monogr.*, 1958, **57**, 393–464.

Leeper, R. The role of motivation in learning: a study of the phenomenon of differential motivational control of the utilization of habits. *J. genet. Psychol.*, 1935, **46**, 3–40.

Levine, S. The role of irrelevant drive stimuli in learning. *J. exp. Psychol.*, 1953, **45**, 410–416.

Levine, S. The effects of a strong irrelevant drive on learning. *Psychol. Rep.*, 1956, **2**, 29–33.

Lewin, K. Das Problem der Willenmessung der Assoziation. *Psychol. Forsch.*, 1922, **1**, 191–302; **2**, 65–140.

Lewis, D. J., Butler, D., & Diamond, A. L. Direct manipulation of the fractional anticipatory goal response. *Psychol. Rep.*, 1958, **4**, 575–578.

Ley, R. Effects of food and water deprivation on the performance of a response motivated by acquired fear. *J. exp. Psychol.*, 1965, **69**, 583–589.

Logan, F. A. The role of delay of reinforcement in determining reaction potential. *J. exp. Psychol.*, 1952, **43**, 393–399.

Logan, F. A. *Incentive*. New Haven: Yale Univer. Press, 1960.

Logan, F. A., Beier, E. M., & Ellis, R. A. Effect of varied reinforcement on speed of locomotion. *J. exp. Psychol.*, 1955, **49**, 260–266.

Logan, F. A., Beier, E. M., & Kincaid, W. D. Extinction following partial and varied reinforcement. *J. exp. Psychol.*, 1956, **52**, 65–70.

Logan, F. A., & Wagner, A. R. *Reward and punishment*. Boston: Allyn & Bacon, 1965.

Marx, M. H. Some relations between frustration and drive. In M. R. Jones (Ed.), *Nebraska symposium on motivation*. Lincoln: Univer. of Nebraska Press, 1956.

Marx, M. H., & Brownstein, A. J. Effects of incentive magnitude on running speeds without competing responses in acquisition and extinction. *J. exp. Psychol.*, 1963, **65**, 192–189.

McDougall, W. *An introduction to social psychology*. Boston: Luce, 1908.

Mendelson, J. Role of hunger in T-maze learning for food by rats. *J. comp. physiol. Psychol.*, 1966, **62**, 341–349.

Mendelson, J. Lateral hypothalamic stimulation in satiated rats: the rewarding effects of self-induced drinking. *Science*, 1967, **157**, 1077–1079.

Meyer, D. R., Cho, C., & Wesemann, A. F. On problems of conditioned discriminated lever-press avoidance responses. *Psychol. Rev.*, 1960, **67**, 224–228.

Miller, N. E. A reply to "sign-gestalt or conditioned reflex." *Psychol. Rev.*, 1935, **42**, 280–292.

Miller, N. E. Studies in fear as an acquirable drive: I. Fear as motivation and fear-reduction as reinforcement in the learning of new responses. *J. exp. Psychol.*, 1948, **38**, 89–101.

Miller, N. E. Some reflections on the law of effect produce a new alternative to drive reduction. In M. R. Jones (Ed.), *Nebraska symposium on motivation*. Lincoln: Univer. of Nebraska Press, 1963.

Miller, N. E., & DeBold, R. C. Classically conditioned tongue-licking and operant bar pressing recorded simultaneously in the rat. *J. comp. physiol. Psychol.*, 1965, **59**, 109–111.

Miller, N. E., Sampliner, R. I., & Woodrow, P. Thirst-reducing effects of water by stomach fistula vs. water by mouth measured by both a consummatory and an instrumental response. *J. comp. physiol. Psychol.*, 1957, **50**, 1–5.

Moltz, H. Latent extinction and the fractional anticipatory response mechanism. *Psychol. Rev.*, 1957, **64**, 229–241.

Montgomery, K. C., & Segall, M. Discrimination learning based upon the exploratory drive. *J. comp. physiol. Psychol.*, 1955, **48**, 132–136.

Morrison, J. H., & Porter, J. J. Magnitude of reward in selective learning. *Psychon. Sci.*, 1965, **3**, 531–532.

Morse, W. H., & Skinner, B. F. Some factors involved in the stimulus control of operant behavior. *J. exp. anal. Behav.*, 1958, **1**, 103–107.

Mowrer, O. H. *Learning theory and behavior*. New York: Wiley, 1960.

Mowrer, O. H., & Keehn, J. D. How are inter-trial "avoidance" responses reinforced? *Psychol. Rev.*, 1958, **65**, 209–221.

Mowrer, O. H., & Lamoreaux, R. R. Avoidance conditioning and signal duration—a study of secondary motivation and reward. *Psychol. Monogr.*, 1942, **54** (Whole no. 247).

Muenzinger, K. F., & Fletcher, F. M. Motivation in learning: VII. The effect of an enforced delay at the point of choice in the visual discrimination habit. *J. comp. Psychol.*, 1937, **23**, 383–392.

Myers, J. L. The effects of delay of reinforcement upon an operant discrimination in the pigeon. *J. exp. Psychol.*, 1958, **55**, 363–368.

Pavlik, W. B., & Reynolds, W. F. Effects of deprivation schedule and reward magnitude on acquisition and extinction performance. *J. comp. physiol. Psychol.*, 1963, **56**, 452–455.

Pereboom, A. C., & Crawford, B. M. Instrumental and competing behavior as a function of trials and reward magnitude. *J. exp. Psychol.*, 1958, **56**, 82–85.

Perin, C. T. Behavioral potentiality as a joint function of the amount of training and the degree of hunger at the time of extinction. *J. exp. Psychol.*, 1942, **30**, 93–113.

Perin, C. T. The effect of delayed reinforcement upon the differentiation of bar responses in white rats. *J. exp. Psychol.*, 1943, **32**, 95–109.

Perkins, C. C., Jr. The relation of secondary reward to gradients of reinforcement. *J. exp. Psychol.*, 1947, **37**, 377–392.

Premack, D. Reversibility of the reinforcement relation. *Science*, 1962, **136**, 255–257.

Ramond, C. K. Performance in instrumental learning as a joint function of delay of reinforcement and time of deprivation. *J. exp. Psychol.*, 1954, **47**, 248–250.

Renner, K. E. Influence of deprivation and availability of goal box cues on the temporal gradient of reinforcement. *J. comp. physiol. Psychol.*, 1963, **56**, 101–104.

Rescorla, R. A., & Solomon, R. L. Two-process learning theory: Relationships between Pavlovian conditioning and instrumental learning. *Psychol. Rev.*, 1967, **74**, 151–182.

Revusky, S. H. Hunger level during food consumption: Effects on subsequent preference. *Psychon. Sci.*, 1967, **7**, 109–110.

Revusky, S. H. Effects of thirst level during consumption of flavored water on subsequent preference. *J. comp. physiol. Psychol.*, 1968, **66**, 777–779.

Reynolds, B., Marx, M. H., & Henderson, R. L. Resistance to extinction as a function of drive-reward interaction. *J. comp. physiol. Psychol.*, 1952, **45**, 36–42.

Reynolds, W. F., & Anderson, J. E. Choice behavior in a T-maze as a function of deprivation period and magnitude of reward. *Psychol. Rep.*, 1961, **8**, 131–134.

Seward, J. P. Reinforcement in terms of association. *Psychol. Rev.*, 1943, **50**, 187–202.

Seward, J. P. An experimental analysis of latent learning. *J. exp. Psychol.*, 1949, **39**, 177–186.

Seward, J. P. Introduction to a theory of motivation in learning. *Psychol. Rev.*, 1952, **59**, 405–413.

Seward, J. P. Drive, incentive, and reinforcement. *Psychol. Rev.*, 1956, **63**, 195–203.

Seward, J. P., & Procter, D. M. Performance as a function of drive, reward, and habit strength. *Amer. J. Psychol.*, 1960, **73**, 448–453.

Sgro, J. A., & Weinstock, S. Effects of delay on subsequent running under immediate reinforcement. *J. exp. Psychol.*, 1963, **66**, 260–263.

Sheffield, F. D. New evidence on the drive-induction theory of reinforcement. In R. N. Haber (Ed.), *Current research in motivation.* New York: Holt, Rinehart and Winston, 1966.

Sheffield, F. D., & Campbell, B. A. The role of experience in the "spontaneous" activity of hungry rats. *J. comp. physiol. Psychol.*, 1954, **47**, 97–100.

Sheffield, F. D., & Roby, T. B. Reward value of a non-nutritive sweet taste. *J. comp. physiol. Psychol.*, 1950, **43**, 471–481.

Sheffield, F. D., Roby, T. B., & Campbell, B. A. Drive reduction versus consummatory behavior as determinants of reinforcement. *J. comp. physiol. Psychol.*, 1954, **47**, 349–355.

Sheffield, F. D., Wulff, J. J., & Backer, R. Reward value of copulation without sex drive reduction. *J. comp. physiol. Psychol.*, 1951, **44**, 3–8.

Siegel, P. S. Alien drive, habit strength, and resistance to extinction. *J. comp. Psychol.*, 1946, **39**, 307–317.

Smith, S., & Guthrie, E. R. *General psychology in terms of behavior.* New York: Appleton-Century-Crofts, 1921.

Solomon, R. L. Punishment. *Amer. Psychologist*, 1964, **19**, 239–253.

Spear, N. E., & Pavlik, W. B. Percentage of reinforcement and reward magnitude effects in a T-maze: between and within subjects. *J. exp. Psychol.*, 1966, **71**, 521–528.

Spence, K. W. The role of secondary reinforcement in delayed reward learning. *Psychol. Rev.*, 1947, **54**, 1–8.

Spence, K. W. Theoretical interpretations of learning. In C. P. Stone (Ed.), *Comparative psychology*, 3rd Ed. Englewood Cliffs, N.J.: Prentice-Hall, 1951.

Spence, K. W. *Behavior theory and conditioning*. New Haven: Yale Univer. Press, 1956.

Spence, K. W. An emotionally based theory of drive (D) and its relation to performance in simple learning situations. *Amer. Psychologist*, 1958, **13**, 131–141.

Tapp, J. T., & Simpson, L. L. Motivational and response factors as determinants of the reinforcing value of light onset. *J. comp. physiol. Psychol.*, 1966, **62**, 13, 143–146.

Teel, K. S. Habit strength as a function of motivation during learning. *J. comp. physiol. Psychol.*, 1952, **45**, 188–191.

Teghtsoonian, R., & Campbell, B. A. Random activity of the rat during food deprivation as a function of environment. *J. comp. physiol. Psychol.*, 1960, **53**, 242–244.

Theios, J., & Dunaway, J. E. One-way versus shuttle avoidance conditioning. *Psychon. Sci.*, 1964, **1**, 251–252.

Thorndike, E. L. *Animal intelligence*. New York: Macmillan, 1911.

Tolman, E. C. *Purposive behavior in animals and men*. New York: Appleton-Century-Crofts, 1932.

Tombaugh, T. N. Resistance to extinction as a function of the interaction between training and extinction delays. *Psychol. Rep.*, 1966, **19**, 791–798.

Trapold, M. A. Reversal of an operant discrimination by non-contingent discrimination reversal training. *Psychon. Sci.*, 1966, **4**, 247–248.

Trapold, M. A., & Bell, J. E. Effect of non-contingent exposure to shifts in reward magnitude in subsequent instrumental runway performance. *Psychol. Rep.*, 1964, **15**, 679–684.

Trapold, M. A., & Fowler, H. Instrumental escape performance as a function of the intensity of noxious stimulation. *J. exp. Psychol.*, 1960, **60**, 323–326.

Treichler, F. R., & Collins, R. W. Comparison of cyclic and continuous deprivation on wheel running. *J. comp. physiol. Psychol.*, 1965, **60**, 447–448.

Verplanck, W. S., & Hayes, J. R. Eating and drinking as a function of maintenance schedule. *J. comp. physiol. Psychol.*, 1953, **46**, 327–333.

Wagner, A. R. Effects of amount and percentage of reinforcement and number of acquisition trials on conditioning and extinction. *J. exp. Psychol.*, 1961, **62**, 234–242.

Wagner, A. R. Conditioned frustration as a learned drive. *J. exp. Psychol.*, 1963, **66**, 142–148.

Warden, C. J., & Haas, E. L. The effect of short intervals of delay in feeding upon speed of maze learning. *J. comp. Psychol.*, 1927, **7**, 107–116.

Watson, J. B. *Psychology from the standpoint of a behaviorist*. Philadelphia: Lippincott, 1919.

Webb, W. B. The motivational aspect of an irrelevant drive in the behavior of the white rat. *J. exp. Psychol.*, 1949, **39**, 1–14.

Williams, S. B. Resistance to extinction as a function of the number of reinforcements. *J. exp. Psychol.*, 1938, **23**, 506–521.

Wist, E. R. Amount, delay, and position of delay of reinforcement as parameters of runway performance. *J. exp. Psychol.*, 1962, **63**, 160–166.

Wist, E. R. Effect of training level at the time of introduction of delay on runway performance. *Psychol. Rep.*, 1963, **12**, 899–911.

Woods, P. J., Davidson, E. H., & Peters, R. J., Jr. Instrumental escape conditioning in a water tank: effects of variations in drive stimulus intensity and reinforcement magnitude. *J. comp. physiol. Psychol.*, 1964, **57**, 466–470.

Yamaguchi, H. G. The effect of continuous, partial, and varied magnitude reinforcement on acquisition and extinction. *J. exp. Psychol.*, 1961, **61**, 319–321.

Young, P. T., & Shuford, E. H., Jr. Quantitative control of motivation through sucrose solutions of different concentrations. *J. comp. physiol. Psychol.*, 1955, **48**, 114–118.

Suggested Readings

Amsel, A. The role of frustrative nonreward in noncontinuous situations. *Psychol. Rev.*, 1958, **55**, 102–119. Frustration treated as an incentive-motivational effect.

Bolles, R. C. *Theory of motivation.* New York: Harper & Row, 1967. A survey of much of the relevant research and a critical view of the drive construct.

Brown, J. S. *The motivation of behavior.* New York: McGraw-Hill, 1961. A survey of relevant research and a partisan view of the drive construct.

Cofer, C. N., & Appley, M. H. *Motivation: theory and research.* New York: Wiley, 1964. A consideration of further topics in motivation and learning not treated here, especially those involved in human motivation.

Lawson, R., & Marx, M. H. Frustration: theory and experiment. *Genet. Psychol. Monogr.*, 1958, **57**, 393–464. A skeptical view of frustration as a motivational effect.

Mowrer, O. H. *Learning theory and behavior.* New York: Wiley, 1960. A provocative treatment of incentive theory as well as the special problem of negative incentives.

Rescorla, R. A., & Solomon, R. L. Two-process learning theory: relationships between Pavlovian conditioning and instrumental learning. *Psychol. Rev.*, 1967, **74**, 151–182. Some new considerations in incentive theory, including one aspect of negative incentives.

II

Perception and Learning

James M. Vanderplas

Washington University

Types of Interactions

Perception and learning, like most other concepts in psychology, have traditionally been treated as separate topics of investigation. But their interaction has long been recognized. The empiricists' position in philosophy, that perceptual experiences arise out of the association, through learning, of basic sensory elements, attests to an assumed interaction of perception and learning. And the opposed philosophical position of the nativistic school, that the organization of sensory elements, as given, determines and limits knowledge, implies an acceptance of an interaction of learning and perception. The fact of this recognition is further supported by the arguments for these opposed positions in philosophy; they have more often been stated in terms of *dependency* than in terms of *interaction*. The empiricist position implies a dependency of perception upon learning, whereas the nativist position implies a dependency of learning upon perception. Both positions, nevertheless, recognize an interaction, with the major disagreement being over the *direction* of the interaction. For a detailed account of the history of the controversy, see Boring (1942, Chaps. 9–13) and Hochberg (1962).

Present-day theorists of learning recognize its interaction with perception by including perceptual relations as partial determinants of learning, and most modern perceptual theorists recognize the interaction by including past experience as a partial determinant of perception. In learning theory, for example, the fundamental concept of stimulus generalization and its use as a basis for an account of transfer of learning clearly imply a dependency of transfer upon the organization of sensory elements. A dog, conditioned to salivate in response to a tone of 1,000 cps, will also respond to other tones, higher or lower in frequency, the strength of the response being related to the difference in frequency between the new tone and the original conditioned stimulus tone. In the Gestalt theory of perception (commonly regarded as nativistic), as an opposite example, past experience or "custom" is included as a factor in determining the mode of perception. A series of words, for instance, printed without spaces between them can nevertheless be grouped or separated by the reader, the perception of individual words being dependent upon the customary mode of organizing them in past experience.

A number of early and recent experiments in psychology will serve to indicate some of the kinds of interactions that might be found between learning and perception. A review of the results of a few of these experiments and some of the interpretations of the results also will serve to introduce some of the problems involved in determining the nature and direction of the interactions. In this review we shall illustrate four types of interactions:

1. The effect of practice on the change of a sensory process—a threshold.
2. The role of perceptual organization in learning.
3. The effects of reward and punishment on perceptual organization.
4. The effect of labeling of stimuli upon later discrimination in instrumental performance.

Effect of Practice on a Sensory Process

The effect of practice on a sensory process is illustrated by an experiment performed by A. W. Volkmann over 100 years ago. While attempting to measure the two-point limen on the skin (the distance between two point-stimuli that is just perceived as two rather than one), Volkmann (1858) noted three remarkable phenomena. First, a striking decrease, with practice, of the threshold occurred in the area of the skin where the stimuli were applied. Second, the corresponding area on the opposite side of the body seemed to develop an almost equal improvement, without specific practice in the (opposite) area. Third, this "acquired sensitivity" decreased or disappeared after a few days. These phenomena were later confirmed in experiments by Dresslar (1894), Messenger (1903), and Boring (1920).

The apparent decrease in the two-point threshold must have been quite puzzling at the time. For this was a period in psychology when a physiological interpretation of perceptual phenomena was common. Johannes Mueller's doctrine of specific energies of nerves was popular among physiologists. The doctrine said, in effect, that there is a correspondence between the nature of the nerves of sense and the perception. Thus, for the two-point limen, the feeling of two points would be said to depend on the density of the distribution of touch receptors in the skin. Where receptors are sparsely populated, the two points would need to be farther apart in order to feel like two points than they would where the receptors are densely populated. The threshold should therefore depend upon the density of population of touch receptors, but certainly not upon the "experience" (practice) that the nerves had had in "feeling" the points!

That the decrease should also occur on the symmetrically opposite area of the body and not in nonsymmetrical areas was equally puzzling. It was not definitely known at the time that opposite members of the peripheral nervous system are represented in symmetrically opposite parts of the brain, and according to the specific energies doctrine one would perhaps be more likely to assume that any "transfer effect" would "spread" more readily to adjacent areas than to areas all the way over on the other side of the body. To confound the result, the fact that the change in sensitivity with practice was somehow also subject to disappearance with disuse was clearly contrary to a peripheral account in terms of the doctrine of specific energies of nerves. Volkmann nevertheless inferred, principally on the basis of the transfer effect, that the change was in the brain, not the skin.

For our present purposes it is important to note that Volkmann did not specify the nature of the change in the brain but that he did specify (by inference) that the change took place there. The fact of a change in the threshold would seem to imply that a perception was somehow subject to change as a result of experience (learning) and disuse of the structure (forgetting.) The account of this change was still, at the time, made in terms of structure, albeit brain structure and not peripheral nerve structure. So the interaction of perception and learning, though factually established in this instance, was accounted for by reference to a perceptual (structural) mechanism.

We may note, parenthetically, that there are two alternative accounts of this interaction. First, the associationist could account easily for Volkmann's finding by saying the "idea" of "twoness," arising from the sensation of twoness on one side of the body, would become associated with the idea of twoness on the opposite side. But he would have difficulty explaining why this should be more likely to occur on symmetrically opposite areas than in adjacent areas. Second, one could postulate that the result was due to improvement in the interpretation of subthreshold stimulation. At distances so small that the two points are felt as one there are still small differences that can be correctly interpreted. These small differences vary considerably from area to area, but they are more likely to be similar in feeling on symmetrically opposite areas.

Role of Perceptual Organization in Learning

The second kind of interaction appears in an extensive series of experiments with chimpanzees. Köhler (1924) confronted his *S*s with a number of problems to solve, one of which required that a pair of sticks be fastened together at the ends to make a single long stick which could be used as a rake to obtain a food container placed outside the animal's cage. Normally, we would expect a chimpanzee to engage in a good deal of trial-and-error behavior before solving this problem, and indeed many of them did in Köhler's experiments. They would try to reach the food without

the sticks and, failing that, would try to use only one of the two sticks as a rake, but to no avail. However, when the sticks were seen by the animal as being able to be fastened together, the solution proceeded forthwith.

These studies by Köhler illustrate an interaction in the direction opposite to that of the one described previously. Although Volkmann's experiment showed that a perception may be modified by learning (practice), Köhler's experiments with the chimpanzees indicate that learning to solve a problem may depend upon the organization of perceptual cues. That is, although the animal may engage in trial-and-error activity, the Gestalt psychologist would argue that the activity will not, by itself, result in learning unless it results in reorganization of the perceptual cues which are important in perception of the relations of the parts (Hilgard, 1948, Chap. 7). Thus, unless the animal perceives the parts of the sticks as being capable of being put together and used as a rake, it will not solve the problem.

We should note that at the time of Köhler's studies (1921, 1924) the school of Gestalt psychology, established by Wertheimer, Koffka, and Köhler, was about eight years old. Köhler's experiments were designed to show that perceptual organization (as opposed to compounded elements) is an important variable in perception and that the same principles that apply to perception also apply to learning and thinking. Later experiments by Köhler (1941) showed that even associative learning, in a paired-associates task, may be strongly influenced by the organization of the associated materials. In these experiments Köhler showed that when a pair of stimulus forms was drawn so that they could fit together (like a jig-saw puzzle), they were more readily associated than when they did not so fit. Thus, the Gestalt perceptual principle of "fittingness" was shown to be appropriate as a principle of learning as well.

Effects of Reward and Punishment on Perceptual Organization

The effect of reward and punishment on perceptual organization is illustrated in an experiment by Schafer and Murphy (1943). Human Ss were shown ambiguous figures consisting of semicircles, the diameter line of which was curved so that it could be seen as a profile of a face. Two such semicircles could be fitted together like pieces of a jig-saw puzzle so the diameter of the resulting circle could be seen as either a left or right profile on a circular ground. Following a number of trials in which rewards (pennies) were given on presentation of one of the semicircles and punishment (removal of pennies) was given on presentation of the other semicircle, the complete ambiguous figure was shown. The face that was reported was the rewarded one on most (80 per cent) of the test trials.

This experiment illustrates an interaction different from the two previous ones we have reviewed. Schafer and Murphy interpreted the effect of the reward as increasing the probability that the rewarded face would be reported as figure (by naming the appropriate half of the ambiguous form as the one recognized). They also inferred from these results that the reward influenced the perception of the figure-ground relationship. Thus, reward, normally considered by learning theorists to be effective in modifying responses alone (in the usual S-R learning paradigm), is shown possibly to be effective in modifying even fundamental perceptions.

The experiment by Schafer and Murphy has been challenged in several later studies (Rock and Fleck, 1950; Smith and Hochberg, 1954; Postman, 1963) on grounds that it was not the *perception* that was altered by reward and punishment, but the *response*, of naming the recognized form. It has also been criticized for the way in which the data were selected for analysis (Solley and Murphy, 1960, pp. 265–270). We shall have more to say later about this

kind of interpretation, because this problem is both an interpretive one and one of experimental design.

Effect of Labeling on Later Discrimination

The fourth kind of interaction, the effect of labeling on later discrimination, is illustrated in an experiment by Birge (1941). Children were first taught to call abstract animal drawings by nonsense names. Three drawings were used, one having one name, the other two both having the same, second name. Let us say, for illustration, that Figure A was called X, and both Figures B and C were called Y. When the names were learned, Ss were next conditioned to reach for a box on which was drawn Figure B. The reaching response was rewarded when the S found a piece of candy under the box. Following the conditioning procedure, a test was made of generalization of the reaching response to each of two boxes on which were drawn Figures A and C, respectively. It was found, remarkably, that generalization from Figure B to Figure C was much greater than from Figure B to Figure A. The figures and the names were counterbalanced across several groups of Ss, so that the generalization would be expected to be equal if it were based on pure stimulus similarity as in the case of classical generalization. Therefore, the greater generalization was to a figure called by the same name in the first part of the experiment, whereas the lesser generalization was to a figure called by a different name.

In this study by Birge, it is shown that stimulus generalization, normally associated with perceptual variables such as physical similarity of the stimuli, may be influenced by the nature of the response process involved. When Birge's Ss learned names for the forms, the naming response, occurring along with the reaching response during the second phase of the experiment, served to mediate or influence positively the generalization of the reaching response from the conditional stimulus form to the other form called by the same name during the first phase of the experiment.

Here, as in the Schafer-Murphy experiment, there is difficulty in reaching complete agreement on the interpretation. It could be argued, for example, that the generalization was not stimulus generalization, but merely transfer of the response, made to the (implicit or covert) form called by the same name. We shall reserve judgment on this question until we have had an opportunity to examine more closely the empirical studies of Chapter 7.

Summary

Now, the preceding four kinds of findings illustrate, in a preliminary way, some of the kinds of interactions one may find of perception and learning and some of the problems of interpretation. We find, first, an interaction of past experience with perceptions arising from direct stimulation; second, we see interactions of perceptual cues with trial-and-error behavior engendered in problem solving; third, we find an interaction of reinforcement, a response-learning principle, with a fundamental figure-ground perceptual relation; and fourth, we see an interaction of a perceptual phenomenon, stimulus generalization, with a principle of transfer mediated in some way by reinforcement of response.

As we have noted with respect to each illustration, although the fact of these interactions is established and recognized, the means by and manner in which they occur are not very clear. The interpretation of the results and the inferences drawn from the interpretation are subject to many disagreements. The nature of the disagreements, in turn, depends upon the theoretical position adopted in interpreting the findings and even upon the definitions adopted for the theory. In order to understand these differences prior to reviewing more extensively the studies dealing with these interactions, we shall find it convenient to look briefly into some of the major definitions and theories of perception and learning.

6

Definitions and Theories

In attempting to deal with the problem of the nature and basis of interactions of learning and perception, we must examine briefly some of the definitions and theories in these two areas. In perception, we shall find that a good deal of effort has gone into the attempt to establish a basis for a definition of perception, whereas in learning much of the effort has been devoted to establishment of underlying mechanisms for many commonly established facts of behavior.

As regards the interactions of learning and perception, the main substance of theoretical discussion revolves about two fundamental questions. The first question concerns the extent and manner of influence of learning or past experience upon perception, the second question concerns the degree to which learning may be understood in terms of perception or as perceptual change (Postman, 1963). The first question is, of course, an empirical one and is partly resolved on the basis of studies to be reviewed in the next chapter. The second question is theoretical and has generated much heated controversy in the literature. Although we cannot resolve this important question at this time, we shall return to it in Chapter 8. The bulk of discussion and experimental effort has been focused primarily upon the first of these two questions.

Definitions and Theories of Perception

In the analysis of the effects of past experience or learning upon perception there is major disagreement over the various usages of the term *perception* and over the experimental procedures that are appropriate in investigation of perceptual processes. For some writers, perception refers to the data of immediate experience or awareness, without specific regard to the nature or source of the data. For others, it refers to a *relation* between agreed sources of data (usually stimulation by physical energy) and an agreed characteristic of the verbal report or behavior. Still other writers employ the term to refer to a process of inference or hypothesis by which the data of experience are interpreted by the perceiver. Still another group of writers, disregarding both the problem of experience and that of inferential constructs, refers to perception merely as a class of experimental procedures for relating some aspect of an independent variable to an arbitrary class of responses. A brief review of representative theories of perception will be helpful in dealing with the experiments to be reviewed in the next chapter.

Perception as a Process

Perhaps the greatest portion of what are called theories of perception deals with the problem of definition—or more properly, with the problem of finding an adequate basis for a formulation of a definition. Most experiments and discussions have dealt with demonstrations of effects of experience or practice upon perception. The experiments have the common property of representing relations between conditions of the experiment (for example, practice, past history, and so on) and responses of S (detection, discrimination, and so on). That these responses have been called perceptual has entailed a great deal of discussion, and that they should be called perceptual has formed a focus of interest and controversy in many of the discussions. For many theorists, *perception*, as a conceptual term, implies something over and above a given class of responses; it implies a process, internal to the perceiver, that is characterized by the response but that does not necessarily determine it under conditions of stimulation. That is, perception may vary with stimulation and at the same time it may have stimulus properties in the sense of being capable of directing or influencing a response (Bevan, 1961). It is therefore a *dispositional* term and is not capable of definition by the usual reductionistic method; that is, it cannot be defined denotatively. Its definition depends partly upon inferences from observable responses, partly upon assumptions or expectations which underlie the references to these relations as perception. It is clear that no single discussion or set of results may be used as an inclusive basis for a definition of perception. Indeed, it is the *totality* of

experiments and assumptions and relations between them that must form the basis of a definition, theory, or model of perception. Of the current formulations no single one is seen as universally adequate, and no single one can be completely adequate. Whether one chooses a physiological model, a phenomenalistic model, a judgmental model, a stimulus-response model, a sensory model, or any other model is at present a matter of personal predilection.

General Theories

Perception as Conscious Content. Stemming from the early empiricist view in philosophy, which claimed that awareness or knowledge of our world comes through the senses, early Es in psychology were concerned primarily with the determination of the content of consciousness. This view came to be known as structuralism. For Wundt and his students the basic problem of psychology was to determine experimentally the elements of consciousness, the manner of connection of these elements to each other, and the laws of their connections. The fundamental unit or element of consciousness, according to this view, is the *sensation;* perception is simply a combination of sensations, joined together according to the laws of attention and association with other sensations, images, and ideas. The attributes of any sensation are describable in terms of their intensity, extent, duration, and clearness (or attensity). Sensations are distinguished from feelings on grounds that feelings do not have all the preceding attributes, whereas sensations do.

Perceptions are classified by the structuralists as being of two kinds: *pure* and *mixed*. A pure perception, such as that of a rose, is simply the total of sensations brought about by the various properties of the object (the rose). A mixed perception is more complicated than a pure perception (as well as being more common) and involves the addition of images arising from past experience. These images of past experience serve to add additional meaning to the pure perception, and they also serve to form a basis for the interaction of learning with perception. The association of pure perceptions with the images of past experience might be termed the basis for the interaction, whereas the admixture or summation of numerous sensations as immediately perceived would distinguish a pure perception from a sensation.

Although perception involves past experience and therefore what some theorists have called "enrichment" (Gibson and Gibson, 1955), basically it is conceived as being derivable from the fundamental sensations or sensory processes, and the focus of the structuralists' attention is on the content of awareness. Their purpose in studying perception is the analysis of awareness or experience by means of introspection.

Perception as Behavior. An alternative way of describing perception and of distinguishing between sensation and perception is to distinguish between the kinds of behavior required of S. In studies in which S is required to report or otherwise respond to the nature and quantity of some stimulus (an energy change), we speak of sensation; in studies which require S to report or respond to some object quality or objective fact which is indicated by the stimulus, we speak of perception. Another way of distinguishing between sensation and perception involves a reference to the kind of organization of behavior about which we speak. In studies where the behavior may be said to be directly related to the quality or intensity of the stimulus, we would speak of sensation. On the other hand, if the behavior were understood to be a function both of the quality and intensity of the stimulus and of some other aspect of the stimulus (such as past experience, repetition of the stimulus, or other organized activity preceding or coincident with the presentation of the stimulus) or of the

perceiver, we would speak of perception. Titchener (1910) distinguished between sensation and perception on the basis that sensation involved an isolated set of attributes immediately described; perception, on the other hand, involved some kind of organization of these attributes in terms of a context of other attributes against which the isolated attributes were encountered. When this context served as a basis for the description of an object or objective fact and if S reported this rather than the basic qualities of the fundamental attributes, Titchener spoke of the "object error." Others have called this the "stimulus error," because the observer attends to and reports the object or the objective fact rather than the stimulus or the simple sensation (Boring, 1942). Thus when a trained observer describes directly the quality and intensity of the stimulus, we would speak of sensation, whereas if he reports the nature and type of object or objective fact, we would speak of perception.

It may be seen from the preceding that sensation and perception, viewed as conscious content or as behavior, may be conceived similarly by two widely divergent views, provided that one can make the translation from one set of terms to another. In describing sensation, the structuralist refers to the content of consciousness itself, assuming the accuracy of the report; the behaviorist refers to the content of the report, assuming that consciousness is an inferred construct. The two views may be made compatible, in part, by the translation from one set of terms to the other.

Perception as Phenomenal Experience. According to the phenomenologist, perception refers to processes of immediate awareness whose characteristics are inferred from the behavior or verbal report by the perceiver and which may or may not influence or modify behavior. It is commonplace for persons to report experiences with no outwardly observable manifestations, and it is perhaps on this basis that perception is regarded by some as inherently "private" and "subjective." The characterization of a "percept," according to this view, must depend on the assumption that either the report of the perceiver accurately reflects the characteristics of the percept or the report furnishes data from which correct inferences may be drawn (and alternative inferences ruled out). A similar distinction is made by the phenomenologist between the experience and the stimulus properties associated with it. Thus, there is neither a direct relation between the properties of the stimulus and the corresponding perception nor a direct relation between the perception and the behavior of S. It is only by indirection that the "phenomenal experience" may be subjected to inquiry.

An interesting and provocative challenge of the phenomenological position was made by Ryle (1948), who claims that an assumption of private awareness, inaccessible to an outsider, commits a logical error and invokes a myth of "the ghost within the machine." Others (for example, Postman, 1963), have also challenged the position as precluding any kind of legitimate science of perception.

With these points of view in mind, we may review briefly some of the major theories of perception. While considering these theories it is well to bear in mind that they are not all completely independent or exclusive and that they may be variously grouped or classified together. Several of the specific theories (for example, adaptation level and psychophysical correspondence) may well be thought of in terms of a general stimulus-response model, differing among themselves in the particular way in which the data are treated.

Specific Theories

Cell-Assembly Theory. According to Hebb (1949) perception may be understood in terms of events in the central nervous system which are correlates of stimulation. These events, which involve the activity of collections of neurons, take place in such a way as to form associations (both sensory-sensory and sensory-motor) which strengthen and facilitate patterns of neural activity, called *cell assemblies* and *phase sequences*. These assemblies and sequences are not necessarily in one-to-one correspondence to stimuli or responses at any given moment, but through repetition of stimulation and response they tend to have relatively stable structure (but with variations around a mean stability). And it is this stability of neural activity which results in the stable perceptions that are experienced. The existence of figure-ground relations is regarded as primary, whereas the existence of identity, discrimination, and similar perception is held to depend upon the establishment of cell assemblies and consistent phase-sequencing of neural patterns, brought about by stimulation and activity.

Sensory-Tonic Field Theory. This theory is intended to account for certain aspects of perception involving motor activity as well as sensory process (Werner and Wapner, 1950). Motor activities, including those involved in postural sets as well as those involved in actual movement, are held by the theory to interact with sensory processes in perception and to be a part of a "total dynamic process," including bodily states and perceived objects. The main attempt of the theory is to provide for consideration of activities, postural sets, and their interactions with stimulation rather than to regard perception as related primarily to sensory activity or associations alone.

Motor Adjustment Theory. An emphasis similar in some respects to that of sensory-tonic theory is involved in the motor adjustment theory of Freeman (1948). The theory holds that the posture or set of the organism, at the time of stimulation, provides a general background of muscular tension and a specific set in individual muscle groups. These develop a pattern of action which interacts with stimulation to determine the nature of the perception. Indeed, it is this action pattern that is the percept, in the sense that it takes place in relation to the external events of stimulation and serves as a basis for the action.

Transaction Theory. According to the transaction theorists (Ittleson and Cantril, 1954; Cantril, 1950; Kilpatrick, 1952) perception is a complex process by which the person attributes significance to events in his environment. This attribution of significance involves the interpretation of stimuli encountered in the environment from the standpoint of expectations and assumptions developed during the person's past attainment of goals. Perception is thus not a passive reception of stimuli which reflect the characteristics of the world but is an active process of interpretation and attribution whose particular aspects are determined by the nature of the person's transactions with the environment. When these transactions are successful in attaining goals his interpretive biases are strengthened with respect to those aspects of the (inferred) world associated with the attainment of the goal. When his transactions are not successful, his biases are weakened with respect to those aspects. The argument of the transactionist is that a given retinal pattern in vision could result from an infinity of objective stimulus forms. The form that is perceived (or inferred) will be that one which has most often in the past been confirmed through other transactions with form (walking about, feeling forms, and so on). Perception is thus necessarily a product of learning and not immediately "given" by the properties of the stimulus and the receptor. They are built up gradually through the reinforcement of assumptions (through the confirmation of inferences, hypotheses, and so on) which in turn are established and maintained through the activities of goal attainment.

Probabilistic Functionalism. This theory emphasizes phenomena commonly associated with "constancy" of objects and object characteristics under changing conditions of stimulation (Brunswick, 1956). Important in the determination of constancy phenomena are "cues," which serve as a basis for constitution by the perceiver of object characteristics. These characteristics, however, are not exact recapitulations of the object but are intermediate between those of the real object and those of the stimuli received by the organism. The validity and reliability of the cues and their relations to the object and the organism determine in part the perception on a probabilistic basis. Perception is thus a compromise between reality and a set of proximal stimuli having no relation to objects.

Adaptation Level Theory. The adaptation level theory emphasizes the judgments or responses that the perceiver makes in relation to the characteristics of objects and events. In proposing the theory, Helson (1964) was attempting to account for judgments of a psychophysical type (brightness, hue, and so on) in terms of the adaptive state of the perceiver as determined by the complexes of stimulation to which he had been exposed prior to the judgmental task as well as by the immediate situation or stimuli. The main thesis of the theory is that adaptation levels, brought about by experience, establish neutral points against which further experiences are judged. The determination of these neutral points (adaptation levels), their changes, and their interactions with present stimuli constitute the basis of research conducted in the framework of the theory. Extensions to areas of social perception, judgments of beauty, value, and the like, led Helson and his followers to regard the theory as generally applicable to all perceptions.

Directive State Theory. According to the directive state theory, perception is based upon both structural factors and behavioral factors. Structural (or autochthonous) factors are those associated with stimulation and their counterparts in receptor and neural processes. Behavioral factors are those associated with past experiences such as needs, values, tensions, attitudes, and the like. The emphasis of the theory, propounded by Bruner and Postman (1949), is on the determination of the effects of these latter factors upon the judgments and actions of the perceiver in relation to the present environment. The theory deals with social phenomena as they relate to perceptual phenomena and as both of these relate to the total personality of the individual.

Psychophysical Correspondence. The general hypothesis underlying the psychophysical correspondence approach states that for every aspect of the perceived world there is a variable associated with the energy flux at the receptor (however complex) with which the perceived property corresponds, under the condition that an appropriate psychophysical correspondence exists. This hypothesis may at first appear to be contrary to hypotheses relating perception to learning. However, according to Gibson (1950), the hypothesis does not deny that experience plays a role in perception, nor does it deny that recall, imagination, attention, set, or other factors associated with learning affect perception. Moreover, it does not necessarily imply that perception is innate. The hypothesis does assert an unfamiliar concept of stimulation; it postulates that stimulus energy may be described in complex, multidimensional terms (what Gibson has called a "flowing sea of energy" in which the perceiver finds himself immersed). These stimuli, of which perception is postulated to be a function, are assumed by Gibson to be changeable in their effects with practice and are assumed to be capable of being "learned" in the sense that more and more of the dimensions and the differences between values of stimuli in a given dimension become discriminated under conditions of learning. The suggestion of the hypothesis is that perception, to the

extent that it is learned, involves learning of a different kind from that which assumes an association between a stimulus and a response. Learning, on this view, implies discriminations of increasing "fineness," the perceived world being more clearly differentiated, abstracted, and selected as a result of repeated stimulation rather than being enriched, supplemented, or built up out of experience without regard to stimulation.

Stimulus-Response Analysis. Graham (1934, 1950, 1952, 1958; Graham and Ratoosh, 1962) has proposed an analysis of perception in terms which are classically behavioristic. Perception, according to this view, is a class of stimulus-response relations which may be embraced by a general expression of the form

$$R = f(a,b,c,\ldots,n,\ldots,t,\ldots,x,y,z)$$

wherein R is the response, and the letters in parentheses denote variables which express the values of stimuli or conditions of which R is a function (f). The first letters of the alphabet refer to values of stimuli (for example, intensity of a light, frequency of a tone, and so on); the last letters refer to conditions of S (physiological states, instructions, past experience, and so on); n and t are number of presentations of the conditions and time, respectively.

In experiments analyzed according to this view, we would expect to find several of the variables being manipulated simultaneously (that is, nonindependently). For example, in the two-point threshold study by Volkmann (1858), the letter a could denote the distance between the points of the aesthesiometer, x could be the instructions, n and t could be the number and time of presentation of the stimuli, and R could be the probability of a judgment "two" or "one." The equation would then reduce to a special form

$$R = f(a,n,t,x)$$

with other terms held constant. In the

Schafer-Murphy experiment a, the value of the stimulus, would be held constant, whereas n, t, and x were varied under conditions assumed to manipulate the past experience y of Ss. The equation would now be rewritten

$$R = f(n,t,x,y)$$

with the term a and others held constant. R, the response, would also be changed to denote the probability of a judgment "left" or "right" as determined by the values of (n,t,x,y).

It is possible to derive other functions from this formulation, particularly what we may call perceptual functions. As an example, consider a psychophysical experiment in which the threshold for identification of words or forms is determined as a function of their meanings or association value or similar characteristics. The critical value of a, the threshold, is now stated as a function of the variable b, the nature of the word; x, the type of subject; y, the instructions; and (R_a), the kind of response, as follows:

$$a = f(b,x,y,R_a)$$

The analysis of perception by this method is at once provocative and challenging. For although it is possible to translate the procedures of perceptual studies into the straightforward language of stimulus-response psychology, the meaning of the translation will depend upon several factors. First, it is necessary to restrict and measure both the independent variables on the right-hand side of the equation and the dependent variable on the left-hand side to specific classes and in terms of numerical values. Second, it is necessary that the responses employed be those which are both measurable and classed as "perceptual." This second requirement is perhaps the most difficult to achieve. However, the analysis does permit at least the partial translation of phenomenalistic studies into behavioral language. The concept of perception may then be thought of as referring

not to an entity or a process but to a special class of functional relations having clearly defined reference variables similar to those in other behavioral concepts. They therefore represent limiting "domains" of responses, variations of stimuli, and conditions of the organism among which relations may be called perceptual.

Definitions and Theories of Learning

In contrast to the disagreement over the usages of the term *perception*, there is little disagreement among investigators of learning over the references or facts denoted by the term *learning*. Although a precise and inclusive definition of learning is not yet possible, most writers in the area are likely to exhibit little or no disagreement with a definition as a "process by which activity originates or is changed through training procedures . . . as distinguished from changes by factors not attributable to training" (Hilgard, 1948, p.4). There is, as we suggested earlier, disagreement over the means by which such changes occur through training and over whether the changes occur through training as distinguished from other factors, such as maturation, fatigue, adaptation, and so on. But the disagreement is more likely to be over questions of translation of the experimental facts or their interpretation by theory than over the fact that learning occurred.

It will be helpful to distinguish several views or theories relating to learning, because at least a part of the problem of interpretation of interactions of learning and perception lies in a distinction between the two terms. Some theorists, for example, regard the basis of change in activities through training to be fundamentally grounded in perceptual (Gestalt psychology) or cognitive (judgmental) changes; other theorists regard the basis of change as grounded strictly in associative, stimulus-response connections.

Problems of Definition

A major problem that arises in an attempt to select one or another definition involves the question of the point of view that we adopt. Should we define our concept as a theoretical one, referring to intervening variables for our definition? Should we refer to a process (which may be the very thing we are trying to determine)? Or should we refer to the procedures we engage in (as is the case in the concepts of length, mass, and time) to quantify the concept? In our opinion, a definition should not preclude investigation of any of these, nor should it restrict us to a particular one.

Although learning often involves behavior which changes during the time period of the conditions of practice, there are cases of practice during which no change in behavior occurs. There are also cases where the conditions of practice are not such as to yield a clear statement about the nature of the behaviors which are to be regarded as practice. Passing a test in history, for example, represents behavior that is not shown by the test score alone to have occurred under the conditions of practice known to have been the reading of the book. If we had a pretest measure of S's knowledge of history, we could compare the performance on the test and the performance on the pretest and show the increase or change in performance. If we had sufficient knowledge of the kinds of responses (observing, verbalizing, note taking, and so on) occurring during the reading of the textbook, we could also specify the behavior that occurred during learning. The fact that neither of these is done (that is, comparison of pretest and test and specification of the responses made during practice) does not, we submit, negate the definition or challenge its validity. If we take the words *change in performance* to include lasting changes measured in terms of pre- and post-test conditions, and if we take the words *conditions of practice* to include instructions to Ss to do certain things (for example, "read this book," "think about that," "anticipate something," or even perhaps "watch the experimenter perform," as was done in the 1960 experiment by Hillix and Marx), we should have no difficulty in encompassing most experiments as "learning" experiments.

If S passes a test, which we are convinced was not possible without some kind of learning, and if we can specify conditions under which such success was made possible, we could describe these conditions as the conditions of practice and passing the test as the change in performance. Such specification, in terms either of description of the conditions or inferences back to the conditions from the performance in an examination of S's behavior or of the instructions, would be sufficient to meet the criterion of the definition. The fact that such specification is not made, however, is not a sufficient criterion for rejection of the definition; it is a criterion related to the design of the experiment, the measure of performance, and the specification of the conditions of practice. It does not negate the definition, but it may well negate the validity of the experimental study. Our definition, therefore, is inclusive, provided that the performance and the conditions of practice are well described. To arrive at a knowledge of learning it is necessary to study performance under conditions where the effects of practice are exactly known. As we shall see, as regards the interaction of perception and learning, not all these conditions have been met. However, a considerable advancement toward the realization of this possibility has been made in recent years.

Following Hilgard (1956), we may say that learning theories divide into two major classes: *stimulus-response* theories and *cognitive* theories. A third class of theory would include those of psychodynamics and functionalism (neither of which is specifically restricted to learning but is intended to encompass other aspects of behavior, for example, motivation, personality, and so on) and the mathematical models (which may be said to be more concerned with derivation of rational *expressions* of learning and the conditions thereof than with accounts in terms of physiological, cognitive, or other factors).

Types of Theories

Stimulus-Response (S-R) Theories. Stimulus response theories include those of Thorndike, Hull, Guthrie, Spence, and Skinner. The basic account of learning by the S-R theorist is in terms of responses to stimuli. Thus, for the S-R theorist what is learned is a system of "habits"; each habit involves a specific response to a specific stimulus or situation, with complex habits being "built up" as a compounding of simple habits. Practice, according to the S-R theorist, results in an assembly of habits which, if they are appropriate to the solution of a new problem, will bring it about. If not, the learner engages in trial-and-error behavior until a solution is reached. The solution, when attained, establishes a new habit, and so forth. Thus, the S-R theorist believes that complex problem-solving and cognitive activity may be deduced from the principles of habit formation.

Cognitive Theories. Cognitive theories include those of Tolman, Köhler and Koffka, and Lewin. Whereas the S-R theorist accounts for learning in terms of chains of stimulus-response connections, the cognitive theorist employs a general concept referring to central brain processes, including memories, expectations, and perceptions as "intermediaries" or as integrators of behavior. What is learned, according to the cognitive theorist, is a system of facts or knowledge about the various aspects of situations within which

action is to take place. Under the aegis of practice, the learner, on this view, accumulates information (right or wrong) which is used in arriving at solutions to problems. Thus, the cognitive theorist would emphasize such concepts as "insight," "perceptual organization," and "structuring" of problems and situations in accounting for the solution to a given problem. He would hold that complex problem solving and cognitive activity are fundamental to learning and not deducible from the principles of habit formation as suggested by the S-R theorist.

Psychodynamics, Functionalism, and Models. A third group of theories would include the psychodynamic theories such as those of Freud and his followers; the functionalistic theories of Dewey, Angell, Carr, and Woodworth; the mathematical theories of Estes, Burke, Bush, and Mosteller; and the game theories of Von Neumann and Morgenstern (Hilgard, 1956, Chap. 1). We shall not, however, concern ourselves here with theories of these kinds, because either they are considerably more general in their considerations of personality, motivation, and so on, or they are concerned with specific aspects of learning not closely related to or interactive with perception.

Classes of Perceptual Processes and Studies

We have seen that perception may be treated in several different ways, and we have pointed out that the interpretation of the nature and direction of the interaction of learning and perception may depend largely upon which method of treatment we adopt. Thus, for example, if we find, as Volkmann did, that the threshold of perception of two-point stimulation *as* two decreases with practice, we might conclude that practice somehow increased S's sensitivity to stimulation without altering the distribution of sense organs on the skin.

On the other hand, we might conclude, as Boring did much later, that the decrease was only an apparent one and that what the practice did was to alter the basis of S's report (his attitude or judgment). In the Schafer-Murphy study, we might regard the reward as somehow reinforcing perception and clarifying the stimulus. But if we note that S learned the name of the fact he later reported, we might easily discount awareness completely and interpret the result as arising from reward of the verbal response. In short, the result would seem to depend on our assumptions about what the experiment meant, and not on what was done!

An attempt to disentangle these postulated effects may be largely fruitless unless we have a very clear idea of the nature of the experimental procedure employed in revealing the results. In our review of studies of interactions in the next chapter, we have classified the experiments rather arbitrarily according to a scheme which will, hopefully, lead to a minimum of disagreement as to what was done and what was found by the investigators.

There are probably as many ways of classifying interactions of perception and learning as there are taxonomists, theorists, and investigators. One way would be in terms of what Gibson (1951) has called theory-bins, listing studies according to the theories to which they are related. We might at first consider classifying them as studies of conscious content, phenomenological studies, physiological studies (cell-assembly, sensory-tonic, motor-adjustment), transactional studies, functionalistic studies, and so on. But, as Gibson has also pointed out, these "bins" do not necessarily reflect the uses to which the theories may be put.

Because our aim is to look at representative empirical studies, rather than studies conducted in accordance with theories, we have found it useful to follow a somewhat different line than that suggested by Gibson. We have classified the studies according to the procedures and the corresponding methods of investigation. This classification does not imply "dimensionality" of the realm of investigations, nor does it imply mutual exclusiveness or exhaustiveness, because this would in itself be a "theory" of classification. Rather, it permits us to discuss both experimental findings and their relations to theory in a way which does not commit them or us to any particular, a priori theoretical bias.

We have chosen, for these reasons, to adopt the following headings under which to present our array:

1. Early demonstrational studies, which introduce some of the problems of the nature and basis of interactions.
2. Sensory deprivation and perceptual development, which includes studies which set a base level for assessment of behavior in the absence of stimulation and the beginnings of development of perceptual function.
3. Figure-ground, which deals with primitive organizational features of perceptions.
4. Detection, concerned with perception of single figures in homogeneous perceptual environments.
5. Discrimination, dealing with perception of differences between figures.
6. Recognition, dealing with temporal aspects of perception involving familiarity.
7. Identification, dealing with specific denotative behavior associated with stimulus properties and past experience or practice.
8. Judgments, dealing with evaluative behavior related to stimulus properties or conditions, such as size, weight, space-distance, and so on.
9. Illusions, dealing with anomalies of perception or perceptions which are distortions of stimulus properties.

7

Empirical Studies

Having reviewed some examples of interactions and some of the definitions and theories which represent the frameworks within which perceptual and learning studies have taken place, we shall in this chapter review representative empirical studies of interactions of perception and learning.

Empirical studies involving interactions of perception and learning have ranged from studies of simple effects of practice upon changes in the threshold of detection of a simple energy change (such as light or sound) to studies of effects of complex past experiences upon changes in judgments of values of objects or events (such as relative size of people or the potential threat of an approaching object). Our interpretation of many of these studies as well as our classification of them may well depend upon which of the definitions or theories (see Chapter 6) we might adopt. For this reason it is well to give brief consideration to our basis of organization of this chapter.

In organizing the studies that we are presenting here, we chose to follow a modified version of a taxonomy originally suggested by Hake (1957), in which experiments are classified as dealing with detection, discrimination, recognition, identification, and judgment, according to the kind of response required of S. We have, for our purposes, added the criterion of the stimulus-response relation involved in the experiment and have chosen to consider certain additional classes. Although such a system of organization may not be universally acceptable, we believe the one selected serves as a reasonable organizing framework based on the kinds of behavior involved and not on any particular theoretical or definitional bias.

Space obviously does not permit us to conduct an exhaustive review in all the areas within which interactions of learning and perception have been found. We have therefore chosen to review representative studies within each of the areas. It is hoped that these representative studies will provide an overview of the experimentation which has been conducted in each of the areas and will provide a reference base for further review by the reader.

Early Demonstrational Studies

Much of the recent and current work on interactions of learning and perception arose out of some early demonstrational studies in which investigators were concerned with the relative effectiveness of the experience of the observer as contrasted with the inherent characteristics of the perceived object. From the assumptions of Gestalt theory, it may be argued that perception is fundamentally based upon the inherent characteristics or "organization" of the stimuli and their interaction with the characteristics of the observer. On this view, past experience as such would not alter perception. There were many attempts by Gestalt psychologists and others to attempt to resolve the issue as to whether perception is basically innate or basically a result of past experience. Gestalt-oriented theorists conducted their studies in such a way as to demonstrate that the "organization" of the stimulus figure is, if not the sole determinant of perception, the most potent. This kind of experiment is represented in a study by Gottschaldt (1926, 1929). Gottschaldt showed his Ss a number of familiar forms, such as a hexagon, a square, or the letter A, both in isolation and in a context in which they were imbedded in a more complex figure. His results indicated that even familiar and so-called good figures would not be seen or recognized when the organizational properties of the figure were such as to overcome the extended effects of past experience in producing the correct perception. He concluded that the organizing principles of the mode of function in the visual system are more potent in perception than factors related to familiarity with common figures.

The opposite point of view was taken by other investigators, one of whom was Djang (1937). He employed a series of irregular figures, some of which he called simple, others of which he called complex. The figures of the "complex" set were drawn so that each of them masked within it a figure of the "simple" set. Half of each of the sets was used in a test series, and the other half was used in a control series. Observers learned one or the other of the simple series of figures by drawing them a number of times in repeated trials. Following learning they were shown the complex figures and were asked whether they saw any of the simple figures masked within them. Differences were significant between the test series and the control series; more simple figures were seen imbedded in the "complex" figures when the figures were from the test series than when they were from the control series.

Taken together, these two representative studies demonstrate, on the one hand, that a great deal of past experience in perceiving familiar figures can be overcome by the clever design of a masking context (Gottschaldt). At the same time, figures imbedded in a masking context may be more readily perceived following practice in drawing the figures (Djang). These studies did not, of course, settle the issue as to whether perception is innate or acquired, nor were they designed to do so, although the investigators perhaps thought they were. They do indicate, however, that there are two factors working in perception: organizational factors, related to the characteristics of the stimuli, and experiential factors, related to the characteristics of the perceiver. Just how these factors operate and how they are related to each other became the topic of further demonstrational studies.

One such study was done by Braly (1933), who was interested in determining whether particular kinds of perceptual experiences influenced new perceptions in any consistent way. His procedure consisted of exposing what he called an impression series of geometrical forms followed by a test series consisting of additional forms of different types interspersed with the impression series. In one of the series, various arrangements of squares were used as an impression series and arrangements of triangles or pentagons were used in the test series. After exposure to the impression series, Ss were asked to draw what they had seen by filling in figures in the test series. The results showed that the presentation of a particular type of figure in the impression series influenced the nature of the reproduction in the test series.

A similar demonstration was later reported by Leeper (1935). He reported that once an observer organizes or interprets stimuli in a particular way, this seems to influence (that is, render difficult) the possible organization of the material in future situations. His materials consisted of two ambiguous figures, one of which was a picture of either an old woman or a young woman, the other of which was a picture of either a pirate or a rabbit. In the exposure phase, Ss were shown only one possible part of the ambiguous figure (for example, the old woman part of one figure and the pirate part of the other). In the test phase, Ss were shown the ambiguous figures in their complete form. The group of Ss was divided into halves, each half being shown one part of the figure, either old woman or young woman and either pirate or rabbit, in counterbalanced fashion. Of the group which saw only the young woman part of the first figure in the exposure phase, none saw the old woman in the ambiguous figure in the test phase. Of the group which was shown the pirate part of the figure in the exposure phase, 96 per cent saw the pirate in the ambiguous figure. Of the group which saw the rabbit part of the figure in the exposure phase, 60 per cent saw the rabbit in the ambiguous figure and 6 per cent saw the pirate. The remainder of this group reported seeing both the rabbit and the pirate in the ambiguous figure.

Now, the two studies by Braly and Leeper carry the investigation a step further than did the two studies by Gottschaldt and Djang, for they begin to specify some of the details of the relation of past experience to perception. It is now possible to compare the relative effects of organization and experience, because the figure is presented under circumstances in which both factors are present in a competitive way.

Another aspect of past experience, in this case the nature of a verbal association to a perceived stimulus and its influence upon the reproduction of a figure, was investigated by Carmichael, Hogan, and Walter (1932). Their Ss were shown a series of figures and were told they would be asked later to reproduce them as accurately as possible. The figures themselves were relatively unstructured. For example, one figure was a trapezoid, another was a pair of circles, side by side with a short line connecting them, and another was a rectangle with an inscribed lozenge. Just prior to exposing each figure a verbal suggestion was given that the figure resembled one or another of two possible objects. It was suggested, for example, that the trapezoid resembled a beehive or a hat; the pair of circles resembled a pair of eyeglasses or a dumbbell; and the rectangle and lozenge resembled curtains in a window or a diamond in a rectangle. Half the group of Ss was given one of the two suggestions for each figure, the other half of the group was given the other suggestion. Although many of the reproduced drawings deviated only slightly from the originals, some of them appeared to show a definite influence of the suggestion; the appearance of the reproduced form resembled more closely the object which was suggested than the original stimulus figure.

Many additional experiments extended the list of types of past experiences and other characteristics of the observer which influence perception. Duncker (1939), for example, showed that matching the color of an object using a colorimeter could be influenced by the shape of the object. If the object was in the form of a donkey cut from a piece of green milliner's cloth, Ss used more red in their matches than if the object was in the form of a leaf, cut from the same bolt of cloth, in which case they used more green in their matches. He also found that Ss reported less "chocolate" flavor in candy from which the color had been removed, although otherwise it was the same. Henle (1942) showed that letters of the alphabet could be seen at lower thresholds of exposure than their reversed images, indicating that experience with the letter-forms served as a determinant of the readiness with which a figure could be perceived. Additional aspects of past experience, giving rise to so-called "dynamic" characteristics of the perceiver, have also been studied with regard to their influence upon perception. Such characteristics as personal values, individual needs, personality, and similar characteristics of the perceiver have been studied as determinants of perception (Bruner and Goodman, 1947; Postman, Bruner, and McGinnies, 1948; Vanderplas and Blake, 1949).

An experiment to illustrate the effect of hunger upon perception was conducted by Levine, Chein, and Murphy (1942). *S*s verbalized an association which was presumably aroused by looking at ambiguous figures exposed on a screen after 1, 3, 6, or 9 hrs. without food. The number of food words associated to the stimuli appeared to increase at the 3- and 6-hr. intervals but appeared to decrease at the 9-hr. interval. These results were obtained with black and white stimuli. With colored stimuli they appeared to increase up to three hours but decreased thereafter. In order to account for the decrease in the food-related associations after the maximum period the authors postulated a need to leave the field in addition to the need of hunger which they used to explain the increase. The hypothesis concerning the need to leave the field, of course, was constructed *post hoc* and was not tested by the experiment.

Sensory Deprivation and Perceptual Development

A topic of considerable interest, particularly to the empiricist, who assumes that all knowledge in the world comes by way of sensory experience, is how these experiences are built up and elaborated in producing the complex perceptions of adulthood. Some light may be shed upon this topic by studies in which *S*s are restricted in their experiences from a very early age. Comparison of the perceptual behavior of *S*s so deprived with the behavior of normal control *S*s has been one way of studying this problem. Another method has included the provision for experimental *S*s to be given additional experiences, with control *S*s being given ordinary experience.

Deprivation Studies in Humans

Studies of sensory deprivation with human *S*s have not been as nicely controlled as one might like them to be, for the obvious reason that it is not socially possible to exercise this degree of visual control within the normal human culture. There are clinical data that provide some information about defects of early and prolonged visual deprivation. These data have come from the study of human *S*s who have been blind from birth and who have had their vision restored by surgery relatively late in life. These persons at the time of restoration of vision may be considered to be completely naive visually but otherwise normal. Senden (1932) provided one of the most complete early accounts of such human *S*s. The evidence, although fragmentary and more suggestive than conclusive, provided a rich source of speculation upon the effects of early deprivation. In an account of the Senden studies Hebb (1949), who incorporated a good deal of this evidence into a theory of perceptual development, divided the processes of these persons into two general areas. The first he called *figural unity*, by which he refers to the mere detection of the existence of an object in the environment, or a figure against a background. The second process, which he calls *identity*, refers to perception of a figure that appears segregated from its background; that is, it is a unitary figure which is also recognized as a member of a *class* of figures. (We shall later call this process *identification*.) As criteria for identity Hebb requires the patient to be able to say at least, "This figure is different from that figure." (That is, he must be able to discriminate two figures which are physically different.) He must also, at a higher level say, "This is [or is not] the same object that I was shown earlier." At a still higher level he must be able to assign a name to the figure—for example, "circle," "square," or "triangle."

The apparent effect of deprivation in Senden's Ss seemed predominantly to be one affecting the process of identity, using Hebb's term, rather than the process of unity. Most of the Ss were capable from the very beginning of perceiving the *fact* of the *existence* of an object, but they required a long period of training before they were able to discriminate, recognize, or identify the objects. Even after the patient had learned to identify an object it was possible that the identity would be disrupted if a change in context was introduced. A patient could learn to identify an object held before him on one occasion but he might fail to recognize it when it was seen in a different context (held in the examiner's hand on one occasion and suspended from a string on another).

In these studies we can see certain distinctions in the processes that are affected by what we might call pure perceptual experiences (those arising out of perception of objects in various contexts associated with past experience). It seems clear here that the presence of an object (unity) is more nearly related to perception alone, whereas its discrimination, recognition, or identification may be associated with processes of learning (past experience, practice, and so on).

At the very least, the evidence provided by the Senden studies would suggest that some aspects of perception considered to be "nativistic" are actually acquired through learning. Hebb takes the position that this learning is equally difficult for the naive adult and for the unstimulated infant.

But even this reasonable inference is subject to dispute in its interpretation. For example, Senden's studies did not have good controls for postoperative difficulties which Ss may have been experiencing. Moreover, it was not shown by Senden that his patients, subjected to prolonged visual deprivation, did not suffer some form of neural deterioration in the visual cortex, deterioration which might have been overcome by experience but which nevertheless existed at the time of the studies. At least some of the inhibitory effects found in these patients might have been due to certain effects associated with the immediate removal of bandages—dazzle, caused by exposure of a dark-adapted eye to intense light; narrowing of the visual field and distracting cramps of the eye muscles in attempting to focus and converge upon the objects. We must keep in mind in evaluating the inference concerning the effect of experience upon perception that in the infant learning itself is slow and difficult and that in the adult the inference is based not only upon the observed difficulty in perceiving objects, but also upon an inference which ignores the lack of necessary controls.

Deprivation Studies in Animals

Deprivation in Chimpanzees. A number of experiments illustrate some of the effects of deprivation using experimental techniques which provide for certain controls not possible in the study of humans. Riesen (1947, 1950) reports results with several chimpanzees raised in complete darkness for varying periods. One chimpanzee was raised in darkness for seven months. Another was also raised in darkness but was given diffuse illumination for 1.5 hrs. each day. A third was allowed normal visual stimulation for 1.5 hrs. each day. This procedure provided for the partial control of possible retinal deterioration and for the control of pattern experiences.

The totally deprived chimpanzee showed signs of structural deficiency which could be attributed to retinal or neural deprivation and deterioration. Neither of the other animals showed such evidence.

The chimpanzee that was given limited but normal experiences did not differ from other chimpanzees raised normally. Both of the other chimpanzees were markedly retarded in even the simplest of visual tasks. One was found to be retarded even in the normal blinking response to a moving object for a period of six days after removal from darkness and the other did not develop the blinking response for about fifteen days. Visual tracking behavior did not occur for one until thirteen days after removal and for the other for thirty days. They were able to track, but they did so in a series of fixations rather than smoothly as normal Ss of similar age could do. Visual pursuit of a moving bottle took one chimpanzee twenty days to develop and the other sixteen days. When the chimpanzees were presented with a large black and yellow striped disk paired with mild electric shock, it took them thirteen and fifteen days to begin to develop a consistent avoidance response.

Nissen, Chow, and Semmes (1951) restricted the tactual experience of a chimpanzee. This animal was deprived of tactual stimulation of the hands, forearms, feet, and legs from the time he was four weeks old until he was thirty-one months. Beginning at the age of fifteen weeks his limbs were encased in cardboard tubes. Movement was partly restricted as well. After his period of confinement the chimpanzee was given a tactual discrimination task. The task consisted of indication by an appropriate head movement which hand had been stimulated. The chimpanzee never showed evidence of having learned which of his hands had been stimulated even after a period of 2,000 trials. A control animal raised normally, attained a level of almost perfect response after some 200 trials. The experimental chimpanzee gave normal performance on a series of visual discrimina-

tion tasks, indicating a modality-specific effect of the deprivation. Because only one experimental and one control animal were used by Nissen, Chow, and Semmes, their conclusions are relatively cautious. That experience plays a role in the development of tactual sensitivity, however, just as it does in visual sensitivity, is fairly clear from even this limited amount of experimentation.

Deprivation in Rats and Birds. Studies of deprivation in animals other than humans and chimpanzees have in general yielded similar results. Hebb (1937) reports an experiment in which rats were raised in darkness and compared with normals on visual discrimination problems. Performance was markedly inferior at the outset of training but approached that of the normally raised rats after approximately 1 hr. of experience with pattern stimulation. Siegel (1953a) performed similar experiments with the ring dove by covering their heads with translucent plastic hoods. Between the ages of eight and twelve weeks the birds were given training in jumping from a perch to a platform with their hoods on. After about 400 trials of this training a window was cut in the hood, allowing monocular vision. The birds were then tested for their ability to discriminate a circle and a triangle. Their performance was inferior to that of normal controls. The normal dove required an average of about seventy-eight trials, whereas the experimental doves required an average of about 127 trials to reach a criterion of nine correct discriminations out of ten.

Figure and Ground Perception

One of the fundamental aspects of perception involves the distinction by the perceiver of *figural* qualities in the perceptual field from *background* qualities in the field. Rubin (1915, 1921) was one of the first to formulate this distinction. He reported that it is possible to see any well-marked part of a visual field as a figure, leaving the rest as background. If a white sheet of paper, for example, has a single splash of black ink upon it, normally the blot ink will be seen as a black figure against a white background. If, on the other hand, half the page were covered with black ink, the other part being white, with an irregular contour separating them, either the black part or the white part could be seen as a figure, with the other part being seen as the background. Rubin classified the experienced differences between figure and background in five ways:

1. The figure is seen as having form, while the background is formless.
2. The background appears to extend continuously behind the figure and is not seen as being interrupted by the figure.
3. The figure appears as an object or a thing, while the background appears more like unformed "stuff" or material.
4. The figure usually tends to appear in front of the background, while the background appears behind the figure.
5. The figure seems to suggest some kind of meaning, whereas the background has no such meaning.

The first three of the preceding characteristics have been usually thought of as properties of fundamental perceptual events; that is, they seem to have primitive characteristics involving unity of a figure as its simplest aspect. A bounded area, for example, will be seen as a unit in front of the background even before the figure is seen to have particular characteristics— that is, before it "looks like something." Hebb (1949) and Senden (1932) have both called attention (Hebb, theoretically, and Senden, empirically) to the fact that even untrained and naive Ss are able to perceive figural qualities before they are able to make the simplest of discriminations. We, of course, would regard studies of this sort as dealing with the perceptual process we have earlier called detection. We would say

that the detection of a figure against a background is one of the most primitive aspects of perception.

That the appearance of figure-ground relations interacts with learning was demonstrated in a somewhat more complicated way in a study by Atkinson and Ammons (1952). These investigators presented to their Ss a Rorschach ink blot and asked them to press a key when they saw a figure that was previously described. One half the Ss were asked to press the key when they saw the face of a cat; the other half of the Ss were asked to press the key when they saw a second figure, such as a motorcycle. The latency of the response, or the time between the opening of the shutter on a projector and S's key pressing response, was recorded. After the first trial he was required to look at a magazine for a few moments to break up his set for the seen figure. He was then given another trial, asked to look again for the figure, and so on for ten trials. The latency curve derived from the two groups of Ss was a typical declining curve of latency as a function of the number of successive exposures, indicating that practice in looking for a specific object in an otherwise unstructured field (the meaningless ink blot) results in a decreasing latency, thus indicating some kind of learning effect. These two investigators also demonstrated that this kind of perception is subject to an interference effect similar to that found in studies of memory. After a brief rest their Ss were given ten additional trials with the same ink blot, but they were asked to signal when they saw a second figure, which was the other figure looked for by the opposite group. The learning curve for the second ten trials was in general higher than that for the first ten trials, thus indicating that looking for one kind of figure for ten trials produces an increase in the latency to find a second figure in a second ten trials.

Another primitive aspect of figure-ground perception involves that of figure-ground reversal. For some figure-ground patterns either part may be seen as figure while the other part is seen as ground. When such a field is viewed for a period of time by S, it is common to find that figure and ground tend to be reported as reversed; that is, the part of the field previously seen as figure may now be seen as ground. With successive or continued exposures of such a field, it is not unusual to find a number of such reversals. That this figure-ground reversal interacts with learning in some way is demonstrated in an experiment by K. T. Brown (1954). Brown exposed continuously a visual field containing a figure that could be seen as rotating in one direction or the other, but the direction of rotation was not determined by the successive time position characteristics of the sort that we would find in ordinary rotation—that is, the rotational direction of the figure was ambiguous. Brown asked his Ss to press a telegraph key each time they saw the figure as reversing its direction. He found that the number of apparent reversals of direction within short (10-sec.) intervals of exposure time increased as a function of the total time period of observation. Similar phenomena, using Lissajous figures displayed on a cathode-ray tube, had been previously reported by Philip and Fisichelli (1945) and by Fisichelli (1947).

The preceding experiments have shown an interaction between a learning or practive effect and figure-ground perception. One aspect of this problem which has remained uninvestigated is the nature and the direction of the interaction. We may ask why it is that the latency for the perception of a particular figure against an ambiguous but complicated background should decrease over the period of observation or why it is that the time interval between reversals should decrease as a function of continued exposure. The Atkinson and Ammons study leaves this question unanswered; the Brown and the Fisichelli studies interpret the effect in terms of processes involving visual adaptation similar to those suggested by the Gestalt psychologists in connection with their studies of visual satiation (Köhler and Wallach, 1944). Gestalt psychologists might agree that exposure of a particular portion of the perceptual field results in satiation (somewhat like fatigue) of the receptors and their counterparts in the central nervous system. This satiation, according to theory, makes impossible the continued perception of a particular field within a given area of the visual field. This theory has received some support from various sources, including those which show that continued exposure of primitive figures such as lines and circles results in their disappearance after a very short time, if the area of exposure is held fixed by precluding the normal random eye movements that occur with continued fixation (for example, Riggs et al., 1953). However, we would caution that on the behavioral level, learning, as we are using the term, is an equally adequate account.

Much of the information in the area encompassed thus far by these studies is of a demonstrational character, and a good deal of the interpretation of the phenomena involved depends on the theoretical position taken by E. A good deal of additional research will be needed in order to shed more light on the underlying processes involved in the interaction of learning with these primitive perceptual phenomena.

Figure and Object Detection

It will be recalled that in using the term *detection* we are referring to the perception of a single object against a homogeneous background. It will also be recalled that the term *learning* refers to the "conditions of practice" and not to other conditions, such as fatigue, adaptation, and so on. To speak, therefore, of interactions of learning and detection is to speak of changes in the perception of single objects which come about as a function of conditions of practice. To speak of this kind of interaction may well involve us in some interesting contradictions of terminology. When we speak of the absolute threshold, for example, we imply the existence of a minimum energy value below which perception does not occur. If we find evidence for a change, either upward or downward in the absolute threshold, we must adduce evidence for some kind of practice condition, and we must also show that the change did not occur as a function of some more straightforward or fundamental effect of adaptation or fatigue or other factors which we say are not associated with learning. As an example, we may cite the traditional studies of light and dark adaptation (for example, Woodworth and Schlosberg, 1955, Chapter 8) in which it is found that the absolute threshold for perception of light changes systematically upward with exposure to a preadapting light field and downward with exposure to total darkness as a function of time. These effects may easily be accounted for by reference to the physiological changes which occur in the retina and not as a function of "practice in detecting" the stimulus. Therefore, in referring to "practice" or "learning" effects, in studies of detection, it is necessary to show changes which occur in addition to or as alternatives to these effects.

One such experiment was conducted by Blackwell (1953). Blackwell modified the traditional psychophysical technique of the method of constant stimuli by using a forced-choice technique in which the stimulus could appear in one of four different places (within a given experiment) or in the same place but over one of four different time intervals. S's task was to indicate on each trial which of four locations or which of four time intervals was the one in which the stimulus was presented. The intensity of the stimulus was also varied from trial to trial and over a series of trials so that the results would yield a "threshold" for a given series of trials. Blackwell was interested in the effect upon the threshold of procedures known to

yield significant relations to practice in performance of verbal and motor tasks, namely, giving S knowledge of the results of his choices. Over several series of trials Blackwell found that his observers' thresholds tended to decrease. The possibility that the decrease in the threshold might be due to a physiological effect such as adaptation was controlled by first preadapting Ss to the background illumination for a period of time necessary to stabilize their adaptation level. Thus, we might reasonably conclude the decrease in threshold is related to a practice effect and not to an increase in "sensitivity." Ss, apparently, were learning something about the way in which they might improve their ability to detect targets. They may have learned, for example, to control their visual accommodation or to fixate an anticipated position of the target; they may also have learned something about the sequences, rhythm, or position of the intervals; or they may have learned not to blink at the wrong time. In general, we might say that they improved their "procedures for responding" to the potential onset of the stimulus. They are thus becoming "better observers" in the same sense that Volkmann's observers learned to distinguish more carefully among the various kinds of sensations arising from two-point stimulation of the skin (see Chapter 5).

Whether or not the change in the threshold is due to a change in sensitivity is not relevant for our purposes. The results of Blackwell's experiments show at least that in the determination of detection thresholds part of the result may be due to factors associated with learning and part may be due to factors associated with sensitivity. It may be that these two kinds of factors interact in such a way that in an ordinary psychophysical experiment they are confounded effects.

Several other experiments illustrate changes in the absolute or detection threshold which may come about under conditions of practice. Verplanck, Cotton, and

Collier (1953) determined the absolute threshold for the detection of light using six dark-adapted Ss. Three Ss were employed using the method of limits; three were employed using the method of constant stimuli. Following an initial determination of their thresholds they were given four daily sessions of threshold determination. On two of the days they received three pairs of descending and ascending series followed by 300 trials of stimulation at a previously determined threshold point and on the other two days they were given sixty stimulations with random variation in brightness followed by 300 stimulations at the previously determined threshold. Following these sessions Ss showed sequences of positive responses at frequencies much greater than chance. It should be recalled that presentations of stimuli at the threshold should, by definition, produce 50 per cent correct responses. That the frequency of such responses was greater than would be predicted by chance is an indirect indication of a decrease in the threshold resulting from the continuing practice sessions.

Another experiment shows a similar interaction. Bruce and Low (1951) measured the threshold for the detection of a gap in a Landholdt C (a standard target for measuring visual acuity) using four gap widths near the threshold value. A large group of aviation cadets was used to make the determination. The cadets were then given a series of training sessions in the recognition of aircraft and ships. The sessions were 40 min. long each day and continued for five days each week for eight weeks. Following training their visual acuity was again measured using the standard procedure. A smaller group of medical students who met the same acuity criteria as the cadets served as control Ss, receiving only the tests of visual acuity. The retest scores for the cadets were significantly higher than those of the medical students, indicating an apparent effect of practice in recognition training upon visual acuity.

Bevan and Zener (1952) trained twelve Ss over four daily sessions in visual form perception. On the first day, Ss were presented twenty-four simple nonmeaningful designs at subthreshold intensities. Illumination was increased until S reported seeing "something" (method of limits). S was then asked to draw what he had seen. The illumination of the projected image was taken to be the threshold of perception of the design indicated by the drawing. The procedure was repeated until accurate reproductions were made by the Ss. This procedure permitted additional thresholds to be measured. One was called the threshold of incomplete perception, the other the threshold of complete perception. On the second and third days additional exposures of the figures were given at intensities above the threshold. Some figures were presented twice, some were presented eight times, and others were presented forty-eight times. On the fourth day the original procedure was repeated, using the original twenty-four designs and twenty new designs as a control. On the final day the thresholds were found to be lower for the designs presented for the first time than they were for the designs presented on the first day. This result the investigators called a *general* practice effect. In addition, figures presented both during the first day and the last day showed a further lowering of the threshold, which the investigators called a *specific* practice effect. With increasing amounts of practice (that is, two, eight, or forty-eight exposures during the second and third days), the threshold showed a downward, negatively accelerated trend.

Object Discrimination

Before reviewing studies of interactions of discrimination and learning, we will do well to clear up a point of possible confusion in the use of the term *discrimination* in the area of perception and the use of the same term in the area of learning. Traditionally, the term *discrimination* referred to behavior associated with the determination of the *difference threshold* or *limen*. The value assigned to the threshold was the value describing the difference between two stimuli which would be reported correctly in 50 per cent of a number of repeated trials. Measurement of the difference limen was usually made in order to determine the relationship between stimulus intensity and "sensation level." This relationship was determined in classical psychophysics by first measuring the absolute threshold (the value of the stimulus that could be "just perceived" 50 per cent of the time) and then measuring successive difference thresholds above the absolute threshold. Each successive difference threshold was added to the preceding one, and the sum of these differences above the absolute threshold designated the sensation level (for a detailed account of the methods used see Woodworth and Schlosberg, 1955).

Discrimination, as the term has been used in studies of learning, differs a great deal from the use of the term in perception. One of the more widespread types of experiments in animal psychology has to do with what is called discrimination learning. The apparatus in such an experiment usually consists of some kind of a starting box and a runway or an open space which the animal must traverse or jump across, and two doors or two alleys opening out of a small chamber or at the end of the open space across which the animal must jump. One of the doors usually leads to some sort of reward such as food, the other to either punishment or no reward. From trial to trial in such an apparatus the animal must choose consistently the pattern or figure on the door leading to reward in order to solve the problem. The doors may differ in terms of brightness or size or pattern, one of which is associated with reward, the other with punishment or no reward. The experiment was originally used for testing the senses of animals. If an animal, for example, were able correctly to choose a white door and avoid a black one, it would be inferred that the animal was able to make the gross brightness discrimination involved. When the animal had learned such a problem, the light door could be darkened somewhat and the black door could be lightened somewhat and he could be tested again. If he learned the new problem it would be inferred that the animal was able to make the more subtle discrimination of shades of gray. Successive problems could be presented requiring the animal to discriminate smaller and smaller differences in brightness between the doors until one had reached the animal's limit of "discrimination." The conduct of the experiment under these circumstances was conceived as one in animal psychophysics.

But we must note here some significant differences between the procedures employed in determining the difference threshold in psychophysics and in conducting an experiment in discrimination learning, even though the latter may be regarded as a psychophysical experiment. In determining the difference threshold, the human S is usually asked to look at a pair of stimuli and tell whether they are different or not. If he answers correctly he is given credit for a correct choice. He is usually informed in advance of the dimension along which the comparison is to be made. In the animal discrimination learning experiment, on the other hand, not only does the animal need to make what we presume is a discrimination, but he must also determine what it is to which he must respond, and he must make the response (running, jumping, or choosing one or the other of the doors). As Woodworth and Schlosberg have pointed out, "it would tax our ingenuity to give an acceptable formula stating exactly what the animal has to learn" (1955, p. 583). They point out that this is a situation in which we cannot say exactly whether the animal must learn (1) the difference between light and dark or (2) the act of running, jumping, or choosing. Although we can say that he must learn to approach one or the other of the objects or that he must acquire an association between the stimulus and the response, we cannot say anything about the basis upon which the presumed association is established.

An excellent example of the difference between discrimination as a perceptual task and as a learning task may be illustrated by a pair of studies (Lawrence, 1952; Baker and Osgood, 1954). In Lawrence's study, animals (rats) were trained on a problem of simultaneous brightness discrimination. In this problem the animals began each trial in a starting box; when the door leading from the starting box was opened, the animal faced a pair of compartments, side by side with a partition between them. One of the alleys was painted a light color, the other was painted a dark color. The animal's task was to choose one or the other of the compartments and enter it. If the animal entered the "correct" compartment, it was rewarded with food. If it entered the other compartment, no reward was given. Lawrence wanted to test the hypothesis that practice on an "easy" discrimination makes it easier to learn a "difficult" discrimination than learning the difficult discrimination from the beginning. Four groups of animals were trained on the test problem after different kinds of pretraining. One group was trained only on the final problem; another group was first trained on a slightly easier problem, then on the final problem; a third group was first given a very easy problem, followed by another easy problem, then on the test problem. The overall result indicated that learning the final problem is more efficient if an easy problem is mastered first. The most efficient of all was the fourth group, for which fewest trials of all were required, which had previously learned a very easy problem followed by a second easy problem and then the final problem.

In the second study, by Baker and Osgood, four groups of human Ss were first trained on problems involving pairs of tones differing in pitch. Although Es said that their experimental design was the same as that of Lawrence, note the difference in procedure during the training. Whereas Lawrence's rats, confronted simultaneously with two brightnesses, were required to choose one or the other of the brightnesses and move to the compartment painted a particular color, Baker and Osgood's human Ss were required to listen to a pair of tones and say whether they were same or different. An interesting result of this study as compared with Lawrence's was that the only evidence of an increase in efficiency in carrying out the difficult discrimination task was observed for the Ss who approached the final discrimination through the gradual series—very easy, easy, then final. The fact that in the Lawrence study Ss had to choose one or the other of two stimuli and respond in a particular way to each distinguishes sharply this procedure from the procedure of Baker and Osgood, in which S is required merely to say "same" or "different." The Baker and Osgood experiment represents the procedures of classical human psychophysics, whereas the Lawrence experiment represents those of traditional animal psychophysics.

Now, as we have already seen, when an S in an experiment is required to make a particular response to a particular stimulus (for example, by saying "that object is an x"), we have chosen to call the experiment one of identification. For our purposes in this section, we shall deal with those studies of discrimination in which there is a clear requirement for S to respond (contingently) to a difference between a pair of stimuli, confining our attention to those studies. We shall reserve review of studies of discrimination learning until we come to the section on studies of identification. We shall also have occasion to discuss some of the issues arising out of these differences in procedure in Chapter 8.

As one example of the interaction of learning and discrimination, we have already cited the study by Volkmann (Chapter 5) of the decrease in the two-point limen under conditions of practice and its transfer to the bilaterally symmetrical area of the body. We have also pointed out, in connection with Volkmann's study, that the decline in the threshold probably did not necessarily represent an increase in sensitivity to differences as such, but rather that it may have represented some form of learning, of consistency of judgment, or of identification of patterns of stimulation that occur as a function of differences in the distances between the points on the skin. A similar form of learning was postulated in connection with the decline in the absolute threshold discussed in the preceding section. Interestingly, more recent experiments conducted to show the influence of training upon discrimination have yielded a variety of ambiguous results. Let us see what some of these results have been.

Much of the work on interaction of learning and discrimination stems from a series of hypotheses advanced by E. J. Gibson (1940). Gibson's hypothesis, developed in connection with studies of verbal learning, involved what has come to be known as "stimulus predifferentiation." This hypothesis was stated, "If differentiation has been set up within a list (involving paired associates), less generalization will occur in learning a new list which includes the same stimulus items paired with different responses; and the trials required to learn the new list will tend to be reduced by a reduction of internal generalization" (Gibson, 1940, p. 222). This hypothesis, which predicts positive transfer to a new list when it is learned following the learning of an old list, states that the transfer will be due to a reduction in the number of "confusions" of items within the list and would be expected to manifest itself in a situation in which generalization of responses are minimized. Gibson's hypothesis has some attractive implications, one of which is that the reduction in the number of intralist confusions results from a change in S's

perception so that the stimulus items in the list are more "distinctive."

Evidence in support of Gibson's hypothesis of stimulus predifferentiation was sought in an experiment by Gagné and Baker (1950). In their experiment Ss were taught to respond by saying a different letter of the alphabet when each of four different lights was presented. They then learned to manipulate a different switch when each of the four different lights appeared. Increases in the rates at which performance improved and reduction of errors in the manipulative task, associated with previous practice in letter naming, were interpreted by the investigators as supporting the view that practice in naming reduced the amount of stimulus generalization by increasing the degree to which Ss were able to differentiate or to distinguish the light stimuli.

However, the stimulus-predifferentiation hypothesis seems also to be supported by an experiment conducted in accordance with an alternative hypothesis, that of the "acquired distinctiveness of cues" (Miller and Dollard, 1941). Lawrence (1949) advanced the hypothesis that transfer occurs on the basis of familiarity with the stimulus and that a mediating process is established during a discrimination task which enhances the distinctiveness of the stimulus cues. Ss were trained first on a simultaneous discrimination learning problem and tested on a successive discrimination learning problem. Three groups of rats were used. One group learned a black-white problem, another learned a rough-smooth problem (roughness was associated with the fineness of a wire-mesh grid laid across the floor), a third learned a wide-narrow problem (the dimension being the width of the alley that they were to enter to obtain food). A test problem was then learned in which two sets of the cue dimensions were present; one of them was relevant, the other was irrelevant. The results indicated that familiarity, in terms of prior learning, with those cues which were relevant to the test discrimination led to faster learning. The interpretation by Lawrence was that a mediating process was established during the learning of the simultaneous discrimination that enhanced the distinctiveness of the cues.

Evidence of an influence of a type quite different from that found in the Gagné and Baker experiment was obtained in the study by Birge (1941) which we reviewed in Chapter 5. Gagné and Baker's results might be interpreted to support the idea that discrimination influences later responses. Birge's evidence seemingly supports the idea that responses influence discrimination. Recall that the groups of children were first taught to call each of three abstract animal forms by name and that the three forms used were clearly different from each other. Ss learned the same name for two of the forms and learned a different, second name for the third form. Following this practice in naming, in the second phase a reaching response was learned for one of the two forms having the same name. The third phase of the study consisted of testing Ss for generalization of the reaching response to the other two forms. Generalization was greater to the form called by the same name than to the one called by a different name. Generalization was also more likely to occur if the children said the name aloud. Birge's conclusion was that the learning of the same name for different forms resulted in "equivalence" of the stimulus cues. The hypothesis, arising out of the hypothesis of equivalence of cues of Miller and Dollard (1941), was that the cue characteristics of stimuli are altered by the labels in such a way as to make them less discriminable. Other studies, along similar lines and stemming from this same hypothesis, have indicated that learning different, and thus distinctive, labels for different stimuli might make them more distinctive and thus reduce the tendency to generalize. The implication of this kind of study (see Goss, 1953, 1955; Goss and Greenfeld, 1958) is that a perceptual task involving discriminative responses (in the sense of discrimination learning) is

dependent upon the same kind of stimulus-response relations as those found in studies of transfer and instrumental conditioning.

These studies illustrate, on the one hand, the role of discrimination in learning and, on the other hand, the role of learning in discrimination. Although they represent opposite sides of the question, they seem, as do others, to show a clear interaction of discrimination and learning. The precise nature of the interaction, however, is far from clear. In the study of Gagné and Baker, for example, the influence of discrimination in producing positive transfer was inferred from the differences in the rates of learning and the errors that Ss made in the overall transfer task. In the Birge study, on the other hand, the effect of labeling upon discrimination was inferred from the differences in generalization of the reaching response from one stimulus to another. Studies in which "pure" discriminations have been employed as part of training (in the psychophysical sense), or studies in which a "pure" discriminative criterion (in the same sense) has been employed, have been few in number, and those studies have yielded negative or ambiguous results. (For a summary and evaluation of most of these studies, see the excellent article by Arnoult, 1957.)

Object Recognition

Studies of interactions between learning and recognition are actually quite few in number. Although many titles of papers in the literature contain the word *recognition*, in many instances the studies deal with what we would call identification. When we refer to recognition we imply a contingency of response upon the presence or absence of a stimulus presented now, and its presence in the past. The response need not require the assignment of a name or execution of a particular motor act, it need only include a reference to the appearance of the stimulus in the past. Many of the studies of recognition fail to support unequivocally the idea that perception interacts with learning.

An excellent example of the study of interaction between learning and recognition may be found in the experiment by Arnoult (1956b). The basis of this study was previous research in the area of transfer of verbal training and the accounts offered by Miller and Dollard (1941) and E. J. Gibson (1940) in terms of the concepts of "distinctiveness" and improved "discriminability," reviewed in the previous section. Arnoult was interested in the extension of these hypotheses to the area of form recognition. Five groups of Ss were first shown a set of eight nonsense shapes, with varying numbers of exposures of each shape (1, 2, 3, 4, 5, 8, 10, or 15). Ss were asked either to

1. Observe them.
2. Learn a nonsense name for each.
3. Learn a girl's name for each.
4. Learn an arbitrary name designated most frequently as a description by an independent group.
5. Assign a name to each shape and repeat it each time the shape was shown.

Following this practice with the shapes, Ss were given a recognition task requiring them to pick from a group of sixteen shapes (eight on which they had practiced and eight new, but similar ones) the ones on which they had previously practiced. Although the recognition scores did not differ significantly as a function of the various conditions of pretraining (observing or naming), Arnoult found a significant increase in recognition as a function of the amount of verbal pretraining.

In a very general way, Arnoult's experiment supports the contention of a number of previous investigators who showed that "predifferentiation" training—involving observing or labeling stimuli—transfers positively to a new task involving the same or similar stimuli but different responses, a condition in which we would ordinarily

predict negative transfer (see Arnoult, 1957). However, in some of these studies it was found that the kind of response involved in the training task resulted in unpredictable amounts of transfer. Arnoult was interested in testing the influence of a label upon recognition, which does not require that S assign a name or label to the stimulus in the transfer task. The finding of a relation between recognitive performance and amount of previous experience (observing or labeling with various meaningful responses) would indicate the effect, but not the locus of the effect. We should also note that a previous experiment by Arnoult (1953) failed to show an effect of predifferentiation practice upon a same-different discrimination task, and it is perhaps partly in the nature of the transfer task that the effect exists. Vanderplas (1958, 1963) has pointed out previously that the relation between the training and the transfer tasks is an important consideration in the transfer effect, and Vanderplas, Sanderson, and Vanderplas (1964) have shown that differences in pretraining may transfer in quite different amounts, depending upon the type of criterion tasks used to obtain the effect. Similar demonstrations by Ellis and Muller (1964) emphasize that the relation between the training task and the transfer task is an important consideration in the transfer effect.

Object Identification and Judgment

In reviewing studies of identification, we are confronted by a difficulty similar to that encountered in our previous review of discrimination and recognition. Many of the studies that we call studies of identification contain in their title the word *recognition*. Most, if not all, of the studies of word recognition are, by our criterion, studies of identification. We noted in our use of the term *recognition*, that no particular response needs to be made to a particular stimulus, but only that the response should refer to the previous appearance of the stimulus. Studies of word recognition, requiring as they do the assignment of a name to the word, thus become by our criterion studies of identification, not recognition.

Most studies illustrating interaction of learning and perception using identification have been conducted using verbal materials. Typical of these is the study by Postman, Bruner, and McGinnies (1948) on the influence of personal values upon the threshold for identification of words. These investigators first administered the Allport-Vernon Study of Values to students and obtained scores on six categories of personal values: theoretical, economic, aesthetic, social, political, and religious. Thirty-six words were then selected as being related to the six value categories (six for each). The words were exposed to Ss tachisto-scopically, in increasing amounts of time until the words were correctly identified. The general finding was that the higher the score on the value category to which the word was related, the lower the threshold time interval. A similar study was carried out by Vanderplas and Blake (1949), using spoken words with auditory intensity as a measure of the threshold, with a similar result. Thus, the identification of a word is demonstrated to be a function of the relation of the "meaning" of the word to the experience of the perceiver.

A study along similar lines, to demonstrate the role of emotional characteristics of the perceiver in identifying words, was carried out by McGinnies (1949). He exposed eighteen words tachistoscopically to sixteen Ss and determined identification for the word thresholds. Eleven of the words were regarded as "neutral," and seven were regarded as "critical," in the sense of being socially taboo or unpleasant (for example, *bitch*, *raped*, *whore*). The threshold for the "critical" words was found to be higher than those for the "neutral" words.

A problem in interpretation of these studies involves the possible confounding of "values" and "critical" characteristics of the words themselves with other variables, such as frequency of experience and reward and punishment of responses of identification. Solomon and Howes (1951), using a procedure similar to that of Postman, Bruner, and McGinnies, determined thresholds for words divided into high and low value ranks and also into high and low frequencies of appearance in printed media. They found that frequency rather than value was more systematically related to the threshold. Postman and Schneider (1951) obtained similar results, but they argued that the effect of frequency is more potent than values at the high-frequency end of the scale, whereas values are more potent for infrequent words.

In an effort to control for effects of past experience with words, Lazarus and McCleary (1951) used nonsense syllables. Ten five-letter syllables were used, five being associated during a pretraining session with electric shocks, five being merely exposed to Ss. Following this treatment, thresholds were obtained and galvanic skin response was determined. The thresholds for the shock-associated syllables were higher than for the control syllables, and the galvanic skin response was greater for the shock than for the nonshock syllables.

Whether the identification threshold is related to perception as such, however, was challenged by Goldiamond and Hawkins (1958). They gave Ss varying numbers of exposures to nonsense syllables and then gave a session in which they told Ss they would expose the syllables at subthreshold values. They actually showed blank slides. The frequencies of identification responses corresponded closely to the frequencies of prior exposure of the syllables.

Scales of Judgment

A good many studies have been made of the development and characteristics of *scales of judgment*. Such scales are employed in psychophysical experiments and *S*s may assign labels which distinguish objects as being light or heavy, large or small, and so on. Evidence for the relation of such scales to learning comes from a number of studies, of which the following by Johnson (1949) is representative.

*S*s were asked to judge sounds as being either "high" or "low" in pitch. Eighteen such sounds were used, ranging from 256 to 4,870 cps, spaced a quarter octave apart. The eighteen sounds were divided into two groups of nine each. For the first part of the experiment, the "upper" set of tones (numbers 10 to 18) was judged, followed by the "lower" set of tones in a second series.

Of first interest is the determination of the "anchor point," or reference point of the series against which *S* judges a tone as being either "high" or "low" in pitch. According to one theory (Helson, 1947), this reference point may be calculated by finding the geometric mean of the frequencies of the nine judged tones. For the first series Johnson found the midpoint to be 13.0, comparing favorably with a theoretical value of 14.6.

Of next interest is the determination of the effect of practice with the "upper" series upon the reference point of the "lower" series. Johnson employed three practice "trials," each consisting of one judgment (high or low) of each of the nine "upper" tones. The empirical reference point was 13.8. He then employed seven trials using the "lower" tones. If practice on the first series had no effect on the judgments of the second series, the theoretical value for the second series would have been 5.0 (the geometric mean of the "lower" tones, ranging from 1 to 9). The obtained values on the first trial of the second series were higher (7.1) than the theoretical value and shifted downward on succeeding trials from 7.1 to 4.8 on the last trial.

This result indicated an effect of practice in judging tones upon the reference point

of succeeding judgments. In two additional experiments, Johnson was able to show similar effects of practice in judging the "lower" series upon the judgments of the "upper" series and was also able to show a systematic effect of amount of practice. Additional studies by Johnson (1955) and Tresselt (1947) show similar effects using weights as stimuli, and studies by Youtz (1948) and by Grant and Berg (1948), show similar effects in problem-solving and card-sorting tasks.

The development of a scale of judgment seems to follow closely the principles of paired-associates verbal learning, with the modifications that the stimuli are physically variable rather than discrete, as is the case with verbal stimuli, and the responses are in terms of ranges of values rather than specific identification responses (Postman, 1963). The degree of improvement of the scale is usually stated in terms of the agreement between the range of stimuli and the range of responses. Thus, if *S* were able to divide his judgments into as many values as there were values of the stimuli, he would be maximally accurate. However, if he classified a large number of stimuli into, say, only three or four ranges (light, medium, medium-heavy, heavy), his accuracy would be poor. The relation of the judgment scale to the stimulus scale, then, may easily be seen to be a function of the stimulus range, the response range, and their relation to each other, as well as the amount and type of practice with the scale.

If we assume that one begins with some psychophysical relationship (such as the Weber-Fechner law), then we could account for shift or modifications of the relation in terms of practice or experience. For example, Johnson (see Postman, 1963, p. 86) assumes a logarithmic relation between the value of the stimulus and a "central effect" of a range of stimuli, the midpoint of any range of judgments being at the geometric mean of the stimulus range, with stimulus frequency being used as a weighting factor. Each judgment by *S* constitutes a trial of practice, and these trials accumulate to a central tendency of judgment against which new stimuli are compared. One determines the value of the midpoint of the scale and its stability by shifting the range of stimuli upward or downward and noting what happens to the range of judgments. Typically, the speed with which shifts occur varies inversely with the number of prior judgments (Postman, 1963, p. 86). Thresholds of differences may be calculated for a series of stimuli and when they are obtained, one finds good agreement with the preceding assumptions. Pitch and weight have been studied with good results; size judgments seem to follow a curvilinear function (Parducci, 1956).

Space and Distance

Since the time of Berkeley (1709) the perception of space and distance has been regarded as being closely related to (if not dependent upon) learning. In his analysis of space perception, Berkeley attempted to show how spatial characteristics were built up out of experience. He argued that distance (and also form and size) are not perceived directly, but are "suggested" to us by associations of the visual sensations with others, including touch sensations, straining of the eyes, and convergence. From experiences of touching, walking, and so on, the visual cues come to possess "meaning," and it is this meaning that is the "perception" of space.

It was perhaps as a result of Berkeley's influence that modern views of space perception include the usual list of visual "cues" for depth—apparent size, color, superposition, shadows, perspective, position, and relative motion—and the list of physiological cues: accommodation, convergence, retinal image size, and blurring of the image.

That the perception of space is related to learning finds support from a great mass of data: the so-called facial vision of the blind, which has been shown to be due to their learned ability to make use of reflected sounds (Cotzin and Dallenback, 1950); the ability of baseball players to catch and hit; and the ability of billiard players, rifle marksmen, and archers to propel their missiles with increasing accuracy as a function of experience.

But, strange as it may seem, little is known in a general way about either the laws or the underlying basis for such improvements or their relation to learning. In an extensive review of the literature on improvement of perceptual judgments as a function of controlled practice or training, Gibson (1953) concluded that, "Theoretical discussions of perceptual learning . . . contribute little to the facts presented . . ." (p. 421) with regard to such improvements. Her appraisal of the various accounts of perceptual learning indicated that its theoretical basis remained obscure. More recently, Wohlwill (1964), in a study of distance judgments, was unable to produce consistent increases in the accuracy of these judgments by using relatively common training techniques such as feedback, correction, and practice with specific responses.

Illusions and Figural Aftereffects

Interesting phenomena involving several types of illusions demonstrate the interaction of learning and perception. In one experiment (Gibson, 1933) Ss were asked to view a straight line through a prism. The prism distorted the line so that it produced an image of a curved line on the retina. After about a 10-min. inspection period the apparent curvature of the lines was reported by Ss to have markedly decreased and the line tended to "straighten out." When the prism was then removed, the line, which was now undistorted and straight, was reported to appear curved in the direction opposite to the original appearance of the curvature when the line was viewed with the prism. Gibson also found that when *S*s viewed a physically curved line without a prism an apparent decrease in curvature also occurred, and a straight line that was observed after prolonged inspection of the curved line seemed also to be curved in the opposite direction. This phenomenon, which has come to be known as a figural aftereffect, was found by Gibson not only in the visual modality, but also in the tactual-kinesthetic modality. *S*s who were asked to run a finger across a curved surface for several minutes were found later to perceive the curved surface as being straight. Subsequent running of the finger across a straight line produced a report of curvature in the opposite direction. For example, if the original curve was convex the straight line appeared to feel concave (with a depression toward the center).

In an extensive series of experiments on numerous kinds of figures, Köhler and Wallach (1944) described a theory based on what they call satiation. Their hypothesis was that when a figure is inspected for some time, the neural correlates of that figure, in the brain, become satiated (that is, relatively incapable of responding to further stimulation). As a consequence of this basic postulate, Köhler and Wallach predicted that figures which are inspected for prolonged periods will produce satiation not only in the immediate area of the inspection, but also in surrounding areas. A straight line, for example, will appear to be displaced from its physical position to a point to either side (or up or down) by an amount which will be determined by its distance from the original line which produced the satiation and by the inspection time. In addition to a number of specially drawn figures which they used to demonstrate the consequences of their neural theory, Köhler and Wallach explained very nicely the results of a well-known experiment on the Müller-Lyer illusion (Judd, 1902, 1905). In Judd's experiments it was found that repeated

settings of the Müller-Lyer illusion resulted in a gradual decrease of the amount of illusion to near zero; that is, the two lines appeared more nearly equal with continued inspection. Köhler and Wallach explain this result by arguing that the amount of satiation built up in the apparently short region of the figure is greater than the amount built in the apparently long region. After a sufficient number of inspections, the short distance is predicted to increase relative to the long distance and the extent of the illusion therefore should diminish. If the illusion is rotated either 180 or 90 degrees the practice effect should disappear, because the area of satiation is no longer being stimulated by various parts of the figure. Köhler and Wallach explain this result as well.

We should note that the Köhler-Wallach paper contains an extensive account of the various illusions and other kinds of figures producing satiation and demonstrating their results, written in such a manner as to demonstrate and support the validity of the theory concerning the details of the brain mechanisms involved. Other investigators, notably Osgood and Hyer (1952), have given a theoretical account of the figural aftereffect based upon assumptions concerning neural action somewhat more like those involved in the traditional accounts of brain physiology. Relying basically on a theory of sensory acuity and neural mechanisms in vision originally proposed by Marshall and Talbot (1942), Osgood and Hyer are able with some cleverness to deduce many of the figural aftereffects otherwise accounted for by Köhler and Wallach. Because our emphasis here is upon the empirical demonstration of the practice effect, we would not defend one or the other of these two theoretical accounts. However, the studies of Judd, Gibson, and Köhler and Wallach all demonstrate a clear interaction of learning and perception.

A number of other experiments have confirmed and extended the work on various illusions, time effects, and so on. Köhler and Fishback (1950) have confirmed and extended the results with the previously mentioned Müller-Lyer illusion. Hammer (1949) studied the extent of the aftereffect as a function of the amount of exposure and found that it reached a maximum after about 1 min., followed by a decrease in the effect. Wertheimer and Leventhal (1958) found evidence of long-term periods of kinesthetic aftereffects, whereas Nachmias (1953) attempted without success to reproduce certain of the paradoxical effects found in visual figural aftereffects. In addition to the visual aftereffect and the kinesthetic aftereffect reported by Gibson, results suggestive of similar effects in auditory perception have also been reported by Krauskopf (1954).

Illusions as Perceptual Learning Phenomena

There has been a tendency on the part of some theorists to do away with the distinction between illusory and nonillusory phenomena in perception, as may be inferred from the treatments given the previously discussed phenomena. We here maintain this distinction, referring to illusions as stimuli or configurations which, by the nature of their design, evoke a non-veridical perceptual response. The distinction is not a sharp one, and any "error" of discrimination, identification, or judgment could be called an illusory perception. When the precise relation between the properties of the stimulus and the response is known, however, we would no longer call the response an illusory one. An illusion, according to this distinction, is an error for which the relationship is not specified. When the relationship is specified, the "error" is merely a response that is functionally related to a known property of the stimulus. In the field of psychophysics, an error is a response which arises with predictable probability as a function of the deviation of a pair of measured stimuli

from identity. In this sense, illusions, as errors, become errors rather than illusions when they "correctly" reflect known properties of the stimulus; in this case the known property is the amount of deviation from measured identity. To illustrate the lack of a sharp distinction between an illusion and an error, consider the Müller-Lyer illusion once again. If the arrows were not fixed to the horizontal lines at the ends and the midpoints, any error in placement of one or the other of the lines after S had reported perceived equality of length of the two lines would simply be noted to be a function of the deviation of the two lines from equality of length. Under these conditions, we would refer to a constant error (left or right) and a variable error, specifying both of these in terms of the postulates of psychophysics. When, however, the arrow points are fixed to the line, we usually find the constant error magnified in the direction of the line to which the arrows are fixed pointing inward. This change or increase in the constant error we call the illusory response, not because we know its basis, but simply because it is outside the bounds of what we would call the constant error arising under conditions where we know the relationship between the true equality of the lines and what we would call the error or deviation from veridicality.

What is important about the preceding distinction, from the standpoint of the interaction of perception and learning, is that it points up clearly the lack of a known basis for identifying the locus of the interaction. This lack of basis is fairly clear in the case of illusions, because it is related to our failure to specify the explicit relations involved in changes of illusions with practice. The lack is not so clear in the case of nonillusory stimuli, because it is not apparent in many cases just what it is that constitutes the explicit relations.

In our discussion of studies of discrimination, for example, it was strongly implied that arguments over whether stimuli are differentiated or whether responses are altered (to discriminated stimuli) may well hinge on the specification of the explicit locus of the effect. But it is not clear from the studies themselves that the locus has been of real concern. These questions become more pronounced in the study of illusions, for the reasons cited, but they are equally persistent ones in the study of non-illusory perceptual phenomena.

8

Persistent Issues:
A Summary and Critique

We may now turn to a brief summary and critique of the interesting and challenging questions that we have seen raised during our discussion of experiments in perception and learning. Our critique may be brief, because although the questions we have raised seem at first to be many, the underlying issues may be seen to be relatively few. Questions of specific techniques or methods employed, although important, often may divert the argument from the central issue. We shall thus concern ourselves here only with what we believe to be the more persistent and central questions. Recent reviews of the area of perceptual learning (Drever, 1960; Gibson, 1963; Wohlwill, 1966) may be consulted for a more detailed review of the focal areas of research and theory related to these questions.

Theoretical Issues

As we have emphasized repeatedly in the foregoing chapters, the fact of an interaction between perception and learning is almost a truism. However, as we have also indicated, the precise nature of the interaction and the direction of influence, of one upon the other, are matters of considerable disagreement among theorists and experimenters alike. Even the fundamental groundwork of theory, which we might hope would tie the areas together, seems more to generate debate than to foster agreement. An excellent example of the persistence of controversy over the treatment of the relation of perception to learning (or vice versa) may be cited. Postman (1963), in reviewing the area of perceptual learning, emphasizes the continuity between the phenomena of perceptual learning and the general field of learning. He advocates strongly the translation of the theoretical terms of the former to those of the latter. Leeper (1963), in a review of the fields of learning, perception, and personality, which appears in the same volume, emphasizes the nature of learning as an end product of perceptual organization. This emphasis, by each theorist, on the translation of the terms of another's field into the terms of his own seems to us to represent a major block to the understanding of the nature and the direction of the interaction. For, on the one hand, we would attempt to understand learning in terms of perception and, on the other hand, we would attempt to understand perception in terms of learning. Such an attempt at understanding does

not seem completely possible at a time
when the separate fields themselves are as
little understood as they are. We would
point out that an understanding of the
interaction between perception and learning
may entail not "bridging laws" between
the fields, as suggested by Postman (1963),
but laws that are (at least relatively)
independent of either of the two fields.

Focal Issues

Most of the questions we have seen raised
in the previous chapters have to do with the
nature and direction of the interaction
between perception and learning. As regards its nature, these questions have been
directed at the specification of the mechanisms underlying the phenomena. For example, in the study by Volkmann (1858)
the question is raised as to whether the
mechanism that accounts for the variation
in threshold with practice is a sensory one
or a judgmental one. As regards its direction, these questions have been directed
either toward specifying the effects of
experiences related to learning (frequency,
reinforcement, labeling, and so on) on
perception or toward specifying the effects
of factors related to perception (figural
organization, satiation effects, and so on)
upon learning. And as we have seen, these
questions have been raised in the specific
contexts of the experiments which were
designed to show the effects. These experiments, organized and designed in this kind
of context, would not seem, from our point
of view, optimally oriented toward either
establishment of "bridging laws" or independent laws of the interactions themselves.
With these points in mind, let us focus more
closely on these persistent questions.

The Nature of Interactions

In asking the question about the nature
of the interaction between perception and

learning—that is, how it takes place—we
are also in a sense asking *if* it does. At the
very least, does the particular study purporting to show the interaction really do
so? Thus, we are asking in a particular
instance whether the variable, to which a
change in a perceptual response is referred,
has been isolated from possible concom-
itant variables, is necessarily related to
the change, or is logically necessary in
accounting for the change.

As we saw in our review of early demonstrational studies, a major portion of the
effort was addressed to the question of
whether past experience influences perception. The translation of past experience, as
a concept, into experimental variables has
been in terms of extremely broad and
heterogeneous operations which have permitted alternative interpretations in almost
every case.

For example, one can wonder whether
past experience results in a change in the
perception itself or whether it results in
changes associated with responses to un-
altered perceptions. Prentice (1954), for
example, challenged the results of the
Carmichael, Hogan, and Walter (1932)
study on grounds that the reproduction of
the figures in their experiment could easily
be accounted for by referring only to the
response of reproduction, which may be
made either to the perceived form or to the
suggested name. Prentice argued that what
was altered by the suggestion of a name
was not the perceived form which was
reproduced, but rather, the response of
reproduction made to the verbal stimulus
consisting of the suggestion by *E*. To test
this alternative hypothesis, Prentice repeated the experiment giving the same
instructions during the exposure phase, but
instead of using reproduction in the test
phase he used a recognition task. His *S*s
were asked whether forms resembling those
which were reproduced by *S*s of the
Carmichael et al. experiment had been seen
previously during the exposure phase. For
each member of the series of forms the

original and two alternative forms, resembling one or the other of the forms suggested by the names, were presented to *S*s. He found practically no errors of recognition of the original figures and no mistaken recognitions of the alternative figures. We are thus left with the question of whether the suggested name altered the perception of the form or whether it served as a stimulus for the response of reproduction.

Some of the other demonstrational studies have been similarly challenged, although along somewhat different lines. Here the question of whether values, needs, and so on, serve to alter perceptions or whether alternative variables might serve more parsimoniously as determinants has been raised. For example, in the study by Bruner and Goodman (1947) of the role of value and need as determinants of size perception, the question has been raised whether sufficient controls were exercised to prevent the operation of certain psychophysical variables (Carter and Schooler, 1949). Whether personal values influence the identification of words, as in a study by Postman, Bruner, and McGinnies (1948), has been questioned, with possible alternatives suggesting that *frequency* of past experience rather than its *nature* (see Postman, 1963) is the more potent variable.

Additional criticisms have been leveled at many of the studies concerning the operation of needs and values in perceptual learning. Pastore (1949) reviewed most of the experiments done to that date and found a number of bases for criticizing the experimental design, statistical treatment, and interpretations of the data. The experiment by Postman, Bruner, and McGinnies (1948) was criticized for the conclusion that "the higher the value represented by a word, the more rapidly it is likely to be recognized" (1948, p. 148). Hochberg and Gleitman (1949) pointed out that the meaning of the words would first need to be known in order for blockage (presumably the factor which raised the thresholds for less valued words) to occur. How this can happen before the words are perceived seems something of a mystery.

Most of the studies of need and value are open to additional criticism on grounds that there are no good criteria for defining just what "needs" and "values" are and how they operate in producing perceptual performance. The concepts of need and value, as they have been used in most studies, do seem to require as much verification as the perceptual performance purported to be determined by the studies. Such fundamental physiological needs as food deprivation, oxygen hunger, thirst, and the like serve reasonably well as first-order definitions of needs. Values, on the other hand, are so diverse from individual to individual that they defy even a reasonable attempt at classification. This should not be understood as denying that the concepts of need and values are useful in understanding perceptual performance, but it is to be understood that these concepts cannot serve as adequate explanatory mechanisms until they themselves are more adequately defined.

The Direction of Interactions

In asking the question of the direction of the interaction of perception and learning, it is asked, essentially, whether perception (or perceptual alteration) influences learning or whether learning influences perception. Here, as with the previous question, it may be asked if there is a directional influence and whether the study purporting to show it really does so. And here also we see similar reservations about the logical necessity of the variables cited in accounting for the obtained results.

As one example, we have seen in the studies of sensory deprivation in animals that rearing in total darkness results in a marked deficit in such performance as form discrimination. For some of the animals, however, physiological damage to the visual system might have accounted for the results. More recent studies have reduced this difficulty in interpretation by stimulating the animal with diffuse light during the deprivation period, thus allowing for stimulation of the retina while depriving the animal of pattern vision (Riesen, 1961; Siegel, 1953a; Siegel, 1953b). On the basis of these studies it may be said that animals reared normally perform better on tasks of discrimination and other tasks than do animals reared under these controlled conditions. However, it may still be questioned whether this superiority of control animals (or, conversely, the inferiority of experimental animals reared in darkness) is due to deficits of perception or whether it is due to retardation of response processes, independent of perception.

It should be recalled that we have distinguished earlier between perceptual learning, consisting of a change in the ability of S to *perceive* differences, and learning, consisting of a change in S's ability to *respond differentially* to already perceived differences. Under conditions where the animal must learn to perceive objects and differentiate them and also to develop the differential response as a part of the task, the two processes are confounded and cannot be disentangled.

A procedure which would disentangle these two processes would require that differential preferences of discrimination be determined which can be measured without requiring acquisition of new instrumental acts. Such a design was artfully contrived in the "visual cliff" demonstrations of Eleanor Gibson and her co-workers (Gibson and Walk, 1956, 1960; Gibson, Walk, Pick, and Tighe, 1958). In these demonstrations Ss are confronted with two patterns of visual stimulation characteristic of a near and a far surface, respectively. This visual appearance is produced by covering an actual valleylike arrangement of apparatus with a sheet of heavy glass. On one side the glass rests upon a horizontal surface; on the other patterned material (wallpaper) is placed flush under the glass

on one side and below the glass on the other side of the "cliff." S is placed on a board at the edge and parallel to the "cliff." The preference of S for the "shallow" side as opposed to the "deep" side forms the basis for inferences concerning S's ability to discriminate depth. Human infants, chickens, lambs, pigs, kittens, and dogs have all been tested on the apparatus, and all consistently show a preference for the shallow side.

Additional examples of the problems involved in specifying the direction of interaction may be cited. The studies on detection that we reviewed illustrate an interaction between learning and detection as indicated by the change in the absolute threshold. Just what the direction of the interaction is, however, is not yet precisely known. In all the studies the decrease in the threshold may have been due to an increase in sensitivity as a result of practice. But it may also have occurred as a result of changes in the observer's more general ability to respond, to take advantage of his knowledge of the experimental procedure, to make sensory-motor adjustments that are conducive to better scores, and so on. Most of the studies of discrimination are similarly subject to alternative interpretation and are beset with methodological difficulties which make it impossible to decide unequivocally for one or the other of the two kinds of hypotheses advanced.

These difficulties of interpretation are especially evident in the studies of "predifferentiation" and the alternatively designed studies of "acquired distinctiveness." We have already mentioned some of the difficulties in Chapter 7 and a few additional comments may be cited here.

There seems to be enough agreement among the results of these studies to say that when the stimuli of training and test tasks are the same, positive results will occur in a task of discrimination learning even though the responses are different, provided that there is no conflict between the responses (for example, checking with a pencil and switch manipulation, as in Gagné and Baker, 1950), or if there is some meaningful relation between, say, a verbal response in the training task and a motor response in the discrimination learning task (for example, a verbal response of "up" and motor response of "moving a lever up" as in McAllister, 1953). But whether the transfer results from "differentiation," as suggested by the predifferentiation hypothesis, or from "enrichment," as suggested by acquired distinctiveness hypothesis, is not clear. In a number of studies it was found that observing or paying attention to cues during pretraining yielded as much or more transfer to a perceptual discrimination or a recognition task (Arnoult, 1953, 1956a; Robinson, 1955; Ellis and Muller, 1964) or to a discrimination learning task involving motor or verbal associations (Baldwin, 1954; Birge, 1941; Campbell and Freeman, 1955; Ellis and Muller, 1964; Goss, 1953). Other studies (Vanderplas and Garvin, 1959; Ellis and Muller, 1964) have found that distinctiveness training may yield greater transfer than observation or attention-to-cues training if the task is a motor or verbal discrimination learning task.

An interesting experiment was conducted by Gibson and Gibson (1955a, 1955b) to show that the response ordinarily associated with a particular stimulus need not necessarily occur or be reinforced. Their human *S*s were shown series of forms which were merely "squiggles" or doodles resembling spiral coils, varying with respect to the number of squiggles and the degree of distortion of the forms. Following presentation of the forms, *S*s were asked to pick out the ones that were "critical" from the original set. As a function of the amount of observational practice that they had in the original series, *S*s were found to pick out the critical forms more accurately.

We are left at this point with a dilemma. Does experience alone with pairs of stimuli, in human psychophysical experiments, result in better discrimination? Or does

practice in making specific discriminative responses to different stimuli result in positive transfer? Must it be one or the other of these? Does the experience result in an increase in perceptual sensitivity, or does it result merely in an increase in the ability of *S* to make differential responses? It is important to note that in those studies conducted in connection with the predifferentiation hypothesis, either experience with stimuli alone or mere discrimination (that is, same or different responses) was required. In both kinds of studies, on the other hand, the response was a differential, but specific, response (that is, a different response was required for each of two or more stimuli). A number of the preceding studies have been conducted to test directly the effect of learning verbal labels for each of several stimuli and the effect of experience with pairs of stimuli upon a more direct test of discrimination, in the same-different sense (Arnoult, 1953; Robinson, 1955; Campbell and Freeman, 1955). But in none of these studies where human psychophysical discrimination has been used as a test of the effect of either predifferentiation or acquired distinctiveness, has clear-cut improvement been found in discrimination.

It may be said that in those studies where *S*s received prior training in labeling, transfer (in a learning sense) has been positive to tasks which involve labeling or motor responses (Goss and Greenfeld, 1958; Vanderplas and Garvin, 1959) but negligible to tasks requiring recognition of discrimination in the psychophysical sense. In those studies in which *S*s received training in observing or discriminating stimuli, transfer has been found positive to tasks of discrimination but negligible to tasks requiring verbal or motor response of a differential sort (Gibson and Gibson, 1955a, 1955b; Goss and Greenfeld, 1958).

The writer and his colleagues (Vanderplas, Sanderson, and Vanderplas, 1964) conducted an experiment in which comparisons were made of transfer to several different kinds of task situations. Although the experimental procedures are too involved to discuss here in detail, it can be said that when prior training was given in either observing, discriminating, or labeling, the amount of transfer (in all cases positive) depended upon the relation of the training task to the test task. When the criterion task involved discrimination, transfer appeared to be as great and positive from a training task involving merely observing or discriminating as it did from one involving labeling. When the criterion task required differential verbal labeling or motor responses (switch manipulation) to each stimulus, transfer appeared to be greater from tasks involving labeling practice than from those involving observing or discriminating alone. The degree of improvement in performance of the criterion task may also depend upon other variables, such as the complexity of the stimuli and their mean-

ingfulness, as well as on the effects of the labels employed or the kinds of responses required (for example, verbal or motor).

A clearer definition of the kinds of perceptual tasks upon which learning has an influence; better criteria for the definition of crucial variables which interact with perception and learning; and improvement of the experimental designs which clearly separate stimulus processes from response processes are all obviously necessary for further and better understanding of the interaction of perception and learning. Studies to date have employed confounded variables, obscure and diffuse data language, and inadequate controls for extraneous effects upon the processes under investigation. We may hope that calling attention to these defects will stimulate further criticism and thought which in turn will result in better handling of both theories and experiments.

Glossary

acquired distinctiveness. The hypothesis of Miller and Dollard that stimuli become more distinctive (that is, that differential responses are more readily made to different stimuli) from the addition of response-produced cues.

behaviorism. The theoretical viewpoint deriving from John B. Watson that the proper study of psychology is behavior, without reference to consciousness or mentalism.

detection. A contingency relation between the presence or absence of a figure and the presence or absence of a response of "I see it" or an equivalent reaction. When the probability of such a response is 0.50, we speak of the detection threshold.

discrimination. A contingency relation between the presence or absence of a measurable difference between two figures and the presence or absence of a response "different" or equivalent. When the probability of the response is 0.50, we speak of a discrimination threshold.

empiricism. The theoretical viewpoint in

philosophy that experience is the sole source of knowledge.

figural aftereffects. Perceptual phenomena illustrating the principle that there is a tendency to maintain stability in the figure-ground relationship.

figure. An inhomogeneity having finite boundaries in an otherwise homogeneous perceptual field.

figure-ground. The principle that perceptions are fundamentally patterned into (1) figure, which stands out, has contour, and appears bounded and finite, and (2) background, which is indistinct and has no clearly shaped or patterned parts.

functionalism. The theoretical viewpoint deriving from Dewey and Angell that the proper subject matter of psychology is mental process or acts and their adaptive significance.

generalization. See stimulus generalization, response generalization.

gestalt. Form, figure, configuration; an integrated whole that defies analysis and is more than the sum of its parts.

identification. A contingency relation between the categorical characteristics of stimuli and the categorical characteristics denoted by responses (for example, a stimulus is a member of class X and a response is "that is an X"; the response is an identification).

innate. Inborn; present at birth; congenital; hereditary; not related to environmental influence or to experience.

judgment. A contingency relation between the value of a stimulus on a magnitude scale (relative or absolute) and a response reflecting a subjective magnitude.

learning. A measured change in behavior that may be attributed to well-defined conditions of practice.

nativism. The theoretical position that knowledge is innate and not related to experience.

perception. A term referring to a multitude of theoretical viewpoints on the relation between the behavior of the organism and its environment. Variously "defined" as knowing objects and events by means of the senses, awareness, sensations to which have been added meanings, discriminative responses, relations between stimuli and responses, and so on.

phi-gamma function. The psychophysical hypothesis that the probability of a perceptual response is a cumulative

normal function of the magnitude of a stimulus.

predifferentiation. A term related to the hypothesis of Eleanor J. Gibson that learning labels for stimuli results in a steepening of generalization gradients such that smaller stimulus differences produce more differential responses than they did prior to such practice.

recognition. A contingency relation between prior exposure of a stimulus and a response denoting previous experience with the stimulus.

response generalization. The principle that following learning of a given response to a stimulus "similar" responses will be elicited upon presentation of the stimulus to which the original response was given.

response-produced cue. A hypothetical construct referring to an aspect of the stimulus situation supposedly produced by the behavior of the organism.

sensation. The structuralist conception of the basic unit of consciousness.

sensory. A term referring to the activity of a sense organ.

stimulus generalization. The principle that following learning of a given response to a given stimulus "similar" stimuli will serve to elicit the response.

References

Arnoult, M. D. Transfer of predifferentiation training in simple and multiple shape discrimination. *J. exp. Psychol.*, 1953, **45**, 401–409.

Arnoult, M. D. Recognition of shapes following paired associates pretraining. In G. Finch and F. Cameron (Eds.), *Symposium on Air Force human engineering, personnel, and training research.* Washington: Nat. Acad. Sci.-Nat. Res. Council Publ. No. 455, 1956a, 1–9.

Arnoult, M. D. Familiarity and recognition of nonsense shapes. *J. exp. Psychol.*, 1956b, **51**, 269–276.

Arnoult, M. D. Stimulus predifferentiation: Some generalizations and hypotheses. *Psychol. Bull.*, 1957, **54**, 340–351.

Atkinson, R. C., & Ammons, R. B. Experiential factors in visual form perception: II. Latency as a function of

repetition. *J. exp. Psychol.*, 1952, **43**, 173–178.

Baker, R. A., & Osgood, S. W. Discrimination transfer along a pitch continuum. *J. exp. Psychol.*, 1954, **48**, 241–246.

Baldwin, R. D. *Discrimination learning as a function of stimulus predifferentiation and mediated association training.* Unpublished doctoral dissertation, State Univer. of Iowa, 1954.

Berkeley, G. Essay towards a new theory of vision, 1709. In *Selections from Berkeley*, Alexander Campbell Fraser, 6th ed. Oxford: Clarendon Press, 1910.

Bevan, W. Perceptual learning: An overview. *J. gen. Psychol.*, 1961, **64**, 69–99.

Bevan, W., & Zener, K. Some influences of past experience upon the perceptual thresholds of visual form. *Amer. J. Psychol.*, 1952, **65**, 434–442.

Birge, J. S. *The role of verbal response in transfer.* Unpublished doctoral dissertation, Yale Univer., 1941.

Blackwell, H. R. Psychophysical thresholds: experimental studies of methods of measurement. *Engng. Res. Bull.,* Univer. of Michigan, 1953, **36**.

Boring, E. G. The control of attitude in psychophysical experiments. *Psychol. Rev.,* 1920, **27**, 440–452.

Boring, E. G. *Sensation and perception in the history of experimental psychology.* New York: Appleton-Century-Crofts, 1942.

Braly, K. W. The influence of past experience in visual perception. *J. exp. Psychol.,* 1933, **16**, 613–643.

Brown, K. T. *Studies of rate of apparent change as a function of observation time, using a new type of ambiguous figure.* Wright Air Devel. Cen., Wright-Patterson AFB, Ohio: WADC Tech. Rept., 54–139, 1954.

Bruce, R. H., & Low, F. N. The effect of practice with brief-exposure techniques upon central and peripheral visual acuity and a search for a brief test of peripheral acuity. *J. exp. Psychol.,* 1951, **41**, 275–280.

Bruner, J. S., & Goodman, C. C. Value and need as organizing factors in perception. *J. abnorm. soc. Psychol.,* 1947, **42**, 33–44.

Bruner, J., & Postman, L. Perception, cognition and behavior. *J. Pers.,* 1949, **18**, 14–31.

Brunswik, E. *Perception and the representative design of psychological experiments.* Berkeley, Calif.: Univer. of California Press, 1956.

Campbell, V., & Freeman, J. T. Some functions of experimentally-induced language in perceptual learning. *Percept. mot. Skills,* 1955, **5**, 71–79.

Cantril, H. *The why of man's experience.* New York: Macmillan, 1950.

Carmichael, L., Hogan, H. G., & Walter, A. A. An experimental study of the effect of language on the reproduction of a visually perceived form. *J. exp. Psychol.,* 1932, **15**, 73–86.

Carter, L. F., & Schooler, K. Value, need, and other factors in perception. *Psychol. Rev.,* 1949, **56**, 200–207.

Cotzin, M., & Dallenbach, K. M. "Facial vision": the role of pitch and loudness in the perception of obstacles by the blind. *Amer. J. Psychol.,* 1950, **63**, 485–515.

Djang, Siao-Sung. The role of past experience in the visual apprehension of masked forms. *J. exp. Psychol.,* 1937, **20**, 29–59.

Dresslar, F. B. Studies in the psychology of touch. *Amer. J. Psychol.,* 1894, **6**, 313–368.

Drever, J. Perceptual learning. *Annu. Rev. Psychol.,* 1960, **11**, 131–160.

Duncker, K. The influence of past experience upon perceptual properties. *Amer. J. Psychol.,* 1939, **52**, 255–265.

Ellis, H. C., & Tenge, R. L. Transfer of predifferentiation training to gradients of generalization in shape recognition. *J. exp. Psychol.,* 1966, **71**, 539–542.

Ellis, H. C., & Muller, D. G. Transfer in perceptual learning following stimulus predifferentiation. *J. exp. Psychol.,* 1964, **68**, 388–395.

Ellis, H. C., Tenge, R. L., Long, K. K., & Pegram, V. G. Evidence for acquired distinctiveness of cues in a perceptual task. *Percept. mtr. Skills,* 1964, **19**, 159–162.

Fisichelli, V. R. Reversible perspective in Lissajou Figures; Some theoretical considerations. *Amer. J. Psychol.,* 1947, **60**, 240–249.

Freeman, G. L. *The energetics of human behavior.* Ithaca, N.Y.: Cornell Univer. Press, 1948.

Gagné, R. M., & Baker, Katherine E. Stimulus pre-differentiation as a factor in transfer of training. *J. exp. Psychol.,* 1950, **40**, 439–451.

Gibson, Eleanor J. A systematic application of the concepts of generalization and differentiation to verbal learning. *Psychol. Rev.,* 1940, **47**, 196–229.

Gibson, Eleanor J. Improvement in perceptual judgments as a function of controlled practice or training. *Psychol. Bull.,* 1953, **50**, 401–431.

Gibson, Eleanor J. Perceptual learning. *Annu. Rev. Psychol.,* 1963, **14**, 29–56.

Gibson, Eleanor J., & Walk, R. D. The effect of prolonged exposure to visually presented patterns on learning to discriminate them. *J. comp. physiol. Psychol.*, 1956, **49**, 239–242.

Gibson, Eleanor J., Walk, R. D., Pick, H. L., Jr., & Tighe, T. J. The effect of prolonged exposure to visual patterns on learning to discriminate similar and different patterns. *J. comp. physiol. Psychol.*, 1958, **51**, 584–587.

Gibson, Eleanor J., & Walk, R. D. The "visual cliff." *Scient. Amer.*, 1960, **202**, 64–71.

Gibson, J. J. Adaptation after-effect, and contrast in the perception of curved lines. *J. exp. Psychol.*, 1933, **16**, 1–31.

Gibson, J. J. *The perception of the visual world.* Boston: Houghton Mifflin, 1950.

Gibson, J. J. Theories in perception. In W. Dennis (Ed.), *Current trends in psychological theory.* Pittsburgh: Univer. of Pittsburgh Press, 1951, 85–110.

Gibson, J. J., & Gibson, Eleanor J. Perceptual learning: Differentiation or enrichment? *Psychol. Rev.*, 1955, **62**, 32–41.

Gibson, J. J., & Gibson, Eleanor J. What is learned in perceptual learning? A reply to Professor Postman. *Psychol. Rev.*, 1955, **62**, 447–450.

Goldiamond, I., & Hawkins, W. F. Vexierversuch: the log relationship between word-frequency and recognition obtained in the absence of stimulus words. *J. exp. Psychol.*, 1958, **56**, 457–463.

Goss, A. E. Transfer as a function of type and amount of preliminary experience with the task stimuli. *J. exp. Psychol.*, 1953, **46**, 419–428.

Goss, A. E. A stimulus-response analysis of the interaction of cue-producing and instrumental responses. *Psychol. Rev.*, 1955, **62**, 20–31.

Goss, A. E., & Greenfeld, N. Transfer to a motor task as influenced by conditions and degree of prior discrimination training. *J. exp. Psychol.*, 1958, **55**, 258–269.

Gottschaldt, K. Ueber den Einfluss der Erfahrung auf die Wahrnehmung von Figuren, I. *Psychol. Forsch.*, 1926, **8**, 261–317.

Gottschaldt, K. Ueber den Einfluss der Erfahrung auf die Wahrnehmung von Figuren, II. *Psychol. Forsch.*, 1929, **12**, 1–87.

Graham, C. H. Psychophysics and behavior. *J. gen. Psychol.*, 1934, **10**, 299–310.

Graham, C. H. Behavior, perception and the psychophysical methods. *Psychol. Rev.*, 1950, **57**, 108–120.

Graham, C. H. Behavior and the psychophysical methods: An analysis of some recent experiments. *Psychol. Rev.*, 1952, **59**, 62–70.

Graham, C. H. Sensation and perception in an objective psychology. *Psychol. Rev.*, 1958, **65**, 65–76.

Graham, C. H., & Ratoosh, P. Notes on some interrelations of sensory psychology, perception, and behavior. In S. Koch (Ed.), *Psychology: A study of a science.* Vol. 4. New York: McGraw-Hill, 1962.

Grant, D. A., & Berg, E. A. A behavioral analysis of reinforcement and ease of shifting to new responses in a Weigeltype card-sorting problem. *J. exp. Psychol.*, 1948, **38**, 404–411.

Hake, H. W. *Contributions of psychology to the study of pattern vision.* Wright Air Devel. Cen. Tech. Rep. No. 57–621, 1957.

Hammer, E. R. Temporal factors in figural after-effects. *Amer. J. Psychol.*, 1949, **62**, 337–354.

Hebb, D. O. The innate organization of visual activity: I. Perception of figures by rats reared in total darkness. *J. genet. Psychol.*, 1937, **51**, 101–126.

Hebb, D. O. *The organization of behavior.* New York: Wiley, 1949.

Helson, H. Adaptation-level as frame of reference for prediction of psycho-physical data. *Amer. J. Psychol.*, 1947, **60**, 1–29.

Helson, H. *Adaptation-level theory.* New York: Harper & Row, 1964.

Henle, Mary. An experimental investigation of past experience as a determinant of visual form perception. *J. exp. Psychol.*, 1942, **30**, 1–22.

Hilgard, E. R. *Theories of learning.* New York: Appleton-Century-Crofts, 1948.

Hilgard, E. R. *Theories of learning* (2nd ed.). New York: Appleton-Century-Crofts, 1956.

Hillix, W. A. & Marx, M. H., Response strengthening by information and effect in human learning. *J. exp. Psychol.*, 1960, **60**, 97–102.

Hochberg, J. Nativism and empiricism in perception. In L. Postman (Ed.), *Psychology in the making.* New York: Knopf, 1962, 255–330.

Hochberg, J. E., & Gleitman, H. Toward a reformulation of the perception-motivation dichotomy. *J. Pers.*, 1949, **18**, 180–191.

Ittelson, W. H., & Cantril, H. *Perception: A transactional approach.* New York: Doubleday, 1954.

Johnson, D. M. Learning function for a change in the scale of judgment. *J. exp. Psychol.*, 1949, **39**, 851–860.

Johnson, D. M. *The psychology of thought and judgment.* New York: Harper & Row, 1955.

Judd, C. H. Practice and its effects on the perception of illusions. *Psychol. Rev.*, 1902, **9**, 27–39.

Judd, C. H. The Müller–Lyer illusion. *Psychol. Monogr.*, 1905, **7**, 29.

Kanfer, F. H. Perception: Identification and instrumental activity. *Psychol. Rev.*, 1956, **63**, 317–329.

Kilpatrick, F. P. (Ed.). *Human behavior from the transactional point of view.* Hanover, N.H.: Inst. for Associated Research, 1952.

Köhler, W. *Intelligenzprufung der Menschenaffen.* Berlin: Springer, 1921.

Köhler, W. *The mentality of apes.* London: Routledge & Kegan, Paul, 1924.

Köhler, W. On the nature of association. *Proc. Amer. Philos. Soc.*, 1941, **84**, 489–502.

Köhler, W., & Fishback, J. The destruction of the Müller–Lyer illusion in repeated trials: II. Satiation patterns and memory traces. *J. exp. Psychol.*, 1950, **40**, 398–410.

Köhler, W., & Wallach, H. Figural aftereffects. An investigation of visual processes. *Proc. Amer. Phil. Soc.*, 1944, **88**, 269–357.

Krauskopf, J. Figural after-effects in auditory space. *Amer. J. Psychol.*, 1954, **67**, 278–287.

Lawrence, D. H. Acquired distinctiveness of cues: I. Transfer between discriminations on the basis of familiarity with the stimulus. *J. exp. Psychol.*, 1949, **39**, 770–784.

Lawrence, D. H. The transfer of a discrimination along a continuum. *J. comp. physiol. Psychol.*, 1952, **45**, 511–516.

Lazarus, R. S., & McCleary, R. A. Autonomic discrimination without awareness: A study of subception. *Psychol. Rev.*, 1951, **58**, 113–122.

Leeper, R. A study of a neglected portion of the field of learning—the development of sensory organization. *J. genet. Psychol.*, 1935, **46**, 41–75.

Leeper, R. W. Learning and the fields of perception, motivation, and personality. In S. Koch (Ed.), *Psychology: A study of a science* (Vol. 5). New York: McGraw-Hill, 1963, pp. 365–487.

Levine, R., Chein, I., & Murphy, G. The relation of the intensity of a need to the amount of perceptual distortion. *J. Psychol.*, 1942, **13**, 283–293.

Marshall, W. H., & Talbot, S. A. Recent evidence for neural mechanisms in vision leading to a general theory of sensory acuity. In H. Klüver (Ed.), *Visual mechanisms. Biol. symposia*, 1942, **7**, 117–164.

McAllister, D. E. The effects of various kinds of relevant verbal pretraining on subsequent motor performance. *J. exp. Psychol.*, 1953, **46**, 329–336.

McGinnies, E. Emotionality and perceptual defense. *Psychol. Rev.*, 1949, **56**, 244–251.

Messenger, J. F. Perception of number through touch. *Psychol. Monogr.*, 1903, No. 17.

Miller, N. E., & Dollard, J. *Social learning and imitation.* New Haven: Yale Univer. Press, 1941.

Mueller, G. E., & Pilzecker, A. Experimentelle Beitrage zur Lehre vom Gedachtniss. *Zeitschrift fur Psychologie Erganzumgsband*, 1900, #1.

Nachmias, J. Figural after-effects in kinesthetic space. *Amer. J. Psychol.*, 1953, **66**, 609–612.

Nissen, H. W., Chow, K. L., & Semmes, J. Effects of restricted opportunity for tactual, kinesthetic, and manipulative experience on the behavior of a chimpanzee. *Amer. J. Psychol.*, 1951, **64**, 485–507.

Osgood, C. E., & Heyer, A. W., Jr. A new interpretation of figural after-effects. *Psychol. Rev.*, 1952, **59**, 98–118.

Parducci, A. Direction of shift in the judgment of single stimuli. *J. exp. Psychol.*, 1956, **51**, 169–178.

Pastore, N. Need as a determinant of perception. *J. Psychol.*, 1949, **28**, 457–476.

Philip, B. R., & Fisichelli, V. R. Effect of speed of rotation and complexity of pattern on the reversals of apparent movement in Lissajou Figures. *Amer. J. Psychol.*, 1945, **58**, 530–539.

Postman, L. Perception and learning. In S. Koch (Ed.), *Psychology: A study of a science* (Vol. 5). New York: Wiley, 1963, pp. 27–103.

Postman, L., & Schneider, B. M. Personal values, visual recognition and recall. *Psychol. Rev.*, 1951, **58**, 271–284.

Postman, L., Bruner, J. S., & McGinnies, E. Personal values as organizing factors in perception. *J. abnorm. soc. Psychol.*, 1948, **43**, 142–154.

Prentice, W. C. H. Visual recognition of verbally labeled figures. *Amer. J. Psychol.* 1954, **67**, 315–320.

Riesen, A. H. The development of visual perception in man and chimpanzee. *Science*, 1947, **106**, 107–108.

Riesen, A. H. Arrested vision. *Scient. Amer.*, 1950, **183**, 16–19.

Riesen, A. H. Stimulation as a requirement for growth and function in behavioral development. In D. W. Fiske and S. R. Maddi (Eds.), *Functions of varied experience.* Homewood, Ill.: Dorsey Press, 1961, pp. 57–80.

Riggs, L. A., Ratliff, F., Cornsweet, J. C., & Cornsweet, T. N. The disappearance of steadily fixated visual test objects. *J. Opt. Soc. Amer.*, 1953, **43**, 495–501.

Robinson, J. S. The effect of learning verbal labels for stimuli on their later discrimination. *J. exp. Psychol.*, 1955, **49**, 112–115.

Rock, I., & Fleck, F. S. A re-examination of the effect of monetary reward and punishment in figure-ground perception. *J. exp. Psychol.*, 1950, **40**, 766–776.

Rubin, E. *Synsoplevede Figurer.* Copenhagen: Gyldendalska, 1915.

Rubin, E. *Visuell wahrgenommene Figuren.* Copenhagen: Gyldendalska, 1921.

Ryle, Gilbert. *The concept of mind.* New York: Barnes and Noble, 1948.

Schafer, R., & Murphy, G. The role of autism in a figure-ground relationship. *J. exp. Psychol.*, 1943, **32**, 335–343.

Senden, M. von. *Raum- und Gestaltauffassung bei operierten Blindgeborenen vor und nach der Operation.* Leipzig: Barth, 1932.

Siegel, A. I. Deprivation of visual form definition in the ring dove: I. Discriminatory learning. *J. comp. physiol. Psychol.*, 1953, **46**, 115–119.

Siegel, A. I. Deprivation of visual form definition in the ring dove: II. Perceptual-motor transfer. *J. comp. physiol. Psychol.*, 1953, **46**, 249–252.

Smith, D. E., & Hochberg, J. E. The effect of "punishment" (electric shock) on figure-ground perception. *J. Psychol.*, 1954, **38**, 83–87.

Solley, C. M., & Murphy, G. *Development of the perceptual world.* New York: Basic Books, Inc., 1960.

Solomon, R. L., & Howes, D. H. Word frequency, personal values, and visual duration thresholds. *Psychol. Rev.*, 1951, **58**, 256–270.

Titchener, E. B. *A textbook of psychology.* New York: Macmillan, 1910.

Tresselt, M. E. The influence of amount of practice upon the formation of a scale of judgement. *J. exp. Psychol.*, 1947, **37**, 251–260.

Vanderplas, J. M. Transfer of training and its relation to perceptual learning and recognition. *Psychol. Rev.*, 1958, **65**, 375–385.

Vanderplas, J. M. Associative processes and task relations in perceptual learning. *Percept. mot. Skills*, 1963, **16**, 501–509.

Vanderplas, J. M., & Blake, R. R. Selective sensitization in auditory perception. *J. Personal.*, 1949, **18**, 252–266.

Vanderplas, J. M., & Garvin, E. A. Complexity, association value and practice as factors in shape recognition following paired-associate training. *J. exp. Psychol.*, 1959, **57**, 155–163.

Vanderplas, J. M., Sanderson, W. A., & Vanderplas, Janet N. Some task-related determinants of transfer in perceptual learning. *Percept. mot. Skills*, 1964, **18**, 71–80.

Verplanck, W. S., Cotton, J. W., & Collier, G. H. Previous training as a determinant of response dependency at the threshold. *J. exp. Psychol.*, 1953, **46**, 10–14.

Volkmann, A. W. Ueber den Einfluss der Uebung auf das Erkennen, raumlicher distanzen. *Beitrage uber die Verls. D. kgl. Sachs Gesellsch. der. Wissensch zu. Leipzig.* 1858, **10**, 38–76.

Werner, H., & Wapner, S. Sensory-tonic field theory of perception. In J. S. Bruner and D. Krech (Eds.), *Perception and personality, a symposium.* Durham, N.C.: Duke Univer. Press, 1950. Pp. 88–107.

Wertheimer, M., & Leventhal, C. M.

"Permanent" satiation phenomena with kinesthetic figural after-effects. *J. exp. Psychol.*, 1958, **55**, 255–257.

Wohlwill, J. F. Changes in distance judgements as a function of corrected and non-corrected practice. *Percept. mot. Skills*, 1964, **19**, 403–413.

Wohlwill, J. F. Perceptual learning. *Annu. Rev. Psychol.*, 1966, **17**, 201–232.

Woodworth, R. S., & Schlosberg, H. *Experimental psychology.* New York: Holt, 1955.

Youtz, R. P. The relation between number of confirmations of one hypothesis and the speed of accepting a new and incompatible hypothesis. *Amer. Psychologist*, 1948, **3**, 248–249.

Suggested Readings

Allport, F. H. *Theories of perception and the concept of structure.* New York: Wiley, 1955. An exhaustive review of the author's own concept, designed to integrate the theories reviewed.

Boring, E. G. *Sensation and perception in the history of experimental psychology.* New York: Appleton-Century-Crofts, 1942. A scholarly review of the historical development of sensation and perception with detailed analyses of both experimental and theoretical aspects of the problems of perception.

Dember, W. N. *Psychology of perception.* New York: Holt, 1960. Chapters 7, 8, 9, and 10 are excellent summaries of effects of learning, motivation, set and past experience, and experience relations in perception.

Epstein, W. *Varieties of perceptual learning.* New York: McGraw-Hill, 1967. This is a survey of theoretical and empirical studies, including recently reported experiments by Ivo Kohler on transformations of the visual world viewed through distorting lenses and prisms. Also an excellent review of the work of Richard Held on adaptation to transformed stimulation.

Forgus, R. H. *Perception.* New York: McGraw-Hill, 1966. Gregory, R. L. *Eye and brain.* New York: McGraw-Hill, 1967. von Fieandt, Kai. *The world of perception.* Homewood, Ill.: Dorsey Press, 1966. These three monographs represent the variety with which authors consider perception and its relation to learning. Forgus treats perception as a process of information extraction, whereas von Fieandt treats it as coding and experiencing of sensory messages. Gregory takes an eclectic view while focusing on

visual perception. He also has an interesting account of several of the classical illusions which relates them to both sensations of depth and to experience.

Helson, H. *Adaptation level theory.* New York: Harper & Row, 1964. A comprehensive survey of adaptation-level theory and applications to a wide variety of psychological problems. The chapters on psychophysical judgment (4), perception (5), and learning and performance (7) are especially recommended.

Hochberg, J. Nativism and empiricism in perception. In L. Postman (Ed.), *Psychology in the making.* New York: Knopf, 1962, 255–330. An extensive review and excellent critique of the historic controversy over the role of experience in the perceptual process.

Leeper, R. W. Learning and the fields of perception, motivation, and personality. In S. Koch (Ed.), *Psychology: A study of a science*, Vol. 5. New York: Wiley, 1965. Pp. 365–487. Postman, L. Perception and learning. In S. Koch (Ed.), op. cit. Pp. 30–113. These two papers illustrate differing views of perceptual learning, from the standpoints of a translation of perceptual phenomena into terms of learning theory and translation of learning phenomena into terms of Gestalt psychology as perceptual organization.

Postman, L. (Ed.). *Psychology in the making.* New York: Knopf, 1962. A collection of original writings on theoretical issues and problems of psychology. The articles on nativism and empiricism in perception, by Julian E. Hochberg; on rewards and punishments in human learning, by Leo Postman; and on repression by D. W. MacKinnon and W. F. Dukes, are especially recommended.

III

Problem Solving and Concept Attainment

Roger L. Dominowski

University of Illinois at Chicago

9

Characteristics of Thinking

In the history of psychology one of the oldest and most persistent problems concerns the nature of thinking. Descartes, often considered the founder of modern psychology, emphasized the problem with his famous *Cogito, ergo sum* (I think, therefore I am). The function of psychology is to describe thinking in behavioral terms and to specify those variables that affect it. The fundamental assumption of this section is that problem solving and conceptual behavior constitute a significant part of what we call thinking. Before we consider these two kinds of activity in detail, we must first examine what we mean by thinking.

When we use the verb *think*, we refer to a variety of activities, including reasoning, recalling, judging, comparing, and discovering. These behaviors have in common two major characteristics, their complexity and the fact that they involve implicit (covert) activity to a great degree. Stressing the *complexity* and *covertness* of thinking has several implications for understanding how psychologists approach this problem.

Complexity

Psychologists agree that thinking is complex behavior. This can be readily observed in the organization of introductory texts. Most writers proceed from simple to complex behavior, and thinking is typically toward the end of the book. The implication is that thinking is in some way built upon simpler processes. In order to think, there must be something to think about or with. Because we reject the notion of innate ideas, thinking must depend on prior experience, specifically learning.

Just as we expect thinking to depend on experience because of its complexity, we also expect it to be characteristic of complex organisms. In fact, most studies on this topic have employed adult human Ss. The question of whether thinking is limited to humans is difficult, and perhaps impossible, to answer. The answer depends on how one defines thinking in very specific terms. If one requires that thinking involve language, there is a severe restriction on the list of organisms than can "think." However, if any kind of implicit responding is allowed in a definition of thinking, then many organisms are "thinkers."

In the present treatment, we will concentrate on studies of adult human Ss for several reasons. First, by any definition, thinking is most characteristic of these organisms. Second, a number of theorists have distinguished between verbal and nonverbal organisms, limiting "true" thinking to those using language. Indeed, many of the tasks used by *E*s require language; alternatively, the type of explanation offered changes as one proceeds from nonverbal to verbal *S*s. Finally, as a practical decision, limiting the presentation will allow a more cohesive description to be developed.

Covert Activity

Thinking is a kind of behavior that cannot be equated with muscular or glandular activity; rather, it is a central process. *Thinking is inferred when there is some delay between the presentation of a stimulus and the occurrence of S's response, and the response is related to but not identical with the stimulus.* For example, after presentation of the stimulus *house*, it would be appropriate to infer thinking if the *S*'s response were *apartment*, but not if his response were *house*. Notice that the appropriateness of the response must be judged by *E*. Thinking is thus a type of mediating process which is postulated by an investigator as an aid to accounting for the S-R relationships observed.

Substitution for Motor Behavior. One way in which thinking functions is to take the place of overt motor activity. This was neatly demonstrated in a study by Duncan (1963). His *S*s were given a rather complex problem to solve, and solution required that a certain number of overt responses be made (turning switches). Most *S*s made many more than the required number, but Duncan found that instructing them to "think" resulted in a large reduction in the number of switch-turns made in solving the problem. It is this ability to consider alternatives without actually trying them as overt responses that we usually attribute to thinkers.

It must be emphasized that thinking does not occur in a vacuum. Although *S* exhibits

little or no motor activity, other measures can be taken. Woodworth and Schlosberg (1954) have reviewed some early evidence regarding slight muscle movements during thinking. In a more recent study, measurements were taken of changes in EEG rhythms during mental tasks (Glanzer, Chapman, Clark, and Bragdon, 1964). Such investigations establish without doubt that thinking involves organismic activity, but, to date, such measures have not provided much insight into the process of thinking.

Research on Thinking

Investigators of thinking have much the same research problems as those interested in other behavior, but certain aspects of the research process stand out. The typical study includes the presentation of a task (problem) selected by *E*, followed eventually by *S*'s successful or unsuccessful attempt to produce the response required by *E*. The point is that relatively few observations may be made between these two occurrences, yet *E*'s interest might be primarily directed toward the behavior occurring during this "empty" interval. Very often, *E* knows only the length of time *S* took to produce the required response. Of course, knowledge of variables which affect the time required for response production has clear implications for understanding the thinking process. That is, knowing what does and what does not change this processing time tells us something about the process itself. Nevertheless, many *E*s prefer to have more obvious data on which to build an account of thinking. By using problems requiring more overt responding by *S*, or by requiring *S* to "think out loud," *E*s try to get more evidence about the thinking process.

Our discussion thus far has dealt with thinking in general terms. The two specific topics of this section, problem solving and concept attainment, need not involve thinking, although they usually do. If problem solving and conceptual behavior can be adequately described without reference to covert representational processes, then they do not involve thinking. As indicated earlier, especially for adult human *S*s, thinking plays an important role in these behaviors. We will now try to define problems and concepts, as well as indicate how they are related to learning.

Learning, Problems, and Concepts

In attempting to distinguish these behaviors, we are engaged in a classification task, and it should be realized that any classification system is basically arbitrary. There does not appear a high level of agreement among psychologists regarding how many behavior categories there should be, much less how these categories should be formed. The situation is one in which similarities will occur among behaviors placed in different categories and differences occur among those in the same category. Nevertheless, the distinctions about to be made do seem to be worthwhile.

To provide a framework for this discussion, let us state that *problem solving may be considered a special form of learning, and concept attainment a special form of problem solving*. This statement is based on the general definition of learning as a relatively permanent change in behavior that occurs as a function of practice. It is clear that, having solved a problem, *S* has learned the solution (Gagné, 1964). However, *E*'s interest in studying problem solving lies not in the demonstration that *S* would have little difficulty in producing the required response if the problem were presented again, but rather in how *S* solves the problem on its first presentation.

Response Discovery

As already implied, the critical behavior in problem solving is *S*'s discovery of the correct response. Underlying this idea is the assumption that *S* has already learned the correct response in some way and has also learned other, now incorrect responses. If simple learning is described as the formation of an association between a stimulus and response, problem solving may be viewed as the discovery of the required response from a set of previously learned associations. Another way to state this distinction is in terms of *E*'s operations. In a simple learning situation, *E* indicates which response is correct for a particular stimulus, then tests *S* by presenting that stimulus again. In problem solving, *E* presents a stimulus (the problem) and usually identifies the possible responses to some extent, but requires *S* to determine which of these responses is correct. Finally, as already noted, the problem is seldom repeated. Alternatively, *S*'s performance on a repetition of the problem situation is an index of the degree to which he had learned the solution (Duncan, 1964).

Concepts

There are a number of different definitions of concepts, varying in the degree to which concepts are considered associative learning. Let us begin with a very simple description of concepts based on operational grounds. *In any conceptual task, a given response will be correct for more than one stimulus*. Of course, the assignment of responses to stimuli is typically not done arbitrarily or randomly, but rather in a systematic fashion. Stimuli for which the same response is correct form a category, and categories are established on the basis of systematic relationships among the attributes of the stimuli. The differences between simple associative learning and concepts are indicated in Table 9-1.

The associative learning task is called paired-associate learning. Each stimulus has a unique correct response, and responses can be arbitrarily or randomly assigned to

Table 9-1   Paired Associates, Concepts, and Arbitrary
                 Groups: Assignments of Responses to Stimuli

Stimuli	Paired Associates	Concept 1	Concept 2	Arbitrary Groups
red large circle	A	A	A	A
red small circle	F	B	C	B
red large square	M	A	B	C
red small square	X	B	D	A
blue large circle	G	A	A	B
blue small circle	D	B	C	C
blue large square	C	A	B	A
blue small square	E	B	D	B

stimuli. Two different concepts are shown. In the first, there are two responses, each assigned to four stimuli according to the rule, "A for large, B for small." In the second, four responses have each been assigned to two stimuli on the basis of "A for large circles, B for large squares, and so on." The final column gives an arbitrary assignment of three responses to the eight stimuli; the response assignments do not appear to be systematically related to any stimulus dimensions or combinations of attributes.

Characteristics of Concepts. Table 9–1 illustrates several important features of concepts that we might consider. First, the description of concept attainment as problem solving is clear; there are many ways in which stimuli may be systematically placed in categories, and S must discover which system is being used. Secondly, what is the difference between concepts and paired-associates? What is the effect of systematic assignment? This can be demonstrated by imagining that a new stimulus, a *green small circle*, is now included. For the paired-associate task, can we predict what the correct response will be for this stimulus? It appears that we cannot, other than that it will probably be a letter. In contrast, for the first concept, we can predict that the

correct response will be B, and, for the second concept, that the response will be C. For the arbitrary assignment, we seem to be in the same position as for paired associates, unable to predict with any certainty what the correct response will be. Thus, concepts, as they reflect the systematic categorization of stimuli, include a kind of predictability not encountered with the other tasks. Finally, the reader should be aware that different ways of systematically grouping stimuli are likely to be different in difficulty, as the studies by Metzger (1958) and by Fallon and Battig (1964) have shown.

Summary of Distinctions

As we have seen, concept attainment constitutes a form of problem solving. Any task will be classified as problem solving if it requires S to discover the correct response, either from alternatives specified by E or from a number of previously learned responses that S must recall in the problem situation. For many simple problems, there is only one presentation—namely, the problem—and S makes only one correct response. In contrast, concept attainment involves the presentation of a number of distinct stimuli, and success often requires that S respond correctly a number of times. Transitional tasks are obviously possible. For example, if several simple problems are presented and their solutions are similar in some respect, performance over the series of problems takes on some of the characteristics of concept attainment.

Concepts and Problems. In the present discussion, concept attainment has been described as a kind of problem solving. This has been done primarily because our review will concentrate on the behavior of adult human Ss. For the concepts in Table 9-1, it is obvious that such Ss have already learned to categorize on the basis of color, size, and shape; thus, their task is one of discovery. For less experienced Ss, concept attainment takes on more of the characteristics of associative learning, and we shall consider such differences in behavior at the end of the chapter on concept attainment. In a somewhat different analysis, Gagné (1964) has proposed that problem solving is the use of concepts, rules, and principles in new situations. This view corresponds with our description of concept attainment by adult human Ss. However, for some of the simple problems we will consider, it is not clear what concepts or rules S might use to discover the solution. It is true that such simple problems assume a certain level of concept attainment (for example, asking S to think of a word makes little sense if S does not know what a word is). What is not clear is that S, in solving such a problem, learns or discovers a generalizable rule than he can use in subsequent problems.

The general features of problem solving and concept attainment should now be apparent. To this point, we have described these behaviors without much concern over the diversity of approaches which psychologists have employed. It is these different approaches that we will now consider, dealing separately with problem solving and concept attainment.

Approaches to Problem Solving

An approach to problem solving is a manner of describing this behavior, simultaneously a choice of language as well as a specification of the important variables affecting this behavior. There are three approaches that we will consider—associative, cognitive-Gestalt, and information processing. The points to consider in evaluating these positions are the extent to which they provide an adequate description of the problem-solving process and the degree to which they suggest further investigation.

Associative Approaches

Perhaps the dominant approach to problem solving is that stemming from learning theory, specifically associative theory. Researchers in this tradition employ behavioristic concepts, S-R language, and attempt to relate problem solving to simple learning as directly as possible. Theoretical essays advocating this position have been written by Kendler and Kendler (1962), Maltzman (1955), and Mednick (1962). The Kendlers' work has been primarily in concept attainment, whereas Mednick proposed an associative theory of creativity, which will be considered later. For the present, we will lean most heavily on Maltzman's essay for a general description.

Habit-Family Hierarchies. The most important feature of the associative approach to problem solving is the notion of the habit family hierarchy, which has been alluded to earlier. This is indicated schematically in Figure 9-1. The external stimulus (S), which we may consider the problem situation, may arouse any of a number of *anticipatory goal responses* (r_g's). Each r_g has stimulus properties (s_g), serving to elicit any of a number of individual responses (R's) leading to a particular goal response

(R_G). As indicated, there may also be a direct association between S and any of the R's. The r_g's may be ordered in terms of their associative strength to S, and R's may be similarly ordered in terms of associative strength to s_g. There is thus a compounding of hierarchies of associative strength within each habit family (R's) and between anticipatory responses for different habit families (r_g's), thus the name *compound habit family hierarchy*. Actually, this description is oversimplified, because there may be other S's present (such as drive stimuli), and any R may be the anticipatory response for another habit family. Nevertheless, it is sufficiently complex to illustrate the associative approach, and probably also complex enough to require an example.

An Example. Assume that S is presented with a boat filling with water through a hole in its bottom and given the problem of keeping the boat from sinking. This represents S. Assume further that two different goals might be anticipated, bailing the boat and plugging the hole; each of these corresponds to r_g. Associated with each r_g is a family of individual responses that might fulfill that function. Thus, bailing can be accomplished by using a pump, bucket, cup, bottle, collander (if one is fast enough), the hands, mouth, and so on. Similarly, the hole could be plugged with a cork, oar, finger, and so on. If these two general goals (bailing versus plugging) differ in strength, and if there is variation in strength among the different responses

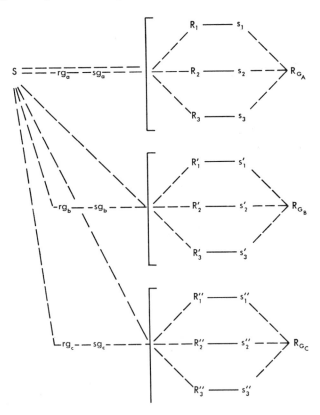

Figure 9-1.   A compound habit family hierarchy produced by a combination of habit family hierarchies. (Reprinted with permission from Maltzmann, I., Thinking: From a behavioristic point of view. *Psychol. Rev.*, 1955, **62**, 275–286.)

which might accomplish each goal, then a compound habit family hierarchy exists.

According to Maltzman a problem exists if the dominant response in the dominant habit family is not correct, and problem solution involves the rearrangement of the habit family hierarchy. The principles of conditioning and extinction are applied, with a very strong emphasis on mediated generalization, that is, generalization employing the r_g-s_g mechanism. This can be illustrated by several examples.

Mediated Generalization. The effective strength (of a response) is a function of both its excitatory potential and its inhibitory potential, which act in opposition to each other. When a response occurs and is successful (reinforced), there is an increase in its excitatory potential, which increases its effective strength. When a response occurs and is unsuccessful (extinguished), there is an increase in its inhibitory potential, which lowers its effective strength. Generalization refers to the fact that changes in the effective strength of one response will also produce changes in the strengths of other responses. Mediated generalization refers to the notion that generalization involves the r_g-s_g mechanism. For example, if bailing with a pump is successful, its strength will be increased; in addition, this increase will generalize to the anticipatory goal response of bailing, and, through it, to other bailing responses. Conversely, should bailing with a pump prove unsuccessful, a decrease in strength will occur for both other bailing responses and the mediating response of bailing itself.

The idea of responses organized into sets and arranged in order of strength implies some of the complexities of problem solving. Assume that, for our example, bailing with a large piece of cardboard is the only way to solve the problem. If S first thinks of bailing, he might look for a pump, but there is none. He tried the bucket, but it has a hole in it, and the bottle does not allow him to work fast enough. These

failures will lower the strength of all bailing responses, and S might switch to trying to plug the hole. He will not solve the problem until this class of responses is extinguished, the idea of bailing recovers some strength, and he discovers the piece of cardboard.

Identification of Response Hierarchies. Maltzman believes that this kind of organization was primarily a function of linguistic responses serving as mediators (r_g's) and that consequently this kind of behavior is limited to articulate organisms (humans). In a more direct way, researchers holding this position have typically employed verbal problems, because it is possible to obtain prior information about the relative strengths of classes of verbal responses. In contrast, for a problem such as saving a sinking boat, it is relatively difficult to obtain this information about the hierarchy of response classes. Although the analysis can be applied to such problems, it is typically an ad hoc description. One way to increase the power of the analysis is to establish a hierarchy in the laboratory, then test predictions about performance in a subsequent task. The research on problem-solving set will serve as an example of this approach.

Although this approach is based primarily on the principles of simple conditioning, it has been extended with some success to a variety of behaviors in the area of thinking. In addition to creativity and concept attainment, the associative approach has been used by Maltzman (1962) to analyze the effects of motivation on thinking, and we will encounter such an analysis in the next chapter. For the present, however, we shall have to be satisfied with this brief exposition and turn to another approach.

Cognitive-Gestalt Approaches

In the history of psychology one finds a systematic antagonism between associative theorists and cognitive theorists. The role of the cognitive theorist was usually held by the Gestalt psychologists, representing a school of thought best known in the area of perception. As such, these approaches tend to dismiss associative theory as either incomplete or irrelevant, emphasizing instead a perceptual analysis of problems.

Cognitive descriptions of problem solving tend to stress the analysis of problem-solving protocols and the use of problems that can be conveniently described in perceptual terms. Great emphasis is given to the directedness of thinking and to the occurrence of insight, which in turn leads to problem solution. This will become apparent in considering Duncker's (1945) example of one solution of the radiation problem.

A Sample Problem. This problem consists of the statement that a tumor exists somewhere in the middle of the body; the instructions are to eliminate the tumor with radiation without damaging other tissues. The protocol described by Duncker consists of a one-sided dialogue between *S* and *E* (*S* does more talking). *S* proposes several possible solutions, such as sending rays through the esophagus, desensitizing the healthy tissue, moving the tumor to the outside of the body, and so on. *E* evaluates these proposals, indicating their inadequacies, and asks questions designed to "direct" *S* in productive ways. Finally, *S* produces the desired solution, to send a broad band of weak rays through the body in such a way that the tumor lies at their intersection and thus receives intensive radiation.

Functional Value. In the analysis of this and other protocols, Duncker's interest lies in the functional value of *S*'s proposals, the general principle that *S* appears to be following in trying to solve the problem. For example, the proposals to "move the tumor to the exterior" or to "expose the tumor by an operation" have the functional value of avoiding contact between the rays

and healthy tissue. Duncker notes that the process of solution consists of successive reformulations of the problem. Thus, the original problem, "destroy only the tumor," is reformulated to "find a way to avoid contact between healthy tissue and the rays" or "minimize the intensity of the rays on the way to the tumor."

Duncker makes several points regarding the functional value of *S*'s proposals. Difficulty in problem solving is viewed as caused by functional fixedness, persisting in following a general principle that cannot work. For example, if avoiding contact is impossible, *S* will fail so long as he persists in thinking of ways to accomplish this. In this context, Duncker distinguishes between "good" and "bad" errors. A good error occurs when *S* correctly identifies the functional value but incorrectly states the specific way in which to accomplish that goal. Bad errors exist when, according to Duncker, "the outward form of an earlier, or an imitated solution is blindly reproduced without functional understanding." Although this distinction seems difficult to state in general terms, it is clear that Duncker rejects the description of problem solving as "meaningless, blind, trial-and-error reactions." *S*'s behavior is directed by a functional value, and solution will occur when the correct reformulation of the problem is realized.

Fixation. A similar position has been taken by Scheerer (1963), who emphasized more of the perceptual aspects of problem solving. According to this view, a problem possesses a certain structure of its own that points the way to solution. Once the correct perception of the requirements of the problem occurs (insight), the solution follows somewhat automatically. Again, Scheerer emphasizes that productive thinking does not involve blind, or random, trial and error. Rather, *S* changes his perception of the problem (reformulates the problem) until the correct perception (insight) occurs. In his discussion of fixation, Scheerer notes that solution will not occur if the problem is misperceived. Further, the problem can be made more difficult by structuring the problem situation in such a way that misperception is more likely. For example, a problem is described which required for its solution the use of a piece of string to tie two sticks together. If the string hung by itself on a nail on the wall, the problem was easy. Solution was much more difficult if the string was a hanger for a sign, mirror, or calendar. The problem situation in the second case emphasized perceiving the string as "something to hang things with," thus making it more difficult to perceive the string as "something to tie things with."

Insight. The stress on the correct perception of the problem implies a certain discontinuity in problem-solving behavior. That is, S, upon attaining insight (correct perception), will suddenly and abruptly solve the problem. This is usually contrasted with the trial-and-error analysis attributed to behavioristic (associative) theorists. As stated by Köhler (1947) this awareness called insight does not develop gradually but suddenly and as a consequence of the dynamics of the situation. Although the concept of insight has been used in an explanatory manner by some writers and has been the focal point of much controversy (see Osgood, 1953), Köhler himself states that insight is used in only a descriptive sense. One way in which this theoretical controversy has been evidenced is in the contrast between "understanding" and "rote memorization." Understanding is typically related to insight, whereas memorization is attributed to the associative position.

"Memorization" vs. "Understanding." A number of studies have been conducted to compare the transfer effects of training by memorization and training by understanding. The question, which stemmed from the theoretical controversy, was, "If one desires

to train someone to solve problems, is it better to teach him a general principle (understanding) or have him learn a solution by rote memorization?" These studies were reviewed by Duncan (1959) and, as a group, they do not lead to a very satisfying conclusion. There is, first of all, some difficulty in specifying the differences between the various methods of understanding and those of memorization. As Osgood (1953) has noted, it is reasonable to state that Ss receiving training by understanding actually learn a general method or principle by rote memorization. Secondly, Duncan's review indicates that training by understanding may take either more or less time than training by memorization and may produce either better, equal or worse performance than memorization on subsequent problems. Although this was originally considered a clear theoretical issue, it appears that ambiguity in defining the issue has led to ambiguous findings.

Comparison of Associative and Cognitive Approaches

Although associative and cognitive approaches appear to be quite different, it is actually rather difficult to specify their differences in a manner suitable for research. Many findings have been interpreted both ways. Indeed, Osgood (1953) has suggested that the major difference between the two approaches might be simply in the kind of language used. Examples can be cited to support this position, which indicates the great difficulty of evaluating theoretical positions. Duncker's analysis of problem solving employs the concept of functional value (the general manner of problem solution); he states that this functional value can be realized in a number of different ways. Thus, in the radiation problem, exposing the tumor or moving it to the exterior of the body are said to have the functional value of avoiding contact between healthy tissue and the rays.

This seems quite similar to Maltzman's concept of the anticipatory goal response and its associated habit family. In fact, Maltzman (1955) noted the similarity of his and Duncker's theories.

Scheerer's example of the two ways of presenting the string (hanging alone or supporting something) was described in perceptual terms. However, it could also be described in associative terms. The string hanging alone, as a stimulus, elicits a particular hierarchy of responses in which, apparently, using the string to tie things together is relatively high in dominance. The stimulus of the string supporting a mirror, in contrast, elicits a different hierarchy of responses, in which the tying response is somewhat lower in dominance. These examples should make clear the interpretive problems involved. The contrast of the two theoretical positions will be completed when we discuss two additional issues, trial-and-error versus insight problem solving and productive versus reproductive problem solving.

Trial-and-Error Processes. As noted in both Duncker's (1945) and Scheerer's (1963) essays, there is in the cognitive view a rejection of trial and error in discussing thinking. In fact, their protest is against explaining problem solving in terms of overt trial-and-error behavior. Because modern associative theorists emphasize covert processes, the contrast between positions is not as sharp as one would expect. If S appears to be doing nothing and then suddenly solves the problem, this could be described as covert trial and error which substitutes for overt behavior, with the "insightful" solution being sudden and smooth because of this previous process. In a paper advocating a trial-and-error approach, Campbell (1960) cites a wide variety of historical evidence in support of his position. Interestingly enough, this evidence of trial and error (at the covert or implicit level) stems from introspective reports of problem solving, a kind of

evidence usually associated with the Gestalt approach.

"Blindness." Cognitive theorists often describe trial and error as blind and/or random, and one tends to get the impression that Ss emit responses in a manner similar to kernels of popcorn erupting from the bottom of a hot pan. This impression is not warranted and thus deserves comment. As Campbell has stated, *describing a response process as blind essentially means that responses are produced without prior knowledge of which ones will be successful.* Campbell notes that this "blindness" can apply to individual responses, short-cut methods, or principles. Thus, in Duncker's example, when S reformulates the problem in a particular way, there is no guarantee that he will be successful, and consequently his behavior can be described as "blind."

The description of trial and error as random typically connotes a situation in which all responses are equally likely and independent of each other. Campbell points out that neither of these conditions is essential to the trial-and-error position, and we should be aware that the notion of the habit family hierarchy contradicts both of these requirements. That is, different responses are clearly not equal in their probability of occurrence, and successive responses are not independent of each other. (A response is more likely to be followed by a response of lower dominance in the same habit family than by other responses.)

It appears that modern associative approaches to problem solving do not possess the characteristics to which the cognitive theorists object. In their emphasis on covert processes, anticipatory responses, and response hierarchies, associative theories such as Maltzman's have accommodated some of the criticisms of cognitive theorists. Campbell (1960) referred to another difference, namely, the connotations of the language used. Associative descriptions tend to characterize S as passive, whereas cognitive descriptions emphasize active processes. This might be just a difference in language rather than in underlying meaning, but it is admittedly difficult to separate one's ideas from the language in which they are expressed. Problem-solving behavior does seem to be active and to exhibit some discontinuities, and it is reasonable to question whether the language and concepts of conditioning constitute the most appropriate way to describe this behavior. We will return to this issue in discussing information-processing approaches.

Productive vs. Reproductive Thinking. A final argument raised by cognitive theorists concerns a distinction between types of problem solving, with the point that associative theories cannot account for one type, productive thinking (Maier, 1940). Reproductive thinking refers to the application of previously acquired experiences that lead to a correct solution in a new situation, and an associative description seems appropriate. In contrast, productive thinking is held to involve the integration of previously unrelated experiences. According to Maier, this integration is produced by a direction that is not itself a habit; direction is often manipulated through hints to the problem solver. The point is that, for productive thinking, having the relevant past experience is not sufficient for solution; direction is also needed. However, Weaver and Madden (1949) and Saugstad (1957) did not find that a hint supposedly giving direction facilitated problem solving. In two separate studies, Raaheim (1962, 1964) found that an added instruction facilitated solution in one case but not in the other. All of these studies used the kinds of problems assumed to involve productive thinking; thus the question regarding the necessity of direction (at least as it involves hints or instructions) remains somewhat open, although the negative findings weaken Maier's argument.

An Associative Analysis. Maltzman (1955) has attempted to deal with Maier's distinc-

tion in associative terms. According to Maltzman, in reproductive problem solving the correct habit family is dominant (either through previous experience or experimental manipulations), and solution consists of extinguishing the initially dominant responses in this one hierarchy. In productive thinking, the correct habit family is initially low in the compound hierarchy, and solution requires both that the correct habit family become dominant (through extinction of more dominant, incorrect habit families) and that the correct responses become dominant within that hierarchy. Although Maltzman's and Maier's formulations are not necessarily equivalent, once again the similarity of the two approaches is demonstrated.

A General Weakness. The comparison of associative and cognitive approaches yields the conclusion that, although the two approaches appear quite different, it is difficult to identify specific, distinctive predictions about problem solving. In those cases that initially seemed promising (methods of understanding, hints), the findings are ambiguous and do not support a strong distinction between theoretical positions. Associative approaches have led to more research, primarily because of the availability of a large number of functional relationships from conditioning studies which could be fairly easily tested in simple problem-solving situations. A weakness in both associative and cognitive-Gestalt approaches lies in their inability to make specific statements about the order of responses in problem solving. Both positions essentially make predictions about the overall level of difficulty of a problem, but neither contains an explicit statement about how the postulated processes operate. Duncker does not state what produces reformulation, and Maltzman speaks only vaguely about an extinction-recovery process governing the order of responding. A useful contrast is provided by the information-processing approaches.

Information-Processing Approaches

A major innovation in the recent study of problem solving is the use of computers to attempt to simulate human behavior. Programming a computer to simulate human problem solving presupposes a theory of human problem solving; our interest lies in examining the characteristics of such programs. It is perhaps necessary to point out that the proposed analogy between computer and human is not in terms of hardware (computer = brain), but in terms of processes. A computer program is a statement of methods for processing information, and the proposal to be evaluated is that human Ss exhibit similar processes. To state this somewhat differently, E states a theory about how humans solve problems, programs a computer to perform according to the theory, and tests the theory by comparing the computer output with that of human Ss. Thus, the computer is a convenient testing device rather than an integral part of the theory. The possible separation of information-processing theory from the use of computers will be seen clearly in studying concept attainment, where information-processing ideas have been widely accepted with relatively little computer simulation actually conducted.

Information, Uncertainty, and Problems. Information is dependent on uncertainty, and uncertainty is an essential ingredient of problems. In one sense, information is that which reduces uncertainty; if one already knows where an object is located, being told where it is provides no information. If, on the other hand, the object might be in any of several locations, then being told its location is obviously informative. In a similar fashion, there must be multiple alternatives for a problem to exist, and problem solving consists of choosing the alternative which meets the problem requirements (Feigenbaum and Feldman, 1963).

Algorithms and Heuristics. Two general methods have been identified for searching through a set of alternatives to solve a problem. *Methods which deliberately consider every possible alternative are called algorithms* (Hovland, 1960). If a solution exists, an algorithmic method will find it, although an enormous number of trials might be required. *A heuristic is any device which drastically limits the search for solutions*, which reduces the number of alternatives to be considered. Heuristics do not guarantee solution, but rather provide solutions that are adequate most of the time (Feigenbaum and Feldman, 1963). Notice that for an algorithm to be successful there must be access to the set of all possible alternatives. If this cannot be achieved, no algorithm is possible; even if access is present, an algorithmic approach is likely to be inefficient, unless the number of alternatives is small. This suggests that the solution to a problem might be a combination of algorithms and heuristics, because one might limit search by a heuristic, then employ an algorithm to evaluate the alternatives specified by the heuristic. One clear assumption of information-processing approaches is that human Ss are largely heuristic problem solvers.

Examples of Heuristics. In the game of chess, a player is faced with a practically uncountable number of possible alternatives if he considers all the possible sequences of moves by himself and his opponent following any given move. There are many possible heuristics, both good and bad, which might be used to limit one's search for the "right" move at any point in the game. A player might limit the depth of his evaluation of a move, perhaps only to his opponent's immediate reply. He might select from only those moves which will capture one of his opponent's pieces, or from only those which will not place any of his pieces in danger of being captured.

Simon and Newell (1964) have presented an explicit theory of problem solving in chess, with particular reference to attempts to produce checkmating combinations. A checking move is one which places the opponent's king under attack; if the attack cannot be escaped or thwarted by other means, checkmate occurs (the attacker wins). The postulated process includes a number of heuristics—for example, "cease exploring any move to which the opponent has more than four replies"; "choose the checking move with the fewest possible replies"; "if a tie occurs on number of replies, choose the move which will produce simultaneous check by two pieces"; and so on. A program incorporating these heuristics performed quite similarly to master chess players in terms of the number of alternatives considered (moves, replies, rejoinders) in finding checkmating combinations. Furthermore, the program missed some combinations, duplicating the "errors" of master players. The degree of correspondence, both in terms of successes and shortcomings, is impressive evidence in favor of the theory.

Generality of the Approach. One should not get the impression that information-processing theories are restricted to chess, because the approach has been applied to other behaviors as well, with notable success in regard to solving problems in logic (Newell, Shaw, and Simon, 1958; Newell and Simon, 1963). Research has concentrated on rather difficult problems involving a succession of discrete steps, although heuristics have been suggested for simple problems (Miller, Galanter, and Pribram, 1960). However, it is true that a program is quite specific and that a theory for solving logic problems is relatively useless as a description of chess playing. It is therefore reasonable to ask whether there are any common features to these attempts, a point we will now consider.

Plans. In all information-processing models, there is *a hierarchical process controlling the order in which a sequence of operations*

will be performed, a plan or executive process (Miller et al., 1960). Planning processes simplify the original problem by eliminating some of the detail. A solution is then sought for the simplified version; if found, it serves as a plan to guide the solution of the original problem (Simon and Newell, 1964). Planning processes are heuristics operating at several levels, generating new or subproblems and relating these to the solution of the total problem. For example, the plan to find a checkmating combination might include capturing the opponent's knight, a subproblem to be solved; a planning process for capturing the knight might generate the problem of capturing another piece; and so on. The implication is quite clear; any single operation can be traced back to a general plan or executive routine.

Means-End Analysis. In means-end analysis both the original problem and any generated subproblems are viewed as consisting of a given situation and a desired situation. Processes are postulated which detect differences between these situations, and with each difference there is associated a set of operators (stored in the solver's memory) which might reduce or remove the difference. Applying this idea, Miller et al. (1960) proposed that the basic functioning unit of behavior is the TOTE unit (Test, Operate, Test, Exit) rather than the S-R association. A test is performed on the given and desired states. If no difference is detected, the process terminates (solution has occurred), but if a difference exists, possibly relevant operators are activated. As each is tried, another test is performed—if no difference, exit; if still a difference, try the next operator. Any operation might result in the generation of a new subproblem, activating new TOTE units. The result is a description of the organism as a hierarchically arranged system of TOTEs.

Stop Rules. An important feature of information-processing descriptions is the specification of stop rules, *heuristics for* *terminating ongoing processes.* Stop rules are incorporated in the TOTE unit (no difference—exit), and a specific example has been previously mentioned, for chess; "cease exploring any move to which the opponent has more than four replies." The specification of stop rules overcomes the weakness indicated for associative and cognitive-Gestalt theories, identifying how *S* switches from one type of response to another.

Comparison with Other Approaches. Information-processing approaches include characteristics of both associative and cognitive Gestalt descriptions. As Newell et al. (1958) have stated, information-processing theories resemble associative theories in the acceptance of mechanisms, but in little else. The "flavor" of information processing is decidedly cognitive. Duncker's (1945) "reformulation of the problem" corresponds to planning processes; means-end analysis is common to both approaches. Heuristics *direct* problem solving, and this behavior is *insightful* in that trial and error is reduced. Associations are not eliminated in information processing, but rather than using them as explanatory devices, interest lies in identifying the processes which operate on associations.

The major advantage of information-processing theories lies in their ability to duplicate, in a predictive sense, response sequences of human *S*s. To some extent, information-processing and associative approaches have had different domains, the former dealing with complex problems, the latter with simple problems. The writer would not presume to suggest an associative description of solving problems in logic. Conversely, heuristics have only been suggested for simple problems. It seems clear that heuristic problem solving will be characteristic of fairly sophisticated *S*s; adult human *S*s would appear to generally fit this description. In the chapter on problem solving, no deliberate attempt has been made to suggest heuristic description

for the problems studied, which have primarily stemmed from associative approaches. However, it might prove quite interesting for the reader to make such an attempt.

Approaches to Concept Attainment

Whereas distinctions are somewhat difficult to make between approaches to problem solving, the task is fairly easy with respect to concept attainment because the definition of concepts is involved. Before considering these definitions, it will be instructive to examine a distinction made by Bruner, Goodnow, and Austin (1956). These investigators distinguish between identity and equivalence categories. *Identity categorization is defined as classifying a variety of stimuli as forms of the same thing.* Thus, a particular person does not always appear as the same stimulus, yet we consider him the same person. Because no stimulus is ever exactly repeated, identity categorization is thus a very basic form of behavior, yet, as Bruner et al. point out, the basis of identity responses is not understood. What are usually considered in concept attainment are equivalence categories, which exist when *S* responds to a set of discriminably different stimuli as the same kind of thing.

The notion of equivalence categories constitutes a definition of concept attainment. As we have seen earlier, a simpler definition is possible. The common response definition does not require any particular kind of response; according to this definition, if *S* learns to say PWX to the stimuli VOF, HAQ, and TUK, the essential conditions of a concept are met. Although this "common response" definition has been used (for example, Kendler, 1961), not many investigators actually use it as a basis for their research. We will therefore consider other definitions of concepts.

Common Attributes

The common attributes definition of concepts conforms to what we earlier called systematic methods of assigning responses to stimuli in a concept task. A concept is said to exist when S makes the same response to discriminable stimuli having some attribute or combination of attributes in common. An example of such a concept is the establishment of categories based on shape, such as square, circle, triangle, and so on. Not all squares are identical or considered identical, but they share the attribute of "squareness." This definition is used by investigators who view concept attainment as related to paired-associate or discrimination learning; it is reflected in the work of Kendler and Kendler (1962) and Underwood (1952), among others.

This approach is characterized by a two-stage associative description. That is, concept attainment is described as an associative process, but rather than involving a simple S-R association, a *mediating* association is involved. The mediating response is concerned with identifying the common attribute. Although Kendler has stated that the mediational mechanism is not necessarily verbal, his work has usually involved verbal mediating responses. Thus, when S learns a common response to a number of stimuli, he does so because these stimuli elicit a common mediating (usually verbal) response. The Kendlers have attempted to contrast this type of learning with simple (S-R) associative learning, and we shall consider this research in the chapter on concept attainment.

This common attribute approach therefore views concept attainment as closely related to standard associative learning but adds the mediating response. Investigators employing this approach tend to manipulate characteristics of the mediating response, such as varying the strength of association between stimuli and the mediating response or determining the effect of changing the mediating response on concept attainment. Although this approach has been quite fruitful, it appears to be somewhat incomplete, in that concepts have been employed that are not based on common attributes. This can be seen in the next approach to concept attainment.

Sorting Rules

The sorting-rule approach states that when S learns a concept, he learns a rule for sorting stimuli into categories. Bruner, Goodnow, and Austin (1956) have emphasized this approach, and it has been stressed in the recent work of Hunt (1962), Neisser, and Weene (1962), and Haygood and Bourne (1965). These latter writers have dealt specifically with various rules that might be employed. The point of this emphasis is that concept attainment is systematic yet need not be based on common attributes. For example, according to one possible sorting rule, red things and square things would be classed together, but red squares would be in a different category. The sorting-rule approach places perhaps the greatest emphasis on transfer of the rule to new stimuli. Where the common-attribute and sorting-rule approaches overlap, they are not incompatible; the major distinction is that the sorting-rule approach includes a greater number of possible concepts.

Because this approach uses the notion of rules, there is a strong emphasis on S's attempts to use or find successful rules. Thus, during the task, S is described as testing hypotheses or using strategies in the attempt to attain the concept. Haygood and Bourne (1965) have perhaps most clearly indicated this emphasis in their construction of a task called rule learning. This is a modification of the typical concept task in which S is required only to identify the rule being used to classify stimuli. It is apparent that the sorting-rule approach is a fairly cognitive one and tends to eliminate research on other than adult human *S*s. It corresponds to the information-processing approach to problem solving.

Concept Names and Verbalization

The most restrictive definition of concept attainment has been stated by Hunt (1962). According to his definition, the term *concept* applies only if *S*, having learned, is able to instruct a human to apply the classification rule, without using examples in his instruction. Further, the rule must apply to appropriate stimuli in any context and be deterministic (each stimulus must be uniquely classified). Some of Hunt's requirements are not different from those used by other investigators, but his statement is clearly the most emphatic. As Hunt has stated, with his definition only human adults and computers can learn concepts. (The computer is capable of printing out instructions to a human.)

The stress on verbalization does not really represent a completely distinct approach to concept attainment. It is largely compatible with sorting rules and essentially compatible with common-attribute approaches. It is the degree of emphasis on verbal responses that is noted here. Similar stress on verbal processes has been indicated by Archer (1964) and Cofer (1960). Ordinarily, stress on verbalization is tied to a position holding that concept attainment clearly and necessarily involves principles other than those found in simple learning situations. (See Hunt, 1962, and Archer, 1964.)

Summary

The various preceding approaches are viewed as basically compatible. Some are more general than others, and S-R mediational approaches may require some modification to fit nicely with sorting rules and an emphasis on verbalization. To a certain extent, the apparent differences may be partly a problem of the language used to describe concept attainment. In the chapter on concept attainment, we will encounter all these approaches. However, the findings in this area are better understood if one accepts the sorting-rule approach.

In the following chapters we shall survey research on problem solving and concept attainment. Emphasis will be given to the methodology employed and to the identification of the most important variables. Although there will be no deliberate attempt to contrast theoretical viewpoints, such comparisons might enter our discussion. It should be realized that experimental findings have an importance independent of *E*'s theoretical position. A finding is often compatible with several different theories and might further be incorporated into a new theory not yet proposed. Thus, the total endeavor consists of two, somewhat orthogonal tasks: identify the relevant variables for these behaviors, and systematize this knowledge into a theory. The following chapters are devoted to the first of these tasks.

10

Problem Solving

To understand the psychology of problem solving, one must have some knowledge of both the manner in which researchers approach their task and what they actually do. We have already examined the variety of descriptions that are applied to problem-solving behavior, and as the research literature is reviewed, it might be both helpful and interesting to try formulating alternative explanations of results in different terms (for example, associative versus computer language). One point to remember is that a researcher's theoretical disposition will determine to some extent the kind of research that he does. At a more empirical level, it is important to realize the limitations of research, to place what is known in the perspective of what we need to know. Therefore, before surveying the major findings, we will engage in a methodological analysis of problem-solving research.

not been what one would call the "standard problem-solving task," although it is true that individual investigators are usually consistent in their choices of problems to study. Some difficulty arises, however, because different investigators do not agree on which problem to employ. Having many different problems makes comparisons of findings very perplexing, as indicated by Duncan's (1959) comments after reviewing the problem-solving literature: "In nearly half of these studies the problem used was devised by the authors and has not yet been used by anyone else. . . . This diversity is a major reason why the area of problem solving seems so chaotic, and is a serious obstacle to systematic progress" (p. 412). Fortunately, recent research appears to be more systematic and restricted largely to a few problems. To aid our understanding of this field, we will examine some of the problems most commonly employed in studies of problem solving.

Experimental Tasks

The study of problem solving has not generally involved long-term, systematic research programs. Consequently, there has

Insight Problems

One type of problem is called an insight problem. As might be expected, these problems were introduced by Gestalt psychologists and are usually described in perceptual terms. A problem exists because of incorrect perception, and solution requires changing one's perception of the situation. These problems typically involve manipulation of certain objects in the environment, although all the problems can be given in paper-and-pencil form (see Duncan, 1959).

Two-String Problem. One insight problem that has been widely studied is the "two-string problem" (Maier, 1933). Imagine a large room completely bare of furniture of any kind except for two strings hung from the ceiling. The problem for S is to think of some way to tie the strings together. However, S is told that if he holds one string and walks toward the other, he cannot reach the second string without letting go of the first. Finally, instructions indicate that an object or some objects are available, depending on the particular variation being used. These objects are usually such things as pliers, switches, paper clips, and so on. Of course, the number and type of objects available can be manipulated and the effect on difficulty determined. Although more than one solution exists for this problem, the solution sometimes considered "best," sometimes the only one allowed, is the "pendulum" solution. This involves tying an object, such as pliers, to the end of one string and causing it to swing. If S then walks to the second string, holds it, and waits for the first string to swing to him, he can grasp both strings and tie them together. This problem is fairly difficult, with approximately 10 per cent of college students unable to solve it within 15 min.

Candle Problems. Another problem of this type is the "candle" problem. In this task, S is seated next to a wall and given a candle, tacks, a small box (for example, a matchbox), and matches. His problem is to attach the candle to the wall, using only the objects provided, in such a way that it burns freely and does not drip wax on the table or floor. Again, several solutions are possible, but interest has centered on one. This solution requires S to attach the box to the wall with some tacks, then mount the candle in or on the box. There are several variations of this problem which differ greatly in difficulty, and we shall consider these later. In general, the candle problem appears to be approximately as difficult as the two-string problem.

There are, of course, other insight problems similar to the two-string and candle problems, but these are sufficient examples of this type. As the examples indicate, insight problems typically involve using a common object in a rather unusual way, because one does not ordinarily use pliers as a pendulum weight or attach match boxes to walls as candle supports. It is this feature that lies at the base of Duncker's (1945) concept of functional fixedness, namely, that the problem will not be solved as long as S continued to perceive the "crucial" object as serving its ordinary function. Obviously, insight problems are excellent tasks to use for studying this phenomenon, and have been used in many such studies, which we shall consider in detail later in this chapter. As a final comment on insight problems, it should be noted that they are long or difficult problems compared to other problems used in the laboratory. With most other problems, the 15-min. time limit ordinarily used with insight problems would be much longer than Ss would need.

Arithmetic Problems

Davis (1966) has identified water-jar problems and arithmetic problems as a separate class, although water-jar problems resemble insight problems in some respects. Arithmetic problems should be familiar to all readers and thus need no further description. Water-jar problems are, in a sense, disguised arithmetic problems. S is given three jars of different sizes and instructed to draw a specified amount of water not equal to the capacity of any jar. For example, given jars holding 3, 4, and 17 pints, respectively, how would you draw exactly 5 pints of water? There are several ways of doing this. One could fill the 17-pint jar, then fill the 4-pint jar from it three times, leaving 5 pints in the large jar. Another way is to fill the 4-pint jar twice, pouring the water into the 17-pint jar, then filling the 3-pint jar from this, leaving 5 pints in the large jar. As one can easily see, this is just a problem in addition and subtraction, and solutions can be written in these terms, for example,

$$17 - 4 - 4 - 4 = 5, \quad 4 + 4 - 3 = 5,$$
or
$$3 + 3 + 3 - 4 = 5.$$

Water-jar problems can be constructed to allow only one solution or to allow two or more solutions of varying complexity, if complexity is defined in terms of the number of steps. Interest lies in which solution is chosen or, more specifically, in whether S will become fixed in using a particular type of solution as he solves a series of water-jar problems. These problems resemble insight problems in that they involve using ordinary objects and were originally presented as concrete problems (S was given the jars, and actually filled them), although they can be presented in paper-and-pencil fashion, as we have just done. A major difference between water-jar and insight problems is that the jars are used in their ordinary function. (In an insight problem, one would probably use a jar as a doorstep.)

Search Problems

A somewhat different kind of problem is exemplified by search tasks, lights-and-switches problems, and jigsaw puzzles. Although there are differences among

them, these tasks have in common the characteristic that the entire problem situation, including alternative responses that S might make, is clearly specified. In search tasks, S must locate one or more of a specified number of alternatives, and the interest is in how many guesses or tries S requires before finding the correct one. (The traditional game of "battleships" has these characteristics.)

In one form of the lights-and-switches problem, S is confronted with a display of lights and switches having multiple connections in both directions. (Each light is connected to several switches, each switch to several lights.) Typically, turning a switch will reverse the state of any light it is connected to (if the light is on, it will turn it off, and vice versa). The problem is to turn on only a specified light, and again the interest lies in the number of switch-turns made before this is accomplished. Jigsaw puzzles have been used in two ways, the obvious one of completing the puzzle and another in which S is given a part of the puzzle and required to find a piece that fits it from among the other pieces. The first task of completing the puzzle actually consists of repeating the part problem many times. The major feature of these tasks, as indicated earlier, is that the alternative responses (even though there might be very many) are specified for S, whose task is to select from them until the correct alternative is chosen.

Verbal Problems

A final class of problems that has widespread use consists of verbal problems. To a degree, these resemble guessing or search tasks, because the limits of the problem are set by the language. (There are only twenty-six letters in English, the population of words is defined, and so on.) However, verbal problems are used in somewhat different fashion, with the main interest directed toward the effects of certain characteristics of the language on *S*'s performance. To state this differently, let us compare the task of guessing a square on a checkerboard with the task of guessing one of the letters of the alphabet. Investigators using the checkerboard task would assume that the sixty-four squares are equally likely alternatives, that *S* is as likely to guess one square as any other. Although there is probably some error in this assumption, it is largely correct; at least, it would be difficult to specify beforehand any reason for one square being easier to locate than any other. In contrast, it is possible to determine, ahead of time, the relative frequencies of the letters of the alphabet. One can then determine if the difficulty of guessing a letter is related to its frequency of occurrence. There is simply no comparable information for the checkerboard problem. Essentially, language provides a well-organized set of habits for which measures are available. The investigator can then relate certain characteristics of this habit structure to the difficulty of solving problems in which these habits are involved.

Anagrams. Although several different verbal problems have been used, the most commonly employed is the anagram or scrambled-word problem. *S* is given a set of letters (the anagram) and instructed to make a word from them. Much research with this problem has involved variation in the language characteristics of both the anagram and the solution word. This constitutes the major part of our knowledge about the effects of the organization and strengths of habit structures on problem solving.

Problem Characteristics

We have now considered the most commonly used types of problems. Let us direct our attention to what appear to be the important characteristics of these problems with respect to the kinds of information we can obtain about problem-solving behavior.

Certainty of Solution

One way in which problems differ is in terms of the degree to which solution is inevitable within a reasonable amount of time. Because all the problems we are considering have definite solutions, one might argue that all are inevitably solvable. Perhaps this is so, given an unlimited amount of time, but it is by no means obvious. More important is the question of solving the problem during the experimental session. One point is clear: the problem must not be so easy that nearly all *S*s solve it very rapidly, nor must it be so difficult that nearly all fail to solve it within the time allotted. The reason for this restriction is straightforward, that one must have differences in performance. Tasks either too easy or too difficult preclude differences in performance and thus will provide no information about behavior.

Specified Responses. Certain tasks are virtually always solved, if *S* merely follows instructions. This will be the case when there are a limited number of possible responses that are specified for *S*. Guessing and search tasks fit this model. There are two points of caution in this respect. First, the number of responses actually made may exceed the number of specified alternatives, if *S* repeats responses. In an unpublished study, the author had *S*s guessing from the letters of the alphabet, for reasons unimportant for our present discussion. Of course, the problem should not take more than twenty-six guesses, yet over ninety responses were made in one case. The second point is related to the first, for if there are very many alternative responses and if *S* cannot remember those already made, the problem may not be readily solvable. Consider a problem with ten lights and ten switches; there are so many possible arrangements of switches on and off that S might leave in utter frustration before arriving at the correct arrangement.

Unlimited Responses. Insight problems serve as the perfect example of a problem in which there is no guarantee that solution will occur. The statement of the problem does not indicate to S what responses he should try, and one may be dealing with a situation having an infinite number of responses. Alternatively, if S restricts himself to certain responses, that response set might not include the correct response. It is for just this reason that hints are sometimes given with insight problems.

Anagrams might appear to be problems that must eventually be solved. If, as is typical, five-letter anagrams are used, there are only 120 ways of writing the letters in order, one of which is the solution. However, Ss do not ordinarily do this, perhaps partly because of the instruction to think of a word. If S is thinking of words, then the correct word must be one S knows. Even if S systematically rearranges the letters, he must recognize the word when he arrives at it. Only if S offers every possible arrangement as a solution does solution become inevitable, and this behavior is very improbable.

Implications for Research. To summarize this discussion, the various problems differ in terms of the likelihood of a solution occurring within the experimental session. As suggested earlier, this is a function of the degree to which the alternative responses are specified for S. This is an issue that could be and should be researched, but very little comparison or analysis of different problems has been attempted. We must simply keep in mind that the problems vary in "basic" difficulty and that certain effects might be related to the general difficulty level of a problem. With respect to the design of experiments, nonsolutions

are troublesome unless they are planned in advance. Obviously, if one is intending to measure something about the solution of the problem and the problem is not solved, information is lost. We shall return to this point in the section on measurement.

Kinds of Intermediate Activity

We are returning here to a question raised in the first chapter: "What does S do from the beginning to the end of the problem?" As noted earlier, thinking is associated with a minimum of overt motor activity. It is clear that motor activity is not necessary for problem solution to occur. Duncan's (1963) Ss were instructed to "do the problem in their heads" and were able to do so. However, the investigator's job is made easier if S engages in motor activity (including talking) during the problem, provided that this does not interfere with S's solution of the problem. If intermediate observations can be made in some detail, E has more information about the behavior under study. An important and difficult problem concerns the relevance of this intermediate activity to problem solving itself, and the investigator must be a careful editor. Consider the example of an S who "doodles" while thinking about a problem; a researcher who tries to interpret the doodles and relate them to the solution process is probably wasting a great deal of time and effort.

There are, of course, situations in which S is forced to make intermediate motor responses. Guessing tasks clearly require guesses, and similar requirements exist for lights-and-switches problems, puzzles, and search tasks. Obviously, these responses, although informative, do not represent all that S is doing while attempting solution. This can be easily illustrated; compare a record of guesses with a record of guesses plus stated reasons for the guesses. It seems fairly certain that the reasons occurred to S even when they were not recorded, thus a record of guesses is not exhaustive, and the same argument can be applied to a record of guesses and reasons. Therefore, although it is useful to obtain these intermediate records, one should not make the mistake of equating all of problem-solving behavior with such responses.

We have already noted the problems which typically involve an intermediate-response record. As stated by Davis (1966), problems such as anagrams, water jars, and insight problems can be solved "in the head." With these problems the typical record is just some measurement of the solution. It is possible to obtain intermediate records, as Duncker (1945) has done with insight problems and as Mayzner, Tresselt, and Helbock (1964) have done with anagrams. However, it is generally true that the only record concerns the solution itself. The point to be kept in mind while reviewing the evidence on problem solving is that the kinds of interpretations that one makes are dependent on the kinds of records obtained about S's behavior.

Instructions

The importance of instructions and the possible effects these might have on behavior have already been touched on, but it seems worthwhile to make an explicit statement. The problem as it is presented includes instructions; they form a significant part of the stimulus situation and should not be dismissed as merely "getting S ready." We will, in this chapter, encounter studies in which instructions are deliberately manipulated, with measurable effects on performance. It has been suggested earlier that differences in difficulty among problems might be due to the degree to which allowable responses are specified, often a function of instructions. It thus seems reasonable to suspect that some discrepancies in the results of various studies might be due to instructional dif-

ferences, at least in part. Unfortunately, complete statements of instructions are not usually included in research reports. In addition to possible differences in instructions as they are written, there can be subtle effects of the manner in which instructions are given to S. Rosenthal (1963, 1966) has conducted extensive research on the effects of experimenter bias, leading to the generalization that Es tend to obtain the results they expect. It should be clearly understood that this is not a result of cheating by the Es, because they are often not aware that they are biasing the results. One source of bias is the way in which E gives instructions, as, for example, by rushing through instructions for an S receiving a problem that E expects to be difficult. The suggestion is that, when different researchers obtain contradictory results, one reason might be differences in their expectations. However, experimenter bias cannot account for large discrepancies in results, and there may be other reasons for contradictory findings, as we shall see in our discussion of measurement.

Measurement

To a certain extent, measurement is determined by the problem one uses. The difference between obtaining intermediate records and just having an overall measure of performance is a difference in measurement, and one we have already considered. In this section, attention will be directed toward the formal aspects of measurement as they are related to problem-solving research.

Number of Problems Used

A researcher very often has a choice about the number of problems that he will employ. For example, with a lights-and-switches apparatus, there are many possible arrangements from which to select a "correct" one. There are hundreds of thousands of words from which anagrams can be constructed, and many ways to make an anagram from any word. The point at issue here is the *generality* of the *results* obtained. An *E* who uses only one problem runs the risk of obtaining a result that holds only for that problem. It should be made clear that there are two distinct aspects of experimentation to be considered. An *E*'s primary responsibility is to conduct a good experiment with the tasks that he uses, to ensure that the results of his experiment are trustworthy. Strictly speaking, the results of any experiment hold only for the conditions actually employed (unless these have been randomly selected from the population of all possible conditions, a procedure almost never used). Nevertheless, *E* will usually make a more general statement of his results, in this case a statement about problem solving generally, rather than about solving the particular problem(s) he employed. Our concern is for the reliability of this general statement.

Generalization of Results. It is clear that a result which holds for two problems is more general than one which holds for only a single problem. As *E* includes more problems, he will either obtain a more general result or determine some of the limitations of the finding. Therefore, although *E* might perform a perfectly sound experiment with a single problem, he will provide more information if he employs more problems.

Another way in which problem selection looms important is in comparing the findings of different studies. This has occurred in anagram research, where a large selection pool of problems exists. There are conflicting results on an interesting question, namely, whether the meaning of an anagram influences its difficulty. In reviewing this research, Johnson (1966) commented, "When one experimenter uses 8 pairs of anagrams and another uses 15, and the

rules for choosing these are not reported, variations in results can occasionally be expected" (p. 375). We are faced, then, with a lack of information which hinders our understanding of problem solving. Any conclusions that are made must be viewed in the light of the generality of the results on which they are based.

Solution Probability Versus Solution Time

There are two basic procedures to be used in planning an experiment. Either *E* can present the problem and measure how long *S* takes to solve it, or he can allow a fixed amount of time for the problem and measure whether or not *S* solves it. The choice of a procedure is related to two points we have previously considered, the basic difficulty of the problem and the number of problems employed. This choice is important because it influences the sensitivity of *E*'s evaluation of his experiment.

The situation can be described in its simplest form. Two conditions have been established by *E*, such as two methods of presenting the problem or two kinds of instructions. (This discussion applies with more than two conditions as well.) A number of *S*s have performed under each condition, and *E* must decide whether performance under one condition is better than under the other. Strictly speaking, *E* needs to know whether average performance differs for the two conditions. Formal statistical procedures are the tools to be used in making this evaluation. The choice of a performance measure affects the choice of a statistical procedure, thus influencing *E*'s conclusion about the experiment.

Single-Problem Experiments. We will consider first the case in which only one problem is used. The least efficient procedure is to present the problem for a fixed time, because only two scores are possible for each S, "solved" or "not solved." The only analysis is to compare the proportions of solvers in the two conditions, which is very insensitive unless large numbers of Ss are run. The efficiency of this procedure depends on the amount of time allowed. Obviously, the time limit must allow some Ss to solve the problem. The procedure is inefficient if a fairly long time is allowed, because E obtains only one gross score from each S. If a short time limit is reasonable, then E can run more Ss and increase the sensitivity of this procedure.

It would appear that measuring solution time is the better procedure, because a large number of possible scores are available. However, a difficulty with this procedure is that every S must be allowed to solve the problem. Because there are limitations on the time of both S and E, it is usually the case that some Ss do not solve before the end of the experimental session. When this occurs, E is faced with a problem to which there is no good solution. The common procedures of replacing Ss who fail to solve or assigning artificial scores can possibly result in either a weak analysis of the experiment or serious bias in the results. If the number of nonsolutions is small, the difficulty can be surmounted, but if many fail to solve, the data are of questionable value.

Interpretation of Solution Time. Even if all Ss solve, there can be questions about the meaning of long solution times. In an experiment, E has manipulated some variable, and one can question whether that variable is still effective after S has worked unsuccessfully for some time. Recall the example of guessing the letters of the alphabet; if S had failed to solve after some time, he tended to repeat previous responses, being unable to remember which had been tried. It seems unlikely that this is related to the reason for S's failure to solve earlier. The suggestion is that a manipulated variable might influence the probability of solving during some initial period of time, but not beyond it.

Solution Probability and Time. Some relevant information is contained in Figure 10-1. These data are based on distributions of solutions over time. The anagram data (Mayzner and Tresselt, 1958) represent two types of problems: easy, based on very frequent (VF) words: and hard, based on very infrequent (VI) words as solutions. The other sets of data are based on pendulum solutions to the two-string problem, with separate distributions for men and women (Duncan, 1962).

Several features of these data are of interest. First, for all sets the probability of solution increases as an approximately linear function of the logarithm of solution time. This means that *successive intervals of time result in progressively smaller increases in solution probability*. This has been interpreted as indicating that, when trying to solve a problem, S has an initial burst of solution attempts, but that the rate of producing new possible solutions decreases as S continues to work on the problem. In addition, as mentioned earlier, S may begin to repeat earlier, unsuccessful solution attempts.

The differential difficulty of the two types of problems is indicated by the time limits employed by the Es (4 min. for anagrams, 15 min. for the insight problem) and, more directly, by the occurrence of much earlier solutions to anagrams than to the insight problem. Perhaps the most important feature of these data is that noted by Duncan (1962). For the anagram data, VF solutions are easier to reach than VI solutions; for the insight problem, men are superior to women. The crucial point is that these differences are evident in early solution times and are essentially unchanged by including longer solution times. This is consistent with the notion that variables might affect only the probability of an early solution.

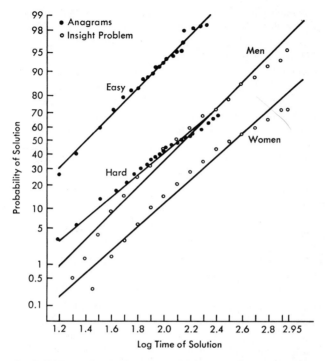

Figure 10-1. Probability of solution as a function of solution time. (Data for the insight problem are reprinted with permission from Duncan, C. P., Probability vs. latency of solution of an insight problem. *Psychol. Rep.*, 1962, **10**, 119–121; anagram data are reprinted with permission from Mayzner, M. S., & Tresselt, M. E. Anagram solution times: A function of letter order and word frequency. *J. exp. Psychol.*, 1958, **56**, 376–379.)

Implications for Research. To summarize, if only one problem is used, the least efficient procedure is to present the problem for a relatively long period of time, counting the number of solvers in different conditions. It would be better to allow less time, because differences between conditions are evident in early solutions and E could then run more Ss (4 Ss per hr. with a 15-min. limit, but 12 Ss per hr. with a 5-min. limit). If E does not choose to do this, he should probably measure solution time. Despite the problems of nonsolvers and the questionable meaning of a long solution time, this measure is more sensitive than just number of solvers after a long working time.

Multiple Problems. It has been previously stated that using multiple problems is

desirable because of the greater generality of results. In some situations, multiple problems probably cannot be used, but with problems such as anagrams, multiple problems are commonly used. Let us consider an example (comparing VF and VI solution words) with respect to measuring performance. Either E can allow S to solve all (or most) problems and measure solution time for each, or E can present each problem for a fixed amount of time and determine the number of problems that S solves. We can compare these two procedures, assuming that E will limit the experimental session for each S.

Statistical Considerations. If solution time is used, E must allow sufficient time for solution to occur in most cases. (Most Es will concede that some problems will be failed.) Allowing a maximum of 4 min. per problem, E could schedule about ten problems in a 30-min. session, because only some problems would take the full 4 min. Each S's score would be his average solution time, which would have to be the median because of some nonsolutions. The median—roughly, the middle score—does not directly reflect the actual values of the other solution times; thus some information is lost. A common result with median solution times is relatively high variability among Ss in the same condition, which lowers the sensitivity of a comparison of conditions.

If E presents each problem for a short time and counts the number of solutions that S achieves, he has several advantages. If 30 sec. are allowed for each problem, E could then schedule about sixty problems in a 30-min. session, increasing the generality of his results to a large degree. Because many problems are attempted, there is a wide range of possible scores (S can solve from nought to sixty problems), and each problem contributes directly to S's score. Finally, with number of solutions as the measure, variability among Ss in the same condition is usually found to be low, which increases the sensitivity of a comparison of conditions.

Using multiple problems is recommended where possible because it *increases* the *generality* of results and the *reliability* of measurement. For example, S's average solution time for ten problems is more reliable than his solution time for only one problem. However, when multiple problems are used, the preferred procedure appears to be presenting each problem for a short time and counting the number of solutions that S achieves, for the reasons previously noted.

Implications for Research. The preceding points about procedure should be kept in mind as we survey the research on problem solving. If, for example, E has concluded that a particular manipulation does not affect problem-solving performance, it is reasonable to ask whether E's procedure was sensitive enough to allow a difference in performance to be detected. When results from different studies conflict, one can frequently resolve the conflict by examining the studies for differences in instructions, number of problems, number of Ss, measurement, and so on. In our survey of the literature, this approach will be presented where it seems applicable.

Types of Research

The basic observation of problem-solving research is that performance on problems varies, and the general goal of research is to account for these differences in difficulty. Sources of variation can be roughly categorized as influences of past experience or current effects, that is, variables occurring while the problem is being solved. Among current effects, the major variable is the manner of problem presentation, which we will consider as a stimulus factor. The influence of past experience will be dealt with in two sections, long-term extra-experimental learning and training given immediately prior to problem presentation. The first of these has been mentioned before, in the discussion of language problems; the idea is essentially that S comes to the problem session with a long history of learning (if he is a college student) and that we try to determine the effects of this experience on his problem-solving behavior. The analysis of training effects is closely tied to this question; if problem solving is related to differences in past experience, then we should be able to change this behavior by appropriate training. We will first examine studies of stimulus factors and past experience (learned responses), because these are simpler from a procedural viewpoint than training studies. In addition, analyses of these effects are a common source of ideas for particular training methods, which dictates the same order of topics. It will be fruitful for the reader, while surveying research on stimulus and response factors, to try to think of training methods suggested by the findings.

Response Characteristics

Measuring the effects of response characteristics requires that E know what responses will occur in the problem situation. For this reason, research on this topic has been performed almost exclusively with guessing or search tasks and verbal problems. Much of this research involves the prior measurement of verbal response hierarchies of various sorts, with E subsequently constructing problems in which the relative strength of the correct response is manipulated. Research with guessing or search tasks has been concerned with a different variable, the number of alternative responses available. We will consider these in turn.

Response Strength

The relative strength of different responses is assumed to correspond to their relative frequencies in a hierarchy. Therefore, any set of responses whose frequencies are known can be used to investigate the effect of response strength. There are two somewhat different sources of frequency information about verbal responses. One source is typified by the gathering of *free-association responses* (for example, Russell and Jenkins, 1954). With this technique, a large number of Ss are presented a number of words, with the instruction to respond with the first word that comes to mind as each stimulus word is shown. By tabulating the frequencies of occurrence of responses to a given stimulus word, a hierarchy of responses is established. This hierarchy can then be employed in a problem-solving situation by presenting S with the stimulus

word and requiring him to guess one of the associates; E can vary the frequency of the associate defined as correct. Obviously, by collecting responses to any type of stimulus, E can obtain a hierarchy for subsequent use in problem-solving situations.

The other source of frequency information for verbal responses stems from extraexperimental language behavior. By sampling from magazines and newspapers, frequency counts have been established for words, letters, and letter combinations. The main source of word frequencies is a book by Thorndike and Lorge (1944); frequencies for letters and letter combinations have been tabulated by Mayzner and Tresselt (1965) and by Underwood and Schulz (1960). It should be noted that association techniques involve spoken frequencies, whereas language samples contain printed frequencies; to date, no combined frequency count is available.

Individual vs. Group Hierarchies. The frequencies obtained by the preceding methods represent the pooled responses of a number of Ss, a hierarchy for the group. When these materials are used in problem-solving studies, it is assumed that this hierarchy applies to individual Ss with some accuracy. This appears to be a reasonable assumption, because when individual and group hierarchies have been compared, they have been found to be similar, though not identical (for example, Duncan, 1960; Cofer, 1958). That is, the order in which an individual S gives a number of responses to a stimulus approximates the order of these responses in terms of frequency of occurrence in the group hierarchy.

Word Frequency Effects. In a relatively free-responding situation, such as free association, Ss tend to give responses in order of their frequencies. Underwood and Schulz (1960) stated this relationship in a general form, called the *spew hypothesis*. This hypothesis, which is testable in a number of situations, states that the order of emission of verbal responses is directly related to their frequencies of occurrence.

Applied to problem solving, the spew hypothesis predicts that problem difficulty will be inversely related to the frequency of the correct response. High-frequency responses should be emitted earlier, resulting in shorter solution times or more solutions; low-frequency responses should occur later, resulting in longer solution times or fewer solutions. With respect to the frequency of words required as solutions, this prediction has been supported by numerous studies.

Anagrams. Using anagram problems, Mayzner and Tresselt (1958) compared solutions varying in frequency from a high of over 100 occurrences per million words (Thorndike-Lorge count) to a low of less than one occurrence per million words. Solution times increased markedly as the frequency of the solution word decreased. Using different procedures and different frequencies, this finding has been replicated repeatedly (for example, Dominowski, 1966, 1967; Mayzner and Tresselt, 1959, 1966).

Further evidence on word-frequency effects with anagrams has been obtained with problems having more than one solution. Johnson and Van Mondfrans (1965) used anagrams having three or more solutions, finding that the order in which the solutions were given was directly related to the frequencies of the words. With double-solution problems, Mayzner and Tresselt (1966) found that the higher-frequency solution was solved far more rapidly than the low-frequency solution in twenty-five of thirty-two comparisons.

Guessing Tasks. Similar evidence regarding word-frequency effects has been obtained with guessing tasks. Duncan (1966b) asked his Ss to think of a word after they were given such information as the first or last letter of the word, the number of letters, or the class (for example, animal names) to which the word belonged. In all cases, more words of high frequency were emitted than words of low frequency. As the specifications of the solution were changed, the number of acceptable solutions varied, but more high-frequency words were given in all cases. Further evidence on the order of responding was obtained with problems having two answers, one a high-frequency word and the other a low-frequency word. When S was instructed to give only one answer, 70 per cent of the answers were high-frequency alternatives. When S attempted to give both answers, 70 per cent of the first answers were high-frequency alternatives. Providing the low-frequency alternative and asking for the high-frequency word did not affect the number of high-frequency words emitted, but providing the high-frequency alternative resulted in a large increase in the number of low-frequency alternatives given.

This study clearly indicates that Ss strongly tend to emit high-frequency responses when given a problem requiring production of a word. In a similar study, Broerse and Zwaan (1966) obtained the same result. Duncan (1966a) reported further evidence on the relationship between frequency and order of responding. Duncan reasoned that if S guesses in order of frequency, performance on a first guess at solution should be better if the correct response is of high frequency than if it is of low frequency. However, on subsequent guesses this difference should be reduced, with a relatively greater gain when trying to guess a low-frequency response. With problems based on the Russell and Jenkins' (1954) norms, Ss were given up to three guesses to discover either the first associate (Group 1) or the second associate (Group 2) of a stimulus word. On the first guess, Group 1 solved many more problems than Group 2, but on guesses 2 and 3, there was no significant difference between the groups, with Group 2 actually doing slightly better. Virtually the same finding is contained in Duncan's (1966b) study presented previously, in that asking S for both solutions increased the number of low-frequency alternatives given more than the number of high-frequency words (compared to performance when S gave only one answer).

Response Sampling. The preceding findings strongly support the spew hypothesis, that the order of responding is directly related to the frequencies of the responses. However, it should be noted that not all problems with high-frequency solutions are solved within the time allowed. As Duncan (1966b) has stated, the spew hypothesis predicts (successfully) that the responses given will occur in order of frequency. But S might respond from an incomplete sample of the population of possible responses, in which case solution will not occur. It would seem to follow that the size of this population might influence the magnitude of the frequency effect by affecting the probability of an "inadequate" sample being used. There is, unfortunately, no direct evidence on this point.

Bigram-Frequency Effects. In addition to studying the effects of word frequency, the frequencies of two-letter sequences (bigrams) have been manipulated in problem situations. There are two reasons for considering words and bigrams separately. First, the populations of words and of bigrams are of very different sizes, especially because bigram variables are typically studied in tasks where one letter of the bigram is given. The issue of incomplete sampling or of the unavailability of certain responses is relevant to this distinction. Quite simply, if S must guess the least frequent letter or the least frequent bigram with a z, the alternatives are few in number and are all available to S. (He could, if asked, enumerate all the alternatives.) In contrast, S might never guess the least frequent five-letter word beginning with g; although it exists in the language, this word might be unavailable to S. One might thus expect frequency effects with

bigrams to be of lesser magnitude than with words.

A second reason for this separate treatment is that most research on bigram-frequency effects has employed a problem having a word and not a bigram as its solution, namely anagrams. The influence of bigram frequency is thus limited to part solutions on intermediate steps in the solution process. This complicates an analysis of bigram-frequency effects, because the relationship between part solutions and the final solution needs to be known.

Guessing from Specified Alternatives. It appears that, when bigrams and words are employed as solutions in similar tasks, the effects of frequency are similar. In a study by Dominowski (1965), S was given a card containing five bigrams having the same first letter and selected to represent different frequency levels. The task was to guess the "correct" bigram; for different groups, different positions in the frequency hierarchy were correct. Over ten such problems, performance first decreased and then improved as the correct bigram occupied a lower position in the hierarchy. Duncan (1967) reported an experiment in which S was shown a stimulus word and five associates and was told to guess (in different conditions) either the first, third, or fifth associate in terms of strength of association. As indicated in Figure 10-2, the results of the two experiments are quite consistent, and they do not correspond to the frequency effects found with word production tasks.

In the studies presented in the previous section, difficulty systematically increased as responses of lower frequency were required. In contrast, Figure 10-2 indicates greatest difficulty for an intermediate position in the frequency hierarchy. The crucial difference appears to be that the responses were provided for S in the Dominowski (1965) and Duncan (1967) experiments, whereas S was required to

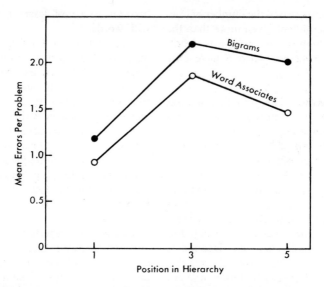

Figure 10-2. Mean errors per problem as a function of position of problem solution in the response hierarchy. (Reprinted with permission from Duncan, C. P. Response hierarchies is problem solving. In C. P. Duncan (Ed.), *Thinking: Current experimental studies.* Philadelphia: Lippincott, 1967. Pp. 18–40. Bigram data from Dominowski, R. L. Problem difficulty as a function of relative frequency of correct responses. *Psychon. Sci.*, 1965, **3**, 417–418.)

produce words as responses in the other studies. *When alternatives are provided it appears easier to identify low-frequency items than to identify items of intermediate strength.* Notice that the curves in Figure 10-2 are not precisely symmetrical. The "identification" hypothesis predicts that the end positions of an ordered sequence will be easier to identify than those in the middle. If this is combined with the spew prediction of greater difficulty with lower frequency, the results can be accounted for. The first position in the frequency hierarchy is favored by both spew and identification predictions, the middle position by neither, and the weakest position by identification but not by spew. One would suspect that the effects of identifying relative strengths would be less if greater emphasis were placed on production of responses, but there is no evidence on this point. The argument is that knowing that the correct response is an infrequent word would be of little help if *S* could not think of the word.

Bigrams in Words. In studies of anagram solving, the bigram-frequency characteristics of solution words have been manipulated. The general rationale is that *S* constructs bigrams as part solutions, and that *S* is more likely to construct a bigram of high frequency than one of low frequency. The results of these manipulations are not completely consistent, and we will not have time to consider them in detail. We can, however, examine some of the interesting aspects of this research.

Measures of Bigram Strength. There has been some disagreement about the most appropriate measure of bigram strength. Although some studies (Mayzner and Tresselt, 1962; Dominowski and Duncan, 1964) have employed the general frequency of a bigram as an index of difficulty, Mayzner and Tresselt (1963, 1966) have argued that the frequencies used should be restricted to the positions the bigrams hold in the solution word. To exemplify their argument briefly, if one wishes to characterize the frequency of the bigram *ke* in the word *joker*, rather than using the frequency of *ke* in the entire language sample, one should use its frequency as the third and fourth letters in five-letter words. Dominowski (1967) has argued that frequencies of any sort should not be used, preferring to measure the *number* of *more frequent bigrams* with the same initial letter as an index of potential interference. According to this view, rather than using a *frequency* as the index of strength for *ke*, one should use its *rank* (based on frequency) among bigrams starting with *k*. To illustrate the difference between the measures, the bigrams *fl* and *ec* both have frequencies of about 720 (Underwood and Schulz, 1960), but *fl* is the most frequent bigram starting with *f*, whereas *ec* is the ninth most frequent bigram starting with *e*. On the basis of the rank measure (but not frequency), *fl* should be easier to produce as a part solution to an anagram than *ec*. Both the frequency measure (when position is considered) and the rank measure have data to support their use. There is a general issue raised here, namely, whether the *strength* of a response is indicated by its *probability* (frequency) or by its *ordinal position* (rank) in a hierarchy of responses. Research on paired-associate learning (see Coleman, 1963) and concept identification (Mednick and Halpern, 1962; Underwood and Richardson, 1956a) indicates that both measures may have merit. Thus the issue is not yet resolved.

Part vs. Whole Solutions. The study of bigram effects in anagram solving points out another question, the relationship between part solutions and the final solution to a problem. Constructing bigrams produces part of a solution, yet instructions direct *S* to think of a word, and the effects of word frequency clearly indicate that *S* does produce whole words. The question concerns when letter-sequence construction ends and word production begins. Both Dominowski (1967, 1968) and Johnson (1966) have suggested that word production probably begins no later than after construction of a bigram (when five-letter words are solutions). We need to know how these two stages fit together in the total solution process; most evidence indicates that word production is more important.

Number of Responses

In the previous section on response strength, it was suggested that the number of responses from which *S* chooses might be an important determinant of problem difficulty. As the number of alternative responses increases, with only one response correct, the probability of selecting the correct response should decrease; thus difficulty should increase. Research with various search tasks has demonstrated repeatedly that *solution time increases as an approximately linear function of the number of alternatives* (Neimark and Wagner, 1964; Solley and Snyder, 1958; Thomas and Solley, 1963). With a lights-and-switches problem, Davis (1967) found that performance deteriorated as a negatively accelerated function of the number of available switches. These findings indicate the reliability of the effects of number of alternative responses. However, in all these tasks, the alternatives were considered equally likely as responses at the outset of the problem; it seems reasonable to exercise caution in generalizing the results to hierarchically arranged response sets.

Application to Anagrams. In an attempt to demonstrate the effect of number of responses with anagrams (considered to involve response hierarchies), Ronning (1965) assumed that *S*'s behavior approximates a process of systematically rearranging the anagram letters until a solution is reached. With five-letter anagrams, there are 120 possible orders of the letters. Ronning's notion was that some of these orders could be ruled out because they start with letters or letter sequences that do not occur at the beginning of English words (*glt*, for example). As more orders can be ruled out, there are fewer "real" alternatives and solution should be easier. Ronning found that high-ruleout problems were solved in less time than low-ruleout problems.

There have been some questions about Ronning's procedure, namely, that words differing in ruleout might also differ in other respects, and that the manner of constructing anagrams was not systematically controlled (Johnson, 1966). The underlying assumption of ruleout, that *S* rearranges the entire anagram until solution is reached, may be questioned, because most evidence indicates that *S*s do not do this. A problem with the ruleout measure is that it gives equal weights to orders ruled out because of initial letters, bigrams, or trigrams; it seems that the effects of these different-sized letter sequences might be different.

Letter-Sequence Information. The number of permissible anagram permutations can be reduced by providing *S* with the anagram plus additional information about the solution. For example, Dominowski (1968) provided as additional information either the position of a letter in the solution word or a bigram of the solution (but not its position in the word). With either kind of information, there are only twenty-four possible letter orders remaining. The results indicated that performance when *S* was told a bigram was much better than that when *S* was given no additional information or was told the position of one letter in the word. As such, the results seriously question the assumption that anagram permutations constitute the alternative responses from which *S* chooses. If this were so, bigram and letter position should facilitate performance equally, but this was not the case. In addition, telling *S* either the first or last bigram produced better performance than giving either the

second or third bigram, which argues against emphasizing only initial letter sequences. The results were reasonably accounted for by assuming that *S* uses the additional information to think of words, because evidence from word recall and recognition indicates that the ends of a word are more important than the middle (Brown and McNeil, 1966).

Response Chains. Although we have considered the effects of the size of the response set from which *S* must select a solution, there is another way in which number of responses has been manipulated. It is possible to vary the number of responses that *S* must chain together in order to solve a problem. Hayes (1965) devised the "spy problem" for this purpose; *S* was told to imagine that he is running a spy ring, and that, for security reasons, not all spies can talk with each other. After learning which other spies each spy could communicate with, *S* had to get a message from one spy to another, solving the problem "in his head." Solution time increased disproportionately with an increase in the number of required steps (for example, a problem with twice the number of steps as another might take six times as long to solve). Similar findings have been reported by Gagné and Smith (1962) with a disk-transfer problem and by Davis (1967) with a lights-and-switches problem.

This concludes our examination of the effects of response characteristics. It is clear that problem difficulty is significantly affected by the strength of the response required, the complexity of the required response, and the number of alternative incorrect responses available. From this research, certain questions stand out as topics for future study, particularly the determination of the most appropriate measure of response strength, the relationship between part and whole solutions, and the possible interaction of response strength and number of alternative responses.

Stimulus Factors

Consideration of stimulus factors involves an assessment of the effects of different methods of presenting a problem. In a total analysis of problem solving, it appears that problem presentation is a relatively minor variable, with some notable exceptions. For problems having "known" response hierarchies, it seems that the strength of the correct response is most important. This should not be interpreted as indicating that problem presentation is unimportant; rather, the variables that have been manipulated as stimulus factors appear to be less effective than those involving response characteristics.

Anagram Characteristics

By definition and according to instructions most commonly used, an anagram is a sequence of letters that can be rearranged to produce a word. The manipulation of anagram characteristics is an attempt to make such rearrangement more or less difficult.

Similarity to Solution. One expects that, as the problem situation becomes more similar to the solution, the difficulty of reaching solution would decrease, because less change would be required to go from the problem to its solution. With respect to anagram solving, probably all judges would agree that the anagram *udgej* would be easier to solve for the word *judge* than the anagram *dejug*. If asked, judges would probably also agree that the second anagram is less similar to the word than the first. The question concerns how to measure this similarity. Mayzner and Tresselt (1958) identified "hard" and "easy" anagram letter orders; although these were distinguished on the basis of judged similarity to the solution, Mayzner and Tresselt did suggest that easy letter

orders probably required fewer letter movements to get from the anagram to the word than hard orders.

Number of Letter Moves. In an attempt to provide a generally applicable measure, Dominowski (1966) suggested that anagram letter orders be characterized by the number of letter moves required, disregarding the spacing between letters and the distance letters are moved. According to this system, for the word *chair*, *hacir* requires one move (*c* to the front), *ciahr* requires two moves (for example, placing *a* and *i* between *h* and *r*). For five-letter words, anagrams requiring from one to three moves were compared. Dominowski found that one-move orders were easiest and that two-move orders were the most difficult. Thus, anagram difficulty is not simply related to the number of moves, and the reason for this is not clear. There are several possible explanations. Perhaps the number of letter moves is too gross a measure, although Dominowski did not find much difference between different orders requiring the same number of moves. However, Hunter (1961) has suggested that the distance moved may be important. The writer has noticed the following interesting occurrence. In constructing anagrams, Ronning (1965) reported that he simply tried to make the anagrams as dissimilar as possible to the solution word. (The letter-moves report was not then available.) The interesting point is that all the anagrams that Ronning constructed required two moves. It appears that judged similarly as well is not simply related to the number of letter moves. Clearly, new ideas regarding this variable would be welcome.

Bigram Frequency. Based on the assumption that greater frequency indicates greater strength, Mayzner and Tresselt (1959) reasoned that anagrams containing high-frequency bigrams should be harder to rearrange than anagrams containing low-frequency bigrams. Their results supported this prediction, and Mayzner and Tresselt (1966) replicated the finding. However, because of the bigram frequency characteristics of the anagram, other investigators have been unable to obtain any effect (Dominowski and Duncan, 1964; Pinckney, 1965; Stachnik, 1963). It appears that the effect is quite small; furthermore, it is not clear to what extent the powerful variable of letter order has been controlled in these studies.

Words as Anagrams. Although the anagrams typically used are nonsense letter sequences, it is possible to present a word as an anagram, with S instructed to make another word from the letters. An example of such a problem is to present *cause*, with S required to solve for *sauce*. The comparison of word and nonsense anagrams stemmed from Gestalt concepts. A word was considered to be an organized perceptual whole, a good Gestalt, whereas a nonsense anagram was poorly organized. Consequently, word anagrams should be harder to solve. It should be realized that investigating this question is quite difficult, because all other known variables must be controlled. There has been some suggestion (Mayzner and Tresselt, 1965) that controls have not been adequate. There have been a number of recent studies in which word anagrams have been found more difficult to solve than nonsense anagrams (Beilin, 1966; Beilin and Horn, 1962; Ekstrand and Dominowski, 1965). Mayzner and Tresselt (1965) reported no difference between the two types of anagrams and suggested that procedural flaws had produced differences in earlier studies. However, Beilin's (1966) study employed the same methodology as Mayzner and Tresselt; thus it appears that this is not the case. Not all investigators of this phenomenon have interpreted it in Gestalt terms. For example, Ekstrand and Dominowski proposed that associations to words consist of words with different letters, whereas associations to nonsense anagrams are more likely to be either sub-

word responses or words containing the letters of the anagram, which would make solution easier. In a related study, Hebert and Rogers (1966) rated nonsense anagrams on pronounceability and found easy-to-pronounce anagrams harder to solve than those hard to pronounce. Because words are easier to pronounce than nonsense anagrams, this might be a reason for their greater difficulty as anagrams. What appear to be needed are some parametric studies of the effects of such variables as meaningfulness and pronounceability of anagrams on solution difficulty.

Presenting Insight Problems

In evaluating the effects of various methods of presenting insight problems, we will be primarily interested in the effects of hints or special instructions and in a special sort of problem, a functional-fixedness problem. Before considering these topics, we can examine briefly a manipulation that has been mentioned earlier. Insight problems can be presented as rather concrete problems with actual objects or as verbal or paper-and-pencil problems. Duncan (1959) has reviewed a number of studies comparing such presentations, and he reached the conclusion that the concreteness of presentation has little effect on problem-solving performance. Because little research has been done on this question recently, we will accept his conclusion and turn to the other topics.

Hints and Instructions. The initial analysis of insight problems assumed that solution required the proper direction of problem-solving efforts. In the previous chapter we noted that the effects of directing instructions and hints are ambiguous, with "direction" often having no effect. Some useful information on this problem was reported by Corman (1957), who found that more explicit instructions about a rule for solving facilitated solving for high-ability Ss but interfered with performance for low-ability Ss. Burke, Maier, and Hoffman (1966) found that hints given at the beginning of the problem were more effective than hints given after some attempts at solution had been made. Perhaps their more important observation was that hints can have several effects, including misleading S; they also noted that hints might be ignored. This points out the problems with research on this manipulation, that the expected effect of a hint is often vague and that it is seldom known to what degree S might instruct himself, in which case hints given by E will be redundant.

Perceptual Functional Fixedness. The common characteristic of insight problems is the requirement of using an object in an unusual function. If the presentation of a problem stresses the ordinary function of this object, it is expected that solution will be more difficult. A number of studies have compared different presentations of the Candle problem, focusing on the use of the box as a support for the candle. Adamson (1952) found that solution was easier if the box was empty when presented, compared to presenting the box full of tacks. The explanation is that presenting the filled box stresses its ordinary function, thus making it more difficult for S to perceive the box as a platform. Glucksberg (1964a) found that nonsolving Ss often either do not report the presence of the box when asked to describe the materials or they describe it in an undifferentiated manner, such as "a box of tacks." This suggests that difficulty in solving is due not to a lack of the correct function for the object, but to the "invisibility" of the object itself. Glucksberg and Weisberg (1966) found that labeling each object separately when presenting the problem with the box filled resulted in much faster solutions, presumably because labeling the box made it available as a separate stimulus.

Effects of Motivation. The difference between the empty- ,and filled-box presenta-

tions has been used to test a prediction from learning theory, and we will examine these studies to illustrate the close relation between learning and problem solving. The learning-theory prediction is that high drive (motivation) will impair performance when the correct response is low in the habit hierarchy (nondominant) but will facilitate performance when the correct response is high in the hierarchy (dominant). Glucksberg (1962, 1964b) reasoned that the box-empty presentation elicits a dominant correct response, while the box-filled presentation involved a nondominant correct response. Drive was manipulated by telling half the Ss (high-drive) that they could win money if they did well, whereas the other half (low-drive) were given no such incentive. The prediction was supported; with the box empty, high-drive Ss performed better than low-drive Ss, but, with the box filled, the difference was reversed. In a similar study in which drive was varied by selecting Ss having different scores on an anxiety scale, Tecce (1965) obtained results only partly supporting the learning-theory prediction. Tecce found that the box-filled presentation was more difficult for both high-anxiety and low-anxiety Ss, but it was no different in difficulty from the box-empty presentation for medium-anxiety Ss. Because the methods of varying drive level differed for these studies, we should exercise caution in comparing the results. Regardless of the exact function involved (an interesting motivational problem), these studies demonstrate the similarity of learning and problem-solving behavior.

Evaluation of Stimulus Factors. In concluding this section on stimulus factors, it seems fair to state that problem difficulty seems more dependent on response characteristics than on variations in problem presentation. Although variation in letter moves for anagrams and the functional-fixedness variations produce large performance differences, most other stimulus variables have relatively small effects. It is also difficult to separate stimulus and response effects in some cases, much as perceptual and learning explanations are often difficult to distinguish. A neat situation would exist if stimulus effects could be described as immediate, perceptual influences on behavior, but many of these effects have been reasonably described in terms of the previously learned responses that are elicited. What appears to be involved here is a distinction between the stimulus as E defines and manipulates it and the stimulus as used by S (which is assumed to be different). This distinction has been clearly made in learning (Underwood, 1963). Because of this lack of identity, it is difficult to evaluate the effects of variation in the stimulus situation (as E defines it).

Training and Transfer

The topics that we have previously considered have all been based essentially on a procedure of having S perform only one task in the laboratory. In the present section, we will examine studies in which E has attempted to influence problem solving by requiring S to perform at least two tasks in the laboratory, with the interest directed toward the transfer from the first to the second tasks. It should be clear that many of the variables that have previously been studied involve transfer from experiences outside the laboratory. For example, in manipulating the frequency of a solution word, E assumes that S has been exposed to the language. The major feature of the research that we will now consider is that E attempts to manipulate directly S's experience prior to attacking a problem.

In order to understand transfer effects in problem solving, certain transfer concepts must be explicated. To restate an earlier point, the study of transfer necessarily involves at least two tasks, and it is performance on the latter or test task that is analyzed. Transfer may be either positive or negative, and we will consider these types separately. Positive transfer occurs when performance on the transfer task is facilitated by prior training; negative transfer occurs when transfer performance is impaired by prior tasks. Of course, it is also possible that transfer performance is unaffected by certain kinds of prior experience, and we will encounter such findings.

Specific vs. General Transfer

A useful distinction that can be made in studying transfer is that between specific and general transfer, which is most easily described by referring to Table 10-1. In the experimental condition, the solution words for two successive problems are associatively related. *White* is the most frequently given response to *black* in free association (Russell and Jenkins, 1954). If E is interested in the effect of solving for one word (*black*) on subsequent solution for a *related* word (*white*), he is interested in *specific* transfer. In contrast, the two solutions for the first control condition are *not obviously related*; if E is interested in the transfer from *rough* to *white* as anagram solutions, this would be *general* transfer. Of course, the two problems are not totally unrelated in the first control condition, because they are problems of the same type. However, it should be clear that there is a factor present in the experimental condition (a specfic association between solutions) that is absent in the first control condition.

Table **10-1**   Examples of Conditions for Studying Specific and General Transfer Using Anagram Problems

Condition	First Problem	Second Problem
Experimental	*balkc-black*	*eiwth-white*
Control₁	*ruohg-rough*	*eiwth-white*
Control₂		*eiwth-white*

If E wishes to determine the effect of solving a first, unrelated problem on solving a second problem, he would compare the two control conditions. If he is studying the effects of a specific association between solutions on transfer, he would compare the experimental condition with the *first* control condition, because that is the only way in which they differ. Perhaps the most important point is that comparing the experimental and second control conditions necessarily yields ambiguous information. If these two conditions differ on the second problem, this might be because the experimental Ss solved a first problem (ignoring the specific association) or because they solved for a related word, or both. To state this differently, if E wishes to study specific transfer, he must compare groups given equal opportunities to show general transfer. This is the reason for comparing the experimental and first control groups to test for specific transfer—both groups have solved a problem before attempting the *white* problem, but only the experimental group has solved for an associated word.

Our discussion of transfer effects will treat general transfer separately from specific positive and negative transfer phenomena. General transfer actually is considered always to be positive, if any transfer occurs. That is, if any changes in performance occur as S solves successive problems of the same type (but without any specific interproblem relationships), we expect S to *improve* his performance as he gets more *practice* at solving problems. This general, positive transfer effect might be termed *learning to solve* and is similar to learning to learn effects found with many standard learning tasks. The evidence regarding learning to solve will be our first transfer topic.

Learning to Solve

It seems a reasonable expectation that S should become a better problem solver as

he gains more experience in solving problems. If we introspect upon our own experiences in playing card games and solving puzzles (jigsaw, crossword), we are likely to conclude that we did learn to solve the problems involved. It is therefore somewhat surprising that many investigators have reported that Ss do not improve their performance over a series of problems. The most common finding with anagrams is that Ss *do not improve their performance with practice* (for example, Dominowski, 1966, 1967, 1968; Mayzner and Tresselt, 1962). Duncan (1961) had Ss solve an unrelated insight problem before attempting the two-string problem, but they did no better than Ss attempting only the two-string problem. With word-guessing problems, no improvement over problems has been observed (Battig, 1957; Duncan, 1966b).

In attempting to account for this lack of general transfer, several points must be considered. First, relatively *little* practice has been given in these studies; E is often testing for improvement over a 30-min. period of problem-solving practice. It seems reasonable that learning to solve might require more practice, perhaps over much longer periods of time. There is simply no evidence regarding this possibility. Secondly, the Ss in most studies are college students, and most of their improvement in problem solving might have occurred before they entered the laboratory. Studies involving children, or developmental studies, might show positive results. Finally, one can ask what S might learn that would help him to solve these problems. In studying general transfer, E tries to eliminate any specific relationship between problems; because solution typically is a relatively short process, there may be nothing to learn about the general type of problems. With problems in which solving consists of a sequence of responses, such as search tasks or the game of twenty questions, Ss have improved over successive problems (Faust, 1958; Neimark, 1961). Using tasks more similar to learning tasks, large amounts of general transfer have been observed (Adams, 1954; Duncan, 1958; Morrisett and Hovland, 1959). It is thus clear that the likelihood of finding general transfer varies considerably with the type of problem and the conditions of practice. If E does not attempt to "teach" problem solving, he is quite likely to find no improvement over problems, especially within a short laboratory session.

Positive Transfer

In contrast to the previous section, the studies we will now consider involve attempts to facilitate problem solving by some kind of prior experience, not necessarily involving problems. Because the type of training procedure and its success have varied with the type of problem used as the transfer task, we will consider insight problems, anagrams, and the training of originality as separate topics.

Insight Problems. Because solving an insight problem involves using an object in an unusual way, several training methods have been used in an attempt to increase the probability of occurrence of the correct response. One method requires S to list uses for an object, with that object subsequently used as a pendulum weight in solving the two-string problem. The notion is that Ss giving "weight" uses for the object should be better solvers, and that listing uses should aid thinking of such as use, but there is little favorable evidence. Although Saugstad (1955) found that Ss giving weight uses were better solvers than those not giving such uses, Staats (1957) found no relationship between giving weight uses and success in solving the problem. Furthermore, Ss who list uses beforehand generally do no better in solving the problem that Ss not given the training (Duncan, 1961).

Facilitation has been achieved by using training procedures in which unusual uses for objects are provided by E. Although the positive transfer produced has not always

been large, the finding has been reported with considerable frequency (Judson, Cofer, and Gelfand, 1956; Maltzman, Brooks, Bogartz, and Summers, 1958; Saugstad and Raaheim, 1957). It seems reasonable to conclude that the effect is small, especially because providing relevant uses has not always facilitated problem solution (Maltzman, Belloni, and Fishbein, 1964).

Some training procedures have involved either very specific demonstrations concerning problem solution or prior work on very similar problems or parts of the transfer problem itself. Saugstad (1957) and Saugstad and Raaheim (1960) reported success with such training, but Hoffman, Burke, and Maier (1963) found that Ss given prior experience on a simpler version of the transfer problem actually performed more poorly than Ss not given such experience. It seems clear that, before even small positive transfer might be expected, the training procedure must become quite specific.

Analysis of Insight Problems. Part of the difficulty in facilitating solution of insight problems seems to lie in a lack of understanding of the behavior involved. Various Es have not agreed about what behavioral components are necessary for solution. Performance on insight problems does not seem to be related to other kinds of behavior. Duncan (1961) found no relationship between performance on one insight problem and performance on another. Danks and Glucksberg (1966) reported no correlation between a measure of creativity and problem-solving performance. Burke and Maier (1965) were unable to predict success on an insight problem with any of eighteen different predictors. Although there is no reason to expect that performance on insight problems should be related to all or even many of these other measures, the striking finding is that it is related to none. The difficulty of facilitating solution of insight problems becomes more understandable when we realize that we are not sure of the characteristics of the behavior involved. With other kinds of problem-solving behavior which seem better described, facilitation has proved easier to produce.

Anagrams. Attempts to facilitate anagram solving has been based on the assumption that S thinks of words in trying to solve. The training procedures essentially consist of methods of increasing the strength of the solutions to the anagrams. Dominowski and Ekstrand (1967) found that Ss who were shown a list of solution words prior to anagram solving performed much better than Ss without such training. Mendelsohn and Griswold (1964, 1966) found similar facilitation, even though the training list also contained distracting words and their Ss were not informed of any connection between the word list and the subsequent anagrams. Dominowski and Ekstrand (1967) also found that prior presentation of words associated with the solutions produced strong positive transfer to anagram solving. It is clear that prior presentation or associative arousal of solutions results in much better anagram performance. Because the rationale of these procedures is similar to that for attempts to facilitate solution of insight problems, the greater effectiveness of the procedures with anagrams seems to be due to the better understanding of the responses involved. Consistent with this position is the fact that some success has been attained in predicting individual differences in anagram performance. (See Johnson, 1966; Mendelsohn, Griswold, and Anderson, 1966.)

Originality Training. There has been a recent upsurge in experimental studies of the production of original or creative responses, a type of behavior similar to problem solving. Perhaps the main difference is that there is often no single, correct response that S must produce in studies of originality, in contrast to typical problem-solving tasks. Because there has

been some controversy over the meanings of the terms *originality* and *creativity*, we should know precisely what the terms mean in the present context. Originality is usually defined in terms of the production of *unique* responses to various task instructions; alternatively, a response is considered more original, as it is given by a smaller proportion of Ss. Both free-association tasks and unusual-uses tasks have been used to measure originality. Although Mednick (1962) has characterized creativity as involving the production of both many responses and unique responses meeting certain criteria, the measure of creativity most commonly used is the *Remote Associates Test* (RAT). Each item on this test consists of three words, and S must think of a fourth word that is associated with all three. As an example of the type of item, for the stimulus set of *rat, blue,* and *cottage,* the answer is *cheese.* It should be noted that there is a specific correct answer for each item of the RAT, a feature which has been criticized (Taft and Rossiter, 1966). Mednick's rationale is that Ss capable of producing many associations (thus, more remote associations) are more likely to generate the required response to a RAT item.

Facilitating RAT Performance. Performance on the RAT has been facilitated in a number of ways. Maltzman, Belloni, and Fishbein (1964) presented associates of solutions to RAT items, with Ss instructed to give a different association to each presentation; RAT performance was an increasing function of the number of presentations. However, Maltzman et al. (1964) found that prior association to non-associates of solutions did not facilitate RAT performance, indicating that the prior training must be rather specifically related to RAT content. This position is supported by Caron, Unger, and Parloff's (1963) finding that repeated presentations of nonassociates for free association did not facilitate RAT performance. Freedman

(1965) suggested that the lack of facilitation was due to the inappropriateness of the training procedure. He argues that success on the RAT requires the production of many associations in a short time, but the training procedure used by Caron et al. (1963) and by Maltzman et al. (1964) required S to give only one association each time a stimulus was presented. Freedman found that Ss who were required to give multiple associations to stimuli during training scored higher on the RAT than Ss who merely defined the words during training, thus supporting his argument.

Training Uncommon Responses. Maltzman's (1960) procedure of repeatedly presenting stimulus words, with S required to give a different association to each presentation, has been found to *increase* the originality of responses on a subsequent free-association test (for example, Caron et al., 1963; Maltzman, Bogartz, and Breger, 1958). The training procedure has also been found to facilitate performance on unusual-uses tests (Maltzman, Simon, Raskin, and Licht, 1960; Rosenbaum, Arenson, and Panman, 1964). There are a great many parameters of the training procedure, such as the number of different stimuli used, the number of repetitions, the number of different responses elicited, and whether S responds or has E provide responses. Maltzman et al. (1960) compared a training procedure involving associating once to each of 125 words with the standard procedure of associating five times to each of twenty-five words, giving a different response each time. Although both methods resulted in greater originality on a subsequent free-association test, only the latter procedure produced improved performance on a subsequent unusual-uses test. Maltzman et al. (1960) found that requiring S to repeat his first response to each stimulus repetition may *inhibit* originality, whereas Freedman (1965) found that providing S with associations had no effect on subsequent RAT performance. Furthermore,

instructions can influence originality; instructing S to be original results in greater originality in free-associating (Maltzman et al., 1958) and in giving unusual uses (Davis and Manske, 1966) when the instructions are given just prior to the test, but similar instructions given only before training do not affect giving unusual uses (Rosenbaum et al., 1964).

Analysis of Originality Training. It is clear that originality can be facilitated, and because of this success, research has progressed toward determining the limits of the effect. Most evidence indicates that facilitation is relatively restricted, because a given training procedure typically facilitates one kind of transfer performance while having no effect on another. This is consistent with other findings of a lack of nonspecific transfer in problem solving. It is worth noting that, with conditions for which training is successful, facilitation occurs even with a two-day interval between training and test (Maltzman et al., 1960). Future research should be directed toward the apparent differences between originality (as on free-association and unusual-uses tests) and creativity (RAT performance), especially because the conceptual derivation of these measures is quite similar.

The findings regarding positive transfer in problem solving quickly dispel any notions about "making people better problem solvers." Such general effects are simply not observed. Rather, in order to facilitate performance, one must know precisely what responses are needed for success and then devise a training procedure which strengthens these responses in a fairly specific manner. Of course, we would expect stronger facilitation with much longer periods of training than are typically studied in experiments.

Negative Transfer: Functional Fixedness

Several instances of negative transfer were presented in the previous section (constituting complete failure of a facilitation procedure); now we will be concerned with deliberate attempts to inhibit problem-solving performance. Just as facilitation training is designed to strengthen relevant responses, negative transfer effects are expected when prior training weakens these responses. There have been relatively few studies of simple negative transfer, thus we will concentrate on a particular kind of inhibition called functional fixedness. We have already encountered "perceptual" functional fixedness; the meaning of the term as it is used here is *inhibition in using an object in one function due to recent use of the object in another function* (Duncker, 1945). The study of functional fixedness has usually involved *S*'s choice of objects in solving the two-string problem.

The basic procedure is illustrated by a study by Birch and Rabinowitz (1951). The two-string problem was given with both a small electric switch and a small relay available as weights for making a pendulum of one string. Prior to the problem, some *S*s used the switch to complete a circuit, some used the relay, and control *S*s did nothing. Those *S*s given circuit-completion experience tended to use the alternative object to solve the two-string problem, whereas control *S*s used each with equal frequency. This demonstrates functional fixedness, and the finding has been replicated (for example, Duvall, 1965).

Limitations on Functional Fixedness. Other research has been directed toward defining the limits of functional fixedness. An important limitation was noted by van de Geer (1957). In the studies presented, transfer was always from an ordinary use of the object to an unusual use, and it appears that functional fixedness will occur only if the transfer task requires an unusual use of the object (Duvall, 1965; van de Geer, 1957). Adamson and Taylor (1954) found that the tendency to use the other object to solve the problem decreased as more time elapsed between training and

problem solution. In a similar study, Flavell, Cooper, and Loiselle (1958) varied the number of unusual uses of an object interpolated between its ordinary use and its use in the solution of the two-string problem and found that functional fixedness decreased as *S*s received more unusual-use training. Therefore, although functional fixedness is a reliable phenomenon, it appears to be limited to inhibition of unusual uses and dissipates with time or other training. These studies share a weakness, namely that measures of solution difficulty are not reported; it would indeed be interesting to know if functionally fixed *S*s take longer to solve the problem. This is clearly the case with perceptual functional fixedness, but information is lacking for the preceding procedure.

Problem-Solving Set

The last of our training-and-transfer topics concerns the effects of problem-solving sets, which are typically established by solving a number of problems which have similar solutions. Set is defined as the tendency to respond with a particular type of response to a problem. To be a separate phenomenon, set must be distinguished from a simple, associative habit. This distinction is in terms of the specificity of reference. That is, standard learning involves the development of a particular response tendency, whereas set refers to a class or group of responses. Thus set responses themselves have the status of anticipatory goal responses in Maltzman's system. If this definition is used (and it seems that this must be done), then some studies of set probably should not be identified as such, because the procedures have established the dominance of a single response rather than that of a class of responses. This seems to be the case with letter-order sets in anagram solving, in which case each anagram can be solved by the same rewriting of the anagram letters (for example, the second letter of the anagram is the first letter of the word, the fourth is the second, and so on). Solving in this case requires simply repeating that particular response, and learning this seems an example of simple learning. It is not surprising that letter-order set has been found to be a very powerful "set" (for example, Maltzman and Morrisett, 1953a). It seems better to restrict the term *set* to classes of responses in order to make it a distinct concept.

Establishing Sets. The development of set is unanimously considered to constitute learning, and much research has been directed toward demonstrating the applicability of learning concepts to problem-solving set. Before considering these studies, the basic procedures for studying set should be described. Most studies of set have employed either water-jar or anagram problems. With water jars, the set established is quite specific (for example, fill the largest jar, then pour water into the middle jar twice, then into the smallest jar.) With anagrams, in addition to letter-order sets, sets involving classes of words (for example, animal names) have been studied. The latter type is probably the best example of a set as distinguished from a simple habit. Most studies have involved an *initial series* of set problems, followed either by a test problem requiring a different solution or by a problem having more than one solution. In the second case, the interest lies in which solution *S* will produce, and such studies often have the same lack as functional fixedness studies, the absence of information regarding solution difficulty.

The extension of learning principles to set phenomena has been reasonably successful. If set is a habit, then it ought to increase in strength as more set problems are given, yielding a type of learning curve. Using water-jar problems, Tressel and Leeds (1953) found that the percentage of set solutions on test problems increased as a negatively accelerated function of the number of training problems, a common form for learning curves. A similar finding was reported by Ray (1965).

Extinction of Sets. Gardner and Runquist (1958) demonstrated several learning phenomena in their study of set. They varied the number of set problems (water jars), arguing that performance on a test problem requiring the set solution should be directly related to the amount of training, and they obtained the predicted result. As a measure of resistance to extinction, they gave a problem requiring a different solution, predicting that performance should be inversely related to amount of training; again they were successful. Solving the extinction problem should reduce habit strength to the same level for all groups. Thus, performance on a postextinction problem requiring the set solution should not be related to amount of set training. This last prediction had only slight support; although differences were not statistically reliable, there was a tendency for better performance to be associated with more training. The results of their experiment are indicated in Figure 10-3. With respect to the effects of extinction, Adamson (1959) also found no differences in postextinction performance between groups given different training. In a follow-up experiment, Runquist and Sexton (1961) obtained evidence of spontaneous recovery of set, further strengthening the learning approach to set.

Some Contradictory Data. In another attempt to relate set to learning, Kendler, Greenberg, and Richman (1952) compared massed and distributed practice during set training. Contrary to the usual finding in learning studies, they found that set was stronger after massed training. It was suggested that developing a set resembled extinction more than acquisition (because extinction usually is more rapid with massed trials), but this position is difficult to reconcile with the other evidence stressing the learning of set. Adamson (1959)

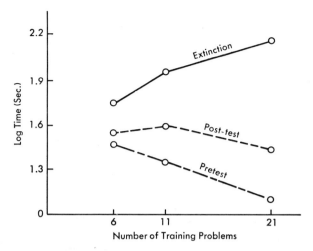

Figure 10-3. Mean log time to solve three test problems as a function of the number of acquisition problems. (Reprinted with permission from Gardner, R. A., & Runquist, W. N. Acquisition and extinction of problem-solving set. *J. exp. Psychol.*, 1958, **55**, 274–277.)

tested another learning principle, that partial reinforcement leads to greater resistance to extinction than continuous reinforcement. During twelve training problems, one group used the same solution for all problems, whereas another group used this solution on six problems, with six problems each having a different solution randomly mixed in the training series. On extinction problems requiring new solutions, the partially reinforced *S*s performed more poorly, supporting the prediction. However, Mayzner (1955) found exactly the opposite result, as did Mayzner and Tresselt (1956). In these studies, reinforcing alternative solutions during training reduced the amount of set. Although the discrepant results regarding partial reinforcement might be due in part to the use of different types of problems in the various studies, Mayzner's work also suggests that describing these procedures as partial reinforcement might be somewhat inappropriate. In the standard learning situation, partial reinforcement involves not reinforcing the correct response on some trials, but no other response is reinforced. In these problem-solving studies, nonreinforcement of the set response was combin-

ed with reinforcement of an incompatible response, and Mayzner and Tresselt clearly conceived of their procedure as developing competing responses.

Effects of Instructions. Maltzman has conducted several experiments investigating the effects of instructions on set performance. In his system, instructions involve arousal of the anticipatory goal response (r_g), and Maltzman has argued that establishment of set in this fashion is nonassociative and thus different from establishing a set through training. It appears that the major difference is that a set established through instructions should be more transient than one established through training. Giving set-inducing instructions does increase the amount of set (Maltzman and Morrisett, 1953b; Maltzman, Eisman, Brooks, and Smith, 1956; Safren, 1962). According to Maltzman, the effects of instructions should depend on when they are given, before training or just prior to the test. In the Maltzman et al. (1956) study, instructions given before training had no effect, but instructions given just before the test were effective. Although this supports his distinction, Maltzman and

Morrisett (1953b) found that pretraining instructions did increase set on a later test. It is thus not clear whether training sets and instructional sets should be conceptually distinguished.

Combining Sets. Using operations considered analogous to combining conditioned stimuli in classical conditioning, Maltzman and Morrisett (1953a) studied the addition and subtraction of sets. Two sets were used, a letter-order set and a "nature" set. (All solutions were "nature" words.) To produce a compound set, the letter-order and nature sets were made congruent. (All anagrams had nature solutions and could be solved by using the same rearrangement of the letters.) After training with either a single set or the compound set, Ss were given multiple-solution problems with either a single or the compound set favoring one of the solutions. Sets were added by training S with just a single set (order or nature), then testing him with the compound set operating. Sets were subtracted in similar fashion, by training with the compound set and then testing with only one set operating.

The results indicated that the greatest number of set solutions occurred when Ss were both trained and tested with the compound set. Adding sets on the test produced more set solutions than training and testing with just a single set. Subtracting sets on the test resulted in fewer set solutions than compound training and testing. One difficulty was that the order set was much stronger than the nature set (because of its extreme specificity), thus the effects of adding and subtracting sets depended on which set was manipulated. For example, the compound set was much stronger than the nature set alone, but there was no significant difference between the compound set and the order set alone. Thus, the manipulation of sets was much more effective when the order set was added to or subtracted from the nature set.

This difference in the strengths of the sets also qualifies a comparison made by Maltzman and Morrisett (1953b). They found that adding the order set to the nature set produced more set solutions than adding nature-set instructions to the nature set. This difference supposedly suggests a difference between training sets and instructional sets (that is, training sets are stronger). However, both the extremely specific character of the order set and the finding that adding the nature set to the order set was no different from adding instructions to the order set mitigate against any firm conclusion.

One final point concerns the generality of problem-solving sets. As might be expected, the more set training is similar to the problems used for testing, the stronger the set is (Maltzman et al., 1956). However, Jacobus and Johnson (1964) demonstrated the formation of a set to adopt a set. They found that Ss who were first given set training with anagrams were more likely to develop a set during subsequent training with water-jar problems than Ss not given the anagram training. This indicates that the effects of set training can extend beyond the particular problems for which set is induced.

Summary

Our survey of research on the solution of simple problems should strengthen the view that learning plays an important role in problem solving. This is evidenced by the fact that the most powerful and reliable effects are observed when E manipulates variables reflecting long-term experience (for example, language variables) or prior training. It seems obvious that a major goal of future research should be the identification of training techniques which will facilitate problem solving; to date, attempts to produce positive transfer have been somewhat unsuccessful.

Because these problems are relatively simple, it seems worthwhile to discuss two points. The first is that their simplicity should not result in the reader considering them as curious experimental tasks of no practical significance. Admittedly, the generality of these findings is unknown, and the analysis of everyday problems is difficult. However, application of the findings should not be considered improbable. There is some evidence suggesting relationships between laboratory performance and everyday behavior. Performance on the RAT has been found to predict successfully scientific productivity in a number of fields (Mednick and Mednick, 1967), a kind of behavior highly valued in our society. Of some interest is the finding of a significant correlation between RAT performance and anagram-solving ability (Mendelsohn and Griswold, 1966). Of course, RAT performance may be related to anagram solving and to scientific productivity for two different reasons, but the following point should not be missed: laboratory behavior does not exist in a vacuum, and

laboratory findings may indeed be verified with more complex, everyday problems.

The second point is related to the first and might explain the difficulty of applying laboratory findings to other situations. It is that little progress has been made in describing the process of problem solving. As we have just seen, success in training problem solving is related to the accuracy of the description. One reason for the lack of adequate theory must be the simplicity of the problems. Solutions are fairly rapid, and the researcher has little additional information to work with. We shall return to this issue later, but for the moment it serves to distinguish this chapter from the next. Concept attainment is a form of problem solving, but the problem is more complex, solution requires more time, and E has available a wealth of additional information. Much more is known about the process of concept attainment, and we will now shift our attention to this body of knowledge.

11

Concept Attainment

Attaining concepts is at once problem solving, learning, and something in addition. It is problem solving for adult human Ss because E usually has chosen a concept that S already knows and must identify during the experimental session. It is learning because measurable changes will occur in S's behavior during the experiment as more trials are given, and these changes will persist. The something extra of concept attainment lies in the fact that S must deal with classes of stimuli rather than with the individual stimuli, that S learns or discovers a rule rather than a solution of limited generality. As in the previous chapter, we will examine the procedures used in conceptual research before surveying the research findings.

In contrast to the variety of problems that were encountered in the previous chapter, there is a high degree of agreement among E's regarding the materials to be used for studying concept attainment. Two types of materials are used, geometric forms and words. When geometric forms are used, concepts are based on combinations of their physical dimensions (size, shape, and so on), whereas verbal concepts are usually based on common associates to a number of words. With either type of

material there are a variety of ways of presenting the materials and measuring S's behavior. It is these which we will now consider.

Task Characteristics

A concept consists of two independent components, the stimulus attributes relevant to the solution of the problem, and the rule for relating those attributes. This leads to three kinds of conceptual tasks, as indicated in Table 11-1.

In attribute identification, S is told the form of the rule (for example, a stimulus must have both attributes to belong to the concept), and S must discover the relevant attributes (for example, red and square). In *rule learning*, the reverse is true, because the relevant attributes are identified for S (for example, *two, large*), and he must discover the rule (for example, either *two* or *large*). In complete learning, S is given a description of the stimuli and told only that a concept exists to be discovered, with neither the relevant attributes nor the form of the rule provided. As Haygood and Bourne (1965) pointed out, most studies of conceptual

Table 11-1   Types of Conceptual Tasks

Task	Relevant Attributes	Rule
Attribute Identification	Unknown	Known
Rule Learning	Known	Unknown
Complete Learning	Unknown	Unknown

behavior have been based on attribute identification, and *E*s have manipulated variables deemed relevant to this task. It should be clear that *S*'s problem is quite different with these tasks. In attribute identification, it may be described as, "I know only one attribute is involved, but which one?" For the rule-learning task, the appropriate question is, "I know that *red* and *square* are being used, but does a stimulus have to be both, or just one, or what?" It should be strongly expected that *S*'s behavior will differ in these tasks, and, consequently, the effects of certain variables will also change.

Description of Stimuli. In all the previously described tasks the stimuli are described for *S*. If this is not done, the task can become very ambiguous, because there are many possible dimensions for any stimulus. Although most *E*s do not use the thickness of ink, smudges, scratches, the length of words, and so on, as dimensions in constructing the task, there is no guarantee that *S* will ignore these if he is not instructed about *E*'s definition of the stimulus dimensions. As Hovland (1952) pointed out, *E* and *S* must be using the same dimensions in order for an analysis of concept attainment to be performed; it is for this reason that the stimulus dimensions are described for *S* prior to his attempting the task. There have been exceptions to this practice with verbal concepts, but in these cases *E* has been interested in the effect of instructions (Underwood and Richardson, 1956b).

Presentation Methods. In any conceptual task, *E* will inform *S* of the category membership of a number of stimuli. With a selection procedure, *S* is allowed to choose the stimuli about which he will obtain information, whereas with a reception procedure, *E* controls which stimuli will be shown. When these procedures have been compared, the selection procedure has been found to result in faster concept attainment than the reception procedure (Duncan, 1964; Hunt, 1965). With the selection procedure, *S* is free to test any hypothesis that he chooses and can switch at any time to another, but the reception procedure forces *S* to adapt his hypothesis to the sequence of stimuli that *E* presents. As Hunt (1965) has noted, this difference requires that concept attainment be described as an active process of testing hypotheses rather than as a passive process of forming associations. As might be expected, when *E* desires to study the strategies that *S*s use in attaining concepts, the selection procedure is used.

Standard Reception Procedure. In a commonly used procedure, each trial consists of the following events: A stimulus is presented, *S* responds by indicating the category to which he thinks the stimulus belongs, and *E* provides some information (feedback) about the correctness of *S*'s response. One of the most important variables in this procedure is the percentage of trials on which feedback is given. Bourne and Pendleton (1958) found that decreasing the percentage of feedback trials resulted in slower attainment of the concept. In most studies feedback is provided on every trial. The completeness or amount of informative feedback also affects performance. For example, if *S* must sort stimuli into four categories and he makes an error in categorizing a stimulus, he will gain information if E says, "Wrong." However, he will gain more information if E tells him the correct category for that stimulus. The latter, more complete feedback produces faster concept attainment (Bourne and Pendleton, 1958).

Temporal Characteristics. Presentation methods differ in terms of the pacing of the task (that is, whether S may work at his own pace versus a pace established by E). Although Bourne, Guy, Dodd, and Justeen (1965) found no difference between control by S or by E of stimulus duration, it seems possible that performance might be impaired in some E-paced tasks. A certain minimum amount of time is required to perceive the stimulus; with S pacing, this is presumably guaranteed, but E might use too fast a pace for S to accomplish this accurately. In addition to variation in stimulus duration, we must also consider two other temporal intervals which can vary.

Feedback and Postfeedback Intervals. The time between S's response and the occurrence of feedback is called the *feedback interval*, whereas the time between the occurence of feedback and the presentation of the next stimulus is the *postfeedback interval*. The importance of variation in these intervals has been investigated, with the finding that the postfeedback interval is of greater importance. In a study by Bourne and Bunderson (1963), S could take as long as he wished to indicate which category he thought was correct for each stimulus, and his response removed the stimulus from view. In different conditions, Ss then had to wait from 0 to 8 sec. before they were informed of the correct response for that stimulus. Results indicated that the length of this delay had no effect on identification of the concept. Although we might expect that longer delays would impair performance, this study indicates that short feedback delays are ineffective.

During the postfeedback interval, S presumably assimilates the information he has received from both the stimulus presentation and feedback. Allowing more than a few seconds after feedback improves performance, but relatively long intervals (ca. 25 sec.) were inferior to moderate intervals (Bourne et al., 1965). These authors suggested that, because neither the stimulus nor the feedback were available during the postfeedback interval, S might begin to forget either or both when the interval became too long. This view was supported by the finding that when the stimulus remained in view during the postfeedback interval, performance improved and was directly related to the length of the postfeedback interval. Keeping the feedback in view had no effect. It should also be noted that providing more than the minimum postfeedback interval produces greater facilitation with more difficult problems. In addition to pointing to a role for forgetting in attaining concepts, these results also relate to the distinction between S- and E-paced procedures. It seems likely that Ss will allow themselves an optimum amount of time for information processing, but some E-paced procedures provide only very short postfeedback intervals (1 or 2 sec.).

Variations of the Reception Procedure. Although the procedure we have been discussing is the one most commonly used. other techniques are also employed. In one variation, the correct category is presented as each stimulus is shown, and S is required to name the concept. A further variation involves the presentation of a series of stimuli with category information that is sufficient to identify the correct concept. Only after the sequence has been presented is S required to respond, either by naming the concept or by categorizing new, test stimuli. Although these methods sometimes vary in pacing, their primary difference lies in what S is asked to do and when he is required to do it. This results in different kinds of information, which we discuss when considering measurement.

List-Learning Technique. A procedure that has been used primarily with verbal materials is basically the standard procedure for paired-associate learning. The entire procedure is automatically paced, usually at a fairly fast rate (for example, 2 sec.). As each stimulus is presented, S tries to give the correct response, after which the correct response is indicated. The main differences between this and the procedures we have previously examined are the use of complete E pacing, the definition of a trial in terms of presenting and responding to a number of stimuli, and, in most cases, the presentation of the same stimuli on successive trials. For example, a list of twenty-four words that can be placed in six categories might be used, with the entire list presented on each trial. Because repeated trials are given, S encounters the same stimulus more than once, which does not occur with the other procedure. The importance of this difference is related to the interpretation of response measures, which we will now consider.

Measurement. In concept attainment studies, three different measures have been used, based on correct categorizing responses, naming the concept, or identifying test stimuli. In comparing these we should keep in mind that concept attainment is considered to be something other than simple associative learning. Therefore, measures of concept attainment should rule out interpretations in terms of simple associative learning if the terms are to be distinct. If the measure is based on naming the concept or on the identification of new test stimuli, then simple associative interpretations are less applicable. This is clearly the case with naming the concept, because this response is different from the S-R pairings presented to S. Although it is possible to argue that test identifications simply reflect stimulus generalization, there is abundant evidence to indicate that any generalization occurring is not that found in simple learning situations.

Responses to Repeated Stimuli. The interpretation of correct responses depends on the method of stimulus presentation. If the response is to a stimulus not previously encountered (as in the studies by Bourne and his colleagues), it has the same characteristics as the identification of a test stimulus. It is when stimuli are repeated that correct responses may not reflect a process different from simple learning. Thus, using the paired-associate procedure, if S responds correctly to a word on trial n, this can reflect nothing more than his having learned that particular response to that particular stimulus. For this reason, S's responses are often scored by concepts rather than by individual stimuli; to be correct, S must respond correctly to all stimuli in the same class on the same trial.

Arbitrary Category Labels. Measurement is also affected by the number of categories that S must use. If two categories are involved, either they are arbitrarily labeled (say, a and b) or S is instructed to discover the name of one of the categories (for example, red squares), in which case stimuli are labeled as belonging or not belonging to the category to be named. We will consider some evidence later in the chapter which indicates that the two methods are not equivalent. If more than two categories are used, then all categories are given arbitrary labels by E; these may be letters, positions (of buttons or sorting boxes), or nonsense syllables. One problem with arbitrary labels is that some of S's efforts must be directed toward learning the labels, as opposed to learning the classification system that they represent. For example, if E is presenting stimuli that can be classed into four categories (red squares, red circles, blue squares, blue circles), these will be labeled in some fashion similar to a, b, c, and d. It is thus possible for S to have discovered the correct categorization system but to make errors because he has not learned the labels completely. (For example, he is not sure whether red squares are a or c and thus sometimes gives the wrong letter.) With simple labels this seems a minor problem, but more complicated labels can require S to devote a large portion of his time to learning them. Richardson and Bergum (1954) have shown that, when nonsense syllables are used as labels, approximately 85 per cent of the time S takes to respond perfectly is due to learning the nonsense syllables rather than identifying the underlying concepts. Because it is concept attainment that is under study, every attempt should be made to reduce the influence of the particular labels that E imposes. In this respect, requiring S to name the concept itself should be used wherever possible.

Conceptual Rules

Concept attainment is essentially the process of discovering or learning the system of classification that has been applied to a population of stimuli. There are numerous ways in which the same stimuli can be classified in accordance with different conceptual rules. We will now consider both the logical status and the relative difficulty of the various rules that have been used in conceptual tasks. This presentation is by no means complete, because we will examine only the more "popular" rules. In discussing the various rules, we are dealing with a situation in which only two categories are involved, with each stimulus either belonging ($+$) or not belonging ($-$) to the category named by the rule. In Table 11-2, the category assignments are based on the relevant attributes *red* and *square*; for purposes of assignment, each stimulus pattern is either red (R) or not red ($\bar{R}$), square (S) or not square ($\bar{S}$).

The rules which describe the various assignments differ in the number of relevant attributes involved (one or two) and in the proportion or the stimulus population that is assigned to the positive category. Although the rules can be stated in terms of symbolic logic, we will use the verbal statement of each rule.

Table **11-2**   Five Conceptual Rules: Methods of Assigning Stimuli to Two Categories

	Stimuli			
Rules	RS	RT($R\bar{S}$)	GS($\bar{R}$S)	GT($\bar{R}\bar{S}$)
Affirmative	$+$	$+$	$-$	$-$
Conjunctive Inclusive	$+$	$-$	$-$	$-$
Disjunctive	$+$	$+$	$+$	$-$
Exclusive Disjunctive	$-$	$+$	$+$	$-$
Conditional	$+$	$-$	$+$	$+$

NOTE. The following abbreviations are used: S = square, T = triangle, R = red, and G = green. The abbreviations in parentheses refer to the logical descriptions of the stimuli. (Adapted with permission from Haygood, R. C., & Bourne, L. E., Jr. Attribute-and-rule learning aspects of conceptual behavior. *Psychol. Rev.*, 1965, **72**, 175–195.)

The *affirmative* rule involves only a single relevant attribute (red); its statement is that all red patterns belong to the concept. Such concepts are most commonly used by associative theorists, probably because they are amenable to associative description. Another frequently used type of rule is the *conjunctive*, which is based on the joint presence of both relevant attributes; only red squares belong to the concept. Notice that, with two-level dimensions, only one-quarter of the stimuli are positive under this rule, which suggests that identifying the concept will depend heavily on encountering positive stimuli. In contrast to this, the *inclusive disjunctive* rule places only one-quarter of the stimuli in the negative category, because all patterns that are red, or square, or both belong to the concept. In this case, we would suspect that encountering negative instances would be very important for identifying the concept.

For the last two rules, stimuli in the positive category do not share common attributes to any great degree. The *exclusive disjunctive* rule states that the concept includes all patterns that are either red or square but not both. The *conditional* rule states that, if a pattern is red, then it must be square to belong to the concept. Notice that, under this rule, patterns having both relevant attributes (RS) and those having neither (R̄S̄) are in the same positive category.

Differences in Rule Difficulty. The preceding and other rules have been compared with all types of conceptual tasks. It has frequently been found that conjunctive concepts are easier to identify than disjunctive concepts (for example, Conant and Trabasso, 1964; Wallace and Sechrest, 1961), and conditional concepts are more difficult than either (Haygood and Bourne, 1965; Neisser and Weene, 1962). It has been suggested that the various rules form a hierarchy based on the complexity of the logical operations involved, and the initial order of difficulty corresponds to this hierarchy (Neisser and Weene, 1962). However, using different logical operators to describe the rules does not result in a hierarchy (Hunt, 1962), and it has been proposed that the differences in difficulty reflect the *S*s' lack of experience with certain rules (for example, exclusive disjunctive, conditional). This is supported by the finding that differences among rules are reduced as *S*s gain more experience in using the rules (Haygood and Bourne, 1965; Wells, 1963). *With sufficient experience, S presumably would be equally facile in using any conceptual rule.*

Rule Familiarity. The notion that rule differences in difficulty reflect differential familiarity indicates the applicability of problem-solving findings to conceptual tasks. In the previous chapter, we reviewed much evidence indicating the strong effect of response frequency on problem difficulty. In this context, certain conceptual rules (for example, affirmative, conjunctive) are more frequently encountered than others and thus are easier to use. Hunt and Hovland (1960) suggested that college-student *S*s will ap-

proach any conceptual task as conjunctive and persist in this attack until it proves ineffective. It has been found that when both conjunctive and disjunctive rules are applicable, *S*s give conjunctive solutions. Appropriate training increases the strength of disjunctive solutions (Wells, 1963).

In addition to considering the overall difficulty of conceptual rules, it is important to note the limitations of our knowledge of the effects of most variables on concept attainment. Most studies have used conjunctive concepts with attribute-identification tasks, and we should not assume that variables will have identical effects with different rules or different tasks. Such generalizations must be tested in future research; our limited information to date indicates that the effects of certain variables do change when a different type of concept is used.

Definition of Terms

In describing conceptual tasks, certain terms have been used repeatedly, and it will be helpful to review their definitions. The stimuli to be categorized are described in terms of dimensions; with geometric forms, these are usually such dimensions as size, position, shape, color, and number. Not all dimensions are used in forming categories; those dimensions important for defining the concept are called relevant, those not used are irrelevant. The particular values on a dimension are called attributes. For example, a stimulus might be described as having the attributes of redness, a value on the dimension of color.

When the task involves just two categories and *S* must give the name of one of these categories, additional terms are used. Stimuli belonging to the category to be named are termed positive instances, whereas those not belonging are called negative instances. The particular attributes used to describe the positive category are described as relevant; this terminology was used in Table 11-2.

Goals of Research

Attaining a concept consists of discovering the method by which stimuli are assigned to categories. Our interest lies in identifying the variables affecting the difficulty of solving this problem and in describing how Ss perform this task, just as in studying the simpler problems of the previous chapter. However, for conceptual behavior, emphasis shifts somewhat. Prior learning is obviously important, as we have seen in considering conceptual rules, and the effect of familiarity will appear at numerous points throughout the chapter. The major differences between this and the previous chapter are that much greater stress is placed on the way in which E provides information about the concept, in contrast to relatively little emphasis on methods of presenting simple problems, and that much more is known about the process of concept attainment.

To state this differently, our survey of the literature will consider the effects of prior experience, stimulus factors, and transfer between concepts. The reader will discover that the section on stimulus information is fairly long, reflecting the importance of this manipulation. Furthermore, there are two sections devoted to processes in concept attainment—namely, the role of memory and strategies, topics only hinted at in our study of simple problems. The attainment of concepts is obviously complex behavior, and it is hoped that our survey will give just credit to researchers' efforts to understand this process.

Concept Dominance

Associative theorists view concept attainment as the formation of a common mediating response to a number of stimuli. A logical variable to manipulate is thus the strength of this mediating response to

instances of the same class. Underwood and Richardson (1956a) developed materials suitable for such a manipulation by measuring the frequencies of occurrence of various *sense-impression* responses to object names. Their Ss were instructed to give a single response to each word, and the dominance of the response is defined in terms of the percentage of Ss giving that response. For example, to the stimulus word *cigar*, 40 per cent said *smelly*, 26 per cent said *brown*, 14 per cent said *long*, and so on. Another technique for measuring dominance involves providing S with a number of sense-impression categories and having him indicate those which apply to each stimulus word (Mayzner, Tresselt, and Blaesing, 1961). In comparison to the associational technique, the judgmental method yields higher dominance values and provides measures for categories of lower dominance (Crouse, 1967). This results because the sense impressions are provided for S and because S is allowed to give a multiple response to each word (compared to just one in the associational method). The judgmental method thus appears to give a more complete description of the dominance of various sense impressions.

Effects of Dominance. It has been repeatedly found that concept attainment is more rapid as the dominance of the correct response increases (for example, Coleman, 1964; Underwood and Richardson, 1956b). In a deviation from the usual paired-associate procedure, Crouse and Duncan (1963) identified the categories by showing S sample instances and required him to sort test instances into the categories defined by the samples. The accuracy of sorting increased with increasing dominance of both the sample and the test instances.

Further research has been directed toward refining our knowledge of the effects of dominance. Mednick and Halpern (1962) compared concepts equal in dominance but differing in *rank*. That is, a particular sense impression might be given by the same percentage of *S*s to two words, but it might be the most frequent response to one word (Rank 1) but only the second most frequent to the other (Rank 2). They found that Rank 1 concepts were attained more readily than Rank 2 concepts. This result raises a question previously encountered in discussing problem solving, namely, how to measure the strength of a response. Dominance is a frequency measure and affects concept attainment when rank is held constant. (Responses, regardless of dominance, are always the most frequent reaction to the stimulus word in the studies mentioned.) On the other hand, concept attainment is affected by the number of stronger responses (0 to 1 for Ranks 1 and 2) when dominance is controlled. This suggests that the strength of a response is a function of both its absolute frequency (dominance) and the number of stronger responses (rank). To date, these two factors have not been compared in a single study.

Speed of attainment also varies with the distribution of dominance within a class (Freedman and Mednick, 1958). That is, two concepts may have equal dominance, but the words in one class may have more similar dominance values than those in the other. For example, with percentages of 45, 40, and 35, the mean dominance is 40, the same as for 65, 40, and 15. Concepts with greater variance in dominance are attained more rapidly, because the inclusion of a very high-dominance member primes the concept response to the instances of lower dominance.

It is obvious that each word elicits more than one sense impression, and it would be expected that if words in different classes shared an irrelevant response, attainment of the concepts would be more difficult. This is in fact the case (Underwood, 1957). In the complement of this statement, concept attainment is facilitated when words not belonging to a given class elicit responses very different from those required for class members (Duncan, 1965; Kendler and Karasik, 1958).

Acquisition of Dominance. Although the preceding studies have used normative materials, Thysell and Schulz (1964) have shown that similar effects occur when associations are established in the laboratory. With nonsense materials, the amount of training with *relevant* and *interfering* associations was varied. To illustrate, the associations *long* and *soft* were established to the stimulus *kalab*, *long* and *thin* to *fetor*, *deep* and *soft* to *hydrax*, *deep* and *thin* to *bezel*. During subsequent concept identification, the categories were *long* and *deep*, thus *soft* and *thin* were interfering associations. Conceptual sorting was facilitated by greater strength of relevant associations and impaired by greater strength of interfering associations.

Preference and Obviousness. With geometric stimuli the relative dominance of different dimensions has not been systematically investigated, although Pishkin (1961) found that *S*s perform better when the concept is based on their preferred dimension (measured independently). One fairly common finding is an order of increasing difficulty for object, form, and number concepts (for example, Heidbreder, 1948; Carlson, 1962), although this is not always the case (Grant and Curran, 1952). Although these differences have sometimes been attributed to variation in the "abstractness" of the concept, they might reflect differences in dominance. A further reason for dimensional differences is the *obviousness* of the dimension. That is, a color dimension consisting of red, green, and blue is more obvious than one consisting of pink, red, and orange. Archer (1962) found that increasing the obviousness of relevant dimensions facilitated performance, but increasing the obviousness of irrelevant dimensions impaired performance. Differences between dimensions are quite often reported and probably reflect differences in dominance and/or obviousness. Both preference and dominance effects illustrate the role of prior learning in concept attainment.

Stimulus Information

Variation in stimulus information can involve changing either the stimulus population, the concept to be attained, or the particular stimuli that S is shown. In the first two cases we are concerned with the amount of relevant and irrelevant information that S must deal with, whereas the last topic refers to differences between positive and negative instances.

Amount of Information

An increase in the number of dimensions on which stimuli vary results in a larger stimulus population and thus requires S to deal with more information in attaining the concept. When adding dimensions, the number of values per dimension is held constant, usually at two values per dimension. It has been consistently found that increasing the number of irrelevant dimensions produces a linear decrement in performance (for example, Bulgarella and Archer, 1962; Bourne, 1957; Walker and Bourne, 1961). These studies used either affirmative or conjunctive concepts, but Haygood and Stevenson (1967) found that the linear effect holds also for conditional and disjunctive concepts. However, the magnitude of the effect varies with the difficulty of the conceptual rule (Figure 11-1). As the rule becomes more difficult, increasing irrelevant dimensions produces greater decrements in performance.

Haygood and Stevenson also found the effect to vary with the task, with increasing irrelevant information impairing complete learning most and rule learning least, with attribute identification affected to an intermediate degree (Figure 11-2). It is reasonable that rule learning should be unaffected by irrelevant information, because the relevant attributes are designated for S prior to the task. With the other tasks, S must discover which dimensions are relevant, thus encountering greater difficulty

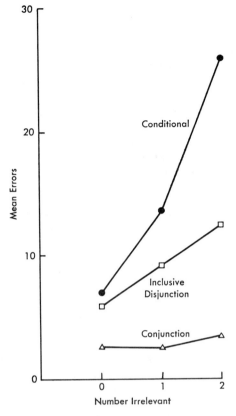

Figure 11-1. Effects of increasing number of irrelevant dimensions for each of three conceptual rules. (Reprinted with permission from Haygood, R. C., & Stevenson, N. Effect of number of irrelevant dimensions in nonconjunctive concept learning. *J. exp. Psychol.*, 1967, **74**, 302–304.)

as the number of dimensions (thus the number of possibilities) increases.

Because increasing the number of relevant dimensions (holding irrelevant information constant) also increases the number of dimensions, similar effects might be expected. Bulgarella and Archer (1962) and Schvaneveldt (1966) confirmed this expectation, finding linear decrements in performance with increasing relevant information. However, Walker and Bourne (1961) found a disproportionate increase in difficulty as the number of relevant dimensions increased. As Bourne (1966) has

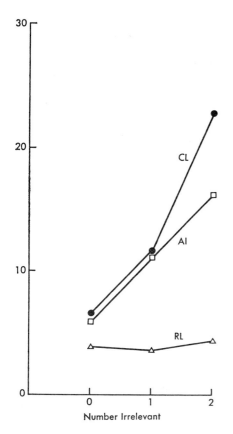

Figure 11-2. Effects of increasing number of irrelevant dimensions for each of three instrumental conditions. (Reprinted with permission from Haygood, R. C., & Stevenson, N. Effect of number of irrelevant dimensions in nonconjunctive concept learning. *J. exp. Psychol.*, 1967, **74**, 302–304.)

of task. There is another way in which the size of the stimulus population can be increased, without changing the number of dimensions. The number of values on each dimension can be increased, producing a direct increase in difficulty (Battig and Bourne, 1961). *Any increase in the size of the stimulus population, either within or between dimensions, impairs attainment of the concept.*

Redundant Information

In discussing the amount of information presented, the dimensions used are orthogonal to each other. That is, each value on a dimension is paired with every value on every other dimension. When certain dimensional values do not observe this rule, some information will be redundant. For example, if squares are always red, triangles always blue, and circles always green, adding the color dimension to the size dimension does not increase the size of the stimulus population and thus provides redundant information. To state this differently, when dimensions overlap in this manner, some stimulus patterns are missing. (There are no green squares, for example.) The amount of redundancy is directly related to the number of overlapping dimensions.

Relevant Redundancy. The overlapping dimensions may either be relevant or irrelevant to attainment of the concept. To illustrate the role of relevant stimulus redundancy, assume that *S* must identify a simple affirmative concept based on shape (square or circle). If the redundant dimension of color is added to shape, the resulting patterns might be red square and blue circle. Notice that with redundancy *S* can solve the concept using either shape or color, because *either dimension leads to the same categorization.* Bourne and Haygood (1959, 1961) and Haygood and Bourne (1967) found that increasing the number

suggested, the probable reason for this difference is that Walker and Bourne increased the number of categories with the number of relevant dimensions, whereas the other investigators held this constant. Increasing the number of categories thus increased difficulty in addition to the effect of number of dimensions.

It thus appears that increasing the number of dimensions (relevant or irrelevant) directly impairs concept identification. The magnitude of the effect varies with the type of concept and with the type of redundant relevant dimensions facilitated performance and that facilitation was greater as the number of independent irrelevant dimensions increased. Peterson (1962) also found increasing relevant redundancy to facilitate concept attainment, noting that few Ss reported the presence of more than one relevant dimension. This suggests that with relevant redundancy, S merely selects one of the redundant dimensions and categorizes on that basis. Because the task is perfectly solvable with no redundancy and because Ss appear not to notice the redundant dimensions, one might wonder how redundancy results in better performance.

Let us assume that the basic task involves one relevant and three irrelevant (and independent) dimensions. If S selects a dimension and tests to determine if it will result in correct categorizations, the chances are 1 in 4 that he will initially select the correct relevant dimension. If two redundant dimensions are added to the relevant dimension, there are now six dimensions, and any one of three will result in correct categorization. Thus, S's chances of selecting a correct dimension are noticeably increased. Furthermore, S is very unlikely to try a new dimension after he finds a correct one, which would account for S not noticing the redundancy.

Irrelevant Redundancy. When the redundant dimensions are irrelevant to attainment of the concept, increasing redundancy results in *impaired* performance. However, the impairment is not as great as when the number of independent irrelevant dimensions is increased. This seems to imply that Ss notice the redundancy and eliminate redundant irrelevant dimensions as a group. It would be interesting to determine if this explanation would be supported by Ss' postexperimental reports, which seems quite likely. Trying one of the redundant dimensions would result in failure, and S would try a different dimension. If this were also a redundant dimension, S might notice

that his categorizations are wrong in the same way as before, check for redundancy, and eliminate the redundant dimensions altogether.

Positive and Negative Information

We have seen earlier that E can provide information about the concept either by presenting stimuli which belong to the concept (positive instances) or by showing stimuli which do not belong (negative instances). There has been a considerable amount of research devoted to comparing the effectiveness of these two types of information, some of which involves comparisons of strategies, which we will consider later.

A thorough analysis of the informational characteristics of positive and negative information was made by Hovland (1952), and we will consider the highlights of his discussion. The primary consideration is whether positive and negative instances are equally informative, and they usually are not. Roughly speaking, the information value of a stimulus is inversely related to the proportion of the stimulus population in its class. Thus, as fewer stimuli are included in a concept, the information value of a positive instance increases and the value of a negative instance decreases. To illustrate this, assume that we are dealing with a population of stimuli consisting of all possible combinations of size (large or small), color (red or blue), and shape (circle or square).

Instances of Affirmative Concepts. If the concept to be identified is affirmative, there are six attributes that could be used as the concept label. With such a concept, positive and negative instances are equally informative. If S sees a large blue circle and is told that it belongs to the concept, there are three possibilities remaining, *large*, *blue*, or *circle*. In similar fashion, if S sees a small red square and is told that it does not belong, again the remaining possibilities are *large*, *blue*, or *circle*. Notice that the remaining possible answers are present in a positive instance but must be inferred from what is not present in a negative instance. Some investigators believe that this difference should be reflected in *S*s' greater difficulty in using information from negative instances, because a "two-step" operation is involved.

Instances of Conjunctive Concepts. With conjunctive concepts, positive instances provide more information that negative instances. For our sample stimulus population, there are twelve possible conjunctive concepts with two relevant attributes. Showing a large blue circle as a positive instance leaves three possibilities (*large circle*, *blue circle*, *large blue figure*). In contrast showing a small red square as negative eliminates only three alternatives (*small square*, *red square*, and *small red figure* must be wrong). A consequence of this difference is that more negative instances must be presented to eliminate all but the correct concept. In this example, five negative instances would be required, but only two positive instances.

Disjunctive Concepts and Negative Instances. The informational difference can be reversed by using a concept in which most stimuli belong, such as the inclusive disjunction (refer to Table 11-2). There are again twelve possible answers at the outset (*red* or *square* or both, *blue* or *circle* or both, *large* or *red* or both, and so on). If a large blue square is presented as a positive instance, only three possibilities are eliminated (*red* or *circle* or both, *red* or *small* or both, *small* or *circle* or both). But, presenting a large red square as a negative instance eliminates nine possibilities, leaving only three (*small* or *blue* or both, *small* or *circle* or both, *blue* or *circle* or both). *Fewer negative instances would be required to specify the concept*, and one would expect that concept attainment would be facilitated by showing negative instances.

Two additional points should be considered before examining the findings. First, positive instances may contain only some of the relevant attributes under certain conceptual rules. With affirmative concepts there is only one relevant attribute, and each positive instance must possess it. Similarly, positive instances of a conjunctive concept must contain both relevant attributes. With disjunctive concepts, however, a positive instance may contain only one of the relevant attributes. For example, a large blue circle belongs to the concept *large* or *red* or both, but does not exemplify both attributes. Therefore, with disjunctive concepts there are two kinds of positive instances—those with both relevant attributes and those with only one. The second point is that it is quite likely that *S*s encounter primarily positive instances in acquiring the concepts they learn prior to entering the laboratory. This experience might result in biases favoring positive instances. Evidence on this point will be presented shortly.

Experimental Evidence. With conjunctive concepts, presenting positive instances leads to better performance than presenting negative instances (Freiburgs and Tulving, 1961; Hovland and Weiss, 1953). This result holds even when equal numbers of positive and negative instances are used, with equal information. In addition, presenting a mixed series of positive and negative instances results in an intermediate level of performance (Hovland and Weiss, 1953). The superior utilization of information from positive instances probably reflects differential transfer from previous concept learning. This is supported by Freiburgs and Tulving's (1961) finding that the difference between positive and negative instances decreases with practice (Figure 11-3). Fryatt and Tulving (1963) have similarly demonstrated that the advantage of all positive instances over mixed presentation can be reduced by practice.

With a simple affirmative concept,

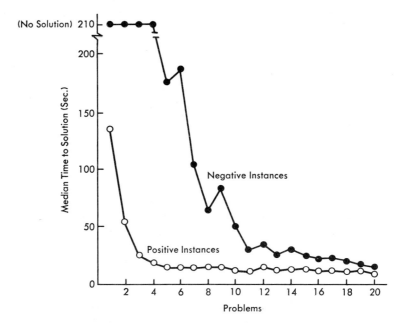

Figure 11-3. Median time to solution of twenty consecutive problems for Ss working with only positive or only negative instances. (Reprinted with permission from Freiburgs, V., & Tulving, E. The effect of practice on utilization of information from positive and negative instances in concept identification. *Canad. J. Psychol.*, 1961, **15**, 101–106.)

Huttenlocher (1962) found positive series superior to negative series, but one kind of mixed series was best of all. Each stimulus series contained only two instances, and best performance occurred when a positive instance followed a negative instance. Because the series was shorter than those used by Hovland and Weiss, and because Huttenlocher's Ss were seventh-graders rather than college students, the difference in results need not be due to a change in conceptual rule. Further research is clearly needed.

There has been little research on this topic with disjunctive concepts. Suggestive evidence has been reported, however, based on studies using the selection procedure. Before S begins selecting instances for testing, E presents an initial instance to start the task. Wallace and Sechrest (1961) found that a positive initial instance facilitated the attainment of conjunctive concepts, but that disjunctive concept at-

tainment was unaffected by the type of initial instance. Wells and Watson (1965) did find that a negative initial instance facilitated attainment of a disjunctive concept, the only type included in their study.

Proportion of Positive Instances. When S is shown both positive and negative instances, the relative proportions can be varied. With conjunctive concepts, Schvaneveldt (1966) has shown that rate of learning is directly related to the proportion of positive instances in a stimulus series. In a study by Mayzner (1962), a sense-impression concept was identified by a variable number of positive instances, and S was required to select a word that matched the concept. As more positive instances were presented, correct matching took less time. Haygood and Devine (1967) found that attainment of biconditional and disjunctive concepts was unaffected by the proportion of positive instances in a series. However, increasing the number of stimuli with both relevant attributes facilitated performance when the proportion of positive instances was held constant.

No general statement can be made regarding the relative effectiveness of positive and negative information. Differences in both information value and effectiveness vary with the type of concept, and the previous experience of S is an important factor. In addition there are some ambiguities with respect to the effects of mixing positive and negative instances. Thus, one must have considerable qualifying information before an accurate statement can be made.

Other Stimulus Characteristics

Variation in stimulus information has almost exclusively involved geometric patterns. These stimuli encompass all dimensions in a single compact figure. From an informational viewpoint, stimulus attributes need not be presented in such fashion; a sequence of six pluses and minuses is equivalent to a geometric form with six attributes. Bourne and Parker (1964) compared unitary figures and distributed displays and found that attainment of a conjunctive concept was more difficult with distributed arrays. Although Laughlin (1965) did not find a difference in difficulty between displays, he did observe greater use of certain strategies with unitary stimulus patterns. Wells (1965) found that when both conjunctive and disjunctive solutions were possible, more conjunctive solutions were given with unitary patterns, but more disjunctive solutions were given with distributed arrays. It thus appears that the way in which visual stimulus information is presented can influence conceptual behavior, although it is not certain that difficulty of concept attainment will be affected.

Relatively little work has included auditory dimensions, but there is some suggestion that auditory and visual dimensions are not equivalent. Lordahl (1961) found that increasing the number of irrelevant auditory dimensions did not impair performance as much as visual irrelevant information does. It was suggested that Ss were less attentive to auditory stimuli. Haygood (1965) found that concepts with relevant visual and auditory dimensions were more difficult than concepts involving only one kind of information. This was attributed to Ss lack of familiarity with audiovisual concepts. Another possibility is that auditory dimensions are less salient or obvious than visual dimensions; to date, little is known on this issue.

The Role of Memory

Concept attainment typically involves the presentation of a number of stimuli over time, and S's probability of responding correctly to any stimulus depends on what he has learned and now remembers from a previous stimulus presentation. What S remembers might be either the attributes of prior stimuli and their classifications or some coded form of this information (his hypotheses). For example, if S uses stimuli to evaluate hypotheses, then he might remember which hypotheses are still tenable and thus need not remember the attributes of prior stimuli. Of course, some combination of these approaches might be used.

Availability of Prior Information

Assuming that S must remember some stimulus information over a series of stimuli, Cahill and Hovland (1960) compared two methods of presentation. With successive presentation, each stimulus was removed as the next stimulus was presented; with simultaneous presentation, stimuli were never removed. Each time a new stimulus was shown, S was required to guess what the concept was. Performance was much superior in the simultaneous condition, and there was strong evidence of memory errors in the successive condition. *Guesses about the concept tended to be incompatible with information contained in previously presented stimuli, and this tendency increased with the remoteness of the stimuli.* That is, S's guess when the ninth stimulus was shown (alone) was least likely to be incompatible with that stimulus' information, more likely to contradict the information in the fifth stimulus, and most likely to contradict the first stimulus' information. This study established both the overall impairment of increased memory load and the loss of stimulus information as a function of the number of following instances. Hunt (1961), using a different method, also found the forgetting of stimulus information to be directly related to the number of subsequent stimuli presented, whereas the number of preceding stimuli had no effect.

Bourne, Goldstein, and Link (1964) noted that simultaneous and successive presentation represented the end points of stimulus availability. In their studies, from nought to ten prior stimuli were allowed to remain in view (for example, in condition 2, when the eighth stimulus was shown, stimuli 6 and 7 were also in view). When S was allowed an unlimited amount of time to respond, greater availability resulted in a linear improvement in performance. With limited time, greater availability first facilitated then impaired somewhat the attainment of the concept. The authors suggested that S had difficulty assimilating all the information in front of him during the short interval.

When S is required to classify each stimulus as it is presented, the instances remaining available may have been either correctly or incorrectly responded to. Pishkin and Wolfgang (1965) found that increasing the availability of incorrectly

sorted instances has no effect on performance, but greater availability of correctly sorted stimuli facilitated attainment of the concept. In this study, if S responded incorrectly in classifying a stimulus, he was not told what the correct response was. Performance is greatly facilitated if this is done (Bourne and Pendleton, 1958; Pishkin, 1967). As a final point on availability, facilitation is much greater as the difficulty of the concept increases (Bourne et al., 1964).

Contiguity of Instances

We have already seen that stimulus information is forgotten as additional stimuli are presented (provided that earlier stimuli are removed). In a related discussion, Underwood (1952) proposed that the ease of attaining concepts is directly related to the contiguity with which instances of the same category occur. The underlying notion is that attaining the concept requires determining the common properties of the class members. As the separation of instances of the same class increases, it becomes less likely that S will remember sufficiently well to discern the common characteristics, thus performance should suffer. It is clear that this prediction is intended to apply to affirmative and conjunctive concepts, in which category members do share common attributes, and research has been restricted to such concepts. A further point to remember is that when instances of the same class are separated, instances from other classes fill the interval.

Effect of Contiguity. The prediction has been tested with both geometric stimuli and verbal materials. Kurtz and Hovland (1956) presented eight instances from each of four categories in either a mixed (low-contiguity) or unmixed (high-contiguity) order. Following this, Ss were required to name the concepts and to identify test instances; although the differences were not large, the high-contiguity presentation resulted in superior performance on both measures. Using the reception procedure in which S attempts to categorize each stimulus as it is presented, both Newman (1956) and Bourne and Jennings (1963) supported the contiguity prediction. In the latter study, five degrees of contiguity were employed, and performance was directly related to the degree of contiguity. Using sense-impression concepts, Schultz, Miller, and Radtke (1963) found performance directly related to contiguity over three levels. The superiority of high-contiguity presentation has thus been demonstrated with both verbal and geometric stimuli.

Alternative Interpretations. Although the effects of contiguity are reliable, there have been some questions concerning their interpretation. One proposal is that although high contiguity might reduce stimulus forgetting, it also provides S with additional information about responding (Dominowski, 1965). With the exception of the Kurtz and Hovland (1956) study, the order of presenting stimuli and the order of testing S's responses have been confounded such that, with high contiguity, the same response is correct several times in succession. It is possible that S would become aware of such response sequences and change his behavior accordingly. The distinction should be made clear; the facilitation resulting from higher contiguity might be due (at least in part) to the additional information about responding that S receives as contiguity increases, rather than to less forgetting of stimulus attributes. The point is that S might guess some correct responses; because S typically receives more information from a correct response, this would facilitate performance. Support for this idea stems from the finding that when one category occurs disproportionately often in a sequence of stimulus presentations, S begins to guess that category more often (Grier and Bornstein, 1966; Mandler, Cowan, and Gold, 1964).

Some recent studies in the writer's laboratory lend support to this idea, although the evidence is not completely clear. When differential responding cues are eliminated (by using the same testing procedure for all levels of contiguity), high contiguity still facilitates the identification of conjunctive categories for geometric forms, although the contiguity effect is slightly greater when differential responding cues are allowed to exist. However, varying contiguity had no effect on the acquisition of sense-impression concepts. These results suggest that the advantage of high contiguity in identifying categories based on perceptible stimulus attributes is independent of differential responding cues, but they cast some doubt on contiguity effects for verbal concepts based on common associates.

Another explanation suggests that contiguity effects may be due not to differences in forgetting, but to differences in the quality of stimulus information that S receives. With high contiguity, successive stimuli belong to the same category, and it is clear that any attributes which change are irrelevant to the concept. In contrast, with low contiguity, successive stimuli belong to different categories, and if several attributes change, it is not clear which are relevant and which are irrelevant. Anderson (1966) has demonstrated that concept attainment is impaired when successive stimuli in different categories differ on both relevant and irrelevant dimensions. Therefore, although high contiguity presentation will usually facilitate concept attainment, we cannot be sure that this is the result of reduced forgetting of stimulus attributes.

Distribution of Practice

A second prediction based on Underwood's (1952) position is that forgetting should occur over time (without introducing "irrelevant" stimuli during the interval). There is some validity to this idea, because, as we have seen, long postfeedback intervals seem to produce forgetting of stimulus information. Underwood's specific prediction concerned the effects of varying the time between trials; in this context, a trial refers to the presentation of a number of stimuli. As the time between trials increases, more forgetting should occur, and attainment of the concept should be impaired. During the intertrial interval, S is kept from rehearsing or processing information in any way, but no unrelated learning materials are given.

No test has supported this prediction, with the typical finding indicating no effect of variation in the intertrial interval (Brown and Archer, 1956; Oseas and Underwood, 1952; Richardson and Bergum, 1954). There is a limitation on these findings, that all of these studies involved more than two categories and thus arbitrary category labels. Because Richardson and Bergum have found that up to 85 per cent of the learning time may be devoted to learning the labels, the tests may not have been sufficiently sensitive.

Stimulus Recall

In all of the preceding studies, forgetting has been inferred either from differences in overall performance or from the kinds of errors that Ss make. There has been one study in which stimulus recall was measured. Trabasso and Bower (1964) presented a series of six stimuli sufficient to define a unique, affirmative concept; Ss were then asked to name the concept and to recall the attributes of each stimulus. The studies of memory errors would lead us to expect that accuracy of recall would increase from the first- to last-presented stimulus. However, Trabasso and Bower obtained a function typical in serial learning; recall was best for the first stimulus, decreased, then increased for the last two stimuli. There are several possible reasons for this discrepancy. Ss were instructed that a test for stimulus

recall would be given and were run through the procedure repeatedly; neither of these conditions held in the study of memory errors (Cahill and Hovland, 1960; Hunt, 1961). Also, the rate of presentation was much faster in the Trabasso and Bower experiment; although the concept was simple (affirmative), performance was not very high. Finally, memory errors may not be due to forgetting stimulus attributes, although this seems quite unlikely.

Suggested Analyses. It should be clear that forgetting plays an important role in concept attainment, even though specifying the precise function is not yet accomplished. Perhaps the emphasis should be placed on remembering, to describe an active process of encoding stimulus information. Restle and Emmerich (1966) have shown that Ss remember stimulus attributes as well as their current working hypothesis, as evidenced by their performance after errors. An error leads S to discard his hypothesis, yet his performance on a subsequent trial far exceeds that predicted by a "no-stimulus-memory" model. These authors believe that a short term memory process is operating, probably involving verbal encoding of stimulus attributes; in addition, they noted the similarity of their results to those on memory span. This illustrates the possibility of a very fruitful line of research. The subprocesses of concept attainment have been studied, in various degrees of isolation, independently of research on concept attainment. The data and theories for short-term memory (for both visual and verbal information) as well as for information processing generally need to be related to concept attainment; Posner (1965) has suggested some promising approaches.

Strategies

We have seen that concept attainment is impaired by increasing memory requirements during the task, and the suggestion has been made that S actively processes information in reaching a solution. A strategy is a systematic plan for obtaining information, which can reduce the memory load (Bruner, Goodnow, and Austin, 1956). The kinds of strategies that S might adopt vary with both the type of concept and the presentation method (selection or reception). To some extent differences in performance observed when concepts and methods are changed might be due to the efficacy with which certain strategies can be used.

Identification of Strategies

The pioneering effort in the study of strategies was made by Bruner et. al. (1956), who identified possible strategies. The underlying assumption is that S tests hypotheses in attaining the concept and that his strategy is directed toward eliminating all but the correct hypothesis. When S is allowed to select instances for testing, there are two basic strategies, focusing and scanning. (Similar strategies hold for the reception procedure.)

Conservative Focusing. A conservative focusing strategy consists of finding a positive instance, then choosing stimuli that differ in only one attribute from the focus instance to determine if a change in category occurs. It should be noted that this refers primarily to attaining a conjunctive concept having two categories, positive and negative. Assume that a large red open circle is found to be positive. A conservative focuser might then select a small red open circle for testing. If this is positive, then the size of the figure must be irrelevant to the concept; if this is negative, then size must be relevant. Under this strategy each card choice would differ in only one attribute from the focus instance. Thus, S starts with an all-encompassing hypothesis (all attributes of the positive instance) and refines his hypothesis by eliminating attributes.

Focus Gambling. A variation of focusing is called focus gambling. With this strategy, S changes two or more attributes in selecting an instance. For example, an instance differing in both size and color might be chosen. If this is also a positive instance, then both attributes are eliminated as irrelevant. The gamble involves the possibility of a category change; if the selected instance is negative, S does not know if one or both of the changed attributes are relevant. There is thus somewhat greater risk involved.

Simultaneous Scanning. The other major strategy is scanning. In simultaneous scanning, S uses each instance to determine which hypotheses are still tenable and which have been eliminated. For example, if a large red open circle is positive, the following two-valued, conjunctive concepts are tenable: large red, large open, large circle, red open, red circle, open circle. An instance is then selected to eliminate as many of these as possible; all remaining hypotheses must be evaluated as each new stimulus is encountered. Bruner et al. (1956) believe that this strategy imposes greater cognitive strain than focusing, because S must remember possible hypotheses and test an instance against all of them.

Successive Scanning. Successive scanning involves choosing one of the possible hypotheses and selecting an instance to test that hypothesis only. For example, S might pick *large red* as his hypothesis, then select large red stimuli (varying on all other attributes) to see if they are positive. Once he encounters a negative instance, that hypothesis is eliminated, and another must be tried. Of course, there is no requirement that S either test all hypotheses or just one, because he might test any number in between. Restle (1962) has considered the possible performance differences associated with the number of hypotheses tested at one time. With the assumptions that S remembers only the hypothesis he is currently testing and that when his current set does not lead to correct categorizations, he draws a new sample (with replacement) from the universe of hypotheses, the number of hypotheses that S samples makes no difference. These assumptions imply that S, once his current hypotheses are abandoned, is back at the beginning of the problem. We will return to this issue shortly.

Relations Among Response Measures. Before considering research on strategies, one further point must be emphasized. Three response processes have been described for concept attainment, strategies, hypotheses, and categorizing responses. A minimal assumption is that Ss' categorizing responses reflect their hypotheses. When this has been tested, the assumption has most often been verified (O'Connell, 1965; Schwartz, 1966); Ss' hypotheses and categorizing responses are closely related in conceptual tasks. The relative effectiveness of different strategies is an empirical matter, because various ways of testing hypotheses need not be differentially difficult (as indicated by common performance measures).

Comparison of Strategies

Bruner et al. (1956) compared focusers and scanners under both selection and reception procedures, systematically finding that focusers attain concepts more readily. Bourne (1963, 1965) has replicated and extended these findings. In his studies, poorer Ss (compared to better Ss) adopted initial hypotheses having fewer attributes included, more often failed to change their hypotheses after categorization errors and made more complex changes in hypotheses. Similar results have been reported by Peterson and Colavita (1964). It is thus well established that Ss who (for unknown reasons) begin with an encompassing hypothesis and test the relevance or irrelevance of attributes will be more successful in attaining a concept. Wickelgren (1964) has shown that attribute testing can be made more likely

by appropriate training, and that such training facilitates subsequent conceptual performance.

It was suggested earlier that differences between conceptual rules might involve strategy variation. Conant and Trabasso (1964) compared conjunctive and disjunctive concepts, finding the latter more difficult. In identifying a disjunctive concept, the most appropriate strategy is negative focusing, that is, starting with a negative instance and testing for the relevance of attributes. Recall that negative instances are more informative with disjunctive concepts, whereas positive instances are more informative with conjunctive rules. Conant and Trabasso found that Ss adopted a positive-focusing strategy much earlier in attaining a conjunctive concept, compared to the adoption of a negative-focusing strategy for disjunctive concepts. Thus, differences in difficulty were reflected in the strategies employed. Wells and Watson (1965) demonstrated that training in the appropriate strategy facilitated disjunctive concept attainment.

Limitations. Although the preceding research indicates that strategies and accuracy of categorizing are related, certain limitations must be pointed out. First, the initial distinction between focusers and scanners is somewhat artificial, because no S must be either one or the other. Bourne's (1965) research describes degrees of using certain strategies. Laughlin (1965, 1966) has developed quantitative measures of focusing and scanning. One result of his research is the demonstration of a correlation (0.54) between the two strategies. Furthermore, increased use of either strategy was correlated with more efficient concept attainment (ca. 0.69). Schwartz (1966) found that use of focusing was unrelated to or was inversely related to overall performance. Thus, there are some inconsistencies which appear to be related to the definitions involved.

A second qualification concerns the effects of certain independent variables on strategies and on measures such as trials to criterion. There are several reports of differential effects. Laughlin (1965, 1966) has found a number of variables to affect the use of focusing but to have no effect on difficulty of attainment (number of card choices to solution); these include two-person groups versus individuals, four-versus two-attribute concepts, and unitary versus distributed stimulus patterns (more focusing in the first of each pair). It appears to be more likely to find a relationship between strategies (focusing) and difficulty when investigating individual differences than when comparing experimental conditions; the theoretical status of strategies is thus somewhat uncertain.

Hypothesis Testing and Memory

The model of hypothesis selection proposed by Restle (1962), as well as others (for example, Bower and Trabasso, 1964), has stimulated research on the role of memory in concept attainment. These models make certain simplifying assumptions, and tests of the models are tests of those assumptions. Some general features of the models, which assume as canning stategy, may be described. It is assumed that S selects a hypothesis and categorizes stimuli on that basis. If his response is correct, S maintains the hypothesis, but, if his response is incorrect, S then resamples from the universe of hypotheses, with replacement. As indicated earlier, such resampling assumes that S has no memory for previous stimuli or hypotheses. A further implication is that, prior to selecting the correct hypothesis, S's performance should be at chance level; upon finding the correct hypothesis, S's performance should be perfect and remain so. There should thus be discontinuity in performance over trials. It should be understood that these are "working" models and that tests of the assumptions are performed for the sensible purpose of refining the models.

Right-Stay, Wrong-Shift. It has been commonly assumed that S will keep a hypothesis if it leads to correct categorizations and abandon it if it leads to an incorrect response. Neither of these assumptions seems to hold completely. Schwartz (1966) found that Ss changed hypotheses on 15 to 50 per cent of the trials following a correct placement. Although Schwartz found that incorrect placements led to hypothesis changes on virtually all trials, others (Bourne, 1965; Peterson and Colavita, 1964) have reported that Ss sometimes do not abandon a disconfirmed hypothesis.

Sampling with Replacement. Much interest has been directed toward the manner in which S selects a new hypothesis after an error. There is abundant evidence that he does *not* sample with replacement. If S were returned to the beginning of the task after any error, then randomly reinforcing his categorizations or changing the concept while he is still making errors should not impede his attainment of the final concept. However, both procedures do interfere (Levine, 1962; Trabasso and Bower, 1966). There is, in addition, independent evidence that Ss remember some prior information. A restatement of the question is thus to determine what and how much S remembers; how must the model be changed to account for the data?

Refining the Models. The answer to the question of how the model must be changed to account for the data is by no means clear, but several attempts have been reported. One possibility is that S remembers the hypothesis he just tried and does not resample it; this is called local nonreplacement (Erickson, 1968). Another possibility is that S eliminates hypotheses (on an error trial) that are inconsistent for that stimulus, a local consistency check. That is, if S has been testing the hypothesis that squares are positive and finds that a red open square is negative, he would also eliminate *red* and *open* when selecting a new hypothesis.

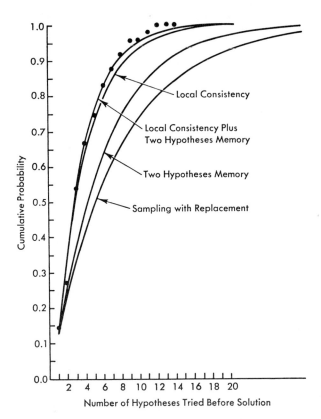

Figure 11-4. Theoretical cumulative distributions of number of hypotheses sampled before solution for various models compared with data from control problem. (Reprinted with permission from Erickson, J. R. Hypothesis sampling in concept identification. *J. exp. Psychol.*, 1968, **76**, 12–18.)

These can be combined, or they can be extended by assuming that S remembers some immediately preceding hypotheses and/or stimuli.

Restle and Emmerich (1966) found their data better accounted for by assuming that S remembered one or two previous stimuli, applying consistency checks to these stimuli. Trabasso and Bower (1966) found that the accuracy of their model increased as retention of more prior stimulus information was included; the best fit occurred with the assumption of retention for about three trials. Erickson (1968) has compared some data with predictions from several models (Figure 11-4). As indicated, models assuming no memory or just hypothesis memory

do not predict very accurately and underestimate the rate of attainment. The best fit occurs when hypothesis memory and local consistency are assumed. Including more memory in the models, either for previous hypotheses or previous stimuli, improves the accuracy of the model. It should be noted that these models have been tested with simple concepts (affirmation) and relatively small stimulus populations; as Erickson (1968) has pointed out, we need to know how increased memory load affects the testing of more complicated hypotheses.

All-or-None Learning. Levine, Miller, and Steinmeyer (1967) have investigated another facet of hypothesis-testing theory, namely, the relationship between hypotheses and correct categorizations over trials. It is assumed that S has never sampled the correct hypothesis if he is still making errors, and that his performance will be perfect once the correct hypothesis is found. There is thus defined a critical point, the trial of the last categorizing error. Prior to this point, S should show no improvement in categorizing, because with the two-category affirmative concepts used, any irrelevant hypothesis is associated with a 0.50 probability of a correct response. Levine (1966) developed a method for determining S's hypothesis without asking for a verbalization. Over a series of trials, only every fifth trial is an outcome trial (S gets feedback); the intervening four trials are "blanks," with S instructed to assume that he is correct if E says nothing. The notion is that S will thus keep the same hypothesis over the four trials, which are specially designed to determine which hypothesis (if any) S is using. Through the mixture of outcome trials and sets of blank trials, information about categorizing and hypotheses is obtained. The relevant data from Levine et al. (1967) are presented in Figure 11-5. Performance is plotted relative to the trial of the last error.

Stationarity. The learning curve is based on S's categorizations on outcome trials. There is no improvement prior to the last error; further, the correct hypothesis almost never occurs before the last error (hypothesis curve). The connection between hypotheses and categorizations is quite nicely demonstrated. Other investigators have also reported no improvement prior to the last error (Trabasso and Bower, 1966). Grier and Bornstein (1966) reported that, with two-valued dimensions, there was no improvement prior to the last error with affirmative concepts, but S's categorizing accuracy did improve with conjunctive concepts. This was attributed to changes in guessing, as noted earlier. With a conjunctive concept, negative stimuli occur more frequently, and S presumably learns to

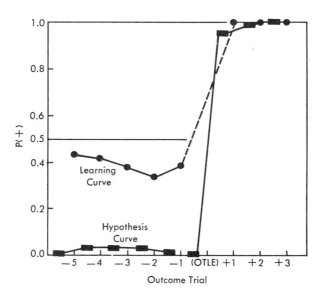

Figure 11-5. Learning and hypothesis curves showing, respectively, the proportion of correct responses on outcome trials and the proportion of correct hypothesis patterns. (Reprinted with permission from Levine, N., Miller, P., & Steinmeyer, C. E. The none-to-all theorem of human discrimination learning. *J. exp. Psychol.*, 1967, **73**, 568–573.)

guess that category more often, thus producing more correct responses.

Whereas correct responding does not increase prior to the last error in most cases, changes do occur in latency of responding during these trials. The underlying assumption is that S's latency is directly related to the size of the hypothesis pool on any trial (Erickson, Zajkowski, and Ehmann, 1966). Latencies tend to decrease over trials prior to the last error, which was interpreted as indicating a reduction in the number of hypotheses possibly under consideration. Of course, this finding does not contradict the notion of sudden attainment of the correct concept, but it is further evidence against the sampling-with-replacement (no memory) model.

The study of strategies implies that concept attainment is something other than the development of associative strength. We have seen that strategies are closely related to remembering, either by adopting a strategy which minimizes memory load (focusing) or by introducing different kinds and/or amounts of memory within a successive scanning strategy. Although our understanding of these processes is by no means complete, the utility of describing concept attainment as an active, information-gathering process seems well established.

Transfer Between Concepts

As in the previous chapter, we will consider two general types of transfer, specific and nonspecific. The latter, learning to solve, has been already encountered throughout the chapter. Improvement in performance over successive tasks is rather commonly observed (for example, Haygood and Bourne, 1965). Furthermore, the relative difficulty of various conditions changes with practice; this is the case when comparing conceptual rules and positive versus negative information. The general trend is toward improved performance with prac-

tice and smaller differences between conditions. Finally, appropriate training in using strategies facilitates subsequent concept attainment. In contrast to the effects observed with the tasks of the previous chapter, conceptual transfer is readily produced. Consistent with our previous analysis, it is not difficult to specify what might be learned over successive conceptual tasks (for example, appropriate strategies) and positive transfer is often the result of increasing the familiarity of an initially weak response (disjunctive rules, using negative information).

The study of specific transfer has been based largely on the theoretical distinction between simple associative learning and mediated learning. The intent has been to design transfer paradigms for which the two approaches make differential predictions. As we shall see, the interpretation of results is not so straightforward.

Reversal and Nonreversal Shifts

The strong positive-transfer effects discussed previously have occurred when S is fully informed that a new task is beginning. In studies comparing different types of shifts, the usual procedure has been to have S learn one concept, then to shift the basis for classification abruptly without informing S of the change. All studies of shifts have employed affirmative concepts, usually with few irrelevant dimensions. The types of shifts are depicted in Figure 11-6; we will first consider just two, reversal and nonreversal shifts.

In a *reversal* shift, the *same dimension is relevant* in both tasks, but the correct responses are reassigned. As indicated in Figure 11-6, shape is relevant to both tasks, but circles are negative in the first task, positive in the second. Contrast this with the nonreversal shift (also called extradimensional). In this case size is relevant in the first task, thus there is a change in the relevant dimension between the two tasks.

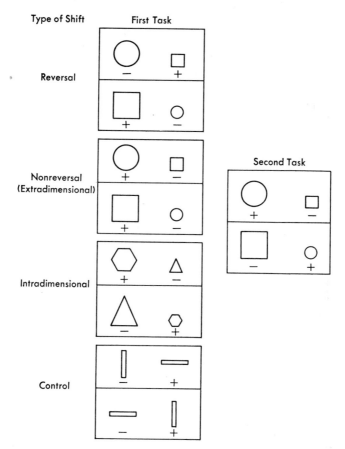

Figure 11-6. Examples of types of shifts between successively learned conceptual tasks.

Note also that, for the examples used, the category assignments are changed for half the stimuli in a nonreversal shift.

Theoretical Relevance. From studies of associative learning, it is well established that negative transfer occurs when S must learn a different response to an "old" stimulus, and the interference is especially pronounced when old responses are reassigned to old stimuli. With this in mind, we can examine the shifts from the viewpoint of simple associative learning. In the reversal shift, the correct response is changed for every stimulus, whereas only half the responses are changed in a non-reversal shift. On this basis, we would expect a nonreversal shift to be easier.

In contrast, if we assume that, during the first task, S acquires a mediating response referring to the relevant dimension, the expectation changes. A reversal shift does not require a change in the mediator, but a nonreversal shift does. We would now expect the reversal shift to be more readily acquired.

Initial Evidence. It has been well established that *adult human Ss learn a reversal shift more readily than a nonreversal shift* (for example, Buss, 1953; Kendler and D'Amato, 1955). *The opposite is true for rats* (Kelleher,

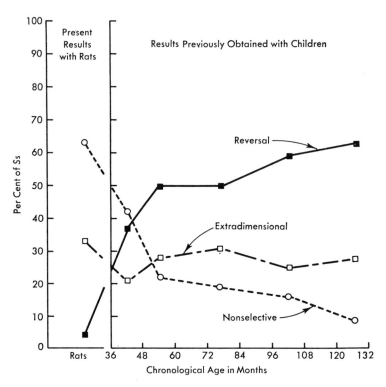

Figure 11-7.   Percentage of Ss responding in each optional shift category for rats and children of different ages. (Reprinted with permission from Kendler, T. S., Kendler, H. H., & Silfen, C. K. Optional shift behavior of albino rats. *Psychon. Sci.*, 1964, **1**, 5–6.)

1956). Using a different technique, *S* is given a second task which can be learned either as a reversal or nonreversal shift. (*E* reinforces whatever choices *S* makes.) With this procedure the percentage of *S*s choosing either shift or responding unsystematically is indicated in Figure 11-7.

The choice data agree with measures of difficulty; for human *S*s, the strength of reversal shift performance increases with age. This is interpreted as indicating the greater use of mediating responses. The nature of these mediators is not universally agreed on. There is some evidence that the mediation is verbal (labeling the correct dimension), but an alternative is that *S* develops a tendency to attend to the relevant characteristics (a perceptual orienting response). There are additional interpretations as well.

Analysis of Shifts. Support for verbal mediators stems essentially from the positive effects of requiring children to label the relevant dimension during the first task. This facilitates reversal shift performance (Kendler, 1964; Kendler and Kendler, 1961; Silverman, 1966). Orienting response theory has also been supported; when the relevant cues maintain the same position in successive tasks, performance is facilitated (Kendler, Glucksberg, and Keston, 1961; Lachman, 1966). A somewhat different verbal interpretation has also been suggested, that transfer is related to the degree of association between relevant cues in successive tasks (as opposed to a dimension-labeling response). In fact, when strong associations exist between successively relevant cues (without involving dimensional changes), acquisition of the second task is faster (Lachman, Meehan, and Bradley, 1965).

Intradimensional Shifts. An extension of the dimensional-mediation approach has involved the use of an intradimensional shift (see Figure 11-6). In this shift, the same relevant dimension is used in both tasks, but there are no reversals of category assignments. As can be seen, this is accomplished by using new values on the relevant dimension, from hexagon and triangle in the first task to circle and square on the second. It is expected that performance on the second task will be best with an intradimensional shift, because S is allowed to use the same mediator (shape) but suffers no interference from changed category assignments. Results have supported this expectation, with intradimensional, reversal, and nonreversal shifts forming an order of increasing difficulty for adult human Ss (Harrow, 1964; Isaacs and Duncan, 1962). The latter authors also attempted to determine whether these shifts produce positive or negative transfer. That is, how does second-task performance after these shifts compare with that of a control group? Isaacs and Duncan argue that previous studies had not used the appropriate control group, namely, one with previous experience in requiring an unrelated concept. Because we know that learning to learn is likely with conceptual tasks, this criticism is quite correct. Isaacs and Duncan used a control group like that in Figure 11-6; in this condition, the stimuli in the first task have different dimensions from those of the second task. The comparison of all four types of shifts indicated that both reversal and nonreversal shifts produce negative transfer relative to the control condition; it was not clear whether the intradimensional shift resulted in positive transfer.

In a related argument, it has been suggested that the reversal-nonreversal reflects interference with the nonreversal shift rather than facilitation of the reversal shift. The proposed reason for this interference is that, for the nonreversal shift, the previous solution is partially reinforced. Recall that only half the category assignments are changed after a nonreversal shift. Because partial reinforcement typically leads to slower extinction in simple learning situations, it is proposed that S will more slowly abandon his previous solution in attaining the second concept. Although it is true that partially reinforcing a currently irrelevant dimension does interfere with concept attainment, this effect holds whether or not that dimension was previously relevant (Abraham, Gormezano, and Wiehe, 1964). Further, the reversal-nonreversal difference holds when partial reinforcement is eliminated (Buss, 1956; Harrow and Friedman, 1958).

Limitations. Although the reversal-nonreversal difference is usually observed with two categories, this is not the case with four categories (Kendler and Mayzner, 1956; Ludvigson and Caul, 1964). Furthermore, the reversal-nonreversal difference can be obtained with nonsense syllables as stimuli (Bogartz, 1965). This is done by simply pairing several nonsense syllables with the same response for each of two responses during the first task. For a reversal shift, the responses are switched; for a nonreversal shift, only half the responses are switched. This led Bogartz to suggest that the typical reversal-nonreversal shift is due to S's being able to use the strategy of "doing the opposite" after a reversal shift. Because this could not be used with four categories, no reversal-nonreversal difference would be expected. As a minimum conclusion, Bogartz's results indicate that dimensional responses are not necessary for a reversal-nonreversal difference to be observed. Finally, Johnson, Fishkin, and Bourne (1966) have shown that this difference obtains only when S is minimally instructed; with more complete instructions the difference disappears. As these findings indicate, the theoretical relevance of shift effects is not as clear as initially envisioned.

Summary and Comment

Research on concept attainment reflects the importance attached to the structure of conceptual tasks. Variation in the amount and type of stimulus information, conceptual rules, and sequences of presentation may all be considered structural manipulations. Further, the study of strategies may be viewed as measuring how S responds to these structural variations. The amount of such research indicates the wide acceptance of the information-processing approach.

The emphasis on information processing should not preclude consideration of the importance of prior experience. Concept dominance and dimensional preferences are important variables and represent the rather simple consequence of prior experience, namely, familiarity. In a similar fashion, certain effects which have been attributed to structural or logical constructs (types of conceptual rules, positive versus negative instances) have been found to diminish with practice, suggesting that differential familiarity is a relevant variable. In addition, transfer effects are quite commonly observed, although some of these are intimately tied to an information-processing approach (for example, teaching strategies).

It seems worthwhile to point out the rather high level of sophistication of research in this area, especially in view of the recency of most of the research. If the reader will scan back through this chapter, he will find a large number of quantitative functional relationships. Quantitative theories have been proposed, and investigators are posing very specific questions for analysis (for example, how are hypothesis memory and attribute memory related?). Perhaps some of this is fortuitous in that psychologists with quantitative interests just happened to work in this area, but it must also be due in part to the fact that researchers have agreed on what they would study: performance on a well-specified task.

In the preceding chapters, the attempt was made to minimize statements of opinion. The presentation, hopefully, describes research and theory as they currently stand. In this final part, some suggestions will be made about how the psychology of thinking might develop and how it ought to proceed.

Theoretical Development. The study of learning, in its broadest sense, has been dominated by associative theory. It is only in recent years that viable alternatives have been proposed, as evidenced by the growth of information-processing approaches. Research on concept attainment is now dominated by information-processing theory, and it is likely that this trend will continue in the near future. Description in terms of hypotheses, strategies, and heuristics provides a basis for dealing with the complexity of thinking, a basis which seems to be lacking in associative language. Of course, all the postulated processes are mediating responses, but the interpretive problem is not solved by such a description; it is, rather, the distinctions and interrelations among the variety of mediating processes that constitute the heart of the matter. A useful theory needs appropriate language.

Consider, for example, the large number of variables that have been found to affect the solution of anagram problems: word frequency, letter moves, bigram variables in the anagram and in the solution, positional variables, relationships among solutions, and differences among Ss (for example, differences in creativity). Programs of research based on S-R, mediational approaches have dealt with most of these variables, but essentially one at a time. A point must be reached when one begins to consider some of these simultaneously. How do they combine to determine problem difficulty? One might simply place them in a multiple prediction equation and leave it at that, but this seems both unlikely and undesirable. The issue here is the sequential order of problem-solving behavior. Information-processing analyses have proved successful in dealing with this issue for conceptual behavior and for the solution of relatively complex problems (chess, logic). The attempt ought to be made to try this approach for simpler problems as well.

Interactions. If theoretical efforts should be directed toward complexity, so also should research design. Experiments having only one independent variable are inefficient, because they provide no information about interactive effects. Statements of interactions are of the form, *the effect of* (variable A) *changes from one level to another of* (variable B). There are numerous reports of interactions in research on concept attainment. The effects of several variables change with the type of rule, the type of stimulus presentation, instructions, practice, and so on. This is important information and represents the empirical side of the effort to deal with the complexity of the behavior under study. Conversely, if no interactions are found, *E*s will demonstrate the generality of their findings. The critical point is that unless *E*s design their studies to investigate interactions, the presence or absence of interactive effects remains unknown, and theoretical development suffers. This criticism applies to the majority of research on simple problems.

Problem Analysis. One reason for the lack of complex designs in studies of simple problems is undoubtedly the variety of tasks that is encountered. When *E* does not have much information about the behavior involved in a task, there is a tendency to restrict the scope of the question for an experiment. Obviously if different *E*s use different tasks, the necessary information for more complex designs accumulates slowly. This is not a call for all *E*s to use the same task, because none of the simple problems possesses the intuitive generality required for such a decision (the concept attainment task apparently does). Rather, relationships among tasks should be investigated.

There are two general approaches to this problem. One is to investigate patterns of individual differences from one problem to the next. To a slight extent this has been done, with discouraging results for insight problems; findings for anagram solving have been more promising. But correlating performance on different problems is not enough; such behavior should also be compared to other, well-specified measures. In this regard it might be fruitful to view simple problem solving as a retrieval process and use the findings of the study of memory to suggest analyses of problem solving.

The second way to consolidate knowledge of different problems is to employ the same independent variables for different tasks. To date, tasks have been created to suit *E*'s special purpose for any experiment. Progress will be made if we could discover how response strength (studied with verbal problems) interacts or combines with number of alternatives (studied with search tasks). To the extent that it is possible, such attempts to validate findings over tasks should be made.

Transfer Effects. A final suggestion is related to the previous comments and concerns what might be the ultimate goal of research, the study of transfer effects. There are two parts to the suggestion. The first recommendation is to study practice effects whenever feasible. For conceptual behavior, interproblem transfer effects are often found, and the effects of other variables change with practice. A reasonable course for any *E* would be to include multiple problems in his research design, to investigate both the overall and interactive effects of practice. For simple problems more deliberate attempts need to be made regarding practice effects. To date, little opportunity for learning to solve has been given, and the typical report of no practice effect is an incidental finding.

The second recommendation is the more difficult to execute, namely, to devise methods for training problem solving. As indicated at several points in the previous chapters, successful training depends on reasonable understanding of the behavior involved. Consequently, adequate problem analysis and theory are prerequisites to such endeavors. The elaboration of a successful training technique represents a tour de force for the theorist, for it indicates that his analysis is specific enough for the technique to be created and accurate enough for the technique to work. In addition, the idea of improving problem solving through training is a research goal with obvious potential benefits in its application.

Glossary

affirmative rule. A conceptual rule stating that stimuli possessing the (one) relevant attribute belong to the concept.

algorithm. Decision processes which are guaranteed to produce a solution, given enough time.

amount of information. Applied to informative feedback, the degree to which E indicates the correct response to S. Applied to stimulus dimensions, the number of dimensions and/or the number of values per dimension.

anagram. A problem requiring S to make a word from a set of letters.

anticipatory goal response. In associative theory, a response with stimulus properties associated with a set or class of particular responses; the r_g–s_g mechanism.

attribute. A characteristic of a stimulus; a value on a dimension, for example, red, square, large, and so on.

attribute identification. A conceptual task in which S is told the rule used to classify stimuli and must discover the attributes to which the rule is applied.

concept. A partition of stimuli into categories based on a rule applied to specified stimulus attributes.

conditional rule. A conceptual rule stating that if a stimulus possesses a specified relevant attribute, then it must possess another specified relevant attribute to belong to the concept.

conjunctive rule. A conceptual rule stating that stimuli possessing all relevant attributes belong to the concept; the "and" rule.

creativity. Generally, the production of uncommon responses meeting specified criteria; in this section, performance on the Remote Associates Test.

dimension. A way in which stimuli vary, for example in size and color.

distribution of practice. A variable referring to the amount of time between successive trials in a learning task.

dominance. For verbal concepts, the percentage of Ss associating a sense-impression adjective (for example, *round*) with an object name (for example, *chair*).

equivalence category. A construct referring to the classification of discriminably different stimuli as members of the same set.

exclusive disjunctive rule. A conceptual rule stating that stimuli possessing one but not more than one relevant attribute belong to the concept.

experimenter bias. The finding that, through subtle influences, Es tend to obtain results consistent with their expectations.

extinction problem. In studies of set, a problem requiring a solution different from that previously successful during a series of training problems.

extradimensional shift. A nonreversal shift.

fixation. In Gestalt descriptions of problem solving, persisting in a misperception of the problem situation.

focusing. A conceptual strategy in which attributes are tested for relevance by selecting stimuli differing in one or more ways from an initially presented instance.

free association. A technique in which S is requested to produce (say or write) any responses that occur to him upon presentation of a stimulus.

functional fixedness. The observation that solving insight problems is made more difficult by either prior use of an object in its usual function or by presentation of the object in its usual function.

functional value. In Gestalt theory, a term referring to the manner in which *S* attempts to solve a problem.

general transfer. A positive transfer effect occurring with practice on tasks of the same type.

habit-family hierarchy. In associative theory, a construct referring to a stimulus which is associated with a number of anticipatory goal responses, each of which serves as a stimulus in association with a set of particular responses.

heuristic. Any device which limits the number of alternatives to be searched in solving a problem.

hypothesis. In concept attainment, usually a guess about the concept.

identity category. A construct referring to the behavior of classifying a variety of stimuli as forms of the same thing.

inclusive disjunctive rules. A conceptual rule stating that stimuli possessing one or more relevant attributes belong to the concept.

information. Technically, that which reduces uncertainty; a measure of the amount of uncertainty present in a set of alternatives.

informative feedback. An operation by *E* indicating the correctness or incorrectness of *S*'s response.

inhibitory potential. A construct referring to a lessening of the effective strength of a response.

insight. Behavior characterized by the sudden occurrence of a problem solution, usually following a period of motor inactivity; in Gestalt theory, the correct reorganization of the perceptual field.

insight problem. A problem requiring *S* to use an object or objects in unusual ways; theoretically, a problem requiring *S* to combine previously unrelated responses.

instance contiguity. The degree to which instances of the same category occur together; the degree to which instances of the same category are not separated by instances of other categories.

intradimensional shift. A transfer paradigm in which the same dimension is relevant in two successive conceptual tasks but in which category assignments are not reversed from the first to the second task.

irrelevant attribute. An attribute not included in the concept definition.

learning. In general terms, a change in behavior that occurs as a function of practice.

local consistency. In concept attainment, the notion that, after an error in categorizing, *S* eliminates hypotheses inconsistent with his current information before selecting a new hypothesis.

mediated generalization. Changes in strength transferring from one response to another through the mechanism of the anticipatory goal response.

mediating response. In general, a response occurring between presentation of a stimulus and occurrence of a terminal motor response; in associative theory, anticipatory goal response.

memory error. A guess about a concept which is inconsistent with previously presented information that is no longer available.

mixed series. In concept attainment, a sequence of stimuli containing both positive and negative instances.

negative instance. A stimulus not belonging to the category selected by *E*.

negative transfer. The finding that performance on a task is impaired by prior training.

nonreversal shift. A transfer paradigm in which a dimension irrelevant in the first conceptual task is relevant in the second task.

object uses task. A test requiring *S* to produce as many uses as possible for a specified object; instructions may request unusual uses; employed as a measure of originality and/or creativity.

originality. The production of uncommon responses in a relatively free-responding situation.

paired-associate task. A task in which *S* is required to learn pairs of verbal items, usually tested by presenting one member of the pair and requiring recall of the other pair member.

plan. Any hierarchical process controlling the order in which a sequence of operations will be performed.

positive instance. A stimulus belonging to the category selected by *E*.

positive transfer. The finding that performance on a task is facilitated by prior training.

postfeedback interval. The amount of time between the occurrence of informative feedback and the presentation of the next stimulus.

problem. A task requiring S to discover a response meeting specified requirements.

productive thinking. The integration of previously unrelated experiences to solve a problem.

reception procedure. For conceptual tasks, a method in which E controls the choice of stimuli about which information will be given.

redundancy. Applied to stimulus dimensions, the perfect covariance of two or more dimensions; that is, values on one dimension are perfectly predictable from knowledge of values of another dimension.

relevant attribute. An attribute used in defining the concept.

Remote Associates Test (RAT). A series of items, each of which requires S to produce a word that is associated with all of three words provided.

reproductive thinking. The application of previously learned responses to solve a problem.

reversal shift. A transfer paradigm in which category assignments are reversed from the first to the second conceptual task.

rule. In conceptual behavior, a statement of the manner in which specified attributes are combined in assigning stimuli to categories. More generally, a statement of the manner in which a problem may be solved.

rule learning. A conceptual task in which S is told the relevant attributes and must discover the rule being applied to them.

sampling with replacement. Applied to conceptual behavior, the theoretical notion that, after an error in categorizing, S randomly selects a new hypothesis from the pool of all possible hypotheses.

scanning. A conceptual strategy in which hypotheses are tested for correctness by selecting stimuli to determine if the hypotheses successfully predict stimulus categorizations.

selection procedure. For conceptual tasks, a method in which S is allowed to choose those stimuli about which information will be given.

set. In problem solving, the tendency to respond from a particular class of responses upon problem presentation.

specific transfer. A positive or negative transfer effect attributed to a specific relationship between the content of two or more successive tasks.

spew hypothesis. The prediction that the order of emission of verbal responses is directly related to their frequencies of occurrence in S's past experience.

stationarity. In concept attainment, the finding that categorizing performance does not improve over trials prior to the trial of the last error.

strategy. A system for gathering and evaluating information about a concept; generally, a planned sequence of steps for solving a problem.

thinking. A type of behavior characterized by a delay between the presentation of a stimulus situation and the occurrence of a response which is related to or changes the stimulus situation.

trial and error. Behavior characterized by a lack of knowledge that a response will be successful.

water-jar problem. A modified arithmetic problem requiring S to obtain a specified quantity by manipulating several different quantities.

References

Abraham, F., Gormezano, I., & Wiehe, R. Discrimination learning as a function of prior relevance of a partially reinforced dimension. *J. exp. Psychol.*, 1964, **67**, 242–249.

Adams, J. A. Multiple versus single problem training in human problem solving. *J. exp. Psychol.*, 1954, **48**, 15–18.

Adamson, R. E. Functional fixedness as related to problem solving: A repetition of three experiments. *J. exp. Psychol.*, 1952, **44**, 288–291.

Adamson, R. E. Inhibitory set in problem solving as related to reinforcement learning. *J. exp. Psychol.*, 1959, **58**, 280–282.

Adamson, R. E., & Taylor, D. W. Functional fixedness as related to elapsed time and to set. *J. exp. Psychol.*, 1954, **47**, 122–126.

Anderson, R. C. Sequence constraints and concept identification. *Psychol. Rep.*, 1966, **19**, 1295–1302.

Archer, E. J. Concept identification as a function of obviousness of relevant and irrelevant information. *J. exp. Psychol.*, 1962, **63**, 616–620.

Archer, E. J. On verbalizations and concepts: Comments on Professor Kendler's paper. In A. W. Melton (Ed.), *Categories of human learning*. New York: Academic Press, 1964. Pp. 237–241.

Battig, W. F. Some factors affecting performance on a word-formation problem. *J. exp. Psychol.*, 1957, **54**, 96–104.

Battig, W. F., & Bourne, L. E., Jr. Concept identification as a function of intra- and interdimensional variability. *J. exp. Psychol.*, 1961, **61**, 329–333.

Beilin, J. Solving words as anagrams: A re-examined issue examined. *Psychon. Sci.*, 1966, **6**, 77–78.

Beilin, H., & Horn, R. Transition probability effects in anagram problem solving. *J. exp. Psychol.*, 1962, **63**, 514–518.

Birch, H. G., & Rabinowitz, H. S. The negative effect of previous experience on productive thinking. *J. exp. Psychol.*, 1951, **41**, 121–125.

Bogartz, W. Effects of reversal and non-reversal shifts with CVC stimuli. *J. verb. Learn. verb. Behav.*, 1965, **4**, 484–488.

Bourne, L. E., Jr. Effects of delay of information feedback and task complexity on the identification of concepts. *J. exp. Psychol.*, 1957, **54**, 201–207.

Bourne, L. E., Jr. Factors affecting strategies used in problems of concept formation. *Amer. J. Psychol.*, 1963, **76**, 229–238.

Bourne, L. E., Jr. Hypotheses and hypothesis shifts in classification learning. *J. gen. Psychol.*, 1965, **72**, 251–261.

Bourne, L. E., Jr. *Human conceptual behavior*. Boston: Allyn & Bacon, 1966.

Bourne, L. E., Jr., & Bunderson, C. V. Effects of delay of informative feedback and length of postfeedback interval on concept identification. *J. exp. Psychol.*, 1963, **65**, 1–5.

Bourne, L. E., Jr., Goldstein, S., & Link, W. E. Concept learning as a function of availability of previously presented information. *J. exp. Psychol.*, 1964, **67**, 439–448.

Bourne, L. E., Jr., Guy, D. E., Dodd, D. H., & Justeen, D. R. Concept identification: The effects of varying length and informational components of the inter-trial interval. *J. exp. Psychol.*, 1965, **69**, 624–629.

Bourne, L. E., Jr., & Haygood, R. C. The role of stimulus redundancy in concept identification. *J. exp. Psychol.*, 1959, **58**, 232–238.

Bourne, L. E., Jr., & Haygood, R. C. Supplementary report: Effect of redundant relevant information upon the identification of concepts. *J. exp. Psychol.*, 1961, **61**, 259–260.

Bourne, L. E., Jr., & Jennings, P. The relationship between response contiguity and classification learning. *J. gen. Psychol.*, 1963, **69**, 335–338.

Bourne, L. E., Jr., & Parker, B. K. Differences among modes for portraying stimulus information in concept identification. *Psychon. Sci.*, 1964, **1**, 209–210.

Bourne, L. E., Jr., & Pendleton, R. B. Concept identification as a function of completeness and probability of information feedback. *J. exp. Psychol.*, 1958, **56**, 413–420.

Bower, G., & Trabasso, T. Concept identification. In R. C. Atkinson (Ed.), *Studies in mathematical psychology*. Stanford: Stanford Univer. Press, 1964. Pp. 32–96.

Broerse, A. C., & Zwaan, E. J. The information value of initial letters in the identification of words. *J. verb. Learn. verb. Behav.*, 1966, **5**, 441–446.

Brown, F. G., & Archer, E. J. Concept identification as a function of task complexity and distribution of practice. *J. exp. Psychol.*, 1956, **52**, 316–321.

Brown, R., & McNeill, D. The "tip of the tongue" phenomenon. *J. verb. Learn. verb. Behav.*, 1966, **5**, 325–337.

Bruner, J. S., Goodnow, J. J., & Austin, G. A. *A study of thinking*. New York: Wiley, 1956.

Bulgarella, R., & Archer, E. J. Concept identification of auditory stimuli as a function of amount of relevant and irrelevant information. *J. exp. Psychol.*, 1962, **63**, 254–257.

Burke, R. J., & Maier, N. R. Attempts to predict success on an insight problem. *Psychol. Rep.*, 1965, **17**, 303–310.

Burke, R. J., Maier, N. R., & Hoffman, R. Functions of hints in individual problem solving. *Amer. J. Psychol.*, 1966, **79**, 389–399.

Buss, A. H. Rigidity as a function of absolute and relational shifts in the learning of successive discriminations. *J. exp. Psychol.*, 1953, **45**, 153–156.

Buss, A. H. Reversal and nonreversal shifts in concept formation with partial reinforcement eliminated. *J. exp. Psychol.*, 1956, **52**, 162–166.

Cahill, H. E., & Hovland, C. I. The role of memory in the acquisition of concepts. *J. exp. Psychol.*, 1960, **59**, 137–144.

Campbell, D. T. Blind variation and selective retention in creative thought as in other knowledge processes. *Psychol. Rev.*, 1960, **67**, 380–400.

Carlson, E. R. Generality of order of concept attainment. *Psychol. Rep.*, 1962, **10**, 375–380.

Caron, A. J., Unger, S. M., & Parloff, M. B. A test of Maltzman's originality training. *J. verb. Learn. verb. Behav.*, 1963, **1**, 436–442.

Cofer, C. N. Comparison of word associations obtained by the method of discrete single word and continued association. *Psychol. Rep.*, 1958, **4**, 507–510.

Cofer, C. N. Experimental studies of the role of verbal processes in concept formation and problem solving. *Ann. N.Y. Acad. Sci.*, 1960, **91**, 94–107.

Coleman, E. B. The association hierarchy as a measure of extra-experimental interference. *J. verb. Learn. verb. Behav.*, 1963, **2**, 417–421.

Coleman, E. B. Verbal concept learning as a function of instructions and dominance level. *J. exp. Psychol.*, 1964, **68**, 213–214.

Conant, M. B., & Trabasso, T. Conjunctive and disjunctive concept formation under equal-information conditions. *J. exp. Psychol.*, 1964, **67**, 250–255.

Corman, B. R. The effect of varying amounts and kinds of information as guidance in problem solving. *Psychol. Monogr.*, 1957, **71** (Whole No. 431).

Crouse, J. H. Response hierarchies measured by two techniques. *J. verb. Learn. verb. Behav.*, 1967, **6**, 169–171.

Crouse, J. H., & Duncan, C. P. Verbal concept sorting as a function of response dominance and sorting method. *J. verb. Learn. verb. Behav.*, 1963, **2**, 480–484.

Danks, J. H., & Glucksberg, S. Asymmetric transfer between the Remote Associates Test and functional fixedness. *Psychol. Rep.*, 1966, **19**, 682.

Davis, G. A. Current status of research and theory in human problem solving. *Psychol. Bull.*, 1966, **66**, 36–54.

Davis, G. A. Detrimental effects of distraction, additional response alternatives, and longer response chains in solving switch-light problems. *J. exp. Psychol.*, 1967, **73**, 45–55.

Davis, G. A., & Manske, M. E. An instructional method for increasing originality. *Psychon. Sci.*, 1966, **6**, 73–74.

Dominowski, R. L. Role of memory in concept learning. *Psychol. Bull.*, 1965, **63**, 271–280.

Dominowski, R. L. Problem difficulty as a function of relative frequency of correct response. *Psychon. Sci.*, 1965, **3**, 417–418.

Dominowski, R. L. Anagram solving as a function of letter moves. *J. verb. Learn. verb. Behav.*, 1966, **5**, 107–111.

Dominowski, R. L., Anagram solving as a function of bigram rank and word frequency. *J. exp. Psychol.*, 1967, **75**, 299–306.

Dominowski, R. L. Anagram solving as a function of letter-sequence information. *J. exp. Psychol.*, 1968, **76**, 78–83.

Dominowski, R. L., & Duncan, C. P. Anagram solving as a function of bigram frequency. *J. verb. Learn. verb. Behav.*, 1964, **3**, 321–325.

Dominowski, R. L., & Ekstrand, B. R. Direct and associative priming in anagram solving. *J. exp. Psychol.*, 1967, **74**, 84–86.

Duncan, C. P. Transfer after training with single versus multiple tasks. *J. exp. Psychol.*, 1958, **55**, 63–72.

Duncan, C. P. Recent research on human problem solving. *Psychol. Bull.*, 1959, **56**, 397–429.

Duncan, C. P. Letter response hierarchies within and among subjects. *Psychol. Rep.*, 1960, **6**, 291–297.

Duncan, C. P. Attempts to influence performance on an insight problem. *Psychol. Rep.*, 1961, **9**, 35–42.

Duncan, C. P. Probability vs. latency of solution of an insight problem. *Psychol. Rep.*, 1962, **10**, 119–121.

Duncan, C. P. Effect of instructions and information on problem solving. *J. exp. Psychol.*, 1963, **65**, 321–327.

Duncan, C. P. Learning to learn in response-discovery and in paired-associate lists. *Amer. J. Psychol.*, 1964a, **77**, 367–379.

Duncan, C. P. Induction of a principle. *Quart. J. Psychol.*, 1964b, **16**, 373–377.

Duncan, C. P. Mediation in verbal concept learning. *J. verb. Learn. verb. Behav.*, 1965, **4**, 1–6.

Duncan, C. P. Problem solving within a verbal response hierarchy. *Psychon. Sci.*, 1966a, **4**, 147–148.

Duncan, C. P. Effect of word frequency on thinking of a word. *J. verb. Learn. verb. Behav.*, 1966b, **5**, 434–440.

Duncan, C. P. Response hierarchies in problem solving. In C. P. Duncan (Ed.), *Thinking: Current experimental studies.* Philadelphia: Lippincott, 1967. Pp. 18–40.

Duncker, K. On problem-solving. *Psychol. Monogr.*, 1945, **58**, 5 (Whole No. 270).

Duvall, A. N. Functional fixedness: A replication study. *Psychol. Rec.*, 1965, **15**, 497–499.

Ekstrand, B. R., & Dominowski, R. L. Solving words as anagrams. *Psychon. Sci.*, 1965, **2**, 239–240.

Erickson, J. R. Hypothesis sampling in concept identification. *J. exp. Psychol.*, 1968, **76**, 12–18.

Erickson, J. R., Zajkowski, M. M., & Ehmann, E. D. All-or-none assumptions in concept identification: Analysis of latency data. *J. exp. Psychol.*, 1966, **72**, 690–697.

Fallon, D., & Battig, W. F. Role of difficulty in rote and concept learning. *J. exp. Psychol.*, 1964, **68**, 85–88.

Faust, W. L. Factors in individual improvement in solving twenty-questions problems. *J. exp. Psychol.*, 1958, **55**, 39–44.

Feigenbaum, E. A., & Feldman, J. (Eds.) *Computers and thought.* New York: McGraw-Hill, 1963.

Flavell, J. H., Cooper, A., & Loiselle, R. H. Effect of the number of pre-utilization functions on functional fixedness in problem solving. *Psychol. Rep.*, 1958, **4**, 343–350.

Freedman, J. L. Increasing creativity by free-association training. *J. exp. Psychol.*, 1965, **69**, 89–91.

Freedman, J. L., & Mednick, S. A. Ease of attainment of concepts as a function of response dominance variance. *J. exp. Psychol.*, 1958, **55**, 463–466.

Freiburgs, V., & Tulving, E. The effect of practice on utilization of information from positive and negative instances in concept identification. *Canad. J. Psychol.*, 1961, **15**, 101–106.

Fryatt, M. J., & Tulving, E. Interproblem transfer in identification of concepts involving positive and negative instances. *Canad. J. Psychol.*, 1963, **17**, 106–117.

Gagné, R. M. Problem solving. In A. W. Melton (Ed.), *Categories of human learning.* New York: Academic Press, 1964. Pp. 294–317.

Gagné, R. M., & Smith, E. C., Jr. A study of the effects of verbalization on problem solving. *J. exp. Psychol.*, 1962, **63**, 12–18.

Gardner, R. A., and Runquist, W. N. Acquisition and extinction of problem-solving set. *J. exp. Psychol.*, 1958, **55**, 274–277.

Glanzer, M., Chapman, R. M., Clark, W. H., & Bragdon, H. R. Changes in two EEG rhythms during mental activity. *J. exp. Psychol.*, 1964, **68**, 273–283.

Glucksberg, S. The influence of strength of drive on functional fixedness and perceptual recognition. *J. exp. Psychol.*, 1962, **63**, 36–41.

Glucksberg, S. Effects of verbal behavior on problem solving: Labeling the functionally fixed object. *Amer. Psychologist*, 1964a, **19**, 575 (Abstract).

Glucksberg, S. Problem solving: Response competition and the influence of drive. *Psychol. Rep.*, 1964b, **15**, 939–942.

Glucksberg, S., & Weisberg, R. W. Verbal behavior and problem solving: Some effects of labeling in a functional fixedness problem. *J. exp. Psychol.*, 1966, **71**, 659–664.

Grant, D. A., & Curran, J. F. Relative

difficulty of number, form, and color concepts of a Weigl-type problem using unsystematic number cards. *J. exp. Psychol.*, 1952, **43**, 408–413.

Grier, J. B., & Bornstein, R. Probability matching in concept identification. *J. exp. Psychol.*, 1966, **71**, 339–342.

Harrow, M. Stimulus aspects responsible for the rapid acquisition of reversal shifts in concept formation. *J. exp. Psychol.*, 1964, **67**, 330–334.

Harrow, M., & Friedman, G. B. Comparing reversal and nonreversal shifts in concept formation with partial reinforcement controlled. *J. exp. Psychol.*, 1958, **55**, 592–598.

Hayes, J. R. Problem topology and the solution process. *J. verb. Learn. verb. Behav.*, 1965, **4**, 371–379.

Haygood, D. H. Audiovisual concept formation. *J. educ. Psychol.*, 1965, **56**, 126–132.

Haygood, R. C., & Bourne, L. E., Jr. Forms of relevant stimulus redundancy in concept identification. *J. exp. Psychol.*, 1964, **67**, 392–397.

Haygood, R. C., & Bourne, L. E., Jr. Attribute- and rule-learning aspects of conceptual behavior. *Psychol. Rev.*, 1965, **72**, 175–195.

Haygood, R. C., & Devine, J. V. Effects of composition of the positive category on concept learning. *J. exp. Psychol.*, 1967, **74**, 230–235.

Haygood, R. C., & Stevenson, M. Effect of number of irrelevant dimensions in nonconjunctive concept learning. *J. exp. Psychol.*, 1967, **74**, 302–304.

Herbert, J. A., & Rogers, C. A., Jr. Anagram solution as a function of pronounceability and difficulty. *Psychon. Sci.*, 1966, **4**, 359–360.

Heidbreder, E. The attainment of concepts: VI. Exploratory experiments on conceptualization at perceptual levels. *J. Psychol.*, 1948, **26**, 193–216.

Hoffman, L. R., Burke, R. J., & Maier, N. R. F. Does training with differential reinforcement on similar problems help in solving a new problem? *Psychol. Rep.* 1963, **13**, 147–154.

Hovland, C. I. A "communication analysis" of concept learning. *Psychol. Rev.*, 1952, **59**, 461–472.

Hovland, C. I. Computer simulation of thinking. *Amer. Psychologist*, 1960, **15**, 687–693.

Hovland, E. I., & Weiss, W. Transmission of information concerning concepts through positive and negative instances. *J. exp. Psychol.*, 1953, **43**, 175–182.

Hunt, E. B. Memory effects in concept learning. *J. exp. Psychol.*, 1961, **62**, 598–604.

Hunt, E. B. *Concept learning: An information processing problem.* New York: Wiley, 1962.

Hunt, E. B. Selection and reception conditions in grammar and concept learning. *J. verb. Learn. verb. Behav.*, 1965, **4**, 211–215.

Hunt, E. B., & Hovland, C. I. Order of consideration of different types of concepts. *J. exp. Psychol.*, 1960, **59**, 220–225.

Hunter, I. M. L. Further studies on anagram solving. *Brit. J. Psychol.*, 1961, **52**, 161–165.

Huttenlocher, J. Some effects of negative instances on the formation of concepts. *Psychol. Rep.*, 1962, **11**, 35–42.

Isaacs, I. D., & Duncan, C. P. Reversal and nonreversal shifts within and between dimensions in concept formation. *J. exp. Psychol.*, 1962, **64**, 580–585.

Jacobus, K. A., & Johnson, N. F. An experimental set to adopt a set. *Psychol. Rep.*, 1964, **15**, 737.

Johnson, D. M. Solution of anagrams. *Psychol. Bull.*, 1966, **66**, 371–384.

Johnson, P. J., Fishkin, A., & Bourne, L. E., Jr. Effects of procedural variables upon reversal and interdimensional shift performance: II. *Psychon. Sci.*, 1966, **4**, 69–70.

Johnson, T. J., & Van Mondfrans, A. P. Order of solutions in ambiguous anagrams as a function of word frequency of the solution words. *Psychon. Sci.*, 1965, **3**, 565–566.

Judson, A. J., Cofer, C. N., & Gelfand, S. Reasoning as an associative process: II. "Direction" in problem solving as a function of prior reinforcement of relevant responses. *Psychol. Rep.*, 1956, **2**, 501–507.

Kelleher, R. T. Discrimination learning as a function of reversal and nonreversal shifts. *J. exp. Psychol.*, 1956, **51**, 379–384.

Kendler, H. H., & D'Amato, M. F. A comparison of reversal shifts and nonreversal shifts in human concept formation behavior. *J. exp. Psychol.*, 1955, **49**, 165–174.

Kendler, H. H., Glucksberg, S., & Keston, R. Perception and mediation in concept learning. *J. exp. Psychol.*, 1961, **61**, 186–191.

Kendler, H. H., Greenberg, A., & Richman, H. The influence of massed and distributed practice on the development of mental set. *J. exp. Psychol.*, 1952, **43**, 21–25.

Kendler, H. H., & Karasik, A. D. Concept formation as a function of competition between response-produced cues. *J. exp. Psychol.*, 1958, **55**, 278–283.

Kendler, H. H., & Kendler, T. S. Effect of verbalization on reversal shifts in children. *Science*, 1961, **134**, 1610–1620.

Kendler, H. H., & Kendler, T. S. Vertical and horizontal processes in problemsolving. *Psychol. Rev.*, 1962, **69**, 1–16.

Kendler, H. H., & Mayzner, M. S., Jr. Reversal and nonreversal shifts in card sorting tests with two or four sorting categories. *J. exp. Psychol.*, 1956, **51**, 244–248.

Kendler, T. S. Concept formation. *Annu. Rev. Psychol.*, 1961, **13**, 447–472.

Kendler, T. S. Verbalization and optional reversal shifts among kindergarten children. *J. verb. Learn. verb. Behav.*, 1964, **3**, 428–436.

Kendler, T. S., Kendler, H., & Silfen, C. K. Optional shift behavior of albino rats. *Psychon. Sci.*, 1964, **1**, 5–6.

Köhler, W. *Gestalt psychology: An introduction to new concepts in modern psychology.* New York: Liveright, 1947.

Kurtz, K. H., & Hovland, C. I. Concept learning with differing sequences of instances. *J. exp. Psychol.*, 1956, **51**, 239–243.

Lachman, R. Range of association level (AL) and observing response (OR) effects in postshift concept attainment. *J. exp. Psychol.*, 1966, **71**, 746–750.

Lachman, R., Meehan, J. T., & Bradley, R. Observing response and word association in concept shifts: Two-choice and four-choice selective learning. *J. Psychol.*, 1965, **59**, 349–357.

Laughlin, P. R. Selection strategies in concept attainment as a function of number of persons and stimulus display. *J. exp. Psychol.*, 1965, **70**, 323–327.

Laughlin, P. R. Selection strategies in concept attainment as a function of number of relevant problem attributes. *J. exp. Psychol.*, 1966, **71**, 773–776.

Levine, M. Cue neutralization: The effects of random reinforcements upon discrimination learning. *J. exp. Psychol.*, 1962, **63**, 438–443.

Levine, M. Hypothesis behavior by humans during discrimination learning. *J. exp. Psychol.*, 1966, **71**, 331–338.

Levine, M., Miller, P., & Steinmeyer, C. H. The none-to-all theorem of human discrimination learning. *J. exp. Psychol.*, 1967, **73**, 568–573.

Lordahl, D. S. Concept identification using simultaneous auditory and visual signals. *J. exp. Psychol.*, 1961, **62**, 283–290.

Ludvigson, H. W., & Caul, W. F. Relative effect of overlearning on reversal and nonreversal shifts with two and four sorting categories. *J. exp. Psychol.*, 1964, **68**, 301–306.

Maier, N. R. F. An aspect of human reasoning. *Brit. J. Psychol.*, 1933, **24**, 144–155.

Maier, N. R. F. The behavior mechanisms concerned with problem solving. *Psychol. Rev.*, 1940, **47**, 43–58.

Maltzman, I. Thinking: From a Behavioristic point of view. *Psychol. Rev.*, 1955, **62**, 275–286.

Maltzman, I. On the training of originality. *Psychol. Rev.*, 1960, **67**, 229–242.

Maltzman, I. Motivation and the direction of thinking. *Psychol. Bull.*, 1962, **59**, 457–467.

Maltzman, I., Belloni, M., & Fishbein, M. Experimental studies of associative variables in originality. *Psychol. Monogr.*, 1964, **78**, 3 (Whole No. 580).

Maltzman, I., Bogartz, W., & Breger, L. A procedure for increasing word association originality and its transfer effects. *J. exp. Psychol.*, 1958, **56**, 392–398.

Maltzman, I., Brooks, L., Bogartz, W., & Summers, S. S. The facilitation of problem solving by prior exposure to uncommon responses. *J. exp. Psychol.*, 1958 **56**, 399–406.

Maltzman, I., Eisman, E., Brooks, L. O., & Smith, W. M. Task instructions for anagrams following different task instructions and training. *J. exp. Psychol.*, 1956, **51**, 418–420.

Maltzman, I., & Morrissett, L., Jr. The effects of single and compound classes of anagrams in set solutions. *J. exp. Psychol.*, 1953a, **45**, 345–350.

Maltzman, I., & Morrissett, L., Jr. Effects of task instructions on solution of different classes of anagrams. *J. exp. Psychol.*, 1953b, **45**, 351–354.

Maltzman, I., Simon, S., Raskin, D., & Licht, L. Experimental studies in the training of originality. *Psychol. Monogr.*, 1960, **74**, 5 (Whole No. 493).

Mandler, G., Cowan, P. A., & Gold, C. Concept learning and probability matching. *J. exp. Psychol.*, 1964, **67**, 514–522.

Mayzner, M. S. The effects of the competition of various strengths of sets in problem solution. *Psychol. Newsltr. NYU*, 1955, **6**, 134–155.

Mayzner, M. S. Verbal concept attainment: A function of the number of positive and negative instances presented. *J. exp. Psychol.*, 1962, **63**, 314–319.

Mayzner, M. S., & Tresselt, M. E. The effect of the competition and generalization of sets with respect to manifest anxiety. *J. gen. Psychol.*, 1956, **55**, 241–247.

Mayzner, M. S., & Tresselt, M. E. Anagram solution times: A function of letter order and word frequency. *J. exp. Psychol.*, 1958, **56**, 376–379.

Mayzner, M. S., & Tresselt, M. E. Anagram solution times: A function of transition probabilities. *J. Psychol.*, 1959, **47**, 117–125.

Mayzner, M. S., & Tresselt, M. E. Anagram solution times: A function of word transition probabilities. *J. exp. Psychol.*, 1962, **63**, 510–513.

Mayzner, M. S., & Tresselt, M. E. Anagram solution times: A function of word length and letter position variables. *J. Psychol.*, 1963, **55**, 469–475.

Mayzner, M. S., & Tresselt, M. E. Solving words as anagrams: An issue reexamined. *Psychon. Sci.*, 1965a, **3**, 363–364.

Mayzner, M. S., & Tresselt, M. E. Tables of single-letter and bigram frequency counts for various word-length and letter-position combinations. *Psychon. Monogr. Suppl.*, 1965b, 1, 2.

Mayzner, M. S., & Tresselt, M. E. Anagram solution times: A function of multiple-solution anagrams. *J. exp. Psychol.*, 1966, **71**, 66–73.

Mayzner, M. S., Tresselt, M. E., & Blaesing, E. A. A comparison of judgmental and associational techniques in developing verbal concept formation materials. *J. Psychol.*, 1961, **51**, 331–342.

Mayzner, M. S., Tresselt, M. E., & Helbock, H. An exploratory study of mediational responses in anagram problem solving. *J. Psychol.*, 1964, **57**, 263–274.

Mednick, S. A. The associative basis of the creative process. *Psychol. Rev.*, 1962, **69**, 220–232.

Mednick, S. A., & Halpern, S. Ease of concept attainment as a function of associative rank. *J. exp. Psychol.*, 1962, **64**, 628–630.

Mednick, S. A., & Mednick, M. T. *Examiner's manual: Remote Associates Test.* Boston: Houghton Mifflin, 1967.

Mendelsohn, G. A., & Griswold, B. B. Differential use of incidental stimuli in problem solving as a function of creativity. *J. abnorm. soc. Psychol.*, 1964, **68**, 431–436.

Mendelsohn, G. A., & Griswold, B. B. Assessed creative potential, vocabulary level, and sex as predictors of the use of incidental cues in verbal problem solving. *J. Person. soc. Psychol.*, 1966, **4**, 423–431.

Mendelsohn, G. A., Griswold, B. B., & Anderson, M. L. Individual differences in anagram-solving ability. *Psychol. Rep.*, 1966, **19**, 799–809.

Metzger, R. A comparison between rote learning and concept formation. *J. exp. Psychol.*, 1958, **56**, 226–231.

Miller, G. A., Galanter, E., & Pribram, K. H. *Plans and the structure of behavior.* New York: Holt, 1960.

Morrissett, L., Jr. & Hovland, C. I. A comparison of three varieties of training in human problem solving. *J. exp. Psychol.*, 1959, **58**, 52–55.

Neimark, E. D. Information-gathering in diagnostic problem-solving. *Psychol. Rec.*, 1961, **11**, 243–248.

Neimark, E. D., & Wagner, H. Information gathering in diagnostic problem solving as a function of number of alternative solutions. *Psychon. Sci.*, 1964, **1**, 329–330.

Neisser, U., & Weene, P. Hierarchies in concept attainment. *J. exp. Psychol.*, 1962, **64**, 640–645.

Newell, A., Shaw, J. C., & Simon, H. A. Elements of a theory of human problem solving. *Psychol. Rev.*, 1958, **65**, 151–166.

Newell, A., & Simon, H. A. GPS, a program that simulates human thought. In E. A. Feigenbaum & J. Feldman (Eds.), *Computers and thought.* New York: McGraw-Hill, 1963. Pp. 279–296.

Newman, S. E. Effects of contiguity and similarity on the learning of concepts. *J. exp. Psychol.*, 1956, **52**, 349–353.

O'Connell, D. C. Concept learning and verbal control under partial reinforcement and subsequent reversal or nonreversal shifts. *J. exp. Psychol.*, 1965, **69**, 144–151.

Oseas, L., & Underwood, B. J. Studies of distributed practice: V. Learning and retention of concepts. *J. exp. Psychol.*, 1952, **43**, 143–148.

Osgood, C. E. *Method and theory in experimental psychology.* New York: Oxford Univer. Press, 1953.

Peterson, M. J. Some effects of the percentage of relevant cues and presentation methods on concept identification. *J. exp. Psychol.*, 1962, **64**, 623–627.

Peterson, M. J., & Colavita, F. B. Strategies, types of solution, and stage of learning. *J. exp. Psychol.*, 1964, **68**, 578–587.

Pinckey, G. A. Transitional probability in anagram solving in a group setting: A replication. *Psychol. Rep.*, 1965, **17**, 369–370.

Pishkin, V. Stimulus and response tendencies in concept identification. *Percept. mot. Skills*, 1961, **13**, 295–304.

Pishkin, V. Availability of feedback-corrected error instances in concept learning. *J. exp. Psychol.*, 1967, **73**, 318–319.

Pishkin, V., & Wolfgang, A. Number and type of available instances in concept learning. *J. exp. Psychol.*, 1965, **69**, 5–8.

Posner, M. I. Memory and thought in human intellectual performance. *Brit. J. Psychol.*, 1965, **56**, 197–215.

Raaheim, K. Problem solving and the awareness of the missing part. *Scand. J. Psychol.*, 1962, **3**, 129–131.

Raaheim, K. Analysis of the missing part in problem situations. *Scand. J. Psychol.*, 1964, **5**, 149–152.

Ray, W. S. Problem-solving set as a function of number of reinforcements. *Psychon. Sci.*, 1965, **3**, 567–568.

Restle, F. The selection of strategies in cue learning. *Psychol. Rev.* 1962, **69**, 329–343.

Restle, F., & Emmerich, D. Memory in concept attainment: Effects of giving several problems concurrently. *J. exp. Psychol.*, 1966, **71**, 794–799.

Richardson, J., & Bergum, B. O. Distributed practice and rote learning in concept formation. *J. exp. Psychol.*, 1954, **47**, 442–446.

Ronning, R. R. Anagram solution times: A function of the "Ruleout" factor. *J. exp. Psychol.*, 1965, **69**, 35–39.

Rosenbaum, M. E., Arenson, S. J., & Panman, R. A. Training and instructions in the facilitation of originality. *J. verb. Learn. verb. Behav.*, 1964, **3**, 50–56.

Rosenthal, R. On the social psychology of the psychological experiment. *Amer. Scientist*, 1963, **51**, 268–283.

Rosenthal, R. *Experimenter effects in behavioral research.* New York: Appleton-Century-Crofts, 1966.

Runquist, W. N., & Sexton, B. Supplementary report: Spontaneous recovery of problem solving set. *J. exp. Psychol.*, 1961, **61**, 351–352.

Russell, W. A., & Jenkins, J. J. The complete Minnesota norms for responses to 100 words from the Kent-Rosanoff word association test. Tech. Rep. No. 11, 1954, Univ. of Minnesota, Contract N8-onr066216, Office of Naval Research.

Safren, M. A. Associations, sets, and the solution of word problems. *J. exp. Psychol.*, 1962, **64**, 40–45.

Saugstad, P. Problem-solving as dependent on availability of functions. *Brit. J. Psychol.*, 1955, **46**, 191–198.

Saugstad, P. An analysis of Maier's pendulum problem. *J. exp. Psychol.*, 1957, **54**, 168–179.

Saugstad, P., & Raaheim, K. Problem solving and the availability of functions. *Acta Psychologia*, 1957, **13**, 263–278.

Saugstad, P., & Raaheim, K. Problem-solving, past experience, and availability of functions. *Brit. J. Psychol.*, 1960, **51**, 97–104.

Scheerer, M. Problem-solving. *Scient. Amer.*, 1963, **208**, 118–128.

Schulz, R. W., Miller, R. L., & Radtke, R. C. The role of instance contiguity and dominance in concept attainment. *J. verb. Learn. verb. Behav.*, 1963, **1**, 432–435.

Schvaneveldt, R. W. Concept identification as a function of probability of positive instances and number of relevant dimensions. *J. exp. Psychol.*, 1966, **72**, 649–654.

Schwartz, S. H. Trial-by-trial analysis of processes in simple and disjunctive concept-attainment tasks. *J. exp. Psychol.*, 1966, **72**, 456–465.

Silverman, I. W. Effect of verbalization on reversal shifts in children: Additional data. *J. exp. child Psychol.*, 1966, **4**, 1–8.

Simon, H. A., & Newell, A. Information processing in computers and man. *Amer. Scientist*, 1964, **52**, 281–300.

Solley, C. M., & Snyder, F. W. Information processing and problem solving. *J. exp. Psychol.*, 1958, **55**, 384–387.

Staats, A. W. Verbal and instrumental response-hierarchies and their relationship to problem solving. *Amer. J. Psychol.*, 1957, **70**, 442–446.

Stachnik, T. Transitional probability in anagram solution in a group setting. *J. Psychol.*, 1963, **55**, 259–261.

Taft, R., & Rossiter, J. T. The Remote Associates Test: Divergent or convergent thinking? *Psychol. Rep.*, 1966, **19**, 1313–1314.

Tecce, J. J. Relationship of anxiety (drive) and response competition in problem solving. *J. abnorm. Psychol.*, 1965, **70**, 465–467.

Thomas, A., & Solley, C. M. Search-discrimination time for missing stimulus information. *J. exp. Psychol.*, 1963, **65**, 501–506.

Thorndike, E. L., & Lorge, I. *A teacher's word book of 30,000 words.* New York: Teacher's Coll., Columbia Univer., 1944.

Thysell, R. V., & Schulz, R. W. Concept-utilization as a function of the strength of relevant and irrelevant associations. *J. verb. Learn. verb. Behav.*, 1964, **3**, 203–208.

Trabasso, T., & Bower, G. Memory in concept identification. *Psychon. Sci.*, 1964, **1**, 133–134.

Trabasso, T., & Bower, G. Presolution dimensional shifts in concept identification: A test of the sampling with replacement axiom in all-or-none models. *J. math. Psychol.*, 1966, **3**, 163–173.

Tresselt, M. E., & Leeds, D. S. The Einstellung effect in immediate and delayed problem solving. *J. gen. Psychol.*, 1953, **49**, 87–95.

Underwood, B. J. An orientation for research on thinking. *Psychol. Rev.*, 1952, **59**, 209–220.

Underwood, B. J. Studies of distributed practice: XV. Verbal concept learning as a function of intralist interference. *J. exp. Psychol.*, 1957, **54**, 33–40.

Underwood, B. J. Stimulus selection in verbal learning. In C. N. Cofer & B. S. Musgrave (Eds.), *Verbal behavior and learning: Problems and processes.* New York: McGraw-Hill, 1963. Pp. 33–47.

Underwood, B. J., & Richardson, J. Some verbal materials for the study of concept formation. *Psychol. Bull.*, 1956a, **53**, 84–95.

Underwood, B. J., & Richardson, J. Verbal concept learning as a function of instructions and dominance level. *J. exp. Psychol.*, 1956b, **51**, 229–238.

Underwood, B. J., & Schulz, R. W. *Meaningfulness* and *verbal learning.* Chicago: Lippincott, 1960.

van de Geer, J. P. *A psychological study of problem solving.* Haarlem: Uitgeverig De Toorts, 1957.

Walker, C. M., & Bourne, L. E., Jr. The identification of concepts as a function of amount of relevant and irrelevant information. *Amer. J. Psychol.*, 1961, **74**, 410–417.

Wallace, J., Jr., & Sechrest, L. Relative difficulty of conjunctive and disjunctive concepts. *J. Psychol. Stud.*, 1961, **12**, 97–104.

Weaver, H. E., & Madden, E. H. "Direction" in problem solving. *J. Psychol.*, 1949, **27**, 331–345.

Wells, H. Effects of transfer and problem structure in disjunctive concept formation. *J. exp. Psychol.*, 1963, **65**, 63–69.

Wells, H. Stimulus compounding and the attainment of conjunctive and disjunctive concepts. *Percept. mot. Skills*, 1965, **21**, 767–770.

Wells, H., & Watson, D. Strategy training and practice in disjunctive concept attainment. *Psychol. Rep.*, 1965, **17**, 925–926.

Wickelgren, W. A. Cues that elicit analytic-deductive methods in concept attainment. *Brit. J. Psychol.*, 1964, **55**, 143–154.

Woodworth, R. S., & Schlosberg, H. *Experimental psychology*. (Rev. ed.) New York: Holt, 1954.

Suggested Readings

Bruner, J. S., Goodnow, J. J., & Austin, G. A. *A study of thinking*. New York: Wiley, 1956. This is an account of a series of exploratory experiments on conceptual behavior, including the initial identification of strategies.

Carroll, J. B. *Language and thought*. Englewood Cliffs, N.J.: Prentice-Hall, 1964. The author provides an introduction to psycholinguistics, with some suggestions regarding the relevance of language to conceptual behavior.

Feigenbaum, E. A., & Feldman, J. (Eds.) *Computers and thought*. New York: McGraw-Hill, 1963. The papers in this volume describe the use of computers for the simulation of human behavior and the development of artificial intelligence.

Hunt, E. B. *Concept learning: An information processing problem*. New York: Wiley, 1962. In this book the attempt is made to bring together the ideas of logic, psychology, and computer science in an analysis of conceptual behavior.

Kleinmuntz, B. (Ed.) *Problem solving: Research, method, and theory*. New York: Wiley, 1966. This book contains a series of symposium papers representing a wide variety of approaches to problem solving and concept attainment.

Kleinmuntz, B. (Ed.) *Concepts and the structure of memory*. New York: Wiley, 1967. The central issue of these symposium papers is the relationship between two areas of research that are usually considered separately. Both the effects of concepts on remembering and the influence of forgetting on concept attainment are considered.

Melton, A. W. (Ed.) *Categories of human learning*. New York: Academic Press, 1964. The contributors to this book wrestle with the problem of trying to provide unambiguous definitions of types of learning, as well as noting the relations among current behavioral categories.

Miller, G. A., Galanter, E., & Pribram, K. H. *Plans and the structure of behavior*. New York: Holt, 1960. The authors propose a purposefully new and distinct approach to psychological theory, stressing the hierarchical organization of information-processes.

Staats, A. W. *Learning language, and cognition*. New York: Holt, 1968. A systematic attempt is made to apply the associative-mediational approach to the broad spectrum of learning; illustrative experiments are presented.

Wallach, M. A., & Kogan, N. *Modes of thinking in young children: A study of the creativity-intelligence distinction*. New York: Holt, 1965. Deriving their impetus from Mednick's theory of creativity, the authors first develop a series of measures of creativity, then examine the correlates of creativity and intelligence in numerous situations.

IV

Learning, Development, and Social Class in the Socialization Process

Edward Zigler

Yale University

12

Sources of Ideas and Evidence: An Evaluative Review [1]

Overview

As the author (Zigler, 1963a) and others (Kendler, 1963; Russell, 1957) have noted, learning theorists and developmental theorists have long been natural enemies. We have argued elsewhere that any adequate theory of human behavior must include both classical developmental and learning constructs (Zigler, 1963a). The purpose of this section is to demonstrate the various and often complementary contributions of the two bodies of theory to a specific area of mutual concern, namely, socialization.

In seeking to illuminate the socialization process, the psychologist must ask such questions as: How does the person change from the tiny, prelinguistic, motorically incompetent organism which we encounter in infancy to that larger, verbal, motorically skilled organism represented in adulthood? How does the dependent and amoral infant develop into the independent, moralistic adult? How do the inaccurate perceptions, the egocentric and illogical thought proc-

esses develop into the accurate perception, the reality-oriented and logical cognitive functioning encountered in maturity? And, ultimately, how do the outcomes of these processes affect the quality of life in the society in which we live?

These and related questions are not the exclusive province of any one approach; rather they afford a singular opportunity for the building of a truly general theory. In the following pages we shall outline briefly some of the schools of thought within the discipline of psychology which have contributed to our thinking about socialization, state the fundamental issues raised by these positions, and suggest a definition of the socialization process. We shall then discuss in detail the contributions of learning and developmental theories to our understanding of socialization in a sampling of particular systems of behavior, and finally we shall discuss the theoretical and practical implications of one important variable, that of social class, for efforts to build a theory of socialization.

[1] Much of the material in this section is to be found in a more comprehensive treatment of socialization by Zigler and Child (1969). The author would like to acknowledge the contribution of Carolyn Pratt in the preparation of this section. Preparation of this work was facilitated by Public Health Service Grant USPHS 1 PO 1 HD-03008-01.

A number of approaches within psychology have contributed to thought about socialization. In this chapter we offer a critical review of the major sources of ideas and evidence, including the psychoanalytic movement, the normative-maturational approach, developmental and cognitive theory, the genetic approach, and various positions within learning theory.

Psychoanalysis

The psychoanalytic movement has had a most significant influence on thinking about the socialization process, and psychoanalysis has contributed a number of hypotheses about the influences of socialization practices on personality. To be sure, these hypotheses are suggested rather than explicitly stated in the psychoanalytic literature, yet their influence has been very great.

As Bronfenbrenner (1963) has noted, it is a grounding in psychoanalytic theory that has led many workers to focus on the general affective quality of the parent-child relationship as the antecedent condition for the development of particular forms of behavior. R. Sears (1959) has also emphasized the great debt that students of personality development and socialization owe to Freud and has pointed out that a truly revolutionary aspect of Freud's thinking was a concern with development. This concern forces one to consider possible forces which underlie the particular changes encountered as the human organism moves from infancy to adulthood. This development and/or change is central to and sometimes treated as synonymous with the socialization process. Many of Freud's concepts—libido, infantile sexuality, the Oedipus and castration complexes—focus attention on the development of relationships within the family. Differences between one family and another then come to be viewed as a major source of variation from person to person in socialization and resulting personality.

The development of psychoanalytic thought in recent decades gives increasingly explicit stress to the importance of social pressures. Emphasis has moved away from Freud's explanatory reliance on biological and instinctual factors toward a greater reliance on environmental and social determinants. Bronfenbrenner (1963) has referred to this shift in emphasis as the "socialization" of Freudian thinking, and one clearly encounters it in the work of such neo-Freudians as Kardiner (1945), Sullivan (1953), Horney (1937), and Erikson (1950).

Criticisms of Psychoanalytic Theory

Despite these theoretical developments, the passage of time has witnessed a diminution of the relative impact of Freudian thought on socialization (Thompson, 1959). Two major facts about Freudian theory, viewed in relation to the total inquiry into socialization and personality development, indicate why this has been the case: (1) the Freudian system has never been developed to the point where it meets the minimal requirements of theory construction allowing for the generation of clearly testable propositions (Jenness, 1962; Rapaport, 1959; Zigler, 1963a); (2) psychoanalytic thought does not deal adequately with a variety of rational and social behaviors that are of central importance to man's socialization, and it is thus a very incomplete approach (Frenkel-Brunswik, 1954; Zigler, 1963a). Despite these handicaps, many researchers have consciously and systematically incorporated Freudian thought into existing frameworks, and in the process have produced hybrid approaches of great value and importance.

The Normative-Maturational Approach

Another source of evidence for students of socialization has been the atheoretical descriptive study of children's behavior, best exemplified by the normative and longitudinal research long so popular among child psychologists in this country. The pattern of such research does not require that it be atheoretical; yet the vast majority of the studies, as published, neither begin with theory nor eventuate in theory, and this feature has led to their being attacked as theoretically sterile (Ausubel, 1958). This attack seems somewhat one-sided. Even the most empirical of these studies have contributed to a sound body of facts concerning a multitude of abilities and age-related behaviors, and, as Anderson (1960a) and Kessen (1960) have argued, the accumulation of such facts about human development is of great clinical and scientific value.

One of the more theoretical representatives of this approach, and at the same time a very prolific empirical researcher, was Gesell; an excellent brief review of his position has been supplied by Stoltz (1958). Gesell's orientation was quite similar to earlier predeterministic views. The growth and change in psychological processes were attributed almost entirely to endogenous regulatory mechanisms. If the behavioral potentialities of the individual are predetermined at the moment of conception, and human growth and development are primarily a flowering or an unfolding process during which these behavioral givens manifest themselves, clearly the most appropriate type of investigation is the normative one in which we carefully chart the sequence in which particular behaviors appear and the precise times at which they emerge.

Criticisms of the Normative-Maturational Approach

Despite Gesell's elaboration of additional concepts, his theory seems to rely very heavily upon the single core construct, maturation, and to offer explanations that are essentially only labels; that is, the norms discovered through empirical investigations are used as explanatory devices. Thus, one discovers that at a certain age children show negativistic behavior, and "explains" their acts by saying that children of this age are in the negativistic stage. The circularity and conceptual inadequacy of such a procedure has frequently been noted (Kessen, 1960; Lewin, 1936).

The extreme maturational position has been severely criticized (Ausubel, 1958; Hunt 1961), and even though the empirical approach associated with it retains great value, it no longer is pursued so actively. The decline of this research activity has serious implications for the child psychologist's orientation to the socialization process. At the height of their influence normative studies provided the age norms which were then employed as the yardstick against which any child's socialization could be assessed. The child psychologist's major job, then, was to discover such norms through the careful point-by-point mapping of socially important behaviors, report these norms to parents, and finally, advise parents on child-rearing practices that would facilitate progression through a series of age-appropriate behaviors. Given such a stance, child psychology was primarily an atheoretical but practical applied discipline, and the socialization process was essentially defined in relation to child-rearing practices.

This approach no longer characterizes child psychology. It has become increasingly obvious that a considerable distance lies between awareness that a child becomes negativistic at about the age of two and understanding of why this should be the case. The child psychologist today is much more interested in developing and testing models or theories which may lead to such understanding than he is in providing parents with advice on how to raise their children. This is probably a healthy development, for the value of advice will surely be greater when it is based on real understanding of the developing child.

Developmental-Cognitive Approach

A particularly important theoretical approach which has also employed normative investigations is that of Piaget and his co-workers (1950, 1962). His system has recently become the focal point of attention for many child psychologists. The popularity of this system is in part attributable to the fact that it includes all the possible factors that could conceivably be advanced to account for human development. Although the maturationist may stress endogenous factors and the environmentalist learning, both can feel comfortable with at least some aspects of Piaget's conceptual rubric. To Piaget development is a function of an internal process, equilibration, which in turn is dependent on activity and experience. Development as conceptualized by Piaget is something quite different from Gesell's maturation, because it is highly influenced by the experiences of the individual which bring out latent contradictions and gaps in his mental structure and thus act as a catalyst for inner reorganization. We thus have here an interactionist position: Piaget's central concepts of accommodation and assimilation refer explicitly to a continuous interaction between organism and environment.

Piaget has concerned himself primarily with developmental changes in cognitive processes, stressing both their reorganization over time and the successive emergence of new structures and operations. Emphasizing the lawfulness and universality of these changes, he has constructed a predominantly descriptive system in which development is portrayed as a succession of stages.

Although the view that the child develops through a series of stages is not unique to Piaget, his particular view is of special importance. As Bronfenbrenner (1963) has noted, Piaget's approach forces us to emphasize systematic properties and their qualitative alterations over the course of development. This emphasis on qualitative changes in the properties of formal systems (for example, cognitive structures) is considerably at odds with the conception of development as a series of quantitative increments along a monotonic scale, a view which inheres in so many of the atheoretical normative studies.

Criticisms of the Developmental-Cognitive Approach

However, stage theory in general and Piaget's stage theory in particular have evoked considerable criticism. It has been charged that (1) stage distinctions are arbitrary, and (2) developmentalists underemphasize cultural and experiential factors. With respect to the first criticism, that of arbitrariness, English (1957) has found little agreement among experts as to the age ranges assigned to commonly designated stages in development and has been forced to conclude that all the present stage distinctions are arbitrary. Thompson (1959) has argued that this arbitrariness stems from the lack of developmental meaningfulness of many of the stage sequences. Thompson has pointed out that what is required are truly developmental stages with important psychological properties which may not be isomorphically coordinated with chronological ages, but which would define identifiable developmental processes related to behavior change. A theoretical critique by Zigler (1963a) shows the emptiness of the age concept and the necessity for truly developmental sequences to be based on psychological process. Piaget's stages generally do appear to meet the criteria of process orientation and developmental meaningfulness noted by Thompson. However, the degree to which Piaget's stages are in keeping with these criteria is clouded by Piaget's practice of stating ages for each stage he describes.

The criticism most frequently leveled against Piaget and other developmentalists is that their approach underemphasizes the importance of cultural and experiential factors in determining the nature of thought and that with proper emphasis on these factors cognitive development will no longer be seen as moving through a series of stages.

Bandura and Walters (1963a) have criticized stage theories on these grounds. These social-learning theorists have argued that it is an error to view behavior as progressing through a relatively fixed sequence of discontinuous stages. They point out that the stage approach, which emphasizes intraindividual variability over time and similarities among individuals at a common age or stage, neglects marked interindividual variability in behavior caused by biological, socioeconomic, cultural, and personality differences. In advancing a position completely antithetical to the stage approach, Bandura and Walters have asserted that the widely differing reinforcement contingencies and social models experienced by children at the same age level result in considerable interindividual variability. Furthermore, because the variety of factors that determine an individual's social-training experiences remains relatively constant throughout much of the child's earlier lifetime, we should expect considerable intraindividual continuity in behavior at successive ages. In common with many other learning theorists Bandura and Walters see the learning process as being qualitatively the same at every point in the life cycle and conclude that only those rarely occurring abrupt alterations in social training would result in the marked changes emphasized by stage theorists. However, this continuity position appears to run headlong into the considerable evidence that there are qualitative changes in thought processes and in the very nature of learning at various times during childhood, two relatively clear instances occurring at approximately eighteen months of age and between five and eight years of age (Bronfenbrenner, 1963; Kendler, 1963; Kendler and Kendler, 1962; Turnure, 1966; Wallach 1963; White, 1963).

Furthermore, the assertion that two children are at the same stage and are thus both employing some common formal psychological features does not mean that both children will emit exactly the same behaviors. It is only the formal, that is, structural, properties of the underlying psychological process that are common. The particular contents of the behavior are determined by the learning phenomena emphasized by Bandura and Walters, with the formal properties of the stage determining the upper limits of what can be learned as well as the particular process that mediates learning itself. As Inhelder (1957) has noted, the structures of thought help shape experience itself as the child apprehends it, and changes in the child's experience which come with changing structure must themselves be considered a crucial factor in the socialization process. The appropriateness of Piaget's constructs and hypotheses for analyzing the child's thinking about his social environment has also been emphasized by Wallach (1963) and Bronfenbrenner (1963). Piaget's applicability may be seen in those efforts that have utilized developmental thinking in dealing with such matters of central concern to students of socialization as dependency, morality, and sex role identification (Kohlberg, 1963a; Kohlberg and Zigler, 1967; Turiel, 1966; Zigler, 1963b).

The developmentalist notion of a fixed sequence of stages in the development of cognition must be antithetical to any purely environmentalistic approach to the development of thought because an important maturational influence seems necessary to explain similar findings repeatedly reported from culturally different populations. It is incorrect, however, to view developmentalists as nativists or pure maturationists who feel that development is uninfluenced by the individual's experiences. As Inhelder (1957) has stated, "structures of thought ... are not innate inasmuch as they are slow to appear and present variations in the average age of appearance depending on the cultural milieu" (p. 157). The disagreements between present-day developmentalists and learning theorists are more apparent than real. Considerable theoretical gains could be attained if both groups turned their attention to the solution of two major problems: (1) the degree to which and the process by which environmental factors influence the rate of development through the sequential stages, and (2) determination of those aspects of behavior which are little influenced by environmental factors and those which are almost completely a product of the individual's particular experiences. The seemingly wide disparity between such learning theorists as Bandura and Walters and such stage theorists as Piaget may be due in considerable part to the fact that they address themselves to quite different realms of behavior rather than to any disagreement about interpretation of the same behavior. Bandura and Walters have concerned themselves with aspects of social behavior observable at any developmental level and varying widely at each level, whereas Piaget has been primarily interested in those formal features of cognitive processes that tend to be characteristic of particular developmental levels.

Numerous studies have by now been directed at resolving for particular topics the problems just suggested. For instance, Ezer (1962) has shown that even with age and intelligence controlled, children with religious training, as compared to children without such training, responded more animistically and anthropomorphically to questions involving physical causality. On the other hand, considerable evidence has been presented that even with training it is extremely difficult to improve the quality of cognitive functioning on Piaget-type tasks (Smedslund, 1961; Turiel, 1966; Wohlwill and Lowe, 1962). In research which also gives us an instance of the use of cross-cultural evidence to test psychological theory, M. Mead (1932) found that contrary to expectations based on Piaget's sequential stage notions, Manus children

analyzed situations in a more logical manner than did their animistic elders. This led her to conclude that animistic thought could not be explained in terms of intellectual immaturity. On the other hand, Piaget's view concerning the development of causal thinking was essentially confirmed in Dennis' (1940) cross-cultural work with Zuni and Navaho children. (In a more recent cross-cultural investigation, however, Dennis [1957] found a much larger percentage of Near Eastern college and high school students than American students responding animistically, and he attributed this to cultural differences in scientific concepts and information.)

Resolution of the problems is also aided by conceptual clarification such as Kohlberg (1966) has provided. Although himself a stage theorist, Kohlberg argues that certain behaviors that have been thought to be sequential are actually a hodgepodge of traits that do not have the character of true developmental dimensions. For example, Piaget has postulated a shift in the course of development from the authority of adults to the authority of peers; shift on this dimension has been found to vary widely as a function of cultural and experiential factors. It does appear in American children but is almost absent among the Swiss. Even in the United States it appears to be heavily influenced by social class, sex, and family variation. Kohlberg points out that there is nothing more cognitively mature or rational about preferring a peer to an adult; such a criterion, not mere correlation with age, is needed to justify conceptualizing a shift as cognitive-developmental in nature. For contrast, Kohlberg calls attention to Piaget's view that with increasing age the bases of a child's moral judgments shift away from consideration of the gross consequences of the act toward consideration of the actor's intentions. This shift does require a change in the logical operations of thought, characterized by increasing differentiation of physical and mental and increasing awareness that values fall into the latter category. One would therefore expect this shift to be a genuine developmental dimension, and cross-cultural evidence confirms the expectation. As Kohlberg notes, the developmental increase in this trait of intentionality has been found in America, Switzerland, Turkey, and China and among the Atayal, the Hopi, the Zuni, the Papago, and the Maya.

The invariance of sequence does not mean that this trait is uninfluenced by environmental factors. For instance, we find earlier intentionality for middle-class than for lower-class children, and this difference does not seem entirely explicable biologically. One environmental influence is easily recognized as likely: that greater intentionality of moral judgment may be characteristically reached by children in a group where it is stronger among adults. But the developmental view calls attention to another environmental influence long neglected by other psychologists which may be much more important; if middle-class children receive more cognitive and social stimulation of development, then they may be expected to reach greater intentionality of moral judgment regardless of what moral judgments they hear expressed by their elders. Cultural differences, Kohlberg argues, may well influence the speed of development toward intentionality and the level generally reached, but they are not likely to alter the direction of development.

A dimension presenting inconsistent cross-cultural findings, such as those of Mead reported earlier, poses more difficulty, and again Kohlberg's analysis is very insightful. Piaget's stages in the child's view of physical causality do appear to reflect a truly cognitive-developmental dimension. Why then does Mead find adults more animistic in their thinking than children? An answer is suggested in Kohlberg's (1966) investigation of the view of dreams among the Atayal, a Malaysian aboriginal group in Formosa. Among middle-class American children the first step away from belief in the reality of dreams occurs before five,

when the child recognizes that dreams are not real events. The next step, achieved shortly thereafter, is that dreams cannot be seen by others. By age six children become aware that dreams take place inside themselves, and by seven they become aware that dreams are thoughts which they themselves produce. In contrast to this Kohlberg found that among the Atayal, adults believe in the reality of dreams. In investigating the development of dream concepts among Atayal children, Kohlberg found that up until the age of eleven they developed (although more slowly) toward a subjective conception of the dream through much the same steps as American children. However, at age eleven and beyond Atayal children and adolescents have a more external view of the dream than do younger children. Kohlberg suggests that it is around age eleven that they first seem really to learn the adult culture's view of the dream.

The implication here is that a normally developing attitude dictated by certain underlying cognitive changes clashes with a particular cultural attitude, and it is the cultural attitude that prevails. It would be extremely interesting to see whether the animistic thought of the adult Manus and the external view of the dream of the adult Atayal have the same formal structure as the superficially similar thoughts of immature children the world over. The developmentalist would predict that they do not and that a more fine-grained analysis of these beliefs would permit a separation of developmental from cultural factors. Thus, the developmentalist would assert that although any inherently developmental attitude could be clouded by a cultural overlay, a thorough examination would reveal features dictated by the individual's developmental structure.

This discussion should make it clear that the developmental approach in general and Piaget's in particular present a number of unresolved issues to the student of socialization. Piaget appears to desert us after the point at which sequentiality and age norms are demonstrated. In spite of a commitment to the importance of the individual, the environment, and the interaction between the two, both the individual and the environment appear to be treated as something of a constant. As others have noted (Hunt, 1961; Wolff, 1960), nothing in Piaget offers much help or encouragement in assessing the effects of either the state of the organism or differences in the environment that give rise to individual differences in development.

Piaget's supporters have failed to appreciate the importance of studies demonstrating that Piaget's age norms do not fit in other cultures. To stress that Piaget is more interested in demonstrating the sequence of such development, rather than the age at which certain behaviors become manifest, is to miss the point of such critical studies. In dealing with socialization we are most intimately concerned with the issue of what conditions give rise to what behaviors and why. This concern is manifested in the study of individual differences, and a system that addresses itself to development but makes no real allowances for such differencies can hardly represent an adequate approach to socialization. The problem may rest in Piaget's own goals. As has frequently been noted (for example, Martin, 1959), Piaget has been more interested in developing an epistemology than a psychology. Or as Kessen (1962) has stated, "it should be noted that Piaget has little interest in individual variation among children in the rate at which they achieve a stage or in their overall capacity during it; he is a student of the development of thinking more than he is a student of children" (p. 77). Nevertheless, students of socialization are indebted to Piaget and other cognitive-developmental thinkers for emphasizing what must certainly be a crucial factor in the socialization process, namely, the cognitive structure with which the individual mediates his experiences.

Two stimulating theoretical papers by Scheerer (1953) and Leeper (1953) suggest the importance of the cognitive structure or the general intellective features of the individual as a determinant in socialization. Evidence in support of this view can be seen in a number of empirical studies. For example, in what must certainly be one of the most ambitious longitudinal investigations of general adjustment ever conducted, Anderson (1960b) found that intelligence in childhood was highly predictive of adjustment both in later childhood and in adulthood. That general intellective level is an important determinant of the outcome of socialization can be seen vividly in the longitudinal studies of retarded and intellectually superior individuals (Charles, 1953; Collman and Newlyn, 1957; E. Miller, 1965; Terman and Oden, 1959). One does not have to be concerned with whether socialization determines the intellect or whether intellect determines socialization in order to conclude that no matter how the intellect evolves, it is an important determinant in the individual's interpretation of his social milieu and thus of considerable import in the socialization process (see Zigler and Harter, 1969).

Genetic Approach

Although there is little question that the bulk of empirical efforts dealing with the socialization process has had a predominantly environmentalistic orientation, we are now witnessing a rekindling of interest in genetic factors. That genetics, with its essential commitment to the phenomenon of variability, has been so little employed by workers committed to the investigation of individual differences is an interesting matter in its own right. The historical factors and the particular values of our society that gave rise to this state of affairs have been discussed by Burton (in press), McKee and Honzik (1962), and Zigler (1966a). That the genetic approach can bring new breadth to our thinking can be

seen in examining cross-cultural social an-
thropological evidence. Differences in behavior uncovered in such investigations are
almost exclusively attributed to external
culture and experiental differences. As
McKee and Honzik (1962) point out, the
assumption that cultural variation reflects
only environmental variation is extremely
dubious if one suspects that the societies
concerned represent different genetic pools.

An extremely telling indictment of an
overly environmentalistic approach to behavior can be found in the recent work of
Thomas, Birch, Chess, Hertzig, and Korn
(1963). These workers correctly point out
that even the developmental-cognitive
approach (discussed earlier), which many
feel emphasizes the genetic aspects of behavior, actually addresses itself to how a
developmental level or stage is important
in structuring the individual's reactions to
his environment. Thus, the concept of
developmental level or stage is more concerned with general laws of responsiveness
and addresses itself to the sequentiality in
which various systematic organizations
make their appearance rather than to the
problem of individuality or uniqueness
of functioning.

A truly genetic approach requires one to
focus upon the initial biological characteristics of the individual as significant factors
in determining the development of psychological individuality. Thomas et al. have
themselves isolated a number of early-
appearing and persisting reactivity patterns
that appear to be responsible for variations
in behavior when environmental factors
remain constant. These authors have
pointed out that the tactics utilized by
socializing agents will have different behavioral results depending on the nature of
the child to whom they are applied.

The need for rescuing this genetic approach from what Bell (1965) refers to as its
excommunication has been asserted cogently by Hirsch (1963), who makes a convincing case for the central role of genetic
factors in understanding of human be-

havior. This is not to say that the genetic
approach has been without active spokes-
men among those interested in human behavior. This approach has continually been
represented as one pole of the nature-nurture
controversy and has represented the theoretical foundation for considerable work
in developmental biology (for example,
Hamburger, 1957), typologic constitutional views from Hippocrates to
Sheldon and Stevens (1942), and a
variety of studies on temperament and
character. [See V. Jones (1954) for a review
of this work.] Although it is true that the
nature-nurture controversy has abated considerably, this does not mean that it was
ever resolved in any very fruitful way. What
appears to have happened in American
psychology in the past two decades is that a
consensus was reached that behavior was
ultimately the product of some "complex
interaction" between these two sets of
forces. Following this consensus the great
majority of American workers continued to
give some lip service to biogenetic factors,
while attending almost exclusively to those
environmentalistic factors that are un-
questionably important determinants of
human behavior.

The pragmatic dangers involved in ignoring genetic factors have been pointed
out by Bruch (1954). Furthermore, the recent work in animal and human behavior
genetics and in ethology (Lorenz, 1952,
1965, 1966; Scott, 1957, 1963; Vandenberg,
1965) is highly relevant to the concerns of
the student of socialization. These workers
are further along than many appreciate in
relating specific behavior to particular interactions between genetic and environmental
factors, and in unraveling the mystery of
how much of the variance in certain behavior can be attributed to each set of factors.
Their efforts have been greatly facilitated
by developments in basic genetics, which
has witnessed a movement away from the
early Mendelian emphasis on the activity of
specific dominant and recessive genes in
favor of polygenic models of inheritance as

well as the development of new statistical approaches (Cattell, 1965).

The relationship between biogenetic and environmental factors is surely complicated and remains baffling. We get some conception of its complexity in the many possible explanatory models that have been enumerated by Cattell (1965). By what route, for example, should genetic characteristics be said to influence environmental determinants of behavior? One possibility is that a person's genetic makeup leads him to create a particular environment for himself. A plausible case for this interpretation is made by Cattell, Blewett, and Beloff (1955) in arguing that people who are aesthetically sensitive—a trait they believe to have a significant inherited component—tend to create a protected, unambitious, aesthetically soothing environment for themselves. Another possibility is that genetically determined characteristics evoke distinctive responses from others and thus elicit rather than create a special environment; an example here is that aggression is often met with aggression (Cattell et al., 1955).

However genetic factors spell themselves out in behavior, a considerable body of literature now exists indicating that such factors are important determinants of individual differences in behavior in infants and young children. As noted by Thomas et al. (1963), such differences have now been found in such specific discrete areas as sensory threshold (Bergman and Escalona, 1949), motility (Fries and Woolf, 1953) perceptual responses (Witkin, Dyk, Faterson, Goodenough, and Karp 1962), sleeping and feeding patterns (Escalona, 1953), drive endowment (Alpert, Newbauer, and Weil, 1956), quality and intensity of emotional tone (Meili, 1959), social responsiveness (Gesell and Ames, 1937), autonomic response patterns (Bridger and Reiser, 1959; Lipton, Steinschneider, and Richmond, 1961), biochemical individuality (Williams, 1956), and electroencephalogenic patterns (Walter, 1953). Although

these differences may in part result from prenatal environment (Pasamanick and Knoblock, 1958; Pasamanick, Knoblock and Lilienfeld, 1956), they certainly indicate that individual differences potentially important for later social behavior are present at birth or shortly thereafter.

Muller (1958), a geneticist considering social behavior from the viewpoint of evolution and the survival value of particular traits, has shown how particular behavior tendencies could have been transmitted genetically along family lines and argues that much of the variance among individuals in aggressiveness, dependence, and other traits may be due to genetic factors. Such human behavior geneticists as Cattell (1965), Cattell, Stice, and Kristy (1957), Eysenck (1954), and Gottesman (1965) have provided considerable evidence that tends to support this interpretation. Employing statistical techniques, which have been referred to as both ingenious and questionable (Vandenberg, 1965), these workers have found a number of primary personality factors, major defenses, and traits to have an important hereditary component.

Tentative though the evidence remains, it is clear that students of socialization can no longer afford to ignore the genetic factor if we are truly to comprehend the socialization process; rather, we may expect to find genetic research increasingly a source of ideas and evidence in the future.

Learning Theory Approaches

For all their importance, the maturational-normative, cognitive-developmental, and genetic approaches must be considered minority positions in the study of socialization. In this section we shall turn our attention to a majority position, namely, the learning theory approach. Socialization phenomena investigated within our society have typically been placed somewhere within this broad theoretical rubric.

This approach is not easy to define. An historical characterization was succinctly given by R. Sears (1959):

It did not stem from the work of any one person. It has not been monolithic, nor has it suffered the stultification of possessing an orthodoxy. Rather, it is the cumulation of that distinctively American behavioral theory that began with Thorndike, became *istic* with Watson, technically sophisticated with Tolman, Guthrie, and Hull, and more precise with Miller, Skinner, and Spence. *Stimulus-response theory* is as good a name for it as any [pp. 42–43].

The specific content varies a good deal, and it is useful to distinguish three major strains of learning theory presently being employed extensively in the investigation of the socialization process.

Neo-Hullian Theory

Perhaps the best known and most influential group of investigators committed to a stimulus-response analysis of socialization are the neo-Hullians (Dollard and Miller, 1950; Nowlis, 1952; R. Sears, Maccoby, and Levin, 1957; R. Sears, et al. 1953; Whiting and Child, 1953), whose theoretical ancestry can be traced directly to the learning work conducted at Yale under the direction of Clark Hull.

Although differing views can be found even among this relatively homogenous group, one does find a common commitment to the applicability of general behavior theory, a tension-reduction approach to the problem of motivation which emphasizes the importance of external reinforcement, and a willingness to include in their theory such intervening variables as needs or motives and expectancies. [See R. Sears (1951), especially on this last point.]

The metamorphosis of Hullian theories in the hands of these workers is of great importance. The relatively new emphasis on mediational variables in the theoretical constructions of such workers as Miller, Dollard, Sears, Mowrer, and Osgood has given considerable new breadth to Hullian learning theory, making it capable of handling many phenomena of central concern to students of socialization.

Social Learning Theory

A learning theory approach noticeably different from the one just described is the social learning position of such workers as Bandura and Walters (Bandura, 1962, 1965; Bandura and Walters, 1959, 1963a; Walters and Brown, 1964; Walters and Parke, 1964). Although continuing to note the importance of external reinforcement in learning, these investigators have tended to emphasize modeling, imitation, and vicarious learning that is somewhat independent of external reinforcement. Their basically parsimonious approach to theory construction has led them to question the value of secondary drive constructs (for example, dependence and aggression) and other intervening variables so important to the neo-Hullians.

The social learning workers also appear to differ from neo-Hullians in what variables interest them in experimental study of learning. As Bronfenbrenner (1963) has pointed out, such workers as Bandura and Walters have "socialized" learning experiments in that they emphasize the social aspect of learning, and, in contrast to the neoclassic learning experiment, they attend explicitly to the sex, age, and occupation of E and to E's attitudes toward S.

Skinnerian Theory

A third learning theory approach to the socialization of the child can be seen in those efforts emanating directly from Skinner's position. This approach to socialization has been presented most clearly and completely by Bijou and Baer (1961) and has become increasingly popular, as can be seen in the many investigations of the acquisition of a variety of behavior of great importance in socialization (Krasner and Ullman, 1965; Ullman and Krasner, 1965). This is certainly the most mechanistic of the stimulus-response approaches in that social behavior is viewed as being completely shaped by reinforcement histories. This approach limits itself to a "functional analysis" framework involving the investigation of the functional relationships between discrete response and stimulus events. The mediational or intervening variables of other learning theorists are seen as excess theoretical baggage. The only aspects of the child thought to be important in determining the functional relationship between a stimulus and a response is his past reinforcement history and relative satiation on the particular reinforcer being dispensed to influence his behavior. Exactly the same paradigm is viewed as operative in the acquisition of all behavior, and the most complex social responses are viewed as products of the learning processes described by Skinner.

Similarities Among Learning Theories

Although pure exponents of each of these three positions can be identified, many students of socialization employ an eclectic learning theory approach that differentially partakes of these various strains, depending upon the particular data to be investigated or explained. There is, of course, a good deal in common among these various approaches. They all tend to an environmentalistic rather than nativistic bias. They are all behavior-oriented in the sense that their ultimate explanatory efforts are directed at understanding circumscribed responses emitted by the child in the presence of designated stimulus configurations. They are all general behavior theorists in viewing their principles as applicable at every ontogenetic level and, in many instances, across

phylogenetic levels as well. All are rigorous and tough-minded in their approach, aiming at precise formulation of their ideas. They share a special respect for experimental method.

Developmental vs. Learning Theories: Sources of Disagreement

Another similarity shared by learning theories is that all have been construed (some more correctly than others) as representing an orientation that stands in opposition to the developmental approach (see Russell, 1957; Zigler, 1963a). The antipathy between learning and developmental thinkers has already been touched upon, and the fundamental differences in the two approaches are of considerable interest to the student of socialization. These differences in approach have been discussed at some length by Russell (1957) and Zigler (1963a). As suggested earlier, a major difference is that learning theorists tend to see behavior as a function of forces applied to the child, whereas developmentalists tend to focus on sequential changes in the psychological structure of the child himself. The changes developmentalists find in formal structure convince them that behavior is mediated by quite different processes at various ages, whereas learning theorists view the same underlying processes as operative throughout the life cycle.

Concern with the developmental problem did lead to a concession by a major learning theorist, Hull; the final postulate of his system (1951, 1952) states that the constant numerical values appearing in equations representing behavioral laws vary in the same individual at different times. In general, learning theorists appear to bridge the gap between principles invariant with age and empirical evidence of change by invoking the concept of maturation. Thus, learning theorists treat maturation as an apparently simple biological given, whereas to the developmentalist it has always been an extremely complex process requiring theoretical illumination in its own right. To learning theorists growth only requires changing parametric values, whereas to the developmentalists growth has to be treated as the central content of the theory. Stated somewhat differently, the learning theorists handle observed changes in the effectiveness of variables at different ages by introducing into their equations or predictions different values for the parameters of interest to them. Developmentalists are interested in a superordinate explanation of all such substitutions of values. Although learning theorists may change the values of their parameters from age to age, developmentalists are concerned with discovering the transition rules for these changes and thus making the change itself, rather than the content of change, the central issue. Learning theorists, committed to the study of general processes that relate the organism to its environment through its past history, continued to remain indifferent to the repeated demonstration of striking changes in behavior that are relatively uninfluenced and unmodifiable by the organism's experiences. This indifference has understandably annoyed the developmentalists. In their turn, though, the latter have been slow to appreciate the importance in the developmental process of the principles emphasized by learning theorists. Even developmentalists of the interactionist persuasion, though giving considerable lip service to the importance of the experiences of the organism, nevertheless tend to treat experience and learning as a constant and give their primary theoretical attention to internal factors in the developmental process.

For a more adequate theory of socialization we must obviously await a genuine synthesis of developmental and learning theory approaches. So far there has been more controversy than synthesis, and the controversy has brought to attention two major issues which we will explore at greater length in the following chapters.

Summary. We have reviewed the contributions of psychoanalytic, normative-maturational, cognitive-developmental, genetic, and learning theory approaches to the study of socialization. Although all approaches continue to contribute to our knowledge of the socialization process, there is now a tendency to abandon atheoretical approaches (for example, normative-maturational) and unarticulated theories (for example, psychoanalytic) in favor of theory-building, as represented by learning and cognitive-developmental approaches. With this emphasis there has been an expansion of areas of interest to encompass a wider range of human behavior and a new attention to genetic factors in the socialization process.

13

Current Issues and Their Implications

Out of the diverse points of view reviewed in Chapter 12, two major issues emerge which appear to be of paramount importance for an understanding or even definition of socialization: (1) whether the human being, child or adult, should be considered an active or passive agent in his socialization, and (2) whether he is to be viewed as essentially positive or negative in nature. As in the preceding chapter, we suggest that thinking about socialization has reflected the implicit assumptions of theories which have been most popular in American psychology. The implications of more recent approaches will be presented as alternatives which must now be considered in the building of a theory of socialization.

Active vs. Passive Views of the Child

A view of human nature as inherently active or passive leads to very different conceptions of the socialization process. If the individual is seen as a passive organism who brings nothing to his environment, then environment and experience must be the focus of attention to understand socialization; on the other hand, if the individual is seen as possessing innate behavioral propensities and the capacity to structure aspects of his own experience, the role of environment is somewhat diminished and the capabilities of the individual become an essential factor in our conception of the socialization process. The contrast, then, is whether the individual is solely acted *on* by his environment or whether he interacts *with* his environment.

The Passive View

The insistence of so many investigators (Harlow, 1953; Kessen, 1963; White, 1960) on treating the child as an active agent, playing an important role in his own development, makes it impossible for us to content ourselves with what has come to be called the "social mold theory" of socialization (Homans, 1950; Wrong, 1961). The view that socialization is essentially the habit-training of a basically passive organism, so well exemplified by the work of Blatz (1944), retains a certain popularity. It is expressed very directly in recent efforts to conceptualize the socialization process within a Skinnerian framework, with its emphasis on shaping behavior through the application of external rewards and punishments (see Bijou and Baer, 1961). It seems to appear in a modified form in the recent work on socialization by Berkowitz (1964a), insofar as he argues against the importance of those nativistic growth gradients that have been emphasized by such self-actualization theorists as Maslow (1954) and Allport (1955). The passive view appears, too, in the statement of basic assumptions in Dager's recent treatment of socialization (1964). One assumption is that the individual is born neither social nor antisocial, but asocial. A second assumption is that we can ignore individual differences due to heredity and other biological factors. Yet Dager presents something of a paradox, because in the postulates that follow his assumptions he insists that the child be considered not a passive agent—as in the classical behaviorism of Watson or in strict cultural determinism—but rather an active agent able to use his existing knowledge in a way original enough to induce change from his previously accepted ways of behaving. Dager also argues that an inherent characteristic of man is his continual effort to put order into his world. These latter views do not appear consistent with any *tabula rasa* approach to socialization, because they appear to postulate basic, inherent attributes that are themselves important in determining how external forces will affect the developing child.

The Active View

The child as an active and positive agent in his own socialization can be found in Parsons' (1958) view that from the very beginning the child "tries to do things" (to maximize his control over his environment). Parsons' view is bolstered by the recent empirical work on infancy. For example, Peiper's research (1963) has made it clear that the behavior of the newborn is

much more competent than had previously been supposed. Kessen (1963), recently reviewing research on infancy, has also emphasized that the underlying conception has been changing from that of an undifferentiated, passive recipient of stimulation to that of an active, competent organism in reciprocal interaction with the environment. Errors following from an extreme passive-child approach are pointed to in the complaint by Bell (1965) and the Wenars (1963) that the literature on child-rearing practices has been built almost entirely on the assumption of a unidirectional effect from parents to offspring. Bell (1965), after noting that the most influential model of the human offspring has been that of a passive recipient of the imprint of the socialization process, has argued that such a passive model is not even appropriate to the interaction of animal young with their environment. Recent publications by Noirot (1964), Rheingold (1963), Ressler (1962, 1963), and Denenberg (1963) clearly show at a subhuman level the importance of the young organism's own behavior in determining the environmental events he experiences. But this newer view has not been universally accepted, and the more passive conception of the child, associated with classical psychoanalysis and American learning theory, continues to find adherents.

The importance of viewing the child in the socialization process as an open system having important inherent characteristics and transacting with the environment rather than being merely a reactor or even an interacter has been emphasized by such thoughtful developmentalists as Anderson (1957) and Harris (1963). The transactional concept underlines the view that the child does things to the environment and is a corrective to the view that behavior is solely reactive or situationally determined.

That a shift in emphasis from a passive to an active view of the child changes our approach to the socialization process has also been noted by R. Brown (1965). Brown, as well as others (for example,

Kohlberg, 1966), has pointed out the inadequacy of those treatments in which socialization is variously conceptualized to be simply the control of impulses, the acquisition of values conforming to norms, or the internalization of parental superego. Such approaches underemphasize the intellectual side of socialization and the active role played by the child. We see in the work of R. Brown (1965) and Kohlberg (1966) how the concept of the active child goes beyond the view that the child influences as well as being influenced. Their emphasis is rather on the importance of the child's intellectual and cognitive characteristics in mediating those external events likely to be important in the socialization process. As Brown points out, before the child can set a positive value on achievement and a negative value on aggression, he must have the cognitive apparatus required to conceptualize achievement and aggression. Such concepts, moreover, are not mechanically stamped in by the socializing agents but must be gradually formed and assimilated to an already ongoing cognitive structure, which is itself changing over time. Thus, the very "same" norm is repeatedly transformed by the child as his cognitive apparatus changes with maturity. This view of the child as an active processor of the society's norms and standards is a far cry from the approach which views socialization as a simple transmission of norms from one generation to the next.

The concept of the active child also forces us to consider those innate biological factors that may play a role in the child's behavior. Criticism of the typical treatment of socialization as abiological has been voiced before (Goodman, 1960; Wrong, 1961). The issue is critical for any comprehensive theory of the socialization process for at least two reasons. Biological factors seem certain to be important in producing individual differences in socialization, and in a variety of subtle as well as obvious ways; a comprehensive theory must be able to deal with these individual differences. Biological factors are certainly important in obvious ways in producing uniformities of socialization as well, but it seems very probable today that subtle processes, challenging to a theory of socialization, are important for uniformities too. An instance is the recent view that the biological programing of the human animal has far more to do with language acquisition than has previously been suspected (Lenneberg, 1967).

Once one considers the biological characteristics of the species, the unique genetic inheritance of the individual, and the everchanging cognitive apparatus with which the developing child mediates his environment, then the socialization process can no longer be viewed as the simple inculcation of conformity to the culture's norms. It is viewed instead as an extremely complex process. The difference here has been articulated in the distinction made by Wrong (1961) between socialization as the "transmission of the culture" and socialization as the "process of becoming human." A view of the child as an active agent in socialization not only requires attention to biological factors, but may itself grow out of attention to biological factors.

Summary. The view of the child as a passive agent in the socialization process, suggested by classical psychoanalysis and American learning theory, has been predominant in thinking about socialization. Cognitive-developmental theory, self-actualization personality theories, and recent advances in behavior genetics have presented a view of the child as an active agent in the socialization process.

Positive vs. Negative Approaches to Man's Inherent Nature

A second issue has been emphasized in other discussions of socialization. This issue also concerns views of human nature which have implications for views of the socialization process. The pertinent views of human nature underlying this issue are more diverse than in the case of the first issue. Several variables in the conception of man can be treated together because they tend to be correlated, a thinker's position on one variable being somewhat predictive of his position on the others, but even more because of the similarity of their implications for a view of socialization. One variable has to do with whether man is thought of as inherently evil or inherently good; this is obviously a question which the scientific temper might want to regard as irrelevant, yet a position on it is implicit in many a piece of scientific research. A second variable is whether man is thought of as innately motivated only by biological drives arising out of physiological functioning of his organs or whether he is thought of as innately motivated also by social motives relating directly to his social interaction. A third variable is whether the goal states in which he finds pleasure are thought to consist only of the reduction of drives (or tension or stimulation) or whether the goal states are also thought to include the production or the creation of something (for example, an object, a social relationship, or an understanding). What is common to these variables in the conception of man may be summed up by saying that each contrasts a negative view with a positive view. These labels are appropriate primarily in relation to implications for socialization. The first-named end of each variable is a view of man's nature that sees it as making socialization difficult: evil must be curbed, biological drives must be forged into tools of society, and drive-reduction must be prevented except when it can serve these ends. The second-named end of each variable is a view that sees man's nature as making socialization easy: the good person will seek to do what is good, the socially-motivated child falls short of adult standards in understanding rather than in motivation, and if the attainment

of understanding is one of his basic goals he is well on his way to remedying the deficiency. These variables, then, all imply a contrast between seeing socialization as imposing conformity and seeing it as facilitating self-actualization.

The Negative View

The negative position has been familiar in discussion of socialization at least since the time of Hobbes, who in effect posed the question of how socialization is possible at all in light of man's base and negative animal nature. Both Wrong (1961) and Parsons (1937) have suggested that the solution of the Hobbesian question is the main problem of socialization. Parsons, for example, has referred to the birth of new generations as a "recurrent barbarian invasion" (noted in R. Brown, 1965). Wrong criticizes our current thinking on the grounds that it does not fully appreciate the base and physiological nature of man's motives, and therefore sees socialization as simple and relatively undemanding. But adherents of the positive view would make just the opposite criticism; that is, current thinking so emphasizes the negative side of human nature that socialization is viewed exclusively as the imposition of restraints.

This negative approach to man is certainly represented in treatments of socialization based on the classical Freudian approach to socialization. Although some (for example, Peller, 1946; Wrong, 1961) find in Freud an emphasis on the positive and self-actualizing, the classical Freudian approach has more often given rise to what Rapaport (1959) has called the "seething cauldron" view, in which man is relentlessly pursued by the demons of the id. In the Hobbesian tradition, Freud believed that society existed primarily to protect men from each other, and that culture was established to assist in preventing the breakthrough of primitive, selfish, or destructive needs. As Merton (1957) has noted, once one accepts this formulation, the social order is assigned the almost totally negative role of blocking or re-channeling man's "imperious biological drives."

Freudian thought is not the only important recent source of this negative approach to man. Behavior theory has been at least as important a source. This theory has tended to attribute major importance to drives that can most easily be considered as strictly physiological and to view behavior as being aroused only under negative circumstances, that is, when the organism is deprived of some essential sustenance. Attempts are made to explain the most complex and intricate human behavior as resulting from such needs and their frustration. Freud and Hull were alike in viewing man's goal as the reduction of tension. This view leads to seeing socialization as a very difficult enterprise in which society seeks to mold a recalcitrant organism. It affects, as Berkowitz (1964a) points out, even a judgment about what types of child-rearing practices will be most conducive to successful socialization.

The Positive View

Recent years have produced a vigorous reaction to this negative tension-reduction view of man. This reaction has been nicely summarized by R. White (1959) in the course of presenting his own argument for recognition of an effectance motive as an important element in the positive nature of man. The reaction can be seen within behavior theory and within psychoanalysis. It is especially in animal experimentation that behavior theorists have demonstrated a growing concern with curiosity, manipulation, exploration, and other features of positive adaptation which are viewed as essentially independent of the biological drives. The psychoanalytic ego psychology of Hartmann and others (Hartmann, 1958; Hartmann, Kriss, and Lowenstein, 1949) advances the view that man's lifelong efforts toward adaptation and mastery cannot be explained solely in terms of the satisfaction of basic drives. These theoreticians argue that no amount of theoretical circumlocution can logically transform libidinal and aggressive drives alone into the total motivation of that primarily reality-adapted organism which is man. They give the adaptive and positive aspects of behavior, represented by the ego, an independent existence rather than viewing the ego as servant of a more basic structure of primitive instincts.

The developmental-cognitive approach to the child has always been antithetical to the Hobbesian conceptualization of man which other approaches have so often found congenial. Developmentalists have generally viewed development, both initially and in its later stages, as a positive process. Growth is conceptualized as the continuous emergence of ever greater adaptive abilities, with the growing organism demonstrating and fulfilling this greater potential at successive stages in his development. The negative approach, whether in its psychoanalytic or its behavioristic version, has always been unacceptable to developmentalists because it seems incompatible with the self-actualizing features so obvious in gross observation of a child's development.

In addition to the developmentalists a group of general personality theorists, including Maslow (1954), Jahoda (1955), Allport (1955), and Rogers (1951), have also emphasized positive intrinsic growth tendencies, and in fact such workers are often referred to as self-actualization theorists. In a recent treatment of socialization Berkowitz (1964a) pointed out how the self-actualization concept, which has much in common with Rousseau's notion of the "noble savage," represents the antithesis of those theoretical efforts congruent with the Hobbesian view of man. Successful socialization is viewed as essentially successful self-actualization. This view may be partly justified by the observation that successful self-actualization generally involves a healthy degree of conformity. However, successful socialization is also viewed as including the maintenance of appropriate autonomy in the face of social pressures. It is defined not as conformity but as the attainment of a transactional relationship in which the individual is able to actualize his own potentialities within the framework of his society. Berkowitz has criticized this point of view as overly optimistic and has argued that it may give rise to child-rearing practices that interfere with successful socialization.

On their face, the self-actualizing and conforming approaches to socialization appear to be completely at odds with one another. The extreme negative orientation views the socialization process as a continuing struggle between society and the individual, with successful socialization representing the defeat of the individual and the victory of society. The extreme positive orientation sees socialization as a relatively effortless developmental process in which the child's inherent growth tendencies give rise to increasingly adaptive and self-fulfilling behavior; here successful socialization has no victim, for it yields both a fully self-realized individual and an improved society.

Despite the vast difference in these two extreme views of socialization, they are surprisingly similar in one important implication. Very demanding criteria have been employed by self-actualization theorists to define the self-actualized and therefore fully socialized individual, so demanding that few people could qualify. This leads to seeing socialization as very difficult after all—the same view that follows so directly from a negative conception of human nature.

This unwitting convergence may arise from error in two implicit assumptions of the self-actualization theorists: that the potential for growth, mastery, or effectiveness is almost unlimited in man and that this potential is the same in every man. Given these assumptions, all individuals can justifiably be evaluated by a single set of ideal criteria. These assumptions are incompatible with the awareness of individual differences which is essential to an adequate understanding of socialization. People may differ in their potential for general adaptation, just as they differ on other continua. So do they differ in what they achieve. Although most people neither lead social movements nor behave like saints, they do meet the demands of society, gain much satisfaction in the process, and often contribute to the welfare of others. Self-actualization, in the extreme form in which it is often defined, really describes just the idealized upper end of a continuum. For an individual not to fit the definition does not mean that he has failed to actualize himself fully any more than his not fitting a definition of the perfect intellectual genius means that he has fallen far short of the intellectual development open to him.

There is nothing inherent in the positive view of man that requires it to remain so alien to the average man. Self-actualization theorists can avoid the dilemma we have been outlining by accepting the premise that individuals have differing potential for social adaptation and social achievement, and that successful socialization consists of adapting at a level appropriate to one's own potential. A modest achievement can itself be viewed as the criterion of socialization, indeed, even of self-actualization, if it represents the fulfillment of the individual's unique potential. For most individuals adjustment to the basic demands of social living is more pertinent than whether their lives resemble those of society's paragons.

Summary. The negative, tension-reduction view of man, contained in American behavior theory and classical psychoanalysis, has been the major approach to socialization. As in the issue of man's active or passive nature, cognitive-developmental and self-actualization personality theories present an alternative to the traditional view, and man is seen as inherently positive, socially motivated, and creative.

Implications for an Understanding of Socialization

In this chapter we have attempted to convey some sense of the conflicting viewpoints that currently characterize thought about socialization. Though we obviously have opinions, our main goal has been to clarify important issues rather than to champion one position. For the purpose of this chapter the essential question is not whether man is basically an active or passive agent or inherently good or bad, but rather whether all possibilities must be considered in arriving at a comprehensive view of socialization. We advocate the broad approach. We need not choose between the active and passive views of man; we need to use them both. The active, mediational cognitive characteristics of the child are important in the socialization process at every stage of development; on the other hand, they do not determine every aspect of the socialized behavior which emerges. What constitutes achievement in one culture, for example, probably has little to do with the active mediational structures of the child and much to do with the particular character and nature of the society. In respect to the process of conceptualizing achievement, the child is an active agent; in respect to the particular content which defines achievement in any society, he is a relatively passive agent. Analogously, that the essential structural syntax of language appears early and seems to have a certain universality (Lenneberg, 1967) is indicative of some sort of biological programing of the organism; but whether that syntax is applied to the French or German language is independent of such biological programing and is instead determined by the society in which the child is reared.

That we need not choose between the positive and negative should also be evident. A child possesses biological appetites and behavioral propensities, continuous expression of which would make any social order impossible. There is an aspect of man that is primitive and gluttonous. This fact directs the student of socialization to concern with the problem of impulse control and to the particular practices employed by the society in blocking or rechanneling individual characteristics that pose a threat for the social order. On the other hand, to say that socialization is nothing more than this is also an error. Observations of the child's desire to become an increasingly effective social being do not seem likely to be illusory. There appear to be inherent forces in the child which align themselves on the side of socializing agents, thus making the child an active and cooperative figure in his own socialization.

How then should we define socialization? In view of the different aspects of the process suggested by the theoretical approaches discussed in Chapter 12, and the conflicting positions on more general issues raised here, a definition is required that is sufficiently inclusive in its terms to admit the possibility of each point of view. We offer, then, this definition: *Socialization is a broad term for the whole process by which an individual develops, through transaction with his environment, his specific patterns of socially relevant behavior and experience.*

14

Variables in the Socialization of Specific Systems of Behavior

The purpose of this chapter is to specify the terms, as much as existing research findings permit, of our definition of socialization. Knowledge relevant to socialization has no sharp boundaries; any complete understanding of socialization would require that we take it as coextensive with human development and consider all the physiological, psychological, cultural, and societal factors that influence development. Nevertheless, certain classes, or systems, of behavior have come to be considered more central than others for an understanding of the development of man's socially relevant behavior. Given our interest in theory construction, we must ask two questions at the outset. (1) Why do we study these particular systems of behavior? (2) What are the implications of our choices for a theory of socialization?

The Choice of Systems of Behavior for Study

Socialization theorists and researchers have expended an extraordinary proportion of their energy investigating certain systems of behavior, for example, oral, excretory, sexual, aggressive, dependency, and achievement. The reasons for selection of these particular classes of behavior for attention are many, but most importantly, they reflect the particular concerns of Freudian, learning, and, to a lesser extent, cognitive-developmental theories. Freudian thought, with its emphasis on the lifelong importance of the conflicts created by society's restraint on the child during the oral, anal, phallic, and genital stages of his development, readily directs attention to the socialization practices surrounding behavior associated with these drives. Learning theory has also influenced the selection of the particular systems of behavior, in that many learning theorists use a tension-reduction model of human behavior with its emphasis on primary and acquired drives. Given a drive approach it makes considerable sense to focus attention on those behavior systems thought to reflect man's important drives.

Implications for a Theory of Socialization

The tendency of socialization theorists to focus on such systems of behavior as orality, toilet training, aggression, and sexual behavior has contributed to the predominance of the negative view of man. To the extent that socialization involves a struggle between the adult and child members of a society, it is on these aspects of behavior that the struggle centers; exclusive attention to them encourages exaggeration of the struggle. A very different picture of socialization might have emerged had the early socialization theorists concentrated instead on the child's acquisition of language.

That could have been an equally appropriate beginning. It is clear that the development of language—and of cognition generally—is a vital factor in determining the course and nature of the child's socialization. Students of cognitive development, having turned their attention to such areas as language, have understandably been impressed by the relative ease of growth and ever greater accomplishment characterizing it in most members of our society. Looking at the two-year-old's command of bladder and bowel, we may find evidence that it was imposed through stern discipline; if we instead look at his command of language, we are more likely to feel that he has gladly seized upon a tool society offered him.

Increasing attention in recent years to cognitive development has indeed encouraged a more positive view of human nature and a greater sense of ease about how socialization is accomplished. This more positive and relaxed view is now extended even to oral, excretory, and sexual behavior in recent advice to parents (Chess, Thomas, and Birch, 1965), as it has been right along by writers such as Gesell and his followers, who have stressed growth and development.

However biased or arbitrary the origins of the conventional classification of behavior systems for socialization research, much research has been directed at the specific effects of hypothesized antecedent variables on these particular systems of behavior. It is beyond the scope of this chapter to provide a comprehensive review of research in all these systems; rather, we have chosen to focus our attention on the systems of aggression, dependency, and achievement. We feel that these three behavior systems, perhaps more than others, provide examples of the way in which various theories—most particularly learning and developmental theory—have produced contributions to a specification of our definition of socialization.

Aggression

Recent years have witnessed a plethora of theoretical and empirical efforts concerned with aggression. Major theoretical statements and reviews have now been presented by Bandura and Walters (1959, 1963a, 1963b), Becker (1964), Berkowitz (1958, 1962, 1964b, 1965), Buss (1961), Feshbach (1964), and Lorenz (1965). Especially pertinent to socialization are Becker's excellent reviews of the child-rearing antecedents of aggressive behavior in children; the reviews by Bandura and Walters presenting a strong case for their modeling and general social-learning approach to the aggressive behavior of children; and the thoughtful statement by Bronfenbrenner and Riccuiti (1960) about theoretical and methodological problems involved in the definition and measurement of aggression in children.

Theoretical Approaches

Aggression is being studied with the help of a variety of theories. Research specifically on its socialization appears to be dominated, as Bronfenbrenner (1963) has noted, by three major viewpoints: Psychoanalytic theory, with its focus on the general affective quality of the parent-child relationships; the fusion of psychoanalytic and learning theory in the drive formulation developed by neo-Hullians (for example, Sears, Whiting, and Child), who have concerned themselves with the effects of parental reward and punishment and have continued to employ the frustration-aggression hypothesis of Dollard, Doob, Miller, Mowrer, and Sears (1939); and the modeling position so forcefully presented by Bandura and Walters (1963a, 1963b). A number of other approaches, however, are also being applied to the aggressive behavior of children, including the maturational, the developmental-cognitive, the genetic, and even the ethological.

As is typically the case in an area where a number of theoretical approaches are vying for ascendancy, the work on aggression is currently characterized by considerable controversy. Adding to the complexity is the fact that certain important empirical findings appear amenable to a variety of theoretical interpretations. Thus, the finding that physical punishment of the child results in greater aggressiveness is consonant with the psychoanalytic view that the type of parent-child relationship reflected here precipitates aggression; with the learning theory drive formulation, inasmuch as such punishment leads to frustration which results in greater aggression; with the modeling formulation inasmuch as the physically punishing parent provides a model emulated by the child in his own agressive behavior; and with the genetic approach, through reasoning we sketched in an earlier chapter.

Innate vs. Acquired Drive

Another continuing problem has been the failure to resolve the question of whether aggression should be considered an innate or acquired drive or not a drive at all. This is no trivial question for the investigator, because his answer to it determines his conception of the socialization process in relation to aggression, the type of evidence he will focus on, and the particular theoretical formulation he is likely

to champion. If one considers aggression an innate drive, this lends credence to the Hobbesian view of man and the position that emphasizes the difficulty of socializing the child. It leads the researcher to focus on whatever appears capable of inhibiting the expression of such a drive. Finally, it leads him to be sympathetic to the frustration-aggression hypothesis inspired by Freud's view that aggression was the "primordial reaction, ... whenever pleasure-seeking or pain-avoiding behavior was blocked" (Dollard et al., 1939, p. 21) and especially to the corollary (N. Miller, 1941) that "the strength of inhibition of any act of aggression varies positively with the amount of punishment anticipated to be a consequence of that act" (p. 33). If one considers aggression as an acquired drive, this generates a different view of its socialization, by focusing on the development of the drive in early childhood (for example, association of the child's aggressive acts with a variety of other primary and secondary reinforcers) and the long-term effects of this early-established acquired drive. A quite different approach is found in the modeling position, which foregoes either drive formulation, views the aggressive acts of the child as similar in nature to any other behavior emitted by the child, and focuses its investigation on the rate and nature of such emissions in relation to the models to which the child has been exposed and the history of positive and negative reinforcers accompanying those acts of the child conceptualized as aggressive.

The Innate Drive Position. We will first consider the innate component. If we adopt the usual assumption that man obeys the same biological laws of evolution as do other animals, then the universality of aggression in animal species and its obvious survival value argue strongly for an innate determinant (Lorenz, 1965; Tinbergen, 1951). Intraspecies variation in aggression occurs in ways indicative of a genetic component; consider, for instance, the striking variation among breeds of dog in the ease with which aggression can be elicited. Genetic influence is also indicated by recent work (Azrin, Hutchison, and Hake, 1963; Ulrich and Azrin, 1962) showing that an intensive aversive stimulus will elicit reflexive fighting in monkeys, mice, and cats. Further, a number of infrahuman studies reviewed by Berkowitz (1962, 1964b, 1965) indicate that direct electrical stimulation of appropriate regions of the brain results in overt aggressive responses (for example, hissing, growling, piloerection, striking with claws) provided that appropriate external stimuli (real or artificial enemies) are present.

That the genetic effects on aggression result partly from genetic effects on general activity level has recently been suggested by Patterson, Littman, and Bricker (1967), and in a discussion of human rather than animal research. They note that a number of studies have consistently found a positive relation between the general activity level of a child and his aggressive output and suggest that a more active organism should be expected to emit many kinds of social act at higher rates. The assumption that some of the variance in aggression must result from physiological-genetic variables is then supported indirectly by a number of studies indicating that infants vary in activity level at birth and that such variations persist for a good number of years (Balint, 1948; Bayley and Schaefer, 1963; Irwin, 1930; Thomas et al., 1963).

These sources of evidence are relevant in evaluating recent efforts to view aggressive behavior as lacking in specificity by deleting "intentionality" from the definition of aggression and conceptualizing aggressive acts as "high magnitude" responses (Bandura and Walters, 1963a, 1963b; Walters, 1966; Walters and Brown, 1964). Robert and Kiess (1964) found that aggression-inducing brain stimulation did not, as that view would suggest, result in

a general arousal state which merely intensifies any response sequence in which the animal is engaging. If the cats were eating when stimulated, they would turn to attack a nearby rat rather than consume their food with increased vigor. At the human level there is some evidence (Sears et al., 1957) that the emotional behavior exhibited by human infants when frustrated may be an unlearned rage response. In keeping with his "high magnitude" concept of aggression, Walters has preferred to interpret such infant behavior as an undifferentiated reaction to stress, which, when intense, is interpreted by adults as rage. The animal evidence may reduce the likelihood that this interpretation will prove to be appropriate.

The Interaction Position. Evidence from lower animals also shows that the aggressive act is far from being purely instinctual or mechanistic. Complex interaction between strength of the innate tendency toward aggression and particular experiences of the organism was demonstrated by King (1957), studying adult aggression of male mice of different inbred strains, with experimental variation of social experiences at different periods after weaning. He showed that the effects of an early experience may be altered, reduced, or eliminated by subsequent experiences, that the effect of early experience may be specific to a given type of adult response, and that the same experience may have different effects on mice of unlike genotypes.

Marked influence of experience on aggression may also be seen in a series of studies of fighting behavior in fish, birds, and mammals conducted by Kuo and reviewed by Becker (1962). Kuo found that specific training in fighting and isolation early in life had a much stronger determining effect on fighting for many species than did nutritional or hormonal variables, and these findings have been confirmed by Bevan, Davis, and Levy (1960). That early isolation increases later aggression is an especially interesting phenomenon which has also been found in mice (Vandenburgh, 1960) and monkeys (Mason, 1960). Extending an interpretation implicit in Kuo's writings, Becker (1962) has explicitly advanced two mechanisms as an explanation of the isolation-aggression phenomenon. Drawing on Hebb's concept, Becker views one mechanism as being the disruption caused by strange stimulation capable of leading either to aggression or to fear; the experience of isolation increases the later occurrence of this mechanism. The second mechanism is inhibitory in its action, and here the mechanism is reduced in the isolated animals; they have not had in early experience the repeated contact with more dominant animals—or possible challengers —which develops inhibitions in normal rearing. Kuo demonstrated the second mechanism directly by forcing aggressive animals into defeat experiences with a trained fighter.

Another study that has demonstrated the importance of both genetic and experiential factors is one by Uyeno (1960), who mated dominant male rats with dominant females, and submissive males with submissive females. Half of the offspring of each group were reared by dominant and half by submissive mothers. Although a clear genetic effect was found, it was also found that rats from dominant parents reared by dominant mothers were less aggressive than those from dominant parents reared by submissive mothers. It would appear that dominant mothers inhibit and submissive mothers facilitate the aggression of their offspring.

Theoretical analyses of aggression and child training very often assume an interaction between genetic and environmental factors, even where there is no direct evidence immediately pertinent to the particular topic being discussed; see, for example, the recent review by Becker (1964). Walters (1966), on the other hand, appears to have totally rejected the importance of innate factors in aggression, although he honestly admits that this rejection is based more on faith than on evidence. Such an article of faith is of course consistent with Walters' rejection of the frustration-aggression hypothesis, which, in its dependence on Freud's "primordial reaction" concept, involves an innate component. As Patterson et al. (1967) point out, the initial formulation of the frustration-aggression hypothesis did not consider the process by which learned aggressive responses come under the control of the stimuli associated with frustration; it thus assumed that an aggressive response to frustration represented an innate stimulus-response relationship.

Opposing the view of Walters is that of Berkowitz (1964b, 1965), who has argued that aggression does have an important innate component. Berkowitz bases his view on the considerable evidence that in some infrahuman species aggressive responses can be released in an animal by certain stimuli without prior observation of aggressive behavior or reward for aggression in the presence of these stimuli. Berkowitz continues to find the frustration-aggression hypothesis valid, but in a modified form; frustration arouses anger and so predisposes a person to respond in an aggressive manner, but whether aggression occurs depends in large part on the presence or absence of appropriate stimuli. He sets the interactionist view of aggression in a broader framework with the following quotation from N. Miller (1964):

It seems highly probable that . . . innate patterns exist, that they play an important role in the development of human social behavior, and that these instinctual patterns are modifiable enough so that they tend to be disguised by learning although they may play crucial roles in motivating, facilitating, and shaping socially learned behavior [p. 160].

This interactionist position should be kept in mind when interpreting many of the following studies which have demonstrated direct learning effects on aggression.

The Acquired Drive Position. Much of the research dealing with socialization of aggression has stemmed from views of aggression as acquired rather than innate. Even the frustration-aggression hypothesis, in the form in which it most influenced research, emphasized learned rather than innate components. Frustration was not viewed as invariably producing aggression; it was instead viewed as giving rise to a general drive which is often followed by aggression, because in the individual's history aggression has led to reducing or removing frustration. Furthermore, because aggression has also been punished, conflict results. This conflict is viewed as producing a drive of its own whose magnitude is determined by the strength of the competing tendencies to be aggressive and to fear being aggressive (R. Sears et al., 1953; Whiting and Child, 1953, Chap. 12). This conflict-produced drive obviously is a resultant of learning, and its multiplicative interaction with aggressive habit is used to explain the greater aggressiveness of children who have been punished for aggression severely but not so severely that aggression is altogether inhibited. As Bandura and Walters (1963b) have noted, a number of theoreticians have now expounded the view that frustration increases motivational level through the addition of conflict-produced, frustration-produced, or "irrelevant" drives (Amsel, 1951, 1958, 1962; Brown and Farber, 1951; Festinger, 1961; Lawson and Marx, 1958). Furthermore, because such drives are often reduced by the aggressive behavior, the aggressive behavior itself takes on the characteristics of a secondary reinforcer, and thus aggression becomes an acquired drive.

The Frustration-Aggression Hypothesis

Whatever the intricacies of the mechanisms mediating the hypothesized frustration-aggression relationship, students of socialization have for many years studied whether the direct frustration of the child results in an increase in aggressive behavior. A number of early studies (summarized in brief form by Radke, 1946) dealing with general variables of parental behavior have reported relationships that might be considered favorable to the view that frustration of the child results in aggression. More recent studies, however, have been much less consistent. Some support for a simple frustration-aggression effect is contained in a study by Goodenough (1931) which shows that, in the early preschool years, the most common sources of anger in children are home situations that interfere with some fairly obvious goal-striving of the child. (However, Goodenough also found, as have other investigators, that not every aggressive act is preceded by a descernible frustration.) Merrill (1946), in a study involving the direct observations of mother-child interactions, finds a positive relationship between the frequency of restricting and controlling behavior by the mother and irritable or complaining behavior by the child. Hartup and Himeno (1959) find an increase in aggressive behavior following a brief period of social isolation (which the authors interpreted as a frustrating condition).

With respect to other potentially frustrating aspects of parental behavior, the following findings are relevant: Lesser (1952), measuring aggression in ten- to thirteen-year-old boys through reports by their agemates, obtains a very marked positive relationship to parental rejection, but to no other aspect of frustration by parents; Wittenborn (1956), employing a measure of children's aggression based on mothers' report, finds a positive correlation with measures (also based on maternal interview) of parental rejection, unsympathetic parental attitude, and severe toilet training. However, these correlations disappear when the measure for one of his two groups is based on an interview with the child. Sears et al. (1953) find no evidence of a relationship between overt aggression of nursery school children and measures of infantile, current, or recent home frustration. Absence of frustration, as measured by current and recent home nurturance, is negatively related with aggression in boys, but the reverse relation is observed with girls. Hollenberg and Sperry (1951), in a study of aggression in doll play done with the same children, find some evidence that fantasy aggression is positively related to a background of home frustration. However, a number of experimental studies which directly manipulated frustration found no relation between frustration and aggression (Jegard and Walters, 1960; Mussen and Rutherford, 1961; Yarrow, 1948).

Clearly, these results do not add up to confirmation of a simple and direct relationship between amount or type of frustration in socialization and strength of chronic aggressive tendency. But we may ask if there is any sound theoretical reason to expect such a relationship. Closer inspection suggests that the answer is no; this expectation seems to have been based on the adoption of a principle of momentary psychodynamics as a principle of learning, without sufficient attention to what previous knowledge about learning would predict.

Sears et al. (1953) have devoted more careful attention to this problem. These researchers point out that the response of others to the child's behavior when frustrated, and his perception of their response, is a crucial factor in determining what the child learns as a result of a given degree of frustration. This view receives support from studies indicating that the relation between frustration and aggression is determined by other personality characteristics of the child, provided we view these personality characteristics as themselves at least partially the products of environmental response to the child's aggression on earlier occasions. Thus, Otis and McCandless (1955) found that the amount of aggressiveness following a potentially frustrating event was greater in children with a dominant "need for power" than in children with a dominant "need for love affection." Children previously classified as "overcontrollers" and "undercontrollers" were compared by Block and Martin (1955) in a frustration situation where they were unable to play with attractive toys, a situation similar to that used by Barker, Dembo, and Lewin (1941). Undercontrollers gave predominantly aggressive responses, whereas overcontrollers played constructively with the less attractive toys that were available. Similarly, Livson and Mussen (1957) found that nursery school children with greater ego control, inferred from behavior in delayed gratification and cosatiation situations, displayed less overt aggression in their social interactions. There also appears to be a cognitive factor determining whether frustration is followed by aggression. Frustration is more likely to be followed by aggression if the frustration is seen as arbitrary rather than reasonable (Burnstein and Worchel, 1962; Kregarman and Worchel, 1962; Pastore, 1952). In sum, we have no reason to expect any simple relation between the amount of frustration experienced by the child and the amount of overt aggression he displays.

Child-rearing Patterns and Aggression: An Alternative to the Frustration-Aggression Hypothesis

Although we must reject a simple frustration-aggression hypothesis, Becker (1964) has noted that there do appear to be some fairly consistent relations between certain broad dimensions of child-rearing and aggression. Two such dimensions we shall consider here are (1) love-oriented vs. power-assertive and (2) restrictive vs. permissive methods of child-rearing.

Love-Oriented vs. Power-Assertive Methods. This dimension is often labeled simply as punitiveness (either general punitiveness or, in some research, punitive treatment of the child's aggression). Love-oriented techniques generally include such positive methods as use of praise and reasoning and such negative methods as showing disappointment with the child and withdrawing love. Power-assertive techniques usually include physical punishment but in some cases have also included yelling, shouting, and verbal threats.

Power-assertive as compared to love-oriented techniques have been found to be correlated with a higher incidence of aggressive behavior at certain ages. For instance, Sears et al. (1953) found that maternal punishment for aggressive behavior was positively related to boys' overt aggression in school. A curvilinear relationship was found for girls, girls of both high- and low-punitive mothers showing the least aggression. Examining some of these same Ss just a year later, Hollenberg and Sperry (1951) found a positive relation between maternal punitiveness and aggression in doll play for both boys and girls. Becker suggested that this indicated that high maternal punitiveness produced strong aggressive reactions in both boys and girls, but that girls inhibited their expression in the schoolroom situation. Sears et al. (1953), Sears (1961), and Nowlis (1953) offer alternative interpretations of the sex differences encountered in studies examining the punitiveness-aggression relation. That the interaction with sex can be complex is indicated by the recent findings of Gordon and Smith (1965) that the stricter the mother, the more aggressive her daughter (provided the mother uses physical punishment), whereas the stricter the mother, the less aggressive her son (especially if she does not use physical punishment). Becker, Peterson, Luria, Shoemaker, and Hellmer (1962), in a study relating maternal punitiveness to teachers' ratings of children's aggression, obtained results completely congruent with those of Sears et al. Ratings of aggression

displayed at home, however, showed positive relations to mothers' punitiveness for both boys and girls. Similar findings with home ratings have been reported by Eron, Banta, Walder, and Laulicht (1961) and Sears et al. (1957). Lefkowitz, Walder, and Eron (1963) found that ratings of aggression were highest where parents reported using physical punishment.

A number of other studies reviewed by Becker (1964) are also consistent with the general finding of a positive relation between parental power assertion and child aggression (Allinsmith, 1960; Hoffman, 1960). However, Becker (1964) has warned that this relation is confounded by the considerable evidence that hostile parents frequently have aggressive children and that such parents tend to use more physical punishment and less reasoning and praise. Thus we cannot be sure whether the relation between parent's punitiveness and child's aggression results from punishment, a combination of punishment and general hostility, or primarily from the general hostility of the parent. Adding to the difficulty of interpreting the punitiveness-aggression relation is the fact that we cannot be sure of the causal direction. Although preferring to view punitiveness as causing aggression, Sears et al. (1957), who assume the importance of an innate component in aggression, raise the possibility that some children, by expressing their innately higher levels of aggressive impulses, bring on themselves greater punishment for aggression. Furthermore, a circular dyadic interaction can be established between parent and child in which the parent's punishment produces in the child more aggression which, in turn, leads to greater punishment. Systematic evidence that the child's aggression may indeed increase parental punitiveness is provided by Hart's (1957) finding that aggression provoked physical punishment threats and ridicule in both authoritarian and nonauthoritarian mothers.

Restrictiveness vs. Permissiveness. Another general dimension of child-rearing that has been found to be related to children's aggression is that of restrictiveness versus permissiveness, typically defined by the general level of restriction and the strictness of enforcement. However, Becker (1964) has pointed out that a major difficulty in integrating the research findings relevant to this dimension has been that its definition has varied widely. Reasonable attention to the complications that result requires extended discussion such as that offered by Becker (1964) and Bandura and Walters (1963b).

Considerable evidence supports the common-sense notion that restrictiveness results in more inhibited and permissiveness results in less inhibited behavior. Several early studies (Radke, 1946; Symonds, 1939) have shown that children with restrictive parents were generally more inhibited than children with dominating parents. More recently, Sears et al. (1957) found that permissiveness was positively related to aggression in both boys and girls at age five and in boys at age twelve. The important longitudinal study of Kagan and Moss (1962) has also indicated that restrictiveness during the first three years had lasting inhibiting effects on both boys and girls. Restricted children were found to be generally less aggressive. Adding credence to the permissiveness-aggression relation are experimental studies which instead of considering parent-child relations have experimentally varied the temporary exposure of children to a permissive adult and have determined the effect on their fantasy or overt aggression (Bach, 1945; Hartup and Himeno, 1959; Hollenberg and Sperry, 1951; Leven and Turgeon, 1957; Pintler, 1945; P. Sears, 1951; Yarrow, 1948).

It now appears that this dimension interacts with that of parental warmth versus hostility, permissiveness resulting in even greater aggression if the parents are themselves hostile. Discipline by such parents is a mixture of general laxity (especially on

the part of the mother) and instances of extremely high punitiveness (usually on the part of the father). Much of the evidence on its nature and effects has come from studies of delinquent children (Bandura and Walters, 1959; Burt, 1929; Glueck and Glueck, 1950; Healy and Bronner, 1926; McCord, McCord, and Zola, 1959). A number of studies of nondelinquent children (reviewed by Becker, 1964) have indicated that a combination of parental hostility and restrictiveness also fosters aggression in children (McCord, McCord, and Howard, 1961; Meyers, 1944; Sears et al., 1957; Sears, 1961). Restrictiveness in "warm" parents, on the other hand, appears to have very different effects. A number of studies indicate that the combination of restrictiveness and warmth results in low overt aggression (Maccoby, 1961; Meyers, 1944; Sears, 1961).

The Modeling Theory of Aggression

Bandura and Walters (1959, 1963a, 1963b) have eschewed dimensions of child-rearing such as we have discussed, and the acquired drives that may arise from them, in favor of a modeling theory of aggression (Bandura and Walters, 1963b; Walters, 1966). Drive theorists have long been aware of a modeling effect and have specifically alluded to the living example of aggression provided by parents who employ physical punishment (Sears et al., 1957). Bandura and Walters make of modeling a prime principle largely intended to replace rather than supplement others. Stated most simply, the imitation or modeling view asserts "that observation of aggressive social models, either in real life or in fantasy productions, increases the probability that the observers will behave in an aggressive manner if the model is rewarded or does not receive punishment for aggressive behavior" (Walters, 1966, p. 60). Bandura and Walters have employed this formulation to interpret much of the child-rearing literature concerned with aggression—saying, for example, that children of punitive parents are aggressive because they model their behavior on that of their parents. They have also done many experiments in which children observe others' behavior and its consequences (controlled by E) and see their outcome as supporting the validity of modeling as the major influence on children's aggressive behavior. The experimental investigations of children's aggression provide the strongest case for the modeling formulation. [See Bandura and Walters (1963a, 1963b) and Walters (1966) for a complete review of this body of work.] In an early study Bandura and Huston (1961) examined the incidental imitative responses of preschool children who had witnessed an adult model make functionless incidental responses, including aggression, while performing a discrimination task. When performing later the same discrimination task, 90 per cent of these children made aggressive responses, whereas none of the control children did. Another study (Bandura, Ross, and Ross, 1961) indicated that the model need not be present for aggression to occur. After observing a model who behaved in either a distinctive aggressive or nonaggressive manner and then experiencing mild frustration, Ss were taken to another room containing a variety of toys. More aggression was displayed by the aggressive-model group than by the nonaggressive-model group and a control group who had no prior exposure to a model; the difference held true both for aggressive acts clearly similar to those of the model and for aggressive acts not obviously imitative. In another study Bandura, Ross, and Ross (1963) found that witnessing aggression in a real adult, in a filmed adult, and in a filmed cartoon all increased the incidence of aggression in children. Further evidence that witnessing aggressive cartoons can increase aggression in children has been provided by Lovaas (1961a) and Mussen and Rutherford (1961).

In all these studies the aggressive behavior of the model goes unpunished and may even lead to definite reward. This variable has itself been subjected to experimental inquiry. The general outcome is to demonstrate a facilitative effect on children's aggression when the model is rewarded and an inhibiting effect when the model is punished.

An interesting experiment by Hicks (1965) suggests the variety of interacting variables that may be found at work when modeling is studied in fine detail. The models in his experiment were all presented by film projection, and for different Ss the model was male or female, peer or adult. The Ss themselves were of both sexes, and their aggressive behavior was measured both immediately afterward and at a later time. Hicks found that the male peer had the most immediate influence in shaping children's aggressive behavior, whereas the adult male had the most lasting effect.

Problems of Interpretation. Although the modeling position has led to impressive and consistent experimental findings, a number of pertinent issues in their interpretation remain unresolved. Bandura and Walters (1963b) have attributed the modeling findings to two different processes each of which results in an increase in the number or intensity of the child's aggressive responses. The first process has to do with the child's learning new responses not previously in his repertory—an effect which can be inferred if the child imitates highly novel aggressive responses exhibited by the model. The second process is disinhibitory; observing an aggressive model weakens the child's inhibitory tendencies and leads him to emit aggressive responses already in his repertory.

The Disinhibitory Effect. Appeal to this second process, a disinhibitory effect, immediately raises the question of what determines the level of the child's aggressive and inhibitory tendencies at the time he encounters the model. Clearly, disinhibitory effects of the aggressive model will depend on the level of the child's existing tendencies to emit aggressive responses and to refrain from doing so. There are a number of possibilities here. One, rejected by Bandura and Walters, is that interindividual variation in tendency to emit aggressive responses reflects variation in innate aggressive drive. A second possibility, which can be found in the work of Bandura and Walters, is that the level of inhibition is determined by the past history of reward and punishment the child has received for behaving aggressively. Thus, Bandura and Walters ascribe the inhibiting effect of seeing an aggressive model punished to its heightening the child's anticipation of punishment. Once the modeling theorists turn their attention to variations in the child's tendency to express or inhibit aggressive behavior, the child's anticipation of punishment for aggression, and the learning histories that give rise to them—as it seems they must do—they appear very similar to the acquired-drive theorists who have preferred to focus on the nature of the parent-child relationship. That Bandura and Walters are at least implicitly aware of this can be seen in their view that we could not completely deduce the disinhibitory effects of viewing an aggressive model unless "we knew the past history of our subjects" (Bandura and Walters, 1963b, p. 372). It would be surprising indeed if an important component of this past history were not the child-rearing practices employed by the parent in socializing the child's aggression.

The Question of "Novelty." The first process to which Bandura and Walters appeal, the learning of novel acts through viewing a model, also raises certain questions. As Patterson et al. (1967) have noted, it is not altogether clear what Bandura and Walters mean by a novel act, whose occurrence they use as a criterion that learning has taken place. Bandura and Walters' novelty criterion appears to rest not so much on the child's emitting novel responses as on his emitting particular aggressive responses at a higher frequency than would be expected in the particular experimental settings employed.

Why Imitate? A more irksome problem here is the question of why the child imitates the model at all. Bandura (1965) has now advanced an explicit theoretical rationale for the modeling-learning effect in which he relies heavily on stimulus contiguity "mediated by cue-producing symbolic responses which exercise discriminative stimulus control over corresponding overt performances" (p. 47). He has also pointed out that both acquisition of a potential response through imitation and the actual performance of that response are influenced by a variety of motivation and reinforcement variables. This theoretical elaboration of what originally appeared to be a simple contiguity theory provides modeling theorists with an answer to the commonsense assertion advanced by Patterson et al. (1967) that not all children imitate all models all the time. Bandura could also reply that new learning through modeling varies from person to person because the perceptual and cognitive aspects of response are influenced by a variety of motivational variables. The point we would make is that such perceptual and cognitive variables as well as the motivational variables are themselves determined by the past learning history of the child as well as by his developmental level.

Thus we see again that the modeling theorist, in attempting to elucidate an extremely interesting effect, has moved from a simple formulation to a much more complex one that shares features with a number of already existing theoretical positions. This movement, and especially the emphasis on the perceptual and cognitive activities of the child, would appear to be a healthy development away from a mechanistic view of modeling and imitation in children. As modeling theorists are aware, much more remains to be done before we can fully determine how exposure to an expressive model will affect the child's aggressiveness.

Other Socializers and Modeling Theory

Applications of modeling theory to data other than those from the laboratory have stressed the role of socializers other than parents—a stress which very readily arises in connection with experiments showing that children's aggression may be influenced by witnessing the behavior of a variety of other people. Modeling theorists have not failed to be concerned with the model provided to the child by his parents but have in addition paid more attention than most psychologists have to the influence of other socializers. Thus, in interpreting the aggression of delinquent children, Bandura and Walters have considered not only the parents' role as models and as direct reinforcers but also the general prevalence of aggressive models in delinquent subcultures. Their approach leads them to suggest that the "crucial psychological process in the development of aggressive antisocial patterns may, in many cases, be identification with an aggressive prototype rather than a hostile reaction to emotional deprivation" (Bandura and Walters, 1963b, p. 370).

This application of modeling theory is very similar to some of the extremely societalistic interpretations of delinquency. Their emphasis on peer relations is surely appropriate. Yet this is a topic on which a modeling interpretation seems to encounter definite difficulties. The frequent association of delinquency with fatherlessness has helped create interest in studying how growing up without a father affects children. A good deal of research has by now been done on this question (Bach, 1946; Bronfenbrenner, 1965; Clausen and Williams, 1963; Gronseth, 1957; Lynn and Sawrey, 1959; Pettigrew, 1964; P. Sears, 1951; Sears, Pintler and Sears, 1946; Stolz, 1954; Tiller, 1957; Wilkins, 1960), and it has resulted in some rather consistent findings. Father absence affects boys more than girls and tends to produce in them during early childhood diminished aggression and generally more effeminate behavior. This early childhood effect of father absence would appear to be quite consistent with modeling theory. However, the long-term effect of father absence, especially in lower class and delinquent subcultures, is not. The long-term effect in boys includes extremely exaggerated aggression which has often been found to be combined with a latent femininity. The most common interpretation has been that such aggression reflects a rebellion against the early protective feminizing environment, a search for masculine identity. It is difficult to see how modeling theory can in itself encompass the findings of exaggerated masculinity in boys who have no masculine model in the home. The modeling theorist could here refer to the contemporary models (for example, peers) in the current social milieu as the aggressive prototypes, but this leaves important questions unanswered: Why for example, do subcultures characterized by father absence value so highly the exaggerated aggressive model? Furthermore, if the aggression here results from imitating the aggression of others, where does the femininity of the same boys come from? It would appear that although modeling plays a role, any complete understanding of exaggerated aggression in adolescence and later life requires more dynamic considerations. Such considerations would include the entire spectrum of child-rearing practices, especially those practices that influence the development of social control. Pertinent here is an especially intriguing study by Wilkins (1960) of the positive relationship between father absence and the incidence of criminality, which may well be considered a form of hypermasculine behavior. His study suggests that the father is important not as an aggressive model but rather for his role in developing the child's social control. The same point emerges from cross-cultural analysis of the incidence of crime (Bacon, Child and Barry, 1963), showing that crime is positively correlated with customs making for the young boy's having no father figure close at hand.

One Area of Agreement: The Role of Reinforcement

There is one principle on which both social learning theorists such as Bandura and Walters (1963a) and the more classical learning theorists can agree. The aggressive responses of children are increased by positive reinforcement of those responses, whether the reinforcement comes from parents, peers, or others.

Comparison of societies, or groups within societies, has repeatedly suggested that overt aggression is higher, and guilt about it is lower, in groups that value and reward aggression than in groups that devalue and punish it. The cultural standards can sometimes be traced to economic needs, household composition, or kinship relationships (Whiting and Whiting, 1960). For instance, children's aggression is more controlled in societies having extended family households than in societies where the nuclear family lives alone; presumably the presence of more people in the dwelling makes children's aggression less tolerable. Interestingly, Roy (1950) found in our own society a direct increase in the permissiveness of child-rearing attitudes as the number of rooms in the house increased. Other studies indicating a dependence of aggression socialization on such features as geography, social organization, and beliefs have been made by Biesheuvel (1959), Havighurst, and Neugarten (1955), LeVine (1960), and Spindler and Spindler (1957). Within our society, subgroups have been found to vary in reinforcement of aggression in their

children (Clausen and Williams, 1963; Davis, 1943; Davis and Dollard, 1940; Davis and Havighurst, 1947).

That positive reinforcement by parents can increase aggression is clear. Lesser (1952) found that aggression toward agemates is positively correlated with parental behavior advising or supporting such aggression. Two studies by Bandura and Walters indicate that parents of aggressive children have given a considerable amount of encouragement and reward for aggression outside the home, whereas the parents of nonaggressive children have tended consistently to discourage aggressive behavior (Bandura and Walters, 1959, 1963c).

Reinforcement contingencies outside the home have also been found to be important determinants of the child's general level of aggression. Thus, Henry and Sharpe (1947) found that children in a highly structured and controlling nursery made fewer aggressive responses than did children in a freer nursery. In an experimental investigation Brown and Elliot (1965) found that the incidence of aggression in nursery school boys was modified when aggression was ignored and responses incompatible with aggression were rewarded. In what is certainly one of the most ambitious investigations ever undertaken of peer reinforcement of aggression, Patterson, Ludwig, and Sonoda (1961) found that the incidence of aggressive acts in children was modified by the positive and negative reinforcers contained in peer responses. A number of experimental studies have now been conducted indicating that children's aggressive responses towards inanimate objects (for example, a Bobo doll) are increased by positive reinforcement and decreased by negative reinforcement (Cowan and Walters, 1963; Davitz, 1952; Hollenberg and Sperry, 1951; Lovaas, 1961b; Patterson et al., 1961).

This body of work indicates that whatever other problems we are confronted with in understanding variations in children's aggression, we can rest assured that the law of effect applies to their actual emission of overt aggressive responses.

Summary. The major contributors to knowledge about aggression have been American behaviorism, modeling theory, psychoanalytic theory, and physiological psychology. There is evidence that aggression has an innate component which is modified by interaction with the environment. Evidence in support of any simple acquired drive position of the behaviorists has been inconsistent. On the other hand, evidence does support a more general relationship between broad dimensions of child-rearing and aggression. Social-modeling theorists argue that aggression is not a drive, but rather results from the imitation of a model. There are impressive findings in support of this view, but serious theoretical problems remain. All learning theories agree that positive reinforcement for aggression increases aggressive responses in children.

Dependence

Two Views of Dependence: Nurturance-Seeking vs. Susceptibility to Social Reinforcement

Recent years have witnessed an upsurge of interest in dependent behavior. A number of reviews are now available of revelant theoretical positions, empirical research, and problems of definition and method (Bandura and Walters, 1963a; Baron, 1966; Hartup, 1963; Parton and Ross, 1965, 1967; Sears, 1963; Stevenson, 1965; Stevenson and Hill, 1966; Walters and Parke, 1964). If we accept Murray's (1938) very useful definition of dependence as behavior which seems to have as its goal the obtaining of nurturance from other people, or which clearly indicates that reliance on the help of others is the individual's dominant method of striving for his goals, we find

that a good deal of the research deals explicitly with dependence. But a good deal of it does not, being directed instead at studying children's susceptibility to social reinforcement. We face at the outset the question of whether to review both kinds of research.

Some seem to think that these two types of study are concerned with different phenotypic expressions of the same underlying needs. Consistent with such a view, although not arguing strongly for it, is the repeated finding that children's dependent behavior and their susceptibility to social influence follow the same developmental course, each decreasing as children grow older. Others, however, have viewed dependence and general reinforcement effects as being somewhat related but nevertheless reflecting some markedly different causal factors. In respect to this position it is certainly true that a rating of the child's general level of dependence has been only one factor among many that have been found related to effectiveness of social reinforcement. Among the many others are the child's level of anxiety or arousal, his social class, his intellectual status, his sex in relation to sex of the reinforcing adult, and the nature of relationship existing between him and the reinforcing adult. Some of these variables have no obvious relation to dependence, and some seem to have a relation to dependence complex enough so as not to provide a ready explanation for the relation with social reinforcement.

We should consider the further possibility that there is really no substantive difference at all between dependence and effectiveness of social reinforcement. Entertaining this possibility leads us to see that the distinction may represent, in part, an intrusion of personal values into scientific work. The concept of dependence certainly has a negative connotation in the context of adult life in our society. Presumably, people in any society would readily see that dependence is inevitable in the helpless infant or the very young child and that in adults a degree of dependence resembling the young child's is entirely unacceptable, so that a movement from dependence toward independence must be a major development trend in the socialization of the individual. With the bias of our social values, though, we often associate the term "dependence" with early periods only and do not recognize that although dependence is of lesser degree in adult life, it is still essential. Perhaps "susceptibility to social reinforcement," then, is just a different label for adult behavior which, in another society, would receive the same label as the dependent behavior of the young child. Certainly susceptibility to social reinforcement does imply that nurturance from others is rewarding, and as Walters and Parke (1964) and Bandura and Walters (1963a) have pointed out, failure of an adult to manifest any such susceptibility would mark him not as an ideal adult but as a sociopathic personality. Has the inconsistency of this with our admiration of rugged individualism led us to adopt two labels, and develop separate research traditions, for a single set of phenomena?

Some parts of the research literature could encourage us, at least momentarily, to make this equation. Many experimental studies of social reinforcement have been explicitly directed at illuminating phenomena of dependence (Gilmore and Zigler, 1964; Hartup, 1958; Stevenson and Fahel, 1961; Zigler, 1963c; Zigler, Hodgden, and Stevenson, 1958). And almost every investigation of social reinforcement throws some light on dependence. Certainly there is much overlap and no reason for regarding the two lines of research as entirely separate.

Yet there is a difference here which goes beyond the focus of a particular age or the value connotation of the behavior studied. On the one hand, the concept of dependence is not defined solely by reference to what is reinforcing, and it includes aspects of behavior not necessarily bearing on social reinforcement. On the other hand, the concept of social reinforcement is associated with research directed partly at topics which certainly may be usefully explored apart from dependence (for example, social attachment, compliance, imitation, and identification), whatever our guesses about the relation of dependence to these topics in an ideal theory. For our purposes here, we have decided to consider only the studies dealing explicitly with dependence and those social reinforcement studies especially relevant to our understanding of dependence.

Theoretical Approaches to Dependence

As in the case of aggression, the work on dependence has centered about a small number of theoretical formulations. Hartup (1963) has pointed out that dependence research has been most influenced by psychoanalysis, on the one hand, and social learning theories, on the other. Researchers influenced by learning theory should, we believe, be further subdivided into two major types: Hullian descendants who have remained committed to the secondary drive approach best exemplified by R. Sears and his coworkers (Sears, 1963; Sears et al., 1953; Sears et al., 1957); and investigators who reject the secondary drive formulation and view dependence as the product of some combination of general anxiety or arousal effects, modeling phenomena, and operant learning through direct reinforcement (see Bandura and Walters, 1963a; Gewirtz, 1954, 1961; Walters and Parke, 1964; Walters and Ray, 1960).

Dependence in Freudian thought is linked to the concept of object relations and the all-important emotional relationship between child and adult. This relationship is not only a prerequisite for maintaining life but also plays a crucial role through identification in the development of the superego or conscience. Within this framework dependence phenomena are thought to be developed in early infancy, during which particular child-rearing practices, especially those dealing with feeding, can produce the oral character.

Is Dependence a Drive?

The current major theoretical controversy about dependence has tended to ignore Freudian thinking, lying rather between the acquired position of the neo-Hullians and those social learning theorists who have argued against the necessity of employing an acquired drive formulation.

The Acquired-Drive View. Within the neo-Hullian position dependent habits are established through the presence and behavior of adults who gratify needs. Through pairings with primary reinforcement, adults take on the characteristics of secondary reinforcers. Once such secondary reinforcing features are established, the child evidences a drive for social reinforcers in their own right, being anxious when deprived of them and being content when they are produced (Hartup, 1963; Walters and Parke, 1964). As we saw in the case of aggression as an acquired drive, however, one neo-Hullian position is that the emergence of dependence as a drive results from early and inevitable frustration of dependent habits. This frustration results in a conflict between previously acquired expectation of reward and a newly acquired expectation of nonreward. Whiting's general formulation that actions followed by both reward and punishment or nonreward become part of an acquired drive system is again employed, with drive strength being viewed as a function of the conflict between the two expectancies. (See the preceding section on aggression.)

The Anxiety Position. Walters and his collaborators (Walters and Ray, 1960; Walters and Parke, 1964) have been especially critical of the view that there is a learned

drive for social reinforcement, whether in the version of Sears and his coworkers (Sears et al., 1953; Sears et al., 1957) or in that of Gewirtz and Baer (1958a, 1958b). Walters and Parke (1964) have employed J. Brown's (1953) conception that the "important motivating component of many of the supposed acquired drives for specific goal objects is actually a learned tendency to be discontented or distressed or anxious in the absence of these goal objects" (p. 12) in coming to the conclusion that dependent behavior may be regarded as habits energized by conditioned emotional responses. This conclusion leads Walters to focus first on the anxiety or arousal itself and then determine specific influences of such states on the child's behavior, for example, faster learning on simple discrimination tasks and increased attention to social cues. As Hartup (1963) has noted, to the extent that Walters thinks that the absence of adult nurturance produces anxiety in the child and this anxiety is reduced by the reinstatement of adult social reinforcement, his position does not differ markedly from that of Sears. The distinction between Walter's view and the drive position rests on the degree to which anxiety aroused by the absence of social reinforcement (as in isolation experiments by Gewirtz and Baer, 1958a, 1958b) results in overt responses other than those directed at securing adult nurturance or social reinforcement.

As Zigler (1964) has noted, regarding an acquired dependence drive as anxiety need not reduce the value of conceptualizing it as a dependence drive. It seems plausible that once certain social reinforcers become effective, their absence or withdrawal should result in the individual's experiencing a state of anxiety which motivates him to perform responses that lead to the reduction of the anxiety. However, the postulation of anxiety does not negate the explanatory value of a dependence drive. A multitude of conditions give rise to anxiety states, and a multitude of responses reduce them. The value of a dependence drive concept lies in its specificity. It suggests one class of events that will give rise to anxiety and, more importantly, names the class of behavior that the individual will then display. Thus a person who has come to value money will become anxious when he finds himself jobless, and one would predict that such a person would become more responsive to that class of reinforcers whose receipt would allay the anxiety. One would not expect him to become more responsive to all reinforcers in an indiscriminate manner. Analogously, the value of the dependence drive concept lies in the specification of a particular class of reinforcers to which the child will display an increased responsivity. Maccoby (1964) has made much the same point in discussing the Gewirtz-Baer findings of an increased effectiveness of social reinforcement following social isolation and Walters' and Ray's attribution of the finding to anxiety arousal.

The Innate Drive View. Accepting the notion of an acquired dependence drive does not imply rejection of an innate dependence drive. The acquired drive might represent an overlay or modification of the child's innate drive for nurturance and human proximity. Parallel issues about innate and acquired drive components and interaction between the two, as we have seen, arise about other systems (for example, aggression) and have received a great deal of attention. Students of dependence and of social reinforcement effects have, in contrast, paid little attention to the importance or even the possibility of an innate element in dependence.

There appears to be several reasons, some substantive and others historical, for this neglect of an innate element in dependence. The very nature of dependent behavior makes it a prime candidate to be conceptualized as acquired rather than innate. Given the classical tension-reduction model so popular in American psychology, there was little need to think of gross dependent behavior (for example, clinging desire for proximity) as reflecting any primary inborn need of the child. It seemed much more parsimonious to view such behaviors as the outgrowth of some combination of satisfaction and frustration by the parent of "truly" primary drives such as hunger and thirst.

The most influential theoretical statements as well as the pioneering research on dependence were made by neo-Hullians using a tension-reduction model. Their greater readiness to postulate an innate component in aggression than in dependence seems attributable to the prominent place they gave to the frustration-aggression hypothesis. This hypothesis, constructed solidly upon Freud's "primordial" reaction, seems to have rendered the Hullians sympathetic to acceptance of an innate component in aggression. That they have displayed no parallel sympathy in discussing dependence may rest upon the fact that there is no counterpart of the original frustration-aggression hypothesis in behaviorists' work on dependence, although Freud's libido theory could have suggested one. Although learning theorists of varying persuasions continue to argue the merits of evoking an acquired drive to explain dependence, almost none seem to think that the innate component is of any great consequence.

Several strands of thinking have recently converged, all encouraging attention to the innate component of dependence. One such line of thought, discussed earlier in this chapter, is the movement away from sole reliance on the tension-reduction model of human behavior toward motivational concepts which include a number of inherent positive drives thought to characterize man (see White, 1959). The latter formulation is obviously more conducive to acceptance of an innate dependence drive than is the classical tension-reduction model. Another pertinent strand of thought is represented by the research of comparative psychologists and ethologists on early attachment and primary socialization in infrahuman species (reviewed recently by Scott, 1963). The research of this sort most widely known to psychologists is that of Harlow (Harlow, 1958, 1961; Harlow and Zimmerman, 1959).

The Attachment Theory. A third strand of thought, the most explicitly relevant one, is exemplified by Bowlby (1958), its leading exponent. He attacks the secondary drive theory of social development and suggests instead that actions typically ascribed to a secondary drive of dependence actually reflect inborn behavior patterns which bind the child to the mother at birth. In advancing this position Bowlby drops the term *emotional dependence* and speaks only of *attachment*. The operational definition of this latter term typically revolves around the tendency of the young to seek the proximity of other members of the species (Schaffer and Emerson, 1964). The class of behavior so defined is obviously more narrow than that of dependence. But attachment, defined in terms of proximity-seeking, clearly falls into the larger category of dependence and seems likely to be very central in understanding the development of dependent behavior generally.

That the interest aroused by Bowlby's views can result in important research findings is shown in the excellent monograph by Schaffer and Emerson (1964). Building on Bowlby's formulation and some of their own earlier work, these investigators in a longitudinal study followed the attachment behavior of infants from the early weeks of life up to eighteen months of age. Their operational measures of attachment comprised the infant's reaction (rated from none to severe) to seven common separation situations (for example, the infant is left alone in a room). The investigators were interested primarily in the age of onset of social attachments, the intensity and objects of such attachments, and finally the variables that might be related to individual differences. Their findings appear to emphasize the importance of innate, genetic, and cognitive-developmental factors in the de-

velopment of dependence—factors that have all been relatively ignored by most students of dependence.

Schaffer and Emerson found conspicuous individual differences. Infants varied in the age at which attachments developed and in the intensity of their attachments. Some infants focused their attachment on one person, whereas others showed attachments to a broad range of individuals. Schaffer and Emerson's investigations of these individual differences appear to have considerable theoretical import. Contrary to the frustration-drive formulation of dependence development (referred to earlier and to be discussed at greater length), the severity of oral and excretory training showed no relation to the child's attachment to mother. The findings also offer little support for the simpler formulation of dependence as an acquired drive based on the association of the mother with the satisfaction of such primary drives as hunger, thirst, and pain withdrawal. Thus, maternal availability, defined by amount of time mother spent with her child, was found to be unrelated to the child's attachment to mother. Schaffer and Emerson did find a relation between the degree of maternal responsiveness to the child's crying and the child's attachment to mother at eighteen months, a relation they interpret as reflecting a "mutual adaptation" based on both the strength of the infant's demands and the degree to which the mother is prepared to respond. The amount of interaction initiated by the mother was also found to be positively related to the child's attachment.

The most important factor in determining attachment, however, appears to be the amount of sensory stimulation another person provides (as measured by his overall responsiveness to the child). The acquired drive theory is especially challenged by the finding that in 39 per cent of the cases the principal object of attachment was not the person mainly responsible for feeding and other care, and in 22 per cent of the cases the principal object of attachment did not participate even to a minor degree in any aspect of the child's physical care. It thus appears that attachments may be formed with individuals not associated with satisfaction of the main biological drives. The data on attachment to people other than the mother also indicate that it is stimulation and attention in general which elicit attachment, and not just the satisfaction of physical needs. Another finding of interest was the discovery that the higher the IQ of the child, the earlier did he form a specific attachment. No other variable investigated was found to be related to the age at onset of specific attachment.

On the basis of these findings, Schaffer and Emerson have advanced an extremely interesting theory of the development of attachment or dependence. They conclude that the attachment need is a primary motivational force giving rise to proximity-seeking, expressed by a variety of behavior patterns that may differ from child to child and from one developmental level to the next. They note that Ainsworth (1963) has identified a large number of such behavior patterns which may be observed to "clock in" at various times of the first year of life. Individual differences in the intensity of the attachment need are viewed as partly a function of environmental factors and partly a function of the inherent characteristics of the individual. They consider this inherent component to be a genetic variation in the infant's threshold of responsiveness in social situations, and they label it "social sensitivity factor." A developmental-cognitive factor is also assumed in order to explain the finding that in the majority of cases specific attachments are formed by the child in the third quarter of the first year. Recalling that Piaget (1953, 1955) has found this to be the period when object conservation is first observed in the child, Schaffer and Emerson argue that specific attachments require a fundamental change in the infant's cognitive structure, that is, in the manner in which perceptions are organized and related to each other as well as to their external sources. Supporting this argument is the relation found between the IQ and the age at onset of specific attachments. Although Schaffer and Emerson clearly view attachment as an inborn primary need, they view the satisfaction of this need as serving a particular requirement of the child, namely, maintaining some level of optimal stimulation. Schaffer and Emerson, finally, advance a three-stage theory of the development of attachment. The first stage is an asocial one in which the infant seeks optimal arousal from all aspects of his enviroment. In the second stage, characterized by indiscriminate attachment behavior, the infant views human beings as particularly satisfying objects and makes special efforts to seek their proximity. The final stage involves a further narrowing in which the child forms attachments to specific persons, presumably those who are good "stimulators."

As noted earlier, this theorizing and the evidence on which it is based differ radically from the theory and evidence presented by Sears and his coworkers (Sears et al., 1953; Sears et al., 1957). However, an important difference in the empirical efforts should be noted. Schaffer and Emerson studied the attachment behavior of children during the first eighteen months of life, whereas the Sears' investigations dealt with the dependent behavior of children considerably older. It may well be that dependent behavior, broadly defined, is primarily determined by an innate need during the very early period of the child's life but is determined later in life by the experiential events on which learning theorists have focused. It would be surprising, however, if the influence of later experiential events was not itself determined by an interaction with the child's innate tendencies.

Schaffer and Emerson, we have seen, offer the child's social-response threshold as the main locus of relevant genetic variation. The necessity for students of socialization to consider genetic variation in the need for attachment is indicated in a study by Freedman (1958). Studying several breeds of dogs, he found that differences among breeds in initial attraction to people greatly influenced the effects of indulgent and disciplinary modes of rearing as measured by the dog's obedience at maturity. Certain features of the current Zeitgeist, especially the greatly increased interest in infant behavior and the growing influence of behavior geneticists, suggest that work on dependence in the future will be much more concerned than in the past with the innate components of this system of behavior.

The Frustration-Dependence Hypothesis

Although the relationship between frustration and dependence has received less attention than the frustration-aggression relation, many investigators of varying theoretical persuasions have dealt with the problem.

Is the development of dependence favored by early rejection or frustration of a child? Research has resulted in a fairly, though not perfectly, consistent correlation in this direction. Sears et al. (1953) found a positive relation between infantile feeding frustration, as measured by rigidity of feeding schedule and severity of weaning, and later dependence in nursery school, as rated by teachers. Smith (1958) has also presented some evidence indicating a positive relation between rigidity of feeding schedules and later dependence. Because these children were generally weaned in infancy, it may be said that later dependence was positively related to infantile frustration; one interpretation would be that infantile frustration establishes a lasting insecurity which motivates dependent strivings.

Sears et al. (1953) also found a positive relation in boys between current frustration or punishment in the home and dependence, and a negative relation in girls. In order to explain these relations, these investigators posited a curvilinear relation between maternal punitiveness and the child's dependence, based on the acquired-drive formulation discussed earlier. The negative relation in girls was then explained in terms of the girls being more identified with the mother, so that the same objective amount of punishment would be more punishing for girls than for boys. [See Walters and Parke (1964) for an alternative interpretation of these findings.] As Hartup (1963) has noted, subsequent studies have provided little further support for the curvilinear hypothesis advanced by Sears et al. However, a number of diverse studies which have investigated the relation between child-rearing practices and dependence have found that punishment or rejection of the child is associated with a greater incidence of dependent behavior either concurrently or later in life (Antonovsky, 1959; Douvan and Adelson, 1958; Kagan and Moss, 1962; Marshall, 1961; McCord, McCord, and Verden, 1962; Sears et al., 1957; Smith, 1958; Watson, 1957; Winder and Rau, 1962; Wittenborn, 1956; see also Stendler, 1952, for discussion of "critical periods" during which frustration of the child is most likely to result in overdependence).

A number of experimental studies have also indicated that frustrating the child by withdrawal of nurturance, or by absence or relative unavailability of adult social reinforcement, results in greater dependence or increased susceptibility to adult social reinforcement (Beller and Haeberle, 1959; Erickson, 1962; Gewirtz, 1954; Gewirtz and Baer, 1958a, 1958b; Hartup, 1958). On the other hand, some child-rearing and experimental studies have either found no relation between frustration and dependence or have found that frustration of the child results in decreased dependence (Bandura and Walters, 1959; Cairns, 1962). Nevertheless, the findings have been consistent enough to have led previous reviewers (Hartup, 1963; Walters and Parke, 1964) to conclude that children who have been deprived or frustrated in their efforts to obtain nurturance show greater dependence and increased susceptibility to social influence. However, the dangers of overgeneralization here have been pointed out by Walters and Parke (1964) and are further indicated by a relatively recent study of Sears (1963), who, although obtaining some support for the frustration-dependence hypothesis, found some quite complex relations between child-rearing practices, sex of the child, and particular classes of dependent behavior.

Also relevant to the frustration-dependence hypothesis is the literature dealing with early deprivation and/or institutionalization (reviews by Casler, 1961; World Health Organization, 1962; Yarrow, 1961, 1964). Wittenborn (1965), who explicitly measured dependent behavior as a consequence of institutionalization, found a significant tendency for adopted children who had lived in the institution for some months to show less dependence at the age of five than children adopted at birth, as determined in parental interview. Results on effects of institutionalization on dependence at later ages show some inconsistency. Congruent with Wittenborn's findings are those of Spitz and Wolf (1946), who describe a generalized apathy in institutional children, which may imply a great reduction in dependence as well as in other forms of social interaction. Goldfarb (1943a 1943b), on the other hand, while stressing the generally low social interaction of institutional children, also provided evidence that these children were in a sense overdependent and displayed a high need for affection and attention. It should be noted that the apathetic or socially unresponsive reaction was found in very young children. This apathetic reaction has been explained by both acquired dependence drive theorists (for example, Sears et al., 1953) and innate dependence drive theorists (Schaffer and Emerson, 1964) as being due to the very unusual circumstances of institutional care in which adult nurturance of the child is insufficient for the typical development of a dependence tendency.

Zigler and his coworkers (Zigler, 1966c), in discussing both institutional and preinstitutional deprivation, offer another resolution of the question whether social deprivation results in a long-lasting increase or decrease in motivation for social reinforcement (that is, dependence). Their view, supported by considerable correlational and experimental evidence, is that severe and early social deprivation has conflicting results: (1) a long-lasting increase in motivation for social reinforcement (a positive reaction tendency), and (2) a reluctance or wariness to interact with strange adults (a negative reaction tendency). How much overt dependence the child exhibits depends on the relative strength of these two tendencies. Of the two, the negative reaction tendency is much more open to modification by situational determinants. Thus the negative reaction tendency of the child is reduced, and he therefore manifests more dependence in interactions with adults he knows are nonpunitive or rewarding.

The research of Zigler and his coworkers, taken in conjunction with relevant research of Stevenson and his coworkers (reviewed in Stevenson, 1965), supports with a variety of evidence the view that early social deprivation (frustration of early nurturance needs) results in a long-lasting increase in the child's dependence or motivation for social reinforcement. The evidence includes a positive relation between the amount of preinstitutional social deprivation experienced by the child and his later motivation for social reinforcement, measured by how long the child will persist on a boring task in order to gain the attention and support of an adult (Zigler, 1961, Zigler, Balla, and Butterfield, 1966); greater motivation for social reinforcement in institutionalized than in noninstitutionalized children (Green and Zigler, 1962; Stevenson and Fahel, 1961; Zigler, 1963c); and greater motivation for social reinforcement in children living in a more socially depriving than in a less socially depriving institution (Butterfield and Zigler, 1965). Two of the studies

(Zigler, Balla and Butterfield, 1966; Zigler and Williams, 1963) provide specific evidence that the amount of preinstitutional social deprivation, in interaction with the deprivation experienced as the result of institutionalization, continues to influence the child's dependence several years later.

The Role of Reinforcement

Whereas the frustration of the child produced by the unavailability of social reinforcement appears to increase his dependence, direct punishment of dependent behavior appears to result in anxiety about being dependent, and consequently in inhibition of overt dependent behavior. Furthermore, as would be expected from all learning-theory formulations, direct positive reinforcement for the child's dependent behavior appears to increase such behavior. As we saw in the Schaffer and Emerson (1964) findings, even in the first eighteen months of life the strength of the infant's attachment to the mother was positively related to the degree of maternal responsiveness. This is consistent with the experimental findings of Rheingold (1956), who performed caretaking acts toward one group of institutionalized children while a control group remained in the usual hospital routine. After a period of eight weeks, the infants who had received the nurturant care of E exceeded the control group in social responsiveness both to E and to a strange examiner.

Beginning with the well-known work of Levy (1943), several studies have indicated that child-rearing characterized by overprotection of the child (a state of affairs in which dependence receives considerable reinforcement) results in increased dependence. Examining clinical case histories, Levy discovered two types of overprotection, each tending to induce a particular mode of dependence. Children of extremely indulgent mothers tended to be aggressive and negativistic in their effort to increase contact with mother. Children of domin-

ant, overpossessive mothers were found to be passively and submissively dependent. A number of studies of overprotection have confirmed, without necessarily making this distinction, that overprotection is associated with greater dependence in children (Kagan and Moss, 1962; Marshall, 1961; Smith, 1958; Stendler, 1954).

Recent research on birth-order effects (reviewed by Warren, 1966) has also lent some tangential support to the view that nurturance and increased reinforcement of dependent behavior increases the incidence of a variety of dependent acts later in life. A number of studies have now indicated that first-borns as compared to later-borns are generally more dependent, that is, show a greater need for affiliation, and are more susceptible to social influence (Becker, Lerner and Carroll, 1964, 1966; Carrigan and Julian, 1966; Schachter, 1959; Staples and Walters, 1961). These findings have typically been attributed to differential dependence training during childhood. Gilmore and Zigler (1964) found some experimental support for the view that first-borns, having received greater social reinforcement earlier in their lives, experience greater frustration than do later-borns in stress situations where social reinforcers should be forthcoming but are not. Gilmore and Zigler have argued that it is in such situations that dependence should be greater in first-borns, and that in situations where social reinforcers are readily available, dependence should be greater in the later born.

More direct evidence for the experience variable assumed here to be responsible is contained in several child-rearing studies indicating that high nurturance or the selective parental reinforcement results in greater dependent behavior (Bandura, 1960; Bandura and Walters, 1959; Finney, 1961; Heathers, 1953; Sears et al., 1957). This efficacy of direct reinforcement has also been found in experimental studies in which the amount of dependence was assessed following reward or punishment of dependent acts (Cairns, 1962; Nelson, 1960).

As Bandura and Walters (1963a) have pointed out in their review of dependent behavior, the withholding of rewards for dependence seems to result in an increase in such behavior, whereas active punishment appears to reduce its incidence. This inhibitive effect of punishment has been found in cross-cultural research; thus, Whiting and Child (1953) found greater dependence anxiety among adults in cultures where dependence was severely treated in childhood than in cultures where dependence was not severely socialized. A high negative relationship between dependence anxiety in adulthood and the degree of indulgence of dependent needs before the beginning of this dependence socialization was also found. Although considerable complexity remains, certain consistencies have been found in the relation between experiences of the child and his later dependent behavior.

Summary. Dependence as a system of behavior is less well defined than aggression. Some investigators treat nurturance-seeking as dependence, whereas others view dependence as susceptibility to social reinforcement. We have concentrated our attention on the former definition. The major theoretical formulations of dependence have come from psychoanalytic theory, neo-Hullian learning theory, and a combination of modeling and operant learning theories. Neo-Hullian theorists see dependence as an acquired drive, whereas social-learning theorists view dependent behavior as a conditioned response to a more general anxiety state. A minority position of increasing importance is the innate attachment-seeking drive proposed by Bowlby and elaborated by Schaffer and Emerson. There is considerable evidence that a frustration-dependence relationship exists, with frustration of the child's efforts to obtain nurturance resulting in increased and persisting dependent behavior. Positive reinforcement for dependent behavior has

been found to increase such behavior, whereas punishment inhibits it.

Achievement

The Problem of Conceptualization: Achievement and Independence

Achievement is often assumed to be closely related to independence (Atkinson, 1954, 1958; Berkowitz, 1964a; Bronfenbrenner and Ricciuti, 1960; Crandall, 1963; Hartup, 1965; McClelland, 1955, 1961; McClelland, Atkinson, Clark and Lowell, 1953). It is tempting to think of achievement as the pole opposite to dependence on a single axis and to seek its genesis in the same set of antecedent conditions that determine level of dependence. McClelland, Atkinson, and their coworkers have indeed postulated that achievement motivation should be determined by socialization practices that emphasize early training for independence.

A number of empirical studies have also suggested a close inverse relation between achievement and dependence. Thus, boys with high projective test scores on achievement were found to be more independent in their problem-solving efforts in school (Winterbottom, 1958) and, in another study, to ask for less aid from their parents and to display greater self-reliance in general (Rosen and D'Anrade, 1959). Further evidence that achievement-oriented children show less overt dependent behavior has been presented by Crandall, Preston, and Rabson (1960) and Crandall and Sinkeldam (1964). Krebs (1958) found that children's achievement tendency was positively related to their maintenance of independence in conformity-evoking situations. Wertheim and Mednick (1958) found an inverse relation between achievement measures and field dependence as measured by the Embedded Figures Test. The inference drawn in this last study is that, as suggested by

McClelland (1955, 1961) and Witkin (Witkin et al., 1962), both achievement motivation and low field dependence originate in parent-child relationships that emphasize independence training. Findings such as these led Blake and Mouton (1959) to suggest that a cluster of variables including achievement motivation, perceptual field independence, social independence, and child-rearing practices would eventually be identified. Evidence supporting the inverse dependence-achievement relationship includes at least one cross-cultural study (McClelland and Friedman, 1952), although a similar cross-cultural study (Child, Storm, and Veroff, 1958) finds no strong confirmation.

It seems reasonable that the diminishing dependence of the child as he grows older involves positive development of more independent modes of responding to the same situations that formerly elicited dependent reactions, and that striving for achievement may be one of those modes. But caution is appropriate here on several grounds: (1) Achievement striving is not the only kind of independent response; many acts which are thoroughly independent seem not at all oriented toward achieving any kind of standard. In a correlational study of self-ratings by college men on many variables of social behavior, Storm, Rosenwald, and Child (1958) did not, indeed, even find that achievement and independence were correlated or had loadings on the same factors, even though each of them showed substantial relations with other variables. (2) The overt dependent behavior of early childhood gives way, not only to clearly independent acts but also to a variety of acts that do not entirely fit that label, for example, more subtle forms of dependence nurturance of younger or more helpless individuals, or cooperative social interaction among equals. (3) Dependence may itself become, even if it usually does not in our society, a main goal of achievement strivings, as when siblings compete to get as much parental attention as possible. (4) Insofar as the payoff for achievement strivings is recognition by others rather than just by oneself, we may view the achievement-oriented adult as still dependent but in a mature rather than an infantile manner.

With these cautions in mind, we would expect that child-rearing practices that produce dependence will not in and of themselves guarantee low achievement motivation, and that the child-rearing antecedents of achievement may well differ greatly from those of low dependence. Similar expectations arise from analyses of dependence and independence advanced by several theorists (Beller, 1955; Hartup, 1963; Heathers, 1955a, 1955b) who, while definitely associating achievement with independence, argue that dependence and independence are orthogonal enough to be considered separate conceptual entities. In their view independence has two criteria: seeking nurturance from others relatively infrequently and showing initiative and achievement-striving. Thus, independence is seen as not only self-reliance but also self-assertion. This conceptualization does not remove all overlap with dependence, but it clearly makes of independence or achievement something much more than simply lack of dependence.

Several different lines of evidence converge in support of the view that achievement and dependence follow, for the most part, separate courses of development, and at any rate are not opposite ends of the same dimension. One line of evidence comes from research on birth order. As we saw, first-borns have frequently been found to be dependent. If dependence were negatively related to achievement, we would expect first-borns to be low achievers. Such is not the case. First-borns as both children and adults have been found to be high achievers as measured by a variety of overt achievement criteria (Altus, 1965; 1966; Sampson and Hancock, 1967; Schachter, 1963; Solomons and Solomons, 1964; Weinberg, 1964). Another type of evidence appears in a recent study by Zigler, Levine, and

Gould (1967). They examined children's mastery motivation across a wide age span by assessing preference for cartoons difficult or easy to understand. We know that dependent behavior declines with age; therefore if dependence is characteristic of the early years and achievement orientation is characteristic of the later years, we should expect the preference for difficult over easy cartoons to be greater at the higher than at the lower ages. Instead, Zigler et al. found a decided preference in this direction to be equal at all ages for both sexes.

The Problem of Measurement

Adding to the difficulty of discovering the antecedents of achievement is the extremely broad spectrum of responses that have been placed in the category of achievement. The achievement literature, consisting of articles which now number in the hundreds, is based on at least three very different measures: (1) preoccupation with achievement in fantasy productions, often referred to as achievement motivation; (2) self-report of achievement-oriented behavior or motivation for it; and (3) overt achievements of extremely diverse types. It relates these diverse measures of achievement to an enormous variety of other variables. It would certainly be surprising if all the findings reported to date could be explained in terms of some single set of antecedent factors.

Achievement Motivation and Fantasy Production. The very nature of the relation between achievement motivation measured through fantasy production (for example, response to TAT cards) and overt achievements or self-reports remains a matter of considerable dispute (Atkinson, 1961; Broverman, Jordan, and Phillips, 1960; Lazarus, 1961, 1966; McClelland, 1956, 1966; Nuttin, 1955; Skolnick, 1966). Although achievement motivation measured through fantasy production has been found to be positively related to overt achievement measures frequently enough to indicate some degree of validity, the relationship has been far from perfect. Not only have many instances of no relationship been found, but the possibility has been raised and some evidence presented that achievement expressed in fantasy represents a substitutive phenomena and thus has an inverse relation to overt achievement (Broverman et al., 1960; Lazarus, 1961, 1966; Nuttin, 1955). A substitutive function of achievement fantasy is suggested by evidence in a cross-cultural study we have already mentioned (Child, Storm, and Veroff, 1958) and in an intensive study of children in a private school in the United States by Sanford, Adkins, Miller, and Cobb (1943). It remains unclear what factors determine whether the relation between achievement motivation measured in fantasy and overt achievement will be positive, negative, or nonexistent. Lazarus (1961, 1966) has both emphasized the complexity of this issue and brought some light to it by drawing a distinction between primary-process fantasy (playful fantasy or reverie) and secondary-process fantasy (problem-solving fantasy). Lazarus argues cogently that the nature of the relation between fantasy and overt achievement will be determined by some combination of such factors as the type of fantasy in which the individual is engaging; the individual's personality characteristics, including his defensive needs; and the individual's perception of the requirements of the situation in which his achievement fantasy is to be assessed. Only with uncertainty can we tentatively take fantasy and overt measures of achievement as two parallel aspects of the same underlying phenomena. (The same observation applies equally to the other systems we have reviewed, but only for this system has a sizeable fraction of the research been confined to a fantasy measure.)

Achievement Motivation and Overt Behavior. Even at the overt level of behavior it is difficult to identify the commonality inherent in all the behavior considered to reflect an achievement orientation. The most influential efforts to bring some unity to this diverse behavioral domain are represented in the definitions of achievement by McClelland, Atkinson, and their coworkers, and Crandall and his coworkers (Crandall, Katkovsky, and Preston, 1960).

McClelland et al. (1953) view the achievement orientation as arising from expectations related to universal experiences in problem-solving, for example, learning to walk, talk, read, write, and so forth. The child is viewed as developing expectations about what walking or other behavior will accomplish for him and deriving pleasure from confirmation of these expectations so long as they retain a certain degree of uncertainty. In order to avoid boredom, the child approaches ever more complex objects or situations, so that mastery is possible but uncertain. Because tasks can be performed either well or badly, the child begins to perceive performance in terms of standards of excellence, and discrepancies from this perceptual frame of reference produce positive effect if performance is above this standard or negative effect if below it. We thus see the child evaluating his own performance, and the crucial aspect of achievement motivation is the presence of effect in connection with evaluation. The child thus comes to evaluate his performance, and experiences pride if the performance exceeds some standard of excellence or shame or guilt if his performance falls beneath this standard.

Crandall et al. (1960) have advanced a definition of achievement behavior involving three criteria: (1) the inferred goal of the behavior, (2) the unique characteristic of the behavior, and (3) the nature of the situations in which the behavior occurs. The goal is the attainment of approval and the avoidance of disapproval, either from the self or from other persons. The unique characteristic which elicits such approval or disapproval is the level of competence

of performance. The major requisite of the situation that calls forth achievement behavior is that it involves activities that permit the individual to apply some standard of excellence to the competence of his behavior. Thus, to Crandall et al., achievement behavior is behavior directed toward the attainment of approval or the avoidance of disapproval for competence of performance in situations to which standards of excellence are relevant.

Crandall (1963) has pointed out that this definition, that of McClelland et al., and other currently accepted definitions have a certain commonality. All agree that situations that evoke achievement motivation are those in which competence of performance is central. Furthermore, the general aim of achievement behavior appears to be that of obtaining positive reinforcement for demonstrated competence. Finally, achievement situations appear to be those which contain cues relevant to a "standard of excellence" that ultimately defines degree of competence or incompetence.

Despite these efforts at definition, the boundaries that delimit achievement behavior remain somewhat unclear. One ambiguity, pointed out by Walters and Parke (1964), relates to the consideration of achievement-oriented acts as instrumental in obtaining social reinforcement or gaining approval. Walters and Parke have argued that conceptualizing such acts as achievement-oriented is an evaluative judgment whose own determinants are unclear, and that they could with equal justice be placed in some other class of behavior, for example, dependence. The problem here is lack of clarity about exactly whose standard of excellence is involved, and about the class of reinforcement (approval from the self or others) thought to be the goal of achievement behavior. The child, for instance, who uses his teacher's standard of excellence, and attempts to meet this standard for no other reason than to obtain the approval of the teacher, may be just as easily considered dependent as achievement-oriented. The school achievement considered in many studies (reviewed by Crandall, 1963) may reflect motives other than achievement. Schoolroom success seems as much determined by the child's "goodness" and desire to conform to external expectations as by his effort toward achieving personal competence defined by an internalized standard of accomplishment or mastery. To consider achievement orientation bound to an internal standard of excellence, with the only relevant reinforcement being that which the child delivers to himself, also poses problems. Children who are independent of the views of others and continue to march to the tune of their own drum are not likely to be viewed as highly achievement-oriented unless their behavior is so considered by the social agents surrounding them. Yet behavior that is agreed to be achievement-oriented can result from a variety of motives, only one of which is genuine motivation for achievement.

As Crandall (1963) has noted, definitions of achievement behavior overlap a number of concepts associated with a positive view of human motivation which have received a great deal of recent attention, such as mastery, effectance, curiosity, exploratory drive, manipulation drive, and the need to know (Hunt, 1960, 1965; Kagan, 1967; Nissen, 1954; White, 1959, 1960). Hunt's formulations are especially relevant. His emphasis on the motivation inherent in the information processing itself, based on something akin to the incongruity-dissonance principle or the discrepancy hypothesis, is reminiscent of McClelland's et al. (1953) concern, in accounting for the development of achievement motivation, with the child's avoiding boredom by dealing with ever more complex objects or situations. Hunt's theoretical synthesis has led him to the opinion that intelligent, self-directed activity which many see as central to an achievement orientation, will be maximized if the environment maintains homeostatic satisfaction, minimizes pain, and does not interfere unduly in the child's determining what he will do. In the following review of empirical research it will be of interest to see whether such relatively laissez-faire child-rearing does result in higher levels of achievement orientation.

Innate vs. Acquired Views of Achievement Motivation

This overlap between achievement and such concepts as effectance and the motivation inherent in information-processing raises the important issue of how much of achievement motivation is innate and how much is acquired. The motivational theorists we have been discussing view the motives for effectance and optimal stimulation as inherent phenomena arising out of the very nature of the human fabric, whereas most influential achievement theorists (see Atkinson, 1960; McClelland et al., 1953) view achievement motivation as an acquired characteristic influenced most heavily by the stress placed on early independence training. The disagreement here may be more apparent than real, arising partly from whether the writer is concentrating on the uniformities among men or on individual differences. Achievement may rest on certain inherent or innate factors, but its precise level or form may be determined largely by experiential factors. It is surprising, however, that the innate components which may determine some of the variation in achievement motivation have received so little attention.

Some empirical evidence as well as some theoretical positions argue for the importance of an innate factor in achievement orientation. We have already mentioned the motivation literature consonant with such a viewpoint. Especially relevant to this issue is the evidence at the infrahuman level that the manipulatory (Harlow, Blezek, and McClearn, 1956) and exploratory

(Nissen, 1954) motives are innate rather than acquired. At the human level Kessen (1963) has reviewed considerable evidence that infants from the very beginning actively organize and structure perception of their surround, and we may well see here early indications of a need for mastery. In observational studies of children during the first eighteen months of life, Stott (1961) and Federov (1961) independently concluded that much of their behavior was directed toward mastery of the environment.

At a theoretical level Nuttin (1955) views the achievement motive as a fundamental need having a biological or constitutional component. As Crandall (1963) has pointed out, Adler (1927), through his concepts of "inferiority complex," "masculine protest," and "striving for superiority," has suggested that the gratification of achievement needs is a basic goal in human behavior. Schachtel (1959) finds in Freud's theoretical writings, in addition to the well-known drive-reduction theory of pleasure, the notion that positive effect arises from expanding encounters with reality and from the development and exercise of growing capacities and skills. But where Schachtel finds in Freud already a basis for an innate view of the achievement motive, White (1960) considers that even the recent psychoanalytic ego psychology would require extensive revision before it could adequately accommodate such inherently positive features of man as the effectance or mastery motive.

None of these theoretical formulations is very clear in suggesting what particular biological characteristics, varying within the human species, account for variation in achievement motivation. One suggestion is contained in the recent findings of Cortes and Gatti (1966) that achievement motivation is positively related to mesomorphy and negatively related to ectomorphy. The authors suggest that the relationship is mediated by the degree of physical energy associated with position on these dimensions of physique. It is but a short step from the variable of physical energy level to the variable of activity level, on which we know individual differences at birth retain some stability thereafter. We have mentioned earlier that activity level has been suggested as the innate component influencing the individual's level of aggression. In its relation to a basic biological mechanism, then, achievement motivation may be more closely related to aggression than to the variable of dependence whose simple inverse it is often considered to be. There is some evidence to support such a view. As Crandall (1963) has pointed out, common observation indicates that the distinction between aggressive and achieving behavior is in many instances subtle and possibly quite subjective. If we grant that high level of early activity may be relevant to later achievement motivation, then it is relevant that Schaefer and Bayley (1963) found that activity level during developmental tests in the first ten to twelve months was associated with unfriendliness, lack of cooperation, distractibility, and inattentiveness up to twelve years. Even more pertinent to an aggression-achievement relation is the surprising finding of Cortes and Gatti (1966) that TAT achievement scores of delinquents average higher than those of nondelinquents. Shaw and Grub (1958) found that overachieving students expressed more hostility than underachievers. In a review of the characteristics of academically proficient children, Crandall (1963) concluded that such children appear to be self-reliant, assertive, competitive, and even aggressive in their everyday academic experiences.

Experience and Achievement

As we have seen, there is some evidence to support the view that innate factors play a significant role in the individual's level of achievement motivation; however, there is also a large body of research findings which support the view that, whatever an individual's innate characteristics, the form achievement behavior takes is determined by his experiences. Experiential factors that have been investigated in relation to achievement behavior include parental permissiveness, restrictiveness, and warmth; direct independence training; direct achievement training; and the child's history of success and failure.

Parent-Child Relationships: Permissiveness, Restrictiveness, Warmth

A number of studies, confirming a suggestion we have cited earlier from Hunt, have indicated that some combination of positive parent-child relations (for example, closeness to and interest in the child, approval of him, and a general permissive attitude) is related to academic achievement (Conklin, 1940; Jones, 1955; Kimball, 1953; Walsh, 1956). Crandall (1963) has pointed out that many of these older studies are marred by a variety of flaws. Yet some more recent and probably more adequate studies also support the view that parental permissiveness and warmth result in higher levels of achievement. As Becker (1964) has noted in summarizing the Kagan and Moss (1962) study, among the lasting effects on children of restrictiveness during the first three years are greater conformity, lowered aggression, lowered dominance, lowered competition with peers, more dependence on adults, and lowered mastery behavior. Contrary to the achievement-aggression relationship we have mentioned, but consistent with the permissiveness-achievement sequence, was the finding by Kagan and Moss that in ages three to six girls who had experienced the most restrictions were high in aggression but low in achievement mastery and in independence. Consistent with both the aggression-achievement and permissiveness-achievement hypotheses are findings of

several studies indicating that permissiveness makes for both aggression and achievement, the latter being variously measured by some combination of self-confidence, independence, curiosity, originality, and imagination (Baldwin, 1948; Raelke, 1946; Symonds, 1939). Watson (1957) investigated the effects of permissiveness versus restrictiveness on children coming from homes characterized by general warmth. He discovered that permissive as compared to restrictive child-rearing resulted in more initiative and independence and higher spontaneity, creativity, and originality. Levin (1958) has found that maximum adult-role-taking (as measured by doll play) occurs in children who have experienced a combination of warmth and permissiveness. As Becker (1964) has pointed out, if adult-role-taking is assumed to reflect a modeling of parent and the learning of adult ways of doing things, Levin's findings are consistent with the greater independence and achievement mastery found to be associated with permissiveness by Watson (1957) and Kagan and Moss (1962).

Contrary to these findings, other studies have indicated that restrictiveness is associated with higher achievement. Watson (1934) found that college students who described their parents' discipline as restrictive reported better grades and stronger ambition than students who described their upbringing as permissive. Consistent with this are the findings of McClelland et al. (1953) in a study of college men. Ss rated their parents on several aspects of child-rearing practices, as did a psychiatrist after extended interviews with Ss. Their ratings were then correlated with Ss' TAT performance. The correlations were consistent in indicating a positive correlation between the achievement measure and general severity of upbringing. Although they point out that the measures of parent behavior were not ideal, McClelland et al. interpret this finding as showing that high achievement tendency is favored by strong parental stress on independent achievement.

In opposition to this, McClelland et al. found that high school boys with strong achievement motivation rated their fathers as less rejecting than did boys with low achievement motivation. Drews and Teahan (1957) found that the mothers of high-achieving junior high school students, as compared to mothers of low achievers, were more authoritarian, restrictive, and reject-ant of their children. However, the general inconsistency of findings in this area is seen in Shaw and Dutton's (1962) report that the mothers of underachieving girls have child-rearing attitudes characterized by authoritarian control. Hoffman, Rosen, and Lippitt (1960) found that boys who perceive their parents as coercive perform more competently in the classroom than those who perceive their parents as more lenient; their conclusion is that parental coercive-ness leads to strong needs for self-assertion. Maccoby (1961) found that boys whose parents had been restrictive in early years (according to interview when the boys were five) were highly motivated to do school work at the age of twelve.

Maternal nurturance has even been claimed to be negatively related to achieve-ment. Crandall, Dewey, Katkovsky, and Preston (1964) found greater academic com-petence in girls whose mothers were rela-tively unaffectionate and low on nurturance. (This finding did not obtain for fathers' relations with their children or for mothers' relations with their sons.) Al-though Crandall (1963) suggests that high academic achievement is associated with such negative parental behavior as rejection, coerciveness, and overprotection, evidence for this view appears to be quite limited. In addition to the permissiveness findings noted earlier, Bronfenbrenner (1961b) found among adolescents of both sexes that rejec-tion, neglect, parental absence, and protec-tiveness were all related to low leadership. Also inconsistent with the view that nega-tive child-rearing practices result in higher achievement is the finding of Bradburn (1963). In a study of adult Turkish males

and their fathers, he found that sons who, for a variety of reasons, were separated from domineering and unaffectionate fathers showed higher TAT achievement scores than those who were not.

Independence Training and Achievement

The child-rearing findings reviewed to this point appear to generate the conclusion that there is no consistent relation between the permissiveness-restrictiveness and par-ental warmth dimensions on the one hand and achievement on the other, as assessed across a wide range of fantasy and overt behavior measures. A somewhat more consistent picture emerges if we turn away from these dimensions to consider parents who themselves value achievement and who actively train their children toward an achievement orientation. Such training appears to be most effective in those instan-ces where the parent is simultaneously neither overindulgent nor overly coercive or dominating. As noted earlier, McClelland, Atkinson, and their coworkers have viewed the genesis of achievement motivation as resting on the child's early independence training. Over a decade ago, however, McClelland (1955) warned that the develop-ment of achievement motivation was also influenced by a number of parental charac-teristics and we should not expect that early independence training would invariably produce higher achievement motivation. The research findings over the years attest to the wisdom inherent in McClelland's warning. There has, of course, been some support of the independence training and achievement hypothesis. More central to the development of an achievement orien-tation, however, appear to be the direct rewards and punishments administered to the child when he performs or does not perform those acts which the parent views as achievements.

The independence training and achievement hypothesis has rested heavily on the findings of Winterbottom (1958), who derived from principles of learning a number of specific hypotheses about variations in socialization which should influence the strength of the achievement motive. Among her independent variables were the mother's demands and rewards for independent accomplishment, the frequency and intensity of such demands and rewards, the mother's restrictions on independent activity, and frequency and intensity of rewards for acceptance of such, and the mother's punitiveness for failure to fulfill demands or accept restrictions. She used as a dependent variable the frequency of achievement-related ideas in stories told by twenty-nine boys aged eight to ten. Her most significant findings were (1) the earlier the age accomplishment demands were made on the child, the greater his later achievement score; (2) the greater the frequency or intensity of rewards for meeting such demands, the greater the child's achievement score; (3) the greater the restrictions on independent activity, the lower the achievement score. These findings are consonant with her predictions. Contrary to prediction, (4) high-achievement children had been subjected to more restrictions at early ages than low-achievement children, but restrictions were fewer than accomplishment demands for this group, whereas this was not true for low-achievement children; (5) high-achievement children had been more frequently and intensely rewarded for acceptance of restrictions than low-achievement children. There were no significant findings with respect to punishment.

The Winterbottom findings thus lend considerable support to the independence training and achievement hypothesis. In a six-year follow-up study Feld (1959) found that the maternal independence training, reported by the mothers at the time of the Winterbottom study, was still predictive of the boys' achievement scores in adolescence. The importance of the early childhood years

in determining achievement orientation can be seen in Feld's somewhat surprising finding that the mothers' reactions to the boys' independence efforts during adolescence were *inversely* related to their sons' achievement scores.

Direct Achievement Training

Relevant evidence from some studies indicates that it is the direct training for achievement rather than general independence training that results in high-achievement motivation. A most pertinent study is that of Rosen and D'Andrade (1959), who explicitly advanced the hypothesis that independence or self-reliance training, when not associated with direct achievement training, is not a sufficient cause of high-achievement motivation. These investigators examined the child-rearing practices of boys who showed either high- or low-achievement motivation as assessed through fantasy productions. Rather than depend on the parents' answers to questionnaires or interviews, Rosen and D'Andrade actually observed and measured the parents' interactions with their children as the children participated in several experimental tasks. They found that the parents of the high- as compared to the low-achievement boys had higher aspirations and expectations and set higher standards for their sons' performances. The differences found between the fathers of high- and low-achievement boys were not as striking as those found between the two groups of mothers. The differences that were found between the two groups of fathers indicated that the fathers of the high- as compared to the low-achievement boys engaged more in both independence and direct achievement training. The fathers of high-achievement boys appeared to Rosen and D'Andrade to be competent men who were willing to take a back seat while their children were performing and who thus encouraged independence along with achievement.

A quite different picture emerges in

Rosen and D'Andrade's comparisons of the mothers of high- and low-achievement motivation boys. Here the emphasis is clearly on direct achievement training rather than on developing the child's independence or general autonomy. The mothers of high- as compared to low-achievement boys were found to be more dominant and expect less self-reliance in their children. However, their aspirations for their sons were higher and their concern over their success greater. The mothers of the high-achievement boys became very involved with their children's performance and, as compared to the mothers of low-achievement boys, were more likely to reward success with approval and to punish failure with hostility. The mothers of high-achievement boys appear to Rosen and D'Andrade to be competent strivers who give their children relatively little option about doing something and doing it well.

A positive relationship between independence training and achievement is challenged by Chance's (1961) research in which children's achievement is measured by academic competence in elementary school. She found early independence training to be negatively associated with this measure. Mothers who fostered dependence rather than independence were found to have children who were especially competent on elementary school achievement tests.

In another study Rosen (1962) found that the values and attitudes permeating the total home atmosphere are also important determinants of the child's achievement level. In this study Rosen employed fantasy measures to assess the achievement motivation of Brazilian boys and obtained socialization data through questionnaires and interviews with the parents. He then compared these data with those obtained from two samples of American children. He found that the achievement motivation scores of U.S. children were much higher than those of their Brazilian counterparts, the difference being especially great at the upper socioeconomic levels. Comparisons of the child-rearing practices reveal that Brazilian parents wait until the child is older before making achievement demands or instituting independence training. The Brazilian parents displayed a high degree of indulgence and affection toward their children in an authoritarian family structure which required obedience and deference, especially in children's behavior toward their fathers. Unlike the American boys, the Brazilian boys did not view their parents as making strong achievement demands of them; they generally believed their parents were satisfied with their performance. The Brazilian boys did report that their parents expected them to become "great" or "important." Rosen suggests that early indulgence may give Brazilian boys unrealistic expectations concerning their own capabilities and that subsequent frustration leads to loss of interest in competition and achievement.

Several early studies have demonstrated the importance of direct achievement training in increasing the overt achievement level of the child. In an experiment by Fales (1937) praise for the specific achievement of putting on and taking off wraps and training in the requisite skills were both found to increase achievement-oriented behavior (refusal of help) in nursery school children. Keister (1937) trained nursing school children to persist at difficult tasks by the use of repeated and specific praise for persistence and reproof for giving up. This training produced increased persistence when children were later tested on similar tasks. Wolf (1938) reports that a high level of persistence in young children is associated with a level of achievement demand from adults that is appropriate to the child's ability. Unreasonable or insufficient demands are associated with low-level persistence. These findings suggest that parental approval-disapproval and the child's success or failure produce a joint effect.

Individual History of Success and Failure

With respect to the success-failure dimension, Pauline Sears (1940) finds that children's level of aspiration in a particular task is largely determined by their histories of success and failure in tasks of the same type. Even though the experiments deal with rather specific learning situations, some generalizations may be drawn from their findings. First, social approval of persistent striving for achievement and disapproval for failure to do so influences the development of this behavior. Second, the development of persistent striving for achievement is also affected by the child's past successes and failures, which must be limited by his capacities and total environment. This latter point is important for our thinking about socialization, in that it emphasizes the importance of the nature of the environment with which the child must cope. For example, parental reinforcement for the child's striving for achievement may fail in its objective if parents permit the child's interaction with his environment to be such that his strivings are uniformly unsuccessful.

Research provides considerable support for these generalizations. A number of studies (reviewed by Cromwell, 1963) have indicated that the child who experiences inordinate amounts of failure adopts a life style oriented toward the avoidance of failure rather than the achievement of success. Several studies (Achenbach, 1966; Gruen and Zigler, 1968; Sanders, Zigler, and Butterfield, 1968; Stevenson and Zigler, 1958; Turnure and Zigler, 1964) also indicate that children who experience a great deal of failure in their everyday lives develop a style of problem-solving characterized by dependence and outer-directedness as well as developing a generally low expectation of success and a resulting willingness to settle for low degrees of accomplishment.

Other Experimental Factors and Achievement Motivation

Parents' attitudes toward their own and their child's achievements, and their direct reinforcement of the child's achievement behavior, are influential in determining the child's achievement level. Thus, Katkovsky, Preston, and Crandall (1964a, 1964b) generally found that the more emphasis parents placed on themselves being intellectually competent, the more likely they were to participate with their children in intellectual pursuits, to encourage their children toward intellectual achievement activities and accomplishments, and to react strongly to their children's achievement efforts. Crandall, Preston, and Rabson (1960) found preschool children's achievement efforts in free play unrelated to general amount of maternal affection and independence training but did find them positively related to direct reward for achievement and for approval-seeking. These findings of Crandall and his coworkers are in general agreement with those of other investigators (Callard, 1964; Kolb, 1965; Mannino, 1962; Morrow and Wilson, 1961).

We also have considerable evidence (reviewed by McClelland, 1955; Berkowitz, 1964a; Crandall, 1963) that achievement level in the individual is positively related to the general cultural evaluation of achievement. However, individuals differ markedly with respect to, for example, achievement motivation, within a single culture. We now turn to the problem of socialization differences within a single society.

Summary. Achievement motivation is often viewed as closely related to independence, but it appears to be a separate system of behavior. The most frequently used measures of achievement motivation are fantasy production and overt behavior. Fantasy production has been found to bear only a weak relationship to overt behavior, which is itself subject to various interpretations. The achievement motive is seen as innate by some theorists and as an acquired drive by others. Evidence for a relationship between achievement motivation and parental permissiveness, restrictiveness, or warmth is inconsistent. Independence training has been found to be related to high achievement motivation, but direct achievement training may be more important in producing such motivation. The child's history of success and failure has been found to determine his level of aspiration, as have positive parental attitudes toward achievement and the general cultural evaluation of achievement.

15

Social Class in the Socialization Process

Thus far we have identified a number of inherited and experiential variables in the socialization process and have attempted to specify, within the scope of existing evidence, the relative importance of these variables for the development of the child's behavior with respect to aggression, dependence, and achievement. However, our concern here is not limited to the basic processes by which socialization occurs; we would also like to know how the resulting behaviors are distributed in society. A global statement such as "positive parental reinforcement for aggressive behavior increases aggression in the child," although a valuable building block in the edifice of socialization theory, tells us little about how many aggressive children (and adults) we may expect to encounter in a given society. Because, by our definition, the individual learns and develops through transaction with other people, it is clear that the characteristics and socialization practices of parents determine, to a large extent, the nature of the socializing transactions the child will experience. Our problem then becomes one of relating particular parent characteristics to socialization practices and child behaviors. There has been much research addressed to this problem, and it is the social

class characteristic of parents and their children which has received the most intensive investigation. In this chapter we shall review studies directed at uncovering social-class variations in children's behavior and in socialization practices among parts of our own society. We shall also present alternative theoretical interpretations of the social-class findings and suggest how these might best be related to the problem of differences in socialization within a society.

The Concept of Social Class

In spite of the multitude of research efforts to use social-class differences as a variable in the socialization process, certain problems of conceptualization and implementation remain which we shall review briefly here. Much of the literature is based on descriptive accounts of widely varying adequacy. These reports have given rise to stereotyped views of the behavior of each class and have fostered a modal-man approach to social-class membership. Thumbnail sketches of what a lower-class or middle-class person "is like" are a familiar part of this literature; see, for example,

Cavan's (1964) sketch of each of six classes from upper-upper down to lower-lower. The word pictures employed to describe a social-class personality inevitably tend to emphasize the homogeneity of behavior within a class and the heterogeneity across classes. Because it is irrelevant to the main purpose, little effort is ordinarily given to discussions of variability within a class or of similarities across classes. In discussing the class personality profiles that have been drawn, Clausen and Williams (1963) have pointed out that although they are largely unsubstantiated, they have resulted "in some remarkably tenacious and persistent stereotypes."

The readiness of so many writers to treat social-class differences in this way is somewhat surprising in light of the very vagueness of the social-class concept. A modal-man approach and emphasis on intergroup variation have a certain plausibility when applied to discrete societies of clearly defined membership and distinguishable from other groups in many obvious ways. They have much less initial plausibility when applied to subgroups of one society, subgroups of uncertain membership with much interaction and mobility, and sharing some common core of history and values

Objection to conceptualizing social classes as discrete groups, each with its own subculture, has frequently been argued at a theoretical level (Brown, 1965, Chap. 3; Cavan, 1964). Objections have also been based on methodological considerations—the lack, for example, of any means of dependably sorting people into classes the way they can be sorted into societies. [See Hoffman and Lippett (1960) and Miller and Swanson (1960) in addition to Brown and Cavan for discussions of the measurement problem involved in social-class categorization.] It is somewhat reassuring to learn that nineteen indexes of socioeconomic class membership are highly correlated, enough to justify speaking, for some purposes, of a single dimension (Kahl and Davis, 1955). On the other hand, they are not identical, and the magnitude of the relationship between social-class membership and particular attitudes and behavior depends on the choice of social-class index. Regardless of how accurately or consistently a position along a social-class dimension is measured, however, there remains the question of whether this dimension should be divided into discrete classes. Certainly there are cultural differences associated with status within every United States community, and attention is called to them by some of the indexes used for social class—occupation, for example, and the specific occupational distinction of white-collar versus blue-collar. But to think that cultural variation is found only among discrete groups and not among levels on a continuously varying dimension is itself an oversimplification resulting from the origin of the culture concept in the ethnography of discrete societies. In dealing with socioeconomic variation, the advantage may sometimes lie with one or another grosser classification, sometimes with a finer measurement. For example, McGrade (1966) recently found that dividing blue- and white-collar workers into four groups rather than two yielded a better understanding of relationships between socioeconomic status and the effectiveness of social reinforcers. Miller and Swanson (1958), on the other hand, found that a finer breakdown of the occupational variable did not enhance the magnitude of relationships they discovered between socioeconomic status and child-rearing practices.

A flexible conception of socioeconomic status, which allows it to be treated as either a continuous dimension or a set of categories, holds the greatest promise of advancing our understanding. We may expect distinctive values from each treatment. Regarding status as a continuous dimension facilitates our relating it to other important dimensions. Breaking it into categories, on the other hand, seems especially valuable for calling attention to distinctive implications of variations in social status that are somewhat independent of the main dimension; an example is Miller and Swanson's account, described later in this chapter, of entrepreneurial versus bureaucratic integration settings.

The Interpretation of Social-Class Findings

Intrasocietal, or social-class, studies are by their nature correlational rather than experimental and share the difficulties implied by this fact. Two main types of interpretations have been employed to explain the social-class findings, the sociogenic and the psychogenic. Sociogenic explanations present the adult personality modal to a class as behavior necessary to successful performance of the role of class member, and child-training practices, if considered at all, as one expression of that modal personality. Psychogenic explanations of social-class differences, as in the case of cross-cultural differences, have relied heavily on the importance of child-rearing practices in producing modal personality characteristics which then have a constraining influence on other behavior. [See Gold (1958) for an interesting example in which the sociogenic and psychogenic interpretations are pitted against each other in an effort to explain social-class differences in aggression.] The psychogenic approach asserts that parents in a particular socioeconomic class employ particular child-rearing practices having a number of resultants in the child's personality, which in turn determines the adult behaviors encountered in that class. The studies encountered in support of this thesis are quite varied. All too rare are studies in which class has been related to child-rearing practices, which in turn have been related to later behavior of the individuals actually subjected to these practices. [See Hoffman (1966), Miller and Swanson (1960), and Sears et al. (1957) for examples of this approach.]

Many scholars have been content to investigate class differences in child-rearing, assuming that these differences would affect later behavior. Others have examined class differences in children's behavior and attributed them without evidence to assumed differences in child-rearing practices. Hoffman and Lippett (1960) have correctly pointed out that studies of the latter type "often involve the theoretical weakness that the breadth of the jump leaves open many possible alternative explanations for any empirical relationships obtained" (p. 950).

We thus see that many social-class studies are vulnerable to a number of theoretical and methodological criticisms. Again, however, the findings themselves are of the utmost interest to the student of socialization, and they form an important body of evidence that must be encompassed by any comprehensive theory of socialization.

Social-Class Variation in Behavior

Given the goals of this chapter, we shall content ourselves with a brief review of studies providing evidence of social-class differences in general attitudes and behavior and theoretically important studies dealing with social-class differences in child-rearing.

Economic and Sociological Correlates of Class. As would be expected, social class has a number of economic and sociological correlates. Cavan (1964) reviews, for instance, American class variation in ethnic background, religious affiliation, house dwelling, type of neighborhood, and amount of education. She also reviews the extensive evidence of class variation in family structure and roles. For example, (1) the middle-class family tends to be more stable than the lower-class family and to be nuclear rather than extended; (2) security of husband's employment varies with social class, as does the likelihood that the wife will not need to be employed; (3) in high-status groups husbands have been found to make more decisions than the wife; in the middle-status (roughly middle-class) group a high degree of equality between husband and wife was found; and in the low-status group the wife was found to be more dominant than in either the high- or middle-status groups (Blood and Wolfe, 1960; Olsen, 1960). Probably related to these characteristics is the finding, with psychological measurement techniques, of greater marital satisfaction in middle-class than in lower-class women (Blood and Wolfe, 1960).

Considerable evidence has now been presented that there are class differences on such broad dimensions of behavior as quality of family relationships, patterns of affection and authority, conceptions of parenthood on the part of parents, perception of parents on the part of children, parents' expectations for the child, general expressive styles, and modal reactions to stress. [See comprehensive reviews of this literature by Clausen and Williams (1963) and Miller and Swanson (1960).]

Class Differences in Parental Values. In a widely noted study of social class and parental values, Kohn (1959a) found that parents of all social classes shared certain values, that is, they thought their children should be honest, happy, considerate, obedient, and dependable. However, Kohn also found differences in parental values related to the parents' socioeconomic class. Middle-class parents were found to emphasize such internalized standards of conduct as honesty and self-control, consideration, and curiosity. Working-class parents emphasized qualities that assure respectability, such as obedience, neatness, and cleanliness.

Working-class mothers have been found to see their role as emphasizing direct responsibility for immediately eliciting specific behavioral conformities from their children, whereas middle-class mothers focus on the child's growth, development, affection, and satisfaction (Duvall, 1946).

Middle-class parents have been found to have more acceptant, egalitarian relationships with their children and to be more accessible to the child than parents in the working class (Maas, 1951). Although the working-class father has been found to be less available and accessible to the child than the middle-class father (Bronfenbrenner, 1961a; Havighurst and Davis, 1955), working-class mothers have been found to expect their husbands to be more directive and to play a larger role in the imposition of constraints (Kohn and Carroll, 1960). Boys from the middle class have been found to perceive their parents as more competent, emotionally secure, accepting, and interested in their child's performance than do lower-class boys, with these class differences being greater for the perception of the father than for that of the mother (Rosen, 1964).

Findings of this sort are not confined to children's relations with their parents. Milner (1951) found that lower-class children were more likely than middle-class children to perceive adults in general as predominantly hostile. In studying retarded children drawn from the lowest segment of the lower socioeconomic class, Shallenberger and Zigler (1961) found that these children were characterized by an atypically high degree of wariness of adults and inferred that this wariness was due to social-class experiences rather than to retardation per se.

Class Differences and Children's "Style" of Life. Social-class differences in children's general approach to problems or "styles" of life have also been found. Alper, Blane, and Abrams (1955) hypothesized that middle-class as compared to lower-class children would be more fearful of getting dirty while engaged in a finger-painting test. This hypothesis was generated from the view of Davis and Havighurst (1946) that middle-class as compared to lower-class children are subjected to earlier and more consistent influences which cause the child to be "orderly, conscientious, responsible, and tame" and from Ericson's (1947) conclusion that middle-class children are "more anxious as a result of these pressures." [The findings of Sears et al. (1957) that middle-class mothers are more permissive in their child-rearing than lower-class mothers would generate a prediction opposite to that of Alper et al.] As predicted, the middle-class children showed a lower tolerance for getting dirty, for staying dirty, and for the materials they produced while dirty. Somewhat related to this is the finding that among both children and adults of the middle as compared to the lower class one encounters a greater readiness to experience guilt (Miller and Swanson, 1960; Zigler and Phillips, 1960). As Clausen and Williams (1963) have pointed out, studies of this type (Davis, 1944; Green, 1946) have given rise to a view that attributes "better adjustment" to the working-class child who is seen as free of the excessive guilt, repressed hostility, and driving anxiety of his middle-class counterpart. Clausen and Williams have noted that contrary to this view, several studies measuring aspects of personality which seem relevant find "better adjustment" in middle-class children (Burchinal, Gardner, and Hawkes, 1958; Sewell and Haller, 1956). Miller and Swanson (1960) have presented some evidence that child-rearing practices in different socioeconomic classes give rise to differences in selection of defense mechanisms. For instance, middle-class children were found to employ repression as a defense more readily, whereas denial was more characteristic of the lower-class child. Miller and Swanson and their students (1956, 1958, 1960) have also demonstrated class differences in broad expressive styles independent of type of defense. The most noteworthy of these is the tendency toward conceptual expression in the middle class and motor expression in the lower class.

Class Differences in Expression of Aggression. Somewhat related to this conceptual-motoric dichotomy are the class differences that have been found in the expression of aggression. Adults of the lower class have often been found to vent their hostility in overt acts of aggression against others, whereas those of higher status are more likely to turn their hostility inward, expressing it in self-deprecatory attitudes and suicide (Gold, 1958; Henry and Short, 1954; Zigler and Phillips, 1960). Among children, McKee and Leader (1955) found lower-class as compared to middle-class children to be both more competitive (defined by acts aimed at excelling or asserting one's own superiority) and aggressive (defined by acts intended to injure another child). Davis (1943) has also found aggression to be more apparent among the lower socioeconomic group. Even in fantasy, according to the evidence of Miller and Swanson and their students, the lower-class child tends to be more aggressive than his middle-class counterpart (Miller and Swanson, 1956, 1960). However, findings on class and aggression have not been completely consistent. Maas (1954), for example, did not find that lower-class adolescent boys were consistently more aggressive than middle-class boys, and Body (1955) found more aggressive behavior in a middle-class than in a lower-class nursery school.

Usually, some combination of psychogenic and sociogenic explanations have been advanced to account for the relationships discovered between social-class status and overt aggression. A popular psychogenic explanation is that class differences in child-rearing give rise to the differences in aggression. Sociogenic explanations have referred to the differing degree to which aggression threatens social relations as structured in various class groups.

Achievement, Independence, and Conformity. Social-class differences have also been found in research on achievement, independence, and conformity. Rosen (1956) found that for the middle-class as compared to the working-class child there is more emphasis on independence in early childhood, higher expectations associated with school performance, a greater belief in the availability of success, and a greater willingness to pursue those activities that make achievement possible. A greater degree of internalization of achievement-striving among middle-class as compared with working-class high school students has been found in two related experiments (Hoffman, Mitsos, and Protz, 1958). Thompson (1959) has inferred that there should be more conformity in middle- than in lower-class adolescents; he does so on the basis of putting together Mussen and Kagan's (1958) finding of conformity positively related to punitive and restrictive child-rearing and Psathas' (1957) evidence that this type of child-rearing characterizes the middle rather than the lower class. Somewhat against the plausibility of this inference, however, is Tuma and Livson's (1960) finding that among middle-class boys greater conformity is found in those of lower status, not those of higher status.

Class and Intelligence: Inheritance vs. Environment

In view of the importance of the intellect in determining the ultimate level of social and personal adjustment, students of socialization should be especially interested in the repeated finding that middle-class children average higher than lower-class children on most general tests of intelligence as well as classroom indexes of school achievement. This finding raises a particularly thorny issue about relationships between class and behavior. It is probably safe to assume that both the individuals' class position and his intellectual level are important determinants of his general behavior. But because these two are substantially correlated with each other, we usually have no way of knowing how much of the apparent dependence of any variable upon one of them should more properly be ascribed

to the other. Where data are gathered to provide this information, we sometimes see things in a new light. Miller and Swanson (1960), for example, give us such information about relationship between class and several other variables, showing that the relationship is sometimes markedly altered when intelligence is controlled. This issue has often been avoided by simply conceptualizing intelligence as almost exclusively determined by environment, and in particular by environmental factors associated with class membership. An equally defensible position (and this is to say that neither extreme is defensible) is that intelligence is almost exclusively determined by genetic factors, and it is the intelligence of the individual and his ancestors (especially his parents) that determines his social class rather than social class determining his intelligence. [The reader should be aware that the intelligence issue is one of the most troublesome in psychology and he is referred to Jones (1954), Tuddenham (1962), and Zigler (1966a) for reviews of evidence and more complete discussions of theoretical problems.]

Thus far it is the former of these two extreme positions that has been more associated with research, and we may distinguish two versions of this extreme environmentalism associated with different kinds of research. The two positions vary in the kind of explanation offered for the very substantial empirical relation between social class and intelligence test scores.

The Unfair Measurement Approach

One position assumes that the average level of intellectual functioning probably does not differ from one class to another and that the observed relation is an artifact of measurement, a product of the unfairness of intelligence tests for lower-class populations (Davis, 1954; Eells, Davis, Havighurst, Herrick, and Tyler, 1951; Haggard, 1954;

Isaacs, 1962). An obvious example is provided by information items such as appear on many intelligence tests. They tend to refer to realms of information to which middle- and upper-class children have been much more exposed than have lower-class children. But research shows much less obvious kinds of unfairness. Evidence is now available that the lower-class child's intelligence tends to be underestimated by our standard intelligence tests (see Zigler, 1966b). It is extremely unlikely, however, that all the social-class variation in test performance is due to test defects and noncognitive differences.

The simple idea of a culture-fair test is illusory. Cattell (1965) correctly pointed out the error of Eells et al. (1951) in rejecting from an intelligence test any items differentiating between social classes. (A culture-fair intelligence test must not only avoid discriminating against the lower class but must also be a fairly good measure of something akin to Spearman's general intelligence.) It makes no sense to construct tests which in the process of partialing out culture also partial out intelligence. Where culture-fair tests have been constructed and applied, however, performance on them has still been found to be significantly related to social-class membership. MacArthur and Elley (1963) found that culture-fair intelligence measure correlated with social status about $+0.22$ to $+0.24$ compared with $+0.30$ to $+0.34$ for traditional intelligence tests.

The Environmental Difference Approach

A quite different environmentalist position is that there are real class differences in intellectual functioning and that these are produced by class differences in environment. Environmental events postulated to explain these differences vary from the very general and sociogenic, on the one hand, to the specific and psychogenic or cognitive, on the other; for example, broad

class attitudes toward intelligence and education (for example, Toby, 1963), general child-rearing practices which favor one cognitive style rather than another (for example, Witkin et al., 1962), specific types of class-related interpersonal communications which result in specific deficits in intellectual functioning (for example, Bernstein, 1961; Hess and Shipman, 1965). Studies associated with this last and most specific example are especially promising and appear to fulfill H. Jones' plea (1954) that we move on from the assertion that the environment influences general intellectual development to the investigation of how particular events impinging on the child influence particular cognitive processes in him.

Social-Class Differences in Child Rearing

Differences in behavior associated with social-class membership are now well documented. There is little agreement, however, on exactly why such differences should exist. As noted earlier, these social-class differences are often explained as resulting from child-rearing practices of the different social classes. This explanation generates the expectation that clear differences among the classes in child-rearing practices would be empirically demonstrable. Although some reviewers (for example, Cavan, 1964) have been able to abstract from a number of studies certain general differences in child-rearing associated with social-class membership, the student of socialization is doomed to disappointment if he expects to encounter a great deal of clarity concerning the relationship between social class and child-rearing practices. The contradictory and inconsistent nature of the findings in this area was recently emphasized by Clausen and Williams (1963). These reviewers argued that much of this inconsistency was due to the focus on specific infant- and child-care practices, often taken out of context, and that greater agreement is to be found when attention is shifted from the more specific, and perhaps more fleeting, to certain more general and enduring dimensions such as quality of family relationships and patterns of affection and authority. Even on these latter dimensions, however, agreement is nowhere as great as would have been expected. For instance, Green (1946), taking a rather broad-gauged approach to middle-class values, goals, and child-rearing practices, came to the conclusion that they are such as should produce an anxiety-ridden, if not imminently neurotic, child. But the conclusion does not necessarily fit the facts; Sewell and Haller (1956, 1959), employing an equally broad-gauged approach, concluded that lower-class children are more anxious than middle-class children, although for reasons other than those advanced by Green to explain the anxieties of the middle-class child.

The Chicago Study. An early and well-known study of social class and child-training is that conducted in Chicago by Davis and Havighurst (1946). These investigators examined class differences in many practices, including those associated with feeding and weaning, toilet training, aggression control, household chores, and techniques of discipline. Davis and Havighurst found that lower-class as compared to middle-class children were breast-fed more frequently, were weaned later, were more often fed on demand, were started on toilet training later and were expected to begin helping in the home at a later age. Middle-class as compared to lower-class children were less severely punished for soiling after toilet training had begun and were more frequently permitted to fight each other so long as they did not hurt each other badly. Middle-class mothers as compared to lower-class mothers were found to mention reward or praise more frequently as a means for getting children to obey. A general conclusion was that the child-rearing practices of the middle class were oriented around restraint and self-discipline, whereas those of the lower class were more permissive.

The Boston Study. This conclusion was challenged by the findings of a study conducted some nine years later in the Boston area (Maccoby and Gibbs, 1954; Sears et al., 1957). No differences in feeding and weaning practices were found between the two social classes. Middle-class as compared to lower-class parents were found to complete bowel training later, to be less severe in their toilet-training procedures, and to be more permissive of their children's aggression when this aggression was directed toward other children or toward themselves. Among disciplinary techniques, scolding statements suggesting withdrawal of love were more frequent in the middle class, whereas physical punishment and deprivation of privileges were more common in the lower class. Middle-class parents were found to be more permissive of the child's sexual behavior, and the relationship between father and child was found to be warmer in the middle- than in the lower-class home. The authors concluded that middle-class parents were generally more permissive, gentler, and warmer toward their children than were working-class parents. In attempting to explain the inconsistency between their Boston study and the Chicago study, Sears et al. asserted that the Chicago data could also be interpreted as showing greater permissiveness on the part of the middle- as compared to the lower-class mother if the behavioral consequences of each particular child-rearing practice were fully considered. In another comparison of the Chicago and Boston studies Havighurst and Davis (1955) concluded that the disagreements between the two studies were substantial and important. They suggested that the inconsistencies may have been due to inadequacies in the sampling procedures in both studies and to changes in child-rearing ideology between 1943 and 1952.

The Eugene, Oregon, Study. In an effort to resolve the disagreement between the Chicago and Boston studies, Littman, Moore, and Pierce-Jones (1957) examined the child-rearing practices of middle- and lower-class parents in Eugene, Oregon. Consistent with the Boston but inconsistent with the Chicago findings were the Eugene data indicating no class differences associated with feeding and weaning practices. Also consistent with the Boston study were the findings that father-child relations were better in the middle than in the lower class and that the middle-class parents were more permissive in regard to the child's sexual behavior. However, in other child-rearing practices the Eugene study supported neither the Chicago nor the Boston study, indicating instead a much greater similarity in child-rearing practices in the two social classes. For example, in the Eugene study no significant class differences were found in toilet training, aggression control, or techniques of discipline. The single indication in the Eugene study that middle-class homes may be more demanding than lower-class homes was the finding that middle-class mothers more frequently complained that household duties required of their children were not carried out. In a thoughtful discussion of the findings of the Chicago, Boston, and Eugene studies taken in toto, Littman et al. (1957) point out that a relatively small percentage of the findings are statistically significant and that of the significant findings many are inconsistent from one study to another; they conclude that there are probably no general or profound differences among classes in socialization practices.

The San Francisco Study. In another effort to resolve the discrepancy between the Chicago and Boston studies, White (1957) compared the child-rearing practices of lower- and middle-class mothers living in the suburban area south of San Francisco, California. She found that middle-class as compared with lower-class mothers were less severe in toilet training, permitted more aggression against the parents, were more responsive to the baby's crying, less often carried through when they told a child to do something, reported more thumb-sucking and less nail-biting, and more often mentioned experts, other mothers, and friends as their sources of ideas on child rearing. This led White to conclude that her study showed more agreement with the Boston study than with the Chicago study, which was conducted a decade earlier than the Boston study. White suggested that the discrepancies between her findings and the Chicago study were due to changes in child-rearing practices that had occurred in the time lapse between the two studies. The White study showed no vast class differences in the child-rearing practices, and the extent to which it supports the Boston study is doubtful. Of the seventeen variables on which White compared the findings of the Chicago, Boston, and California studies, there were fourteen on which no significant differences between the classes were found in the California study. Of the three variables on which significant class differences were found in the California study, one finding—that middle-class parents reported more thumb-sucking—was in agreement with the Chicago study. The finding that working-class mothers were more severe in toilet training was in agreement with both the Chicago and Boston studies (but in disagreement with the Eugene study). The finding that middle-class mothers reported more permissiveness for aggression against the parents was in agreement with the Boston study (but in disagreement with the Eugene study). Furthermore, the California study disagreed with the Boston study in that the California study found no social-class differences related to how much the mother keeps track of the child, permission for aggression against other children, or punishment for aggression against parents.

It thus appears that most of the agreement between the California and Boston studies consists of finding that the social classes do not differ on a sizable number of child-rearing practices. Rather than supporting the conclusion of either the Chicago or Boston studies, then, the California study lends further credence to the Littman et al. conclusion that class differences in child rearing are less than would be expected from either the Chicago or Boston study. Because the important theoretical issue in this matter is not social-class differences in child rearing per se, but rather such differences as the antecedents of later differences in behavior encountered in the two social classes, it is of interest to note that White found no significant class differences in such actual behaviors of the children as dependence behavior reported by the mother, performance on the Draw-a-Man test, the ability to delay gratification, aggression in doll play, or in personality ratings made on the children.

The Detroit Study. Another important investigation of child-rearing differences between middle and lower class was the large-scale study conducted in Detroit by Miller and Swanson (1958). In this, as well as in a later investigation (1960), Miller and Swanson advanced the interesting argument that a variety of changes in our society, including those in immigration patterns, ratio of urban to rural dwellers, and the general nature and complexity of our economic institutions, have changed the meaning of social-class membership. As a result of such changes, social-class membership no longer implies any underlying set of values, attitudes, goals, and life styles. Homogeneity, they argue, is found instead in what they call an "integration setting," which cuts across social-class lines. Thus, to Miller and Swanson child-rearing practices are not directed so much toward inculcating values and behavior germane to the social class as toward developing a personality consonant with success in the family's particular integration setting.

Two types of integration setting have been conceptualized by Miller and Swanson

—the entrepreneurial and the bureaucratic. Membership in the entrepreneurial setting is characterized by involvement in an economic organization having the following features: small size, simple division of labor, relatively small capitalization, and provision for income mobility through risk-taking and competition. The social situations encountered in such a setting are referred to by Miller and Swanson as "individuated," because they tend to isolate people from one another and from the controlling influences of shared cultural norms. According to Miller and Swanson, "Children reared in individuated and entrepreneurial homes will be encouraged to be highly rational, to exercise great self-control, to be self-reliant, and to assume an active, manipulative stance toward their environment" (p. 57). They classified a family as entrepreneurial if the husband met any one of the following characteristics: (1) was self-employed; (2) gained at least half his income in the form of profits, fees, or commissions; or (3) worked in an organization having only two levels of supervision. These criteria alone would exclude most of those members of the lower class who seemed to Miller and Swanson to share the entrepreneurial orientation; they therefore added a fourth criterion, that a family would be considered entrepreneurial if either wife or husband were born on a farm or outside the United States.

Families not classified as entrepreneurial were classified as bureaucratic and thought of as being typically involved in an economic setting characterized by substantially capitalized large organizations employing many kinds of specialists. For the bureaucratic family incomes are in the form of wages or salary, and mobility comes through specialized training rather than through success in taking risks. These families are viewed as being involved in a welfare bureaucracy in which the organization provides support in meeting their personal crises and offers continuity of employment and income despite fluctuations in the business cycle. According to Miller and Swanson, "Children reared in welfare-bureaucratic homes will be encouraged to be accommodative, to allow their impulses some spontaneous expression, and to seek direction from the organizational programs in which they participate" (p. 58).

Miller and Swanson examined child-rearing practices as a function of both social class and integration setting. A surprisingly small number of differences in child rearing were found to be associated with either social class or integration setting. Miller and Swanson then looked at differences between groups defined by both class and integration setting, for example, entrepreneurial middles versus bureaucratic lowers, and related these differences to the findings of the Chicago and Boston studies. Although their findings were generally quite disparate from those of the Chicago study, they concluded that comparisons between the entrepreneurial middle class and the lower class of either integration setting tended to resemble the Chicago findings; comparisons between bureaucratic middles and entrepreneurial lowers showed some resemblance to the Boston findings. In both instances, however, a great deal of the resemblance pertained to variables on which the finding was of no class difference. Miller and Swanson, then, do present some limited evidence indicating that integration setting influences child-rearing practices and that considering integration setting may reduce somewhat the disagreement found among studies of child-rearing practices and social class. The evidence is not, however, sufficient to justify one's taking serious issue with the negative conclusion of Littman et al. (1957) about important general differences among classes in socialization practices.

Other Social-Class and Child-Rearing Studies. Some investigators of social-class differences have concentrated on broad dimensions of child rearing (for example, restrictive versus permissive) rather than on specific infant- and child-care practices. Thus, Klatskin, Jackson, and Wilkin (1956) found some interesting trends in child-rearing styles associated with social-class membership, although these trends were generally not statistically significant. Upper-middle-class mothers showed more optimal child-rearing practices (neither too rigid nor overpermissive) related to feeding, sleeping, toileting, and so on, than did either lower-middle-class or upper-lower-class mothers. Lower-middle-class mothers were the most likely to have rigid practices. What most characterized upper-lower-class mothers was that they showed no consistent pattern, but varied in optimal, rigid, or overpermissive behavior from one aspect of training to another.

A number of studies employing some combination of the broad-gauged and specific approaches have indicated that the middle-class parent is generally more permissive than the lower-class parent. Klatskin (1952), although finding no class differences in permissiveness in regard to feeding, or in the degree to which fathers participated in child care, did find more leniency among the upper-middle-class group than in the lower-middle or upper-lower in toilet training, type of discipline imposed on the child, and disapproval of the child's behavior. Elder (1962) also found that lower-class parents were more autocratic and authoritarian than middle-class parents. The finding that lower-class mothers used more forceful and punitive methods of discipline than middle-class mothers (Bayley and Schaefer, 1960) is consistent with the findings of certain studies noted earlier (Sears et al., 1957; White, 1957).

However, whether one chooses to look at specific practices or broad dimensions, the assertion that middle-class parents are more permissive than lower-class parents needs some qualification. For instance, Psathas (1957) obtained evidence that lower-class parents were more permissive with their adolescent children than were

middle-class parents, who more closely su-
pervised the activities of their adolescent
sons and daughters. Kohn (1959a), who
studied a large group of working- and
middle-class parents of fifth-grade children,
found similar amounts and types of punishment in the two social classes. (He did find,
however, that working-class parents punished the child on the basis of the consequences of the child's disobedience, whereas
middle-class parents punished on the basis
of their perceptions of the child's intent.)
It thus appears that even on broad dimensions of child rearing, findings about social
class and child rearing are far from consistent. Indeed, the very meaningfulness of
such broad dimensions as "permissiveness"
has been questioned by Kohn (1959b), and
the conceptual difficulties that inhere in
abstracting such broad dimensions from
particular child-rearing practices have been
cogently discussed by Littman et al. (1957).

Methodological Problems

Inconsistencies among studies have sometimes been attributed to the general inadequacy of the survey technique on which
they have depended. The parent interview
has very uncertain validity as an indicator
of actual child-rearing practices. Although
there is evidence that the interview technique may sometimes provide accurate
information concerning child-rearing practices (for example, Klatskin, 1952), a
growing body of evidence on the social
desirability factor in subjective reports
Christie and Lindauer, 1963; Edwards, 1957;
Marlowe and Crowne, 1961; Taylor, 1961)
suggests that some of the supposed class
differences in child rearing, as well as some
of the inconsistencies across studies, may
actually relate to variations in the parents'
sensitivity to what constitutes a socially
desirable statement about child rearing.

Inconsistencies have also been attributed
to the fact that various studies are based on
data collected at different times. Variations

in findings do indeed seem likely to reflect,
in part, real changes in practice occurring
differently at different class levels. That the
advice experts give to parents on how to
raise their children has changed over the
years has been documented by Stendler
(1950) and Wolfenstein (1953). Bronfenbrenner (1958) reanalyzed some of the studies of social class and child-rearing practices
we have described, and demonstrated, particularly for the middle class, a high degree
of correspondence between child-rearing
practices reported and expert advice prevailing at the time. Thus, Bronfenbrenner
managed to reduce the inconsistency among
studies.

In view of the significance of the time
variable and the possibly contaminating
effect of the interview technique, a recent
study by Waters and Crandall (1964) on
social class and maternal behavior is of
special importance. Employing home visit
data collected at the Fels Institute on
children between three and five years old,
they examined the relationship between
nine types of observed maternal behavior
and social-class membership at three periods: 1940, 1950, and 1960. No significant
relationships were found between social
class and nurturant maternal behavior,
defined by the variables of babying and
protectiveness, at any of the three times.
Social class was also found to bear little
relation to affectionate maternal behavior,
defined by the variables of affectionateness
and direction of criticism (approval); the
only significant relationship found with
these two variables was that in 1940 maternal approval was positively correlated
with social status. Maternal coerciveness,
defined by the variables of coerciveness of
suggestions and severity of penalties, was
found to be somewhat more associated
with socioeconomic class. In the 1960 sample
both variables were found to be negatively
correlated with social status, coerciveness
being higher in the lower class. The maternal behavior variable most consistently
related to socioeconomic class was found

to be restrictiveness of regulations; at all three time periods the lower the family status, the more a mother tended to impose restrictive regulations on her child's behavior. The variables of clarity of policy and accelerational attempt were found to be positively related to social class in 1940 but not in the two subsequent time periods. Altogether, of the twenty-seven correlations (nine variables at three time periods) nine were significant, and in no instance did a significant result at one period reverse a significant result of another period. In comparing their results with those of earlier investigations, Waters and Crandall noted differences in the nature of their sample and also pointed out that their results tend to disagree with those of studies employing the interview technique but to agree with those of other studies employing direct observation.

Waters and Crandall report some consistent changes in maternal behavior. Regardless of social class, mothers became progressively less coercive between 1940 and 1960. Nurturant and affectionate behavior exhibited a curvilinear trend between 1940 and 1960; babying, protectiveness, affection, and approval peaked in 1950, at the height of the "permissive era," were lower in 1940, and were lowest in 1960. Consistent with the Waters and Crandall finding of reduced coerciveness is the Klatskin et al. (1956) finding of greater permissiveness of mothers regardless of social class between approximately 1940 and 1950, though Klatskin et al. dealt with the first year of life instead of the fourth and fifth.

The discovery that there are trends in child-rearing practices that cut across social-class membership does little to illuminate the central issue of class differences. The principal contribution of the excellent study by Waters and Crandall is to suggest that we may have a very different understanding of class differences when we have better knowledge based on direct observation. For the present a further point that we would emphasize along with Littman et al.

(1957) is that even in those instances where a statistically significant relationship between social class and child-rearing practices has been found, the mean difference between populations has been so small, compared with the great overlap in the distributions and the large spread of each distribution, that the discovered difference is often relatively trivial in predictive and explanatory power.

Other Interpretations of Social-Class Differences

In the explanation of adult behavior, elements in psychological thought so diverse as the Freudian and the Watsonian have stressed an influence of child training of a direct sort: punishment of aggression producing fear of being aggressive, indiscriminate punishment and rejection producing indiscriminate anxiety, and so on. Our present knowledge of American child-rearing practices in relation to social class does not justify great confidence in considering such influences to be the major source of large and consistent variation among classes in adult behavior. Further research may possibly alter the position, but we cannot confidently predict that now. Child training may be less important in these ways than often supposed, or its most important influences in relation to social class may be of the more complicated kinds suggested by the developmental approach we shall consider later.

However we define socialization, we are likely to regard it as a lifelong process. An alternative to the special stress on childhood socialization is stress on this continuing nature of socialization or on its special importance at other portions of the life cycle. Such emphases are made by a number of writers who are in other respects quite different from one another. One of these is Erikson (1950); while continuing to regard the early years as specially important, he views the individual's behavior as the outcome of a series of conflicts or crises which occur throughout the life span and argues the need for equally explicit attention to all periods. Social-learning theorists (for example, Bandura and Walters, 1959) have emphasized the importance of "models" whose behavior is imitated. This approach suggests that in adulthood the behavior of models in the individual's present environment will be of prime importance. Instrumental-learning theorists (Bijou and Baer, 1961) have emphasized reinforcement contingencies as the ultimate determinant of the individual's social behavior. Within this framework paramount importance would be given to the individual's relatively recent history of rewards and punishments accompanying the particular social behavior of interest. Finally, more sociological thinkers (Brim and Wheeler, 1966), calling attention to the fact that socialization is a lifelong process, have emphasized its continuing importance through adulthood; the individual never ceases to adopt new social roles, and most of the pertinent socialization occurs around the time of adoption and not decades in advance.

Sociogenic vs. Psychogenic Interpretations

The Sociogenic Analysis. Views that stress socialization in adulthood for the roles then assumed may, indeed, not be phrased in a psychogenic manner at all, but rather in a completely sociogenic manner. As Allport (1950, 1966) has put it, the approach tends to be one in which an individual's personality becomes an appendage to demography, with behavior being determined not so much by the integrated structure within the skin as by the person's assigned roles as a member of a group. It is not surprising that sociologists and anthropologists have a preference for explanations in terms of social forces external to the

organism, whereas psychologically oriented personality theorists have a preference for explanations in terms of internal psychodynamics. The social-class variable, by its very nature, is more conducive to the sociogenic than to the psychogenic approach. Such indexes of class membership as amount of education, occupation, and type of dwelling are not psychological in nature. Their direct reference is to the individual's social status in a broad sense, not to his psychological characteristics. It is for this very reason that a social-class typology lends itself far better to a sociological than to a psychological analysis. However, just as a psychological analysis of some variation in behavior is often unpalatable to a physiologist, so is a sociological analysis often unpalatable to a psychologist. Each discipline tends to prefer its own level of conceptual analysis, and there may be no differences among them in inherent validity.

The Psychogenic Analysis. When a psychologist is confronted with the evidence that a sociological variable (such as social class or particular dwelling zone within a city) is related to a psychological variable (such as particular forms of mental aberrations or disturbed behavior), he does not feel that he has "explained" the relationship until he reduces the sociological variable by conceptualizing it as a set of psychological events that could cause the behavior being explained. At a psychological level of analysis social-class membership or residence within a particular zone of a city cannot be viewed as the cause of a higher prevalence of a particular form of disturbed behavior. Instead, some social-psychological concomitants of these sociological variables, such as particular forms of family interactions (Myers and Roberts, 1959) or the individual's personal isolation (Rose, 1955), are advanced as the psychological mechanisms actually mediating the relationship between social-status variables and resultant psychological events.

An implication is that to the psychologist discovery of a relationship between social-class membership and some particular behavior is in itself empty or meaningless, and he feels a need to reduce social class to some psychologically more meaningful set of events. The discovered relationship between social class and behavior is likely to be neutral with respect to directing the psychologist to particular social-psychological processes mediating the relationship. The possibilities clearly are myriad, and it would appear that the one that has captured the most interest is the hypothesis that class differences in adult behavior are mediated by class differences in child-rearing practices. But the reason for this seems to lie more in the history of psychology than in relationships established empirically.

Social-Ecological vs. Genetic Interpretations

Relationships established on the social level leave open a broad spectrum of possible interpretations ranging from the social-ecological, on the one hand, to the genetic, on the other.

The Social-Ecological Analysis. The social-ecological extreme illustrates the tendency to seek psychological mediators for relationships first observed at a social level. Aberle (1961), Barry, Child, and Bacon (1959) and Miller and Swanson (1960) have all presented social-ecological accounts of class differences and have suggested psychological interpretations, although the empirical context has been largely, except for Miller and Swanson, intersocietal variation rather than intrasocietal. All these investigators are concerned with an economic influence on socialization and personality, and in what might be called an implicit Marxist approach they especially stress the economy.

A society requires individuals capable of performing the necessary economic functions and will tend to select socialization practices that favor values and behavior contributing to that capability. Child rearing need not be viewed as the main cause of adult behavior. It may be viewed as simply one device helping to guarantee that individuals will have characteristics appropriate for the niche they will fill in the economy.

This point of view is seen most clearly in the work of Miller and Swanson (1958, 1960), whose concept of the integration setting represents a particularly interesting effort to reduce the class concept to a psychologically more meaningful level. To Miller and Swanson the American economic system has changed so that members of a single class may differ widely in the pressures their economic function exerts on personality type. Whether a family is engaged in entrepreneurial or bureaucratic activities, as we have indicated earlier, is the difference these authors view as determining the socialization practices engaged in by the family. We thus see here an effort to mediate class differences in behavior by calling into play the economically oriented concept of integration settings and by viewing socialization as directed toward producing individuals with social-psychological characteristics in keeping with their particular integration settings.

The Genetic View. At the opposite end of some ecological-individualistic continuum of interpretations of social-class variation in human behavior is the genetic point of view. In its immature stage, psychology tended to seek single causes of behavior. A genetic influence was then easy to dismiss because no one need go beyond his own daily experience to establish beyond question that behavioral differences are not solely of genetic origin. Continuing neglect, when psychology is more mature, probably has other origins as well. The egalitarian tradition of the United States has doubtless contributed to the absence of research on possible genetic influences on social-class differences, and to the near absence even of the discussion that might lead up to it.

Gottesman (1965) has recently published a valuable paper which helps fill this gap. He points out that social-class differences are differences between populations rather than individuals and that whenever there is a sizable degree of reproductive isolation between populations, the relative frequencies with which the different forms of genes occur in their gene pools will differ. Basing his views on the clear fact of assortative mating within social classes and the evidence of definite genetic influence on some aspects of personality (see Vandenberg, 1965), Gottesman argues that some social-class differences in behavior may rest partially on a genetic basis rather than on the wholly environmental basis often supposed. His view has probably been the one generally held among psychologists so far as intelligence is concerned, but he argues that it may properly apply to many other variables as well. Although the hypothesis is speculative, as Gottesman points out, it may well merit more attention than it has received to date.

The Developmental Interpretation

Falling somewhere between the social-economic-ecological interpretation of social-class differences in behavior and the genetic interpretation is the developmental viewpoint advanced by Zigler and his coworkers (Katz and Zigler, 1967; Kohlberg and Zigler, 1967; Phillips and Zigler, 1961, 1964; Zigler, 1963b). Building loosely on the theoretical approaches of Piaget (1950, 1953, 1955, 1962) and Werner (1948), these investigators have suggested that behavioral differences between the lower and middle classes are due to the differing developmental characteristics of individuals within the two classes. The argument here is that the developmental progression of individuals in the lower class is on the average slower and more limited than that of individuals in the middle class, and that differences in behavior between the classes from childhood on are due to the fact that comparisons are being made between groups of individuals who are of different average developmental levels. The developmental approach purposely has remained ambiguous in respect to the causes of differences in the rate of development and in the upper levels achieved. At the present time these differences can be attributed to genetic factors, to differences in environmental inputs, or, perhaps most reasonably, to some interaction between these two sets of factors.

In keeping with Piaget's thinking, the developmental approach to social-class differences has emphasized the formal cognitive characteristics of the individual as a crucial mediating structure in the person's intercourse with his environment. If social classes differ greatly in the distribution of formal cognitive structure or developmental level of their members, we would expect to discover social-class differences in behavior. Although differences in the rate of cognitive development associated with class membership are now well documented, as noted earlier, their role in producing class differences in behavior has been largely ignored. Although to Piaget developmental level or stage is defined almost completely in terms of the formal cognitive processes manifested, American psychologists have tended to broaden the definition of developmental level to include a wide array of social-competence indexes indicative of personal and social maturity, reflecting not only intelligence but a variety of personal styles, social values, and psychological orientations that also appear capable of being ordered along a developmental continuum (Phillips and Zigler, 1964; Zigler and

Phillips, 1960, 1962). Within the developmental framework it is not an individual's prestige, the general culture of the class sharing it, nor the various roles he occupies that are emphasized as direct determinants of behavior but rather his internal psychological structure. The most extreme version of this would stress, instead of the sociogenic view of the individual's cognitive structure as entirely a product of class membership, a notion that the cognitive structure a person has attained is the sole determinant of his future class membership—is the sole determinant, that is, of what culture he will be comfortable with or will join in creating. The truth obviously lies somewhere between these two theoretical extremes, and presumably neither extreme has any adherents.

In the less extreme and more tenable form in which it is actually encountered, the developmental approach seems to be a legitimate attempt to understand some of the effects of the sociological variable of social-class membership in terms of the psychological variable of personal developmental level. On an empirical level it should be noted that each concept, that is, social class and developmental level, can be separately and reliably defined. In instances where social class largely determines developmental level or vice versa, measures of the two would be highly correlated. The two would, no doubt, always retain sufficient independence to permit determining how much of the variance in any other variable can be attributed to one and how much to the other. We know that relationships of a certain magnitude have been found between social class and particular behavioral variables. If the magnitude of these relationships is enhanced by substituting developmental level for social class, then the developmental interpretation of social-class differences in behavior takes on some added credence. If the magnitude of the relationships is reduced, then the developmental argument is weakened. In tests of this sort a uniform outcome is not

to be expected for all variables. If such a program were carried out, we would probably discover that developmental level mediated some relationships between class and behavior but did not mediate others. The explanation for relationships not mediated by developmental level would then become the domain of a variety of other theoretical approaches alluded to earlier.

At a theoretical level the developmental approach has the advantage of allowing the utilization of a somewhat untidy but nevertheless broad body of research on developmental processes. This body of work places a number of restraints on developmentalists' efforts to explain social-class differences and, of more importance, dictates the particular relationships that should be found between social class and certain behavior. Thus the developmental approach is receptive to certain relationships but not to others. If, for example, members of the lower class are on the average characterized by a lower developmental level than members of the middle class, then the two classes should be distinguished on a variety of specific variables associated with developmental level. Several of the class differences in behavior noted earlier conform to this expectation. For instance, the greater guilt, self-derogation, and intropunitiveness up to and including suicide (Henry and Short, 1954; Miller and Swanson, 1960; Zigler and Phillips, 1960) found in individuals of the middle as compared to the lower class are predictable from developmental theorizing. As Phillips and Rabinovitch (1958) have pointed out, such "turning against the self" implies an introjection of social standards more characteristic of higher than of lower levels of development. Evidence that an increasing capacity for guilt accompanies increasing cognitive growth and development has been presented recently by Katz and Zigler (1967).

A particularly striking instance in which a social class–behavior relationship is children's transgressions in terms of the immediate consequences of the child's actions, whereas middle-class parents tend to respond in terms of the child's intent in acting as he does. As Kohn points out, this distinction is quite in keeping with the developmental distinction made in Piaget's (1962) discussion of moral realism.

Also consistent with the developmental interpretation of social-class differences in behavior are the general findings that lower-class persons are somewhat more ready to resort to physical punishment, are more physicalistic in their choice of occupations, and engage in more acting-out up to and including homicide, whereas middle-class persons tend to be more obsessive and ideational (Henry and Short, 1954, Miller and Swanson, 1960; Phillips and Zigler, 1964; Zigler and Phillips, 1960). This contrast in life style corresponds closely to an important dimension in development, namely, the action-thought dimension. Developmental theorists of both psycho-analytic (Freud, 1952; Hartmann, 1952; Kris, 1950; Rapaport, 1951) and non-psychoanalytic persuasion (Lewin, 1936; Piaget, 1951; Werner, 1948) have suggested that primitive, developmentally early behavior is marked by immediate, direct, and unmodulated response to external stimuli and internal need. In contrast, higher levels of maturation are characterized by the appearance of indirect, ideational, conceptual, and symbolic or verbal response. The developmental action-thought dimension offers a clear alternative to the sociogenic interpretation which would view the greater acting-out of lower-class individuals as a direct product of their conformity to lower-class culture. According to developmental interpretation both the individual's acting-out and the lower-class culture which encourages it would be viewed as reflecting the developmental characteristics of class members.

Similar disagreement between the external-sociogenic emphasis and the internal-developmental emphasis arises in considering class differences in the incentive value of being correct—a motivational characteristic especially significant in the socialization process. Considerable evidence has now been presented either indicating or suggesting that middle-class children are more motivated to be correct for the sheer sake of correctness than are lower-class children (Cameron and Storm, 1965; A. Davis, 1944; Douvan, 1956; Ericson, 1947; Terrell, Durkin, and Wiesley, 1959; Zigler and deLabry, 1962; Zigler and Kanzer, 1962). Zigler and Kanzer, for instance, studying seven-year-old children, found that the verbal reinforcers most effective with the lower class were those indicating personal praise ("good" and "fine"), whereas the verbal reinforcers most effective with the middle class were those indicating their behavior was correct ("right" and "correct"). Two quite different interpretations can be applied to this finding. A somewhat sociogenic interpretation would be that "being right" is a value that is held in higher regard in the middle than in the lower socioeconomic class, and therefore for the middle-class seven-year-olds as compared to the lower-class seven-year-olds, "being right" had more frequently been associated with secondary and primary reinforcers.

An alternative explanation would employ the concept of a developmentally changing hierarchy of reinforcers. As has been suggested by Beller (1955), Gewirtz (1954), and Heathers (1955a), the effectiveness of attention and praise as reinforcers diminishes with maturity, whereas the reinforcement inherent in the information that one is correct progressively increases in effectiveness. This shift is away from reinforcement by others and toward reinforcement by self and appears to be central to the child's progress from dependence to independence.

Although the child's social experience obviously remains relevant, this explanation does not attribute special importance to the type of reward customary in the consistent with developmental thought is Kohn's finding (1959a, 1959b) that working-class parents tend to respond to their child's environment; it stresses instead the child's cognitive ability—specifically, his ability to comprehend a verbal stimulus as a cue for self-reinforcement and to be able to administer this type of reinforcement. This ability requires that the child differentiate himself from others and comprehend that his success is a direct outgrowth of his own efforts; it also involves the maturity required for the rather complicated process of taking the self as an object that can either be rewarded (and hence feel proud) or punished (and hence feel ashamed or guilty).

Such a process is a far cry from that earlier period in life when the efficacy of a social reinforcer is probably dependent on its close relationship to primary reinforcers and a wide array of social stimuli influences behavior in a relatively undifferentiated hedonistic way involving little or no central mediation. At an earlier age the child might respond to the spoken word "good" as a reinforcer in some such direct way without the involvement of complex processes that might later make "good" and a variety of other words and gestures equivalent because of their common implications.

At this later age reinforcers which consist of praise (words such as "good" and "fine") would be conceptualized, in a developmental view, as conveying information to the child on how the speaker feels toward the responses the child has made. When the child is able to feel that powerful adults are pleased with him, he may anticipate further reward from them. At a later developmental level, however, the child becomes more liberated from concern with the feelings of social agents, and the task of obtaining primary reinforcers from them normally becomes less urgent. He becomes a more autonomous agent primarily interested in obtaining mastery over his world. The motive of effectiveness be-comes central, and he becomes interested in the quality of his own performance. His concern is not limited to how social agents feel about him but is extended to how he feels about himself. How he feels about himself, moreover, is determined by the success he encounters in dealing with the continuous problems presented by the environment. What he is now interested in is whether he is doing things correctly, whether he is right. Thus social agents and the social reinforcers they dispense take on new meaning. At this stage the social reinforcer signifying successful coping by the child is the one he values most; the feelings of the social agent, though related, recede in importance.

When this reasoning is applied to the finding that seven-year-old middle-class children are more motivated to receive reinforcers indicating correctness than are seven-year-old lower-class children, it suggests that the latter children are developmentally lower than the former in not having made a transition in which reinforcers signifying correctness replace reinforcers signifying praise in the reinforcer hierarchy.

Related to this argument is the work of several investigators (Davis, 1941, 1943; Terrell et al., 1959; Zigler and deLabry, 1962) indicating that lower-class children are less influenced than middle-class children by abstract, symbolic rewards. This would obviously be expected if the lower-class child were indeed developmentally lower than the middle-class child of the same chronological age. Some recent studies (McGrade, 1966; Rosenhan and Greenwald, 1965) have failed to support the reinforcer-hierarchy interpretation of social-class differences in preferences for particular classes of verbal reinforcers. Yet so many findings are consistent with this interpretation and with the more general developmental approach of which it is a part that further investigation of their implications and validity is clearly called for.

Summary and Conclusions

None of the various explanatory constructs that we have examined—the specific child-training practices, the social-ecological-economic, the genetic, the developmental—appears capable of singlehandedly accounting for all the behavioral correlates of social-class membership. The positions probably differ in the contribution each can make in isolation, and this depends on the general state of knowledge at the time. We think, for instance, that isolated emphasis on child-training practices out of context is probably of limited value and that the lesson it can teach is if anything too well learned today. We think, too, that the developmental approach offers today some rather novel understanding even when considered in isolation. But we may be confident that with real interlocking of the various explanations a still better understanding will be attained.

We have attempted to demonstrate in the preceding pages that socialization must concern us as a practical and intellectual problem. In practical terms, parents need and are constantly seeking advice from psychologists on how best to rear their children to be adequate, or better than adequate, members of society. As we pointed out earlier, the value of psychologists' advice will surely be greater when it is based on real understanding of the developing child and of the nature of the process of socialization. In the search for understanding of the socialization process, we are confronted with a truly formidable intellectual problem. As we have indicated, at issue are the students' fundamental beliefs about the nature of man—beliefs that are implicit in the theories with which we work and that, if not self-consciously examined, may distort at the outset our attempts at building a theory of socialization. It must also be clear that, given the scope of the problem, no one approach within psychology will be adequate to meet the challenge posed by the phenomenon of socialization; we have tried to demonstrate the extent to which many theoretical approaches have contributed to our understanding of this process. In the case of developmental and learning theory, long held to be natural enemies, we have seen that each has made significant contributions toward a theory of socialization and that in fact it is often possible to integrate the two approaches to their mutual enhancement.

Even, however, were we blessed with conceptual clarity and intradisciplinary harmony, the sheer magnitude of the problem of socialization—which we have earlier characterized as coextensive with human development—is staggering. We have attempted to review evidence concerning a very small number of potentially relevant variables with respect to a small number of potentially significant systems of behavior. Within this narrow range, results still were often contradictory and inconclusive. When we examined the role of social class in the search for systematic differences in socialization practices at the societal level, we found that evidence was again inconsistent. Thus, even with concerted effort at the theoretical level, the problem of fully comprehending the socialization process will remain an intellectual challenge for some time to come.

Glossary

animism. The belief that all objects in nature, both animate and inanimate, are possessed of spirits or souls.

anthropomorphism. The attribution of human characteristics, especially mental, to other beings besides men (for example, animals or nonliving objects).

endogenous. Originating in the individual's own psychodynamics rather than through external causes.

growth gradients. Series of stages or degrees of maturity by which a child progresses toward a higher level of behavior (Gesell).

isomorphic. Being of identical or similar shape or structure.

nativistic. Present in the individual at birth.

ontogenesis. The origin and development in the individual of some specific organ or function.

orthogonal. Completely independent (for example, two variables having zero correlation are orthogonal).

phenotype. The visible characteristic of an organism.

phylogenesis. The evolution of a race or genetically related group of organisms, as distinct from the development of the individual organism.

References

Aberle, D. F. Culture and socialization. In F. L. K. Hsu (Ed.), *Psychological anthropology: Approaches to culture and personality.* Homewood, Ill.: Dorsey Press, 1961. Pp. 381–399.

Achenbach, T. M. Cue-learning and problem-learning strategies in children. Unpublished doctoral dissertation, Univer. of Minnesota, 1966.

Adler, A. *The practice and theory of individual psychology.* New York: Harcourt, Brace, 1927.

Ainsworth, M. D. The development of mother-infant interaction among the Ganda. In B. Foss (Ed.), *Determinants of infant behavior*, Vol. II. London: Methuen, 1963.

Allinsmith, B. B. Expressive styles: II. Directness with which anger is expressed. In D. R. Miller & G. E. Swanson (Eds.), *Inner conflict and defense.* New York: Holt, 1960. Pp. 315–336.

Allport, G. W. Review of S. A. Stouffer et al., *The American soldier. J. abnorm. soc. Psychol.,* 1950, **45**, 168–172.

Allport, G. W. *Becoming.* New Haven: Yale Univer. Press, 1955.

Allport, G. W. Traits revisited. *Amer. Psychologist,* 1966, **21**, 1–10.

Alper, T. G., Blane, H. T., & Abrams, B. K. Reactions of middle and lower class children to finger paints. *J. abnorm. soc. Psychol.,* 1955, **51**, 439–448.

Alpert, A., Neubauer, P. W., & Weil, A. P. Unusual variation in drive endowment. *Psychoanal. Stud. Child,* 1956, **11**, 125–163.

Altus, W. D. Birth order and academic primogeniture. *J. Pers. soc. Psychol.,* 1965, **2**, 872–876.

Altus, W. D. Birth order and its sequelae. *Science,* 1966, **151**, 44–49.

Amsel, A. A three-factor theory of inhibition: An addition to Hull's two-factor theory. *Amer. Psychologist,* 1951, **6**, 487 (abstract).

Amsel, A. The role of frustrative nonreward in noncontinuous reward situations. *Psychol. Bull.,* 1958, **15**, 102–119.

Amsel, A. Frustrative nonreward in partial reinforcement and discrimination learning: Some recent history and a theoretical extension. *Psychol. Rev.,* 1962, **69**, 306–328.

Anderson, J. E. Dynamics of development: Systems in process. In D. B. Harris (Ed.), *The concept of development.* Minneapolis: Univer. of Minnesota Press, 1957. Pp. 25–46.

Anderson, J. E. Child development research: The next twenty-five years. *Child Developm.,* 1960a, **31**, 191–199.

Anderson, J. E. The prediction of adjustment over time. In I. Iscoe & H. W. Stevenson (Eds.), *Personality development in children.* Austin: Univer. of Texas Press, 1960b. Pp. 28–72.

Antonovsky, H. F. A contribution to research in the area of the mother-child relationships. *Child Developm.,* 1959, **30**, 37–51.

Atkinson, J. W. Explorations using imaginative thought to assess the strength of human motives. In M. R. Jones (Ed.), *Nebraska Symposium on Motivation,* 1954. Lincoln: Univer. of Nebraska Press. Pp. 56–112.

Atkinson, J. W. (Eds.). *Motives in fantasy, action, and society.* Princeton, N.J.: Van Nostrand, 1958.

Atkinson, J. W. Personality dynamics. *Annu. Rev. Psychol.,* 1960, **2**, 255–291.

Atkinson, J. W. Discussion of Dr. Lazarus' paper. In J. Kagan & G. S. Lesser

(Eds.), *Contemporary issues in thematic apperceptive methods.* Springfield, Ill.: Charles C. Thomas, 1961. Pp. 72–82.

Ausubel, D. *Theories and problems of child development.* New York: Grune & Stratton, 1958.

Azrin, N. H., Hutchison, R., & Hake, D. Pain induced fighting in the squirrel monkey. *J. exp. Anal. Behav.*, 1963, **6**, 620.

Bach, G. R. Young children's play fantasies. *Psychol. Monogr.*, 1945, **59**, No. 2 (Whole No. 272).

Bach, G. R. Father-fantasies and father-typing in father-separated children. *Child Developm.*, 1946, **17**, 63–79.

Bacon, M. K., Child, I. L., & Barry, H. III. A cross-cultural study of correlates of crime. *J. abnorm. soc. Psychol.*, 1963, **66**, 291–300.

Baldwin, A. L. Socialization and the parent-child relationship. *Child Developm.*, 1948, **19**, 127–136.

Balint, M. Individual differences of behavior in early infancy: An objective method for recording. *J. genet. Psychol.*, 1948, **73**, 57–79.

Bandura, A. Relationship of family patterns to child behavior disorders. Progress Report, U.S.P.H. Research Grant M-1734. Stanford Univer., 1960.

Bandura, A. Social learning through imitation. In M. R. Jones (Ed.), *Nebraska Symposium on Motivation,* 1962. Lincoln: Univer. of Nebraska Press. Pp. 211–269.

Bandura, A. Vicarious processes: A case of no-trial learning. In L. Berkowitz (Ed.), *Advances in experimental social psychology,* Vol. II. New York: Academic Press, 1965. Pp. 3–55.

Bandura, A., & Huston, A. Identification as a process of incidental learning. *J. abnorm. soc. Psychol.*, 1961, **63**, 311–318.

Bandura, A., Ross, D., & Ross, S. A. Transmission of aggression through imitation of aggressive models. *J. abnorm. soc. Psychol.*, 1961, **63**, 575–582.

Bandura, A., Ross, D., & Ross, S. A. Imitation of film-mediated aggressive models. *J. abnorm. soc. Psychol.*, 1963, **66**, 3–11.

Bandura, A., & Walters, R. H. *Adolescent aggression.* New York: Ronald Press, 1959.

Bandura, A., & Walters, R. H. *Social learning and personality development.* New York: Holt, 1963a.

Bandura, A., & Walters, R. H. Aggression. In *Child psychology. National society for the study of education,* Part I. Chicago: National Society for the Study of Education, 1963b. Pp. 364–415.

Bandura, A., & Walters, R. H. *The social learning of deviant behavior: A behavioristic approach to socialization.* New York: Holt, 1963c.

Barker, R. G., Dembo, T., & Lewin, K. Frustration and regression: An experiment with young children. *Univer. of Iowa Studies in Child Welfare,* 1941, **18**, 1–314.

Baron, R. M. Social reinforcement effects as a function of social reinforcement history. *Psychol. Rev.*, 1966, **73**, 527–539.

Barry, H., III, Child, I. L., & Bacon, M. K. Relation of child training to subsistence economy. *Amer. Anthropologist,* 1959, **61**, 51–63.

Bayley, N., & Schaefer, E. Relationships between socio-economic variables and the behavior of mothers toward young children. *J. genet. Psychol.*, 1960, **96**, 61–77.

Bayley, N., & Schaefer, E. Maternal behavior, child behavior, and their inter-correlations from infancy through adolescence. *Monogr. Soc. Res. Child Developm.*, 1963, **29** (6, Whole No. 97).

Becker, S. W., Lerner, M. J., & Carroll, J. Conformity as a function of birth order, payoff, and type of group pressure. *J. abnorm. soc. Psychol.*, 1964, **69**, 318–323.

Becker, S. W., Lerner, M. J., & Carroll, J. Conformity as a function of birth order and type of group pressure. *J. Pers. soc. Psychol.*, 1966, **3**, 242–244.

Becker, W. C. Developmental psychology. *Annu. Rev. Psychol.*, 1962, **13**, 1–34.

Becker, W. C. Consequences of different kinds of parental discipline. In M. L. Hoffman & L. W. Hoffman (Eds.), *Review of child development research,* Vol. I. New York: Russell Sage, 1964. Pp. 169–208.

Becker, W. C., Peterson, D. R., Luria, Z., Shoemaker, D. J., & Hellmer, L. A. Relations of factors derived from parent-interview ratings to behavior problems of five-year-olds. *Child Developm.*, 1962, **33**, 509–535.

Bell, R. Q. Developmental psychology. *Annu. Rev. Psychol.*, 1965, **16**, 1–38.

Beller, E. Dependency and independence in young children. *J. genet. Psychol.*, 1955, **87**, 25–35.

Beller, E. K., & Haeberle, A. W. Dependency and the frustration-aggression hypothesis. Paper read at Eastern Psychological Association meetings, 1959.

Bergman, P., & Escalona, S. Unusual sensitivities in very young children. *Psychoanal. Stud. Child*, 1949, **3–4**, 333–352.

Berkowitz, L. The expression and reduction of hostility. *Psychol. Bull.*, 1958, **55**, 257–283.

Berkowitz, L. *Aggression: A social psychological analysis.* New York: McGraw-Hill, 1962.

Berkowitz, L. *The development of motives and values in the child.* New York: Basic Books, 1964a.

Berkowitz, L. Aggressive cues in aggressive behavior and hostility catharsis. *Psychol. Rev.*, 1964b, **71**, 104–122.

Berkowitz, L. The concept of aggressive drive: Some additional considerations. In L. Berkowitz (Ed.), *Advances in experimental social psychology*, Vol. II. New York: Academic Press, 1965. Pp. 301–329.

Bernstein, B. Social class and linguistic development: A theory of social learning. In A. H. Halsey, J. Floud & C. A. Anderson (Eds.), *Education, economy and society.* New York: Free Press, 1961. Pp. 288–314.

Bevan, W., Daves, W. F., & Levy, G. W. The relation of castration, androgen therapy and pre-test fighting experience to competitive aggression in male C57 BL110 mice. *Anim. Behav.*, 1960, **8**, 6–12.

Biesheuvel, S. Race, culture and personality: The Hoernlé Memorial Lecture, 1959. Johannesburg, South African Institute of Race Relations.

Bijou, S., & Baer, D. M. *Child development.* New York: Appleton-Century-Crofts, 1961.

Blake, R. R., & Mouton, J. S. Personality. *Annu. Rev. Psychol.*, 1959, **10**, 203–233.

Blatz, W. *Understanding the young child.* New York: Morrow, 1944.

Block, J. & Martin, B. Predicting the behavior of children under frustration. *J. abnorm. soc. Psychol.*, 1955, **51**, 281–285.

Blood, R. O., & Wolfe, D. M. *Husbands and wives, the dynamics of married living.* New York: Free Press, 1960.

Body, M. K. Patterns of aggression in the nursery school. *Child Developm.*, 1955, **26**, 3–12.

Bowlby, J. The nature of the child's tie to his mother. *Int. J. Psychoanal.*, 1958, **39**, 350–373.

Bradburn, N. M. N achievement and father dominance in Turkey. *J. abnorm. soc. Psychol.*, 1963, **67**, 464–468.

Bridger, W. H., & Reiser, M. F. Psychophysiologic studies of the neonate. *Psychosomatic Medicine*, 1959, **21**, 265.

Brim, O. G., Jr., & Wheeler, S. *Socialization after childhood: Two essays.* New York: Wiley, 1966.

Bronfenbrenner, U. Socialization and social class through time and space. In E. Maccoby, T. Newcomb, & E. Hartley (Eds.), *Readings in social psychology* (3rd ed.). New York: Holt, 1958. Pp. 400–425.

Bronfenbrenner, U. The changing American child—a speculative analysis. *J. soc. Issues*, 1961a, **17**, 6–18.

Bronfenbrenner, U. Some familial antecedents of responsibility and leadership in adolescents. In L. Petrullo & B. M. Bass (Eds.), *Leadership and interpersonal behavior.* New York: Holt, 1961b. Pp. 239–271.

Bronfenbrenner, U. Developmental theory in transition. In *Child Psychology. National society for the study of education*, Part I. Chicago: National Society for the Study of Education, 1963. Pp. 517–542.

Bronfenbrenner, U. The psychological costs of quality and equality in education. In M. Tumin & M. Bressler (Eds.), *Quality and equality in education*, preprint, 1965.

Bronfenbrenner, U., & Ricciuti, H. N. The appraisal of personality characteristics in children. In P. Mussen (Ed.), *Handbook of research methods in child development.* New York: Wiley, 1960. Pp. 770–817.

Broverman, D. M., Jordan, E. J., & Phillips, L. Achievement motivation in fantasy and behavior. *J. abnorm. soc. Psychol.*, 1960, **60**, 374–378.

Brown, J. S. Problems presented by the concept of acquired drives. In *Current theory and research in motivation: A symposium.* Lincoln: Univer. of Nebraska Press, 1953. Pp. 1–21.

Brown, J. S., & Farber, I. E. Emotions conceptualized as intervening variables with suggestions toward a theory of frustration. *Psychol. Bull.*, 1951, **68**, 465–495.

Brown, P., & Elliott, R. Control of aggression in a nursery school class. *J. exp. child Psychol.*, 1965, **2**, 103–107.

Brown, R. *Social Psychology.* New York: Free Press, 1965.

Bruch, H. Parent education or the illusion of omnipotence. *Amer. J. Orthopsychiat.*, 1954, **27**, 723–732.

Burchinal, L. G., Gardner, B., & Hawkes, G. R. Children's personality adjustment and the socioeconomic status in their families. *J. genet. Psychol.*, 1958, **92**, 149–590.

Burnstein, E., & Worchel, P. Arbitrariness of frustration and its consequences for aggression in a social situation. *J. Pers.*, 1962, **30**, 528–540.

Burt, C. *The young delinquent.* New York: Appleton-Century-Crofts, 1929.

Burton, R. V. Social development. In D. L. Sells (Ed.), *International encyclopedia of the social sciences.* New York: Macmillan, 1968. Pp. 534–544.

Buss, A. H. *The psychology of aggression.* New York: Wiley, 1961.

Butterfield, E. C., & Zigler, E. The effects of success and failure on the discrimination learning of normal and retarded children. *J. abnorm. Psychol.*, 1965, **70**, 25–31.

Cairns, R. B. Antecedents of social reinforcer effectiveness. Unpublished manuscript, Indiana Univer., 1962.

Callard, E. D. Achievement motive in the four-year-old child and its relationship to achievement expectancies of the mother. Unpublished doctoral dissertation, Univer. of Michigan, 1964.

Cameron, A., & Storm, T. Achievement motivation in Canadian Indian middle-

and working-class children. *Psychol. Rep.*, 1965, **16**, 459–463.

Carrigan, W. C., & Julian, J. W. Sex and birth-order differences in conformity as a function of need affiliation arousal. *J. Pers. soc. Psychol.*, 1966, **3**, 479–493.

Casler, L. Maternal deprivation: A critical review of the literature. *Monogr. Soc. Res. Child Developm.*, 1961, **26** (2, Whole No. 80.)

Cattell, R. B. Methodological and conceptual advances in evaluating hereditary and environmental influences and their interaction. In S. G. Vandenberg (Ed.), *Methods and goals in human behavior genetics.* New York: Academic Press, 1965. Pp. 95–139.

Cattell, R. B., Blewett, D. B., & Beloff, J. R. The inheritance of personality: A multiple variance analysis of approximate nature-nurture ratios for primary personality factors in Q-data. *Am. J. hum. Genet.*, 1955, **7**, 122–146.

Cattell, R. B., Stice, G., & Kristy, N. A first approximation to nature-nurture ratios for eleven primary personality factors in objective tests. *J. abnorm. soc. Psychol.*, 1957, **54**, 143–159.

Cavan, R. S. Subcultural variations and mobility. In H. T. Christensen (Ed.), *Handbook of marriage and the family.* Chicago: Rand McNally, 1964. Pp. 535–581.

Chance, J. E. Independency training and first graders' achievement. *J. consult. Psychol.*, 1961, **25**, 149–154.

Charles, D. C. Ability and accomplishment of persons earlier judged mentally deficient. *Genet. Psychol. Monogr.*, 1953, **47**, 3–71.

Chess, S., Thomas, A., & Birch, H. G. *Your child is a person.* New York: Viking, 1965.

Child, I. L., Storm, T., & Veroff, J. Achievement themes in folktales related to socialization practices. In J. W. Atkinson (Ed.), *Motives in fantasy, action, and society.* Princeton, N.J.: Van Nostrand, 1958. Pp. 479–492.

Christie, R., & Lindauer, F. Personality structure. *Annu. Rev. Psychol.*, 1963, **14**, 201–207.

Clausen, J. A., & Williams, J. R. Sociological correlates of child behavior. In

Child psychology. National society for the study of education, Part I. Chicago: National Society for the Study of Education, 1963. Pp. 62–107.

Collmann, R. D., & Newlyn, D. Leisure activities of educationally subnormal and other ex-pupils in England. *Amer. J. ment. Defic.*, 1957, **62**, 464–469.

Conklin, A. Failures of highly intelligent pupils. Teachers College Contributions to Education No. 792. New York: Teachers College, Columbia Univer., 1940.

Cortes, J. B., & Gatti, F. M. Physique and motivation. *J. Consult. Psychol.*, 1966, **30**, 408–413.

Cowan, P. A., & Walters, R. H. Studies of reinforcement of aggression: I. Effects of scheduling. *Child Developm.*, 1963, **34**, 543–551.

Crandall, V. J. Achievement. In *Child psychology. National society for the study of education*, Part I. Chicago: National Society for the Study of Education, 1963. Pp. 416–460.

Crandall, V. J., Dewey, R., Katkovsky, W., & Preston, A. Parents' attitudes and behaviors and grade-school children's academic achievements. *J. genet. Psychol.*, 1964, **104**, 53–66.

Crandall, V., Katkovsky, W., & Preston, A. A conceptual formulation of some research on children's achievement development. *Child Developm.*, 1960, **31**, 787–797.

Crandall, V. J., Preston, A., & Rabson, A. Maternal reactions and the development of independence and achievement behavior in young children. *Child Developm.*, 1960, **31**, 243–251.

Crandall, V. J., & Sinkeldam, C. Children's dependent and achievement behaviors in social situations and their perceptual field dependence. *J. Pers.*, 1964, **32**, 1–22.

Cromwell, R. L. A social learning approach to mental retardation. In N. R. Ellis (Ed.), *Handbook of mental deficiency*. New York: McGraw-Hill, 1963. Pp. 41–91.

Dager, E. Z. Socialization and personality development in the child. In H. T. Christensen (Ed.), *Handbook of marriage and the family*. Chicago: Rand McNally, 1964. Pp. 740–781.

Davis, A. American status systems and the socialization of the child. *Amer. sociol. Rev.*, 1941, **6**, 234–254.

Davis, A. Child training and social class. In R. Barker, J. Kounin, & M. Wright (Eds.), *Child behavior and development*. New York: McGraw-Hill, 1943. Pp. 607–619.

Davis, A. Socialization and adolescent personality. In *society for the study of education*, Part I. Chicago: National Society for the Study of Education, 1944. Pp. 198–216.

Davis, A. Social-class influences upon mental problem-solving. In W. E. Martin & C. B. Stendler (Eds.), *Readings in child development*. New York: Harcourt, Brace, 1954. Pp. 104–114.

Davis, A., & Dollard, J. *Children of bondage*. Washington: American Council on Education, 1940.

Davis, A., & Havighurst, R. J. Social class and color differences in child rearing. *Amer. Sociol. Rev.*, 1946, **11**, 698–710.

Davis, A., & Havighurst, R. J. *The father of the man*. Boston: Houghton Mifflin, 1947.

Davitz, J. L. The effects of previous training on post-frustration behavior. *J. abnorm. soc. Psychol.*, 1952, **47**, 309–315.

Denenberg, V. H. Early experience and emotional development. *Scientific American*, 1963, **208**, 138–146.

Dennis, W. Piaget's questions applied to Zuni and Navaho children. *Psychol. Bull.*, 1940, **38**, 520.

Dennis, W. Animistic thinking among college and high school students in the Near East. *J. educ. Psychol.*, 1957, **48**, 193–198.

Dollard, J., Doob, L. W., Miller, N. E., Mowrer, O. H., & Sears, R. R. *Frustration and aggression*. New Haven: Yale Univer. Press, 1939.

Dollard, J., & Miller, N. E. *Personality and psychotherapy: An analysis of learning, thinking, and culture*. New York: McGraw-Hill, 1950.

Douvan, E. Social status and success striving. *J. abnorm. soc. Psychol.*, 1956, **52**, 219–223.

Douvan, E., & Adelson, J. The psychodynamics of social mobility in adolescent boys. *J. abnorm. soc. Psychol.*, 1958, **56**, 31–44.

Drews, E., & Teahan, J. Parental attitudes and academic achievement. *J. clin. Psychol.*, 1957, **13**, 328–332.

Duvall, E. M. Conceptions of parenthood. *Amer. J. Sociol.*, 1946, **53**, 193–203.

Edwards, A. *The social desirability variable in personality assessment and research.* New York: Dryden Press, 1957.

Eells, K., Davis, A., Havighurst, R. J., Herrick, V. E., & Tyler, R. W. *Intelligence and cultural differences.* Chicago: Univer. of Chicago Press, 1951.

Elder, G. H., Jr. Structural variations in the child rearing relationship. *Sociometry*, 1962, **25**, 241–262.

English, H. B. Chronological divisions of the life span. *J. educ. Psychol.*, 1957, **48**, 437–439.

Erickson, M. T. Effects of social deprivation and satiation on verbal conditioning in children. *J. comp. physiol. Psychol.*, 1962, **55**, 953–958.

Ericson, M. Social status' and child rearing practices. In T. M. Newcomb & E. L. Hartley (Eds.), *Readings in social psychology.* New York: Holt, 1947.

Erikson, E. H. *Childhood and society.* New York: Norton, 1950.

Eron, L. D., Banta, T. J., Walder, L. O., & Laulicht, J. H. Comparison of data obtained from mothers and fathers on child rearing practices and their relation to child aggression. *Child Developm.*, 1961, **32**, 457–572.

Escalona, S. Emotional development in the first year of life. In J. E. Milton & M. D. Stenn (Eds.), *Problems of infancy and childhood.* New York: Josiah Macy, Jr., Foundation, 1953.

Eysenck, H. J. Zue theorie der personlichkeitsmessung. *Zeitschrift Diagnotische Psychologie und Personlichkeitsforschung*, 1954, **2**, 87–101, 171–187.

Ezer, M. The effect of religion upon children's responses to questions involving physical causality. In Judy F. Rosenblith & W. Allinsmith (Eds.), *The causes of behavior: Readings in child development and educational psychology.* Boston: Allyn & Bacon, 1962. Pp. 481–487.

Fales, E. Genesis of level of aspiration in children from one and one-half to three years of age. Unpublished manuscript, 1937. [Described by Lewin, K., Dembo, T., Festinger, L., & Sears, P. S. Level of aspiration. In J. McV. Hunt (Ed.), *Personality and the behavior disorders*, Vol. I. New York: Ronald, 1944. Pp. 354–355.]

Federov, V. K. On some physiological mechanisms in the initial period of child's mental life. *Voprosy Psikhologii*, 1961, **4**, 101–107. (Based on partial oral translation.)

Feld, S. Need achievement and test anxiety in children and maternal attitudes and behaviors toward independent accomplishments: A longitudinal study. Paper read at the meeting of the American Psychological Association, Cincinnati, 1959.

Feshbach, S. The function of aggression and the regulation of aggressive drive. *Psychol. Rev.*, 1964, **71**, 257–272.

Festinger, L. The psychological effects of insufficient rewards. *Amer. Psychologist*, 1961, **16**, 1–11.

Finney, J. C. Some maternal influences on children's personality and character. *Genet. Psychol. Monogr.*, 1961, **63**, 199–278.

Freedman, D. G. Constitutional and environmental interactions in rearing of four breeds of dogs. *Science*, 1958, **127**, 585–586.

Frenkel-Brunswik, E. Psychoanalysis and the unity of science. *Proceedings of the American Academy of Arts and Sciences*, 1954, **80**, 271–350.

Freud, A. The mutual influences in the development of ego and id: Introduction to the discussion. *Psychoanal. Stud. Child*, 1952, **7**, 42–50.

Fries, M., & Woolf, P. Some hypotheses on the role of congenital activity type in development. *Psychoanal. Stud. Child*, 1953, **8**, 48.

Gesell, A. Early evidences of individuality in the human infant. *Sci. Mon.*, New York, 1937, **45**, 217–225.

Gewirtz, J. Three determinants of attention seeking in young children. *Monogr. Soc. Res. Child Developm.*, 1954, **19** (2, Whole No. 59).

Gewirtz, J. A learning analysis of the effects of normal stimulation, privation, and deprivation on the acquisition of social motivation and attachment. In B. M. Foss (Ed.), *Determinants of infant behavior*, New York: Wiley, 1961.

Gewirtz, J., & Baer, D. M. The effects of brief social deprivation on behaviors for a social reinforcer. *J. abnorm. soc. Psychol.*, 1958a, **56**, 49–56.

Gewirtz, J., & Baer, D. M. Deprivation and satiation of social reinforcers as drive conditions. *J. abnorm. soc. Psychol.*, 1958b, **57**, 165–172.

Gilmore, J. B., & Zigler, E. Birth order and social reinforcer effectiveness in children. *Child Developm.*, 1964, **35**, 193–200.

Glueck, S., & Glueck, E. T. *Unraveling juvenile delinquency.* Cambridge, Mass.: Harvard Univer. Press, 1950.

Gold, M. Suicide, homicide, and the socialization of aggression. *Amer. J. Sociol.*, 1958, **63**, 651–661.

Goldfarb, W. The effects of early institutional care on adolescent personality. *J. exp. Educ.*, 1943a, **12**, 106–129.

Goldfarb, W. Infant rearing and problem behavior. *Amer. J. Orthopsychiat.*, 1943b, **13**, 249–265.

Goodenough, F. L. *Anger in young children.* Univer. of Minnesota Institute of Child Welfare Monogr. No. 9. Minneapolis: Univer. of Minnesota, 1931.

Goodman, P. Growing up absurd. *Dissent*, 1960, **7**, 121–136.

Gordon, J. E., & Smith, E. Children's aggression, parental attitudes, and the effects of an affiliation-arousing story. *J. Pers. soc. Psychol.*, 1965, **1**, 654–659.

Gottesman, I. I. Personality and natural selection. In S. G. Vandenberg (Ed.), *Methods and goals in human behavior genetics.* New York: Academic Press, 1965. Pp. 63–80.

Green, A. W. Middle-class male child and neurosis. *Amer. sociol. Rev.*, 1946, **11**, 31–41.

Green, C., & Zigler, E. Social deprivation and the performance of feeble-minded and normal children on a satiation-type task. *Child Developm.*, 1962, **33**, 499–508.

Gronseth, E. The impact of father absence in sailor families upon the personality structure and social adjustment of adult sailor sons. Part I. In N. Anderson (Ed.), *Studies of the family*, Vol. II. Gottingen:

Vandenhoeck & Reprecht, 1957. Pp. 97–114.

Gruen, G., & Zigler, E. Expectancy of success and the probability learning of middle-class, lower-class, and retarded children. *J. abnorm. Psychol.*, 1968, **73**, 343–352.

Haggard, E. A. Social-status and intelligence: An experimental study of certain cultural determinants of measured intelligence. *Genet. psychol. Monogr.*, 1954, **49**, 141–186.

Hamburger, V. The concept of "development" in biology. In D. B. Harris (Ed.), *The concept of development.* Minneapolis: Univer. of Minnesota Press, 1957. Pp. 49–58.

Harlow, H. Mice, monkeys, men and motives. *Psychol. Rev.*, 1953, **60**, 23–32.

Harlow, H. The nature of love. *Amer. Psychologist*, 1958, **13**, 673–685.

Harlow, H. The development of affectional patterns in infant monkeys. In B. Foss (Ed.), *Determinants of infant behaviour.* London: Methuen, 1961. Pp. 75–88.

Harlow, H., Blezek, N. C., & McClearn, G. E. Manipulatory motivation in the infant rhesus monkey. *J. comp. physiol. Psychol.*, 1956, **49**, 444–448.

Harlow, H., & Zimmerman, R. R. Affectional responses in the infant monkey. *Science*, 1959, **130**, 421–432.

Harris, D. B. Child psychology and the concept of development. In D. S. Palermo & L. P. Lipsitt (Eds.), *Research readings in child psychology.* New York: Holt, 1963. Pp. 21–31.

Hart, I. Maternal child rearing practices and authoritarian ideology. *J. abnorm. soc. Psychol.*, 1957, **55**, 232–237.

Hartmann, H. Mutual influences in the development of ego and id. *Psychoanal. Stud. Child*, 1952, **7**, 9–30.

Hartmann, H. *Ego psychology and the problem of adaptation* (trans. by D. Rapaport). New York: International Universities Press, 1958.

Hartmann, H., Kris, E., & Lowenstein, R. Notes on the theory of aggression. *Psychoanal. Stud. Child*, 1949, **3–4**, 9–36.

Hartup, W. W. Nurturance and nurturance-withdrawal in relation to the dependency behavior of young children. *Child Developm.*, 1958, **29**, 191–201.

Hartup, W. W. Dependence and independence. In *Child psychology. National society for the study of education*, Part I. Chicago: National Society for the Study of Education, 1963. Pp. 333–364.

Hartup, W. W. Early pressures in child development. *Young Children*, 1965, **20**, 270–283.

Hartup, W. W., & Himeno, Y. Social isolation vs. interaction with adults in relation to aggression in preschool children. *J. abnorm. soc. Psychol.*, 1959, **59**, 17–22.

Havighurst, R. J., & Davis, A. A comparison of the Chicago and Harvard studies of social class differences in child rearing. *Amer. sociol. Rev.*, 1955, **20**, 438–442.

Havighurst, R. J., & Neugarten, B. L. *American Indian and white children: A sociopsychological investigation*. Chicago: Univer. of Chicago Press, 1955.

Healy, W., & Bronner, A. F. *Delinquents and criminals: Their making and unmaking*. New York: Macmillan, 1926.

Heathers, G. Emotional dependence and independence in a physical threat situation. *Child Developm.*, 1953, **24**, 169–179.

Heathers, G. Emotional dependence and independence in nursery school play. *J. genet. Psychol.*, 1955a, **87**, 37–57.

Heathers, G. Acquiring dependence and independence: A theoretical orientation. *J. genet. Psychol.*, 1955b, **87**, 277–291.

Henry, A. F., & Short, J. F. *Suicide and homicide: Some economic, sociological, and psychological aspects of aggression*. New York: Free Press, 1954.

Henry, M. A., & Sharpe, D. F. Some influential factors in the determination of aggressive behavior in preschool children. *Child Developm.*, 1947, **18**, 11–28.

Hess, R. D., & Shipman, V. C. Early experience and the socialization of cognitive modes in children. *Child Developm.*, 1965, **36**, 869–886.

Hicks, D. J. Imitation and retention of film-mediated aggressive peer and adult models. *J. Pers. soc. Psychol.*, 1965, **2**, 97–100.

Hirsch, J. Behavior genetics and individuality understood. *Science*, 1963, **142**, 1436–1442.

Hoffman, Lois W., & Lippitt, R. The measurement of family life variables. In P. H. Mussen (Ed.), *Handbook of research methods in child development*. New York: Wiley, 1960. Pp. 945–1013.

Hoffman, L. W., Rosen, S., & Lippitt, R. Parental coerciveness, child autonomy, and child's role at school. *Sociometry*, 1960, **23**, 15–22.

Hoffman, M. L. Power assertion by the parent and its impact on the child. *Child Developm.*, 1960, **31**, 129–143.

Hoffman, M. L. Parental practices and the development of internal social control. Paper presented at the 1966 Midwestern Meeting of the Society for Research in Child Development, Bowling Green State Univer., Bowling Green, Ohio.

Hoffman, M. L., Mitsos, S. B., & Protz, R. E. Achievement striving, social class and test anxiety. *J. Abnorm. soc. Psychol.*, 1958, **56**, 401–403.

Hollenberg, E., & Sperry, M. Some antecedents of aggression and effects of frustration in doll play. *Pers.*, 1951, **1**, 32–43.

Homans, G. C. *The human group*. New York: Harcourt, Brace, 1950.

Horney, K. *The neurotic personality of our time*. New York: Norton, 1937.

Hull, C. L. *Essentials of behavior*. New Haven: Yale Univer. Press, 1951.

Hull, C. L. *A behavior system: An introduction to behavior theory concerning the individual organism*. New Haven: Yale Univer. Press, 1952.

Hunt, J. McV. Experience and the development of motivation: Some reinterpretations. *Child Developm.*, 1960, **31**, 489–504.

Hunt, J. McV. *Intelligence and experience*. New York: Ronald, 1961.

Hunt, J. McV. Intrinsic motivation and its role in psychological development. In M. R. Jones (Ed.), *Nebraska Symposium on Motivation*, 1965, Lincoln: Univer. of Nebraska Press. Pp. 189–283.

Inhelder, B. Developmental psychology. *Annu. Rev. Psychol.*, 1957, **8**, 139–162.

Irwin, O. C. The amount and nature of activity of new born infants during the first ten days of life. *Genet. Psychol. Monogr.*, 1930, **8**, 1–92.

Isaacs, J. T. Frequency curves and the ability of nations. *Brit. J. statist. Psychol.*, 1962, **15**, 76–79.

Jahoda, M. Toward a social psychology of mental health. In A. M. Rose (Ed.), *Mental health and mental disorder.* New York: Norton, 1955. Pp. 556–577.

Jegard, S. F., & Walters, R. H. A study of some determinants of aggression in young children. *Child Developm.*, 1960, **31**, 739–748.

Jenness, A. Personality dynamics. *Annu. Rev. Psychol.*, 1962, **13**, 479–514.

Jones, E. The probation student: What he is like and what can be done about it. *J. educ. Res.*, 1955, **49**, 93–102.

Jones, H. E. The environment and mental development. In L. Carmichael (Ed.), *Manual of child psychology* (2nd ed.). New York: Wiley, 1954. Pp. 631–696.

Jones, V. Character development in children—an objective approach. In L. Carmichael (Ed.), *Manual of child psychology* (2nd ed.). New York: Wiley, 1954. Pp. 781–832.

Kagan, J. On the need for relativism. *Amer. Psychologist*, 1967, **22**, 131–143.

Kagan, J., & Moss, H. A. *Birth to maturity: The Fels study of psychological development.* New York: Wiley, 1962.

Kahl, J. A., & Davis, J. A. A comparison of indexes of socioeconomic status. *Amer. sociol. Rev.*, 1955, **20**, 317–325.

Kardiner, A. *The psychological frontiers of society.* New York: Columbia Univer. Press, 1945.

Katkovsky, W., Preston, A., & Crandall, V. J. Parents' attitudes toward their personal achievements and toward the achievement behaviors of their children. *J. genet. Psychol.*, 1964a, **104**, 67–82.

Katkovsky, W., Preston, A., & Crandall, V. J. Parents' achievement attitudes and their behavior with their children in achievement situation. *J. genet. Psychol.*, 1964b, **104**, 105–121.

Katz, P., & Zigler, E. Self-image disparity: A developmental approach. *J. Pers. soc. Psychol.*, 1967, **5**, 186–195.

Keister, M. E. The behavior of young children in failure, *Univer. Iowa Stud. Child Welfare*, 1937, **14**, 27–82.

Kendler, H., & Kendler, T. Vertical and horizontal processes in problem solving. *Psychol. Rev.*, 1962, **69**, 1–16.

Kendler, T. The development of mediating responses in children. *Monogr. Soc. Res. Child Developm.*, 1963, **28** (2, Whole No. 86).

Kessen, W. Research design in the study of developmental problems. In P. Mussen (Ed.), *Handbook of research methods in child development.* New York: Wiley, 1960. Pp. 36–70.

Kessen, W. "Stage" and "structure" in the study of children. *Monogr. Soc. Res. Child Developm.*, 1962, **27** (2, Whole No. 83).

Kessen, W. Research in the psychological development of infants: An overview. *Merrill-Palmer Quarterly*, 1963, **9**, 83–94.

Kimball, B. Case studies in educational failure during adolescence. *Amer. J. Orthopsychiat.*, 1953, **23**, 406–415.

King, J. A. Relationships between early social experience and adult aggressive behavior in inbred mice. *J. genet. Psychol.*, 1957, **90**, 151–166.

Klatskin, E. H. Shifts in child care practices in three social classes under an infant care program of flexible methodology. *Amer. J. Orthopsychiat.*, 1952, **22**, 52–61.

Klatskin, E. H., Jackson, E. B., & Wilkin, L. C. The influence of degree of flexibility in maternal child care practices on early child behavior. *Amer. J. Orthopsychiat.*, 1956, **26**, 79–93.

Kohlberg, L. The development of children's orientations toward a moral order: I. Sequence in the development of moral thought. *Vita Humana*, 1963, **6**, 11–33.

Kohlberg, L. A cognitive-developmental approach to socialization—morality and psychosexuality. Paper presented at the 1966 Midwestern Meeting of the Society for Research in Child Development, Bowling Green State Univer., Bowling Green, Ohio.

Kohlberg, L., & Zigler, E. The impact of cognitive maturity on the development of sex-role attitudes in the years four to eight. *Genet. Psychol. Monogr.*, 1967, **75**, 89–165.

Kohn, M. L. Social class and parental values. *Amer. J. Sociol.*, 1959a, **64**, 337–351.

Kohn, M. L. Social class and the exercise of parental authority. *Amer. sociol. Rev.*, 1959b, **24**, 352–366.

Kohn, M. L., & Carroll, E. E. Social class and the allocation of parental responsibilities. *Sociometry*, 1960, **23**, 372–392.

Kolb, D. A. Achievement motivation training for under-achieving high school boys. *J. Pers. soc. Psychol.*, 1965, **2**, 783–792.

Krasner, L., & Ullmann, L. P. (Eds.). *Research in behavior modification*. New York: Holt, 1965.

Krebs, A. M. Two determinants of conformity: Age of independence and training and n achievement. *J. abnorm. soc. Psychol.*, 1958, **56**, 130–131.

Kregarman, J. J., & Worchel, P. Arbitrariness of frustration and aggression. *J. abnorm. soc. Psychol.*, 1962, **55**, 369–372.

Kris, H. Notes on the development and on some current problems of psychoanalytic child psychology. *Psychoanal. Stud. Child*, 1950, **5**, 34–62.

Lawson, R., & Marx, M. H. Frustration: Theory and experiment. *Genet. Psychol. Monogr.*, 1958, **57**, 393–464.

Lazarus, R. S. A substitutive-defensive conception of apperceptive fantasy. In J. Kagan & G. S. Lesser (Eds.), *Contemporary issues in thematic apperceptive methods*. Springfield, Ill.: Charles Thomas, 1961. Pp. 51–71.

Lazarus, R. S. Story telling and the measurement of motivation: The direct versus substitutive controversy. *J. consult. Psychol.*, 1966, **30**, 483–487.

Leeper, R. W. What contributions might cognitive learning theory make to our understanding of personality? *J. Pers.*, 1953, **22**, 32–41.

Lefkowitz, M. M., Walder, L. O., & Eron, L. D. Punishment, identification and aggression. *Merrill-Palmer Quarterly*, 1963, **9**, 159–174.

Lenneberg, E. H. *Biological foundations of language*. New York: Wiley, 1967.

Lesser, G. S. Maternal attitudes and practices and the aggressive behavior of children. Unpublished doctoral dissertation, Yale Univer., 1952.

Levin, H. Permissive childrearing and adult role behavior. In D. E. Dulony, R. L. DeValois, D. C. Beardsley, &

M. R. Winterbottom (Eds.), *Contributions to modern psychology*. New York: Oxford Univer. Press, 1958. Pp. 307–312.

Levin, H., & Turgeon, V. The influence of the mother's pressures on children's doll-play aggression. *J. abnorm. soc. Psychol.*, 1957, **55**, 304–308.

LeVine, R. A. The internalization of social values in stateless societies. *Human Organization*, 1960, **19**, 51–58.

Levy, D. M. *Maternal overprotection*. New York: Columbia Univer. Press, 1943.

Lewin, K. *A dynamic theory of personality*. New York: McGraw-Hill, 1936.

Lipton, E. L., Steinschneider, A., & Richmond, J. B. Autonomic function in the neonate: IV. Individual differences in cardiac reactivity. *Psychosom. Med.*, 1961, **23**, 472–484.

Littman, R. A., Moore, R. C. A., & Pierce-Jones, J. Social class differences in child rearing: A third community for comparison with Chicago and Newton. *Amer. Sociol. Rev.*, 1957, **22**, 694–704.

Livson, N., & Mussen, P. H. The relation of ego control to overt aggression and dependency, *J. Abnorm. soc. Psychol.*, 1957, **55**, 66–71.

Lorenz, K. *King Solomon's ring*. New York: Crowell, 1952.

Lorenz, K. *Evolution and modification of behavior*. Chicago: Univer. of Chicago Press, 1965.

Lorenz, K. *On aggression* (1965). (Trans. by M. K. Wilson). New York: Harcourt, Brace, 1966.

Lovaas, O. I. Effect of exposure to symbolic aggression on aggressive behavior. *Child Developm.*, 1961a, **32**, 37–44.

Lovaas, O. I. Interaction between verbal and nonverbal behavior. *Child Developm.*, 1961b, **32**, 329–336.

Lynn, D. B., & Sawrey, W. L. The effects of father-absence on Norwegian boys and girls. *J. abnorm. soc. Psychol.*, 1959, **59**, 258–262.

Maas, H. S. Some social class differences in the family systems and group relations of pre- and early adolescents. *Child Developm.*, 1951, **22**, 145–152.

Maas, H. S. The role of member in clubs of lower-class and middle-class adolescents. *Child Developm.*, 1954, **25**, 241–252.

MacArthur, R. S., & Elley, W. B. The reduction of socio-economic bias in intelligence testing. *Brit. J. educ. Psychol.*, 1963, **33**, 107–119.

Maccoby, E. E. The taking of adult roles in middle childhood. *J. abnorm. soc. Psychol.*, 1961, **63**, 493–503.

Maccoby, E. E. Developmental psychology. *Annu. Rev. Psychol.*, 1964, **15**, 203–251.

Maccoby, E. E., & Gibbs, P. K. Methods of child rearing in two social classes. In W. E. Martin and Celia B. Stendler (Eds.), *Readings in child development*. New York: Harcourt, Brace, 1954. Pp. 380–396.

Mannino, F. V. Family factors related to school persistence. *J. educ. Sociol.*, 1962, **35**, 193–202.

Marlowe, D., & Crowne, D. Social desirability and response to perceived situational demands. *J. consult. Psychol.*, 1961, **25**, 109–115.

Marshall, H. R. Relations between home experiences and children's use of language in play interactions with peers. *Psychol. Monogr.*, 1961, **75**, 5 (Whole No. 509).

Martin, W. Rediscovering the mind of the child: A significant trend in research in child development. *Merrill-Palmer Quarterly*, 1959, **6**, 67–76.

Maslow, A. H. *Motivation and personality*. New York: Harper & Row, 1954.

Mason, W. A. The effects of social restrictions on the behavior of rhesus monkeys: I. Free social behavior. *J. comp. physiol. Psychol.*, 1960, **53**, 582–589.

McClelland, D. C. Some social consequences of achievement motivation. In M. R. Jones (Ed.), *Nebraska Symposium on Motivation*, 1955, Lincoln: Univer. of Nebraska Press, Pp. 41–65.

McClelland, D. C. Personality. *Annu. Rev. Psychol.*, 1956, **7**, 39–63.

McClelland, D. C. *The achieving society*. Princeton, N.J.: Van Nostrand, 1961.

McClelland, D. C. Longitudinal trends in the relation of thought to action. *J. consult. Psychol.*, 1966, **30**, 479–483.

McClelland, D. C., Atkinson, J. W., Clark, R. A., & Lowell, E. L. *The achievement motive*. New York: Appleton-Century-Crofts, 1953.

McClelland, D. C., & Friedman, G. A. A cross-cultural study of the relationship between child-training practices and achievement motivation appearing in folk tales. In G. E. Swanson, T. M. Newcomb, & E. H. Hartley (Eds.), *Readings in social psychology*. New York: Holt, 1952. Pp. 243–249.

McCord, W., McCord, J., & Howard, A. Familial correlates of aggression in nondelinquent male children. *J. abnorm. soc. Psychol.*, 1961, **62**, 79–93.

McCord, W., McCord, J., & Verden, P. Familial and behavioral correlates of dependency in male children. *Child Developm.*, 1962, **33**, 313–326.

McCord, W., McCord, J., & Zola, I. K. *Origins of crime*. New York: Columbia Univer. Press, 1959.

McGrade, Betty J. Effectiveness of verbal reinforcers in relation to age and social class. *J. Pers. Soc. Psychol.*, 1966, **4**, 555–560.

McKee, J. P., & Honzik, M. P. The sucking behavior of mammals: An illustration of the nature-nurture question. In L. Postman (Ed.), *Psychology in the making*. New York: Knopf, 1962. Pp. 585–661.

McKee, J. P., & Leader, F. The relationship of socioeconomic status and aggression to the competitive behavior of preschool children. *Child Developm.*, 1955, **26**, 135–142.

Mead, M. An investigation of the thought of primitive children, with special reference to animism. *J. royal anthropol. Inst.*, 1932, **62**, 173–190.

Meili, R. A longitudinal study of personality development. In L. Jessner & E. Pavenstedt (Eds.), *Dynamic psychopathology in childhood*. New York: Grune & Stratton, 1959. Pp. 106–123.

Merrill, B. Relation of mother-child interaction to children's social behavior. Unpublished Doctoral Dissertation, State Univ. Iowa, 1946.

Merton, R. K. *Social theory and social class* (2nd ed.). New York: Free Press, 1957.

Meyers, C. E. The effect of conflicting authority on the child. *University of Iowa Studies in Child Welfare*, 1944, **20**, No. 409, 31–98.

Miller, D. R., & Swanson, G. E. The study of conflict. In M. R. Jones (Ed.), *Nebraska Symposium on Motivation*, 1956, Lincoln: Univer. of Nebraska Press. Pp. 137–174.

Miller, D. R., & Swanson, G. E. *The changing American parent.* New York: Wiley, 1958.

Miller, D. R., & Swanson, G. E. *Inner conflict and defense.* New York: Holt, 1960.

Miller, E. L. Ability and social adjustment at midlife of persons earlier judged mentally deficient. *Genet. Psychol. Monogr.*, 1965, **72**, 139–198.

Miller, N. E. The frustration-aggression hypothesis. *Psychol. Rev.*, 1941, **48**, 337–342.

Miller, N. E. Some implications of modern behavior theory for personality change and psychotherapy. In P. Worchel & D. Byrne (Eds.), *Personality change.* New York: Wiley, 1964.

Milner, E. A. A study of the relationships between reading readiness in grade one school children and patterns of parent-child interaction. *Child Developm.*, 1951, **22**, 95–112.

Morrow, W. R., & Wilson, R. R. Family relations of bright high-achieving and under-achieving high school boys. *Child Developm.*, 1961, **32**, 501–510.

Muller, H. J. Human values in relation to evolution. *Science*, 1958, **127**, 625–629.

Murray, H. A. *Explorations in personality.* New York: Oxford Univer. Press, 1938.

Mussenn, P. H., & Kagan, J. Group conformity and perceptions of parents. *Child Developm.*, 1958, **29**, 57–60.

Mussen, P. H., & Rutherford, E. Effects of aggressive cartoons on children's aggressive play. *J. abnorm. soc. Psychol.*, 1961, **62**, 461–465.

Myers, J. K., & Roberts, B. H. *Family and class dynamics in mental illness.* New York: Wiley, 1959.

Nelson, E. A. The effects of reward and punishment of dependency on subsequent behavior. Unpublished manuscript, Stanford Univ., 1960.

Nissen, H. W. The nature of the drive as innate determinant of behavioral organization. In M. R. Jones (Ed.), *Nebraska Symposium on Motivation*, 1954, Lincoln: Univer. of Nebraska Press. Pp. 28–32.

Noirot, C. E. Changes in responsiveness to young in the adult mouse: The effect of external stimuli. *J. comp. physiol. Psychol.*, 1964, **57**, 97–99.

Nowlis, V. The search for significant concepts in a study of parent-child relationships. *Amer. J. Orthopsychiat.*, 1952, **22**, 286–299.

Nowlis, V. The development and modification of motivational systems in personality. In *Current theory and research in motivation: A symposium.* Lincoln: Univer. of Nebraska Press, 1953. Pp. 114–138.

Nuttin, J. Personality. *Annu. Rev. Psychol.*, 1955, **6**, 161–186.

Olsen, M. E. Distribution of family responsibilities and social stratification, *Marriage and Family Living*, 1960, **22**, 60–65.

Otis, N. B., & McCandless, B. Responses to repeated frustrations of young children differentiated according to need area. *J. abnorm. soc. Psychol.*, 1955, **50**, 349–353.

Parsons, T. *The structure of social action.* New York: McGraw-Hill, 1937.

Parsons, T. Social structure and the development of personality: Freud's contribution to the integration of psychology and sociology. *Psychiatry*, 1958, **21**, 321–340.

Parton, D. A., & Ross, A. O. Social reinforcement of children's motor behavior: A review. *Psychol. Bull.*, 1965, **64**, 65–73.

Parton, D. A., & Ross, A. O. A reply to "The use of rate as a measure of response in studies of social reinforcement." *Psychol. Bull.*, 1967, **67**, 323–325.

Pasamanick, B., & Knobloch, H. The contribution of some organic factors to school retardation in Negro children. *J. Negro Educ.*, 1958, **27**, 4–9.

Pasamanick, B., Knobloch, H., & Lilienfeld, A. M. Socionomic status and some precursors of neuropsychiatric disorder. *Amer. J. Orthopsychiat.*, 1956, **26**, 594–601.

Pastore, N. The role of arbitrariness in the frustration-aggression hypothesis. *J. abnorm. soc. Psychol.*, 1952, **47**, 728–731.

Patterson, G. R., Littman, R. A., & Bricker, W. Assertive behavior in children: A step toward a theory of aggression. *Monogr. Soc. Res. in Child Developm.*, 1967, **32** (5, Whole No. 113).

Patterson, G. R., Ludwig, M., & Sonoda, B. Reinforcement of aggression in children. Unpublished manuscript, Univer. of Oregon, 1961.

Peiper, A. *Cerebral function in infancy and childhood.* New York: Consultants Bureau, 1963.

Peller, L. E. Incentives to development and means of early education. *Psychoanal. Stud. Child,* 1946, **2**, 397–415.

Pettigrew, T. F. *A profile of the Negro American.* Princeton, N.J.: Van Nostrand, 1964.

Phillips, L., & Rabinovitch, M. S. Social role and patterns of symptomatic behaviors. *J. abnorm. soc. Psychol.*, 1958, **57**, 181–186.

Phillips, L., & Zigler, E. Social competence: The action-thought parameter and vicariousness in normal and pathological behaviors. *J. abnorm. soc. Psychol.*, 1961, **63**, 137–146.

Phillips, L., & Zigler, E. Role orientation, the action-thought parameter and outcome in psychiatric disorder. *J. abnorm. soc. Psychol.*, 1964, **68**, 381–389.

Piaget, J. *The psychology of intelligence.* New York: Harcourt, Brace, 1950.

Piaget, J. Principal factors in determining evolution from childhood to adult life. In D. Rapaport (Ed.), *Organization and pathology of thought.* New York: Columbia Univer. Press, 1951. Pp. 154–175.

Piaget, J. *The origin of intelligence in the child.* London: Routledge, 1953.

Piaget, J. *The child's construction of reality.* London: Routledge, 1955.

Piaget, J. *The moral judgment of the child* (trans. by M. Gabaith). New York: Collier, 1962.

Pintler, M. H. Doll play as a function of experimenter-child interaction and initial organization of materials. *Child Developm.*, 1945, **16**, 145–166.

Psather, G. Ethnicity, social class, and adolescent independence from parental control. *Amer. sociol. Rev.*, 1957, **22**, 415–423.

Radke, M. Relation of parental authority to children's behavior and attitudes. *University of Minnesota Institute of Child Welfare Monographs*, 1946, No. 22.

Raelke, M. J. *The relation of parental authority to children's behavior and attitudes.* Minneapolis: Univer. of Minnesota Press, 1946.

Rapaport, D. Toward a theory of thinking. In D. Rapaport (Ed.), *Organization and pathology of thought.* New York: Columbia Univer. Press, 1951. Pp. 689–730.

Rapaport, D. The structure of psychoanalytic theory. In S. Koch (Ed.), *Psychology: A study of a science*, Vol. III. New York: McGraw-Hill, 1959. Pp. 55–183.

Ressler, R. H. Parental handling in two strains of mice reared by foster parents. *Science*, 1962, **137**, 129–130.

Ressler, R. H. Genotype-correlated parental influences in two strains of mice. *J. comp. physiol. Psychol.*, 1963, **56**, 882–886.

Rheingold, H. L. The modification of social responsiveness in institutional babies. *Monographs of the Society for Research in Child Development*, 1956, **21** (2, Whole No. 63).

Rheingold, H. L. (Ed.). *Maternal behavior in mammals.* New York: Wiley, 1963.

Roberts, W. W., & Kiess, H. O. Motivational properties of hypothalamic aggression in cats. *J. comp. physiol. Psychol.*, 1964, **58**, 187–193.

Rogers, C. *Client-centered therapy.* Boston: Houghton Mifflin, 1951.

Rose, A. M. (Ed.). *Mental health and mental disorder.* New York: Norton, 1955.

Rosen, B. C. The achievement syndrome: A psycho-cultural dimension of social stratification. *Amer. sociol. Rev.*, 1956, **21**, 203–211.

Rosen, B. C. Socialization and achievement motivation in Brazil. *Sociol., Rev.*, 1962, **27**, 612–624.

Rosen, B. C. Social class and the child's perception of the parent. *Child Developm.*, 1964, **35**, 1147–1153.

Rosen, B. C., & D'Andrade, R. The psychosocial origins of achievement motivation. *Sociometry*, 1959, **22**, 185–218.

Rosenhan, D., & Greenwald, J. The effects of age, sex and socioeconomic class on responsiveness to two classes of verbal reinforcement. *J. Pers.*, 1965, **33**, 108–121.

Roy, K. Parents' attitudes toward their children. *J. Home Econom.*, 1950, **42**, 652–653.

Russell, W. A. An experimental psychology of development: Pipe dream or possibility? In D. B. Harris (Ed.), *The concept of development*. Minneapolis: Univer. of Minnesota Press, 1957. Pp. 162–174.

Sampson, E. E., & Hancock, F. T. An examination of the relationship between ordinal position, personality and conformity: An extensive replication, and partial verification. *J. Pers. soc. Psychol.*, 1967, **5**, 398–408.

Sanders, B., Zigler, E., & Butterfield, E. C. Outer-directedness in the discrimination learning of normal and mentally retarded children. *J. Abnorm. Psychol.*, 1968, **73**, 368–375.

Sanford, R. N., Adkins, M. M., Miller, R. B., & Cobb, E. Physique, personality and scholarship. *Monogr. Soc. Res. Child Developm.*, 1943, **8**, No. 1.

Schachtel, E. *Metamorphosis: On the development of affect, perception, attention, and memory.* New York: Basic Books, 1959.

Schachter, S. *The psychology of affiliation.* Stanford, Calif.: Stanford Univer. Press, 1959.

Schachter, S. Birth order, eminence and higher education. *Amer. sociol. Rev.*, 1963, **28**, 757–768.

Schaefer, E. S., & Bayley, N. Maternal behavior, child behavior, and their intercorrelations from infancy through adolescence. *Monographs of the Society for Research in Child Development*, 1963, **28** (3, Whole No. 87).

Schaffer, H. R., & Emerson, P. E. The development of social attachments in infancy. *Monogr. Soc. Res. Child Developm.*, 1964, **29**, 5–77.

Scheerer, M. Personality functioning and cognitive psychology. *J. Pers.*, 1953, **22**, 1–17.

Scott, J. P. The genetic and environmental differentiation of behavior. In D. B. Harris (Ed.), *The concept of develop-ment.* Minneapolis: Univer. of Minnesota Press, 1957. Pp. 59–77.

Scott, J. P. The process of primary socialization in canine and human infants. *Monogr. Soc. Res. Child Developm.*, 1963, **28** (1, Whole No. 85).

Sears, P. S. Levels of aspiration in academically successful and unsuccessful children. *J. soc. Psychol.*, 1940, **35**, 498–536.

Sears, P. S. Doll-play aggression in normal young children: Influence of sex, age, sibling status, father's absence. *Psychol. Monogr.*, 1951, **65**, 6 (Whole No. 323).

Sears, R. R. A theoretical framework for personality and social behavior. *Amer. Psychologist*, 1951, **6**, 476–483.

Sears, R. R. Personality theory: The next forty years. *Monogr. Soc. Res. Child Developm.*, 1959, **24**, 37–50.

Sears, R. R. The relation of early socialization experiences to aggression in middle childhood. *J. abnorm. soc. Psychol.*, 1961, **63**, 466–492.

Sears, R. R. Dependency motivation. *Nebraska Symposium on Motivation*, 1963, **11**, 25–65.

Sears, R. R., Maccoby, E. E., & Levin, H. *Patterns of child-rearing.* New York: Harper & Row, 1957.

Sears, R. R., Pintler, M. H., & Sears, Pauline S. Effects of father-separation on pre-school children's doll play aggression. *Child Developm.*, 1946, **17**, 219–243.

Sears, R. R., Whiting, J. W. M., Nowlis, V., & Sears, P. S. Some child-rearing antecedents of aggression and dependency in young children. *Genet. Psychol. Monogr.*, 1953, **47**, 135–236.

Sewell, W. H., & Haller, A. O. Social status and the personality adjustment of the child. *Sociometry*, 1956, **9**, 114–125.

Sewell, W. H., & Haller, A. O. Factors in the relationship between social status and the personality adjustment of the child. *Amer. Sociol. Rev.*, 1959, **24**, 511–520.

Shallenberger, P., & Zigler, E. Rigidity, negative reaction tendencies, and co-satiation effects in normal and feeble-minded children. *J. abnorm. soc. Psychol.*, 1961, **63**, 20–26.

Shaw, M. C., & Dutton, B. E. The use of the parent attitude research inventory with the parents of bright academic underachievers. *J. educ. Psychol.*, 1962, **53**, 203–208.

Shaw, M., & Grubb, J. Hostility and able high school underachievers. *J. counsel. Psychol.*, 1958, **5**, 263–266.

Sheldon, W. H., & Stevens, S. S. *The varieties of temperament.* New York: Harper & Row, 1942.

Skolnick, A. Motivational imagery and behavior over twenty years. *J. consult. Psychol.*, 1966, **30**, 463–478.

Smedslund, J. The acquisition of conservation of substance and weight in children. *J. Scandinav. Psychol.*, 1961, **2**, 71–87.

Smith, H. T. A comparison of interview and observation measures of mother behavior. *J. abnorm. soc. Psychol.*, 1958, **57**, 278–282.

Solomons, G., & Solomons, H. C. Factors affecting motor performance in four-month-old infants. *Child Developm.*, 1964, **35**, 1283–1296.

Spindler, G. D., & Spindler, L. S. American Indian personality types and their sociocultural roots. *Ann. Amer. Acad. of Polit. Soc. Sci.*, 1957, **311**, 147–157.

Spitz, R. A., & Wolf, K. M. Anaclitic depression. In Anna Freud and others (Eds.), *The psychoanalytic study of the child*, Vol. II. New York: International Universities Press, 1946. Pp. 313–342.

Staples, F., & Walters, R. Anxiety, birth order and susceptibility to social influence. *J. abnorm. soc. Psychol.*, 1961, **62**, 716–720.

Stendler, C. Sixty years of child training practices. *J. Pediat.*, 1950, **36**, 122–134.

Stendler, C. Critical periods in socialization and overdependency. *Child Developm.*, 1952, **23**, 3–12.

Stendler, C. Possible causes of over-dependency in young children. *Child Developm.*, 1954, **25**, 125–146.

Stevenson, H. W. Social reinforcement of children's behavior. In L. P. Lipsitt & C. C. Spiker (Eds.), *Advances in child development*, Vol. II. New York: Academic Press, 1965. Pp. 97–126.

Stevenson, H. W., & Fahel, L. The effect of social reinforcement on the performance of institutionalized and noninstitutionalized normal and feeble-minded children. *J. Pers.*, 1961, **29**, 136–147.

Stevenson, H. W., & Hill, K. T. The use of rate as a measure of response in studies of social reinforcement. *Psychol. Bull.*, 1966, **66**, 321–326.

Stevenson, H. W., & Zigler, E. Probability learning in children. *J. exp. Psychol.*, 1958, **56**, 185–192.

Stoltz, L. M. *Father relations of warborn children.* Palo Alto, Calif.: Stanford Univer. Press, 1954.

Stoltz, L. M. Youth: The Gesell Institute and its latest study. *Contemp. Psychol.*, 1958, **3**, 10–15.

Storm, T., Rosenwald, G. C., & Child, I. L. A factor analysis of self-ratings on social behavior. *J. Soc. Psychol.*, 1958, **48**, 45–49.

Stott, D. H. An empirical approach to motivation based on the behavior of a young child. *J. child Psychol. Psychiat.*, 1961, **2**, 97–117.

Sullivan, H. A. *The interpersonal theory of psychiatry.* New York: Norton, 1953.

Symonds, P. M. *The psychology of parent-child relationships.* New York: Appleton-Century-Crofts, 1939.

Taylor, J. What do attitude scales measure: The problem of social desirability. *J. abnorm. soc. Psychol.*, 1961, **62**, 386–390.

Terman, L. M., & Oden, M. M. *The gifted group at mid-life.* Stanford, Calif.: Stanford Univer. Press, 1959.

Terrell, G., Jr., Durkin, K., & Wiesley, M. Social class and the nature of the incentive in discrimination learning. *J. abnorm. soc. Psychol.*, 1959, **59**, 270–272.

Thomas, A., Birch, H. G., Chess, S., Hertzig, M. E., & Korn, S. *Behavioral individuality in early childhood.* New York: New York Univer. Press, 1963.

Thompson, G. G. Developmental psychology. *Annu. Rev. Psychol.*, 1959, **10**, 1–42.

Tiller, P. O. Father absence and personality development of children in sailor families: A preliminary research report, Part II. In N. Anderson (Ed.), *Studies of the family*, Vol. II. Göttingen: Vandenhoeck & Reprecht, 1957. Pp. 115–137.

Tinbergen, N. *The study of instinct.* Oxford: Clarendon Press, 1951.

Toby, J. Orientation to education as a factor in the school maladjustment of lower-class children. In N. J. Smelser & W. T. Smelser (Eds.), *Personality and social systems.* New York: Wiley, 1963. Pp. 549–558.

Tuddenham, R. D. The nature and measurement of intelligence. In L. Postman (Ed.), *Psychology in the making.* New York: Knopf, 1962. Pp. 469–525.

Tuma, E., & Livson, N. Family socio-economic status and adolescent attitudes to authority. *Child Developm.*, 1960, **31**, 387–399.

Turiel, E. An experimental test of the sequentiality of developmental stages in the child's moral judgments. *J. Pers. soc. Psychol.*, 1966, **3**, 611–618.

Turnure, J. E. Children's reactions to distractions: A developmental approach. Unpublished doctoral dissertation, Yale Univer., 1966.

Turnure, J. E., & Zigler, E. Outer-directedness in the problem solving of normal and retarded children. *J. abnorm. soc. Psychol.*, 1964, **69**, 427–436.

Ullmann, L. P., & Krasner, L. (Eds.). *Case studies in behavior modification.* New York: Holt, 1965.

Ulrich, R. E., & Azrin, N. H. Reflexive fighting in response to aversive stimulation. *J. exp. Anal. Behav.*, 1962, **5**, 511–520.

Uyeno, E. J. Hereditary and environment aspects of dominant behavior in the albino rat. *J. comp. physiol. Psychol.*, 1960, **53**, 138–141.

Vandenberg, S. G. (Ed.). *Methods and goals in human behavior genetics.* New York: Academic Press, 1965.

Vandenburgh, J. G. Eosinophil response to aggressive behavior in CFW albino mice. *Anim. Behav.*, 1960, **8**, 13–18.

Wallach, M. Research on children's thinking. In *Child psychology. National society for the study of education*, Part I. Chicago: National Society for the Study of Education, 1963. Pp. 236–276.

Walsh, A. *Self-concepts of bright boys with learning difficulties.* New York: Teachers College, Columbia Univer., 1956.

Walter, G. Electroencephalographic development of children. In J. M. Tanner & B. Inhelder (Eds.), *Discussions on child development.* New York: International Universities Press, 1953.

Walters, R. H. Implications of laboratory studies on aggression for the control and regulation of violence. *Ann. Amer. Acad. Polit. Soc. Sci.*, 1966, **364**, 60–72.

Walters, R. H., & Brown, M. A test of the high-magnitude theory of aggression. *J. exp. Child Psychol.*, 1964, **1**, 376–387.

Walters, R. H., & Parke, R. D. Social motivation, dependency, and susceptibility to social influence. In L. Berkowitz (Ed.), *Advances in experimental social psychology*, Vol. I. New York: Academic Press, 1964. Pp. 232–276.

Walters, R. H., & Ray, E. Anxiety, social isolation and reinforcer effectiveness. *J. Pers.*, 1960, **28**, 354–367.

Warren, J. R. Birth order and social behavior. *Psychol. Bull.*, 1966, **65**, 38–49.

Waters, E., & Crandall, V. J. Social class and observed maternal behavior from 1940 to 1960. *Child Developm.*, 1964, **35**, 1021–1032.

Watson, G. A comparison of the effects of lax versus strict home training. *J. soc. Psychol.*, 1934, **5**, 102–105.

Watson, G. Some personality differences in children related to strict or permissive parental discipline. *J. Psychol.*, 1957, **44**, 227–249.

Weinberg, C. Family background and deviance or conformity to school expectations. *J. Marriage Fam.*, 1964, **26**, 89–91.

Wenar, C., & Wenar, S. C. The short term prospective model, the illusion of time, and the tabula rasa child. *Child Developm.*, 1963, **34**, 697–708.

Werner, H. *Comparative psychology of mental development* (2nd ed.). Chicago: Follett, 1948.

Wertheim, J., & Mednick, S. A. The achievement motive and field independence. *Journal of Consulting Psychology*, 1958, **22**, 38.

White, M. Social class, child rearing practices and child behavior. *Amer. sociol. Rev.*, 1957, **22**, 704–712.

White, R. Motivation reconsidered: The concept of competence. *Psychol. Rev.*, 1959, **66**, 297–333.

White, R. Competence and the psychosexual stages of development. In M. R. Jones (Ed.), *Nebraska Symposium on Motivation*, 1960, Lincoln: Univer. of Nebraska Press. Pp. 97–141.

White, S. H. Learning. In *Child psychology. National society for the study of education.*

Chicago: National Society for the Study of Education, Part I, 1963. Pp. 196–235.

Whiting, J. W. M., & Child, I. L. *Child training and personality: A cross-cultural study*. New Haven: Yale Univer. Press, 1953.

Whiting, J. W. M., & Whiting, B. Contributions of anthropology to the methods of studying child rearing. In P. L. Mussen (Ed.), *Handbook of research methods in child development*. New York: Wiley, 1960. Pp. 918–944.

Wilkins, L. T. Delinquent generations. *Home office research unit, research report*, No. 3. London: Her Majesty's Stationery Office, 1960.

Williams, R. V. *Biochemical individuality*. New York: Wiley, 1956.

Winder, C. L., & Rau, L. Parental attitudes associated with social deviance in preadolescent boys. *J. abnorm. soc. Psychol.*, 1962, **64**, 418–424.

Winterbottom, M. The relation of need for achievement in learning experiences in independence and mastery. In J. Atkinson (Ed.), *Motives in fantasy, action, and society*. Princeton, N.J.: Van Nostrand, 1958. Pp. 453–478.

Witkin, H. A., Dyk, R. B., Faterson, H. F., Goodenough, D. R., & Karp, S. A. *Psychological differentiation*. New York: Wiley, 1962.

Wittenborn, J. R. A study of adoptive children: III. Relationships between some aspects of development and some aspects of environment for adoptive children. *Psychol. Monogr.*, 1956, **70** (3, Whole No. 410).

Wohlwill, J. F., & Lowe, R. C. Experimental analysis of the development of the conservation of number. *Child Developm.*, 1962, **33**, 153–167.

Wolf, T. H. The effect of praise and competition on the persisting behavior of kindergarten children. *University of Minnesota Institute of Child Welfare Monographs*, 1938, No. 15.

Wolfenstein, M. Trends in infant care. *Amer. J. Orthopsychiat.*, 1953, **23**, 120–130.

Wolff, P. The developmental psychologies of Jean Piaget and psychoanalysis. *Psychol. Issues*, 1960, **2**, 1 (Whole No. 5).

World Health Organization. Deprivation of maternal care. Public Health Paper No. 14. Geneva: Author, 1962.

Wrong, D. H. The oversocialized conception of man in modern sociology. *Amer. Sociol. Rev.*, 1961, **26**, 183–193.

Yarrow, L. J. The effects of antecedent frustration on projective play. *Psychological Monogr.*, 1948, **62** (6, Whole No. 293).

Yarrow, L. J. Maternal deprivation: Toward an empirical and conceptual reevaluation. *Psychol. Bull.*, 1961, **58**, 459–490.

Yarrow, L. J. Separation from parents during early childhood. In M. L. Hoffman & L. W. Hoffman (Eds.), *Review of child development research*, Vol. I. New York: Russell Sage, 1964. Pp. 89–137.

Zigler, E. Social deprivation and rigidity in the performance of feebleminded children. *J. abnorm. soc. Psychol.*, 1961, **62**, 413–421.

Zigler, E. Metatheoretical issues in developmental psychology. In M. H. Marx (Ed.), *Theories in contemporary psychology*. New York: Macmillan, 1963a. Pp. 341–369.

Zigler, E. Social reinforcement, environment, and the child. *Amer. J. Orthopsychiat.*, 1963b, **33**, 614–623.

Zigler, E. Rigidity and social reinforcement effects in the performance of institutionalized and noninstitutionalized normal and retarded children. *J. Pers.*, 1963c, **31**, 258–269.

Zigler, E. The effect of social reinforcement on normal and socially deprived children. *J. Genet. Psychol.*, 1964, **104**, 235–242.

Zigler, E. Mental retardation: Current issues and approaches. In L. W. Hoffman & M. L. Hoffman (Eds.), *Review of child development research*, Vol. II. New York: Russell Sage, 1966a. Pp. 107–168.

Zigler, E. Discussion of psychosocial and cultural deprivation in psychobiological development. In H. W. Magoun (Moderator), *Deprivation in psycho-biological development*. Washington, D.C.: Pan American Health Organization, Pan American Sanitary Bureau, Regional Office of the World Health Organization, Scientific Publication No. 134, 1966b. Pp. 66–71.

Zigler, E. Research in personality structure in the retardate. In N. R. Ellis (Ed.), *International review of research in mental retardation*, Vol. I. New York: Academic Press, 1966c. Pp. 77–108.

Zigler, E., & Child, I. Socialization. In G. Lindsey & E. Aronson (Eds.), *The Handbook of Social Psychology*. Reading, Mass.: Addison-Wesley, 1969. Pp. 450–589.

Zigler, E., Balla, D., & Butterfield, E. C. The effects of preinstitutional social deprivation upon changes in intelligence and social deprivation. Unpublished manuscript, Yale Univer., 1966.

Zigler, R., & deLabry, J. Concept-switching in middle-class, lower-class, and retarded children. *J. abnorm. soc. Psychol.*, 1962, **65**, 267–273.

Zigler, E., & Harter, S. Socialization of the mentally retarded. In D. A. Goslin & D. C. Glass (Eds.), *Handbook of socialization theory and research*. New York: Rand McNally, 1969. Pp. 1065–1102.

Zigler, E., Hodgden, L., & Stevenson, H. W. The effect of support on the performance of normal and feeble-minded children. *J. Pers.*, 1958, **26**, 106–122.

Zigler, E., & Kanzer, P. The effectiveness of two classes of verbal reinforcers on the performance of middle- and lower-class children. *J. Pers.*, 1962, **30**, 157–163.

Zigler, E., Levine, J., & Gould, L. Cognitive challenge as a factor in children's humor appreciation. *J. Pers. soc. Psychol.*, 1967, **6**, 332–336.

Zigler, E., & Phillips, L. Social effectiveness of symptomatic behaviors. *J. abnorm. soc. Psychol.*, 1960, **61**, 231–238.

Zigler, E., & Phillips, L. Social competence and the process-reactive distinction in psychopathology. *J. abnorm. soc. Psychol.*, 1962, **65**, 215–222.

Zigler, E., & Williams, J. Institutionalization and the effectiveness of social reinforcement: A three-year follow-up study. *J. abnorm. soc. Psychol.*, 1963, **66**, 197–205.

Suggested Readings

THEORETICAL APPROACHES TO THE SOCIALIZATION PROCESS

Bandura, A., & Walters, R. H. *Social learning and personality development*. New York: Holt, 1963. In this work the authors present their social learning theory, which emphasizes the role of modelling, imitation, and vicarious experience in the learning process. A number of experimental studies are reviewed.

Bijou, S., & Baer, D. M. *Child development*. New York: Appleton-Century-Crofts, 1961. This is a clear and complete statement of the Skinnerian approach to socialization, in which social behavior is viewed as being shaped by the individual's reinforcement history.

Vandenberg, S. G. (Ed.). *Methods and goals in human behavior genetics*. New York: Academic Press, 1965. The papers collected in this volume provide an overview of recent developments in the methods and theory of human behavior genetics.

Zigler, E. Metatheoretical issues in developmental psychology. In M. H. Marx (Ed.), *Theories in contemporary psychology*. New York: Macmillan, 1963. Pp. 341–369. The author discusses the current state of cognitive-developmental theory and argues that the inclusion of certain learning theory concepts and methods is desirable for developmental theory construction.

SOCIALIZATION OF SPECIFIC SYSTEMS OF BEHAVIOR

Crandall, V. J. Achievement. In *Child psychology. National society for the study of education*, Part I. Chicago: National Society for the Study of Education, 1963. Pp. 416–460. The author discusses theoretical and methodological problems in the definition of achievement and provides a comprehensive review of research in this area.

Kohlberg, L. Development of moral character and moral ideology. In M. L. Hoffman & L. W. Hoffman (Eds.), *Review of child development research*, Vol. I. New York: Russell Sage Foundation, 1964. Pp. 383–433. Various theoretical approaches to the development of moral thought and behavior are presented here and major evidence is reviewed. The author presents his own cognitive-developmental approach to moral thinking.

McClelland, D. C., Atkinson, J. W., Clark, R. A., & Lowell, E. L. *The achievement motive*. New York: Appleton-Century-Crofts, 1953. The authors present a view of achievement motivation in which the child's evaluation of his own performance and the effect connected with his evaluation is crucial. Achievement orientation is seen as bound to an internal standard of excellence, with the only relevant reinforcement being that which the child delivers to himself.

Schaffer, H. R., & Emerson, P. E. The development of social attachments in infancy. *Monogr. Soc. Res. Child Developm.*, 1964, **29**, 5–77. The investigators are interested in the age of onset of social attachments, the intensity and objects of such attachments and the variables that might be related to individual differences. Their findings emphasize the importance of innate, genetic and cognitive-developmental factors in the development of dependence.

SOCIAL CLASS IN THE SOCIALIZATION PROCESS

Bronfenbrenner, U. Socialization and social class through time and space. In E. Maccoby, T. Newcomb, & E. Hartley (Eds.), *Readings in social psychology* (3rd ed.). New York: Holt, 1958. Pp. 400–425. Several studies of social class and child-rearing practices are reanalysed by the author, who reduces inconsistencies among studies by taking into account trends in child-rearing advice prevailing at the time various studies were conducted.

Littman, R. A., Moore, R. C. A., & Pierce-Jones, J. Social class differences in child rearing: A third community for comparison with Chicago and Newton. *Amer. sociol. Rev.*, 1957, **22**, 694–704. Child-rearing practices of middle- and lower-class parents in Eugene, Oregon are examined. The findings are compared with those of Davis and Havighurst in Chicago and Sears et al. in the Boston area, and the authors conclude that there are no general or consistently significant differences among classes in socialization practices.

Sears, R. R., Maccoby, E. E., & Levin, H. *Patterns of child-rearing*. New York: Harper & Row, 1957. The relation of social-class differences in the Boston area to differences in maternal child-rearing practices and to differences in the child's subsequent behavior are examined with respect to several behavior systems. The authors conclude that middle-class parents are more permissive, gentle, and warm than are lower-class parents.

V

Comparative Psychology of Learning

Kenneth H. Brookshire

Franklin and Marshall College

16

Definitions and Problems[1]

Definitions

Comparative psychology is the study of the similarities and differences in behavior among animal forms; however, a definition of the comparative psychology of *learning* is more difficult, because psychologists do not agree on the aims and goals of learning research that utilizes animals. Broadly speaking, there are three divergent approaches to the use of animals for behavioral research in learning. Each stems from a different historical tradition in psychology or zoology, and the kinds of generalizations which are made from the data collected by each approach are quite dissimilar.

The Animal as a "Representative" or "Convenient" Preparation for the Study of Learning

One approach that is quite prevalent in the psychology of learning is to start with the assumption, explicit or implicit, that learn-

[1] The preparation of this paper was supported by an award under the Fullbright-Hays program, 1965–1966, and by Research Grant MH 05874 from the National Institute of Health.

ing processes are essentially identical in all animal forms. This assumption is not always put in written form by the researcher when he discusses the results of his experiments with animals, but occasionally psychologists have been brave. For example, Dollard and Miller (1950) state as their rationale for using experiments on animals as a means to interpret human behavior:

The basic facts and concepts can best be introduced by the discussion of a simple experiment on albino rats. In using the results from an experiment of this kind, we are working on the hypothesis that people have all the learning capacities of rats so that any general phenomena of learning found in rats will also be found in people, although, of course, people may display additional phenomena not found in rats [p. 63].

Or again, writers of textbooks of comparative psychology have occasionally allowed this assumption to creep into their interpretation of the data of animal behavior. For example, a recent text by Ratner and Denny (1964) has a chapter titled "Generality of Conditioning," which has as its summary statement the following:

It can be said that conditioning, establishing new associations between stimuli and

291

responses, is neither a simple learning process nor a special kind of learning which is divorced from other learnings. The generality of conditioning is seen in terms of the variety of stimuli that can be used in establishing the associations, the variety of responses conditioned, and *the range of species and ages over which conditioning occurs* [p. 533, italics added].

The essential feature of these two positions is the assumption that there is uniformity in the laws of learning across species, or that even if certain higher forms possess learning processes not found in lower forms, these new processes are simply additive and in no way distort or modify basic learning functions. For example, emergent processes would not be expected to modify the conditions under which classical conditioning or instrumental conditioning or simple discrimination learning would occur. Psychologists who subscribe to this approach often have selected the laboratory rat as a subject for study. The rat can be considered a "representative" preparation for the study of learning, because it is a mammal and therefore an example from among the higher forms of animal life. Or alternatively, the laboratory rat can be considered a "convenient" preparation for the study of learning, on the grounds that humans are unusually poor organisms for scientific study because they bring to the test situation a wealth of past experience which interferes with proper experimentation and because they cannot be subjected to the rather extreme environmental conditions necessary for the study of certain learning phenomena. In contrast, the rat is a simpler organism, its past environment can be controlled, and it can be manipulated in ways which would be considered inhumane if the experiment were carried out on humans. Moreover, a particular animal form may seem to be a convenient preparation in another sense, that is, the animal may possess special characteristics which make it ideal for a particular sort of learning study. (The dog, for example, has characteristics which make

it ideal for the study of classical salivary conditioning, and pigeons are considered ideal for operant conditioning work because they exhibit very high and quite stable response rates in the Skinner box.)

In other words, the preceding point of view (which will be called the uniformity point of view) is one which uses animals to study learning processes but does not study learning processes in animals. It is not comparative psychology in the sense in which biologists use the term comparative anatomy, because it tends to concentrate investigation on a very small number of animal forms and thus cannot be said to study the similarities and differences in behavior among species; it assumes that phyletic status is at best a minor variable in the study of learning. Interestingly enough, it also holds a disadvantage unique to its own purposes. From the uniformity point of view the species of greatest interest usually is the human being (cf. Dollard and Miller, 1950), yet by searching for an "ideal preparation" it has reduced the scope of anthropocentric-oriented research by placing emphasis on simple learning processes (the processes which can be observed in lower animals) and ignoring the more complex ones of man. For example, the number of studies on two-choice discrimination learning in the albino rat far exceeds the number of studies on human concept formation. It is unlikely that the proportion of studies in these two subareas of learning is consistent with their relative importance in understanding learned human behavior.

The Animal as an Analytical Tool for the Study of Learning

A second approach to the study of animal behavior is one which assumes that a direct comparison of learning processes among different animal forms can make unique and important contributions to our understanding of the phenomena of learning. *E*s using this approach expect to find some differences either in the manner or the extent to which animals may learn. These differences can be used to study the neurophysiological and biochemical bases of learning through the method of correlation with neural structure or process, or they can be used to provide a more detailed, more accurate, theoretical analysis of learning (theoretical in the sense of using intervening variables) by permitting us to formulate different explanatory constructs for different groups of animal forms. The precise manner in which the animal is used as an analytical tool varies among investigators. Thus, it is possible to define four subtypes of investigation within this general approach.

The Study of Quantitative Differences in Learning Ability (A Task-Oriented Approach). One way in which different species can be compared is to devise a learning task, simple or complex, and then measure the speed or degree of learning on that problem found in the animal forms under investigation. The emphasis of this approach is a quantitative one; that is, it assumes that all animals studied will learn the problem at hand but at different rates or to different asymptotic levels. After enough animal forms have been tested on such a problem, presumably a chart could be drawn showing a hierarchical relationship among animal species for learning. This chart could then be compared with phyletic status and some deductions made concerning the relationship between evolution and learning ability. In addition, investigators using this approach would hope that some understanding of "intelligence" could be gained by comparing the neurophysiological and biochemical characteristics of animal species showing different learning ability. For reasons that will be discussed in Chapter 17, this approach has yielded data which up to the present time are primarily descriptive.

The Study of Quantitative Differences in Learning Function (A Process-Oriented Approach). A second strategy of the comparative psychologist differs from the previous one in a rather critical way. Instead of being task-oriented, this approach seeks to detect species differences in learning processes. Thus, the dependent variable under investigation is not performance per se on a single preselected learning task, but instead the way in which performance varies as a function of the parameters of the learning task. For example, we know that performance in a learning situation varies as a function of the magnitude of the conditioned stimulus, the temporal relationship between the conditioned and unconditioned stimuli, the reinforcement schedule presented to S, and a host of other variables. Furthermore, for most of these variables a quantitative relationship can be established between each of these variables, as they are independently manipulated in the experimental situation, and some measured aspect of performance. The goal of the comparative psychologist using this second approach is the detection of species differences in these quantitative relationships. Results utilizing this approach will be discussed in Chapter 17, but it can be said in advance that little work has been done from this point of view. The immediate gain to the science of comparative psychology would seem to be mostly descriptive, because it is difficult to imagine how such differences fashion within any interpretative scheme of the comparative psychology of learning. From the point of view of a theoretical analysis of learning, establishing quantitative differences in learning function or process would at best amount to changing the fixed constant in a series of equations describing the relationship between independent and dependent variables.

The Study of Qualitative Differences in Learning Ability (A Task-Oriented Approach). A third strategy used by comparative-oriented investigators has been to search for a "breaking point" in the phyletic scale for the observation of a particular type of learning. Thus, a search has been made for the simplest animal form which will demonstrate any learning at all, and with higher forms a search has been made for the phyletic emergence of more complex sorts of learning. This approach remains task-oriented in the sense that the investigator predefines learning in terms of a specific set of experiental contingencies and then searches for the presence or absence of adaptable behavior by different animal forms. But although this approach is task-oriented, its aim is distinctly different from that of the approach previously discussed, for it seeks what Bitterman (1965) has called a "phylogenetic filter" which will permit a natural separation of the neurophysiological and biochemical conditions necessary and sufficient for the demonstration of a given type of learning. The notion of a phylogenetic filter is an interesting one, for it represents an alternative to the method of extirpation or the method of electrical stimulation in the analysis of brain function; that is, it is a "natural" way to manipulate structural components of the brain. It would seem to be particularly useful in the analysis of simple learning (for example, classical conditioning), because the phylogenetic filter in this instance would permit the detection of the simplest (least complicated) nervous system which is capable of demonstrating learning. Such a nervous system would seem to be an "ideal preparation" for studying the neurological and biochemical bases of learning. Because science has thrived by making generalizations from the analysis of simple phenomena, this would seem to be a good strategy —a good strategy, at least, for determining the minimal requirements for learning to develop. But caution must be exercised in generalizing to other animal forms on that basis alone. It is quite possible that higher forms (more complicated organisms), although they also demonstrate the ability to learn, utilize different mechanisms.

The Study of Qualitative Differences in Learning Function (A Process-Oriented Approach). A fourth way in which animals may be used as an analytical tool for the study of learning is one which attempts to detect instances within the phyletic scale where learning functions; that is, functions describing the influence of one or more independent variables upon learning vary not in degree but in kind. The goal of this approach is the comparison across classes of animals of explanations of learning and not comparisons of learning itself. If learning functions differ qualitatively among animal forms, then it would appear that either a neurophysiological or a theoretical (in terms of "learning constructs" such as habit strength or reactive inhibition) explanation of learning would not be "phyletically" valid, the uniformity hypothesis would have to be rejected, and the theoretical analysis of learning would become pluralistic. Although such a view is not widely held by psychologists today, it is not such an unrealistic one, because it is clear that species differences in neural structure alone (notwithstanding more subtle divergencies) are very wide indeed. Consider, for example, the central nervous systems of the common earthworm and the rhesus monkey. Such wide variation in nervous structure would seem to hint strongly that functional variations in learning could occur.

This approach, by seeking qualitative differences in learning function, can also be thought of as an example of Bitterman's method of phylogenetic filtration. The filtration in this case is not merely for the presence of learning but for the separation, in different animal forms, of the type of relationship between an independent variable, or set of independent variables, and the dependent variables used to assess learning.

The Animal as an Instrument for the Study of Species-Specific Patterns of Learned Behavior

Primarily through the work of the European ethologists (a group interested in animal behavior but whose formal training has been in zoology) we have come to recognize that many animal forms exhibit complex behavior patterns which are quite uncommon throughout the phyletic scale and in some cases are even unique to a given species. At one time these behavior patterns were considered to be instinctive, that is, purely a product of the genetic characteristics of the organism. However, after detailed study by the ethologists (recently with the help of a small group of American psychologists), it has become evident that at least a certain proportion of these complex behavior patterns depend partially on experience. This is not to deny the strong influence of phylogenetic and ontogenetic variables in the control of such behavior, but so long as an experience factor is involved in the development of such responses, they must be considered a proper part of the comparative psychology of learning. Although ethological work has developed within a quite strong theoretical framework (based primarily on evolutionary theory), its implications for the comparative psychology of learning would seem more restrictive because the discovery of "unique processes" argues against phyletic generalization. Although this may be the case, the contribution is not an unimportant one because, as we will see from Chapter 19, it sheds new light on the broad theoretical issues of learning. The fact that species-specific learned behavior exists has led some psychologists to explain it away by appealing to its characteristic of uniqueness. Because this "special" learned behavior is not generally found in the animal kingdom, and because psychologists are interested in establishing a general theory of learning, there has been some disposition to exclude these phenomena from the population of phenomena to be considered by the learning theorist. But to exclude the data on imprinting or on compass reactions in animals, for example, from theoretical consideration does not make them disappear, and the question remains whether the data of learn-

ing should determine the breadth of a learning theory or whether the learning theory should determine the breadth of the data to be considered.

Problems

Before we begin to consider the data of the comparative psychology of learning, it might be useful to point out more explicitly several overriding issues with which the data will deal. These issues stem largely from the fact that there are divergent viewpoints regarding the proper aims and goals of the study of animal behavior. The divergent viewpoints discussed in the previous section have led more or less directly to the elaboration of three basic issues. A brief discussion of these issues follows, but to a large extent their resolution will depend upon an analysis of the actual data of comparative psychology.

Problem 1: Is the Learning Process Uniform Throughout the Phyletic Scale? Clearly the problem of the uniformity of the learning process represents the point of disagreement between the uniformity approach, mentioned earlier, and the approach of other investigators of animal behavior. It is a very important question, for its answer may imply that (1) the construction of a unitary learning theory across species is inappropriate and should be abandoned, or (2) learning is not a proper subject for the comparative psychologist, who should return to the study of species differences in behaviors which do not involve an experience factor. Happily, this question seems to be one which can be answered empirically, and in the succeeding chapters we will look at some data which bear upon this issue.

Notice that if the answer to problem 1 is yes, then we must assume that structural differences in neural tissue, and biochemical variation as well, among animal forms are simply differences in "extent of process."

(That is, we must assume that learning processes are uniform throughout the phyletic scale and are merely additive, with more processes occurring in higher forms than in lower forms.) The alternative is to assume that processes (or the physiological substrate of learning) interact to produce new behavioral functions.

If the answer to problem 1 is no, then do we have in reality a psychology of learning which has been confounded by the utilization of data from different animal forms while at the same time being generalized to other untested and probably inappropriate animal forms? For example, modern textbooks on learning (e.g., Kimble, 1961) represent an attempted integration of the results of learning experiments which have been conducted on rats, pigeons, monkeys, and human beings. (Occasionally there is reference made to one of a few other common animals such as the cat.) Whether such an integration is proper remains in some doubt. But an even riskier assumption is that one can apply the principles of learning abstracted from experiments on mammals to the learned behavior of other animal classes (for example, Pisces, Amphibia, or Aves).

But the problem here is not so much one to be attributed to textbook writers as to the researchers in the field of learning. Bitterman (1960) has estimated that about 90 per cent of the studies on animal learning have been done with the rat as S. Thus, the grounds for generalization of learning principles to all animal forms is rather shaky at best.

Problem 2: Can There Be a Comparative Psychology of Learning? A persistent and perplexing methodological problem which has concerned many investigators and has been cause for the development of a very pessimistic view of the comparative psychology of learning among others is portrayed by the following example. If an E wishes to assess differences in learning between an experimental group and a control group of rats, the usual procedure is to attempt to equate (or at least counterbalance) the conditions under which the two groups will be tested. In testing the effects of a drug on learned behavior, for example, E would select his experimental and control groups from the same population of Ss, often balancing for sex and litter affiliation. He would rear the animals under identical conditions, and he would test them with the same set of procedures. Thus, the learning situation for the two groups would be identical, as would be the conditions for reinforcement, the intensity of the CS, the temporal relationship between the CS and US, and so on. By presenting the same set of conditions to Ss in both groups and by making the assumption that the Ss in both groups will react to those conditions in a similar fashion because of their similar genetic and experiential backgrounds, he can assess the effects of the drug on learned behavior in a reasonably direct and forthright fashion. But the E who attempts to assess differences in learned behavior between two groups of Ss which differ in *phyletic* status does not have the right to make the same assumptions concerning the reactions of his two groups to the experimental procedures. Suppose he were comparing the learned behavior of a rat and a bird. Because the maternal behavior of the animals of the class Mammalia and class Aves differs markedly, the early experience of the Ss in his two groups cannot be said to be equivalent. Furthermore, the effects of rearing Ss in a controlled environment such as the laboratory may be quite different for different species. This is enough of a problem, but consider the difficulties which would be encountered in attempting to provide equivalent testing conditions for animals as divergent as these two:

1. In experiments on learning it is usually necessary to provide a set of conditions which will produce a motivational state in the animal. How do you make a bird equally hungry as a rat which has been deprived for 24 hrs.? And even if

you could accomplish this, what amount of food would be equivalent to 1 gram of standard rat diet?

2. What stimulus could you select to be used as the CS in your learning experiment which would be equivalent for two species with such different perceptual capacities?

3. How would you handle the problem of the differential response repertoire of the two animal forms?

Clearly it would be impossible to establish the same CR in birds and rats, and even if you could, it would not be possible to assume that the CR was equally prepotent in the two species studied.

One solution to this problem, and it appears to be a good one, has been suggested by Bitterman (1960). Bitterman states that, in the case where animals of different species are to be compared, "while the prospects for control by equation are slim indeed, there is available a perfectly suitable alternative, which we may speak of as *control by systematic variation.*" Control by systematic variation is, in essence, a procedure where the limits of applicability of the learning phenomenon under investigation are assessed along those parameters of the test situation which are known to be unequatable across species. Thus, for example, if E feels that he cannot equate motivation level across phyletic status, he can observe the learning process under widely varying levels of motivation and observe to what extent learning is changed. If learning does not vary in a qualitative way as motivation varies, it would seem fair to conclude that observed species differences in process are not the result of capriciously selected levels of motivation. Similar reasoning could be applied to the other critical but unequatable parameters of the test situation in which two species are compared. Control by systematic variation, in addition, would seem to be a procedure appropriate for producing valid measurements of learning differences across species when other comparative psychological approaches are used. For example, quantitative differences in

learning ability become meaningful only when the limits of the test parameters for a given learning problem have been assessed. If E were interested in comparing the rate of aquisition of the conditioned response in varying animal forms, he could only properly do so if he measured rate of acquisition of a widely varying sample of conditioned responses to a set of quite diverse conditioned stimuli and unconditioned stimuli and made these measurements under different motivational conditions, different intertrial and interstimulus intervals, and so on. Control by systematic variation obviates problem 2, but only at great expense, because it requires that the program of research of the comparative psychologist be expanded well beyond the broadly defined area previously mentioned to include the manipulation, in every experiment undertaken, of a set of unequatable parameters that are not of primary interest to him but that must be manipulated purely in the interest of interpretation. This enormous task has rarely been completed in comparative psychology, even for purposes of the interpretation of a single behavioral phenomenon. Thus, most of the results in the chapters which follow, whether they have yielded species differences or not, must be interpreted with caution. They can only be regarded as suggestive, and a more confident interpretation must await future, and hopefully more systematically varied, work.

Problem 3: What Are the Relative Merits of the Ethological and Experimental Approaches to the Analysis of Learned Behavior Among Species? Previous reference has been made to the ethological approach as one which studies species-specific behavior patterns in great detail. This approach can contribute to a general understanding of the comparative psychology of learning by detecting learning processes which may be highly unusual or unique. These processes may have escaped the notice of the American comparative psychologist whose investigations typically are extensions of the experimental method as it is applied in psychology as a whole. Such methods involve, among other things, the notion of hypothesis testing and direct manipulation of the independent variables to be investigated in an experiment. But to vary purposely independent variables in a systematic way implies that E already knows what variables are important. Because the ethologist observes the behavior of organisms in their natural habitat, and because he makes relatively little attempt to control that environment, he is more likely to discover instances of the operation of new variables, perhaps ones that are highly specific to a given species, on learned behavior. In general, the goals of the two groups, although approached from entirely different theoretical perspectives, seem to be compatible, because both recognize the need for comparing the behavior of different animal forms and both attempt to make interspecies generalizations. In terms of methods, however, they are at once both complementary and incompatible. The divergent methods which each used do in fact broaden the range of data within the general field of comparative psychology of learning, but they complicate attempts at theoretical interpretation.

The remaining chapters of this section will present a description of some representative research problems undertaken within each of the five major strategies discussed in the foregoing pages. The coverage will be instructive (hopefully) but not exhaustive.

Quantitative Differences in Learning Ability and Function

Learning Ability

Classical Conditioning

Early Research. Razran (1933) summarized the rate of classical conditioning among various animals according to Table 17-1.

We can now add considerably more data to Razran's table on the basis of more recent studies. Table 17-2 depicts the performance of a number of animals for which rate of classical conditioning has been assessed since 1933. Only those cases where performance across trials were reported are presented in Table 17-2, so that reasonably direct interspecies comparisons could be made.

The construction of such tables as these can be done, at best, only by overlooking many procedural differences between each study, differences which amount to unsystematic parametric control for purposes of comparative assessment. For example, *E*s have not used the same intertrial intervals or the same interstimulus (CS-US) intervals in work with different animals; the latter are specified in Tables 17-1 and 17-2 in order to show the range of values that have been employed. In addition, *E*s have not trained their *S*s to the same learning cri-

terion, nor have they always presented their data in a way suitable for comparison with other studies.

But even if we ignore these difficulties, which at least in theory are correctable through greater attention to systematization of procedure in future work, the tables show some more basic problems with this approach to comparative psychology.

1. Intraspecies variability is, in some cases, so large that interspecies comparisons (especially with small sample sizes) are not as meaningful as we should like. Crustaceans (Mikhailoffa, 1920) varied from 34 to 1,112 trials in making an initial withdrawal CR. For horseshoe crabs (Smith and Baker, 1960), the number of trials required to meet an 85 per cent learning criterion ranged from 80 to 480 trials among only eight experimental *S*s. And albino rats are absurdly inconsistent in the development of classically conditioned leg flexion responses. Among twenty *S*s tested under identical conditions, King (1968) has found instances where as many as nineteen CRs occurred within the first thirty trials, whereas other animals produced no greater than thirty-six conditioned responses over 800 trials. (That is, the latter *S*s must be considered, essentially, to be conditioning "failures.")

2. Ordering the data of Table 17-2 is complicated because of an apparent difference in the difficulty of forming autonomic CRs and skeletal CRs: vasomotor responses are formed more rapidly in rabbits (Fromer, 1963) and in humans (Shmavonian, 1959) than skeletal CRs such as the eyelid reflex. In fact, Newton and Gantt (1966) have reported statistically significant cardiac conditioning in dogs after only one trial. And Kappauf and Schlosberg (1937) observed that when respiratory responses and leg flexions were conditioned simultaneously in rats, respiratory CRs developed much more quickly.

3. There are certain instances where the very nature of the CR is in question. Studies on cardiac conditioning in the rat have produced both reliable accelerative (Black and Black, 1967) and reliable decelerative (Holdstock and Schwartzbaum, 1965) CRs. Until the reasons for these discrepant results are understood, interspecies comparisons are premature.

4. Another problem regarding the question of conditioned response definition involves an apparent difference in the conditionability of "discrete" and "diffuse" skeletal movements. Whereas fish (cf. Noble et al., 1959) learn a diffuse CR in sixty to eighty trials, rabbits (cf. Schneiderman and Gormezano, 1964) require four to nine times as long to learn a CR involving extension of the nictitating membrane (even under optimal interstimulus intervals of 0.25 to 0.50 sec.). Although it is possible that other unequated variables can account for a part of these discrepancies, it stretches the imagination to attempt to account for the greater efficacy of CR acquisition in fish without appealing to the nature of the response. This point is supported further by the observations of numerous investigators that prior to the emergence of a specific CR (for example, leg flexion) in classical conditioning, Ss demonstrate widespread bodily reaction to the CS (cf. Schlosberg, 1937). Thus, a diffuse CR comparable to that reported in Table 17-2 for fish indeed occurs in mammals as well, but typically it has been ignored in favor of the measurement of a more precise (and more easily defined) CR. This biases the results in our table against those animal forms in which E has *chosen* to measure specific CRs.

5. Even conditioned responses which would appear to be sufficiently similar to be acceptable for species comparisons are, on closer examination, open to question. In the rabbit, for example, the conditioned eyelid response develops to the 70 per cent level after 656 trials (Schneiderman et al., 1962), but the conditioned extension of the nictitating membrane of the eye develops (under virtually identical test conditions) to the same level after only 350 trials (Schneiderman and Gormezano, 1964). Moreover, it appears that it is not safe to assume that the "conditioned eyelid response" is in fact the same thing in different mammals. Figure 17-1 shows records of eyelid conditioning in the dog, monkey, and man. Kimble (1961) has suggested that these CRs are qualitatively different from one another and that the shorter latencies for dog and monkey imply that the responses are voluntary.

These considerations make it extremely difficult to support the contention that the quest for quantitative differences in the rate of acquisition of classically conditioned responses will permit a systematic ordering of species in terms of learning ability.

Trial-and-Error Learning

If the measurement of the rate of learning of a simple CR is unacceptable for comparison of learning ability among different animals, then perhaps a more indirect method of assessing behavior patterns during learning would produce better results. Hamilton (1911, 1916) reasoned that if animals were given a more complicated problem in which to seek reinforcement, and if the problem were partially insolvable, we might be able to detect species differences based on the nature of adjustment made by the Ss to the situation. Thus, he trained animals to select one of four doors arranged in a semicircle opposite the starting point of a discrimination apparatus.

Table **17-1** A Comparison of Rate of Acquisition Among Animals from the Results of Some Early Classical Conditioning Studies (Adapted from Razran, 1933)

Name of Organism	E	N	CS	CS-US Interval (sec.)	UCS	CR	Trials to First CR	
							Minimum	Maximum
Crustaceans (Paguri striati)	Mikhailoff (1920a)	14	Light	Simultaneous	Tactile	Withdrawal	34	1,112
Cephalopods (Eledone moschatoe)	Mikhailoff (1920b; 1921)	6	Light	Simultaneous	Tactile	Change in body color	175	912
Urochords (Ascidiacea)	Kreps (1925)	3	Light	5–10	Tactile	Body contraction	11	15
Fish	Froloff (1925)	Unspecified	Light and sound	5–10	Electric shock	Dorsal-fin response	5	30
Pigeons	Popov (1922; 1930)	13	Various	1–14	Electric shock	Leg flexion	30	90 (Three conditioning failures)
Guinea Pigs	Upton (1929)	4	Sound	6 respiration cycles	Electric shock	Respiration change	238	263
Cats	Wever (1930)	3	Sound	5	Electric shock	Respiration change	19	128
Sheep	Liddell and Anderson (1928)	6	Sound	2–10	Electric shock	Leg flexion	3	7

Table 17-2   A Comparison of Rate of Acquisition Among Animals from the Results of Some More Recent Classical Conditioning Studies

Name of Organism	E	N	CS	CS-US Interval (sec.)	UCS	CR	Level of Learning*	Group Mean Trials to Level of Learning
Crab (Limulus polyphemus)	Smith and Baker (1960)	8	Light	10	Electric shock	Tail-spine movement	85%	220 Range: 80–480
Fish (Mollienisia sp.)	Noble, Gruender, and Meyer (1959)	15	Incr. in illumination	2.0	Electric shock	Diffuse movement	80% / 90%	20 / 60
Fish (Tilapia macrocephala)	Gonzales, Eskin, and Bitterman (AJP, 1963)	15	Light	4.5	Electric shock	Diffuse movement	Asymptotic magnitude increase	80
Fish (Notemigonus crysolecus)	Scarborough and Addison (1962)	14	Light	4.0	Electric shock	Diffuse movement	90%	80
Fish (Betta splendens)	Adler and Hogan (1963)	5	Weak shock	Simultaneous	S's mirror image	Gill membrane extension	Two successive CRs	86 Range: 50–130
Frog (Rana p. pipiens)	Goldstein, Sepinwall, and Spies (1964)	26	Tactile (to nostril)	2.0 (trace)	Tactile (no cornea)	Eyelid response	60%	75
Rat (newborn)	Caldwell and Werboff (1962)	8	Vibratactile	1.2 or 2.4	Electric shock	Leg flexion	30%	30
Rat (adult)	Kappauf and Schlosberg (1937)	2	Buzzer	0.67	Electric shock	Leg flexion	45%	135
Rat	Holdstock and Schwartzbaum	4	Clicks	5.0	Electric shock	Heart rate (decrease)	−30 bpm	72
Rat	Black and Black (1967)	20	White noise	5.0	Electric shock	Heart rate (increase)	+30 bpm	10
Rabbit	Schneiderman, Fuentes, and Gormezano (1962)	12	Tone	0.5	Puff of nitrogen	Eyelid response	70%	656
Rabbit	Deaux and Gormezano (1963)	6	Tone	0.5	Puff of nitrogen	Eyeball retraction	85%	560
Rabbit	Gormezano et al. (1962)	12	Tone	0.5	Puff of nitrogen	Nictitating membrane	90%	420

Rabbit	Schneiderman and Gormezano (1964)	12	Tone	0.5	Puff of nitrogen	Nicitating membrane	90%	560
Rabbit	Schneiderman and Gormezano (1964)	12	Tone	0.25	Puff of nitrogen	Nicitating membrane	70%	350
Rabbit	Prokasy and Papsdorff (1965)	15	Tone	0.40	Puff of nitrogen	Nicitating membrane	90%	280
Rabbit	Prokasy and Papsdorff (1965)	15	Tone	2.50	Puff of nitrogen	Nicitating membrane	90%	568
							60%	142
							60%	568
Rabbit	Fromer (1963; Expt. 1)	6	Tone vs. light (Diff. CR)	12.0	Electric shock	Vasomotor response	80% (Spaced trials)	32
Dog	Church and Black (1958)	28	Tone	5.0 or 20.0	Electric shock	Heart rate (increase)	+30 bpm	6
Pig	Noble and Adams (1963; Expt. 1)	10	Increase in illumination	2.0	Electric shock	Diffuse movement	50%	15
Pig	Liddell, James, and Anderson (1934)	Un-specified	Tone	2.0, 5.0, or 10.0	Electric shock	Leg flexion	Four successive CRs	20
Sheep	Liddell, James, and Anderson (1934)	Un-specified	Tone	10.0	Electric shock	Leg flexion	Four successive CRs	36
Monkey	Noble and Harding (1963)	13	Increase in illumination	2.0	Electric shock	Diffuse movement	50%	30
Man	McAllister (1953)	45	Tone	0.45	Puff of air	Eyelid response	40%	18
Man	Kimble, Mann, and Dufort (1955)	18	Light	0.50	Puff of air	Eyelid response	90%	60
Man	Moore and Gormezano (1961)	24	Illumination change	0.50 or 3.0	Puff of nitrogen	Eyelid response	90%	30
Man	Shmavonian (1959)	13	Tone	10.0	Electric shock	Vasomotor response	Asymptotic amplitude change	6

* "Level of learning" is the mean percentage CRs displayed by the total sample of Ss under the conditions described, unless otherwise noted.

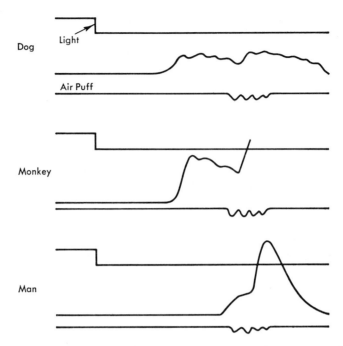

Figure 17-1. Tracings of records obtained from dog, monkey, and man in an eyelid-conditioning situation. The original records were photographs obtained with Dodge's photochronographic procedure. In such records, eyelid closures appear as upward excursions of the response line. Note especially that the amount by which the airpuff is anticipated is much less for man than for the dog or monkey. This suggests that the responses in the upper records are voluntary. (Reprinted with permission from Kimble, G. A. *Hilgard and Marquis' conditioning and learning*. New York: Appleton-Century-Crofts, 1961.)

The size of the apparatus and the reinforcement were adjusted to the species being studied, but the simplicity of the task permitted all animals to be tested on the same "problem." The problem for S was to select the single door on each trial which permitted access to the reinforcement. The problem was "insolvable" to the extent that no door was consistently reinforced (that is, each door was reinforced on 25 per cent of the trials). However, the problem was "partially solvable" in the sense that the same door was never correct on two consecutive trials. Thus, Ss could learn to avoid the door which was correct on the immediately preceding trial; furthermore, Ss could learn to eliminate perseverative responses to a single door.

Hamilton selected out those trials on which three or more responses were made by each S and then assigned the S's response for each trial to one of five categories:

Type A: All three possible doors are tried, once each; no response is made to the "impossible" door (that is, the door correct on the preceding trial).

Type B: All four doors are tried, once each in an irregular order.

Type C: All four doors are tried in a regular sequence, from one side to the other, but without any repeated responses.

Type D: The same door is tried more than once but the two attempts are not successive.

Type E: All other response sequences involving three or more responses (for

Table **17-3**   Distribution of Classified Reaction Sequences by
Different Animals in the Hamilton Multiple-Choice Apparatus

Ss	N	Avg. Age	Percentage Reaction Sequences					Combined A + B + C	Combined D + E
			A	B	C	D	E		
Humans	8	Fourteen yrs.	76	20	2	2	0	98	2
Humans	17	Seven yrs.	33	3	32	24	8	68	32
Human Infant	1	Twenty-six mo.	16	5	19	26	34	40	60
Nonhuman Primates	5	Adult	22	20	20	25	13	62	38
Nonhuman Primates	2	1.5 yrs.	15	23	31	18	13	69	31
Dogs	2	Adult	12	22	0	34	32	34	66
Dogs	8	Fifty-three days	14	10	14	23	39	38	62
Cats	3	Adult	9	20	4	27	40	33	67
Cats (Warren, 1959)	5	150 days	4	16	11	15	54	31	69
Cats	2	Sixty-three days	7	11	0	14	68	18	82
Rats	17	Adult	12	8	8	17	55	28	72
Gophers	6	Adult	7	2	2	8	81	11	89
Chickens (Warren, 1959)	7	Twenty-eight days	7	10	15	12	56	32	68

(Adapted from Hamilton, 1911 and 1916.)

example, S makes two consecutive responses to the same door, or alternates repetitively between two incorrect doors, and so on).

Table 17-3 shows a summary of Hamilton's data, excluding a number of species where only a single S was tested. Some additional data by Warren (1959) also are presented.

Hamilton did not provide us with a statistical analysis of his data, but it does seem that we can reach a few conclusions from the information provided in the table. (1) All species tested perform at a level above chance (that is, they showed adaptive behavior). If Ss had selected the doors in a totally random fashion, we would expect

the combined A, B, and C response sequences to yield 9.4 per cent of the total. No animals performed, as a group, at this level, and only gophers approached it. (2) With the exception of the primates, there is remarkably little difference in the percentage of Type A reactions among animals as diverse as chickens and dogs. Thus, it seems that this measure is an insensitive one for a very large range of the animal kingdom. Moreover, the degree of response perseveration (measured by Reaction Types D and E) is reasonably consistent among nonprimate species. Only gophers seem to show an atypically large amount of perseveration.

The analysis of error sequences in multiple-choice learning would appear to escape a number of objections usually resurrected when learning is compared across species (for example, objections having to do with the relationship between species characteristics and problem difficulty). However, the general conclusion forced upon us by Hamilton's and Warren's data is that the very abstract nature of the task makes it unsuitable as a test of learning ability among lower mammalian and inframammalian forms. In addition, the task does not discriminate well in regard to perseverative errors, primarily because of a "ceiling effect" related to the complexity of the problem. The test may make useful discriminations among higher mammals and, within species, among developmental stages (Harlow, 1959), however. It is unfortunate that we have so little data on which to judge its adequacy in this regard (but see Warren and Warren, 1966, for an instance of the test's inability to discriminate among developmental stages in cats).

Learning Sets

Both rate of learning of a simple CR and error patterns on a more complicated multiple-choice task have been found to be less than completely suitable as indexes for the comparative study of learning ability. A third candidate has been offered by Harlow (1959), who has suggested that a distinction can be made between intraproblem learning (for example, acquisition of a discrimination habit) and interproblem learning (for example, improvement of learning across a number of discrimination problems by means of a concept or a "strategy"). The term *learning set* has been applied by Harlow to this type of interproblem improvement, and he has suggested that a learning set is not merely an instance of transfer of training. In the typical learning set paradigm, S is given successive discrimination problems involving pairs of stimulus objects differing in multiple characteristics. In each pair, one object is consistently rewarded while the second is consistently nonrewarded. A single discrimination problem may be presented for a fixed number of trials or until S has met a predetermined learning criterion. In either case, a succession of problems is presented and performance is compared across problems. Figure 17-2 shows the performance of monkeys on 450 such discrimination problems of eight trials each. Notice that Ss perform consistently at chance on trial 1, even after 450 problems, obviating the possibility that improvement is based on stimulus generalization between successive problems. For the first fifty problems the monkeys show *gradual* improvement from trials 1 to 8, but only reach a final performance level of about 63 per cent correct responses on trial 8. However, after 400 discrimination problems improvement over trials is much more rapid, and the performance level on trial 8 is above 90 per cent. This improvement, from the first fifty to the last fifty discrimination problems, is the evidence for learning set. Animals are said to be "learning how to learn."

It has been suggested that the rate of learning set formation may be a suitable measure for a quantitative differentiation of learning ability or intelligence among animal forms (especially among higher mammals), on the grounds that interproblem improvement of learning performance is not evidently tied closely to the sensory, motivational, or motor characteristics of the organism in the way in which discrimination learning necessarily is. It is as though interproblem learning "transcends" the problems themselves. Although this may be a possibility, there is certainly at least one sense in which discrimination learning sets (such as that displayed in Figure 17-2) are not independent of sensory capacity, and that is in the phyletic sense: the species being tested must have a sufficiently sophisticated sensory apparatus to permit the practical presentation of a large number of discrimination problems which are sufficiently different to prevent stimulus generalization. As a consequence, the lowest

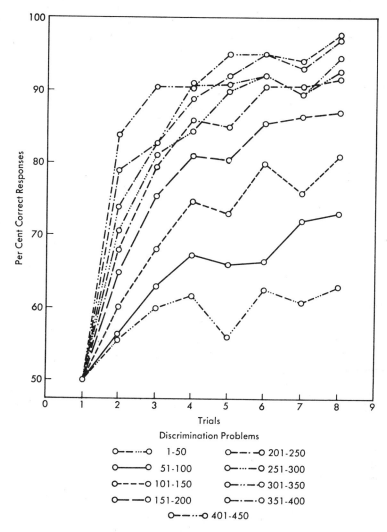

Figure 17-2. Learning set curves with trials as the parameter. (Reprinted with permission from Harlow, H. F. Learning set and error factor theory. In S. Koch (Ed.), *Psychology: A study of science.* Vol. 2. New York: McGraw-Hill, 1959.)

forms in which discrimination learning sets have been demonstrated are rats (Tyrrell, 1963), raccoons (Shell and Riopelle, 1957), weasels (Doty, Jones and Doty, 1967), and pigeons (Zeigler, 1961), all of which seem to show a capacity for learning set information equal to, or better than, domestic cats (Warren and Baron, 1956). It is not likely that animals below the classes Mammalia and Aves would be suitable *S*s for discrim-

ination learning set experimentation; consequently, the list of species comparisons necessarily will remain truncated at the low end of the phyletic scale.

Warren (1965b) has described the learning set performance of certain species of primates, carnivores, and rodents over six-trial discrimination problems according to Figure 17-3. (Data on tree shrews by Leonard et al, 1966, have been added.) The

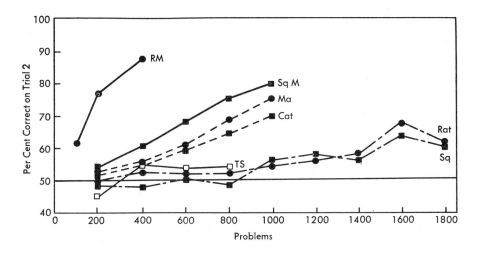

Figure 17-3. Discrimination learning set formation by various mammals: Rhesus monkeys, squirrel monkeys, marmosets, cats, tree shrews, rats, and squirrels. (Adapted with permission from Warren, J. M. Primate learning in comparative perspective. In A. M. Schrier, H. F. Harlow, & F. Stollnitz (Eds.), *Behavior of nonhuman primates*. Vol. 1. New York: Academic Press, 1965b.)

measure of the learning set was performance *trial 2 only* of each problem. All the species presented showed some evidence of learning set formation, although the relative performance of cats and rats was not equivalent, as described previously (probably because of the shorter number of trials per problem). The capacity for learning set formation progresses in an orderly fashion consistent with phyletic status.

The data of Figure 17-3 are impressive, but we must not be misled into thinking they are necessarily a uniquely useful tool to assess learning ability. Although there are instances where animals can show discrimination learning but are incapable of forming sets (for example, infant rhesus monkeys; Harlow, 1959, p. 505), it is nevertheless true that the development of a learning set depends on the performance of *S*s on each individual discrimination problem. Two lines of evidence support this contention. (1) Hayes, Thompson, and Hayes (1953) found that a chimpanzee trained at a fixed rate of two trials per problem remained at a chance level of perform-

ance for 300 problems but improved rapidly when shifted to ten trials per problem, where *intra*problem learning could occur. Thus, no interproblem learning occurred without intraproblem learning. Levine, Levinson, and Harlow (1959) have shown that learning set development is similar, for a fixed total number of trials, with problems ranging from three to twelve trials per problem. This suggests that for experimentally naive adult primates, with stimuli varying in multiple characteristics, three-trial problems are sufficient for both intra- and interproblem learning. (2) The discriminability of the stimuli used in learning set problems has been found to play an important role. Kay and Oldfield-Box (1965), as well as Tyrrell (1963), have shown that more discriminable stereometric (three-dimensional) stimuli may permit faster development of learning sets in rats than planometric stimuli. Also, Shepp and Schrier (in Shepp, 1967) have noted that learning set formation is completely absent in monkeys given 120 ten-trial discrimination problems with only a single stimulus dimension relevant for solution of the problem (rather than multiple dimensions, as employed by Levine, Levinson and Harlow); the same monkeys failed to show intraproblem improvement as well. Thus, although many other variables (Miles, 1965) contribute to the formation of learning sets, it remains possible that when "equivalent" learning set experiments are conducted on different species, the dominant variable influencing rate of acquisition of the learning set is not phyletic status per se but the S's discrimination capacities for the particular stimuli employed. Whereas an orderly progression of simple discrimination learning ability, "in the abstract," is not found to occur as a function of phyletic status (Warren, 1965a), both intra- and interspecies variations in learning indeed are found in relation to the particular cues relevant to solution of a particular discrimination task. Because discrimination learning sets necessarily restrict the appropriate or practical cue dimensions to a very few which can possibly permit extensive manipulation over problems, it is not unreasonable to suppose that this operates as a bias among the species tested—especially in view of the fact that the cue dimensions invariably selected have been, anthropocentrically, visual ones. For example, comparisons between monkeys and cats are rendered suspect, because color vision and stereopsis are not equivalent in these two animals. Similarly, species differences in regard to other visual cues are not difficult to imagine.

Learning Function

Efficiency of learning varies as a function of a host of independent variables, such as the properties of the CS and US, the intertrial interval, and so on. Thus, it is possible to plot in graphic form a function relating the quantitative values of any critical independent variable to some dependent variable which reflects efficiency of learning. For

example, Figure 17-4 presents the relationship between CS-US interval and the degree of classical conditioning of the finger withdrawal response in human Ss. It is apparent that an interval of 0.5 sec. produces maximal conditioning. Simultaneous or backward CS-US arrangements produce little, if any, conditioning.

Now, from the previous discussion in this chapter it would appear that a quantification of species differences in learning ability is made virtually meaningless because learning depends on an adventitious interaction of many variables, and the exact manner of each of these variables is not known across species. This brings us to the point of departure of the present approach. Let us suppose that in fact the operation of a single independent variable on learning is not universal but varies as a function of species. If this is so, then it should be possible, through experimentation, to determine a family of functions relating the variable in question to learning for different animals. In this way, we will have supplied phyletic information regarding the degree of quantitative precision of any proposed set of mathematical learning principles (cf. Hull, 1943), and as well we will have perhaps improved the possibility of making truly meaningful interspecies comparisons of learning ability. We could then compare animals' learning under the most advantageous conditions for each species, and so approach, for each, their true learning "capacities." Thus, in the study of interspecies learning ability, no attempt would be made to equate learning tasks, which would be meaningless in a functional sense anyway, but rather the task would presumably incorporate conditions for optimal learning.

Although this approach could provide some important data for the comparative study of learning, there has been little effort directed toward its goals. One exception is the attempt to determine the optimal CS-US interval for classical conditioning in different species. From Figure 17-4 it is apparent

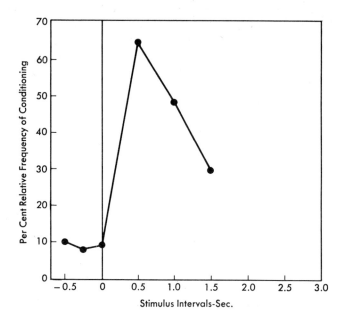

Figure 17-4.   Average frequency of CRs as a function of CS-US interval. (Adapted with permission from Spooner, A., & Kellogg, W. N. The backward-conditioning curve. *Amer. J. Psychol.*, 1947, **60**, 321–334.)

that the optimal CS-US interval for human *S*s is around 0.5 sec. This is true for short-latency responses, such as the eyeblink and finger withdrawal, but longer latency responses, such as GSR or pupillary dilation, require somewhat longer CS-US intervals (up to 3 sec.) for optimal learning (Jones, 1962). This fact shows us, immediately, that we cannot expect the optimal CS–US interval to vary in an orderly fashion phylogenetically, because results for any species will depend upon the *response* chosen for conditioning as well as the genetic characteristics of the organism. Nevertheless, it is possible to present the data of Table 17-4 with the admonition that the reader should pay very close attention to the particular stimuli and responses studied in each animal.

The table is brief to the point of frustration, but it is a beginning. Of course, it also represents only one of many variables which affect the rate of conditioning, and it is to be hoped that parametric analysis

will come to the field of comparative psychology; without it, we are doomed to imprecision and overgeneralization.

Even within Table 17-4 there are certain difficulties of which we must be aware:

1. The optimum CS-US interval may increase as a function of the number of training trials which *E* selects. Jones (1962) has hypothesized that early in training the efficiency of performance is affected chiefly by the temporal contiguity of CS and UR; later in training the contiguity of CR and US is most critical. Noble and Adams (1963), Boneau (1958), and Jones (1961) have obtained data which confirm this prediction.

2. There is some evidence that CS-US interval and distribution of practice interact in the determination of probability of CR, at least in some species of fish (Klinman and Bitterman, 1963).

3. It is unclear whether the *test* of the effects of various CS-US intervals should be made by (a) simply determining the

Table **17-4**   Optimal CS-US Interval in Various Animals and with Various CRs

Es	Animal	CS	US	CR	Optimal CS-US Interval (sec.)
Noble, Gruender, and Meyer (1959)	Fish	Light	Shock	Diffuse body movements	2.00
Caldwell and Werboff (1962)	Rat (newborn)	Vibro-tactile	Shock	Foreleg flexion	0.60–2.40
Kappauf and Schlosberg (1937)	Rat	Tone	Shock	Respiratory change	0.67–1
Black and Black (1957)	Rat	White noise	Shock	Heart-rate increase	5
Schneiderman and Gormezano (1964)	Rabbit	Tone	Puff of nitrogen	Nictitating membrane	0.25
Prokasy and Papsdorf (1965)	Rabbit	Tone	Puff of nitrogen	Nictitating membrane	0.40
Black, Carlson, and Solomon (1962)	Dog	Tone	Shock	Heart-rate increase	5–10
Noble and Adams (1963)	Pig	Light	Shock	Diffuse body movements	2 (Trials 1–15) 8 or greater (Trials 16–30)
Noble and Harding (1963)	Monkey (Rhesus)	Light	Shock	Diffuse body movements	2
Pennypacker and Cook (1967)	Monkey (Squirrel)	Tone	Air puff	Eyeblink	4 or greater
Spooner and Kellogg (1947)	Human	Tone	Shock	Finger withdrawal	0.50
McAllister (1953)	Human	Tone	Air puff	Eyeblink	0.45
Gerall and Woodward (1958)	Human	Tone	Shock	Pupil dilation	1.50

frequency of occurrence of a CR within each CS-US training trial, or (b) presenting Ss with CS-only test trials which are equal in length regardless of the CS-US interval under which conditioning is being carried out. Bitterman (1964) has argued in favor of the second procedure, but it is at once clear that although this equates for "response opportunity" on critical test trials, it does so in a biased fashion: the CS-only test period usually employed is one which is slightly longer than the largest CS-US interval under study, thus permitting the data to be confounded by false or sham CRs (that is, CRs which normally would be considered intertrial responses). Moreover, such a procedure tends to favor long-latency CRs over short-latency CRs, and it favors CRs to those CSs for which CS-onset is not a very distinctive cue. On the other hand, procedure (a) has the simplicity of determining the effectiveness of various CS-US intervals for the observance of an overt CR. It is less theoretical and ignores the operation of a number of potential interacting variables, but it does describe, for comparative purposes, the conditions under which learning is most efficiently demonstrated during ordinary acquisition trials.

Qualitative Differences in Learning Ability and Function

Learning Ability

Classical Conditioning

From Chapter 17 it is clear that all verte-brates can acquire a classically conditioned response, and there is some evidence that crustaceans and cephalopods also are con-ditionable. A great deal of interest has developed recently as to the "breaking point" in the phyletic scale regarding the observation of this presumably "simple" form of learning. The research has been concentrated almost exclusively on the relatively simpler metazoa, from the phyla Annelida and Platyhelminthes. There re-mains some distant possibility that even simpler organisms can acquire classical CRs, but to this date we have no scienti-fically acceptable evidence in support of such a contention.

Annelida. Ratner and Miller (1959a) have observed classically conditioned withdrawal responses in the earthworm, *Lumbricus terrestris*. The Ss were placed in a plastic tube, and after a 20-min. dark adaptation period an experimental group received 100 CS (vibration)–US (light) paired presenta-

tions. Control groups received an equal number of trials containing (1) CS only (Group V), (2) US only for ten consecutive trials and CS only for five subsequent trials (Group L), or (3) neither CS nor US (Group R). The experimental group then received thirty additional extinction trials on which the US was omitted. Ratner and Miller found that Ss which experienced CS-US pairings showed an increase in the probability of response to the CS during acquisition training and a diminution of responding during the thirty extinction trials. Control groups made some responses to the CS but at frequencies much lower than the experimental group and with prob-abilities that decreased over the 100 train-ing trials.

Unfortunately, Ratner and Miller did not include the most appropriate control procedure for classical conditioning, namely a procedure where Ss would be given 100 random (noncontingent) presentations of both CS and US (Rescorla, 1967). Moreover true conditioning implies that the CR is made specifically to the CS and not to other, dissimilar, stimuli. Again, we have no information pertaining to this from the Ratner and Miller study.

Subsequent work (Peeke, Herz, and Wyers, 1967) has included these control procedures. In addition, there is some indirect evidence in support of a learning interpretation of the Ratner and Miller data. In a second study, Ratner and Miller (1959b) have shown that responses to the CS are more frequent when the conditioning trials are spaced (90 sec. ITI) than when they are massed (10 sec. ITI). Longer ITIs produce more frequent responses to the US only but not the CS only (Ratner and Miller, 1959b; Ratner and Stein, 1965), supporting the proposition that the Ss are not merely demonstrating sensitization during spaced-trial CS-US presentations. Removal of the supra- and subpharyngeal ganglia abolished differential CRs under spaced conditions but not under massed conditions (Ratner, 1962; Ratner and Miller, 1959b), suggesting that massed-trial CRs may be partly or wholly the result of sensitization or some other pseudoconditioning phenomenon, whereas spaced-trial CRs, because they are susceptible to destruction by surgical insult to the S's nervous system, more likely are an indication of learning. This interpretation is supported by the observation that following a 20-min. rest period after the eightieth conditioning trial, spaced-practice Ss showed about 90 per cent retention of CRs whereas massed-practice Ss (normals or surgically treated) fell to a performance level equivalent to nonconditioned control groups (that is, showed no retention of the putative CR at all).

Wyers, Peeke, and Herz (1964) tested the effect of partial reinforcement on acquisition and extinction of a classically conditioned CR. Figure 18-1 presents the results which they obtained for groups of Ss given 100 per cent reinforcement (Group C), 50 per cent reinforcement (Group P), or control presentations of CS only (Group V) or US only (Group 2). Reinforcement schedule did not affect the frequency of CRs during acquisition, but Ss receiving partial (50 per cent) reinforcement responded

more vigorously during extinction. It is unclear, however, whether this phenomenon represents an instance of the Partial Reinforcement Effect (PRE) observed in higher forms or whether it is merely an indirect reflection of the greater efficacy of conditioning in earthworms under spaced rather than massed practice: Ss in Group C received a reinforced trial every 15 sec., whereas Ss in Group P received a reinforced trial every 30 sec., during acquisition training.

There is good reason to remain cautious concerning the evidence in support of classical conditioning in annelids. Evans (1966a) has presented two excellent examples of how behavioral modifications in nereid worms might easily be mistaken for conditioning in the absence of appropriate control procedures. In one experiment Ss received fifty paired presentations of a CS (decrease in illumination) and a US (electric shock). One control group (Group B), often used in conditioning experiments, received an equal number of trials on which the CS was presented alone. A second control group (Group C), however, received fifty presentations of both the CS and the US, but the stimuli were not temporally contiguous (the US preceded the CS by 40 sec.). Figure 18-2 shows the reactions of the Ss to the CS. If the experiment had contained only Groups A and B, the results might have been interpreted as providing evidence for conditioning. But together with a second experiment showing that electric shock is effective in increasing the probability of a subsequent withdrawal response to illumination change, the performance of Group C suggests that the responses are produced purely by sensitization. Group C actually responded more frequently to the CS than Group A, an effect predictable from the hypothesis of sensitization, because the CS followed shock by 90 sec. (the intertrial interval) for Group A but only by 40 sec. for Group C. If shock sensitizes worms to respond to a subsequently presented CS, then we

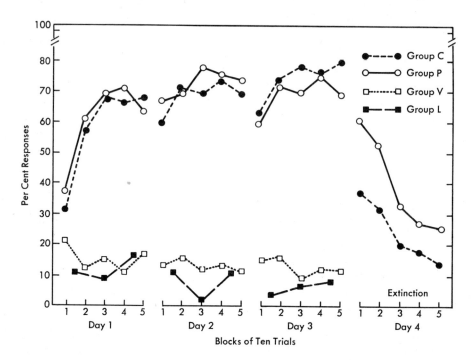

Figure 18-1. Classical conditioning of earthworms. Comparison of the percentage of responses by blocks of trials over three days of conditioning and one day of extinction. Group C (100 per cent reinforcement), Group P (50 per cent reinforcement), and Group V (sensitization control) are presented in terms of ten-trial blocks. Group L (pseudoconditioning control) is presented in terms of five-trial blocks. (Reprinted with permission from Wyers, E. J., Peeke, H. V. S., & Herz, M. J. Partial reinforcement and resistance to extinction in the earthworm. *J. comp. physiol. Psychol.*, 1964, **57**, 113–116.)

would predict that the effect would be greater with a shorter US-CS interval.

Evans (1966a) also found that feeding sensitizes nereid worms to subsequent increases in illumination and that in conditioning experiments where light serves as a CS and food presentation serves as a US, the increased probability of a conditioned approach response found by previous investigators (Copeland, 1930; Copeland and Brown, 1934) can be produced equally well by feeding the Ss between trials as by pairing the stimuli according to the usual forward conditioning paradigm.

Platyhelminthes. The member of the phylum platyhelminthes that has been used exclusively by the psychologist to study classical

conditioning has been the planarian. Thompson and McConnell (1955), using the species *Dugesia dorotocephala*, were the first to present plausible evidence of classical conditioning. They placed individual planaria in a plastic trough filled with water. At each end of the trough was an electrode through which could be passed a DC electric current. When S was "gliding" in the trough, a trial could be started: for the conditioning group (E) the CS was a 3-sec. bright light and the US was a 1-sec. shock, coterminous. A light control group (LC) received only the 3-sec. light but no shock, in order to assess the cumulative effects of the CS alone; a shock control group (SC) received only the 1-sec. US, in order to test for sensitization; and a "spontaneous

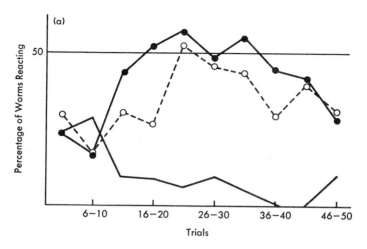

Figure 18-2. "Conditioning" in nereid worms. Percentage of worms reacting to sudden decreases in illumination (CS) presented alone (solid line), paired with electric shock in a forward conditioning procedure (dashed line), and with electric shocks presented in a backward conditioning procedure (interrupted line). (Reprinted with permission from Evans, S. M. Non-associative behavioural modifications in the polychaete Nereis diversicolor. *Anim. Behav.*, 1966a, **14**, 107–119.)

response" control group (RC) received neither the CS nor the US. Over the course of 150 massed trials, Thompson and McConnell observed that the number of responses to the CS (or a "mock" CS in Group RC) was distributed according to Figure 18-3. The responses of Group SC, not shown, decreased over trials, presumably reducing the possibility that the data for the experimental group can be explained on the basis of sensitization.

Two things are immediately evident from Figure 18-3. First, planaria respond to the CS alone, and thus light serves as a weak US; second, the level of conditioning effected by 150 massed trials, although significant in the statistical sense, is modest. These facts have led several investigators (Cummings and Moreland, 1959; Halas, James, and Knutson, 1962; Halas, James, and Stone, 1961) to question whether the behavior change which occurred in Thompson and McConnell's experimental group was true conditioning. On theoretical grounds there is no reason for such hesitancy. The fact that the level of responding

to the CS after 150 trials was only 43 per cent is not unexpected in such a simple organism, especially because the procedure of massed trial presentation was unlikely to produce optimal learning. Moreover, there are instances in higher forms (for example, Deaux and Gormezano, 1963) where CRs also develop very slowly. The observation that the CS (light) was not neutral (that is, elicited responses when presented alone) is at best an example of the need for adequate controls in studies of classical conditioning. Typically, psychologists describe the stimulus which serves as the CS as "neutral"; of course, it is not. The CS usually elicits responses in its own right and often elicits responses similar to the CR to be studied (Kimble, 1961). The critical point to be made is that classical conditioning is merely a phenomenon with a descriptive definition: it refers to an increase in the probability of a response to a particular CS which depends on US contingency. As such, it is only necessary to show that the responses observed are not the result of noncontingent

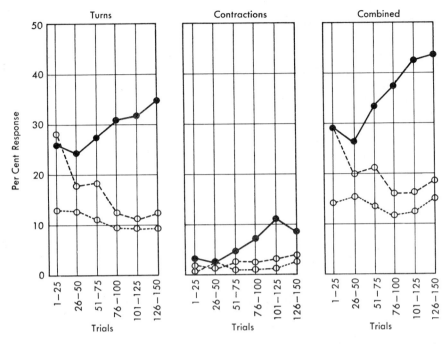

Figure 18-3.   Classical conditioning in planarians. Percentage of turns, contractions, and combined responses for Groups E (solid line), LC (interrupted line), and RC (dotted line). (Reprinted with permission from Thompson, R., & McConnell, J. Classical conditioning in the planarian, *Dugesia dorotocephala. J. comp. physiol. Psychol.*, 1955, **48**, 65–68.)

presentations of CS and US (Rescorla, 1967) and are specific to the CS (that is, do not occur to other, dissimilar, stimuli). Kimble (1961) has described sensitization (or "alpha conditioning") as the augmentation of the response to the CS through a conditioning procedure. If we accept this definition, then studies of classical conditioning in planaria could never be considered "true" conditioning, because the light CS and the shock US elicit the same UR. But it is not clear that this sort of artificial differentiation should be made, for it has been based on evidence such as that by Grant and Adams (1944) showing that fifty habituation trials (that is, light CS presented alone) dramatically reduced the number of eyelid CRs when an air puff was used as the US. It was assumed that the CRs to the light (which occasionally

elicits an unconditioned eyeblink response) had been sensitized, and that "true learning" had not taken place. But it is now known that habituation of many CSs used in conditioning studies also renders them considerably less effective in eliciting a CR (Carlton and Vogel, 1967; Lubow, 1965; Lubow and Moore, 1959), whether or not the CS is capable of eliciting the same UR as the US. Thus, although the observation that the CS is not neutral is not itself sufficient to describe the Thompson and McConnell data as representing something other than conditioning, it is true that they did not include control groups which would rule out other interpretations of the data; neither Group LC nor Group SC received an equal number of noncontingent CSs and USs, and no test was made of the possible CRs to other stimuli than the light CS.

Notwithstanding definitional problems, it remains possible that the data of Thompson and McConnell are nonreplicable or, somehow, misleading. Apparently, there are no serious replication difficulties (Corning, 1964a; Baxter and Kimmel, 1963; Jacobson, Horowitz, and Fried, 1967; Halas, James, and Knutson, 1962; Griffard, 1963; Crawford, King, and Siebert, 1965), although it is true that control Ss consistently show some responses to the CS (but significantly less than experimental groups). James and Halas (1964) attempted to detect the presence of classical conditioning by assessing resistance to extinction in groups of planaria given CS-US pairings or controls. They found an equal and high level of responding during extinction trials by both "conditioned" and control Ss and interpreted this as indicating that Ss had not learned. However, the interpretation of these data is rendered difcult, because the Es (1) used a confounded conditioning procedure (Ss were trained in large groups, not individually, and were tested for extinction in a different apparatus), (2) did not observe CRs during acquisition, and (3) failed to replicate their own (and other) control data. Baxter and Kimmel (1963) and Kimmel and Yaremko (1966) also observed resistance to extinction and found that Ss in the experimental group showed "immediate" extinction (that is, the percentage CRs dropped to the level of the control group within the first block of extinction trials). However, these data on extinction cannot be used as critical evidence against the notion that planaria can be conditioned, because the definition of classical conditioning ultimately must be in terms of the acquisition of a response, not in the peculiarities of its disappearance. At best the data from Kimmel's laboratory suggest that the functional properties of experimental extinction vary among species and/or among test conditions.

But even if it is assumed that the replicated data on classical conditioning in planaria may still represent pseudoconditioning or sensitization, more demanding tests can be made. Vattano and Hullett (1964) were able to show that forward pairing of a CS and US produced more CRs than either a backward sequence or simultaneous presentation. Baxter and Kimmel (1963) found that noncontingent CS and US presentations (cf. Rescorla, 1967) did not increase the probability of a response to the CS. And finally, Kimmel and Harrell (1964, 1966); Griffard and Pierce (1964); and Jacobson, Horowitz, and Fried (1967) have shown differential conditioning in the planarian, suggesting that the CRs observed in previous work are, in fact, stimulus-specific. Figure 18-4 shows an impressive demonstration of differential conditioning in individual Ss.

It is true that the situations and stimuli used by investigators to measure classical conditioning in planaria have less than ideal characteristics for experimentation. When a DC electric shock is used as the US, conditioning is much more rapid when S is oriented toward the cathode (Barnes and Katzung, 1963), confirming the observation that the sensory threshold to shock is lower with orientation in this direction (Viaud, 1954). The responsivity of Ss to light varies as a function of the animal's size and the wave form of the US (Best and Elshtain, 1966; Best, Elshtain, and Wilson, 1967) as well as temperature, trough shape, and dark adaptation (Van Deventer and Ratner, 1964). Finally, there is evidence that there is differential responsivity to light between species of planaria (DeBold, Thompson, and Laudraitis, 1965; Reynierse, 1967). In view of considerations such as these, it is at once clear why the results from different experiments on classical conditioning in planaria sometimes seem disparate and why we must exercise some caution in interpreting them. Even after more than a decade of intensive research effort, the issue is not settled to the satisfaction of all investigators (Jensen, 1965). Nevertheless, the weight of evidence seems to suggest that the phylum Annelida can be conditioned, if testing conditions are optimal. It is evident, also, that this statement could never be made regarding an animal form whose sensory and motor characteristics are so little known, until a substantial amount of well-controlled and systematic research had been done.

Instrumental Conditioning

Because the conditions considered to be necessary and sufficient for classical conditioning and instrumental conditioning are not identical, many psychologists (cf.

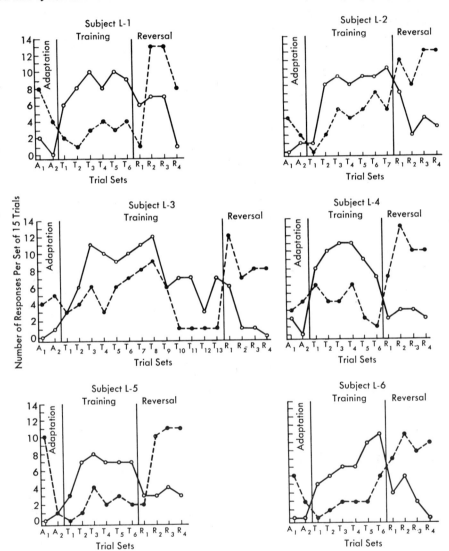

Figure 18-4. Differential classical conditioning in the planarian. Responses of planaria to light (continuous line) and to vibration (dashed line) during differential conditioning. *Ss* L-1 to L-6 received reinforcement to light; *Ss* V-1 to V-6 received reinforcement to vibration. (Reprinted with permission from Jacobson, A. L., Horowitz, S. D., & Fried, C. Classical conditioning, pseudoconditioning, or sensitization in the planarian. *J. comp. physiol. Psychol.*, 1967, **64**, 73–79.)

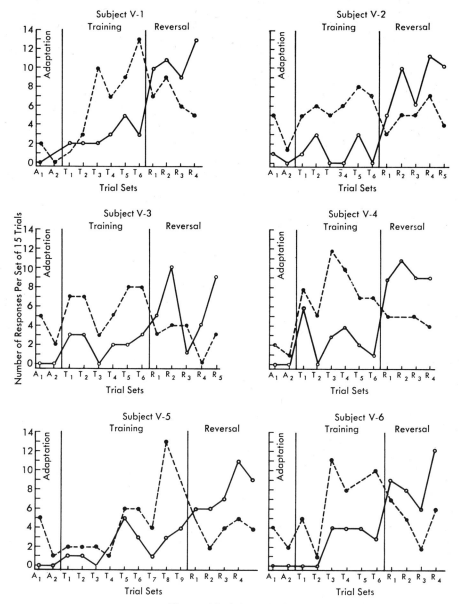

Figure 18–4 (cont'd.).

Kimble, 1961, p. 78) have chosen to regard the two as representing different "kinds" of learning. If this is so, then it is possible that the "breaking point" in the phyletic scale is different for instrumental conditioning than for classical conditioning. It may be, for example, that planaria are capable of learning when a classical conditioning procedure is used but not under an instrumental conditioning procedure. In fact, if we could demonstrate this conclusively, we would have strong evidence to support the contention that there is indeed more than one learning process in animals, because it is difficult to imagine why a single learning process would produce a behavioral change when one conditioning paradigm, but not another, is used.

Let us be quick to note, however, that a single failure to produce instrumental learning in some given lower form is not a conclusive indication that the animal cannot learn, for it may simply be the result of an unfortunate selection of test conditions by the E. There are many examples, even in mammals, where learning is drastically impaired by the introduction of "disruptive" variables. This point is particularly important when we understand that very little is known about the sensory and motor characteristics of simple animals. Moreover, there is an unfortunate statistical difficulty in the attempt to establish a phyletic filter for ability to learn, and this is that the scientist is faced, ultimately, with the prospect of trying to "prove the null hypothesis," a logically and mathematically impossible task. Practically, we say that "Species Y cannot learn" when we have performed experiments on learning in which there is no evidence which demands an associationistic explanation and when the psychological research community has lost its enthusiasm for further work. But we must remember to be humble, for we may have demonstrated merely the limitations of the comparative psychologist rather than the limitations of the species under study.

Annelida. Nereid worms show an avoidance response to shock which could be interpreted as instrumental learning. When the worm is introduced into a glass tube, it crawls rapidly to the opposite end and then searches around the mouth of the tube or leaves it altogether. However, if S is given an electric shock at the end of the tube, it shows, on successive trials, a tendency to "reverse," that is, leave the tube by means of the entrance. Evans (1963a, 1966b) has found some very interesting characteristics associated with this response. Nereid

worms will demonstrate a progressive increase in avoidance responding when trials are spaced (ITI = 30 min.) or when trials are massed (ITI < 1 min.). Although the response appears to be the same under both practice conditions, there is evidence that the processes on which the response is based are in fact different. When trials are massed, Ss are unable to retain the avoidance response beyond 6 hrs., show the development of the response both when the supraoesophageal ganglion is removed and when the punishment is applied outside the apparatus (either between trials or before training). On the other hand, with spaced trials the avoidance response occurs in normal but not in decerebrate worms. This evidence suggests, but does not demonstrate conclusively, that associative avoidance learning may occur but only under conditions of spaced practice. When trials are massed, avoidance learning is masked by sensitization of an unlearned reversal response which occurs naturally among nereid worms subjected to confined spaces. The use of the term *masking* is peculiar here, because under both conditions the responses are apparently identical. But the number of trials to meet a learning criterion is less in the case of sensitization (twenty-one and a half trials under massed practice and fifty trials under spaced practice).

There is some support for this interpretation of avoidance learning from observations of the behavior of nereid worms in T-mazes (Evans, 1963b). *Nereis virens*, the species in which avoidance "reversal" responses were studied, can learn to discriminate between the arms of a T-maze when one arm leads to a positively reinforcing darkened chamber and the other arm leads to electric shock punishment under conditions of spaced practice (ITI = 5 min.). Moreover, Ss do not demonstrate learning if they are not given access to the darkened chamber, obviating the possibility that the Ss are merely reacting to an aversive situation with biased responses. Interesting, also, are the following results: the average number of trials to criterion was 58.2 (similar to that found for "reversal" avoidance responses), and decerebrate worms were unable to learn the T-maze discrimination. Thus, it appears that a critical variable for observing instrumental learning (rather than sensitization) in worms receiving electric shock punishment is the intertrial interval.

The common earthworm, *Lumbricus terrestris*, also can learn a T-maze discrimination habit (Schmidt, 1955; Bharucha-Reid, 1956; Datta, 1962), when the ITI is at least 5 min. but less than 25 min. However, Datta found no evidence of retention of the habit after fifteen days of rest, suggesting that learning is much less stable than that usually found in mammals. On the other hand, the earthworm shows an increased capacity for discrimination learning following mere exposure, without reinforcement, in the T-maze—the so-called latent learning effect (Bharucha-Reid, 1956); and overtraining of a discrimination habit facilitates discrimination-reversal learning (Datta, 1962). Both of these effects have been assumed to reflect rather complex learning mechanisms and thus are paradoxical in view of the instability of T-maze learning.

Reynierse and Ratner (1964) have shown also that the locomotor response latencies of earthworms in an alley decrease when the *S*s approach a moist environment but will increase when the moist environment is removed. There is a need, however, to show that this behavior is contingent upon goal box reinforcement and is not, simply, the demonstration of increased activity or increased vigor following a period (5 min.) in an environment to which the *S*s are biologically suited (cf. Reynierse, Halliday, and Nelson, 1958).

Platyhelminthes. There is good evidence that planaria are capable of modest instrumental learning. Lee (1963) has shown operant conditioning in the planarian. He trained *Cura foremani* to break a narrow beam of light directed at a photoelectric cell in order to turn off an intense and aversive light source for 15 min. Yoked control *S*s received identical light stimulation but could not determine the presence or absence of the light by responding. Lee tested eight experimental *S*s and eight yoked controls. The data for one pair of *S*s is presented in Figure 18-5. The experimental *S*s showed a greater response rate during acquisition than the yoked controls, and demonstrated extinction and reconditioning. All eight experimental *S*s responded at higher rates during acquisition than any control *S* and showed progressively shorter response latencies over time, demonstrating the dependence of the CR on the reinforcement contingency. Additional control groups, exposed to continuous darkness, continuous light, or alternating light-dark periods, responded at about the same rate as the yoked controls. Lee's results have been replicated by Best (1965) and by Crawford and Skeen (1967), the latter showing that the phenomenon will occur with shorter reinforcement periods (darkness) and even when the photobeam which defines the response is greater in intensity than the background illumination (that is, when negatively phototropic *S*s must approach an even more aversive environment to make the operant response).

Planaria can also acquire a discrimination habit. Best and Rubenstein (1962) trained *S*s to discriminate between the light and dark arms of a Y-maze for water reinforcement (flooding of a noxious dry maze). Figure 18-6 presents the proportion of correct responses for four planaria over twelve blocks of six trials each. Although the behavior of the *S*s deviates significantly from chance, the performance is modest by mammalian standards. Corning (1964b), in a similarly conceived experiment, found that ten of seventeen *S*s attained a learning criterion of nine out of ten correct choices (on consecutive trials) when presented with a right-left discrimination in a T-maze.

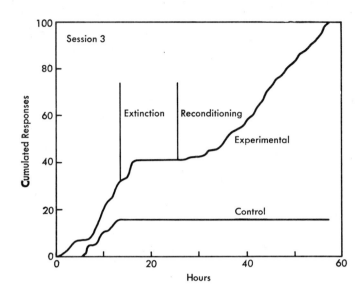

Figure 18-5.   Operant conditioning in the planarian. Cumulated responses as a function of time in hours from the beginning of the experiment. Data for an experimental
and yoked control *S* are shown. The period for which the extinction procedure was
followed is marked on the experimental curve. (Reprinted with permission from Lee,
R. M. Conditioning of a free operant response in planaria. *Science*. 1963. **139**, 1048–1049.)

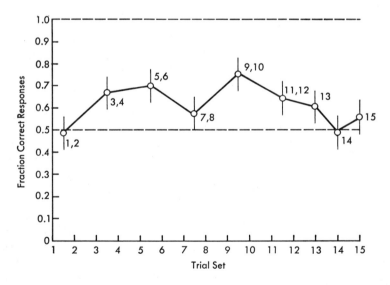

Figure 18-6.   Instrumental learning in the planarian. Mean proportion of correct
responses scored in various trial sets by *Cura foremani* in a rim maze with both position and light-dark cues. (Reprinted with permission from Best, J. B., & Rubenstein, I. Maze
learning and associated behavior in planaria. *J. comp. physiol. Psychol.*, 1962, **55**, 560–566.)

Paramecia. Despite early claims that protazoa can learn (Smith, 1908; Day and Bentley, 1911; French, 1940), recent experimental evidence casts considerable doubt on the validity of this assumption and shows again the importance of an adequate experimental design in assessing learning in lower forms. Two examples will suffice.

Bramstedt (1935, 1939) studied paramecia in a half-light, half-dark, water-filled well. When the lighted half was heated and the darkened half was cooled, the paramecia tended to remain in the cool side. When the temperature of the two sides was again equalized, the Ss continued to avoid the lighted, previously heated side, whereas control Ss showed no preference. Bramstedt interpreted these data as indicating that paramecia can learn an avoidance response. Furthermore, by reversing the light and dark halves after heating and cooling, and by mixing the contents of the well, it appeared that Bramstedt had ruled out alternative explanations of the behavior, such as residual thermal CO_2 or O_2 gradients.

However, two direct attempts (Best, 1954; Mirsky and Katz, 1958) to replicate this learning phenomenon have been unsuccessful, and it is difficult to conclude that learning has been demonstrated. The question remains, of course, as to why Bramstedt obtained the results that he reported. Best (1954) has shown that following exposure to heat, but not in association with light, paramecia are temporarily photosensitized ("temperature shock"). Although Best observed the sensitization effect for only a duration of 30 to 45 sec., it is probable that the somewhat longer lasting "avoidance behavior" observed by Bramstedt was merely a fortuitous consequence of sensitization and not learning at all.

Gelber (1952) sought to demonstrate approach learning in paramecia by baiting a platinum wire with bacteria and lowering it into a culture of Ss. After forty trials she found that the number of paramecia adhering to the wire or within an adjacent area was considerably larger than a nonreinforced control group which received forty trials on which a sterile platinum wire was inserted into the culture. Moreover, the difference in "approach behavior" between the reinforced and nonreinforced groups persisted through two additional test trials on which a sterile platinum wire was inserted into both cultures.

However, there is now evidence which permits us to make a more parsimonious interpretation of these data than that of associative learning. Jensen (1957a) repeated Gelber's procedure, except that after the fortieth trial he measured the bacterial count both adjacent to the sterile platinum wire and from points several millimeters away. He found that the forty training trials resulted in a high concentration of bacteria in the vicinity of the wire but very few in the periphery. In a separate experiment he observed that the addition of bacteria increased the general attachment of paramecia even without training. Moreover, Katz and Deterline (1958) have shown that an untrained group of paramecia, but with bacteria introduced on the fortieth trial only, also were located in the vicinity of the sterile wire on a subsequent test trial. And observations made between the training trials of Ss which received reinforcements indicated that the paramecia remained in the center of the well, where the bacteria-laden wire was lowered, and thus could not be described as showing "approach behavior" to the CS at all. Jensen (1957b, 1959) has suggested that the behavior of paramecia under conditions such as these is influenced by a phenomenon related to the animal's metabolism. When deprived Ss enter a zone rich in food bacteria, they secrete acidic products which reduce subsequent activity and increase the probability of attachment to any object contacted. This explanation possibly can account for other phenomena associated with approach behavior in paramecia, such as superior "retention" after 3 hrs. by Ss receiving spaced practice (Gelber, 1958): the massed practice group became satiated, their metabolism was lowered, and subsequent attachment was reduced relative to the spaced practice group. Altogether, the application of the concept of instrumental learning to the behavior of paramecia seems unjustified experimentally at this time.

Formation of "Strategies" for Discrimination Learning

From Chapter 17 it is apparent that most mammals can form discrimination learning sets. On a set of two-choice problems with differential visual cues, their performance improves in the sense that on successive problems Ss show an increasingly larger percentage of correct responses after the first trial of any particular problem. In addition, subhuman primates, such as the rhesus monkey, exhibit "one-trial learning" after extended practice; that is, when presented with a new discrimination problem, they show virtually complete mastery after the first "information" trial. A number of theories have been proposed to account for the data on learning sets. For example, one theory (Riopelle, 1953) describes the improvement of Ss on successive problems as the result of transfer suppression. It is assumed that animals bring many erroneous or irrelevant tendencies (such as position habits or stimulus preferences) to the test situation and that these must be extinguished or suppressed before proficient performance will emerge. Over successive problems the suppression of these "biased responses" is transferred, permitting more and more efficient learning.

Another, quite different, interpretation of learning sets which has been suggested is that Ss acquire a proficient "win-stay, lose-shift" strategy over successive problems (Levine, 1959; Schusterman, 1962). The strategy, or hypothesis, is strengthened both by the consistent reinforcement of a cue within any discrimination problem and

also by the consistent applicability of the same strategy among successive problems.

If animals can develop a "win-stay, lose-shift" strategy, and if they can apply this strategy to successive discrimination problems such as those presented in the study of learning sets, then it should be possible to demonstrate transfer between different problem types so long as the particular strategy remains appropriate. Schusterman (1964) has tested this assumption using chimpanzees as Ss. He trained one group of Ss to learn a two-choice discrimination reversal habit. (That is, after S had learned to select stimulus A of pair A and B, stimulus A was nonrewarded and stimulus B was rewarded; on learning then to select B, stimulus A was again designated as correct, and so on.) Another group of chimpanzees learn a set of discrimination problems (that is, learning set paradigm). Both of these procedures presumably could lead to the formation of a "win-stay, lose-shift" strategy, yet the discrimination reversal (DR) training would not permit the development of transfer suppression, because the stimuli were not varied from problem to problem. (One exception to this is that positional, that is, right versus left, biases should be suppressed.) Following the fifty DR or fifty discrimination problems, Schusterman tested both groups on a series of four-trial discrimination problems. Figure 18-7 presents the results. Where as naive control Ss exhibited the normal learning set function (gradual improvement over successive problems) and while the Ss given prior learning set training (Group MD) showed the expected positive transfer to the new discrimination problems, the interesting feature of the curves is that prior DR training also permitted positive transfer. Indeed, the transfer was at least as good as that of group MD. This is consistent with the proposition that transfer can be effected by a nonspecific learning mechanism such as a strategy.

Further support for the concept of a "win-stay, lose-shift" strategy has been

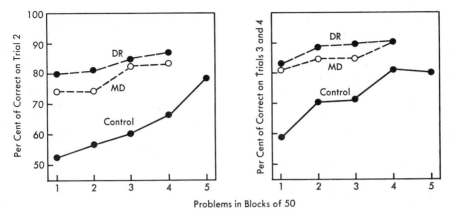

Figure 18-7. Strategy formation in the chimpanzee. The left panel presents percentage of correct responses on Trial 2 and the right panel presents percentage of correct responses on Trials 3 and 4 combined, when Ss are given successive discrimination-reversal (DR) training or multiple discrimination training (MD) prior to training on 250 four-trial discrimination problems. (Adapted with permission from Schusterman, R. J. Successive discrimination-reversal training and multiple discrimination training in one-trial learning by chimpanzees. *J. comp. physiol. Psychol.*, 1964, **58**, 153–156.)

provided by Schrier (1966), who has found that macaque monkeys also show the transfer of a "win-stay, lose-shift" strategy and in both directions: from DR tasks to learning-set tasks and from learning-set tasks to DR tasks. Squirrel monkeys (Rumbaugh and Prim, 1964) also show the phenomenon, but it breaks down when three-trial DR problems are presented to the Ss. Three-trial DR problems are not solvable by squirrel monkeys, and thus this evidence confirms the hypothesis that the acquisition and maintenance of the strategy depends on learning about the reinforcement contingencies for each stimulus. In fact, the monkeys trained on three-trial DR problems actually were inferior to untrained control Ss when both groups were given a set of discrimination learning-set problems, suggesting that in the absence of detectably consistent reinforcement contingencies Ss not only fail to learn the "win-stay, lose-shift" strategy but also acquire alternative, inappropriate strategies or rely more heavily upon stronger response biases or stimulus preferences than they normally would. This concept of "inappropriate" strategies

also has been studied by Schusterman (1962). Schusterman has shown that training on single alternation problems, where a win-shift, lose-stay strategy would be appropriate, does not improve subsequent performance on discrimination learning-set problems.

If strategy formation is a useful way to explain long-term transfer effects in animals, it most certainly is not a panacea. For example, there are instances (see Shepp and Schrier; in Shepp, 1967) where negative transfer is observed between successive discrimination problems, even though S is successful in solving each individual problem and although each problem is one to which a win-stay, lose-stay strategy could be applied. Shepp and Schrier found that if rhesus monkeys were trained on three successive discrimination problems in which the relevant stimulus dimension is alternated (for example, on problem 1, form is relevant; on problem 2, color is relevant; and on problem 3, form) Ss made more errors on problem 3 than on problem 1. This indicates that attentional factors play a role in transfer of discrimination learning, at least over short runs of transfer problems, and these attentional factors can effectively mask or prevent the development of strategy learning. It would be interesting to look at the transfer results for a longer set of such problems (Schusterman presented his Ss with fifty DR problems), in order to see whether strategy formation would override the negative transfer effect observed by Shepp and Schrier.

Recently, Warren (1966) has introduced an exciting new prospect for those psychologists interested in detecting phyletic filters for learning ability. Using Schusterman's method he has found that whereas rhesus monkeys indeed show positive transfer from DR to visual discrimination learning-set problems (and in fact will do so even when the DR problems involve a nonvisual position discrimination), domestic cats do not. Thus, referring to Chapter 17, we are faced with the following unusual circumstance: both primates and cats are able to acquire learning sets, but they apparently do so through the utilization of different learning mechanisms. Although it is premature at this time to do more than speculate, cats might develop learning sets through transfer suppression whereas monkeys might develop them through the formation of strategies. This sort of analysis might also clarify why monkeys are capable of true one-trial learning (that is, when presented with a new discrimination problem after considerable learning-set training, they exhibit virtually perfect performance on trial 2) whereas other subhuman mammals do not. That is, the superior performance of primates reflects the operation of a different mechanism. If this is the case, however, it would also raise another serious objection to any attempts to compare learning-set performances quantitatively among species (as in Chapter 17).

It remains unclear whether the formation of strategies in discrimination learning will continue to show phyletic trends after more experiments are performed. At the present time the most serious limitation regarding

the efficacy of this type of analytic tool is that it rests on a rather sparse amount of data. However, it may very well turn out that comparative analyses of intertask transfer provide a profitable method of looking for a phyletic filter for complex learning rather than the classical methods which have concentrated upon single, so-called symbolic problem solving such as the solution of oddity problems, delayed response, double alternation, and so on (Warren, 1965b).

Another example of differential strategy formation among cats and monkeys can be seen from an experiment by Warren (1965b). The Ss were given a set of eighty discrimination-discrimination reversal problems. Each problem consisted of presenting Ss with stimulus objects, one of which was rewarded until the S learned to choose it consistently. Then the problem was reversed, that is, the previously nonrewarded stimulus was made the correct one. Both the monkeys and the cats were divided into two groups. Each S received the initial discrimination training for each of the eighty problems with a white tray holding the stimulus objects; when the DR training for each problem was instituted, the white tray was replaced by a black one before the first reversal trial, providing a cue for the change in the reinforcement contingency. Figure 18-8 presents the mean intraproblem DR learning for the cats and monkeys on problems 61 through 80. Both monkeys and cats clearly utilized the cue provided by changing the color of the tray, because neither shows a negative transfer effect on trial 1. If Ss had ignored the tray color, they would be expected to select the correct stimulus on trial 1 of the DR virtually none of the time.

But although tray color functioned as an effective cue for both species, it appears that the cue served the development of a different strategy for each. Monkeys used the cue as a signal to reverse their discrimination habit, whereas cats used the cue to suppress previous learning. The performance of the cats

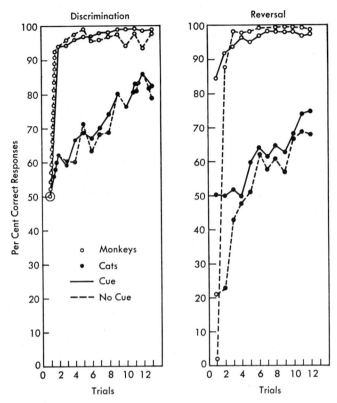

Figure 18-8. Intraproblem learning curves for cats and rhesus monkeys trained on discrimination reversal to food and nonfood signs. (Reprinted with permission from Warren, J. M. Primate learning in comparative perspective. In A. M. Schrier, H. F. Harlow, & F.Stollnitz (Eds.), *Behavior of nonhuman primates.* Vol. 1. New York: Academic Press, 1965b.)

does not suggest the operation of a "win-stay, lose-shift" strategy conditioned to the cue; it suggests that as soon as the tray-color cue appeared, the cat responded as if totally naive. It had developed a strategy, but not the same strategy utilized by monkeys.

Learning Function

If animals differ qualitatively in their ability to demonstrate certain types of learning (for example, classical conditioning, "win-stay, lose-shift" strategy formation, and so on), it is possible that they may also behave in qualitatively different ways to systematic changes in certain independent variables of which learning is a function. The research strategy here is as follows: because all animals above platyhelminthes are, apparently, capable of learning, it is probable (although not certain) that the most straightforward (and sufficient) conditions for simple learning—the variables which function in the "laws of association" —are critical and cannot vary from species to species in any but a quantitative way. It is also probable that even quantitative variation is restricted within reasonably narrow ranges (CS-US interval, ITI, US intensity, and so on). However, there are a host of more complex (and sometimes seemingly "paradoxical") relationships between certain variables and performance on learning tasks. This latter class of variables defines conditions that are not necessarily critical for learning per se but that influence the manner in which learned responses are manifested. Interest has centered recently on the question of whether this class of variables exerts the same sort of influence on behavior in different animals, or whether the functional relationships described for the higher mammals are simply nonexistent or different in kind in lower classes.

To this date the types of functional relationships studied in a comparative psychological way fall into two broad classes, (1) reinforcement functions and (2) transfer-learning functions. In the first case the general question is whether phenomena related to the precise manner of presentation of positive reinforcement in instrumental learning are consistent throughout the phyletic scale. In the second case the question is whether transfer of learning, specifically discrimination learning, follows the same laws in lower animal forms as in mammals.

Reinforcement Functions

By the "weak law of effect," reinforcement is necessary for instrumental learning. However, it appears that the manner in which reinforcement functions to modify learned behavior varies by animal class. Two examples of this are (1) behavior following inconsistency of reinforcement, and (2) the effects of nonsequential reinforcement variables (for example, amount of reward).

Inconsistency of Reinforcement: Probability Learning. When an animal is given a two-choice discrimination problem, the typical procedure is consistently to reward one of the alternatives (stimulus A) and consistently not to reward the other (stimulus B). Under such conditions, animals throughout

a wide array of classes learn to select the "correct" stimulus virtually all the time. Suppose, however, that the animal is given a choice between two alternatives, but a response to one of the alternatives is more consistently rewarded than a response to the other. On a given trial one, and only one, stimulus is correct, but E has arranged the reinforcement schedule so that the probability of reward (on trial n) is, for example, 0.70 for stimulus A and 0.30 for stimulus B. Under such circumstances what will the animal do?

Notice that the "rational" solution to this problem is to select stimulus A all the time anyway, because this insures that the response will be rewarded precisely 70 per cent of the time. Any response to stimulus B, in the absence of "special knowledge," will reduce the overall probability of reinforcement from 70 per cent toward chance (50 per cent). For example, if S selected stimulus A 70 per cent of the time and stimulus B 30 per cent of the time, the probability of reinforcement would be $(0.70 \times 0.70) + (0.30 \times 0.30) = 0.58$.

The actual behavior of different animals when faced with this problem is interesting. Human Ss typically "match" their responses to the reward probability ratio; that is, if stimulus A is rewarded 70 per cent of the time and stimulus B 30 per cent of the time (a so-called 70:30 problem), they will select stimulus A on 70 per cent of the trials (Grant, Hake, and Hornseth, 1951). Moreover, there is evidence that they do so by adopting "game" strategies based on the supposition that the problem "really has a solution" (Goodnow, 1955).

Subhuman mammals, however, tend to "maximize," that is, they are disposed to select stimulus A on virtually every trial, and they do so whether training is carried out under a "noncorrection" or "correction" procedure. When a noncorrection procedure is used, S simply fails to receive a reward if it makes the wrong choice on a given trial. When a correction procedure is used, S is permitted to reselect the correct stimulus after making an error, thereby insuring that the frequency of reinforcement in fact will correspond to the probability of reinforcement for each stimulus predetermined by E. There are certain occasions when individual mammalian S do not "maximize," but when this occurs, they show a strong tendency to select alternatives on the basis of "strategies." Rats and cats, for example, tend to perseverate to the stimulus reinforced on the preceding trial (Bitterman, 1965, Warren and Beck, 1966); monkeys tend to alternate responses after reinforcement (Wilson, Oscar, and Bitterman, 1964).

In addition, there is evidence that when mammals exhibit "maximizing," they do so with rather large variations in the number of trials necessary for asymptotic performance: both cats and monkeys require considerably more trials to reach asymptote than rats (Poland and Warren, 1967), suggesting that maximizing is achieved in mammals only after other game strategies are extinguished. Because the cats and monkeys used in probability learning experiments have been "sophisticated" Ss trained on a variety of other discrimination problems involving consistent reinforcement) they had had considerably greater opportunity to develop game strategies based on previous reinforcement experience than rats, who were tested as experimentally naive Ss. The extremely persistent demonstration of game strategies by human Ss also is consistent with the notion that previous reinforcement experience can modify the S's method of attacking a probability learning problem. Even rats can be speeded up in the formation of maximizing behavior by purposely rearing them in an environment affording only inconsistent reinforcement (Solomon, 1962). Under such conditions Ss maximized, apparently, after approximately thirty-six to fifty trials, whereas in a similar experiment but with Ss reared in an ordinary laboratory environment (Bitterman, Wodinsky, and Candland, 1958) they required about 120 trials

to maximize. It would appear that the specially reared rats were even less disposed than control rats to seek a solution which would afford consistent reinforcement (that is, they did not attempt game-strategy solutions at all).

Two final points must be mentioned regarding mammalian performance on probability learning problems. First, there is evidence (Solomon, 1962; Wright, 1967) that rats reach asymptotic performance on probability learning tasks much more slowly under conditions of low drive level. Although this would appear to be far from surprising, it can lead to some difficulty of interpretation; it can dispose investigators to identify mistakenly unstabilized behavior as matching behavior. The only acceptable method of preventing this is to increase the number of training trials to the point where there can be no doubt that each S is individually exhibiting asymptotic performance (Uhl, 1963). Second, probability-learning experiments with animals have utilized both visual (color or brightness cues) and spatial (right position versus left position) discrimination problems. There seems to be some evidence to suggest that spatial probability learning problems dispose mammals to maximize, whereas visual problems lead more often to the development of "strategies" (see Warren and Beck, 1966; Wilson, Oscar and Bitterman, 1964). The basis for this difference is not entirely clear, but it will appear again with the study of sub-mammalian forms.

If the characteristic reaction of mammals to a probability learning problem is either to "maximize" or to "match nonrandomly" (respond by using systematized game strategies), what might the behavior of lower forms be like? In extensive studies on goldfish (Behrend and Bitterman, 1966) and African mouthbreeders (Bitterman, Wodinsky and Candland, 1958; Behrend and Bitterman, 1961; Behrend, Bauman and Bitterman, 1965; Marrone and Evans, 1966), utilizing both visual and spatial problems, the evidence suggests strongly that

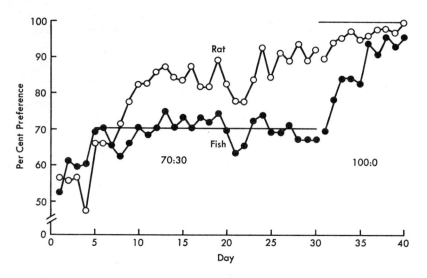

Figure 18-9. Probability matching by the fish on a 70:30 visual discrimination problem. (Reprinted with permission from Bitterman, M. E., Wodinsky, J., & Candland, D. K. Some comparative psychology. *Amer. J. Psychol.*, 1958., **71**, 94–110.)

a third type of reaction takes place, random matching. If fish are trained, say, in a 70:30 visual discrimination problem, they respond to each stimulus in proportions consistent with the reinforcement probabilities. But the critical feature of the fish is not that they "match," for humans and monkeys and cats sometimes do that; it is that the matching behavior is random. (Fish do not seem to employ strategies, but respond sequentially as though the response on each trial is completely unrelated to responses on the immediately preceding trials.) Figure 18-9 presents an instance of this behavior together with corresponding data for the rat. It should be noted that this behavior in the fish usually, though not always (Marrone and Evans, 1966), depends upon the use of the correction method of testing.

When fish exhibit random matching in a two-choice probability learning situation, the question immediately arises of whether the fish discriminate the differential probabilities associated with each stimulus or whether they respond simply on the basis of the differential frequency of reinforce-

ment. In an experiment where probability and frequency of reinforcement were varied independently, the fish demonstrated that probability of reinforcement had a much more powerful effect on behavior than frequency (Behrend, Bauman and Bitterman, 1965) but frequency also had an independent effect. Moreover, other evidence (Gonzalez, Eskin, and Bitterman, 1961) suggests that the fish is particularly sensitive to sheer frequency of reinforcement. Thus, it is not possible to argue that random matching is a product of the fish's failure to discriminate one of the features of the reinforcement conditions. It seems, instead, that fish merely react to reinforcement contingencies in a different way.

Bitterman (1966) has argued that curves of random matching in the fish are based on the behavior of individual Ss, and he has presented data showing that each individual fish selects stimulus A in a 70:30 problem almost precisely 70 per cent of the time. Recently, Weitzman (1967) has found that although fish match as a group, some individual Ss deviate from true matching.

Table **18-1**   Behavior of a Variety of Animals on Probability-Learning
Problems

| | | Asymptotic Performance | |
		Random Matching	Maximizing or Non-random Matching
Animal	*E*		
Human	Grant, Hake, and Hornseth, 1951 Anderson and Grant, 1957		V, S
Monkey	Wilson, Oscar, and Bitterman, 1964 Warren and Beck, 1966		V, S
Cat	Poland and Warren, 1967		V, S
Rat	Bitterman, Wodinsky, and Candland, 1958		V, S
Pigeon	Graf, Bullock, and Bitterman, 1964	V	S
Turtle	Kirk and Bitterman, 1965	V	S
Decorticated Rat	Gonzalez, Roberts, and Bitterman, 1964	V	S
Fish	Bitterman, Wodinsky, and Candland, 1958	V, S	
Cockroach	Longo, 1964	S*	

Adapted from Bitterman, 1965.
V = visual problems; S = spatial problems.
* The cockroach has been tested only on a spatial learning problem.

Nevertheless, this latter criterion is of secondary importance. There is still no evidence that fish "maximize," nor has there been presented any evidence that fish show systematic response tendencies in probability-learning situations. The minimal conclusion is that fish usually show matching behavior and never show systematic response tendencies related to behavior on previous trials. Mammals, on the other hand, usually show maximizing and rarely, if ever, show truly random sequential behavior on consecutive trials.

Other nonmammalian species also have been found to demonstrate random matching on probability learning tasks. Table 18-1 includes the results for an arthropod (cockroach), a reptile (turtle), and a bird (pigeon), as well as for rats that had been decorticated in infancy. Random matching is found for all nonmammalian species tested on visual problems, but not on spatial problems. Thus, the reinforcement functions observed seem to depend not only on phyletic status but also on problem type. The sig-

nificance of this finding is not fully understood. It is possible that, as Bitterman (1965, p.408) has suggested, "new modes of adjustment appear earlier in spatial than in visual contexts as we ascend the phyletic scale." However, other interpretations are possible, such as that the relative dominance of spatial preferences or biases in certain animals affects choice behavior. In the former case we must assume that pigeons, turtles, and decorticated rats are representatives of a separate class of animals, a class which shows both types of adjustment to probability learning problems. In the latter case we might be able to interpret the performance of these animals as being essentially "fishlike," except that a strong disposition for the development of positional biases interferes with the emergence of random matching on spatial problems. Only further research will resolve this question.

Inconsistency of Reinforcement: Partial Reinforcement Effect (PRE). When resistance to extinction is measured in the rat, following continuous (100 per cent) or partial (say, 50 per cent) reinforcement of an instrumental response, it has been found repeatedly that resistance is greater under partial reinforcement (Jenkins and Stanley, 1950; Lewis, 1960). This phenomenon (the PRE) is exhibited in rats even when the total number of acquisition trials is equated between groups (and therefore the partially reinforced Ss have received fewer rewards), when Ss have been trained under a discrete-trial procedure, and when trials have been spaced by as much as 24 hrs. (Bitterman, Wodinsky, and Candland, 1958; Weinstock, 1954).

Pigeons (Roberts, Bullock, and Bitterman, 1963) and turtles (Gonzalez and Bitterman, 1962; Murillo, Diercks, and Capaldi, 1961; Wise and Gallagher, 1964) also show the PRE; however, until recently there seemed to be some evidence that fish do not, at least under the "ordinary" procedure where training trials (but not reinforcements) are equated. In fact, resistance to extinction seemed to be greater for continuously reinforced Ss than partially reinforced Ss. This had been found with massed practice (Wodinsky and Bitterman, 1959), spaced practice (Longo and Bitterman, 1960), short or long periods of acquisition training (Wodinsky and Bitterman, 1960), and under various drive levels (Longo and Bitterman, 1960). However, when groups had been equated for reinforcements (that is, when the partial reinforce-

ment group had received more training trials), the PRE did seem to occur (Gonzalez Eskin, and Bitterman, 1962). Table 18-2 shows the implications of these two procedures: rats demonstrate greater resistance to extinction even when, through partial reinforcement training, they have experienced less rewards than a continuously reinforced control group. Greater resistance to extinction is found in fish only when Ss actually receive more training trials. Both effects are "paradoxical" if one assumes, simplistically, that reward strengthens a habit whereas nonreward weakens it, but the species difference here suggests that the processes underlying extinction may not be equivalent in fish and rats. Additional support for this contention is available from two further observations on fish. First, whereas resistance to extinction in rats is greater after random 50 per cent reinforcement than after alternating 50 per cent reinforcement (Tyler, Wortz, and Bitterman, 1953), fish do not exhibit differential extinction following these two reinforcement procedures (Gonzalez, Eskin, and Bitterman, 1961). This suggests that rats are sensitive to the reinforcement characteristics of sequences of trials but fish are not, and that the unpatterned nature of the training sequence is at least partially responsible for resistance to extinction in the rat but not in the fish. Moreover, the differential sensitivity of rats and fish to reinforcement contingencies on consecutive

Table **18-2**   An Example of Two Partial Reinforcement Procedures
Used for Experimentation with Rats and Fish

	Control Group (Continuous Reinforcement)	50 Per Cent Partial Reinforcement	
		Equated Trials	Equated Reinforcements
Number of Training Trials	100	100	200
Number of Reinforcements	100	50	100
Number of Nonreinforcements	0	50	100

Rats typically show the PRE under both partial reinforcement schedules; fish typically show the PRE only with equated reinforcements.

trials may partly explain their behavior in probability learning experiments: detection of sequences of reinforcement by rats contributes to "strategy formation" whereas this is not true for fish.

Second, Gonzalez, Behrend, and Bitterman (1965) were unable to find the PRE in fish (*even with equated reinforcement*) when *S*s were trained with a 24-hr. intertrial interval. Rats, however, show the PRE under the same training schedule (Weinstock, 1954). This implies that even when the PRE is found in fish, it somehow is the product of a process based on successive reinforcement contingencies which must be temporally contiguous. This is not the case with the rat.

Recently there have been two reports of instances where the PRE had occurred in fish with equated trials, obviating the simplistic notion implied in Table 18-2. If *S*s are trained under a 50 per cent "partial delay" of reward procedure (that is, on 50 per cent of the trials responses are rewarded immediately and on 50 per cent of the trials they are delayed by 30 sec.), a PRE-like phenomenon emerges (Gonzalez, Behrend, and Bitterman, 1965). However, it should be noted that because all instrumental responses during training are in fact rewarded, it is uncertain whether the mechanisms responsible for greater resistance to extinction are the same as those which operate to produce the "typical" PRE effect (that is, where some proportion of responses are not reinforced at all during training). For example, Schoonard and Lawrence (1962) found that rats which received 100 per cent delay of reward trials extinguished a running response more slowly than groups which received either 0 per cent or 30 per cent delay of reward trials. This suggests that the difference in resistance to extinction following partial delay is not produced by sequential reinforcement patterns at all, because it does not depend on the intermixing of two types (delay and nondelay) of trials, as does the PRE. In a second report Gonzalez and Bitterman (1967) have noted

that the typical (equated trials) PRE is obtained under rather unique conditions where training involves an instrumental response of low effort, and where the response is followed by very large rewards. It appears, then, that together with the knowledge that an equated-reinforcements PRE occurs readily in the fish, the issue is not whether fish display the PRE but why it is that they do so under a very restricted (and sometimes unusual) set of conditions as compared with mammals, birds, and reptiles. More will be said about this later, but it seems fair to conclude that the data at least support the contention that the processes responsible for the PRE in the fish and the rat may not be the same, for they apparently are not influenced in a parallel fashion by the same set of independent variables.

Nonsequential Reinforcement Functions: Amount of Reinforcement. It is well known that rats respond to changes in the magnitude of reward by shifting their behavior accordingly (Crespi, 1942; Zeaman, 1949). If two groups of *S*s are trained in an alley under high and low reward conditions until they reach asymptotic running speed, and if at this point the magnitude of reward for each group is shifted to the other value, then each group responds as in Figure 18-10. Three aspects of the results are worth noting: (1) both groups of *S*s shift their running speed in the direction predicted by the performance of preshift animals; (2) the shift is very rapid, taking only three or four trials until a new asymptote is reached; and (3) there are both positive and negative contrast effects such that *S*s "overshoot" the predictions based on preshift performance.

Fish do not show the same behavior following reward shifts. Lowes and Bitterman (1967) trained goldfish to respond to an illuminated target for high and low rewards. After the fish had reached asymptotic performance, the reward values were reversed. In Figure 18-11 is presented the postshift

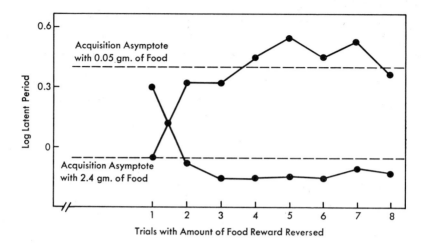

Figure 18-10.   The effect of a change in food reward upon the latency of a running response by rats. The acquisition asymptote is estimated from latencies on the last several trials before the shift in amount of reward. Note that the change in amount of food employed as a reinforcer produces an immediate shift on Trial 2 after only a single trial with the new amount. (Reprinted with permission from Kimble, G. A. *Hilgard and Marquis' Conditioning and Learning.* New York: Appleton-Century-Crofts, 1961.)

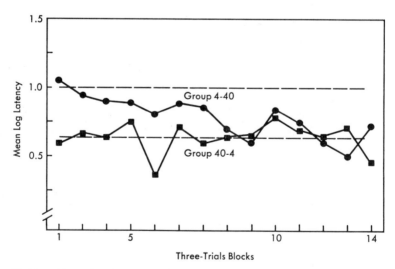

Figure 18-11.   Mean log latency of an instrumental response in the goldfish as a function of amount of reward. Group 40-4 was shifted from forty to four worms on Trial Block 1; Group 4-40 was shifted from four to forty worms at the same time. The dashed lines indicate averaged performance of nonshifted fish: the upper line for *S*s receiving four worms throughout, the lower line for *S*s receiving forty worms throughout. (Adapted with permission from Lowes, G., & Bitterman, M. E. Reward and learning in the goldfish. *Science,* 1967, **157,** 455–457.)

performance of these Ss. Interestingly, the fish did not show postshift behavior at all consistent with that of rats. First, their response times were modified only when magnitude of reward was increased but not when it was decreased. Second, the single instance of a change in response time can be characterized as a gradual one. And third, no contrast effects were noted.

These results suggest that magnitude of reinforcement is a more powerful variable for the fish than for the rat, and that reinforcement is capable of sustaining learned behavior independently and in spite of

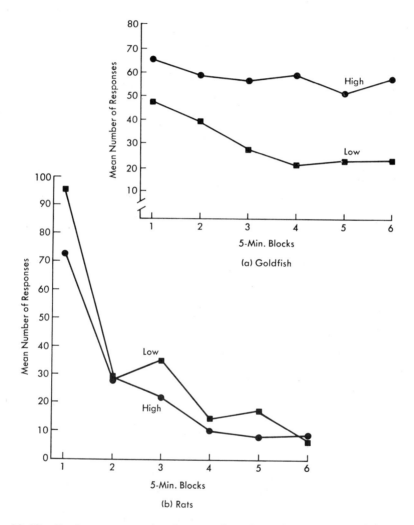

Figure 18-12. Resistance to extinction as a function of magnitude of training reinforcement: (a) goldfish and (b) rats. Ss were *trained* under low and high reinforcement. During extinction goldfish make a greater number of responses when training involves high reinforcement magnitude. Just the opposite occurs in rats. (Adapted with permission from Gonzales, R. C., Holmes, N. K., & Bitterman, M. E. Resistance to extinction in the goldfish as a function of frequency and amount of reward. *Amer. J. Phsyiol.*, 1967a, **80**, 269–275.)

sequential reward contingencies in fish but not in rats. Additional support for this contention comes from a study by Gonzalez and Bitterman (1967), in which fish were trained to press a target for either high or low food reward (consistent reinforcement). After training, both groups were subjected to experimental extinction, and it was found that resistance to extinction was greater for the high reward group. Just the opposite occurs with rats (Hulse, 1958; Wagner, 1961). Again, it seems that large rewards sustain learned behavior in the fish but provide the opportunity for contrast effects in the rat.

The observed greater resistance to extinction of fish under high-reward training conditions is not limited to discrete-trials experiments. Figure 18-12 presents similar results, for fish and rats, where Ss were trained in a free-operant conditioning situation with equated reinforcements per training session. Although the effective differences in magnitude of reinforcement cannot be justifiably equated, it is evident that resistance to extinction is positively related

to reward magnitude in fish but apparently inversely related to reward magnitude in rats.

Nonsequential Reinforcement Functions: Frequency of Reinforcement. The greater dependence of the fish on the magnitude of reinforcement is consistent with the observation that the behavior of fish, also, is more closely tied to the frequency of reinforcement than is the case with rats. Gonzalez, Eskin, and Bitterman (1961) trained African mouthbreeders and rats to make an instrumental conditioned response for continuous reinforcement, After training, Ss were extinguished, reconditioned, extinguished, and so on, until they had experienced six extinction sessions. Then, Ss from both species were given zero, three, or six sessions of reconditioning, twenty trials (and twenty reinforcements) per session. In Figure 18-13 are presented the results: for fish, resistance to extinction is a direct function of the frequency of reinforcement during interpolated retraining; for rats, resistance to extinction is

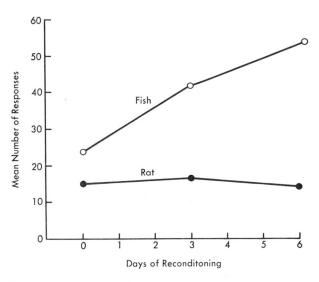

Figure 18-13.   Resistance to extinction in fish and rats as a function of the amount of interpolated retraining. (Adapted with permission from Gonzalez, R. C., Eskin, R. M., & Bitterman, M. E. Alternating and random partial reinforcement in the fish, with some observations on symptotic resistance to extinction. *Amer. J. Psychol.*, 1961, **74**, 561–568.)

independent of frequency of reinforcement. In a similar experiment on goldfish, but using a free-operant procedure, the same phenomenon was found (Gonzalez, Holmes, and Bitterman, 1967a). *S*s receiving alternating periods of training and extinction showed greater resistance to extinction if they received twenty reinforcements during a given retraining period than if they received only ten reinforcements. Again, no evidence was found that fish can learn to behave during extinction trials in a manner independent of the immediately preceding reinforcement contingencies.

Inconsistent Reinforcement: A Reconsideration. The experiments which show the effects of amount and frequency of reinforcement on fish may provide a key to the nature of the class differences found for probability learning and partial reinforcement. At first glance it would appear that the essential distinction is that the performance of fish is tied closely to the nonsequential parameters of reinforcement (magnitude, frequency, and possibly others) and that these variables are sufficiently powerful to outweigh any modest ability the fish might have to respond to the ordering of reinforcement and nonreinforcement over blocks of trials. On the other hand, mammals (particularly rats, on which most investigators have been centered) tend to behave on the basis of reinforcement patterns, especially after extensive training.

But we must be cautious. All the evidence, even for fish, is not yet in. We need to know whether differences in magnitude and/or frequency of reinforcement are sufficient to explain random probability matching or whether they merely can modify it. We need to know whether other animal classes which show random matching or which fail to exhibit the PRE also behave toward reward magnitude and frequency in a manner like fish. In addition, we must determine whether the observed effects of these reinforcement variables imply species (or class) differences in function which are qualitative or quantitative. For example, the observation that fish can exhibit the PRE under "optimal" conditions could be taken to mean that the processes responsible for the PRE differ only quantitatively between fish and rats; alternatively, the fact that the PRE in fish occurs only under a particular and narrow set of circumstances could be interpreted as suggesting that it is only analogous to the PRE in rats, that is, that it is an artifact produced by a happy combination of variables but does not imply the operation of a process of the sort proposed as an explanation for the PRE in mammals.

Transfer-Learning Functions

Let us now consider a different class of experiments, where the procedural details of the application of reinforcement are not under scrutiny. If a mammal is trained in the ordinary way (that is, under consistent reinforcement contingencies) to discriminate between two stimuli A and B, where A is rewarded and B is not rewarded, it is possible to study the nature of the transfer of that discrimination habit to other discrimination problems. One method of study already has been discussed in an earlier section, namely, the development and transfer of learning sets. A simpler sort of transfer paradigm involves discrimination-reversal learning (where, following initial acquisition, the *E* makes B the rewarded stimulus and A is now unrewarded). The comparative psychologist has investigated in particular two variants of discrimination-reversal learning: (1) the course of transfer during a succession of many discrimination reversals, where first A is rewarded, then B, then A again, and so on, and (2) the effects of overtraining on the *S*'s ability either to reverse the discrimination habit or to shift his response to a stimulus alternative involving a different stimulus dimension ("extradimensional" or ED shift).

Successive Discrimination Reversals. Suppose a mammal such as the rat is trained to discriminate A from B. A is rewarded until S meets a learning criterion, then B is rewarded until the same learning criterion is met, then A again, and so on. (A variant of this procedure is to train Ss on each reversal problem for a fixed number of trials, instead of to a learning criterion.) If we plot the mean number of errors made by the Ss as a function of the ordinal number of the reversal problem, we typically obtain performance functions such as those depicted in Figure 18-14. R_0 refers to performance on the initial discrimination problem, and R_1, R_2, and so on, indicate in turn the reversal problems in consecutive order.

Several aspects of these functions in Figure 18-14 are worth pointing out. First, the animals make more errors on the first reversal problem than they do on the initial discrimination problem (R_0). This is clearly a negative transfer effect, which can be understood as an instance of proactive interference. Second, there is recovery from the negative transfer effect (for example, when, as in R_3 of Figure 18-14, performance returns to the level of R_0). This would seem to represent a process of "unlearning": Ss become able to ignore what they had learned on the previous problem and therefore treat the next reversal problem as though it were unrelated to their previous experience. Third, after further experience with reversal problems, Ss perform in a manner *superior* to initial learning. In fact, on some occasions, as in Figure 18-14 (for spatial problems), they can learn a reversal problem after making only one error (which is necessary for informational purposes). This third effect is not merely

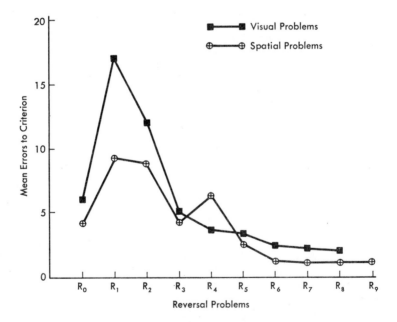

Figure 18-14. The course of reversal learning for spatial (a) and visual (b) discrimination problems in the rat. Mean number of errors made for initial learning (Ro) and each successive reversal (R_1, R_2, etc.). (Adapted with permission from Dufort, R. H., Guttman, N., & Kimble, G. A. One-trial discrimination reversal in the white rat. *J. comp. physiol. Psychol.*, 1954, **47**, 248–249, and Gatling, F. The effect of repeated stimulus reversals on learning in the rat. *J. comp. physiol. Psychol.*, 1952, **45**, 347–351.)

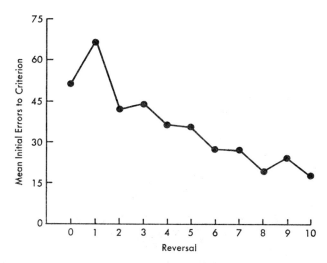

Figure 18-15. Successive discrimination-reversal learning in turtles (visual task). (Reprinted with permission from Holmes, P. A., & Bitterman, M. E. Spatial and visual habit reversal in the turtle. *J. comp. physiol. Psychol.*, 1966, **62**, 328–331.)

the result of the destruction of proactive interference; it represents positive transfer and can be explained only by assuming that, in some sense, *S* has "learned how to learn," that is, that a "game strategy" has been adopted or that a mediated attentional process is at work (cf. Mackintosh, McGonigle, Holgate, and Vanderver, 1968).

The data in Figure 18-14 are for the rat (Dufort, Guttman, and Kimble, 1954; Mackintosh et al., 1968), but similar curves have been generated by a large number of other mammals: chimpanzees (Schusterman, 1964); rhesus monkeys (Rothblat and Wilson, pers. comm.); cats (Warren, 1966); sea lions (Schusterman, 1966); opossums (Friedman and Marshall, 1965); and raccoons (Warren and Warren, 1962). It seems reasonably unlikely that each of the three aspects of the curves of Figure 18-14 could not be found in other mammalian forms if we persisted in looking for them. Furthermore, they occur under testing conditions utilizing visual, spatial, or tactual cues.

Pigeons (Bullock and Bitterman, 1962; Stearns and Bitterman, 1965) and chickens

(Bacon, Warren, and Schein, 1962; Warren et al., 1960), as well as a number of other avian species (Gonzalez, Berger, and Bitterman, 1966; Gossette, 1967) also show the progressive improvement characterized by Figure 18-14. And recently an instance of the same performance pattern has been found in a reptile (Holmes and Bitterman, 1966; see Figure 18-15). However, there are instances with birds, particularly when the discrimination problem involves discriminative key-pecking in an operant-conditioning box under the "correction" method where the positive transfer limb of the curve is difficult to obtain (Figure 18-16). This does not mean that positive transfer cannot be found in these birds (Gossette and Cohen, 1966). It merely is pointed out to show two things: first, it is necessary, as always, to remain cautious in extrapolating from one or a few experiments regarding the question of whether a given behavioral trait is "present" or "absent" in a given species; and second, this fact will be useful later on in our attempt to provide a functional analysis of reversal learning.

There seems to be sufficient evidence now

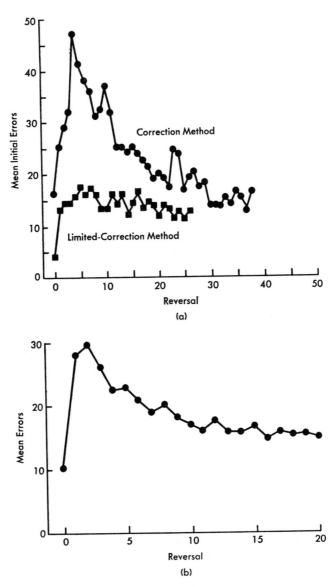

Figure 18-16. (a) Performance of pigeons on successive reversals of a visual discrimination problem. (b) Performance on a similar problem by quail. (Adapted with permission from Stearns, E. M., & Bitterman, M. E. A comparison of discriminative learning in pigeons. *Amer. J. Psychol.*, 1965, **78**, 48–56; and Gonzalez, R. C., Berger, B. D., & Bitterman, M. E. Improvement in habit-reversal as a function of amount of training per reversal and other variables. *Amer. J. Psychol.*, 1966, **79**, 517–530.)

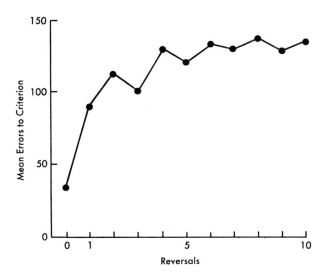

Figure 18-17.   Mean errors to criterion in an original red-green discrimination and a series of ten reversals by fish. (Adapted with permission from Behrend, E. R., & Bitterman, M. E. Further experiments on habit reversal in the fish. *Psychon. Sci.*, 1967, **8**, 363–364.)

that fish (goldfish and African mouthbreeders: Behrend, Domesick, and Bitterman, 1965; paradise fish: Warren, 1960) show a negative transfer effect, but no progressive improvement, on successive reversal problems. After extensive research it appears that this phenomenon occurs in fish whether they are trained on visual (Behrend, Domesick, and Bitterman, 1965) or spatial (Behrend and Bitterman, 1967) problems, whether the correction (Bitterman, Wodinsky, and Candland, 1958) or noncorrection (Warren, 1960) method of reinforcement presentation is used, and whether Ss are trained on each reversal problem for a fixed number of trials (Behrend and Bitterman, 1967) or to a learning criterion (Warren, 1960). Figure 18-17 shows a typical learning pattern for the fish. Even after as many as twenty reversal problems there is no indication of improvement, even though (and this is a crucial point) the Ss show *within-problem* improvement, that is, they do learn each successive discrimination problem. Whatever processes are operating in higher forms to produce progressive

improvement in reversal learning, they seem to be either absent in fish or masked by other mechanisms.

Two further experiments by Bitterman and his collaborators may help us determine the nature of the functional difference between fish and higher vertebrates. In the first experiment, Gonzalez, Holmes, and Bitterman (1967b) trained goldfish and rats to make an instrumental response for food reinforcement and then subjected them to a series of extinction sessions separated by retraining sessions in which Ss received a constant thirty reinforcements. They found that resistance to extinction over sessions followed the course shown in Figure 18-18. The results indicate that rats come to show extinction behavior that is more abrupt and is independent of interpolated retraining, whereas fish do not. The goldfish in this experiment continue to behave in a manner consistent with the number of rewarded trials immediately preceding it. This suggests that, as in studies of reward functions (in the preceding chapter), the fish is unable to "free" itself from the effect of sheer

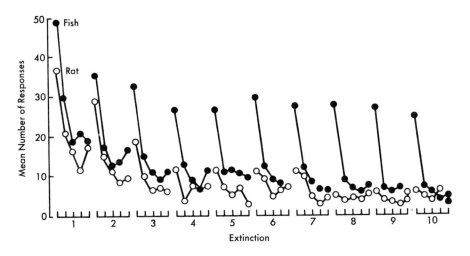

Figure 18-18.   Course of extinction in fish and rat plotted in terms of mean number of responses for successive 3-min. periods in each of ten 15-min. extinction sessions separated by one or more retraining sessions. (Reprinted with permission from Gonzalez, R. C., Holmes, N. K., & Bitterman, M. E. Asymptotic resistance to extinction in fish and rat as a function of interpolated retraining. *J. comp. physiol. Psychol.*, 1967b, **63**, 342–344.)

frequency of reinforcement. Thus, the failure of fish to "recover" from the negative transfer effect in discrimination reversal studies can be explained, in part, on the basis of the direct and permanent relationship between reinforcement and extinction of a learned discriminative response in the fish. This relationship is absent in rats (and presumably in other higher vertebrates).

Further supportive evidence for this interpretation comes from an experiment by Gonzalez, Behrend, and Bitterman (1967). Pigeons and goldfish were trained to make a visual discrimination and then were given eighty-trial reversal problems every two days. As expected, pigeons showed recovery from negative transfer (but apparently no positive transfer), whereas fish did not. To assess the degree of proactive interference displayed by each species, a "memory" score was computed on the basis of the carryover of correct responses from day 1 to day 2 within a given reversal problem. It was found that fish, but not pigeons, retained maximal

proactive interference throughout the series of reversals, suggesting that the recovery from the negative transfer effect in reversal learning by higher vertebrates is indeed the product of a "forgetting" or a "masking" of the effects of immediately preceding reinforcements. Of course, this can explain only the development of independence from processes which free Ss from a negative transfer effect (which is the only instance of progressive improvement normally found in pigeons using the "correction" method and a key-peck discrimination problem); when *positive* transfer effects are found (that is, when reversal performance is superior to performance on R_0), the differential progress of proactive interference is not a sufficient explanation (Mackintosh et al., 1968). It seems evident, then, that fish differ from higher vertebrates in at least two ways. First, they cannot develop a process that frees them from the proactive interference which disrupts performance during early reversal learning, and second, they cannot develop a second-order "strategy" or "attentional mechanism" that will permit them to utilize reversal-learning cues to their advantage. Instead, fish behavior appears to remain tied to reinforcement contingencies in a direct and unmodifiable way, unlike the behavior of higher vertebrates.

Invertebrates also do not show progressive improvement in reversal learning. In fact, they do not even show the negative transfer effect typically displayed by fish. There is some indication that isopods (Thompson, 1957), annelids (Datta, 1962), and arthropods (Longo, 1964) are able to solve each consecutive reversal problem with slightly fewer errors, but when these Ss are compared with control Ss, trained on the same discrimination problem but not subjected to reversal learning until they have received a large amount of overtraining, it appears that the very modest improvement can be attributed to some factor having to do with habituation to the test environment. The control Ss showed reversal improvement equivalent to Ss that had had a *series* of reversal problems! The retention of invertebrates, including crustaceans (Datta, Milstein, and Bitterman, 1960), from one test period to another, is minimal by mammalian standards; for example, the mean errors by crabs on trial 1 of ten successive reversal problems fell almost precisely at chance (Datta et al., 1960), and a similar result has been found for an annelid, the earthworm (Datta, 1962). Thus, although these invertebrates can learn a discrimination reversal problem (their within-problems performance improves over trials), there is little evidence for any of the between-problems phenomena typically found in mammals—the negative transfer effect, recovery from negative transfer, and progressive positive transfer.

Suppose we assume that the reversal-learning behavior of mammals such as the rat is the result of the processes of proactive interference, inhibition of proactive interference, and strategy-learning. If this is so, then we can say that fish display only the first of these processes and invertebrates do not display any of them. Whether these processes are absent in lower forms, or whether they are merely masked by other variables, is a question to be answered only by further research. However, one bit of evidence providing weak support for the view that the processes may be absent in precortical animals is supplied by Gonzalez, Roberts, and Bitterman (1964), who were able to prevent the occurrence of progressive improvement in the reversal learning of rats by making extensive cortical lesions in these Ss during infancy. But the prevention of progressive improvement occurred only for *visual* discrimination-reversal learning and, inexplicably, not for *spatial* discrimination-reversal learning.

Effects of Overtraining on Discrimination Reversal and Extradimensional (ED) Shifts. Reid (1953) trained rats on a black-white discrimination task in a Y-maze. Once the Ss had met the learning criterion, they were divided into two equivalent groups. One group was placed immediately on a reversal problem (that is, whereas the white stimulus had been rewarded previously, during reversal training the black stimulus was rewarded). The second group received an additional 150 training trials on the original problem before reversal was initiated. These 150 additional trials were called "overtraining," because the animals had already demonstrated that they had learned the discrimination by having met the learning criterion. Reid found that overtrained rats learned the reversal problem in fewer trials than the control group. Clearly, this result (called the overtraining reversal effect, or ORE) is paradoxical if one assumes, simplistically, that the strength of a discriminative response is related to frequency of reinforcement, and it has usually been taken to imply the necessity for a "two-stage" or "mediational" theory of discrimination learning.

Since Reid's initial experiment was published, a large number of studies of the ORE have been undertaken using rats as Ss (for reviews of this literature, see Mackintosh, 1965a; Paul, 1965; Sperling, 1965), and it is now clear that the ORE is not replicable in the general sense; that is, the phenomenon is not found in all experiments involving discriminative responses in the rat (Clayton, 1963; D'Amato and Jagoda, 1962; D'Amato and Schiff, 1965; Erlebacher, 1963; Hill and Spear, 1963). Consequently, an attempt has been made by several investigators to ascertain the conditions necessary for the appearance of the ORE—but, with less than signal success. No proposal has been offered for which there is not at least one instance of contradictory evidence. Nevertheless, it seems fair to assert that the more than twenty studies which have shown an ORE (in rats alone) are sufficient to establish it as a real phenomenon; and it is not abusing the literature too badly to suggest that it is most likely to appear when (1) the discrimination task involves additional, irrelevant cues (for example, when S must discriminate between two stimuli differing in form, both forms are presented in two colors that vary randomly between trials; Mackintosh, 1965b), (2) when the discrimination problem is difficult or the relevant cue is one to which S does not normally attend (Lovejoy, 1966), and (3) when large rewards are used (Theios and Blosser, 1965). If these conditions are met, the probability of obtaining the ORE in rats is very high, if less than certain.

There seems to be universal agreement that a "two-stage" theory is necessary to explain the ORE (cf. Kendler and Kendler, 1966; Mackintosh, 1965a) and although several have been proposed, they have in common the notion that discrimination training strengthens not only a particular instrumental response but also a mediation variable (for example, "attention") which makes the relevant stimulus dimension more salient than other irrelevant aspects of the environment. It is proposed that the mediation variable is acquired more slowly than the instrumental response and continues to be strengthened during overtraining. Thus, reversal learning is made easier for overtrained animals because they have acquired a set to attend to the relevant stimulus dimension (for example, "form") and must merely adjust their instrumental responses to conform to a new reinforcement contingency within that dimension.

The same general two-stage theory makes another prediction. Suppose S is trained on a discrimination problem where the discriminanda have two dimensions, call them R and I, where R is relevant and I is irrelevant. It should follow that overtraining on dimension R not only should facilitate learning a reversal problem (where R is still relevant and I is still irrelevant), but also should retard learning of an extradimensional (ED) shift problem, where R is now irrelevant and I is relevant. This is to be expected because Ss will have learned a set which is no longer appropriate and which actually interferes with acquisition of a new conditioned response.

Overtraining facilitates reversal learning by human Ss when the problem involves discrimination of nonsense syllables (Mandler and Heinemann, 1956), meaningful words (Holborn and Boe, 1965), colored forms (Uhl, 1966), or when it is a simple conditional discrimination (Hergenhahn, Capehart, and Sitterley, 1966). Children also show the ORE with visual discrimination problems (Eimas, 1966; Furth and Youniss, 1964; Tighe and Tighe, 1965). On the other hand, for human adults overtraining also facilitates ED shift performance, when the relevant and irrelevant stimuli are held constant from original learning to transfer learning (Shift ED_c in Wolff, 1967). This finding is not strictly inconsistent with the prediction of mediation theories (Zeaman and House, 1963), because the particular transfer paradigm employed is a confounded test. (The problem here is that during transfer learning Ss receive partial reinforcement for the previously rewarded cue, thus confounding the design.) But more important for our purposes is the fact that the finding is not in agreement with some of the work on subhuman forms.

Overtraining does not facilitate reversal learning, nor does it impair ED shifts, in either monkeys (Cross and Boyer, 1966; Cross, Fickling, Carpenter, and Brown, 1964; Tighe, 1965) or cats (Beck, Warren, and Sterner, 1966; Hirayoshi and Warren, 1967). This is true regardless of the maturity of the animals or the degree of prior discrimination training they have experienced ("experimental sophistication"). On the other hand, rats demonstrate the ORE under at least some conditions, and there is evidence, as well, that overtraining retards the learning of an ED shift problem (Mackintosh, 1962, 1964; but see also Tighe, Brown, and Youngs, 1965). This lack of phyletic continuity may be taken to mean that the mediation mechanisms responsible for overtraining effects may be different in different species. Alternatively, it might be that overtraining effects such as the ORE are merely masked in cats and monkeys by the operation of another, stronger process on discriminative behavior. But it is unclear what this process might be. There is some evidence that prior training on learning set problems may reduce or eliminate the differential degree of difficulty usually found between discrimination reversal and ED shift problems (Coutant and Warren, 1966); if this is so, then it could be argued that formation of a learning set (or long-term game strategy) might outweigh an attentional mediation process in determining the facility with which cats and monkeys respond to reversal and ED shift problems. But animals which have had no opportunity to develop such strategies also have failed to demonstrate the ORE (D'Amato, 1965).

The class Aves (more specifically, pigeons and chickens) also shows the ORE but, as in the rat, the effect is only obtained under a restricted set of conditions. (Positive results: Mackintosh, 1965b; Williams, 1967. Negative results: Brookshire, Warren, and Ball, 1961; Mackintosh, 1965b; Schade

and Bitterman, 1965; Warren, Brookshire, Ball, and Reynolds, 1960.) It appears that the ORE is more likely to appear when the discrimination problem is a difficult one (for example, shape discrimination) than when it is an easy one (for example, a brightness discrimination or a spatial discrimination). Furthermore, overtraining often retards the learning of an ED shift (Brookshire, Warren, and Ball, 1962; Schade and Bitterman, 1965).

The inconsistency of the results for rats and birds has led one mediation theorist (Mackintosh, 1965b) to postulate that the ORE will be found only under conditions that optimize the development of a dimensional set during the overtraining period. These conditions presumably include (1) the inclusion of irrelevant stimulus dimensions (which prevent the set from reaching asymptote prior to the overtraining period), and (2) the use of a "nondominant" stimulus dimension for discrimination training (which permits the development of the set in the first place). This theory can predict some of the negative results for rats and birds by making the assumption that rats are "spatially oriented" animals, whereas birds are "visually oriented" animals. Thus, the ORE should not appear when rats are given uncomplicated spatial problems or when birds are given uncomplicated visual problems. Although these results are usually found, the Mackintosh attentional theory fails to predict some of the other details of experiments on this topic. For example, if the Mackintosh hypothesis is correct, one should predict that, at a minimum, the ratio of errors to criterion on the initial (pretransfer) visual discrimination problem and on the initial spatial discrimination problem should be considerably larger in rats than in birds (because of the presumed difference in attentional sets prior to training), yet the ratios are nearly identical (Brookshire, Warren, and Ball, 1962). Furthermore, if birds are visually oriented, then overtraining on a visual problem should have little effect on an ED shift but overtraining on a spatial problem should retard an ED shift. Precisely the opposite is found (Brookshire, Warren, and Ball, 1962). Moreover, if animals develop dimensional sets, then a confounded set of discrimination problems which involves sometimes reversals and sometimes ED shifts should produce, over problems, one of two results, either (1) *S*s should not show progressive improvement at all (because the development of an attentional set is not strictly adaptive), or (2) *S*s should display improvement in reversal learning but at the expense of increased difficulty in ED shifting. An experiment by Schade and Bitterman (1966) has found that with pigeons neither of these predictions is upheld—*S*s showed progressive improvement on both reversal and ED shift problems. Thus, the pigeon apparently possesses a mediation mechanism other than an attentional set, and if this is so, then this second mechanism probably influences behavior following overtraining as well.

Neither paradise fish (Warren, 1960) nor goldfish (Mackintosh, Mackintosh, Safriel-Jorne, and Sutherland, 1966) have been observed to show the ORE, but it is unfortunate that we have so little data on which to make a judgment. Nonetheless, the failure to find the ORE in fish is consistent with the absence of improvement in successive discrimination reversals in these animals and strengthens the hypothesis that mediation mechanisms are absent in these simple vertebrates.

The octopus, on the other hand, behaves in a fashion similar to rats and birds. Mackintosh and Mackintosh (1963) have found the ORE in these animals, and Mackintsoh and Holgate (1965) have observed impairment of an ED shift following overtraining. These data from an invertebrate make it very clear that we are unlikely to find any simple phyletic regularity in regard to the possession of mediation mechanisms and confirms the impression developed in the consideration of the data on successive discrimination reversals that even so simple an operation as the introduction of overtraining trials may alter or influence several different mechanisms in different animals. Consider the summary represented by Table 18-3. Although the table ignores certain fine points on each of the three phenomena depicted, it may nevertheless be instructive. If further research fails to provide exceptions, it would appear that there are several different patterns of behavior displayed by the animals summarized, and it is extremely unlikely that a single hypothesized mechanism

Table **18-3** Behavior of Different Animals, Following Overtraining, on Discrimination Reversal and ED Shift Problems

	Overtraining Reversal Effect (Facilitation Effect)	Effect of Overtraining on ED Shifts* (Retardation Effect)
Human Adults	+	0
Human Children	+	No Data
Monkeys	0	0
Cats	0	No Data
Rats	+	+
Birds	+	+
Fish	0	No Data
Octopuses	+	+

+ = transfer consistent with attention theory is found; 0 = transfer inconsistent with attention theory is found.
* See Wolff (1967) for a description of different ED shift paradigms.

(however complicated its action) can account for all the data.

There is another problem we have left unattended so far. When the ORE is not observed, either of two possible behavior outcomes remain: (1) overtraining does not alter reversal learning at all, or (2) overtraining retards reversal learning. To this date little attention has been given to the conditions under which either of these two possibilities will occur (but see Mackintosh, 1965a) and to their relationship to phyletic status. Until this is done, it will be impossible to evaluate effectively the ORE itself, for behavior during transfer learning obviously depends on whether there exists an interaction with variables inclining S to show perseverative behavior during reversal which might mask attentional processes while leading us to believe they do not exist.

Ethological Considerations

Up to this point we have discussed the topics of learning ability and learning function among different animals almost exclusively as though we can give an adequate account of them simply by judicious use of the hypothetico-deductive method. That is, emphasis has been placed on the assumption that we can fashion experiments, based on theoretical considerations, which will tell us how animals learn and how they differ in learning—if only we are ingenious enough in our method of design.

Ethology has contributed to the comparative psychology of learning by forcing us to admit that such an approach is limited in the absence of an understanding of the instinctive patterns and ecology of each species. This understanding is obtainable only through naturalistic observation. Also, it begins with description of ongoing behavior rather than experimental modification or control of it (although experimentation may follow). When there are variations in the momentary behavioral repertoire of two species, there is a good chance that this will influence the way in which we must think about learning in each of them. Let us consider three examples of how this is so.

Interferences of Learning Created by Species-Specific Responses: Instinctive Drift

Regardless of the assumptions we might wish to make concerning the equivalent of reinforcement contingencies in different animals (see Chapter 18), it nevertheless is true that within a given species it is not possible to predict in the abstract how the learning of a given response will progress over time or over trials. Some responses, if they are learned under conditions favoring the emergence of competing instinctive responses, may decay, or "drift" over time. Breland and Breland (1961, 1966) have catalogued a large number of instances of this phenomenon during attempts to develop instrumental responses in animals for commercial purposes. Consider the following examples.

Instinctive Drift in Raccoons. The Brelands (1961) have reported an attempt to train raccoons to put money (two coins) in a "piggy bank" (metal container) by reinforcing Ss for this act with food. In principle, the technique used was similar to that which the comparative psychologist might use to train pigeons to peck a key or rats to press a lever. However, the following account describes the difficulties they encountered.

We started out by reinforcing him for picking up a single coin. Then the metal container was introduced, with the requirement that he drop the coin into the container. Here we ran into the first bit of difficulty: he seemed to have a great deal of trouble letting go of the coin. He would rub it up against the inside of the container, pull it back out, and clutch it firmly for several seconds. However, he would finally turn it loose and receive his food reinforcement. Then the final contingency: we put him on a ratio of 2, requiring that he pick up both coins and put them in the container.

Now the raccoon really had problems (and so did we). Not only could he not let go of the coins, but he spent seconds, even minutes, rubbing them together (in a most miserly fashion), and dipping them into the container. He carried on this behavior to such an extent that the practical application we had in mind—a display featuring a raccoon putting money in a piggy bank— simply was not feasible. The rubbing behavior became worse and worse as time went on, in spite of nonreinforcement [Breland and Breland, 1961, p. 682].

Instinctive Drift in Pigs. The Brelands tried a similar training procedure with pigs. They attempted to reward the animal for picking up four or five wooden coins and depositing them in a large "piggy bank" 6 ft. away. However, although the animals usually started out in the early stages of training in a quite promising fashion, after a while the following problem developed:

Over a period of weeks the behavior would become slower and slower. He might run over eagerly for each dollar, but on the way back, instead of carrying the dollar and depositing it simply and cleanly, he would repeatedly drop it, root it, drop it again, root it along the way, pick it up, toss it up in the air, drop it, root it some more, and so on.

We thought this behavior might simply be the dilly-dallying of an animal on a low drive. However, the behavior persisted and gained in strength in spite of a severely increased drive—he finally went through the ratios so slowly that he did not get enough to eat in the course of a day. Finally it would take the pig about 10 minutes to transport four coins a distance of about 6 feet. This problem behavior developed repeatedly in successive pigs [Breland and Breland, 1961, p. 683].

It should be noted that the instinctive "washing behavior" of the raccoon and the instinctive "rooting behavior" of the pig, although interfering with the learning of the particular responses under study, do not interfere with all learned behavior, and both animals have been successfully trained on other problems (Breland and Breland, 1966). But it is clear that we can predict whether learning will occur and be maintained only after we have an understanding of the ethology of the organism—and consequently of the degree to which instinctive responses will intrude on learned responses.

Phylogenetic and Ontogenetic Determinants of Learning Function: Imprinting

There seems to be reasonably good evidence to support the proposition that specific animals, at specific stages of development, can profit from experience according to principles that are not only dissimilar to those found in other species but also dissimilar to those found in the same species at another age. This class of behavior has been termed *imprinting* and is exemplified by the following experimental demonstration (Hess, 1959). Ducklings were hatched in the dark and kept isolated until 16 hrs.

old. Then they were released in a circular track around which a decoy could be rotated. It was found that (1) the duckling would "follow" the decoy when it was moving, and (2) at a later time the animal would continue to follow the decoy and show a preference for models similar to the imprinted decoy.

One very important characteristic of the imprinting was that it would only occur during a restricted developmental period, called the *critical period*. Figure 19-1 depicts the critical period for the ducklings in Hess's experiment. The optimal age for the development of this particular attachment was 16 hrs. and virtually no imprinting occurred after 32 hrs.

The fact that imprinted following occurs only during a temporally short critical period has led investigators (e.g., Hess, 1964) to suggest that this learned response cannot be considered to be merely an instance of ordinary classical or instrumental conditioning, because conditioning usually can be affected in animals over a very wide developmental range (see Warren, 1965a). But there are even more cogent reasons to

believe that the imprinted following response is a different sort of learning phenomenon:

1. In order to effect conditioning, there must be a selective pairing of a stimulus and a response. The stimulus is considered to be "neutral" (that is, it does not normally elicit the CR) prior to training. In imprinting, an S-R bond is simply strengthened through practice. In other words, whereas in conditioning there are two functionally separate external stimuli necessary (serving as cue and as reinforcement), in imprinting there is only one. This has led Hinde, Thorpe, and Vince (1965) to characterize imprinting as "self-reinforced learning."

2. There is evidence (Hess, 1962; Thompson and Dubanoski, 1964) that imprinting follows a "law of effort," such that it improves not only with additional practice but also with the effortfulness of the response. Conditioning ordinarily does not.

3. Klopfer (1967) has found that the retention of an imprinted response is related to the perceptual preference of the *S*s toward the imprinted stimulus. Whereas

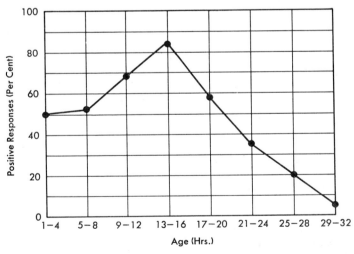

Figure 19-1. The critical period for ducklings. The per cent following responses made by *S*s that had been imprinted at different ages, calculated in hours from the time of hatching. (Reprinted with permission from Hess, E. Imprinting. *Science*, 1959, **130**, 133–140.)

during the initial training period two stimuli might evoke equal amounts of following in ducklings, the amount of following on subsequent retention tests varies with the characteristics of the stimulus. This suggests that although the following response is indeed learned, its evocation is partly controlled by nonassociative factors. The characteristics of the CS used in conditioning experiments, on the other hand, may have an effect on whether the CR will be observed, but this, typically, is in evidence during the acquisition period itself.

4. There is some evidence (Jaynes, 1958) that retention of imprinting depends on the amount of initial practice (a characteristic of other learning phenomena). It is possible to argue, however, that under optimal conditions imprinting is surprisingly well retained (Hess, 1964), although not irreversible, as claimed initially by Lorenz (1935). There are insufficient data at this time to ascertain whether retention of an imprinted response follows different laws than retention of classical and instrumental conditioned responses, but the fact that the response attachment seems to follow the principle of primacy (the first stimulus-response attachment seems to prevent further attachments; Hess, 1962), rather than the principle of recency, suggests that this might very well be the case.

Imprinting does not occur in all animal forms, the types of imprinted responses vary widely, and there are species differences in the length and time of the critical period. It seems unlikely that these important factors can be ignored for long by the student of the comparative psychology of learning.

Phylogenetic Determinants of Specific Learning Patterns: Navigation in Birds

It is well known that migratory birds follow rather specific "flyways" when moving from one geographical area to another in the spring and fall, and that a very large proportion of any species finds its way to the same nesting area year after year. In addition, one of the most amazing feats of navigation is that displayed by homing pigeons, which have been able to return to their own loft after being displaced from it by hundreds of miles. Although it is possible to argue that seasonal migratory tendencies are a product of rather simple and innate mechanisms such as sun-compass orientation (for example, the animal can sense direction, but no more, from the sun and then flies, say, "southwest") and a tendency to be influenced in flight by the topography of the area (rivers, coastlines, mountain ridges, and so on.), a more complicated set of principles appears to be necessary to explain homing in birds, for homing implies not only that the animal be able to tell direction but that he be able to establish, as a ship's navigator does, his "present position" in relation to his goal. The difference is to be seen if one contemplates being lost in a forest. It is one thing to determine (by means of the sun, for instance) which way is east and which way is west; it is quite another to determine whether home is to the east or to the west. Homing pigeons are able to do this, and it is now becoming apparent that they do so by means of two learning mechanisms, one utilizing the sun as a cue and the other landmarks. Consider the following experiment, conducted by G. V. T. Matthews (1963). Pigeons were removed from a loft near Cambridge, England, and released at a point 25 miles away. Figure 19-2 shows the "vanishing point" (the point where, with binoculars, the bird could no longer be seen from the site of release) for the birds on each of six successive trials from the same release point. The data indicate three things. First, the birds were disoriented on trial 1 (although they did eventually find the home loft); second, their ability to orient properly improved dramatically over the six trials; and third, since trial 6 occurred on an overcast

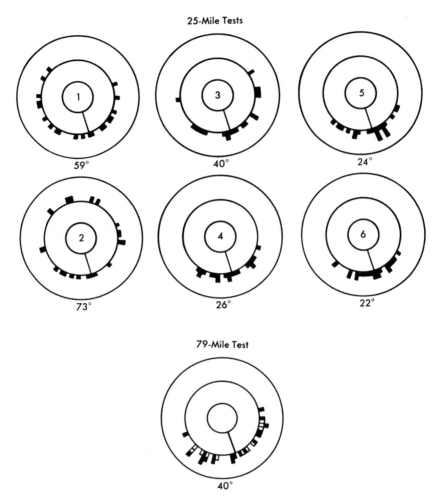

Figure 19-2. Matthews' experiment on homing in pigeons. Vanishing points in successive releases at the same point twenty-five miles away. Each 5° block represents the bearing on which a bird was lost from sight. The figure to the right of each circle is the average deviation of these bearings from that of home (indicated by the radial line). The central figure is the number of the test. Landmarks had been learned by Test 6 but not on Test 1. At a later date the same birds were released seventy-nine miles from home and showed good orientation on the first trial. (Reprinted with permission from Matthews, G. V. T. The orientation of pigeons as affected by the learning of landmarks and by the distance of displacement. *Anim. Behav.*, 1963, **11,** 310–317.)

day, their ability to show good orientation did not require the use of the sun as a cue. This suggests that the birds used landmarks as cues to home more efficiently, that they learned to use the landmarks, and that the learning required very few trials.

Following trials 1 to 6, the same birds were released at points 2.5, 5.0, and 10.0 miles from home—*in any direction*—and the data regarding "vanishing points" indicated that homing remained quite accurate, even though the compass direction toward home was usually quite different from the SSW flight required on trials 1 to 6. The birds evidently had learned, on trials 1 to 6, enough about the landmarks within a radius of 10 miles of Cambridge to be able to display good navigation.

Next, Matthews released these same birds from sites at distances 23 to 35 miles from Cambridge but again in different directions. The result was random scattering. Apparently, the animals had not learned enough about landmarks to be able to use them effectively at distances much greater than 10 to 20 miles from the loft.

Finally, a release was made from a new site at a distance of 79 miles, over twice as far from the loft than the birds had ever been before. Figure 19-2 presents the results for this test; the vanishing point was found to be in the general direction of the loft, even though at 23 or 35 miles this had not been the case. Considering especially the fact that the environment must have been unfamiliar to the birds, it seems clear that they used some other set of cues, such as the sun, for purposes of orientation. The ability of the animals to make the discrimination of the arc angle, altitude, and movement of the sun necessary to "compute" the directional relationship between the release site and the loft has been tested by Meyer (1964, 1966). He found that pigeons can make discriminations which, by estimation, ought to permit them to detect 30- to 60-mile displacements, a fact which is remarkably consistent with Matthews' data. Matthews' pigeons (in the absence of learned landmarks) could orientate quite well at 79 miles, but not at 23 to 35 miles.

A reasonable assumption from this and other experiments is that two learning mechanisms operate in bird navigation, and that one of them (based on the use of the sun as a cue) is quite unusual. Although it is not known whether the processes involved in such learning are unique, the behavior which is learned is quite remarkable. It involves the possibility that the animal learns and remembers the details of the

sun's arc at the point of the home loft, that he corrects his memory as the seasons change, and that he can utilize this remembered information for purposes of navigation over unfamiliar terrain. Certainly there is reason to believe that our understanding of animal learning might be broadened by the study of specific learning patterns such as this, even though the problems of experimental control associated with such work are awesome to contemplate.

Conclusion

Early work by comparative psychologists was oriented toward determining the relationship between learning ability and phyletic status. The underlying assumption was that "intelligence" is correlated with the complexity of the nervous system, and it was anticipated, therefore, that the extent to which an animal could solve problems would be related to its evolutionary history. It is now known that such an undertaking is methodologically suspect; more important, it is probably unwise to assume that learning is always the best way for an animal to cope with its environment. Many organisms have evolved in such a way that they have extremely efficient genetically controlled behavior patterns for handling the exigencies of life without recourse to what we, anthropocentrically, call learning. Thus, it is unclear why one should expect that more complex organisms always will exhibit more efficient, or a broader array of, association mechanisms.

Recent evidence (cited in Chapters 18 and 19) suggests that there is a far more critical way in which comparative psychology may contribute to our understanding of learning. We can no longer assume that all animals learn in the same fashion, and it appears that it will be necessary for us to determine the extent to which different adaptive processes exist in different taxa before we can hope to formulate a general theory of learning.

Glossary

correction method. One of two training techniques used in discrimination learning experiments. Suppose *S* is presented with two stimuli, A and B. Under the correction method, if A is correct but *S* selects B, the trial continues and *S* is permitted to choose again between A and B until it receives reinforcement. In other words, a "trial" is defined as the presentation of the discrimination task *until* S *makes a correct response* (see *noncorrection method*).

extradimensional (ED) shift problem. A discrimination problem in which the stimulus dimension relevant for solution has been changed. For example, if the discrimination stimuli vary in the dimensions of color and form, and if *S* has already solved the problem for color, a new problem in which *S* must attend to form but no longer to color is called an ED shift problem.

habituation. A relatively permanent decrement in the response to a stimulus which occurs upon repeated presentation of the stimulus. Habituation is thought to be a primitive form of learning. If habituation occurs to a stimulus that is later used as the CS for classical conditioning, the CR is retarded in its development.

maximizing. A term used in probability learning experiments to depict behavior which produces the greatest probability of reward. Thus, in a two-choice discrimination problem with different probabilities of reward for the two stimuli, *S*s maximize by always selecting the stimulus for which the probability of reinforcement is greater.

noncorrection method. One of the training techniques used in discrimination learning experiments. Suppose *S* is presented with two stimuli, A and B. Under the noncorrection method, if A is correct but *S* selects B, the trial is considered to be concluded, an error is recorded, and the next trial is begun. (That is, A and B may now be presented in different contexts; whereas A may have been on the left before, it may now be on the right.) Thus, a trial is defined as the presentation of the problem *until* S

makes a single choice, regardless of whether the choice is right or wrong (see *correction method*).

nonrandom matching. A term used in probability learning experiments which describes the choice behavior toward stimuli as corresponding to probability of reward. However, the matching behavior is the product of systematic responses sequences (for example, a win-stay, lose-shift strategy; position preference; stimulus perseveration; and so on). The response on any trial n, therefore, is not random (see *random matching*).

perseveration. Repetition of a response to a stimulus in a discrimination problem even though the response is inappropriate in terms of the conditions of reinforcement.

pharyngeal ganglia. Two masses of nervous cells in the anterior portion of annelids, particularly marine annelids such as *Nereis.* These ganglia have been regarded as a primitive brain and function both as sensory and motor centers and as a source for the production of hormones.

pseudoconditioning. A general term referring to an increase in the strength of a response to a CS which depends only upon prior experience with a US.

random matching. A term used in probability learning experiments to depict choice behavior toward each stimulus which corresponds to the probability of reinforcement. For example, if Stimulus A is rewarded 70 per cent of the time and stimulus B is rewarded 30 per cent of the time, *S* would exhibit matching if it selected the two stimuli in a ratio of 70:30. The *S* would be considered to be exhibiting random matching if no systematic response sequences could be found (see *nonrandom matching*).

sensitization. An increase in the strength of an unlearned response (UR) to a CS when a US is contingent upon CS presentation. Sensitization is sometimes called alpha conditioning; it is presumed to differ from "true" conditioning in that it is really a UR which is being strengthened, not a CR.

yoked-control condition. A procedure used in instrumental learning studies to determine whether the putative conditioned response is in fact the result of the temporal contiguity of reinforcement rather than some other condition of the experimental procedure. A yoked-control *S* is paired with an experimental *S* in the following way: when the experimental *S* makes a CR, *E* has programmed the study so that both *S*s receive reinforcement. Thus, the experimental *S* can "control" his reinforcements by his own behavior; the yoked *S* cannot. If the yoked *S* develops the same response, then that response cannot be a CR; that is, it is not the result of an association with reinforcement.

References

Adler, N., & Hogan, J. A. Classical conditioning and punishment of an instinctive response in *Betta splendens, Anim. Behav.*, 1963, **11**, 351–354.

Anderson, N. H., & Grant, D. A. A test of a statistical learning theory model for two-choice behavior with double stimulus events. *J. exp. Psychol.*, 1957, **54**, 305–317.

Bacon, H. R., Warren, J. M., & Schein, M. W. Non-spatial reversal learning in chickens. *Anim. Behav.*, 1962, **10**, 239–243.

Barnes, C. D., & Katzung, B. G. Stimulus polarity and conditioning in planaria. *Science*, 1963, **141**, 728–730.

Baxter, R., & Kimmell, H. D. Conditioning and extinction in the planarian. *Amer. J. Psychol.*, 1963, **76**, 665–669.

Beck, C. H., Warren, J. M., & Sterner, R. Overtraining and reversal learning by cats and rhesus monkeys. *J. comp. physiol. Psychol.*, 1966, **62**, 332–335.

Behrend, E. R., Bauman, B. A., Bitterman, M. E. Probability-discrimination in the fish. *Amer. J. Psychol.*, 1965, **78**, 83–89.

Behrend, E. R., & Bitterman, M. E. Probability matching in the fish. *Amer. J. Psychol.*, 1961, **74**, 542–551.

Behrend, E. R., & Bitterman, M. E. Probability matching in the goldfish. *Psychon. Sci.*, 1966, **6**, 327–328.

Behrend, E. R., & Bitterman, M. E. Further experiments on habit reversal in the fish. *Psychon. Sci.*, 1967, **8**, 363–364.

Behrend, E. R., Domesick, V. B., & Bitterman, M. E. Habit reversal in the fish. *J. comp. physiol. Psychol.*, 1965, **60**, 407–411.

Best, J. B. The photosensitization of *Paramecia aurelia* by temperature shock: A study of a reported conditioned response in unicellular organisms. *J. exp. Zool.*, 1954, **126**, 87–100.

Best, J. B. Behaviour of planaria in instrumental learning paradigms. *Anim. Behav.*, Suppl. 1, 1965, 69–75.

Best, J. B., & Elshtain, E. Unconditioned response to electric shock: Mechanism in planarians. *Science*, 1966, **151**, 707–709.

Best, J. B., Elshtain, E., & Wilson, D. D. Single monophasic square-wave electric pulse excitation of the planarian *Dugesia dorotocephala. J. comp. physiol. Psychol.*, 1967, **63**, 198–207.

Best, J. B., & Rubenstein, I. Maze learning and associated behavior in planaria. *J. comp. physiol. Psychol.*, 1962, **55**, 560–566.

Bharucha-Reid, R. P. Latent learning in earthworms. *Science*, 1956, **123**, 222.

Bitterman, M. E. Toward a comparative psychology of learning. *Amer. Psychol.*, 1960, **15**, 704–712.

Bitterman, M. E. Classical conditioning in the goldfish as a function of the CS-US interval. *J. comp. physiol. Psychol.*, 1964, **58**, 359–366.

Bitterman, M. E. Phyletic differences in learning. *Amer. Psychol.*, 1965, **20**, 396–410.

Bitterman, M. E., Wodinsky, J., & Candland, D. K. Some comparative psychology. *Amer. J. Psychol.*, 1958, **71**, 94–110.

Black, R. W., & Black, P. E. Heart rate conditioning as a function of interstimulus interval in rats. *Psychon. Sci.*, 1967, **8**, 219–220.

Black, A. H., Carlson, N. J., & Solomon, R. L. Exploratory studies of the conditioning of autonomic responses in curarized dogs. *Psychol. Monogr.*, 1962, **76**, No. 29.

Boneau, C. A. The interstimulus interval and the latency of the conditioned eyelid response. *J. exp. Psychol.*, 1958, **56**, 464–472.

Bramstedt, F. Dressurversache mit Paramecium candatum and stylouchia mytilus. *Z. vergl. Physiol.*, 1935, **22**, 490–516.

Bramstedt, F. Uber die Dressurfahigkeit der Ciliaten. *Verhandlungen Deutschen Gesellschaft*, 1939, **41**, 111–132.

Braungart, D. C., & Buddeke, R. *An introduction to animal biology* (6th Edition). St. Louis: Mosby, 1964.

Breland, K., & Breland, M. The misbehavior of organisms. *Amer. Psychol.*, 1961, **16**, 681–684.

Breland, K., & Breland, M. *Animal Behavior*. New York: Macmillan, 1966.

Brookshire, K. H., Warren, J. M., & Ball, G. G. Reversal and transfer learning following overtraining in rat and chicken. *J. comp. physiol. Psychol.*, 1961, **54**, 98–102.

Bullock, D. H., & Bitterman, M. E. Habit reversal in the pigeon. *J. comp. physiol. Psychol.*, 1962, **55**, 958–962.

Caldwell, D. F., & Werboff, J. Classical conditioning in newborn rats. *Science*, 1962, **136**, 1118–1119.

Carleton, P. L., & Vogel, J. R. Habituation and conditioning. *J. comp. physiol. Psychol.*, 1967, **63**, 348–351.

Church, R. M., & Black, A. H. Latency of the conditioned heart rate as a function of the CS–US interval. *J. comp. physiol. Psychol.*, 1958, **51**, 478–482.

Clayton, K. N. Reversal performance by rats following overlearning with and without irrelevant stimuli. *J. exp. Psychol.*, 1963, **66**, 255–259.

Copeland, M. An apparent conditioned response in *Nereis virens*. *J. comp. Psychol.*, 1930, **10**, 339–354.

Copeland, M., & Brown, F. A. Modification of behavior in *Nereis virens*. *Biol. Bull. mar. biol. Lab., Woods Hole*, 1934, **67**, 356–364.

Corning, W. C. The effect of classical conditioning on nucleic acid quantity and metabolism in planarians. *Dissert. Abstracts*, 1964, **25**, 2026–2027. (a)

Corning, W. C. Evidence of right-left discrimination in planarians. *J. Psychol.*, 1964, **58**, 131–139. (b)

Coutant, L. W., & Warren, J. M. Reversal and nonreversal shifts by cats and rhesus monkeys. *J. comp. physiol. Psychol.*, 1966, **61**, 484–487.

Crawford, F. T., King, F. J., & Siebert, L. E. Amino acid analysis of planarians following conditioning. *Psychon. Sci.*, 1965, **2**, 49–50.

Crawford, F. T., & Skeen, L. C. Operant responding in the planarian: A replication study. *Psychol. Rep.*, 1967, **20**, 1023–1027.

Crespi, L. P. Amount of reinforcement and the level of performance. *Psychol. Rev.*, 1942, **51**, 341–357.

Cross, H. A., & Boyer, W. N. Influence of overlearning on single habit reversal in naive rhesus monkeys. *Psychon. Sci.*, 1966, **4**, 245–246.

Cross, H. A., Fickling, R. M., Carpenter, J. B., & Brown, L. T. Discrimination reversal performances in squirrel monkeys as a function of prereversal experience and overlearning. *Psychon. Sci.*, 1964, **1**, 353–354.

Cummings, S. B., & Moreland, C. C. Sensitization versus conditioning in planaria: Some methodological considerations. *Amer. Psychol.*, 1959, **14**, 410.

D'Amato, M. R. The overlearning reversal effect in monkeys provided a salient irrelevant dimension. *Psychon. Sci.*, 1965, **3**, 21–22.

D'Amato, M. R., & Jagoda, H. Overlearning and position reversal. *J. exp. Psychol.*, 1962, **64**, 117–122.

D'Amato, M. R., & Schiff, D. Overlearning and brightness-discrimination reversal. *J. exp. Psychol.*, 1965, **69**, 375–381.

Datta, L-E.G. Learning in the earthworm, *Lumbricus terrestris*. *Amer. J. Psychol.*, 1962, **75**, 531–553.

Datta, L-E.G., Millstein, S., & Bitterman, M. E. Habit reversal in the crab. *J. comp. physiol. Psychol.*, 1960, **53**, 275–278.

Day, L. M., & Bentley, M. A note on learning in Paramecium. *J. anim. Behav.*, 1911, **1**, 67–73.

Deaux, E. B., & Gormezano, I. Eyeball

retraction: Classical conditioning and extinction in the albino rabbit. *Science*, 1963, **141**, 630–631.

DeBold, R. C., Thompson, W. R., & Landraitis, C. Differences in responses to light between two species of planaria: *Dugesia tigrina* and *D. dorotocephala*. *Psychon. Sci.*, 1965, **2**, 79–80.

Dollard, J., & Miller, N. E. *Personality and psychotherapy*. New York: McGraw-Hill, 1950.

Doty, B. A., Jones, C. N., & Doty, L. A. Learning-set formation by mink, ferrets, skunks, and cats. *Science*, 1967, **155**, 1579–1580.

Dufort, R. H., Guttman, N., & Kimble, G. A. One-trial discrimination reversal in the white rat. *J. comp. physiol. Psychol.*, 1954, **47**, 248–249.

Eimas, P. D. Effects of overtraining, irrelevant stimuli, and training task on reversal discrimination learning in children. *J. exp. Child Psychol.*, 1966, **3**, 315–323.

Erlebacher, A. Reversal learning in rats as a function of percentage of reinforcement and degree of learning. *J. exp. Psychol.*, 1963, **66**, 84–90.

Evans, S. M. The effect of brain extirpation on learning and retention in *Nereid* polychaetes. *Anim. Behav.*, 1963a, **11**, 172–178.

Evans, S. M. Behavior of the polychaete *Nereis* in T-mazes. *Anim. Behav.*, 1963b, **11**, 397–392.

Evans, S. M. Non-associative behavioural modifications in the polychaete *Nereis diversicolor*. *Anim. Behav.*, 1966a, **14**, 107–119.

Evans, S. M. Non-associative avoidance learning in *Nereid* polychaetes. *Anim. Behav.*, 1966b, **14**, 102–106.

French, J. W. Trial and error learning in *Paramecium*. *J. exp. Psychol.*, 1940, **26**, 609–613.

Friedman, H., & Marshall, D. A. Position reversal training in the Virginia opossum: evidence for the acquisition of a learning set. *Quart. J. exp. Psychol.*, 1965, **17**, 250–254.

Froloff, J. P. Bedingte Reflexe bei Fischen. I. Mitteilung. *Pflug. Arch. ges. Physiol.*, 1925, **208**, 261–271.

Fromer, R. Conditioned vasomotor re-

sponses in the rabbit. *J. comp. physiol. Psychol.*, 1963, **56**, 1050–1055.

Furth, H. G., & Youniss, J. Effect of overtraining on three discrimination shifts in children. *J. comp. physiol. Psychol.*, 1964, **57**, 290–293.

Gelber, B. Investigations of the behavior of *Paramecium aurelia*: I. Modification of behavior after training with reinforcement. *J. comp. physiol. Psychol.*, 1952, **45**, 58–65.

Gelber, B. Retention in *Paramecium aurelia*. *J. comp. physiol. Psychol.*, 1958, **51**, 110–115.

Gerall, A. A., & Woodward, J. K. Conditioning of the human pupillary dilation response as a function of CS-UCS interval. *J. exp. Psychol.*, 1958, **55**, 501–507.

Goldstein, A. C., Spies, G., & Sepinwall, J. Conditioning of the nictitating membrane in the frog, *Rana p. pipiens*. *J. comp. physiol. Psychol.*, 1964, **57**, 456–458.

Gonzalez, R. C., Behrend, E. R., & Bitterman, M. E. Partial reinforcement in the fish: Experiments with spaced trials and partial delay. *Amer. J. Psychol.*, 1965, **78**, 198–207.

Gonzalez, R. C., Behrend, E. R., & Bitterman, M. E. Reversal learning and forgetting in bird and fish. *Science*, 1967, **158**, 519–521.

Gonzalez, R. C., Berger, B. D., & Bitterman, M. E. Improvement in habit-reversal as a function of amount of training per reversal and other variables. *Amer. J. Psychol.*, 1966, **79**, 517–530.

Gonzalez, R. C., & Bitterman, M. E. A further study of partial reinforcement in the turtle. *Quart. J. exp. Psychol.*, 1962, **14**, 109–112.

Gonzalez, R. C., & Bitterman, M. E. Partial reinforcement effect in the goldfish as a function of amount of reward. *J. comp. physiol. Psychol.*, 1967, **64**, 163–167.

Gonzalez, R. C., Eskin, R. M., & Bitterman, M. E. Alternating and random partial reinforcement in the fish, with some observations on asymptotic resistance to extinction. *Amer. J. Psychol.*, 1961, **74**, 561–568.

Gonzalez, R. C., Eskin, R. M., & Bitterman, M. E. Extinction in the fish after partial and consistent reinforcement with number of reinforcements equated. *J. comp. physiol. Psychol.*, 1962, **55**, 381–386.

Gonzalez, R. C., Eskin, R. M., & Bitterman, M. E. Further experiments on partial reinforcement in the fish. *Amer. J. Psychol.*, 1963, **76**, 366–375.

Gonzalez, R. C., Holmes, N. K., & Bitterman, M. E. Resistance to extinction in the goldfish as a function of frequency and amount of reward. *Amer. J. Psychol.*, 1967, **80**, 269–275. (a)

Gonzalez, R. C., Holmes, N. K., & Bitterman, M. E. Asymptotic resistance to extinction in fish and rat as a function of interpolated retraining. *J. comp. physiol. Psychol.*, 1967, **63**, 342–344. (b)

Gonzalez, R. C., Roberts, W. A., & Bitterman, M. E. Learning in adult rats with extensive cortical lesions made in infancy. *Amer. J. Psychol.*, 1964, **77**, 547–562.

Goodnow, J. J. Determinants of choice-distribution in two-choice situations. *Amer. J. Psychol.*, 1955, **68**, 106–116.

Gormezano, I., Schneiderman, N., Deaux, E. B., & Fuentes, I. Nictitating membrane: classical conditioning and extinction in the albino rabbit. *Science*, 1962, **138**, 33–34.

Gossette, R. L. Successive discrimination reversal (SDR) performances of four avian species on a brightness discrimination task. *Psychon. Sci.*, 1967, **8**, 17–18.

Gossette, R. L., & Cohen, H. Error reduction by pigeons on a spatial successive reversal task under conditions of non-correction. *Psychol. Rep.*, 1966, **18**, 367–370.

Graf, V., Bullock, D. H., & Bitterman, M. E. Further experiments on probability-matching in the pigeon. *J. exp. anal. Behav.*, 1964, **7**, 151–157.

Grant, D. A., & Adams, J. K. "Alpha" conditioning in the eyelid. *J. exp. Psychol.*, 1944, **34**, 136–142.

Grant, D. A., Hake, H. W., & Hornseth, J. P. Acquisition and extinction of a verbal conditioned response with differing percentages of reinforcement. *J. exp. Psychol.*, 1951, **42**, 1–5.

Griffard, C. D. Classical conditioning of the planarian *Phagocata gracilis* to

waterflow. *J. comp. physiol. Psychol.*, 1963, **56**, 597–600.

Griffard, C. D., & Pierce, J. T. Conditioned discrimination in the planarian. *Science*, 1964, **144**, 1472–1473.

Halas, E. S., James, R. L., & Knutson, C. S. An attempt at classical conditioning in the planarian. *J. comp. physiol. Psychol.*, 1962, **55**, 969–971.

Halas, E. S., James, R. L., & Stone, L. A. Types of responses elicited in planaria by light. *J. comp. physiol. Psychol.*, 1961, **54**, 302–305.

Hamilton, G. V. A study of trial-and-error reactions in mammals. *J. anim. Behav.*, 1911, **1**, 33–66.

Hamilton, G. V. A study of perseverance reaction in primates and rodents, *Behav. Monogr.*, 1916, **3**, 1–65.

Harlow, H. F. The development of learning in the rhesus monkey. *Amer. Sci.*, 1959, **47**, 459–479.

Harlow, H. F. Learning set and error factor theory. In S. Koch (Ed.), *Psychology: A study of a science.* Vol. 2. New York: McGraw-Hill, 1959.

Hayes, K. J., Thompson, R., & Hayes, C. Discrimination learning sets. *J. comp. physiol. Psychol.*, 1953, **46**, 99–104.

Hergenhahn, B. R., Capehart, J., & Sitterley, T. E. Overlearning reversal effect on a conditional discrimination task. *Psychol. Rep.*, 1966, **18**, 809–810.

Hess, E. Imprinting. *Science*, 1959, **130**, 133–140.

Hess, E. H. Ethology: An approach toward the complete analysis of behavior. In *New Directions in Psychology*. New York: Holt, 1962.

Hess, E. H. Imprinting in birds. *Science*, 1964, **146**, 1128–1139.

Hill, W. F., & Spear, N. C. A replication of overlearning and reversal in a T-maze. *J. exp. Psychol.*, 1963, **65**, 317.

Hinde, R. A. *Animal Behavior.* New York: McGraw-Hill, 1966.

Hinde, R. A., Thorpe, W. H., & Vince, M. A. The following response of young coots and moorhens. *Behaviour*, 1956, **9**, 214–242.

Hirayoshi, I., & Warren, J. M. Overtraining and reversal learning by experimentally naive kittens. *J. comp. physiol. Psychol.*, 1967, **64**, 507–510.

Holborn, S., & Boe, E. The effect of over-learning on transfer of training. *Quart. J. exp. Psychol.*, 1965, **27**, 178–180.

Holdstock, T. L., & Schwartzbaum, J. S. Classical conditioning of heart rate and galvanic skin response in the rat. *Psychophysiology*, 1965, **2**, 25–38.

Holmes, P. A., & Bitterman, M. E. Spatial and visual habit reversal in the turtle. *J. comp. physiol. Psychol.*, 1966, **62**, 328–331.

Hull, C. L. *Principles of Behavior.* New York: Appleton-Century-Crofts, 1943.

Hulse, S. H., Jr. Amount and percentage of reinforcement and duration of goal confinement in conditioning and extinction. *J. exp. Psychol.*, 1958, **56**, 48–57.

Jacobson, A. L., Horowitz, S. D., & Fried, C. Classical conditioning, pseudo-conditioning, or sensitization in the planarian. *J. comp. physiol. Psychol.*, 1967, **64**, 73–79.

James, R. L., & Halas, E. S. No difference in extinction behavior following various types and amounts of training. *Psychol. Rec.*, 1964, **14**, 1–11.

Jaynes, J. Imprinting: The interaction of learned and innate behavior: III. Practice effects on performance, retention, and fear. *J. comp. physiol. Psychol.*, 1958, **51**, 234–237.

Jenkins, W. O., & Stanley, J. C. Partial reinforcement: A review and critique. *Psychol. Bull.*, 1950, **47**, 193–234.

Jensen, D. D. Experiments on "learning" in paramecium. *Science*, 1957a, **125**, 191–192.

Jensen, D. D. More on "learning" in Paramecia. *Science*, 1957b, **126**, 1341–1342.

Jensen, D. D. A theory of the behavior of *Paramecium aurelia* and behavioral effects of feeding, fission, and ultraviolet microbeam irradiation. *Behaviour*, 1959, **15**, 82–122.

Jensen, D. D. Paramecia, planaria and pseudo-learning. *Anim. Behav.*, Suppl. 1, 1965, 9–20.

Jones, J. E. The CS-UCS interval in conditioning short- and long-latency responses. *J. exp. Psychol.*, 1961, **62**, 612–617.

Jones, J. E. Contiguity and reinforcement in relation to ·CS–UCS intervals in classical average conditioning. *Psychol. Rev.*, 1962, **69**, 176–186.

Kappauf, W. E., & Schlosberg, H. Conditioned responses in the white rat. III. Conditioning as a function of the length of the period of delay. *J. genet. Psychol.*, 1937, **50**, 27–153.

Katz, M. S., & Deterline, W. A. Apparent learning in the Paramecium. *J. comp. physiol. Psychol.*, 1958, **51**, 243–247.

Kay, H., & Oldfield-Box, H. A study of learning sets in rats with an apparatus using 3-D shapes. *Anim. Behaviour*, 1965, **13**, 19–24.

Kendler, H. H., & Kendler, T. S. Selective attention versus mediation: Some comments on Mackintosh's analysis of two-stage models of discrimination learning. *Psychol. Bull.*, 1966, **66**, 282–288.

Kimble, G. A. *Hilgard and Marquis' conditioning and learning.* (2nd Ed.) New York: Appleton-Century-Crofts, 1961.

Kimmel, H. D., & Harrell, V. L. Differential conditioning in the planarian. *Psychon. Sci.*, 1964, **1**, 227–228.

Kimmel, H. D., & Harrell. V. L. Further study of differential conditioning in the planarian. *Psychon. Sci.*, 1966, **5**, 285–286.

Kimble, G. A., Mann, L. I., & Dufort, R. H. Classical and instrumental eyelid conditioning. *J. exp. Psychol.*, 1955, **49**, 407–417.

Kimmel, H. D., & Yaremko, R. M. Effect of partial reinforcement on acquisition and extinction of classical conditioning in the planarian. *J. comp. physiol. Psychol.*, 1966, **61**, 299–301.

King, A. P. Personal communication, 1968.

Kirk, K. L., & Bitterman, M. E. Probability-learning by the turtle. *Science*, 1956, **148**, 1484–1485.

Klinman, Cynthia S., & Bitterman, M. E. Classical conditioning in the fish: The CS–US interval. *J. comp. physiol. Psychol.*, 1963, **56**, 578–583.

Klopfer, P. H. Stimulus preferences and imprinting. *Science*, 1967, **156**, 1394–1396.

Kreps, E. M. [The reactions of Ascidiacea to external stimulation.] *Arkhiv Biolog. Nauk*, 1925, **25**, 197–200.

Lee, R. M. Conditioning of a free operant response in planaria. *Science*, 1963, **139**, 1048–1049.

Leonard, C., Schneider, G., & Gross. C. G. Performance on learning set and delayed-response tasks by tree shrews, *J. comp. physiol. Psychol.*, 1966, **62**, 501–504.

Levine, M. A model of hypothesis behavior in discrimination learning set. *Psychol. Rev.*, 1959, **66**, 353–366.

Levine, M., Levinson, B., & Harlow, H. F. Trials per problem as a variable in the acquisition of discrimination learning set. *J. comp. physiol. Psychol.*, 1959, **52**, 396–398.

Lewis, D. J. Partial reinforcement: A selective review of the literature since 1950. *Psychol. Bull.*, 1960, **57**, 1–28.

Liddell, H. S., & Anderson, O. D. Certain characteristics of the formation of conditioned responses in sheep. *Proc. Soc. exp. Biol. Med.*, 1928, **26**, 81–82.

Liddell, H. S., James, W. T., & Anderson, O. D. The comparative physiology of the conditioned motor reflex. *Comp. Psychol. Monogr.*, 1934, **11**, 1–89.

Longo, N. Probability-learning and habit reversal in the cockroach. *Amer. J. Psychol.*, 1964, **77**, 29–41.

Longo, N., & Bitterman, M. E. The effect of partial reinforcement with spaced practice on resistance to extinction in the fish. *J. comp. physiol. Psychol.*, 1960, **53**, 169–172.

Lorenz, K. Z. Der Kumpan in der Umwelt des Vogels. *J. Ornithol.*, 1935, **83**, 137–213.

Lovejoy, E. Analysis of the overlearning reversal effect. *Psychol. Rev.*, 1966, **73**, 87–103.

Lowes, G., & Bitterman, M. E. Reward and learning in the goldfish. *Science*, 1967, **157**, 455–457.

Lubow, R. E. Latent inhibition: Effects of frequency of nonreinforced pre-exposure of the CS. *J. comp. physiol. Psychol.*, 1965, **60**, 454–457.

Lubow, R. E., & Moore, A. V. Latent inhibition: The effect of nonreinforced pre-exposure to the conditional stimulus. *J. comp. physiol. Psychol.*, 1959, **52**, 415–419.

McAllister, W. R. Eyelid conditioning as a function of the CS-US interval. *J. exp. Psychol.*, 1953, **45**, 417–422.

Mackintosh, N. J. The effects of over-training on a reversal and a nonreversal shift. *J. comp. physiol. Psychol.*, 1962, **55**, 555–559.

Mackintosh, N. J. Overtraining and transfer within and between dimensions in the rat. *Quart. J. exp. Psychol.*, 1964, **16**, 250–256.

Mackintosh, N. J. Selective attention in animal discrimination learning. *Psychol. Bull.*, 1965a, **64**, 124–150.

Mackintosh, N. J. Overtraining, reversal, and extinction in rats and chicks. *J. comp. physiol. Psychol.*, 1965b, **59**, 31–36.

Mackintosh, N. J., & Holgate, V. Overtraining and the extinction of a discrimination in octopus. *J. comp. physiol. Psychol.*, 1965, **60**, 260–262.

Mackintosh, N. J., & Mackintosh, J. Reversal learning in octopus *vulgaris Lamarck* with and without irrelevant cues. *Quart. J. exp. Psychol.*, 1963, **15**, 236–242.

Mackintosh, N. J., Mackintosh, J., Safriel-Jorne, O., & Sutherland, N. S. Overtraining, reversal and extinction in the goldfish. *Anim. Behav.*, 1966, **14**, 314–318.

Mackintosh, N. J., McGonigle, B., Holgate, V., & Vanderver, V. Factors underlying improvement in serial reversal learning. *Canad. J. Psychol.*, 1968, **22**, 85–95.

Mandler, G., & Heinemann, S. H. Effect of overlearning of a verbal response on transfer of training. *J. exp. Psychol.*, 1956, **52**, 39–46.

Marrone, R., & Evans, S. Two-choice probability learning in fish. *Psychon. Sci.*, 1966, **5**, 327–328.

Matthews, G. V. T. The orientation of pigeons as affected by the learning of landmarks and by the distance of displacement. *Anim. Behav.*, 1963, **11**, 310–317.

Meyer, M. E. Discriminative basis for astronavigation in birds. *J. comp. physiol. Psychol.*, 1964, **58**, 403–406.

Meyer, M. E. The internal clock hypothesis for astro-navigation in homing pigeons. *Psychon. Sci.*, 1966, **5**, 259–260.

Mikhailoff, S. Experiences réflexologiques. L'activité neuropsychique (formation des réflexes associés) est-elle possible sans l'écorce cérébrale? *Bull. Inst. Oceanogra.*, 1920a, No. 375, 1–11.

Mikhailoff, S. Experiences réflexologiques (deuxième communication préliminaire). Experiences nouvelles sur *Eledone moschata. Bull. Inst. Oceanogra.*, 1920b, No. 379, 1–8.

Mikhailoff, S. Experiences réflexologiques (troisième communication préliminaire). Experiences nouvelles sur Eledone moschata. *Bull. Inst. Oceanogra.*, 1921, No. 398, 1–11.

Miles, R. C. Discrimination-learning sets. In A. M. Schrier, H. F. Harlow, & F. Stollnitz (Eds.), *Behavior of nonhuman primates.* Vol. 1. New York: Academic Press, 1965.

Mirsky, A. F., & Katz, M. S. Avoidance "conditioning" in paramecia. *Science,* 1958, **127**, 1498–1499.

Moore, J. W., & Gormezano, I. Yoked comparisons of instrumental and classical eyelid conditioning. *J. exp. Psychol.,* 1961, **62**, 552–559.

Murillo, N. R., Diercks, J. K., & Capaldi, E. J. Performance of the turtle, *Pseudomys scripta troostii,* in a partial reinforcement situation. *J. comp. physiol. Psychol.,* 1961, **54**, 204–206.

Newton, J. E. O., & Gantt, W. H. One-trial cardiac conditioning in dogs. *Conditional Reflex: A Pavlovian Journal of Research & Therapy,* 1966, **1**, 251–265.

Noble, M., & Adams, C. K. Conditioning in pigs as a function of the interval between CS and US. *J. comp. physiol. Psychol.,* 1963, **56**, 215–219.

Noble, M., Gruender, A., & Meyer, D. R. Conditioning in fish (*Mollienisia sp.*) as a function of the interval between CS and US. *J. comp. physiol. Psychol.,* 1959, **52**, 236–239.

Noble, M., & Harding, G. E. Conditioning in rhesus monkeys as a function of the interval between CS and US. *J. comp. physiol. Psychol.,* 1963, **56**, 220–224.

Paul, C. Effects of overlearning upon single habit reversal in rats. *Psychol. Bull.,* 1965, **63**, 65–72.

Peeke, H. V. S., Herz, M. J., & Wyers, E. J. Forward conditioning, backward conditioning, and pseudoconditioning sensitization in the earthworm (*Lumbri-cus terrestris*). *J. comp. physiol. Psychol.,* 1967, **64**, 534–536.

Pennypacker, H. S., & Cook, W. A. Acquisition and extinction of the conditioned eyelid response in the squirrel monkey as functions of the CS-US interval. *Psychol. Rep.,* 1967, **20**, 1235–1243.

Poland, S. F., & Warren, J. M. Spatial probability learning by cats. *Psychon. Sci.,* 1967, **8**, 487–488.

Popov, N. A. (Conditioned reflexes in birds and the problem of the space analyzer.) *Izvest. Aberbayd. Gosndar. Univers.,* 1922, **2**, 105–154.

Popov, N. A. [Conditioned and unconditioned reflexes in birds in connection with the doctrine of dominance.] *Psikhologia,* 1930, **3**, 85–117.

Prokasy, W. F., & Papsdorf, J. D. Effects of increasing the interstimulus interval during classical conditioning of the albino rabbit. *J. comp. physiol. Psychol.,* 1965, **60**, 249–252.

Ratner, S. C. Conditioning of decerebrate worms, *Lumbricus terrestris. J. comp. physiol. Psychol.,* 1962, **55**, 174–177.

Ratner, S. C., & Denny, M. R. *Comparative psychology.* Homewood, Ill.: Dorsey, 1964.

Ratner, S. C., & Miller, K. R. Classical conditioning in earthworms, *Lumbricus terrestris. J. comp. physiol. Psychol.,* 1959a, **52**, 102–105.

Ratner, S. C., & Miller, K. R. Effects of spacing of training and ganglia removal on conditioning in earthworms. *J. comp. physiol. Psychol.,* 1959b, **52**, 667–672.

Ratner, S. C., & Stein, D. G. Responses of worms to light as a function of intertrial interval and ganglion removal. *J. comp. physiol. Psychol.,* 1965, **59**, 301–305.

Razran, G. H. S. Conditioned responses in animals other than dogs. *Psychol. Bull.,* 1933, **30**, 261–324.

Reid, L. S. The development of non-continuity behavior through continuity learning. *J. exp. Psychol.,* 1953, **46**, 107–112.

Rescorla, R. A. Pavlovian conditioning and its proper control procedures. *Psychol. Rev.,* 1967, **74**, 71–80.

Reynierse, J. H. Reactions to light in four

species of planaria. *J. comp. physiol. Psychol.*, 1967, **63**, 366–368.

Reynierse, J. H., Halliday, R. A., & Nelson, M. R. Nonassociative factors inhibiting earthworm straight-alley performance. *J. comp. physiol. Psychol.*, 1968, **65**, 160–163.

Reynierse, J. H., & Ratner, S. C. Acquisition and extinction in the earthworm, *Lumbricus terrestris. Psychol. Rec.*, 1964, **14**, 383–387.

Riopelle, A. J. Transfer suppression and learning sets. *J. comp. physiol. Psychol.*, 1953, **46**, 108–114.

Roberts, W. A., Bullock, D. H., & Bitterman, M. E. Resistance to extinction in the pigeon after partially reinforced instrumental training under discrete-trials conditions. *Amer. J. Psychol.*, 1963, **76**, 353–365.

Rothblat, L. A., & Wilson, W. A., Jr. Intradimensional and extradimensional shifts in the monkey within and across sensory modalities. (pers. comm.)

Rumbaugh, D. M., & Prim, M. M. Temporary interference of insolvable discrimination reversal training upon learning set in the squirrel monkey. *J. comp. physiol. Psychol.*, 1964, **57**, 302–304.

Scarborough, B. B., & Addison, R. G. Conditioning in fish: Effects of X-irradiation. *Science*, 1962, **136**, 712–713.

Schade, A. F., & Bitterman, M. E. The relative difficulty of reversal and dimensional shifting as a function of overlearning. *Psychon. Sci.*, 1965, **3**, 283–284.

Schade, A. F., & Bitterman, M. E. Improvement in habit reversal as related to dimensional set. *J. comp. physiol. Psychol.*, 1966, **62**, 43–48.

Schlosberg, H. The relationship between success and the laws of conditioning. *Psychol. Rev.*, 1937, **44**, 379–394.

Schmidt, H., Jr. Behavior of two species of worms in the same maze. *Science*, 1955, **121**, 341–342.

Schneiderman, N., Fuentes, I., & Gormezano, I. Acquisition and extinction of the classically conditioned eyelid response in the albino rabbit. *Science*, 1962, **136**, 650–652.

Schneiderman, N., & Gormezano, I. Conditioning of the nictitating membrane of the rabbit as a function of CS–US interval. *J. comp. physiol. Psychol.*, 1964, **57**, 188–195.

Schoonard, J., & Lawrence, D. H. Resistance to extinction as a function of the number of delay of reward trials. *Psychol. Rep.*, 1962, **11**, 275–278.

Schrier, A. M. Transfer by macaque monkeys between learning-set and repeated-reversal tasks. *Percept. mot. Skills*, 1966, **23**, 787–792.

Schusterman, R. J. Transfer effects of successive discrimination-reversal training in chimpanzees. *Science*, 1962, **137**, 422–423.

Schusterman, R. J. Successive discrimination-reversal training and multiple discrimination training in one-trial learning by chimpanzees. *J. comp. physiol. Psychol.*, 1964, **58**, 153–156.

Schusterman, R. J. Serial discrimination: reversal learning with and without errors by the California Sea Lion. *J. exp. Anal. Behav.*, 1966, **9**, 593–600.

Shell, W. F., & Riopelle, A. J. Multiple discrimination learning in raccoons. *J. comp. physiol. Psychol.*, 1957, **50**, 585–587.

Shepp, B. E. Studies in discriminative learning and transfer in normal and retarded children. *Progress Report No. 1*, August, 1967, Brown University, Research Grant No. HD-01349, National Institute of Child Health and Human Development.

Shmavonian, B. M. Methodological study of vasomotor conditioning in human subjects. *J. comp. physiol. Psychol.*, 1959, **52**, 315–321.

Skinner, B. F. The phylogeny and ontogeny of behavior. *Science*, 1966, **153**, 1205–1213.

Smith, J. C., & Baker, H. D. Conditioning in the horseshoe crab. *J. comp. physiol. Psychol.*, 1960, **53**, 279–281.

Smith, S. The limits of educability in Paramecium. *J. comp. Neurol. Psychol.*, 1908, **18**, 499–510.

Solomon, S. Effects of variations in rearing, drive level, and training procedure on performance in probability learning tasks. *Psychol. Rep.*, 1962, **10**, 679–689.

Sperling, S. E. Reversal learning and resistance to extinction: A review of the rat literature. *Psychol. Bull.*, 1965, **63**, 281–297.

Spooner, A., & Kellogg, W. N. The backward-conditioning curve. *Amer. J. Psychol.*, 1947, **60**, 321–334.

Stearns, E. M., & Bitterman, M. E. A comparison of key-pecking with an ingestive technique for the study of discriminative learning in pigeons. *Amer. J. Psychol.*, 1965, **78**, 48–56.

Theios, J., & Blosser, D. The overlearning reversal effect and magnitude of reward. *J. comp. physiol. Psychol.*, 1965, **59**, 252–257.

Thompson, R. Successive reversal of a position habit in an invertebrate. *Science*, 1957, **126**, 163–164.

Thompson, R., & McConnell, J. Classical conditioning in the planarian, *Dugesia dorotocephela*. *J. comp. physiol. Psychol.*, 1955, **48**, 65–68.

Thompson, W. R., & Dubanoski, R. A. Imprinting and the "Law of effort." *Anim. Behav.*, 1964, **12**, 213–218.

Thorpe, W. H., & Davenport, D. (Eds.) Learning and associated phenomena in invertebrates. *Anim. Behav. Supp.*, No. 1, 1965.

Tighe, T. J. Effect of overtraining on reversal and extradimensional shifts. *J. exp. Psychol.*, 1965, **70**, 13–17.

Tighe, T. J., Brown, P. L., & Youngs, E. A. The effect of overtraining on the shift behavior of albino rats. *Psychon. Sci.*, 1965, **2**, 141–142.

Tighe, L. S., & Tighe, T. J. Overtraining and discrimination shift behavior in children. *Psychon. Sci.*, 1965, **2**, 365–366.

Tyler, D. W., Wortz, E. C., & Bitterman, M. E. The effect of random and alternating partial reinforcement on resistance to extinction in the rat. *Amer. J. Psychol.*, 1953, **66**, 57–65.

Tyrrell, D. J. The formation of object discrimination learning sets by rats. Paper read at East. Psychol. Assn., New York, 1963.

Uhl, C. N. Two-choice probability learning in the rat as a function of incentive, probability of reinforcement, and training procedure. *J. exp. Psychol.*, 1963, **66**, 443–449.

Uhl, N. Intradimensional and extradimensional shifts as a function of amount of training and similarity between training and shift stimuli. *J. exp. Psychol.*, 1966, **72**, 429–433.

Upton, M. Auditory sensitivity of guinea pigs. *Amer. J. Psychol.*, 1929, **41**, 412–421.

Van Deventer, J. M., & Ratner, S. C. Variables affecting the frequency of response of planaria to light. *J. comp. physiol. Psychol.*, 1964, **57**, 407–411.

Vattano, F. J., & Hullett, J. H. Learning in planarians as a function of inter-stimulus interval. *Psychon. Sci.*, 1964, **1**, 331–332.

Viaud, G. Conception nouvelle du galvanotropisme animal. Experience sur les planaries. *Experientia*, 1954, **10**, 233–242.

Wagner, A. R. Effect of amount and percentage of reinforcement and number of extinction trials on conditioning and extinction. *J. exp. Psychol.*, 1961, **62**, 234–242.

Warren, J. M. Perseverative reactions in chicks and kittens. *J. Psychol.*, 1959, **47**, 9–12.

Warren, J. M. Reversal learning by paradise fish (*Macropodus opercularis*). *J. comp. physiol. Psychol.*, 1960, **53**, 376–378.

Warren, J. M. The comparative psychology of learning. *Annu. Rev. Psychol.*, 1965a, **16**, 95–118.

Warren, J. M. Primate learning in comparative perspective. In A. M. Schrier, H. F. Harlow, & F. Stollnitz (Eds.), *Behavior of nonhuman primates*. Vol. 1. New York: Academic Press, 1965b.

Warren, J. M. Reversal learning and the formation of learning sets by cats and rhesus monkeys. *J. comp. physiol. Psychol.*, 1966, **61**, 421–428.

Warren, J. M., & Baron, A. The formation of learning sets by cats. *J. comp. physiol. Psychol.*, 1956, **49**, 227–231.

Warren, J. M., & Beck, C. H. Visual probability learning by cats. *J. comp. physiol. Psychol.*, 1966, **61**, 316–318.

Warren, J. M., Brookshire, K. H., Ball, G. G., & Reynolds, D. V. Reversal learning by White Leghorn chicks. *J. comp. physiol. Psychol.*, 1960, **53**, 371–375.

Warren, J. M., & Warren, H. B. Reversal learning by horse and raccoon. *J. genet. Psychol.*, 1962, **100**, 215–220.

Warren, J. M., & Warren, Helen B. Performance of immature and adult cats on the Hamilton search test. *Psychon. Sci.*, 1966, **6**, 5–6.

Weinstock, S. Resistance to extinction of a running response following partial reinforcement under widely spaced trials. *J. comp. physiol. Psychol.*, 1954, **47**, 318–322.

Weitzman, R. A. Positional matching in rats and fish. *J. comp. physiol. Psychol.*, 1967, **63**, 54–59.

Wever, E. G. The upper limit of hearing in the cat. *J. comp. Psychol.*, 1930, **10**, 221–233.

Williams, D. I. The overtraining reversal effect in the pigeon. *Psychon. Sci.*, 1967, **7**, 261–262.

Wilson, W. A., Oscar, M., & Bitterman, M. E. Probability-learning in the monkey. *Quart. J. exp. Psychol.*, 1964, **16**, 163–165.

Wise, L., & Gallagher, D. P. Partial reinforcement of a discriminative response in the turtle. *J. comp. physiol. Psychol.*, 1964, **57**, 311–313.

Wodinsky, J., & Bitterman, M. E. Partial reinforcement in the fish. *Amer. J. Psychol.*, 1959, **72**, 184–199.

Wodinsky, J., & Bitterman, M. E. Resistance to extinction in the fish after extensive training with partial reinforcement. *Amer. J. Psychol.*, 1960, **73**, 429–434.

Wolff, J. L. Concept-shift and discrimination-reversal learning in humans. *Psychol. Bull.*, 1967, **68**, 369–408.

Wright, R. L., Motivational effects in probability learning. *Psychon. Sci.*, 1967, **7**, 329–330.

Wyers, E. J., Peeke, H. V. S., & Herz, M. J. Partial reinforcement and resistance to extinction in the earthworm. *J. comp. physiol. Psychol.*, 1964, **57**, 113–116.

Zeaman, D. Response latency as a function of the amount of reinforcement. *J. exp. Psychol.*, 1949, **39**, 466–483.

Zeaman, D., & House, B. J. The role of attention in retardate discrimination learning. In N. R. Ellis (Ed.), *Handbook of mental deficiency*. New York: McGraw-Hill, 1963.

Zeigler, H. P. Learning set formation in pigeons. *J. comp. physiol. Psychol.*, 1961, **54**, 252–254.

Suggested Readings

Bitterman, M. E. Toward a comparative psychology of learning. *Amer. Psychol.*, 1960, **15**, 704–712. An approach to the general question of the benefits and limitations of the study of learning at different phyletic levels.

Braungart, D. C., & Buddeke, R. *An introduction to animal biology.* (6th ed.) St. Louis: Mosby, 1964. An elementary textbook which gives a good description of the classification scheme of the chief groups of animals (pp. 405–409).

Hinde, R. A. *Animal behaviour.* New York: McGraw-Hill, 1966. An interesting attempt to synthesize the data from the ethological and comparative psychological points of view.

Skinner, B. F. The phylogeny and ontogeny of behavior. *Science*, 1966, **153**, 1205–1213. An approach to the general question of the benefits and limitations of the study of learning at different phyletic levels.

Thorpe, W. H., & Davenport, D. Learning and associated phenomena in invertebrates. *Anim. Behav. Supp.*, No. 1, 1965. The proceedings of a conference held at Cambridge, England. Many of the papers presented point up important methodological considerations for the study of learning in lower forms.

Warren, J. M. Primate learning in comparative perspective. In A. M. Schrier, H. F. Harlow, & F. Stollnitz (Eds.), *Behavior of nonhuman primates.* Vol. 1. New York: Academic Press, 1965. This source contains a review of quantitative comparisons of learning ability among taxa, and it considers a number of types of learning task which were ignored in this book, for example, simple discrimination learning, double alternation, delayed response, and so on.

VI

The Physiology of Conditioning

Shepard Siegel

McMaster University

Neurophysiological Background[1]

Traditionally, the biological systems important for the behavior of organisms have been divided into three broad (but not always mutually exclusive) categories. There are those structures that detect stimulation, in the environment or within the organism, and transduce it into a form coded for transmission in the organism. These are the *receptors*.

There are those systems important for the organism's responses to stimuli. These are the *effectors*. The secretory activity of the glands, the contraction of striated voluntary and smooth involuntary muscle, all involve actions of effector tissue.

The third system involves those structures important for the transmission of information from receptors to effectors. This is the organism's *nervous system*. In this system stimulation provided by the receptors is somehow analyzed and integrated with other information stored within the organism. Responses are emitted on the basis of activities within the system.

Psychologists interested in studying the conditioning process have typically studied response variables as a function of stimulus variables. Changes in the nervous system during the learning process, although not ignored, have been relegated to a position of secondary importance. The learner is the "black box"—the automaton whose behavior is to be studied, but whose workings are irrelevant to the study of learning.

Why Open the "Black Box"?

Few investigators would deny that the rat which has learned to turn right in a T-maze to receive food, the dog who salivates when it hears a tone, the student who knows how to do problems of integral calculus, all are different physiologically from their experimentally naive or unschooled peers. Pinning down what these changes are, however, has proved to be an elusive problem. It is only recently that technological advancements have enabled researchers to peer within the black box to investigate what goes on during learning.

The question can reasonably be raised, "why open the black box?" Cannot psychology flourish as an experimental science without entering into the study of neurophysiological mechanisms of behavior;

[1] Preparation of this paper was supported in part by Grant MH–13479 from the National Institute of Mental Health, Public Health Service.

indeed, would not the premature combination of these two nascent disciplines mutually impede their progress (Skinner, 1938)? Perhaps, but I think not. The glimpses we have into the black box are too intriguing to ignore until a more opportune moment.

Consider a series of experiments by Gelber (1952, 1958). She demonstrated that paramecia would tend to congregate around a platinum wire if that wire had previously provided a source of nutriment. That is, paramecia could change their normal behavior of avoiding a solid object and actually adhere to it if the presentation of the object had been associated with food. Furthermore, this new response was retained for several hours. It would appear, on the basis of Gelber's data, that this single-celled organism, the most primitive of all animals, can change its behavior as a result of reinforced practice; that is, according to the commonly accepted definition (Kimble, 1961), it can learn. It should be noted that the question of learning in the paramecium is not settled; indeed, it appears likely that Gelber's results may be artifact of her procedure (Jensen, 1957; Katz and Deterline, 1958), and not a demonstration of unicellular learning.

Although an unambiguous answer has yet to be found to the question, "Can the paramecium learn?" researchers other than Gelber have provided data in the affirmative (Day and Bentley, 1911; French, 1940; Smith, 1908). Consider the implications of such findings. Most investigators concerned with physiological correlates of learning speak of the importance of the highest cortical functions (for example, Pavlov, 1927), or the importance of lower brain centers (for example, Gastaut, 1958), or even the spinal cord (for example, Dykman and Shurrager, 1956). They stress complex interactions between various parts of the brain (for example, Penfield, 1958), neuronal interactions in the central nervous system (Hebb, 1949), and chemical (for example, Katz and Halstead, 1950) or structural (for example,

Eccles, 1953) changes within the central nervous system concurrent with the learning process, to name (and oversimplify) just a few. Yet the lowly paramecium is excluded from all these processes. It has no cells specialized for nervous function—it is but a single cell. Yet, perhaps, it too can learn. If so, learning may not necessarily depend on the nervous system. The basic learning process may involve molecular processes within the cell. One cannot help but contemplate the implications for the infinitely more complex, billion-celled mammalian organism. To discover the nature of the basic learning process, we must open the black box.

The tremendous information storage capacity of the single cell is dramatically demonstrated with a more familiar illustration. The single cell, the zygote, formed at conception by the union of the egg and sperm, is barely more than 0.1 mm. in diameter. Yet, within this tiny space a tremendous amount of information is stored. "Every individual's supply of genes, the bearers of hereditary factors, is given him once and for all and unalterably at conception" (Kuhlen and Thompson, 1963). Somewhere in the molecular structure of this barely visible cell lies the blueprint for the development of the fully formed neonate, and perhaps factors that significantly affect postnatal physical and psychological development.

It is just recently that investigators have begun studying the chemistry of learning, the intracellular activities which, perhaps, *are* learning. Most of the research, however, has involved the study of intercellular interactions in familiar multicelled organisms during the learning process, and hence it is in this area that the present discussion primarily rests.

The Neuron

It is not within the scope of this chapter to give the reader anything approximating an adequate review of neurophysiology. Nevertheless, a very brief and admittedly simplified outline of the basics at this point will aid in understanding the following chapters.

Structure of the Neuron

Nervous tissue, like all biological tissue, is made up of cells. Single nerve cells are called neurons. A schematic diagram of a neuron is shown in Figure 20-1. The neuron

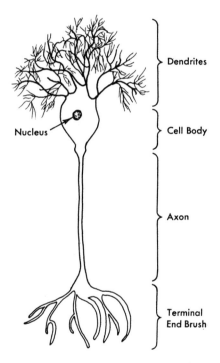

Figure 20-1. Schematic diagram of a neuron.

may be divided into three parts. The first part, the dendrites, receives excitation from other nerve cells. This excitation is transmitted down the second part, the cell body (or soma), to the third part, the axon. From the tip of the axon (the terminal end brush or telodendria) the propagated electrical activity is transmitted, by a process to be

described shortly, across a small gap (the synapse) to dendrites of other neurons.

Neurons differ greatly in shape, size of components, and exact topographic features Figure 20-2 illustrates a variety of neurons.

Electrical Activity of the Neuron

The neuron, like all cells, is enclosed in a covering, or membrane. Cell membranes play a crucial role in cell metabolism; they let certain nutritive substances into the cell and permit potentially harmful substances to pass out of the cell. In the neuron the membrane plays an additional role—it is of primary importance in the propagation of neural impulses.

The membranes of many cells are such that the cell is normally kept in a state of polarization. That is, the membrane is selectively permeable so that certain charged ions are kept from getting inside the cell, and others are kept within the cell, the result being a disparity in the electrical charge on each side of the membrane. If we were to hook up a voltmeter with one side of the instrument connected to the inside of the neural membrane and the other side to the outside, we would measure a voltage difference of about 50 to 100 mv. In other words, the outside of the membrane is 50 to 100 mv more positive than the inside. This is the *resting potential* of the neuron.

This resting potential probably results from the fact that the membrane of the neuron is relatively impermeable to sodium ions (Na+), keeping them outside the neuron, but it permits most other ions to pass through. The excess of sodium ions on the outside of the membrane results in the relative negativity of the inside of the membrane.

If an area of a neuron is irritated with a stimulus of sufficient intensity (mechanical, chemical, or electrical), a small area of the membrane, coinciding with the point of irritation, becomes depolarized—the resting

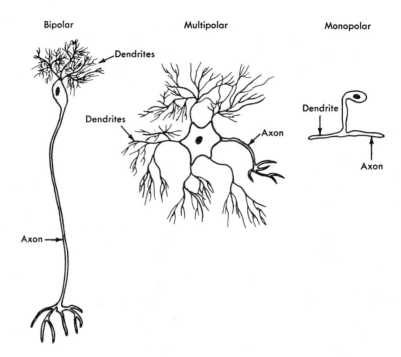

Figure 20-2.   Several types of neurons.

potential breaks down. It is thought that, for just a few milliseconds, the small area of the membrane becomes permeable to sodium ions and they pass into the neuron. Indeed, for an instant, the resting potential is reversed, and the inside of the membrane becomes more positive than the outside. For example, a resting potential of -60 mv may change to a potential of about $+30$ mv. Such a temporary reversal of polarity of a small area of the neuron is called a *spike potential.*

An important feature of the spike potential is its "all-or-nothing" character. Given that a neuron is stimulated with a suprathreshold stimulus, a spike is produced. The amplitude of the spike depends on a number of different factors: size and type of neuron, chemical environment at the time of stimulation, metabolic state, and so on. Notable by their absence on this list are any references to features of the stimulus that initiate the spike. The spike, then, if initi-

ated at all, has parameters that are independent of those of the initiating stimulus.

The spike potential is the basic neural impulse. If a stimulus of sufficient intensity to initiate a spike is applied to a neuron, the spike produced is propagated down the length of the cell.

The neural impulse, then, is not analagous to an electric current in a wire. It is not a continuous, "*flowing*" phenomenon. It is not transmitted at anything near the speed of an electric current (over 300 million m. per sec.). Rather, the area of membrane depolarization is transmitted down the length of the neuron, in an undiminished, undistorted form, at a speed ranging from one meter per second to over 100 m per sec. The exact transmission speed depends on the neuron's diameter, metabolic state, and numerous environmental factors. Once a spike is initiated, its propagation speed, like its other parameters, is independent of the magnitude of the initiating stimulus.

The energy for the transmission of the neural impulse comes not from the stimulus that initiates the impulse, but rather from metabolic processes within the neuron.

Interactions Among Neurons

The human brain consists of about ten billion neurons. Each of them receives information (in the form of electrical impulses) from many others, and similarly transmits information to many others. As a rule, the terminal endbrushes of neurons do not touch the dendrites of the neurons with which they communicate. Rather, the structures are separated by a very small space (about 20 mμ). It is this small area, called the synapse, that is the location of neuronal interaction.

It should be mentioned that although most synapses involve near contact with axon terminal endbrushes and dendrites, there are some in which the axon terminal endbrushes connect with the cell body of another neuron. The former are called axo-dendritic synapses, and the latter are called axo-somatic synapses. Figure 20-3 indicates a possible configuration of three neurons and their synaptic contacts.

At one time there was some controversy about the basic mechanism of synaptic

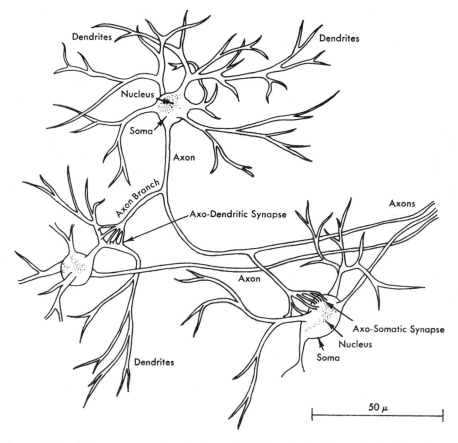

Figure 20-3. Three neurons (semischematic). (Reprinted with permission from Stevens, C. F. *Neurophysiology: A primer.* New York: Wiley, 1966.)

transmission: how does the nerve impulse continue to be propagated beyond the synapse? Synaptic transmission is now generally conceded to be a chemical process. The arrival of the neural impulse at the end of the axon of the presynaptic neuron acts to release a chemical which affects the ion permeability of the postsynaptic neuron. If the postsynaptic neuron becomes sufficiently depolarized, a spike is generated in it.

However, another type of event sometimes occurs at the synapse. The effect of the synaptic chemical reactions may serve to decrease even further the permeability of the postsynaptic neural membrane to sodium ions, to make the outside of the membrane even more positive than it normally is, that is, to hyperpolarize the membrane. In such cases it is more difficult for other presynaptic neurons to excite this hyperpolarized postsynaptic neuron. Therefore, synaptic events include not only excitatory effects transmitted from the presynaptic neuron to the postsynaptic neuron but also inhibitory effects—the activity of a presynaptic neuron may act to inhibit neuronal transmission in a postsynaptic neuron.

Why are some neuronal contacts excitatory (depolarizing) and others inhibitory (hyperpolarizing)? The basis of this difference is not yet clear. The distinction probably does not lie in the composition of the chemical transmitter, because it is known that the same transmitter substance may produce excitatory effects in some synapses and inhibitory effects in others. It is thought that the answer may be in the exact structure of various postsynaptic neural membranes and/or in the topographic arrangement of the structures of the neurons at the synapse. Also, there is some recent evidence to indicate that the frequency of neural firing in the presynaptic neuron may code the excitatory or inhibitory nature of the synaptic event (Wachtel and Kandel, 1967).

Many presynaptic neurons (perhaps thousands) synapse with a single postsynaptic neuron. Because most neurons have only one axon, the incoming information (both excitatory and inhibitory) from all these sources must be integrated in arriving at a single output. The process by which this occurs is called *spatial summation.*

When a chemical transmitter substance is released at the synapse, a postsynaptic potential (abbreviated PSP) is generated in the postsynaptic neuron. This may be either an excitatory postsynaptic potential (EPSP) or inhibitory postsynaptic potential (IPSP), depending on whether the postsynaptic neuron is depolarized or hyperpolarized.

Typically, only one EPSP is not of sufficient intensity to generate a spike in the postsynaptic neuron. Each chemical reaction occurring at the synapse creates a small, nonpropagated potential called a *local potential.* The magnitude of the local potential is proportional to the quantity of transmitter substance released at the synapse. If an EPSP is initiated in the dendritic area of a postsynaptic neuron, it quickly reaches a peak of maximum magnitude and gradually tapers off. A second EPSP may be generated in this same location and adds to what remained of the first EPSP, and so on. Eventually, the summated EPSPs may become great enough to generate a spike in the postsynaptic neuron.

At any one synapse, there may be IPSPs generated, in addition to EPSPs. The effect of these IPSPs is opposite to that of the EPSPs. These sum in a roughly algebraic manner, and the net result of this process determines whether spikes will be propagated down the postsynaptic neuron.

Nervous System Control Mechanisms

The concept of neural inhibition, postulated in the nineteenth century, was not readily accepted by physiologists. It was difficult to conceive how the basically excitatory neural impulse could also exert inhibitory influences. It remained for the brilliant experimentation and uncanny speculation of Sir Charles Sherrington (1947) forcefully to demonstrate the existence of neural inhibition, and to suggest the new dimensions it added to nervous system functioning. Investigators have recently localized the synapse as the site of the phenomenon and are now further investigating its mechanisms. (The history of the development of the concept of neural inhibition may be found in Diamond, Balvin, and Diamond, 1963.)

To understand the current picture of nervous system control mechanisms more completely, another concept in addition to neural inhibition must be introduced. This is the *centrifugal control* of incoming information. Centrifugal control (literally, "a force exerted outward from the center") refers to the modification by higher brain centers of incoming neural impulses at lower levels of the nervous system.

Centrifugal control is a recent concept of neurophysiology. Sensory information coming into the brain was previously considered simply to travel along ascending (afferent) pathways, usually terminating at the supposed seat of mammalian neural integration, the cerebral cortex. The only descending (efferent) pathways that were recognized were those carrying information to the effectors, Early in the twentieth century, it was recognized that many afferent relay nuclei (lumps of cell bodies within the central nervous system) received synaptic connections from neural pathways initiated from above. Therefore, our current picture of nervous control mechanisms indicates that the brain is not simply a passive receiver of incoming sensory information, but can actively modify its input via centrifugal control. Such descending efferent pathways have been identified in virtually all sensory modalities (see review by Livingston, 1959.)

How far down do these descending control systems reach? Evidence indicates that for most modalities they start in the cortex, synapse with many sensory relay nuclei in lower brain centers, and extend right to the receptors. Moreover, a given receptor system of sensory nucleus may receive centrifugal control from several different sources. These descending pathways typically exert a tonic, inhibitory influence. However, when one considers that the net effect of centrifugal-control adjustments at lower sensory nuclei or even at receptors may effectively involve either amplification or attenuation of the sensory information that reaches higher levels of the brain, the potential for flexibility in nervous system functioning becomes apparent.

21

Habituation

The first time an organism is presented with a novel stimulus, it engages in a complex of motor and autonomic activities, known collectively as the "what-is-it? reaction" or the "orientation reaction" (Pavlov, 1927; Sokolov 1963). If the stimulus is repetitively presented, the organism's initial orientation reaction gradually decreases in intensity. This decrease in responsiveness to a repetitively presented stimulus is called *habituation*. If we consider learning as a response modification resulting from experience, then habituation must be considered as a form of learning—indeed, as perhaps the simplest form of learning.

Whereas we usually think of the conditioning process as consisting of training *S*s to learn the significance of a stimulus (CS), it could reasonably also consist of training *S*s to learn the *insignificance* of a stimulus. Certainly this "negative learning" (Hernández-Péon, 1960) is clearly displayed during experimental extinction, in which a response learned to a previously reinforced stimulus decreases in strength as that stimulus is repetitively presented without reinforcement. There is a growing body of literature suggesting that nonreinforced presentations of a stimulus to an experimen-

tally naive organism prior to conditioning make it more difficult for that organism later to learn the significance of that stimulus during conditioning (Carlton and Vogel, 1967; Lubow, 1965; Lubow and Moore, 1959). Recent investigations have recognized the value of studying habituation as a learning phenomenon (for example, Thompson and Spencer, 1966), and it has been suggested that inasmuch as learning and habituation both involve response modification as a function of experience, they can be incorporated into a more global concept, such as "behavioral plasticity" (James, 1890; Konorski, 1948).

Cortical Arousal and Habituation

One of the characteristics of the orientation response is an "activation pattern" (Rheinberger and Jasper, 1937) in the electrical activity of the cortex. That is, when an organism is presented with a novel stimulus, tracings of cortical electrical activity tend to change in the direction of faster and lower amplitude waves. This may be seen in the first tracing of Figure 21-1. Cortical arousal tends to decrease, both in magnitude and duration, as the stimulus is repetitively presented (second tracing of Figure 21-1). That this is not simply a receptor fatigue phenomenon can be demonstrated by changing the characteristics of the habituated stimulus (that is, from a tone burst of 500 cps to one of 100 cps); the original orientation pattern returns (third tracing of Figure 21-1).

In the human the electrical activity of the cortex is typically measured by means of electrodes affixed to the scalp, and the tracing obtained is called an electroencephalograph (EEG). In the normal, relaxed state the human EEG exhibits a prominent "alpha rhythm," an approximately sinusoidal activity in the range of 8 to 13 cps. The alpha rhythm becomes arrested, or "blocked," when S is suddenly presented with a novel stimulus. This "alpha blocking" response is one characteristic of the human orientation reaction, and it has been shown to habituate (for example, Sokolov, 1960), much as the arousal reaction habituates in animals. That is, an external

stimulus which initially blocks the alpha activity of the EEG will, with repeated presentations, fail to induce alpha blocking.

Evoked Responses and Habituation

When a receptor is stimulated, the physical energy (light, sound, and so on) is transduced into neural impulses. These impulses travel through rather diffuse neural pathways into and through the central nervous system. Information about the parameters of the stimulus initiating this neural activity is coded by the duration of trains of neural impulses, frequency of impulse propagation, the threshold characteristics of the transmitting neurons, and the locus of these sensory pathways and their synaptic connections in the central nervous system.

If a recording electrode is placed in the appropriate areas of the nervous system, electrical activity associated with the sensory, exteroceptive stimulus can be recorded. Typically, such electrodes sample the activity of thousands of neurons at the

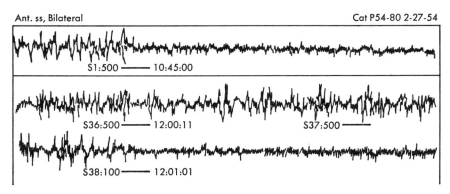

Ant. ss, Bilateral   Cat P54-80 2-27-54

S1:500 ——— 10:45:00

S36:500 ——— 12:00:11   S37:500 ———

S38:100 ——— 12:01:01

Figure 21-1. Cortical electrograms from the suprasylvian gyrus of a normal cat showing typical habituation of the arousal reaction to a 500-cycle tone after about thirty trials. In the first tracing the response to the first presentation of the 500-cycle tone is shown (SI:500). The solid bar shows the duration of the stimulus followed by the time in hours, minutes, and seconds (10:45:00). In the second tracing is shown the thirty-sixth and thirty-seventh trials (S36 and S37). Then a novel tone of 100 cycles is presented in the thirty-eighth trial (S38:100!). The figures at the right above the EEG traces indicate the duration of the activation in each trial. (Adapted with permission from Sharpless, S., & Jasper, H. H. Habituation of the arousal reaction. *Brain.* 1956, **79**, 655–680.)

same time, and the recording obtained, because it is evoked by the sensory stimulus, is called an *evoked response*.

Neurophysiological studies of habituation frequently involve measuring evoked responses to punctuate stimuli, such as clicks that are repetitively presented to an organism. Parameters of the evoked responses have been noted to change as the duration of presentation of the noninformative background stimulus increases, and the organism is presumably becoming more habituated to it.

Consider the experimental situation utilized by Hernández-Peón, Jouvet, and Sherrer (1957). Their Ss, cats, were exposed to constant, repetitive, background stimulation of tone bursts, each of 0.05 sec. duration, presented at the rate of one per sec. In such a situation the vibrating cone of

the loudspeaker delivering the acoustic stimulus produces successive compressions and rarefactions of the air. These vibrate the eardrum of the organism's outer ear, and the vibratory stimulation is ultimately transduced into neural impulses in the cochlea. The impulses travel into the brain via the cochlear division of the auditory nerve, and terminate in either the dorsal or ventral cochlear nucleus in the medulla. There are synaptic connections with other neurons which carry the acoustically derived neural information to higher parts of the central nervous system, but it is in the cochlear nuclei that the first synaptic connections in the brain occur, and it is here that Hernández-Peón et al. (1957) analyzed the evoked responses to the tone bursts.

A sample of the results of the experiment are shown in Figure 21-2. As may be seen,

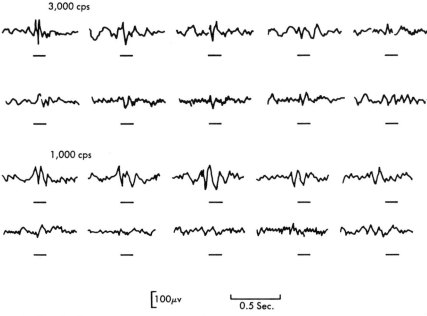

3,000 cps

1,000 cps

$\left[100\mu v\right.$ 0.5 Sec.

Figure 21-2. Auditory responses in cochlear nucleus. Both series show the decrement observed during twenty successive acoustic stimuli: the upper row are responses to the first five stimuli, and the lower row responses to the last five successive stimuli in each series. The upper series shows the decrement in response magnitude to a tone of 3,000 cps. The lower series shows the responses obtained immediately after, by changing the frequency of the tone to 1,000 cps. (Reprinted with permission from Hernández-Peón, R., Jouvet, M., & Scherrer, H. Auditory potentials at cochlear nucleus during acoustic habituation. *Acta neurol. Latinoamer,*. 1957, **3**, 144–156.)

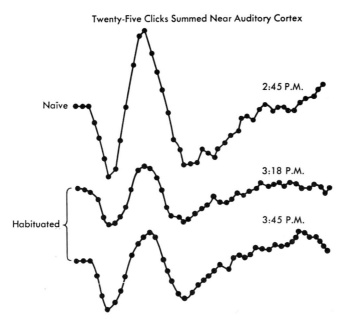

Twenty-Five Clicks Summed Near Auditory Cortex

Naïve

2:45 P.M.

3:18 P.M.

Habituated

3:45 P.M.

Figure 21-3. Average evoked response to a click recorded from the temporal lobe of the monkey. (Adapted with permission from Galambos, R., & Sheatz, G. C. An electro-encephalographic study of classical conditioning. *Amer. J. Physiol.*, 1962, **203**, 173–184.)

the evoked response to the 3,000 cps tone bursts decreased in amplitude during twenty successive presentations. When the nature of the repetitive stimulus was changed (to 1,000 cps), the evoked response was dishabituated; it returned to its original full amplitude and had to be rehabituated. Hence, it would appear that the process involved is not simply one of receptor fatigue.

Changes in the auditory evoked-response amplitude with repetitive stimulus presentations have been noted at many relay nuclei in the classical auditory system higher than the cochlear nuclei. (See Hernández-Peón, 1960.) Also, clear pictures of evoked responses can now be obtained by using recently developed computer "averaging" techniques. Any given number of evoked responses can be sampled. Nonsystematic components of the waveform cancel out, and a clear picture of the evoked response remains. Figure 21-3 indicates averaged

evoked responses, measured from the auditory cortex, clearly demonstrating the habituation phenomenon.

The Neurophysiology of Habituation

To understand physiological interpretations of habituation, we must first examine the receptor systems through which the noninformative stimuli are introduced into an organism's central nervous system. Because most research has concerned auditory habituation, our discussion centers primarily about the auditory system.

As mentioned previously, the vibratory patterns set up in the air by an acoustic stimulus are ultimately transduced into neural impulses in the cochlea of the inner ear. Figure 21-4, representing a cross section of the ear, indicates how this comes about.

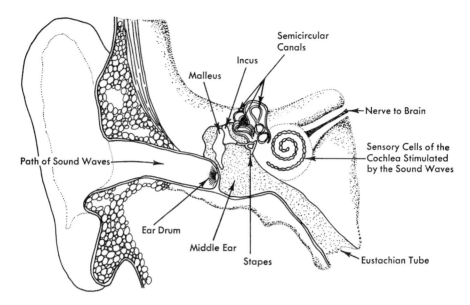

Figure 21-4.   A schematic drawing of the ear. (Adapted with permission from Davis, H. (Ed.). *Hearing and Deafness.* New York : Holt, 1947.)

The sound waves vibrate the ear drum of the outer ear. The inner part of the eardrum is attached to a tiny bone, the *malleus*, which is one of the three bones, or ossicles, that together form the ossicular chain of the middle ear. The malleus is attached to the central ossicle, the *incus*, which, in turn, is attached to the terminal ossicle, the *stapes*. These three articulate with each other such that the vibration imparted to the malleus by the eardrum is transmitted to the stapes. The stapes makes contact with the *oval window*, a membrane covering the end of the cochlea in the inner ear. The role of the cochlea in audition is complicated and fascinating (see von Békésy, 1960). For our purposes, however, it is enough to understand that the vibrations imparted to the oval window by the ossicular chain set into motion fluid in the cochlea. This fluid distorts *hair cells* in the cochlea, which act in a manner analogous to a piezoelectric crystal in a phonograph cartridge; when the hair cells are subject to distortion, they produce a small electric potential, which ultimately produces

neural impulses in the auditory nerve, and this neural coding of auditory information is carried into the central nervous system.

Peripheral Mechanisms

We can discuss one theoretical interpretation of habituation without following the neural impulse any further. It has been proposed that the attenuation of incoming, redundant auditory information takes place right at the ear. There are two small muscles in the middle ear, the *stapedius* and the *tensor tympani*. The stapedius is attached to the stapes near its junction with the incus. The tensor tympani is attached to the malleus. When these muscles contract, they tend to dampen the activity of the ossicular chain, decreasing the intensity of vibration delivered to the oval window of the cochlea. It had been assumed that these muscles reflexively contract to sudden, loud stimuli, thereby protecting the delicate receptor system in the cochlea from potentially excessive vibratory stimulation. Recent evidence concerning the relatively long response latency for these muscles indicates that their protective action is probably quite limited (Wersall, 1958); however, the fact that these muscles can attenuate incoming auditory stimulation has suggested to some researchers that they play an important role in auditory habituation (Alcaraz, Pacheco, and Guzmán-Flores, 1962; Guzmán-Flores, 1961; Guzmán-Flores, Alcaraz, and Harmony, 1960). These investigators have proposed that contractions of these small, intrinsic ear muscles become temporally conditioned during the experimental habituation procedure. When two stimuli are presented in close temporal contiguity a number of times, the requirements for the classical conditioning paradigm are satisfied, and, typically, the first stimulus (the conditioned stimulus or CS) eventually elicits a response (the conditioned response or CR) originally associated with the second stimulus (the unconditioned stimulus or UCS). Traditionally, both these stimuli have been exteroceptive; for example, Pavlov (1927) often used a light as the CS and food as the UCS. However, it has been known for some time that "temporal conditioning" is possible (see review by Dmitriev and Kochigina, 1959), in which the passage of time alone serves as an effective CS. In the temporal conditioning paradigm a UCS is presented at regular intervals. Eventually, a CR is observed to occur just prior to the regular UCS delivery. In this situation the passage of a regular interval of time serves as the CS. Therefore, it might be expected that the middle ear muscles, which reflexively contract to each repetitively presented tone burst or click in the experimental habituation situation, become conditioned to the interval between successive acoustic stimuli presentations; "the process . . . the increased contraction on the inner muscles, is a type of learning, in the sense that the animal is in some way expecting the next click" (Guzmán-Flores, 1961, p. 347). The result of this conditioning would be to attenuate the intensity of acoustic stimulation getting into the cochlea and being transduced into neural impulses, reflected by a decrease in evoked-response amplitude.

Implicit in this interpretation of evoked-response changes during habituation is the assumption that contraction of the middle ear muscles can be conditioned. It would appear that this is the case. Although no attempt at temporal conditioning of these muscles has been made, indirect measurement of their activity during the pairing of a CS (light flash) with a UCS (loud horn blast) indicated that anticipatory contractions of the middle ear muscles to the CS occurred after several pairings (Simmons, Galambos, and Rupert, 1959).

If the middle ear muscles play a crucial role in the evoked-response correlates of habituation, rendering these muscles nonfunctional should eliminate evoked-response habituation. Investigations of this topic have yielded equivocal results. Habituation has been studied after immobilizing the middle ear muscles with a muscle relaxant drug and after surgical interference with the operation of the muscles. Some investigators have reported that no habituation occurs in the absence of middle ear muscles (Alcaraz, Pacheco, and Guzmán-Flores, 1962; Guzmán-Flores, 1961). Furthermore, it has been reported that if evoked-response habituation is permitted to occur in an S with intact middle ear muscles and then a muscle relaxant is intravenously injected, the evoked response increases in amplitude to its prehabituation level in several areas of the auditory pathway (Guzmán Flores, Alcaraz, and Harmony, 1960).

One investigation (Moushegian, Rupert, Marsh, and Galambos, 1961) suggests that the previously reported failures to obtain evoked-response habituation in Ss deprived of middle ear muscles may be due to the limited length of the habituation sessions used, a maximum of six hours. Moushegian et al. (1961) apparently demonstrated evoked-response habituation, at least in the auditory cortex, when S deprived of its middle ear muscles was exposed to the iterative stimulation for a much longer period of time—ten days or more.

If temporal conditioning of the middle ear muscles plays an important role in evoked-response habituation, no such habituation should be obtained in the situation in which temporal conditioning could not occur. If the interval between successive acoustic stimuli presentations were random rather than constant, the interval could not serve as an effective conditioned stimulus for the middle ear muscle contraction. In fact, auditory habituation at the level of the cochlear nucleus apparently occurs whether the interval between successive acoustic stimuli is random or regular (Webster, Dunlop, Simons, and Aitkin, 1965).

Before concluding the discussion of peripheral mechanisms of habituation, it should be mentioned that such interpretations of the phenomenon are not confined to evoked-response habituation of the auditory system. There is some evidence that pupillary contraction plays a role in visual evoked-response habituation analogues to that proposed for the middle ear muscles in auditory evoked-response habituation (Fernandez-Guardiola, Roldan, Fanjul, and Castell, 1961; Naquet, Regis, Fischer-Williams, and Fernandez-Guardiola, 1960).

Central Theories

In contrast with the peripheral interpretation of habituation are a group of central or "centrifugal" theories. These attribute the evoked-response habituation decrement to inhibitory centrifugal influences at relay nuclei in the auditory pathway (see Chapter 20).

Figure 21-5 is a schematic representation of the auditory pathways in a typical mammalian brain. As may be seen, incoming (ascending) auditory information may be modified at any number of points by centrifugal (descending) influences. As mentioned

previously, evoked-response habituation has been observed at the level of the first sensory synapse—the cochlear nucleus (for example, Hernández-Peón et al., 1957). Thus these centrifugal influences must exert their effects here (as well, perhaps, as at other locations).

There is ample neuroanatomical evidence (for example, Brodal, 1957) indicating that centrifugal fibres terminate at the cochlear nucleus and at other auditory relay nuclei in the brain, but the origin of these pathways is still a matter of investigation.

There are many findings implicating the *reticular formation*, an area in the core of the brain stem, in the habituation phenomenon (Hernández-Peón, 1960; Hernández-Peón, 1966). In support of this position it has been reported that when an animal is subjected to barbiturate anesthesia, which presumably inhibits activity of the reticular formation, no evoked-response habituation occurs (for example, Gershuni et al., 1960; Hernández-Peón et al., 1957). However, acoustic habituation in the anesthetized preparation has recently been noted by others (Webster et al., 1965). In any event, it seems that the results of studies investigating auditory habituation in the anaesthetized S will not be crucial for central versus peripheral interpretations of acoustic habituation, because the barbiturates, in addition to their reticular formation effects, apparently also block the action of the middle ear muscles (Carmel and Starr, 1963). More significant findings relating the reticular formation to habituation are provided by studies demonstrating that electrical stimulation of a number of sites in the reticular formation reduces the amplitude of an evoked potential elicited by peripheral stimulation of a number of sensory modalities (Granit, 1955; Hagbarth and Fex, 1959; Hagbarth and Kerr, 1954; Hernández-Peón and Hagbarth, 1955); therefore stimulation of the reticular formation can produce a habituation-like evoked-response decrement. Furthermore, reticular formation lesions may present

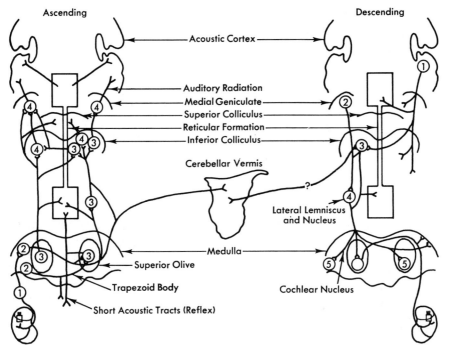

Figure 21-5. Diagram of the auditory pathways in a typical mammalian brain. Numbers refer to first-order neuron, second-order neuron, etc. (Reprinted with permission from Galambos, R. Some recent experiments on the neurophysiology of hearing. *Ann. otal. Rhinol. Laryngol.*, 1956, **65**, 1053–1059.)

evoked-response habituation (for example, Hernández-Péon et al 1958), with the sensory modality so affected dependent on the locus of the lesion (Hernández-Peón, 1960). There is also some evidence to indicate that the electrical activity of the reticular formation undergoes changes during habituation (Huttenlocher, 1960).

Centrifugal inhibitory influences other than those extending from the reticular formation to the level of the first sensory relay nucleus have been implicated in the auditory habituation phenomenon. A descending pathway has been identified which arises in the olivary complex of the brain stem and extends to the hair cells in the cochlea. This pathway is one of those schematically represented in Figure 21-5. It is called the *olivocochlear bundle*, and was first described by Rasmussen (1946). Electrical stimulation of the olivocochlear

bundle reduces the magnitude of the evoked response to auditory stimulation right at the round window of the cochlea (see Figure 21-4), as well as at a number of auditory relay stations in the brain (Galambos, 1956). The possibility exists that these evoked-response diminutions may be due to the effects of olivocochlear bundle stimulation on the middle ear muscles, because Hugelin, Dumont, and Paillas (1960) found that the suppression of acoustic evoked potentials induced by olivocochlear bundle stimulation was much attenuated in cats in which the middle ear muscles were removed. The role of such findings in auditory habituation is open to question, however, because, as mentioned previously, habituation has been noted in the preparation deprived of middle ear muscles if the period of iterative stimulation is sufficiently prolonged (Moushegian et al., 1961).

Other investigators (see Desmedt, 1960) have emphasized the role of still different centrifugal pathways in auditory habituation. These pathways have their origin in the cerebral cortex, rather than the reticular formation, and descend to the cochlear nucleus. Because these pathways have no reticular formation involvement, they form the "Centrifugal Extrareticular Auditory Control System." One such centrifugal influence is in close proximity to the classical ascending auditory pathway (Desmedt, 1960). Another extrareticular descending pathway has also been delineated (Zimmerman, Chamber, and Liu, 1964) which does not lie in proximity to the classical auditory pathway.

Thus, there are many descending pathways, reticular and extrareticular, that could conceivably act on incoming afferent signals at many points in the ascending sensory pathway. Only further research can indicate which ones are crucial for habituation phenomenon, or, as is probably the case, their interactive effects in contributing to habituation.

Finally, it should be pointed out that results of recent investigations of evoked-response habituation suggest that earlier findings may be criticized for methodological inadequacies—especially failure to control the experimental Ss' orientation in the sound field and the possibility of biased data-sampling techniques (see Horn, 1965; Marsh and Worden, 1964; Simmons and Beatty, 1964; Worden, 1966). These procedural problems may have tended to overemphasize the magnitude of acoustic evoked-response habituation, especially at the lower levels of the auditory pathway. Further research with sophisticated methodological and data-analysis techniques will undoubtedly indicate the bases and significance of evoked-response habituation.

22

Learning

Because behavior results from activity within the nervous system, behavior changes as a function of experience also presumably have a neural basis. Without getting into problems of definition, we may note that the behavior changes that are a function of experience are commonly referred to as *learning*. Although we have already categorized habituation as a form of "negative learning," learning traditionally refers to the behavioral plasticity involved in the acquisition of new response tendencies, rather than imply the elimination of initial response tendencies.

Investigators have used many methods in an attempt to comprehend what happens inside the "black box" during learning. Some have studied the ongoing electrical events arising from neural activity in the relatively intact electrical organism, correlating such recorded electrical activity with learning phenomena. Previously mentioned investigations of cortical arousal and evoked potentials during habituation utilized this technique. Other investigations have involved studying the effects of experimentally introduced stimulation of the nervous system. Previously mentioned studies in which evoked-response changes were correlated

with electrical stimulation of the reticular formation provide examples of this stimulation technique, combined with the previously mentioned recording technique. Typically, the stimulation is electrical, although recently chemical stimulation has also been used. Another method involves the destruction (lesion) or removal (ablation) of populations of neural tissue in an attempt to investigate the role of specific central nervous system deficits in learning. Studies mentioned earlier, in which evoked-response habituation was studied subsequent to reticular formation lesions in an attempt to elucidate the role of the reticular formation in habituation, provide examples of the use of this technique. Some *E*s have limited their investigations of the neurophysiology of learning to phylogenetically primitive organisms or surgically simplified specimens in an attempt to understand neural processes underlying learning in the relatively uncomplicated preparation as a prelude to the considerably more complex analysis of mammalian learning. Recently, there has been a good deal of work involving the chemical changes within the organism that appear to be correlated with learning. The contributions of these diverse attacks on what is perhaps the central problem in psychology will be discussed in detail.

Electrophysiological Correlates of Learning

In an attempt to elucidate the structures involved in learning, a number of investigations have involved recording the electrical activity of potentially significant neural structures while the organism is undergoing conditioning procedures (see Morrell, 1961).

The Cortical Arousal Pattern. It was mentioned in the previous section that one component of the "orientation response" to a novel stimulus is the cortical arousal pattern; cortical electrical activity changes in the direction of higher frequency, lower amplitude waves. As the novel stimulus is repetitively presented, the magnitude of the cortical arousal response decreases (Figure 21-1). If a stimulus to which S is habituated (that is, the stimulus elicits little or no cortical arousal) is made the CS in the classical conditioning paradigm (that is, it is now followed by a noxious or appetitive UCS), it will begin again to elicit a cortical arousal response (for reviews, see Diamond and Chow, 1962; Morrell, 1961; Wells, 1963). One example of this type of experiment will be discussed to illustrate the procedure and general findings. Doty (1958) presented an auditory stimulus to a cat many times until the cortical arousal response to this stimulus was habituated. This auditory stimulus was now paired with an electric shock to the animal's paw. After a few such pairings the auditory stimulus again elicited the cortical arousal pattern. This cortical conditioned response (CR) occurred after many fewer pairings than that required for the overt motor CR of leg flexion. Furthermore, when the CS was presented without the UCS after the acquisition of both the cortical CR and motor CR, the cortical CR was found to be much more resistant to extinction than the motor response.

There is some question about whether this type of apparent cortical conditioning really represents learning in the traditional sense or merely sensitization or pseudoconditioning (see Diamond and Chow, 1962). Furthermore, although the cortical arousal response anticipates the motor CR during acquisition, this should not be taken as a reflection of a causal relationship. Cortical arousal may be temporarily eliminated by drugs (for example, atropine or bulbocapnine), and Ss so treated show normal elaboration of motor CRs (Beck and Doty, 1957; Key and Bradley, 1959).

Finally, it should be noted that the phenomenon of cortical arousal patterns correlated with conditioning procedures is not completely reliable, and the exact conditions under which it can and cannot be obtained are not yet well delineated (Gastaut et al., 1957).

Despite difficulties in interpretation, mentioned previously, some investigators have suggested that cortical arousal changes during conditioning are an indication of some internal excitatory tendency intimately tied to the conditioning process (Lynn, 1966). Another aspect of the EEG has been intepreted as indicative of an internal inhibitory tendency—these are low-frequency (3 to 5 per sec.) high-voltage waves, sometimes called *hypersynchronous slow waves*. An overview of the research literature (Gastaut, 1957) substantiates this position by reviewing findings which indicate that, during extinction of a CR, the same CS which elicited high-frequency, low-amplitude activity characteristic of the arousal reaction during acquisition comes to elicit the high-amplitude, low-frequency activity characteristic of hypersynchronous slow waves. Furthermore, hypersynchronous slow waves are elicited by the nonreinforced (negative) stimulus in the differential classical conditioning procedure, much as the arousal pattern is elicited by the reinforced (positive) CS. Another behavioral inhibitory state has been termed *inhibition of delay* (Pavlov, 1927). With a sufficiently prolonged CS–UCS interval, the CR does not occur until near the end of the interval, the CR presumably being inhibited during the earlier part of the interval. Hypersynchronous slow waves occurring during the inhibition of delay period have been noted by several investigators (for example, Morrell and Ross, 1953; Rowland and Gluck, 1960).

Although there is probably more general agreement that slow waves are indicative of a conditional inhibitory state than that the arousal pattern is indicative of a conditional excitatory state, it should be noted that the evidence is not entirely unequivocal (Grossman, 1967, pp. 656–659).

Labeled Rhythms. Another approach to exploring neural correlates of learning has utilized the technique of *labeled rhythms.* The dominant rhythm in the human EEG is the alpha rhythm, consisting of activity in the range of 8 to 13 cps. Other species also have characteristic dominant rhythms of the EEG: about 5 cps for the rabbit, 15 to 20 cps for the cat, and so on. If iterative, punctate stimulation is presented to an organism (for example, flickering light, clicks, repetitive electrical stimulation of the skin), the dominant pattern of electrical activity in some areas of the brain becomes "driven" by this peripheral stimulation; that is, it adopts the dominant frequency which is synchronized with the recurrent stimulation. By using such stimulation as a CS, it is possible to detect changes in these labeled rhythms in parts of the nervous system during the acquisition of the learned response:

The recurrent conditioned stimulus has been termed a "tracer conditioned stimulus" (TCS) because the neural signals evoked may be followed through the brain somewhat as a radioactive tracer may be followed through a chemical process [John and Killam, 1959].

This experiment of John and Killam is a widely cited example of the use of labeled rhythms in studies of learning. They used a light flickering at the rate of 10 cps as the CS in an avoidance learning situation. The *S*s (cats) had electrodes implanted in a number of cortical and subcortical locations. Prior to conditioning, presentation of the flicker stimulus produced labeled rhythms in most of the brain areas sampled. After a large number of nonreinforced presentations of the CS, this "photic driving" habituated, that is, it was drastically reduced or eliminated in all areas. When the flicker now was made into a CS in the avoidance conditioning paradigm, labeled rhythms reappeared at all recording sites. As training progressed, the amplitude and location of the labeled rhythms changed, with characteristic patterns associated with the first avoidance CR and asymptotic avoidance performance. There is some evidence suggesting that the distribution and magnitude of labeled rhythm changes during conditioning is somewhat different for the instrumental appetitive conditioning situation than for the avoidance conditioning situation (John and Killam, 1960).

Other investigators using the labeled rhythm technique (for example, Liberson and Ellen, 1960; McAdam, Snodgrass, Knott, and Ingram, 1961; Stern, Vlett, and Sines, 1960) have obtained conflicting findings and have used experimental designs that are not strictly comparable. As pointed out by Morrell (1961) and Grossman (1967) it is not yet clear whether the findings from investigations using labeled rhythms represent: (1) some general changes in the arousal of the organism during the conditioning process; (2) an epiphenomenon associated with the use of a tracer CS frequency not readily distinguishable from the normal frequency of the electrical activity of the brain, compounded by excessive use of subjective data-analysis techniques; or (3) an actual indication of the information-processing and coding that goes on during learning.

Evoked Responses. The use of evoked responses in studies of habituation has already been mentioned. In the *S* whose evoked response to a peripheral stimulus is of diminished amplitude because of habituation, it will quickly increase in amplitude again if the peripheral stimulus precedes the delivery of a noxious electric shock or puff of air, or appetitive UCS. (See Morrell, 1961, for review.) In some cases, evoked-response increases during conditioning have been noted in *S*s not subjected to the habituation experience prior to conditioning (Galambos, 1958; Gerken and Neff, 1963). There is some evidence that the amplitude changes are highly correlated with the occurrence of overt CRs (for example, Hernández-Peón et al., 1956), although the amplitude of the evoked response tends to decrease again with overtraining (Hearst, et al., 1960; Roitbak, 1960).

An interesting finding was reported by Jouvet and Hernández-Peón (1957). They paired a CS (clicks) with a UCS (shock to the limb). Click-evoked potentials were noted in the motor areas of the cortex about the time that the overt motors CRs were first evidenced.

Extinction of a CR results in diminution of evoked responses to the CS (for example, Galambos, Sheatz, and Vernier, 1956), the decline in amplitude taking place relatively rapidly (for example, Galambos and Sheatz, 1962) and occasionally continuing for days (for example, Galambos et al., 1956). Alternating periods of acquisition and extinction produce corresponding periods of evoked-response increase and decrease (for example, Galambos et al., 1956; Marsh, McCarthy, Sheatz, and Galambos, 1961).

A large research literature has accumulated relating evoked-response changes, both cortical and subcortical, with conditioning phenomena (see Morrell, 1961). These must be viewed with the same reservations as those findings dealing with evoked response changes during habituation. Frequently, the lack of attention to *S*'s orientation to the source of the CS presentation and less than rigorous data-sampling and analysis techniques may have led to exaggerated conclusions.

Conditioning Electrophysiological Responses

According to Pavlov, the formation of a CR represented the development of a temporary neural connection between that part of the cortex involved in processing the CS input ("auditory analyzer," "visual analyzer," and so on) and another part of the cortex aroused by the UCS. The actual anatomical and physiological basis for the existence of these CS and UCS cerebral centers and the development of connections between them was not specified. More recently, many investigators have attempted "to make use of the electrical activity of the cortex itself as a means of making a more direct study of neurophysiological mechanisms underlying the formation of temporary connections in the brain" (Morrell and Jasper, 1956, p. 201).

Conditioning of the electrical activity of the cortex was first reported by Durup and Fessard (1935). They were examining the EEG response of a cat to a visual stimulus and photographing the display of cortical electrical activity from a cathode-ray oscilloscope. The apparatus was set up so that the camera shutter was operated just prior to stimulus presentation. Because of an apparatus failure, the camera operated on some occasions without presentation of the visual stimulus, but on these occasions an EEG arousal response was recorded which was similar to that obtained when the visual stimulus was presented. Because the camera shutter operation did not elicit such an EEG alteration prior to its pairings with the visual stimulus, Durup and Fessard suggested that it acquired this property by classical conditioning, the shutter operation being the CS and light presentation being the UCS. Repeated operation of the camera shutter without light presentation led to a diminution of shutter-produced EEG alteration, which, the authors proposed, represented extinction of the CR.

The original finding of Durup and Fessard was serendipitous, a fortuitous combination of apparatus failure and astute researchers, but it was soon replicated under more rigorous conditions (for example, Cruikshank, 1937; Jasper and Cruikshank, 1937; Loomis, Harvey, and Hobart, 1936). A detailed summary of the vast research literature in this area may be found in the reviews by Morrell (1961) and Grossman (1967, pp. 670–691).

Sensory-Sensory Conditioning

The type of conditioning procedure in which different sensory stimuli serve as CS and UCS and the responses being measured are EEG alterations is sometimes referred to as *sensory-sensory conditioning*. An elaborate series of sensory-sensory conditioning experiments was conducted by Jasper and Shagass (1941). Using a tone to which the EEG alpha block was habituated as the CS and light as the UCS, they demonstrated the development of EEG CRs with nearly all types of Pavlovian forward-conditioning paradigms: simple conditioning (simultaneous CS and UCS presentations), delayed conditioning (CS onset substantially prior to UCS onset, with simultaneous termination of both stimuli), trace conditioning (CS offset prior to UCS onset), temporal conditioning (temporal interval between successive UCS presentations serving as the CS), and discriminative conditioning (one CS pitch being followed by the UCS and another CS pitch not being followed by the UCS). Moreover, Jasper and Shagass demonstrated *backward conditioning* (UCS presented prior to CS). Pavlov (1927) reported an inability to obtain backward CRs, a finding later confirmed by a number of subsequent investigations addressed to the specific question of the possibility of backward conditioning (for example, Cason, 1935; Portet, 1938). Indeed, several investigators have suggested that the result of the backward-conditioning procedure actually is to condition a response antagonistic to the CR (Barlow, 1956; Konorski, 1948; Rescorla, 1967).

Backward conditioning is a control frequently used to assess the role of pseudo-conditioning or sensitization in apparent conditioning (for example, Kalish, 1954; Wagner, Siegel, and Fein, 1967). That EEG conditioning was obtained with the backward-conditioning paradigm suggests that the phenomenon represents a sensitized response to the CS, rather than a true CR. The nature of the acquisition of the conditioned alpha-block response has also suggested to some investigators that it possesses properties more characteristic of a sensitized response than a learned response. Usually, the alpha-block CR reaches its maximal strength very shortly after the start of acquisition—much sooner than overt CRs are demonstrated in a typical conditioning procedure, and the response tends to become weaker with extended training (for example, Knott and Henry, 1941). Furthermore, the alpha-block CR usually does not occur with great frequency, and it often tends to be unstable, even after many conditioning trials, with only a few CS-alone trials being required to produce complete extinction (for example, Albino and Burnand, 1964; Shagass and Johnson, 1943; Travis and Egan, 1938). Recent research indicates that it is possible to obtain what looks like alpha-block conditioning without actually pairing the CS and UCS, but by interpolating forty UCS- (light) alone presentations between a CS- (tone) alone habituation session and a final CS-alone test session (Milstein, 1965). Furthermore, the frequency and magnitude of CS-induced alpha blocking obtained under these noncontingent conditions is the same as that later obtained in the same *S*s with the usual contingent conditioning procedure. Because the effect need not necessarily depend on CS and UCS contingency, its status as a true learning phenomenon is subject to question.

In contrast with these findings of Milstein (1965) are those of Putney (1966), who compared tone-elicited alpha blocking during noncontingent pseudoconditioning sessions and contingent-conditioning sessions in nine *S*s. "Pseudoconditioning was a tenable explanation of anticipatory supression for only four subjects. . . . All other subjects demonstrated that noncontingent light (UCS) presentations had less effect on tone blocking than paired conditioning trials did" (Putney, 1966).

Further evidence contrary to interpretations of apparent sensory-sensory conditioning as a sensitization effect is provided by studies indicating that the CR can be highly selective to a particular CS (see Jasper and Shagass 1941; Morrell and Jasper, 1956). For example, as mentioned earlier, Jasper and Shagass reported discriminative alpha-block conditioning; a CS (−) of 500 cps did not elicit a conditioned alpha-block response, but a CS (+) of 700 cps reliably did so. If the tone-elicited EEG alteration simply represented increased cortical excitability following the introduction of the novel stimulus (the visual UCS), or a dishabituation of the habituated EEG response to the tone CS caused by the novel stimulus, it would not be expected that the obtained alpha blockage would be selectively produced by a CS of one pitch and not by one 200 cps lower.

Other findings contrary to sensitization interpretations of apparent sensory-sensory conditioning may be found in studies in which the UCR is a synchronization and augmentation of EEG activity, rather than a desynchronized arousal response. In one group of experiments reported by Morrell and Jasper (1956), the UCS employed was a light that flickered at a rate in the same frequency range as the dominant activity of the EEG of the monkey *S*s. The resulting UCR was not the usual cortical arousal pattern, but rather the photic driving response described earlier; the EEG pattern in the occipital area of the cortex became augmented and synchronized with the visual flicker stimulus. The auditory CS used elicited the usual alpha-blocking response when it was first presented prior to conditioning. However, when this original response was habituated and the auditory CS was paired with the

flicker UCS, CRs similar to the UCRs of photic driving were recorded. It may be argued that because the CS elicited a response after conditioning that was unlike its response prior to habituation and its pairing with the UCS, the EEG alterations cannot be ascribed to sensitization. Moreover, the frequency-specific CR was highly selective to the CS used during training, and was not obtained with an auditory stimulus of a different pitch. However, in contrast with the results from the typical conditioning procedure, the nature of the CR changed during the course of training; the frequency specific CR grew weaker and gave way to a desynchronized cortical arousal response. According to Morrell and Jasper the loss of the frequency-specific CR and adoption of a desynchronized response, although "somewhat surprising," may be an artifact of the electronic characteristics of their apparatus, They suggested that a detailed computer analysis of the EEG records would reveal a synchronized anticipatory response to be present even in the late stages of conditioning. They conclude, "The localized occipital frequency specific, repetitive discharge which, following paired trials, is elicited by a previously ineffective stimulus and is subject to differentiation, we regard as an objective trace in cortical activity of a conditioned temporary connection" (Morrell and Jasper, 1956, p. 214).

These basic findings of Morrell and Jasper have been essentially replicated (for example, Morrell, Naquet, and Gastaut, 1957; Yoshii and Hockaday, 1958). Subsequent research which subjected to detailed computer analysis the desynchronized EEG response that develops after the frequency-specific CR indicated that, contrary to Morrell and Jasper's original speculation, there was no evidence of frequency-specific activity hidden in the desynchronized arousal pattern (Morrell, Barlow, and Brazier, 1960), and Morrell has revised his earlier position that frequency-specific CRs represent the temporary cortical connection about which Pavlov spoke (Morrell, 1959).

Some attempts have been made to consider the two different types of CRs as representative of different stages in the conditioning process (for example, Yoshii et al., 1960).

In summary, results of studies investigating the conditioning of electrophysiological responses did not live up to original expectations as "a direct study of neurophysiological mechanisms underlying the formation of temporary connections in the brain" (Morrell and Jasper, 1956, p. 201). The field has been plagued by conflicting findings concerning the role of sensitization in the phenomenon, and "the data available are still scattered, fragmentary and incomplete" (Galambos and Morgan, 1960, p. 1484). Perhaps recent research involving the conditioning of the activity of single neurons (for example, Morrell, 1960), and attempts at operant conditioning of neural unit activity (Olds and Olds, 1961) will, when sufficiently elaborated with further research, make a more substantial advance toward fulfilling the original expectations of this type of conditioning procedure.

Intraneural Conditioning

Another approach to exploring the neurophysiological mechanisms of learning has been to bypass the afferent input to the central nervous system when presenting the CS and/or UCS and instead to use direct electrical stimulation of relevant brain structures. In terminology proposed by Gantt (1937) this would represent "intraneural" conditioning, indicating that the conditioning stimuli originate in the central nervous system. This is in contrast to the more customary "extraneural" conditioning situation in which the conditioning stimuli originate outside the Ss central nervous system. For example, instead of using light as an extraneural CS, direct stimulation of sensory areas of the brain (for example, occipital cortex) may be used as an intraneural CS; instead of using peripheral shock to a limb as a UCS for extraneurally

elicited flexion response, electrical stimulation of a motor area of the brain may be used, which intraneurally elicits a similar flexion response. In some studies both the CS and UCS have consisted of brain stimulation, each in a different area. If Pavlov's ephemeral "temporary connection" between the cortical CS analyzer and the cortical UCS area of excitation were responsible for overt conditioning, having both cerebral foci under the control of E would appear to offer an excellent opportunity for exploration of this connection.

Early Research. Several early investigations of intraneural conditioning achieved success with a central CS and peripheral UCS. The investigations of Loucks indicated that electrical stimulation in a variety of cortical areas could serve as an effective CS for conditioning of limb flexion (Loucks, 1933, 1935) and salivation (Loucks, 1938). The effectiveness of cortical stimulation as a CS for instrumental as well as classical conditioning was subsequently verified (Doty and Rutledge, 1959; Doty, Rutledge, and Larson, 1956; Rutledge and Doty, 1955). It appears that this conditioning technique was rather commonplace in Giurgea's laboratory in Rumania (see Grossman, 1967, pp. 776–785). Rate of conditioning when using a cortical CS is approximately equivalent to that obtained with a peripheral CS. Furthermore, discriminations can be established such that Ss will respond to stimulation delivered to one area of the cortex and not another and possibly even to cortical stimuli of one frequency and not another (Doty, Rutledge, and Larson, 1956).

The central nervous system is covered by a layered membrane, the meninges. It is conceivable that an artifact of cortical stimulation is meningeal stimulation, which might result in the sensation of pain, effectively making the internal cortical CS an external tactile or irritative stimulus. However, meningeal stimulation results in a galvanic skin response (Spiegel and

Hunsicker, 1936), but stimulation of the sensory cortex does not (Langworthy and Richter, 1930). Most of the effective cortical CSs of Doty et al. (1956) did not elicit galvanic skin responses, indicating that such stimuli had minimal meningeal involvement. Furthermore, Doty et al. (1956) demonstrated conditioning to a cortical CS in a cat with surgically denervated meninges.

In the well-trained S, if the area of cortical stimulation is either undercut or cortically circumscribed, postoperative testing reveals some loss of the CR, but undercutting was found to be more detrimental than cortical circumspection (Doty and Rutledge, 1959).

Recent research indicates that subcortical stimulation in a number of areas can serve as an effective CS (Nielson, Doty, and Rutledge, 1958; Neilson, Knight, and Porter, 1962; Morgenson and Morrison, 1962).

Many investigators have attempted to demonstrate conditioning with direct electrical stimulation of the cortex as the UCS. Unsuccessful attempts were reported by Loucks (1933; 1935). He paired an external CS (buzzer) with electrical stimulation of the motor cortex, which elicited a stereotype leg flexion response in dogs. Even after as many as 600 trials no CRs were obtained. Masserman (1943) reported an inability to condition a motor response elicited by electrical stimulation of the cerebellum. Loucks asserted that the UCR elicited by direct cortical stimulation did not possess any affective qualities, rendering it ineffective as a conditionable response. In cases in which successful conditioning was reported with central nervous system stimulation as the UCS (Brogden and Gantt, 1942; Gantt, 1937; Gantt and Loucks, 1938; Loucks and Gantt, 1938; Segundo, Roig, and Sommer-Smith, 1959), it is likely that stimulation involved sensory as well as motor components (Grossman, 1967, pp. 770–774).

These findings have been interpreted as supporting the proposition that some sort of reward, motivation, or drive reduction is necessary for learning, and mere CS-UCS contiguity is not enough. Thus, according to Loucks (1935), his experiments reveal "the serious inadequacy of those formulations of learning or conditioning built solely upon the principle of association by contiguity" (p. 35). Spence (1951) has suggested that failures at conditioning cortically elicited responses "lend strong support ... to the view that reinforcement plays a critical role in the acquisition of conditioned responses involving skeletal systems" (p. 710). Mowrer (1960) has asserted that Loucks' research demonstrates that "a reflex response made to a stimulus which cannot arouse pain (and fear) is utterly incapable of occurring anticipatorily, to a signal" (p. 240).

Eastern European Research. It was of great theoretical significance when it became apparent to Western researchers that intraneural UCs had frequently and successfully been employed by Eastern European investigators (Giurgea, 1953; Giurgea and Raiciulescu, 1959; Nikolaeva, 1955, 1957; Tchilingaryan, 1963). A collaboration between one of these investigators, G. Giurgea, and R. W. Doty resulted in a demonstration in an American laboratory of the effectiveness of cortical UCSs (Doty and Giurgea, 1961). Indeed, this investigation by Doty and Giurgea demonstrated conditioning when both the CS and UCS were stimulation of distinct cortical areas. Conditioning with a cortically elicited UCR does not appear to be a result of sensitization or pseudoconditioning, for it can be specific to a given CS; simple discriminations can be formed between CSs delivered to different cortical areas (Doty and Giurgea, 1961), and between different, peripheral auditory stimuli (Thomas, 1967; Wagner, Thomas, and Norton, 1967). Furthermore, if two different CSs are each paired with electrical stimulation of two distinct cortical points, so that one CS is always paired with one intraneurally elicited UCR (for example, right forelimb flexion) and the second CS is paired with the second intraneurally elicited UCR (for example, right hindlimb flexion), a complex differentiation will be formed so that each CS tends to elicit its appropriate CR. This has been demonstrated with both intraneural (Doty and Giurgea, 1961) and extraneural (Wagner et al., 1967) CSs.

Why did the early investigations of Loucks fail to demonstrate conditioning with a cortical UCS and later investigations achieve success? Doty and Giurgea suggest that the intertrial interval may be crucial, conditioning being obtained with an intertrial interval of at least 3 min., with shorter intervals (such as the 0.5 to 2 min. used by Loucks) being too brief to be conducive to the formation of CRs. There is certainly some evidence that such short intertrial intervals may have a detrimental effect with more customary classical conditioning procedures. (See review by Beecroft, 1966, pp. 100–104.) Furthermore, research on conditioning a motor response elicited by brain stimulation indicates that CRs elaborated with well-spaced trials become unstable when the interval between trials is reduced to about 2 min. or less (Giurgea, 1953; Giurgea and Raiciulescu, 1959).

Evidence concerning the presumed nonmotivational aspects of electrical stimulation of the motor cortex has been gathered from a number of different sources—neuroanatomical considerations, general observations of animals subjected to motor cortical stimulation, and introspective reports of humans undergoing such stimulation. Doty and Giurgea (1961) attempted an objective assessment of the affective qualities of the electrical stimulation of the cortex. They trained several of their Ss in an instrumental-learning situation in which successful operation of a manipulandum was effective in delivering food reward. When this instrumental response stabilized, motor cortical stimulation was additionally made contingent on manipulation operation. In most cases the addition of this contingency did not change the rate of instrumental

responding, neither decreasing it nor increasing it, which suggested that the cortical UCS was neither aversive nor rewarding.

Recent Research. A most ingenious series of experiments from Wagner's laboratory (Thomas, 1967; Wagner et al., 1967), however, has identified a probable source of motivation in this type of conditioning situation. It appears that the presence of an anticipatory flexion response serves to prepare the animal for the unconditioned flexion response, decreasing the imbalance and the need for sudden postural adjustments that a sudden, unsignaled, cortically evoked limb flexion would entail. Thus, Wagner et al. observed that, in the well-conditioned dog, presenting the cortical UCS alone elicited flexion responses that were much more abrupt and less well integrated than those obtained when the UCS was signaled by an auditory CS. In fact, sometimes the unsignaled UCS resulted in the dog's completely losing its balance. In addition, several animals conditioned with a cortical UCS to flex a limb were subsequently trained in an instrumental situation in which responses to either of two panels would be equally effective in delivering food reward. An additional contingency was added when the panel-pressing response stabilized; presentations of the auditory CS followed by the cortical UCS (in accordance with the prior classical conditioning condition) were associated with responses to one of the two panels, and presentations of the UCS alone were associated with responses to the other panel. The Ss demonstrated a preference for responding more to the panel that produced the signaled UCS than to the panel that produced the unsignaled UCS. This preference is congruent with the assumption that the CS allows S to prepare for the UCS and questions the notion that conditioning of a cortically elicited response is unmotivated.

Additional evidence concerning the balance-maintenance motivational component in this type of conditioning is the correlation observed by Wagner et al. (1967) between the amount of conditioned leg flexion obtained and the Ss' posture during conditioning sessions. In cases which conditioned leg flexion would be of minimal utility in maintaining a dog's balance when the cortical UCS is presented (that is, S remains seated throughout the conditioning session), little or no evidence of conditioning was obtained. Conditioning was more likely to be obtained in animals not allowed to remain seated during the conditioning sessions, in which case the unconditioned flexion response was observed to require drastic and sudden postural adjustments for the maintenance of balance.

The work of Thomas (1967) experimentally demonstrated the role of preparatory postural adjustments as a basis for motivation in experiments employing a cortical UCS:

The experimental manipulation was based on a premise regarding the value of a postural preparatory response under different required postures. When a dog is standing on all four limbs and one limb is lifted, it must, in order to remain upright, shift its center of gravity toward the remaining sources of support, i.e., the remaining limbs. If the limbs are widely separated a grosser weight shift is required than if the limbs are narrowly spaced. It is reasonable that the grosser the shift required, the greater the utility of (and incentive for) a preparatory postural adjustment. Thus, it might be expected that subjects required to adopt a stance in which the limbs are widely separated would evidence more conditioned responding than subjects required to adopt a narrow stance [pp. 4–5].

The expectation was confirmed. Four dogs trained to lift their right rear leg with limbs widely spaced demonstrated a greater degree of conditioning than four dogs trained with limbs narrowly spaced. Conditioning was assessed by a number of different measures, ranging from observed full leg-lifting to subtle limb movements automatically detected by sensitive strain gauges.

Findings such as these on the role of postural adjustments in conditioning a motor response evoked by brain stimulation are especially significant because, in an early failure to condition cortically evoked limb flexion (Loucks, 1933), the animals were completely suspended in a hammock during the conditioning session, which eliminated the necessity for any postural adjustment to maintain balance when limb flexion was produced. As recently suggested (Wagner et al., 1967), eliminating this source of motivation may have accounted for Louck's reported inability to obtain conditioning.

It would appear, then, that the phenomenon of conditioning a motor response to a cortical UCS is not crucial to the general question of the necessity of motivation in conditioning, contrary to the earlier statements of Loucks (1935), Spence (1951), Mowrer (1960), and Doty and Guirgea (1961), among others. Instead, a clear motivational component has been isolated in this type of conditioning procedure, Furthermore, it is intriguing to speculate on the more general implications for theories of learning of these findings clarifying the motivational aspect of conditioning with a cortically evoked UCR: "these studies would also indicate that it may be profitable, in general, to question the degree to which behavior changes observed in classical conditioning situations are influenced by available instrumental contingencies" (Wagner et al., 1967).

The Threshold Probe. Before concluding the discussion of interneural learning, it should be mentioned that this type of situation has provided an interesting technique useful for assessing excitatory and inhibitory tendencies accruing to the positive and negative stimuli in the classical conditioning situation. The technique employed, termed the *threshold probe* by Thomas (1967), involves presentation of the cortical UCS at intensities known to be less than fully effective in eliciting the motor response. For example, if an isolated electrical stimulation of 1.0 ma intensity applied to the motor cortex reliably produces discrete limb flexion in the dog, a lower value of electrical stimulation can be determined (for example, 0.30 ma) which will elicit the motor response only 50 per cent of the time. This less than fully effective value of stimulation, called the threshold value of the UCS, can be determined by a modified version of one of the classical psychophysical techniques. Following the original work of Nikolaeva (1955, 1957) and Tchilingaryan (1963), Thomas' (1967) research included an extensive analysis of responses to threshold values of a cortical UCS when such low-level stimulation was presented alone, when it was preceded by a positive auditory CS (that is, a CS with a history of being followed by a UCS of suprathreshold intensity), and by a negative auditory CS (that is, a CS with a history of not being followed by a UCS). Thomas reported that the threshold value of the UCS typically elicited a motor response considerably more than 50 per cent of the time when it was preceded by a positive CS, and considerably less than 50 per cent of the time when it was preceded by a negative CS. Thus, the absolute threshold for responding to the cortical UCS is affected by the excitatory or inhibitory states developed by the preceding peripheral CS. Such threshold modifications during conditioning may represent a more sensitive measure of learning than can be obtained by simply tabulating overt CRs. Furthermore, such a technique for assessing the degree of conditioning may be applicable to extraneural as well as intraneural conditioning, and provides a means of investigating theoretical interpretations of learning incorporating such heretofore covert variables as "response thresholds," and "distribution of response tendencies" (for example, Hull, 1943).

Electroconvulsive Shock and Consolidation

It is obvious that without memory there can be no learning. The improvement in performance that results from practice is based on the residual benefits of previous practice. The mechanisms of learning and memory, if not coincidental, must certainly be closely related.

A number of theoretical interpretations of learning have incorporated both concepts, learning and memory, by postulating two different types of neurologically distinct events occurring during acquisition. The first is a chemical or structural modification of relatively short duration which results, functionally, in a facilitation of neural transmission between the central CS and UCS "analyzers." This hypothesized temporary connection, which represents short-term memory, is presumably reversible. Only with repeated practice does this connection become permanent and stable, converting the previous short-term memory into long-term memory. It is this long-term, distinct manner of responding to a CS that is commonly referred to as learning. The process by which the initial short-term memory is converted into a more enduring memory trace has been termed *consolidation* (DeCamp, 1915; Müller and Pilzaker, 1900).

One line of evidence substantiating this two-process interpretation of simple learning has been termed the *fragility of the nascent engram* (Meldrum, 1966). It has been known for some time that if an organism's central nervous system is subjected to gross physiological insult (for example, anoxia, concussion, deep anesthesia, epileptic seizure, pharmacologically or electrically induced convulsive states, and so on), memory of events occurring just before the trauma is profoundly impaired, whereas learning that has taken place well before the trauma is relatively unaffected (Burnham, 1903; McDougall, 1901). It seems that the trauma affects consolidation but not long-term memory.

The bulk of the experimental work on consolidation interpretations of learning has been obtained in brain stimulation experiments in which electrical stimulation is applied at various stages of the acquisition process. The nature of the stimulation is quite different from that used in the previously described research on interneural conditioning. Large current values are used, more than 30 ma with small animals to over 500 ma in man, compared with the less than 2 ma employed in previously discussed brain stimulation research. Such stimulation, when delivered through a pair of electrodes placed on either side of an organism's head, typically induces a convulsive state, and such stimulation is referred to as electroconvulsive shock (ECS).

The earliest use of ECS was in the clinical setting. It has been employed in psychiatric practice for some time, and investigations of the effects of ECS on psychiatric patients indicated that it interfered with the retention of material that the patients had learned prior to the treatment (for example, Williams, 1950; Zubin and Barrera, 1941).

Subsequent systematic investigations of ECS and consolidation conducted with animal Ss have substantiated and extended the findings of the earlier clinical investigations (for reviews, see Glickman, 1961; Grossman, 1967, Chapter 14). It has been found in a large number of investigations that animals receiving ECS after each acquisition trial in a simple learning situation learn more slowly than control animals receiving no ECS, or receiving painful shocks to areas other than the head. The sooner after each acquisition trial the ECS is given, the more deleterious is its effect on performance. For example, in a study by Duncan (1949), rats subjected to ECS 20 sec. after each trial in an avoidance-conditioning situation showed little or no improvement in avoidance performance with practice. Other independent groups of Ss receiving the ECS from 40 sec. to 15 min.

after each trial learned successively faster, but still not as fast as control Ss. When the delivery of the ECS was delayed for 1 hr. or more after each trial, Ss learned as rapidly as control animals:

The results were interpreted in terms of a consolidation theory. It was suggested that newly-learned material undergoes a period of consolidation or perseveration. Early in this period a cerebral electroshock may practically wipe out the effect of learning. The material rapidly becomes more resistant to such disruption; at the end of an hour no retroactive effect of cerebral electroshock was found [Duncan, 1949, p. 44].

The fact that the ECS appears to be aversive (for example, Gallinek, 1956) has suggested to some investigators that the important effect of the ECS may not lie in disruption of neural activity, and findings demonstrating the detrimental effects of the ECS on learning may be irrelevant to consolidation interpretations of learning. That is, the ECS may simply serve as a punishment for engaging in behavior that immediately preceded the ECS (Coons and Miller, 1960), or it may initiate a number of responses which become conditioned to the training situation but are incompatible with the response being trained (Adams and Lewis, 1962a, 1962b; Lewis and Adams, 1963). Although it is probably true that the punishing and emotional attributes of the ECS account for some of its deleterious effects on acquisition, there is a good deal of evidence indicating that these factors are not solely responsible for the obtained amnesic effects (see McGaugh, 1965); it appears that some sort of functional disruption of consolidation occurs also.

Anodal Polarization

Another quite different form of electrical stimulation of the brain has been used in investigations of the neural basis of memory and learning. Low-level (2 to 10 μa) direct anodal current can be applied to the motor cortex of an animal, the intensity of the current being insufficient to elicit a motor response. Under certain circumstances, a "dominant focus of excitation" is created in this situation, and the presentation of a peripheral sensory stimulus (for example, tone, light, and so on) during the period of anodal stimulation results in a motor response appropriate to the area stimulated. That is, application of a peripheral stimulus during a period of anodal polarization can somehow initiate neural activity which summates with the anodal stimulation, resulting in a behavioral response.

Rusinov (1953) reported that, in rabbits, after limb movements were obtained by pairing anodal stimulation with sensory stimulation, and the anodal stimulation was terminated, the sensory stimulus alone could evoke the limb movement for a period of approximately 0.5 hr. Because, prior to its pairing with the anodal stimulation, presentation of the sensory stimulus alone did not result in limb movement, Rusinov suggested that the pairing resulted in the formation of a temporary connection between two areas of the brain, the "motor analyzer" and the "auditory analyzer."

Although most of the research on anodal polarization has been conducted in the Soviet Union (see review by Rusinov and Rabinovitch, 1958), the basic phenomena have been replicated in Western laboratories (see Morrell, 1961). It appears that the postpolarization motor responses elicited by the sensory stimulus are highly specific to that sensory stimulus presented during the period of polarization:

During the period of current flow, the polarized region appeared to be sensitized in a nonspecific manner so that any transitory event such as a handclap, extraneous noise, a puff of air to the animal's face, entrance of the experimenter into the recording cage or a tone or light stimulus would trigger the appropriate behavioral response. The increased sensitivity which persisted for a short time (about 20 minutes) after the termination of current flow, however, was selective rather than diffuse. In the postpolarization interval, behavioral responses appeared only upon presentation of those stimuli which had been administered during the actual current flow and were absent during administration of signals of the same or other modalities having no prior association with the anodal current. This was true even when such "differential" signals were more intense (louder or brighter) than those presented during polarization provided that all the test stimuli were familiar to the animal as a result of exposure before polarization to the point of electrographic habituation. Although such findings do not rule out simple threshold differences between polarization and postpolarization periods, they do indicate that the selective sensitivity is a function of the past history of a signal rather than an incident characteristic at the moment of presentation [Morrell, 1961, p. 470].

The duration of the lasting effects of anodal polarization (a few hours at the most) is strikingly similar to the period of consolidation as suggested by the ECS experiments described previously. It would appear that the anodal-polarization technique provides a unique opportunity for studying the morphological and chemical changes and single-unit activity associated with the formation of temporary connections. Potentially, it could provide fruitful insights into the physiological nature of short-term memory and perhaps long-term consolidation.

Brain Lesions and Conditioning

Before the development of sophisticated bioelectronic techniques, researchers interested in studying the neurophysiology of conditioning primarily used the method of lesioning. This involved destroying a specified area of neural tissue and comparing the behavior of the lesioned preparation with that of an intact organism or with the prelesion behavior of the operated organism. Ideally, such a technique would isolate neuroanatomical structure or structures essential for learning.

At first, such experimentally inflicted brain injury had to be confined to readily accessible structures, primarily areas of the cortex. With the development of stereotaxic techniques (Horsley and Clarke, 1908) the door was opened for investigation of the effects of reasonably well-delineated subcortical lesions with very minimal cortical involvement. A description of the use of stereotaxic techniques may be found in Thompson (1967, pp. 45–49). More recently lesioning techniques have been developed which involve X-rays, high-speed electron beams, ultrasonic sound, and radio-frequency waves.

Methodological Difficulties. It should be noted that interpretation of results from lesioning experiments is more complex than at first appears. Does the lesion affect learning in general, or are the effects of the lesion limited to the training situation used in a specific experiment? Perhaps the effects of the lesion are due to the gross physiological insult inflicted on S (anesthetization, loss of blood, general tissue and bone damage, and so on), and these factors, rather than the removal of a specific section of neural tissue, account for postoperative deficits. Perhaps the lesion's primary effect is to cause sensory or motor defects, which may affect performance but are unrelated to some central learning mechanism. If a lesion in a specific area leads to some deficit, what accounts for the deficit, the locus of the lesion or its magnitude? Perhaps the destruction of an equivalent amount of neural tissue in a different area would have similar effects. Are deficits observed in an S with a lesion in a given area due to impair-

ment of function in the lesioned area or due to the interruption of an ascending or descending centrifugal control influence terminating in a quite different area? Obviously, lesion experiments require a good deal in the way of careful design and appropriate comparison groups before unambiguous conclusions can be drawn.

The research literature on brain lesions and learning is voluminous. We shall concentrate on only the major findings.

Cortical Mechanisms

The outer rind of the brain, the cerebral cortex, has been the most thoroughly investigated area of the brain. Its orderly phylogenetic development has suggested to investigators that it accounts for phylogenetically more complex aspects of behavioral plasticity. Its accessibility has further served to encourage research.

Even the scholarly neurology textbooks emerge from their morass of appellations when introducing the reader to the cerebral cortex:

This is the region of the brain with which we must eventually come to deal when considering the highest thought processes, memory, speech, and consciousness. It is therefore the portion of the brain which must study itself. Its accomplishments, if listed, would include all the artifacts of civilization, including the libraries and the contents of the printed pages they contain [Ranson and Clark, 1959, p. 347].

Needless to say, cortical mechanisms have played a major role in theoretical interpretations of the physiology of learning. The analysis of the role of the cortex in learning naturally followed from Pavlov's investigations of salivary conditioning. Indeed, the subtitle of Pavlov's (1927) famous work *Conditioned Reflexes* is *An Investigation of the Physiological Activity of the Cerebral Cortex*, and Pavlov's theory of conditioning was based on hypothesized cortical processes. As the organism conditioned, connections were formed between CS and UCS centers in the cortex. The precise anatomical location of these cortical centers was not specified.

There has been a good deal of research investigating the effects of cortical lesions on learning (see Grossman, 1967, pp. 698–741). Although lesions in certain areas of the cortex may impair retention of a previously learned response, no area of the cortex appears so crucial for learning that its removal precludes conditioning.

Pavlov's commitment to the cortex as the location of neuronal processes involved in conditioning was supported by then available research findings demonstrating an inability to obtain conditioning in a dog deprived of its cortex. Subsequent research indicated that conditioning could occur in the radically decorticated organism (Lebeninskaia and Rosenthal, 1935; Poltyrew and Zeliony, 1930), but the influence of Pavlov's theory of conditioning was so strong that learning was attributed to a tiny bit of remaining cortical tissue that survived the surgery. However, other investigations which used completely decorticated animals demonstrated that such preparations could demonstrate conditioning (Bromiley, 1948; Culler and Mettler, 1934; Girden, Mettler, Finch, and Culler, 1936; Poltyrew, 1936; Ten Cate, 1934; Zeliony and Kadykov, 1938). Sensory and motor deficits and affective abnormalties do limit the responsiveness of the decorticate organism, but there is little evidence suggesting that processes involved in conditioning are substantially affected by removal of the cortex.

It is of course possible that many areas of the brain, cortical and subcortical, functioning in relatively independent ways, may underlie the elaboration of CRs. The physiological processes involved in the acquisition of learned responses may be quite different in the organism deprived of its cortex than in the intact organism (see Culler, Coakley, Shurrager, and Ades,

1939; Girden et al., 1936). Nevertheless, a physiological theory of conditioning such as Pavlov's, based wholly on cortical processes, is not substantiated by the data now available.

Subcortical Mechanisms

Results of investigations of the effects of subcortical lesions on conditioning provide further demonstrations of the elusive nature of the engram. Interpretation of the effects of subcortical lesions are complicated not only by the sensory, motor, and emotional changes that may result from such lesions (as is sometimes the case with cortical lesions), but also by the motivational changes that a subcortically lesioned preparation may undergo.

Despite these problems of interpretation, a vast research literature has grown concerning the effects of subcortical lesions on learning (see Grossman, 1967, pp. 741–768). On the whole, such research has provided additional evidence of the brain's indomitability. Although there has been some suggestion that one or other subcortical area is crucial for the formation of a simple CR, notably various parts of the midbrain reticular formation (Doty, Beck, and Kooi, 1959; Hernández-Peón et al., 1958), the majority of the investigations have revealed little evidence for the existence of an area indispensable for the acquisition of CRs. Indeed, it has been reported that in a chronically decerebrate cat, even with a complete transection as low as the pontile level, it is possible to demonstrate eyelid conditioning (Bard, in discussion following Bard and Macht, 1958).

Spinal Mechanisms

Brain lesions, be they highly specific to well-delineated areas or more extensive, involving complete decortication or even more global decerebration, have failed to reveal a "center" for conditioning. No area of the brain yet investigated has been unequivocally demonstrated to be necessary for simple conditioning. Indeed, one might question whether the brain itself is necessary for conditioning. Perhaps the spinal cord is all that is required in the way of central nervous system tissue for conditioning to occur.

Demonstrations of classical conditioning in S with a central nervous system transection such that the spinal cord is neurally isolated would provide a potentially useful situation for investigating the neurophysiological bases of learning. If learning can proceed without the brain's participation, it would be possible to study learning phenomena in a considerably less complex preparation than the normal intact mammal. The neurology of the spinal cord is much better understood than that of the brain—its structure is less intricate, and its synaptic mechanisms have been more intensively studied.

The question of spinal conditioning has been debated since the original reports of its existence by Shurrager and his associates (Shurrager and Culler, 1938, 1941; Shurrager and Shurrager, 1941, 1946). These investigators reported conditioning in at least some acute spinal dogs, using a CS consisting of electrical or tactile stimulation of the tail and a UCS consisting of a strong shock to the paw. The CR and UCR consisted of a twitch of an isolated hind limb flexor muscle.

Kellogg and his colleagues (Kellogg, 1947; Kellogg, Deese, and Pronko, 1946; Kellogg, Deese, Pronko, and Feinberg, 1947) have suggested that the apparent conditioning obtained in Shurrager's laboratory represented a sensitization or pseudoconditioning rather than a learning phenomenon. Kellogg attempted conditioning with chronic spinal animals. He used a UCS of a strong electric shock to one hind limb and a CS consisting of a weak shock to the opposite hind limb. Gross flexion responses of the limb receiving the UCS

were monitored. No evidence of conditioned limb flexion was obtained in these studies.

It is possible that these reported failures to obtain spinal conditioning were due to the nature of the CS used, weak hind limb shock. This CS may have reflexively elicited extension of the opposite hind limb, which was receiving the strong shock UCS, thereby interfering with the observation of flexion CRs. Also, the use of a gross response measure such as overt leg flexion may fail to reveal spinal conditioning, whereas the use of a more sensitive measure (such as the isolated muscle twitch used in studies reporting successful spinal conditioning) may indicate the existence of the phenomenon.

A more recent investigation (Dykman and Shurrager, 1956) indicated that, under appropriate conditions, spinal conditioning could be obtained in situations in which the CR consisted of overt limb flexion rather than the more subtle muscle twitch.

The issue of the existence and reliability of spinal conditioning is still open. Further research with more standardized methodology is needed before the question of the indispensability of the brain for simple learning can be answered. As has been suggested (Forbes and Mahan, 1963; Thompson, 1967), the primary value of such research probably does not lie in elucidating the normal learning process of the intact organism, but rather in providing a greatly simplified neural system where the physiological bases of conditioning can be subjected to detailed analyses.

The Primitive System as a Model

As is obvious from the preceding discussion, the analysis of the physiological bases of learning in the mammalian organism is exceedingly complex. Attempts at investigating the intact or semi-intact mammalian organism have, in many cases, yielded ambiguous findings. Perhaps new insights into the mechanisms of conditioning can be obtained by opening a less complex black box, that is, by investigating the control correlates of conditioning in a phylogenetically primitive organism with a relatively simple nervous system (see Bullock, 1966). Such a research strategy might not only result in inherently interesting comparative data, but might also provide an informed basis for inferences concerning the physiological correlates of behavioral plasticity in evolutionarily more advanced and morphologically more complex species.

Basic Methodology. Horridge (1962) pointed out the problems involved in attempting to study the physiological correlates of learning in the complex organism, and the advantages of investigating the process in phylogenetically primitive species:

The electrophysiological and chemical analysis of the changes which occur during learning in higher animals is hampered and delayed by the immense complexity of the regions of the nervous system so far suspected to be the site of the changes lying behind the learnt behaviour. In the animals normally used for training experiments it is possible that many thousands of nerve cells are involved in every simple response. At any one time only a few cells can be observed and there remain an undeterminable number of possible combinations of activity. A change, even when experimentally found to occur during learning, cannot therefore be identified as the primary change or even as a relevant one. Perhaps on this account theories of the mechanisms which lie behind learning tend to be based on changes in patterns of activity of many cells, as if these were the cause, rather than the effect, of the primary change. It may therefore be profitable to turn to the lower animals, or parts of them, in search of preparations showing a form of learning which, while still having the essential attribute of being

associative, can be studied in a ganglion containing relatively few cells and having relatively simple sensory inflow [Horridge, 1962, p. 33].

Headless Insects. Horridge's research provided a good deal of impetus for the primitive-organism approach to the study of the mechanisms of learning. He demonstrated apparent avoidance conditioning in headless cockroaches (*Periplaneta americana*) and locusts (*Schistocerca gregaria*). In these insects, different segmental ganglia control the movement of each section of the body in an independent and autonomous manner (Roeder, 1963). Decapitating the insect removes the largest ganglion, the "brain." Such headless insects can live for many days. Horridge removed all but one appendage, a leg in a thoracic segment, of these headless insects. This preparation was suspended over a dish of saline solution, and an electric circuit was wired such that if the thoracic leg extended into the saline it received a shock. A yoked control procedure was employed by Horridge. Every time a shock was delivered to the leg of an experimental cockroach because it made contact with the liquid, a shock was also delivered to the leg of a concurrently run control cockroach, but without any reference to the position of the control preparation's leg. The conditioning situation used by Horridge is illustrated in Figure 22-1. Both experimental and control *S*s received the same number and pattern of shocks, but these shocks were paired with extension of the leg into the saline for experimental *S*s and were uncorrelated with leg position for the control *S*s. Following this initial training phase, a testing phase was given to all the insects in which the shock was wired such that each *S* would receive the shock only when its leg made contact with the saline. The experimental headless cockroaches, previously shocked for this response, made many fewer leg extensions into the solution than the yoked-control headless cockroaches, who previously received

A (Train)

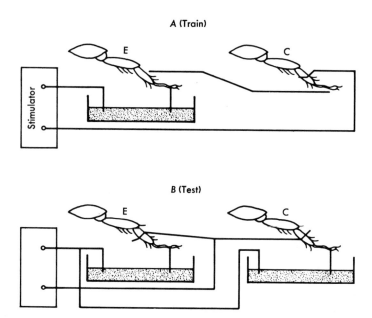

B (Test)

Figure 22-1. The arrangement of the stimulating leads for the experimental (E) and control (C) insects in Horridge's investigations. (A) during the initial training the two preparations are arranged in series so that both E and C insects receive shocks when E lowers its leg beyond the critical point. (B) In the testing phase, the insects are connected in parallel to the stimulator so that either receives a shock separately if it lowers its leg beyond the critical point. (Reprinted with permission from Horridge, G. A. Learning of leg position by the ventral nerve cord of headless insects. *Proceedings Roy. Soc.* (London), *Series B*, 1962, **157**, 33–52.)

shocks not systematically related to their leg position.

The findings of Horridge have been replicated by Eisenstein and Cohen (1965). Eisenstein and Cohen demonstrated avoidance conditioning of a thoracic leg in decapitated cockroaches in which the thoracic ganglion associated with the conditioned leg was surgically isolated from the other segmental ganglia, sparing only the neural connections between the thoracic ganglion and its thoracic appendage. The yoked-control technique was also used by Eisenstein and Cohen.

The potential of such findings is great. The only neural tissue participating in these demonstrations of learning involves a single ganglion and connections between this ganglion and the conditioned appendage. Such a preparation is obviously much more amenable to detailed investigation than the immeasurably more complex mammalian nervous system. Current research efforts are directed toward analyzing biochemical changes in segmental ganglia associated with experimental and yoked control legs within the same insect (as described in Bullock, 1966).

Eisenstein and Cohen also prepared several "ganglionless" Ss. The segmental ganglion associated with the conditioned leg was removed, leaving only the appendage, its musculature, and peripheral neural tissue. Surprisingly, this preparation did receive fewer and fewer shocks during the training session. In fact, the learning curve for the avoidance response was essentially unaffected by removal of the ganglion. However, no differences were obtained between experimental ganglionless Ss, who were shocked for leg extension, and yoked control ganglionless Ss, who received the same number and patterns of shocks un-correlated with leg position. Whether these findings represent a type of nonassociative behavioral plasticity unique to this degang-lionated preparation, or an artifact of the techniques employed, is still a matter of speculation. Recent criticisms of the yoked-control design (Church, 1964) have argued that this control technique may yield ambiguous results if any source of random error, such as individual differences, is present. Several investigators have com-mented on the wide range of individual differences obtained in the headless-insect conditioning situation (Horridge, 1962; Hoyle, 1965).

Hoyle pointed out that this ostensibly simple headless-insect conditioning prep-aration is really quite complicated. The learned response, leg withdrawal, may result from either increased discharge in any one or more of eleven extensor muscles, de-creased discharge in any one or more of nine flexor muscles, or some combination of activity of both types of muscles. In an attempt to simplify the neural analysis of this type of learning situation, Hoyle con-ducted an elegant series of experiments of conditioning in the headless locust. Rath-er than measuring overt leg withdrawal, Hoyle measured muscle junctions potentials from identified leg muscles cells. The con-ditioned leg itself was fixed. It was assumed that the intracellular response measured signaled leg withdrawal in Horridge's insect conditioning situation. Whereas Horridge and Eisenstein and Cohen shocked the insect's leg each time it touched the saline, Hoyle stimulated an afferent nerve each time the measured intracellular firing rate fell below a specified criterion level. Using this operant procedure, it was possible to increase the spontaneous discharge frequen-cy of the monitored cell. The yoked-con-trol technique which was used indicated that noncontingent afferent nerve shocks had no systematic effects on the discharge frequency of this cell.

The importance to general physiology of this insect phenomenon is that it provides the promise of a preparation which will permit a study of the cellular changes involved in long-term changes in the nervous system. All forms of learning must involve long-term changes, and although it is not hard to conceive of ways in which they could conceivably occur (modern models range from reverberatory neuronal circuits to changes in the neuronal nucleic acid structure) no actual examples are known. The present work has narrowed down a phenomenon of long-term central neuronal change to a situation in which it is fairly readily reproducible in material available to many workers and in which the final indicator is a single cell whose effects are easily tapped [Hoyle, 1965, p. 230].

Mollusks. Investigations of the intracellular indexes of learning have been conducted in a quite different situation by Kandel and Tauc (1964, 1965a, 1965b). They utilized the abdominal ganglion of a marine mol-lusk, the sea slug (*Aplysia depilans*). This ganglion contains relatively few nerve cells (about a thousand), most of which are large, readily identifiable, accessible, and rather easily subjected to microelectrode recording techniques (see Kandel and Spencer, 1968; Kandel and Tauc, 1965a).

In one experiment (Kandel and Tauc, 1965a), two afferent nerves were electrically stimulated. The stimulation parameters were selected so that stimulation of one nerve (the CS) produced an intracellularly recorded EPSP (see Chapter 20), and stimu-lation of the second input nerve (the UCS) produced a burst of spikes. This intracellular conditioning situation is illustrated in Figure 22-2. The two stimuli were paired once every 10 sec. with the CS preceding the UCS by 200 to 300 millisec. In several of the cells sampled, the EPSP induced by the CS was facilitated during pairing, with this facilitation persisting for some time (ap-proximately 40 min.) after the pairing pro-cedure was terminated. In some cases the CS-induced EPSP was sufficiently aug-mented during pairing to produce a spike

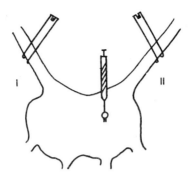

Figure 22-2. Experimental arrangement used by Kandel and Tauc in their demonstration of heterosynaptic facilitation. The CS consisted of electrical stimulation of the input nerve of a ganglion (I) of sufficient strength to produce an intracellularly recorded EPSP. The UCS was electrical stimulation of greater strength delivered to another input nerve (II), causing an intracellularly recorded spike potential. (Reprinted with permission from Kandel, E. R., & Tauc, L. Heterosynaptic facilitation in neurones of the abdominal ganglion of *Aplysia Depilans. J. Physiol.*, 1965a, **181**, 1–27.)

potential (see Figure 22–2). This EPSP facilitation produced by pairing two stimuli to two different nerve cells, was termed *heterosynaptic facilitation.*

In some of the cells sampled by Kandel and Tauc (1965a), unpaired presentations of the CS and UCS also produced heterosynaptic facilitation. Of the remaining cells, however, a facilitation was found only in the paired paradigm, indicating, in these cases at least, an intracellular analogue of classical conditioning.

Obviously, this approach to the analysis of conditioning at the cellular level can provide a tremendous amount of information about the biochemical and morphological changes that accompany simple learning. Research workers are currently attempting to use such a simplified preparation to study the physiological bases of learning (Kandel and Spencer, 1968), and an initial attempt at a simple theoretical interpretation of the mechanisms of the heterosynaptic facilitation phenomenon has been presented (Kandel and Tauc, 1965b). A model has been postulated in which activation of the UCS pathway affects the synaptic terminals of the CS pathway so that CS stimulation leads to increasing amounts of transmitter substance being

released, resulting in a facilitated EPSP, and even CS-induced spikes, with practice.

Planaria. Another primitive organism which has received a great deal of attention by psychologists interested in physiological mechanisms of learning is the flatworm, planaria. Flatworms represent the most primitive species that, like higher forms, are bilaterally symmetrical, have a distinct ventral and dorsal surface, and possess a degree of encephalization, or collection of neurons in the anterior end or head. Thompson and McConnell (1955) reported that planaria were capable of a simple conditioning. Using light as a CS and electric shock as a UCS, a stereotyped body movement initially elicited only by the UCS was eventually elicited by the CS. Subsequent investigations of learning in planaria have obtained dramatic findings ostensibly concerning the biochemistry of learning (for example, Corning and John, 1961). More recently, it has been suggested that apparent planarian learning is an ephemeral phenomenon (for example, Bennett and Calvin, 1964) and may be an artifact of the procedures employed (Brown, Dustman, and Beck, 1966; Jensen, 1965; van Deventer and Ratner, 1964). Moreover, lack of objective response-scoring techniques may play a significant role in apparent planarian learning (Rosenthal and Halas, 1962). Those studies which have obtained data on neurochemical bases of learning using planaria may suffer from inadequate controls (for example, Hartry, Keith-Lee, and Morton, 1964) or statistical inadequacies (for example, Gaito and Zavala, 1964).

In summary, the study of primitive organisms in an attempt to elucidate the bases of learning in complex species is relatively new. Its findings are intriguing and inherently interesting, but its significance for mammalian learning remains to be determined.

Physiological Theories of Learning

Physiological theories of learning may, as suggested by Altman (1966), be divided into three categories: interneuronal, intraneuronal, and extraneuronal.

Interneuronal Theories

Interneuronal theories of learning postulate a changed relationship between neurons as a function of repeated stimulation during practice, The earliest physiological theories of learning were interneuronal theories. Grossman (1967) describes the physiological learning theory of Tanzi (1893). Tanzi suggested that repeated neural firing increases the volume of the neuron, bringing its conducting processes in closer proximity with those of adjacent cells. This change would serve to facilitate interneuronal transmission and provide a mechanism of memory and learning.

There have been many interpretations of learning subsequent to Tanzi's early formulation which have also postulated mechanisms with changed neuronal interrelations but which have taken account of later findings concerning neuronal anatomy and physiology. Thus, enlargement of synaptic

terminals or some other structural or chemical alteration at the synapse has been suggested by several theorists to provide a neural basis for behavioral plasticity (for example, Eccles, 1953; Hebb, 1949; Milner, 1957; Young, 1951). Such facilitation of synaptic transmission with repeated stimulation has been demonstrated (for example, Eccles and Rall, 1951; Lloyd, 1949). This phenomenon has been termed *homosynaptic facilitation*, and its mechanisms may be quite similar to that of heterosynaptic facilitation, discussed previously. There is also some neuroanatomical evidence suggesting structural changes at the synapse associated with repeated neural stimulation (Hill, 1950a, 1950b; Hill and Keynes, 1949); such structural changes could account for homosynaptic facilitation.

Fuller discussions of these interneuronal interpretations of learning may be found in Grossman (1967, Chap. 16).

Intraneuronal Theories

Some of the more exciting research on the physiological bases of learning has concerned the chemical processes within the cell which may underlie behavioral plasticity. The early formulations of intracellular interpretations of learning were based on alteration of protein chemistry with practice (Katz and Halstead, 1950; Monne, 1948). More recently, RNA and DNA changes have been postulated to be of primary importance (for example, Hyden, 1961; Gaito, 1963).

These biochemical interpretations of learning have led to a good deal of speculation and a number of conflicting findings concerning the chemical transfer of learned responses from one organism to another (see reviews by Booth, 1967; Grossman, 1967, Chap. 16).

Extraneuronal Theories

Surprising as it may seem, most of the cells in the central nervous system are not nerve cells, but small, nonneuronal, *glial* cells. Indeed, only about 10 per cent of the cells in the brain are neurons, the remaining 90 per cent glial cells (Nurnberger, 1958). The roles of glial cells are not well understood. It was originally thought that they were nothing more than the supporting tissue of the nervous system, analogous to the connective tissue of other organs (Glees, 1955), but it is difficult to imagine that nine-tenths of the cells in the brain are designed merely to passively support the remaining active one tenth. Some recent evidence suggests that glial cells play an important metabolic and regulatory role in nervous functioning (Hamberger and Hydén, 1963; Hydén and Lange, 1962).

Of special interest are findings indicating that experience can affect cortical glial development (Altman and Das, 1964) and theoretical analyses of the role of these extraneuronal structures in learning (Galambos, 1961). Galambos has suggested that glial cells play a crucial role in the learning process, the function of the neurons being merely to transmit passively the information synthesized by the glial cells.

Conclusion

The conviction that learning has a physiological basis may be found in the earliest theoretical formulations of learning. Pavlov considered the formation of new connections in the brain to be responsible for learning:

It appears that the cells predominantly excited at a given time become foci attracting to themselves nervous impulses aroused by new stimuli—impulses which on repetition tend to follow the same path and so to establish conditioned reflexes [Pavlov, 1927, p. 38].

Thorndike's earliest formulations also employed a neurophysiological model:

When any neurone or neurone group is stimulated and transmits to or discharges into or connects with a second neurone or neurone group, it will, when later stimulated again in the same way, have an increased tendency to transmit to the same second neurone group as before, provided the act that resulted in the first instance brought a pleasant or at least indifferent mental state. If, on the contrary, the result in the first case was discomfort, the tendency to such transmission will be lessened [Thorndike, 1905, p. 165].

Hull's theoretical interpretation of learning (for example, Hull, 1943) was not a physiological theory, but he was not opposed to speculation about the neural substrates of learning.

These early attempts at physiological interpretation of learning often postulated a nervous system that would obey behavioral principles, but with minimal reference to the actual physiological and anatomical realities of the behaving organism. Such approaches lead Skinner (1938) to deprecate the then available physiological interpretations of learning:

The traditional "CNS" might be said to stand for Conceptual Nervous System [p. 421].

The gain to the science of behavior from neurological hypotheses in the past is, I believe, quite certainly outweighed by all the misdirected experimentation and bootless theorizing that have arisen from the same source [p. 426].

However, contemporary theories that attempt to interpret learning at a physiological level have a vast amount of recently collected physiological data to draw on. The integration of physiology and learning psychology is clearly an exciting and ambitious undertaking, but also quite a realistic one.

Glossary

ablation. Removal of area of the central nervous system, usually in an attempt to investigate the significance of that area.

axon. A process extending from the cell body, which carries neural impulses away from the cell body to other cells.

central nervous system (CNS). The brain and spinal cord.

centrifugal control. Influence exerted by higher brain centers on lower centers of the central nervous system or peripheral nervous system.

cochlea. the fluid-filled structure of the inner ear, containing hair cells which transduce sound vibrations into neural impulses.

dendrite. A process extending from the body of a neuron that receives excitatory or inhibitory impulses from other neurons.

effector. A structure specialized for response, that is, a muscle or gland.

EPSP. See excitatory postsynaptic potential.

evoked response. Distinctive pattern of electrical activity recorded in the nervous system and initiated by punctate, peripheral stimulation.

excitatory postsynaptic potential (EPSP). Depolarization of nerve cell bodies and dendrites as a result of chemical events at the synapse.

ganglion. A collection of nerve cell bodies outside the central nervous system (within the central nervous system such a collection is usually called a *nucleus*).

glial cells. Numerous, non-neural cells within the central nervous system.

habituation. Process of decrease in strength of an initial response to a repetitively presented stimulus.

incus. One of the three small bones making up the ossicular chain in the middle ear (the others are the *malleus* and *stapes*) which conducts the air vibrations caused by auditory stimulation from the eardrum to the cochlea.

inhibitory postsynaptic potential (IPSP). Increase in polarization of nerve cell body and dendrites as a result of chemical events at the synapse.

IPSP. See inhibitory postsynaptic potential.

lesion. Destruction of area of central nervous system, usually in an attempt to investigate the significance of that area.

malleus. One of the three small bones making up the ossicular chain in the middle ear (the others are the *incus* and *stapes*) which conducts the air vibrations caused by auditory stimulation from the eardrum to the cochlea.

meninges. The layered membrane covering of the central nervous system.

neuron. A nerve cell.

nucleus. (1) The central body within any cell, containing the basic mechanisms for cell metabolism and reproduction. (2) The name given to a collection of nerve cell bodies within the central nervous system (outside the central nervous system, such a collection is usually called a *ganglion*).

ossicles. The three small bones in the middle ear which articulate with each other such that they transmit sound vibrations from the outer ear to the inner ear.

oval window. The membrane which separates the middle ear from the cochlea of the inner ear.

peripheral nervous system. Areas of the nervous system other than the brain and spinal cord.

polarization. A disparity in the electrical charge on each side of the cell membrane.

pseudoconditioning. Responses to a conditioned stimulus that resemble conditioned responses but do not result specifically from prior pairing of the conditioned stimulus with an unconditioned stimulus.

receptors. Structures specialized for transducing various forms of energy (light, heat, sound, and so on) into neural impulses.

resting potential. The normal state of polarization of a cell.

reticular formation. Core of tissue in the brain stem thought to be important in attention and arousal.

sensitization. Augmentation of an initially

small unconditioned response to a conditioned stimulus by repeated presentations of the unconditioned stimulus. Unlike true conditioned responses, development of the sensitized response does not require pairing of the conditioned stimulus and the unconditioned stimulus.

soma. The body of a neuron.

spike potential. The reversal of nerve cell polarization that is the basic neural impulse.

stapedius. A small muscle in the middle ear which is attached to the stapes near its junction with the incus.

stapes. One of the three small bones making up the ossicular chain in the middle ear (the others are the *malleus* and *incus*) which conducts the air vibrations caused by auditory stimulation from the eardrum to the cochlea.

synapse. The small gap separating neurons from each other, or from receptor or effector cells.

synaptic transmission. The chemical process by which neural impulses interact with each other at the synapse.

telodendria. Endings on the axon of a nerve cell.

tensor tympani. Small muscle in the middle ear which is attached to the malleus.

References

Adams, H. E., & Lewis, D. J. Electroconvulsive shock, retrograde amnesia, and competing responses. *J. comp. physiol. Psychol.*, 1962a, **55**, 299–301.

Adams, H. E., & Lewis, D. J. Retrograde amnesia and competing responses. *J. comp. physiol. Psychol.*, 1962b, **55**, 302–305.

Albino, R., & Burnand, G. Conditioning of the alpha rhythm in man. *J. exp. Psychol.*, 1964, **67**, 539–544.

Alcaraz, M., Pacheco, P., & Guzmán-Flores, C. Changes in acoustic habituation following severance of the intrinsic ear muscles in chronic preparations. *Acta physiol Latinoam.*, 1962, **12**, 1–7.

Altman, J. *Organic foundations of animal behavior.* New York: Holt, 1966.

Altman, J., & Das, G. D. Autoradiographic examination of the effects of enriched environment on the rate of glial multiplication in the adult rat brain. *Nature*, 1964, **204**, 1161–1163.

Bard, P., & Macht, M. B. The behaviour of chronically decerebrate cats. In *Neurological Basis of Behavior.* London: Churchill, 1958.

Barlow, J. A. Secondary motivation through classical conditioning: A reconsideration of the nature of backward conditioning. *Psychol. Rev.*, 1956, **63**, 406–408.

Beck, E. C., & Doty, R. W. Conditioned flexion reflexes acquired during combined catelepsy and de-efferentiation.

J. comp. physiol. Psychol., 1957, **50**, 211–216.

Beecroft, R. S. *Classical conditioning.* Goleta, California: Psychonomic Press, 1966.

Bennett, E. L., & Calvin, M. Failure to train planarians reliably. *Neurosci. Res. Prog. Bull.*, 1964, **2**, 3–12.

Booth, D. A. Vertebrate brain ribonucleic acids and memory retention. *Psychol. Bull.*, 1967, **68**, 149–177.

Brodal, A. *The reticular formation of the brain stem, anatomical aspects and functional correlations.* London: Oliver and Boyd, 1957.

Brogden, W. J., & Gantt, W. H. Intraneural conditioning: cerebellar conditioned reflexes. *Arch. Neurol. Psychiat.*, 1942, **48**, 437–455.

Bromiley, R. B. Conditioned response in a dog after removal of neocortex. *J. comp. physiol. Psychol.*, 1948, **41**, 102–110.

Brown, H. M., Dustman, R. E., & Beck, E. C. Experimental procedures contributing to "learning" in regenerated planaria. *Physiol. Behav.*, 1966, **1**, 245–249.

Bullock, T. H. (ed.) Simple systems for the study of learning mechanisms. *Neurosci. Res. Prog. Bull.*, 1966, **4**, 105–233.

Burnham, W. H. Retroactive amnesia: Illustrative cases and a tentative explanation. *Amer. J. Psychol.*, 1903, **14**, 382–396.

Carlton, P. L., & Vogel, J. R. Habituation

and conditioning. *J. comp. physiol. Psychol.*, 1967, **63**, 348–351.

Carmel, P. W., & Starr, A. Acoustic and nonacoustic factors modifying middle-ear muscle activity in waking cats. *J. Neurophysiol.*, 1963, **26**, 598–616.

Cason, H. Backward conditioned eyelid reactions. *J. exp. Psychol.*, 1935, **18**, 599–611.

Church, R. M. Systematic effect of random error in the yoked control design. *Psychol. Bull.*, 1964, **62**, 122–131.

Coons, E. E., & Miller, N. E. Conflict versus consolidation of memory traces to explain "retrograde amnesia" produced by ECS. *J. comp. physiol. Psychol.*, 1960, **53**, 524–531.

Corning, W. C., & John, E. R. Effect of ribonuclease on retention of conditioned response in regenerated planarians. *Science*, 1961, **134**, 1363–1365.

Cruikshank, R. M. Human occipital brain potentials as affected by intensity-duration variables of visual stimulation. *J. exp. Psychol.*, 1937, **21**, 625–641.

Culler, E. A., Coakley, J. D., Shurrager, P. S., & Ades, H. W. Differential effects of curare upon higher and lower levels of the central nervous system. *Amer. J. Psychol.*, 1939, **52**, 266–273.

Culler, E. A., & Mettler, F. A. Conditioned behavior in a decorticate dog. *J. comp. Psychol.*, 1934, **18**, 291–303.

Day, L. M., & Bentley, M. Note on learning in *Paramecium*. *J. anim. Behav.*, 1911, **1**, 67–73.

De Camp, J. E. A study of retroactive inhibition. *Psychol. Monogr.*, 1915, **19**, (Whole no. 84).

Desmedt, J. E. Neurophysiological mechanisms controlling acoustic input. In G. L. Rasmussen & W. F. Windle (Eds.), *Neural mechanisms of the auditory and vestibular systems*. Springfield, Ill.: Charles C Thomas, 1960.

Diamond, S., Balvin, R. S., & Diamond, Florence R. *Inhibition and choice*. New York: Harper & Row, 1963.

Diamond, I. T., & Chow, K. L. Biological psychology. In S. Koch (Ed.), *Psychology: A study of a science*. Vol. 4. New York: McGraw-Hill, 1962.

Dmitriev, A. S., & Kochigina, A. M. The importance of time as a stimulus of conditioned reflex activity. *Psychol. Bull.*, 1959, **56**, 106–132.

Doty, R. W. Discussion of Gastaut's paper. In H. H. Jasper et al. (Eds.), *The reticular formation of the brain*. Boston: Little, Brown, 1958.

Doty, R. W., Beck, E. C., & Kooi, K. A. Effect of brainstem lesions on conditioned responses of cats. *Exp. Neurol.*, 1959, **1**, 360–385.

Doty, R. W., & Giurgea, C. Conditioned reflexes established by coupling electrical excitation of two cortical areas. In J. F. Delafrasnaye et al. (Eds.), *Brain mechanisms and learning*. Oxford: Blackwell Scientific Publications, 1961.

Doty, R. W., & Rutledge, L. T. "Generalization" between cortically and peripherally applied stimuli eliciting conditioned reflexes. *J. Neurophysiol.*, 1959, **22**, 428–435.

Doty, R. W., Rutledge, L. T., & Larson, R. M. Conditioned reflexes established to electrical stimulation of cat cerebral cortex. *J. Neurophysiol.*, 1956, **19**, 401–415.

Duncan, C. P. The retroactive effect of electroshock on learning. *J. comp. physiol. Psychol.*, 1949, **42**, 32–44.

Durup, G., & Fessard, A. L'électroencéphalogramme de l'homme. *Année Psychol.*, 1935, **36**, 1–32.

Dykman, R. A., & Shurrager, P. S. Successive and maintained conditioning in spinal carnivores. *J. comp. physiol. Psychol.*, 1956, **49**, 27–35.

Eccles, J. C. *The neurophysiological bases of mind*. Oxford: Clarendon Press, 1953.

Eccles, J. C., & Rall, W. Effects induced in a monosynaptic reflex path by its activation. *J. Neurophysiol.*, 1951, **14**, 353–376.

Eisenstein, E. M., & Cohen, M. J. Learning in an isolated prothoracic insect ganglion. *Anim. Behav.*, 1965, **13**, 104–108.

Fernández-Guardiola, A., Roldán, R. E., Fanjul, M. L., & Castell, S. C. Role of the pupillary mechanism in the process of habituation of the visual pathways. *Electroenceph. clin. Neurophysiol.*, 1961, **13**, 564–576.

Forbes, A., & Mahan, Clare. Attempts to train the spinal cord. *J. comp. physiol. Psychol.*, 1963, **56**, 36–40.

French, J. W. V. Trial-and-error learning in *Paramecium. J. exp. Psychol.*, 1940, **26**, 609–613.

Gaito, J. DNA and RNA as memory molecules. *Psychol. Rev.*, 1963, **70**, 471–480.

Gaito, J., & Zavata, A. Neurochemistry and learning. *Psychol. Bull.*, 1964, **61**, 45–62.

Galambos, R. Some recent experiments on the neurophysiology of hearing. *Annu. Octol. Rhinol. Laryngol.*, 1956, **65**, 1053–1059.

Galambos, R. Neural mechanisms in audition. *Laryngoscope*, 1958, **68**, 388–401.

Galambos, R. A glia-neural theory of brain function. *Proc. nat. acad. Sci.*, 1961, **47**, 129–136.

Galambos, R., & Morgan, C. T. The neural basis of learning. In H. W. Magoun & V. E. Hall (Eds.), *Handbook of physiology*, Vol. 3. Washington, D.C.: American Physiological Society, 1960.

Galambos, R., & Sheatz, G. S. An electro-encephalograph study of classical conditioning. *Amer. J. Physiol.*, 1962, **203**, 173–184.

Galambos, R., Sheatz, G. S., & Vernier, V. G. Electrophysiological correlates of a conditioned response in cats. *Science*, 1956, **123**, 376–377.

Gallinek, A. Fear and anxiety in the course of electroshock therapy. *Amer. J. Psychiat.*, 1956, **113**, 428–434.

Gantt, W. H. Contributions to the physiology of the conditioned reflex. *Arch. Neurol. Psychiat.*, 1937, **37**, 848–855.

Gantt, W. H., & Loucks, R. B. Posterior nerve function as tested by the conditioned reflex method. *Amer. J. Physiol.*, 1938, **123**, 74–75. (Abstract)

Gastaut, H. État actuel des connaissances sur l'électroencéphalographie du conditionnement. *Electroenceph. clin. Neurophysiol.*, 1957, Suppl. 6, 133–160.

Gastaut, H. Some aspects of the neurophysiological basis of conditioned reflexes and behavior. In *Ciba Foundation symposium on the neurological bases of behavior*. London: Churchill, 1958.

Gastaut, H., Jus, A., Jus, C., Morrell, F., Storm van Leeuwen, W., Dongier, S.,

Naquet, R., Regis, H., Roger, A., Bekkering, D., Kamp, A., & Werre, J. Étude topographique des réactions d'électroencéphalographique conditionées chez l'homme. *Electroenceph. clin. Neurophysiol.*, 1957, **8**, 1–34.

Gelber, Beatrice. Investigations of the behavior of *Paramecium aurelia:* I. Modification of behavior after training with reinforcement. *J. comp. physiol. Psychol.*, 1952, **45**, 58–65.

Gelber, Beatrice. Retention in *Paramecium aurelia. J. comp. physiol. Psychol.*, 1958, **51**, 110–115.

Gerken, G. M., & Neff, W. D. Experimental procedures affecting evoked responses recorded from the auditory cortex. *Electroenceph. clin. Neurophysiol.*, 1963, **15**, 947–957.

Gershuni, G. V., Kozhevnikov, V. A., Maruseva, A. M., Avakyan, R. V., Radionova, E. A., Altman, J. A., & Soroko, V. I. Modifications in electrical responses of the auditory system in different states of the higher nervous activity. In H. H. Jasper & G. D. Smirnov (Eds.), *The Moscow colloquium on electroencephalography of higher nervous activity. Electroenceph. clin. Neurophysiol.*, 1960, Suppl. 13, 115–124.

Girden, E., Mettler, F. A., Finch, G., & Culler, E. Conditioned responses in a decorticate dog to acoustic, thermal, and tactile stimulation. *J. comp. Psychol.*, 1936, **21**, 367–385.

Giurgea, C. *Elaborarea reflexului condition-at prin excitarea directa a scoartei cerebrale.* Bucharest: Editura Academiei Rep. Pop. Romane, 1953.

Giurgea, C., & Raiciulescu, N. Étude électroencéphalographique du réflexe conditionnel à l'excitation électrique corticale directe. In L. van Bogaert (Ed.), *Proceedings of the First International Congress of Neurological Sciences.* Vol. 3. London: Pergamon Press, 1959.

Glees, P. *Neuroglia, morphology and function.* Springfield, Ill.: Charles C Thomas, 1955.

Glickman, S. E. Perseverative neural processes and consolidation of the memory trace. *Psychol. Bull.*, 1961, **58**, 218–233.

Granit, R. *Receptors and sensory perception.* New Haven: Yale Univer. Press, 1955.

Grossman, S. P. *A textbook of physiological psychology.* New York: Wiley, 1967.

Guzmán-Flores, C. Discussion of Neff, W. D., Discrimination capacity of different divisions of the auditory system. In M. A. B. Brazier (Ed.), *Brain and behavior,* Vol. 1. Washington, D.C.: Amer. Inst. Biol. Sciences, 1961. Pp. 232–240.

Guzmán-Flores, C., Alcaraz, M., & Harmony, T. Role of the intrinsic ear muscles in the process of acoustic habituation. *Biol. Inst. Estud. med. biol. (Mex.),* 1960, **18**, 135–140.

Hagbarth, K. E., & Fex, J. Centrifugal influences on single unit activity in spinal sensory paths. *J. Neurophysiol.,* 1959, **22**, 329–338.

Hagbarth, K. E., & Kerr, D. I. B. Central influences on spinal afferent conduction. *J. Neurophysiol.,* 1954, **18**, 388–411.

Hamberger, A., & Hydén, H. Inverse enzymatic changes in glia during increased function and hypoxia. *J. cell Biol.,* 1963, **16**, 521–525.

Hartry, A. L., Keith-Lee, P., & Morton, W. D. Planaria: memory transfer through cannibalism reexamined. *Science,* 1964, **146**, 274–275.

Hearst, E., Beer, B., Sheatz, G., & Galambos, R. Some electrophysiological correlates of conditioning in the monkey. *Electroenceph. clin. Neurophysiol.,* 1960, **12**, 137–152.

Hebb, D. O. *The organization of behavior: A neuropsychological theory.* New York: Wiley, 1949.

Hernández-Peón, R. Neurophysiological correlates of habituation and other manifestations of plastic inhibition (internal inhibition). In H. H. Jasper & G. D. Smirnov (Eds.), *The Moscow colloquium on electroencephalography of higher nervous activity. Electroenceph. clin. Neurophysiol.,* 1960, Suppl. 13, 101–114.

Hernández-Peón, R. Physiological mechanisms in attention. In R. W. Russell (Ed.), *Frontiers in physiological psychology.* New York: Academic Press, 1966.

Hernández-Peón, R., Alcocer-Cuarón, C., Lavín, A., & Santibañez, G. Centrifugal suppression of induced activity of the olfactory bulb during distraction and olfactory habituation, 1958. Cited in Hernández-Peón, R. Neurophysiological correlates of habituation and other manifestations of plastic inhibition (internal inhibition). In H. H. Jasper & G. D. Smirnov (Eds.), *The Moscow colloquium on electroencephalography of higher nervous activity. Electroenceph. clin. Neurophysiol.,* 1960, Suppl. 13.

Hernández-Peón, R., Brust-Carmona, H., Eckhaus, E., Lopez-Mendoza, E., & Alcocer-Cuarón, C. Effects of cortical and subcortical lesions on salivary conditioned response. *Acta neurol. Latinoam.,* 1958, **4**, 111–120.

Hernández-Peón, R., Guzmán-Flores, C., Alcaraz, M., & Fernández-Guardiola, A. Photic potentials in the visual pathway during attention and photic habituation. *Fed. Proc.,* 1956, **15**, 91–92.

Hernández-Peón, R., & Hagbarth, K. E. Interaction between afferent and cortically induced reticular responses. *J. Neurophysiol.,* 1955, **18**, 44–45.

Hernández-Peón, R., Jouvet, M., & Scherrer, H. Auditory potentials at the cochlear nucleus during acoustic habituation. *Acta neurol. Latinoam.,* 1957, **3**, 144–156.

Hill, D. K. The effect of stimulation on the opacity of a crustacean nerve trunk and its relation to fiber diameter. *J. Physiol.,* 1950a, **111**, 283–303.

Horn, G. Physiological and psychological aspects of selective perception. In D. S. Lehrman, et al. (Eds.) *Advances in the study of behaviour,* 1965, New York: Academic Press.

Hill, D. K. The volume changes resulting from stimulation of a giant nerve fiber. *J. Physiol.,* 1950b, **111**, 304–327.

Hill, D. K., & Keynes, R. D. Opacity changes in stimulated nerve. *J. Physiol.,* 1949, **108**, 278–281.

Horridge, G. A. Learning of leg position by the ventral nerve cord in headless insects. *Proc. roy. Soc. (London), Series B,* 1962, **157**, 33–52.

Horsley, V., & Clarke, R. H. The structure and functions of the cerebellum examined by a new method. *Brain,* 1908, **31**, 45–124.

Hoyle, G. Neurophysiological studies on "learning" in headless insects. In J. E. Treherne & J. W. L. Beament (Eds.), *The physiology of the insect central nervous system*, New York: Academic Press, 1965.

Hugelin, A., Dumont, S., & Paillas, N. Tympanic muscles and control of auditory input during arousal. *Science*, 1960, **131**, 1371–1372.

Hull, C. L. *The principles of behavior*. New York: Appleton-Century-Crofts, 1943.

Huttenlocher, P. R. Effects of state of arousal on click responses in the mesencephalic reticular formation *Electroenceph. clin. Neurophysiol.*, 1960, **12**, 819–827.

Hydén, H. Biochemical aspects of brain activity. In S. Farber & R. Wilson (Eds.), *Control of the mind, Part 1*. New York: McGraw-Hill, 1961.

Hydén, H., & Lange, P. A kinetic study of the neuronglia relationships. *J. cell Biol.*, 1962, **13**, 233–237.

James, W. *The principles of psychology*. New York: Holt, 1890.

Jasper, H. H., & Cruikshank, R. M. Electroencephalography. II: Visual stimulation and the after image as affecting the occipital alpha rhythm. *J. gen. Psychol.*, 1937, **17**, 29–48.

Jasper, H. H., & Shagass, C. Conditioning the occipital alpha rhythm in man. *J. exp. Psychol.*, 1941, **28**, 373–388.

Jensen, D. D. Experiments on "learning" in Paramecium. *Science*, 1957, **125**, 191–192.

Jensen, D. D. Paramecia, planaria, and pseudo-learning. *Learning and associated phenomena in invertebrates. Animal Behaviour Supplement*, 1965, No. 1, 9–20.

John, E. R., & Killam, K. F. Electrophysiological correlates of avoidance conditioning in the cat. *J. Pharm. exp. Therap.*, 1959, **125**, 252–274.

John, E. R., & Killam, K. F. Electrophysiological correlates of differential approach-avoidance conditioning in cats. *J. nerv. ment. Dis.*, 1960, **136**, 183–201.

Jouvet, M., & Hernández-Peón, R. The neurophysiological mechanisms concerning habituation, attention and conditioning. *Electroenceph. clin. Neurophysiol.*, 1957, Suppl. 6, 39–49.

Kalish, H. I. Strength of fear as a function of the number of acquisition and extinction trials. *J. exp. Psychol.*, 1954, **47**, 1–9.

Kandel, E. R., & Spencer, W. A. Cellular neurophysiological approaches in the study of learning. *Physiol. Rev.*, 1968, **48**, 65–134.

Kandel, E. R., & Tauc, L. Mechanism of prolonged heterosynaptic facilitation. *Nature*, 1964, 145–147.

Kandel, E. R., & Tauc, L. Heterosynaptic facilitation in neurones of the abdominal ganglion of *Aplysia depilans*. *J. Physiol.*, 1965a, **181**, 1–27.

Kandel, E. R., & Tauc, L. Mechanism of heterosynaptic facilitation in the giant cell of the abdominal ganglion of *Aplysia depilans*. *J. Physiol.*, 1965b, **181**, 28–47.

Katz, M. S., & Deterline, W. A. Apparent learning in the paramecium. *J. comp. physiol. Psychol.*, 1958, **51**, 243–247.

Katz, J. J., & Halstead, W. C. Protein organization and mental function. *Comp. Psychol. Monogr.*, 1950, **20**, 1–38.

Kellogg, W. N. Is "spinal conditioning" conditioning? *J. exp. Psychol.*, 1947, **37**, 263–265.

Kellogg, W. N., Deese, J., & Pronko, N. H. On the behavior of the lumbospinal dog. *J. exp. Psychol.*, 1946, **36**, 503–511.

Kellogg, W. N., Deese, J., Pronko, N. H., & Feinberg, M. An attempt to condition the chronic spinal dog. *J. exp. Psychol.*, 1947, **37**, 99–117.

Key, B. J., & Bradley, P. B. The effect of drugs on conditioned arousal responses. *Electroenceph. clin. Neurophysiol.*, 1959, **11**, 841. (Abstract.)

Kimble, G. A. *Hilgard and Marquis' conditioning and learning*. New York: Appleton-Century-Crofts, 1961.

Knott, J. R., & Henry, C. E. The conditioning of the blocking of the alpha rhythm of the human electroencephalogram. *J. exp. Psychol.*, 1941, **28**, 134–144.

Konorski, J. *Conditioned reflexes and neuron organization*. New York: Cambridge Univer. Press, 1948.

Kuhlen, R. G. & Thompson, G. G. *Psychological studies of human development*. (2nd ed.) New York: Appleton-Century-Crofts, 1963.

Langworthy, O. R., & Richter, C. P. The influence of efferent cerebral pathways upon the sympathetic nervous system. *Brain*, 1930, **53**, 178–193.

Lebedinskaia, S. I., & Rosenthal, J. S. Reactions of a dog after removal of the cerebral hemispheres. *Brain*, 1935, **58**, 412–419.

Lewis, D. J., & Adams, H. E. Retrograde amnesia from conditioned competing responses. *Science*, 1963, **141**, 516–517.

Liberson, W. T., & Ellen, P. Conditioning of the driven brain wave rhythm in the cortex and hippocampus of the rat. In J. Wortis (Ed.), *Recent advances in biological psychiatry*. New York: Grune and Stratton, 1960.

Livingston, R. B. Central control of receptors and sensory transmission systems. In J. Field, H. W. Magoun, & V. E. Hall (Eds.), *Handbook of Physiology*. Vol. 1. Baltimore: Williams and Wilkins, 1959.

Lloyd, D. P. C. Post-tetanic potentiation of response in monosynaptic reflex pathways of the spinal cord. *J. gen. Physiol.*, 1949, **33**, 147–170.

Loomis, A. L., Harvey, E. N., & Hobart, G. A. Electrical potentials of the human brain. *J. exp. Psychol.*, 1936, **19**, 249–279.

Loucks, R. B. Preliminary report of a technique for stimulation or destruction of tissues beneath the integument and the establishing of conditioned reactions with faradization of the cerebral cortex. *J. comp. Psychol.*, 1933, **16**, 439–444.

Loucks, R. B. The experimental delimitation of neural structures essential for learning: the attempt to condition striped muscle responses with faradization of the sigmoid gyri. *J. Psychol.*, 1935, **1**, 5–44.

Loucks, R. B. Studies of neural structures essential for learning. II: The conditioning of salivary and striped muscle responses to faradization of cortical sensory elements and action of sleep upon such mechanisms. *J. comp. Psychol.*, 1938, **25**, 315–332.

Loucks, R. B., & Gantt, W. H. The conditioning of striped muscle responses based on faradic stimulation of dorsal roots and dorsal columns of the spinal cord. *J. comp. Psychol.*, 1938, **25**, 415–426.

Lubow, R. E. Latent inhibition: effects of frequency of nonreinforced preexposure of the CS. *J. comp. physiol. Psychol.*, 1965, **60**, 454–457.

Lubow, R. E., & Moore, A. U. Latent inhibition: the effect of nonreinforced preexposure to the conditional stimulus. *J. comp. physiol. Psychol.*, 1959, **52**, 415–419.

Lynn, R. *Attention, arousal and the orientation reaction*. New York: Pergamon Press, 1966.

Marsh, J. T., McCarthy, D. A., Sheatz, G., & Galambos, R. Amplitude changes in evoked auditory potentials during habituation and conditioning. *Electroenceph. clin. Neurophysiol.*, 1961, **137**, 280–282.

Marsh, J. T., & Worden, F. G. Auditory potentials during acoustic habituation: cochlear nucleus, cerebellum, and auditory cortex. *Electroenceph. clin. Neurophysiol.*, 1964, **17**, 685–692.

Masserman, J. H. *Behavior and neurosis*. Chicago: Univer. of Chicago Press, 1943.

McAdam, D., Snodgrass, L., Knott, J. R., & Ingram, W. R. Some preliminary observations of electrical changes in deep brain structures during acquisition of a classical conditioned response. *Electroenceph. clin. Neurophysiol.*, 1961, **13**, 146. (Abstract.)

McDougall, W. Experimentelle Beiträge zur Lehre von Gedächniss: Von G. E. Müller und A. Pilzecker. *Mind*, 1901, **10**, 388–394.

McGaugh, J. L. Facilitation and impairment of memory storage processes. In D. P. Kimble (Ed.), *The anatomy of memory*. Palo Alto, California: Science and Behavior Books, 1965.

Meldrum, B. S. Electrical signals in the brain and the cellular mechanism of learning. In D. Richter (Ed.), *Aspects of learning and memory*. New York: Basic Books, 1966.

Milner, P. M. The cell assembly: Mark II. *Psychol. Rev.*, 1957, **64**, 242–252.

Milstein, V. Contingent alpha blocking: conditioning or sensitization? *Electroenceph. clin. Neurophysiol.*, 1965, **18**, 272–277.

Monne, L. Functioning of the cytoplasm. In F. F. Nord (Ed.), *Advances in enzymology*. Vol. 8. New York: Interscience, 1948.

Morgenson, G. J., & Morrison, M. J. Avoidance responses to "reward" stimulation of the brain. *J. comp. physiol.* 1962, **55**, 691–694.

Morrell, F. Electroencephalographic studies of conditioned learning. In Mary A. B. Brazier (Ed.), *The central nervous system and behavior*, 2nd. conference. New York: Josiah Macy, Jr., Foundation, 1959.

Morrell, F. Microelectrode and steady potential studies suggesting a dendridic locus of closure. In H. H. Jasper & G. D. Smirnov (Eds.), *The Moscow colloquium on electroencephalography of higher nervous activity. Electroenceph. clin. Neurophysiol.*, 1960, Suppl. 13, 65–80.

Morrell, F. Electrophysiological contributions to the neural basis of learning. *Physiol. Rev.*, 1961, **41**, 443–494.

Morrell, F., Barlow, J., & Brazier, Mary A. B. Analysis of conditioned repetitive response by means of the average response computer. In J. Wortis (Ed.), *Recent advances in biological psychiatry*. New York: Grune and Stratton, 1960.

Morrell, F., & Jasper, H. H. Electrographic studies of the formation of temporary connections in the brain. *Electroenceph. clin. Neurophysiol.*, 1956, **8**, 210–215.

Morrell, F., Naquet, R., & Gastaut, H. Evolution of some electrical signs of conditioning. I. Normal cat and rabbit. *J. Neurophysiol.*, 1957, **20**, 574–587.

Morrell, F., & Ross, M. Central inhibition in cortical conditioned reflexes. *Arch. Neurol. Psychiat.*, 1953, **70**, 611–616.

Moushegian, G., Rupert, A., Marsh, J. T., & Galambos, R. Evoked cortical potentials in absence of middle ear muscles. *Science*, 1961, **133**, 582–583.

Mowrer, O. H. *Learning theory and behavior*. New York: Wiley, 1960.

Muller, G. E., & Pilzecker, A. Experimentelle Beiträge zur Lehre vom Gedächtnis. *Z. Psychol.*, 1900, Suppl. 1.

Naquet, R., Regis, H., Fischer-Williams, M., & Fernández-Guardiola, A. Variation in the responses evoked by light along specific sensory pathways. *Brain*, 1960, **83**, 52–56.

Nielson, H. C., Doty, R. W., & Rutledge, L. T. Motivational and perceptual aspects of subcortical stimulation in cats. *Amer. J. Physiol.*, 1958, **194**, 427–432.

Nielson, H. C., Knight, J. M., & Porter, P. B. Subcortical conditioning, generalizations and transfer. *J. comp. physiol. Psychol.*, 1962, **55**, 168–173.

Nikolaeva, N. I. Changes in the excitability of various regions of the cerebral cortex in the presence of the formation of motor conditioned reflexes. *Fiziol. Zh. SSSR (Sech. physiol. J. USSR)*, 1955, **41**, 19–24. (Translated as Report Number 62–15057, Office of Technical Services, United States Department of Commerce, Washington, D.C.)

Nikolaeva, N. I. Summation of stimuli in the cerebral cortex. *Fiziol. Zh. SSSR (Sech. physiol. J. USSR)*, 1957, **43**, 27–34.

Nurnberger, J. I. Direct enumeration of cells of the brain. In W. F., Windle (Ed.), *Biology of neuroglia*. Springfield, Ill.: Charles C Thomas, 1958.

Olds, J., & Olds, Marianne E. Interference and learning in paleocortical systems. In J. F. Delafrasnaye et al. (Eds.), *Brain mechanisms and learning*. Oxford: Blackwell Scientific Publications, 1961.

Pavlov, I. P. *Conditioned reflexes*. London: Oxford Univer. Press, 1927.

Penfield, W. Centrencephalic integrating system. *Brain*, 1958, **81**, 231–234.

Poltyrew, S. S. Die Rolle der Ronde und Subrindeknoten in der Bildung der bedingten Reflexe. *Z. Biol.*, 1936, **97**, 180–186.

Poltyrew, S. S., & Zeliony, G. P. Grosshirnrinde und Assoziations-funktion. *Z. Biol.*, 1930, **90**, 157–160.

Porter, J. M., Jr. Backward conditioning of the eyelid response. *J. exp. Psychol.*, 1938, **23**, 403–410.

Putney, R. T. A quantitative evaluation of conditioned blocking enhancement, and inhibition of reinforcement of the alpha rhythm. Unpublished doctoral dissertation, Univer. of Missouri, 1966.

Ranson, S. W., & Clark, S. L. *The anatomy of the nervous system*. Philadephia: Saunders, 1959.

Rasmussen, G. L. The olivary peduncle and other fibre projections of the superior olivary complex. *J. comp. Neurol.*, 1946, **84**, 141–219.

Rescorla, R. A. Pavlovian conditioning and its proper control procedures. *Psychol. Rev.*, 1967, **74**, 71–80.

Rheinberger, M., & Jasper, H. H. The electrical activity of the cerebral cortex in the unanesthetized cat. *Amer. J. Physiol.*, 1937, **119**, 186–196.

Roeder, K. D. *Nerve cells and insect behavior.* Cambridge, Mass.: Harvard Univer. Press, 1963.

Roitbak, A. I. Electrical phenomena in the cerebral cortex during extinction of the orienting and conditioned reflexes. In H. H. Jasper & G. D. Smirnov (Eds.), *The Moscow colloquium on electroencephalography of higher nervous activity. Electroenceph. clin. Neurophysiol.*, 1960, Suppl. 13, 101–114.

Rosenthal, R., & Halas, E. S. Experimenter effect in the study of invertebrate behavior. *Psychol. Rep.*, 1962, **11**, 251–256.

Rowland, V., & Gluck, H. Electrographic arousal and its inhibition as studied by auditory conditioning. In J. Wortis (Ed.), *Recent advances in biological psychiatry.* New York: Grune and Stratton, 1960.

Rusinov, V. S. An electrophysiological analysis of the connecting function in the cerebral cortex in the presence of a dominant region area. *Abstr. Communications XIV Internat. Physiol. Cong.*, Montreal, 1953, 719–720.

Rusinov, V. S., & Rabinovitch, M. Y. Electroencephalographic researches in the laboratories and clinics of the Soviet Union. *Electroenceph. clin. Neurophysiol.*, 1958, Suppl. 8.

Rutledge, L. T., & Doty, R. W. Differential action of chlorpromazine on conditioned responses to peripheral versus direct cortical stimuli. *Fed. Proc.*, 1955, **14**, 126.

Segundo, J. R., Roig, J. A., & Sommer-Smith, J. A. Conditioning of reticular formation stimulation effects. *Electroenceph. clin. Neurophysiol.*, 1959, **11**, 471–484.

Shagass, C., & Johnson, E. P. The course of acquisition of a conditioned response of the occipital alpha rhythm. *J. exp. Psychol.*, 1943, **33**, 201–209.

Sherrington, C. B. *The integrative action of the nervous system.* New Haven: Yale Univer. Press, 1947.

Shurrager, P. S., & Culler, E. A. Phenomena allied to conditioning in the spinal dog. *Amer. J. Physiol.*, 1938, **123**, 186–187.

Shurrager, P. S., & Culler, E. A. Conditioned extinction of a reflex in the spinal dog. *J. exp. Psychol.*, 1941, **28**, 287–303.

Shurrager, P. S., & Shurrager, Harriet C. Converting a spinal CR into a reflex. *J. exp. Psychol.*, 1941, **29**, 217–224.

Shurrager, P. S., & Shurrager, Harriet C. The rate of learning measured at a single synapse. *J. exp. Psychol.*, 1946, **36**, 247–254.

Simmons, F. B., & Beatty, D. L. Sound field variability: Some measurements from the cat. *Electroenceph. clin. Neurophysiol.*, 1964, **17**, 332–334.

Simmons, F. B., Galambos, R., & Rupert, A. Conditioned response of middle ear muscles. *Amer. J. Physiol.*, 1959, **197**, 537–538.

Skinner, B. F. *The behavior of organisms; an experimental analysis.* New York: Appleton-Century-Crotts, 1938.

Smith, S. The limits of educability in Paramecium. *J. comp. Neurol. Psychol.*, 1908, **18**, 499–510.

Sokolov, E. N. Neuronal models of the orienting reflex. In Mary A. B. Brazier (Ed.), *The central nervous system and behavior.* New York: Josiah Macy, Jr., Foundation, 1960.

Sokolov, E. N. Higher nervous functions: the orienting reflex. *Annu. Rev. Physiol.*, 1963, **25**, 545–580.

Spence, K. W. Theoretical interpretations of learning. In S. S. Stevens (Ed.), *Handbook of experimental psychology.* New York: Wiley, 1951.

Spence, K. W. *Behavior theory and conditioning.* New Haven: Yale Univer. Press, 1956.

Spiegel, E. A., & Hunsicker, W. C. The conduction of cortical impulses to the autonomic system. *J. nerv. ment. Dis.*, 1936, **83**, 249–273.

Stern, J. A., Ulett, G. A., & Sines, J. O.

Electrocortical changes during conditioning. In J. Wortis, (Ed.), *Recent advances in biological psychiatry.* New York: Grune and Stratton, 1960.

Tanzi, E. I fattie la induzime ell odierne istologia del sistema nervoso. *Rev. sper. Freniat.*, 1893, **19**, 419–472.

Tchilingaryan, L. I. Changes in excitability of the motor area of the cerebral cortex during extinction of a conditioned reflex elaborated by direct electric stimulation of that area. In E. Gutman & P. Hnik (Eds.), *Central and peripheral mechanisms of motor functions: Proceedings of the conference,* Prague: Czechoslovak Academy of Sciences, 1963.

Ten Cate, J. Konnen die bedingten Reaktionen sich auch ausserhalb der Grosshirnrinde bilden? *Arch. Neerl. Physiol.*, 1934, **19**, 469–481.

Thomas, E. The role of postural adjustments in conditioning with electrical stimulation of the motor cortex as US. Unpublished doctoral dissertation. Yale Univer. 1967.

Thompson, R., & McConnell, J. V. Classical conditioning in the planarian, Dugesia dorotocephala. *J. comp. physiol. Psychol.*, 1955, **48**, 65–68.

Thompson, R. F. *Foundations of physiological psychology.* New York: Harper & Row, 1967.

Thompson, R. F., & Spencer, W. A. Habituation: a model phenomenon for the study of neuronal substrates of behavior. *Psychol. Rev.*, 1966, **173**, 16–43.

Thorndike, E. L. *The elements of psychology.* New York: Seiler, 1905.

Travis, L. E., & Egan, J. P. Conditioning of the electrical response of the cortex. *J. exp. Psychol.*, 1938, **22**, 524–531.

Van-Deventer, J. M., & Ratner, S. C. Variables affecting the frequency of response of planaria to light. *J. comp. physiol. Psychol.*, 1964, **57**, 407–411.

von Békésy, G. *Experiments in hearing.* New York: McGraw-Hill, 1960.

Wachtel, H., & Kandel, E. R. A direct synaptic connection mediating both excitation and inhibition. *Science*, 1967, **158**, 1206–1208.

Wagner, A. R., Siegel, Linda S., & Fein, Greta G. Extinction of conditioned fear as a function of percentage of reinforcement. *J. comp. physiol. Psychol.*, 1967, **63**, 160–164.

Wagner, A. R., Thomas, E., & Norton, T. Conditioning with electrical stimulation of the motor cortex: evidence of a possible source of motivation. *J. comp. physiol. Psychol.*, 1967, **64**, 191–199.

Webster, W. R., Dunlop, C. W., Simons, L. A., & Aitkin, L. M. Auditory habituation: a test of a centrifugal and a peripheral theory. *Science*, 1965, **148**, 654–655.

Wells, C. E. Electroencephalographic correlates of conditioned responses. In G. H. Glasser (Ed.), *EEG and behavior.* New York: Basic Books, 1963.

Wersall, R. The tympanic muscles and their reflexes. *Acta oto-laryng. Suppl.* 139, 1958.

Williams, M. Memory studies in electric convulsive therapy. *J. Neurol. Neurosurg. Psychiat.*, 1950, **13**, 30–35.

Worden, F. G. Attention and auditory electrophysiology. In E. Stellar, & J. M. Sprague (Eds.), Progress in physiological psychology, Vol. 1. New York: Academic Press, 1966.

Yoshii, N., & Hockaday, W. J. Conditioning of frequency-characteristic repetitive electroencephalographic response with intermittent photic stimulation. *Electroenceph. clin. Neurophysiol.*, 1958, **10**, 487–502.

Yoshii, N., Matsumoto, J., Ogura, H., Shimokokochi, M., Yamaguchi, Y., & Yamasaki, H. Conditioned reflex and electroencephalography. In H. H. Jasper & G. D. Smirnov (Eds.), *The Moscow colloquium on electroencephalography of higher nervous activity. Electroenceph. clin. Neurophysiol.*, 1960, Suppl. 13, 199–210.

Young, J. Z. Growth and plasticity in the nervous system. *Proc. roy. Soc. (London), Series B,* 1951, **139**, 18–37.

Zeliony, G. P., & Kadykov, B. I. (Contribution to the study of conditioned reflexes in the dog after cortical extirpation). *Eksp. Med., Kharkov,* 31–34. (*Psychol. Abstr.*, 1938, **12**, No. 5829).

Zimmerman, E. Z., Chambers, W. W., & Liu, C. N. An experimental study of the anatomical organization of the corticobulbar system in the albino rat. *J. comp. Neurol.*, 1964, **123**, 301–324.

Zubin, J., & Barrera, S. E. Effect of electrical convulsive therapy on memory. *Proc. Soc. exp. Biol. Med.*, 1941, **48**, 596–597. (Abstract.)

Suggested Readings

Galambos, R., & Morgan, C. T. The neural basis of learning. In H. W. Magoun, & V. E. Hall (Eds.), *Handbook of physiology*, Vol. 3. Washington, D.C.: American Physiological Society, 1960. A brief review of research findings and theoretical contributions.

Grossman, S. P. *A textbook of physiological psychology*. New York: Wiley, 1967, Part 4. An extensive review of electrophysiological correlates of learning (Chapter 12), findings obtained from stimulation and lesion experiments (Chapter 13), data and theoretical issues concerning memory consolidation (Chapter 14), and physiological and biochemical theories of learning (Chapters 15 and 16).

Kandel, R. R., & Spencer, W. A. Cellular neurophysiological approaches in the study of learning. *Physiol. Rev.*, 1968, **48**, 65–134. An exhaustive outline and evaluation of research of the neural correlates of learning at the cellular level, with special emphasis on the use of simplified preparations.

Morrell, F. Electrophysiological contributions to the neural basis of learning. *Physiol. Rev.*, 1961, **41**, 443–494. An excellent review of the literature concerning electrophysiological correlates of learning.

Stevens, C. F. *Neurophysiology: A primer*. New York: Wiley, 1967. A short (less than 175 pages), easy-to-understand introduction to the basics of neurophysiology.

Thompson, R. F. *Foundations of physiological psychology*. New York: Harper & Row, 1967. A recent text which summarizes a good deal of relevant background material and contains several sections outlining various approaches to physiological interpretations of learning.

Index

Subjects indexed refer to a substantive discussion, a definition (*def.*), or a glossary item (*gl.*). Names of authors are included here only for individual work of substance or significance. Complete reference lists appear on pages 47–53, 99–104, 182–191, 269–286, 355–364, 406–415.